8th edition

FINNEY AND MILLER'S PRINCIPLES OF ACCOUNTING

introductory

Glenn L. Johnson, ph.d.

Washington State University

James A. Gentry, Jr., ph.d., cpa

Emory University

PRENTICE-HALL, INC., ENGLEWOOD CLIFFS, NEW JERSEY 07632

Library of Congress Cataloging in Publication Data

FINNEY, HARRY ANSON, 1886–
    Finney and Miller's Principles of accounting—introductory.

    1. Accounting. I. Miller, Herbert E., joint author.
II. Johnson, Glenn Laurence, 1934– III. Gentry,
James A. IV. Title V. Title: Principles of
accounting—introductory.
HF5635.F538 1980   657   79–20369
ISBN 0–13–317370–4

Editorial/production supervision by Barbara Alexander

Interior design by Ben Kahn

Cover design by Jerry Pfeifer

Manufacturing buyer: Ed Leone

Printed in the United States of America

10 9 8 7 6 5 4 3 2 1

PRENTICE-HALL INTERNATIONAL, INC., *London*
PRENTICE-HALL OF AUSTRALIA PTY. LIMITED, *Sydney*
PRENTICE-HALL OF CANADA, LTD., *Toronto*
PRENTICE-HALL OF INDIA PRIVATE LIMITED, *New Delhi*
PRENTICE-HALL OF JAPAN, INC., *Tokyo*
PRENTICE-HALL OF SOUTHEAST ASIA PTE. LTD., *Singapore*
WHITEHALL BOOKS LIMITED, *Wellington, New Zealand*

CONTENTS

3

PROCESSING ECONOMIC DATA   62

Purpose of chapter / The value of understanding the accounting process / The accounting system / The recording process / The account / The debit-credit recording plan / Revenue and expense account / Dividends account / Summary of debit-credit plan / Equality of debits and credits / Recording transactions / Chart of accounts / Account balances / Alternative account form / The ledger / The journal / Journal illustrated / Advantages of the journal / Posting / The trial balance / Uses of the trial balance / Compound journal entries / Important terms and concepts in chapter 3 / Demonstration problem for review and self-study / Instructions
Chart of accounts

4

INCOME MEASUREMENT   98

Purpose of chapter / Emphasis on income measurement / Nature of net income / The accounting period / Fiscal-period (periodicity) assumption / Revenue-recognition assumption / How is revenue measured? / Matching assumption / How is expense measured? / Relation of cost to assets and expenses / Adjusting entries / Accrual versus cash accounting / Accrual accounting applied to business transactions / Unadjusted trial balance / Required adjustments to year-end balances / Adjusted trial balance / Income statement / Nonoperating items / Extraordinary items / Important terms and concepts in chapter 4 / Demonstration problem for review and self-study / Instructions

5

COMPLETION OF THE ACCOUNTING CYCLE   136

Purpose of chapter / Sequence of accounting procedures / Closing entries / Illustration of closing entries / Trial balance after closing / Possible additional steps in the accounting cycle / Worksheet / Illustrative worksheet / Statements prepared from worksheet / Adjusting entries prepared from worksheet / Closing entries prepared from worksheet / The accounting cycle / Further analysis of adjusting entries / Principal types of adjusting entries / Important terms and concepts in chapter 5 / Demonstration problem for review and self-study / Instructions

6

CASH AND MARKETABLE SECURITIES 172

Purpose of chapter / What is cash? / Reporting cash balances / Control of cash / Internal control / Cash receipts / Cash disbursements / Cash over and short account / Petty cash / Opening a bank account / Deposits / Maintaining a record of the bank balance / The bank statement / Reconciling the bank account / Certified checks / Adjustments after reconciliation / Payroll bank account / Dividend bank account / Bank overdrafts / Classification of investments / Investments classified as current assets / Investments classified as noncurrent assets / Cost of marketable securities / Revenue from marketable securities / Valuation of marketable securities / Valuation at lower of cost or market / Valuation at cost / Valuation at market / Sale of marketable securities / Important terms and concepts in chapter 6 / Demonstration problem for review and self-study / Instructions

Introduction / Compound interest / Present value / Present value of annuity

7

RECEIVABLES AND PAYABLES 209

Purpose of chapter / What are receivables? / Accounts receivable / Trade discounts / Cash discounts / Returns and allowances / Discounts on returned sales / Freight paid and discount taken by customer / Sales discounts on customers' partial payment / Bad debts / Allowance for uncollectibles / Nature of allowance account / Estimating bad debts / Writing off uncollectible accounts / Bad debt recoveries / Direct write-off of bad debts / Credit balances in customers' accounts / Accounts receivable from installment sales / Notes receivable / Maturity / Interest and notes receivable valuation / Recording trade notes receivable / Interest calculations for less than one year / End-of-period adjustments / Dishonored notes / Discounting notes receivable / Classification of receivables / Classes of liabilities / Current liabilities / Accounts payable / Recording purchase liabilities / Short-term notes payable / End-of-period adjustments / Other short-term liabilities / Important terms and concepts in chapter 7 / Demonstration problem for review and self-study / Instructions

Control procedures / Gross earnings / F.I.C.A. taxes / Self-employed persons / Federal unemployment insurance taxes / State unemployment compensation taxes / Federal income tax withholding / Other payroll deductions / Federal Fair Labor Standards Act / Payroll procedures / Wage-payment reports to employees

the balance sheet / Recording treasury stock acquisitions / Disposal of treasury shares / Dividend restrictions resulting from treasury stock acquisitions / Reporting stockholders' equity by sources / Charges to "capital in excess" accounts / Donated capital / Appraisal increments / Earnings per share / Important terms and concepts in chapter 12 / Demonstration problem for review and self-study / Instructions

13

STOCK INVESTMENTS AND CONSOLIDATED STATEMENTS   396

Purpose of chapter / Acquisition of stock / Recording the purchase of stock / Accounting for stock investments subsequent to acquisition / Cost method / Equity method / Use of the cost and equity methods / Market-value method / Lower-of-cost-or-market method / Parent-subsidiary relationship / Consolidated financial statements / Purchase versus pooling of interests / Acquisition treated as a purchase / Purchase of wholly owned subsidiary / Purchase of subsidiary stock at book value / Purchase price in excess of book value / Acquisition treated as pooling of interests / Consolidated statements after acquisition / Acquisition treated as a purchase / Acquisition treated as a pooling of interests / Minority interest / Intercompany sales and profits in inventory / Subsequent realization of intercompany profit / Limitations of usefulness of consolidated statements / Important terms and concepts in chapter 13 / Demonstration problem for review and self-study / Instructions

14

OTHER FORMS OF BUSINESS ORGANIZATIONS   432

Purpose of chapter / Capital and drawing accounts / Working papers and financial statements / Closing the books / Nature of a partnership / Partnership versus a corporation / Capital and drawing accounts / Loan accounts / Opening the books / The profit and loss ratio / Working papers and statements / Closing the books / Allocation of earnings and losses / Basis of illustrations / Salaries and interest in excess of net income / Admission of a new partner / Purchase of interest of old partner / Liquidation of a partnership / Disposal of assets / Division of the gain or loss / Distribution of cash / Partner with a debit balance / Incorporation of a partnership / Important terms and concepts in chapter 14 / Demonstration problem for review and self-study / Instructions

stages of completion / Illustration—goods in process at beginning and end of period / Interdepartmental transfers / Actual factory overhead / Percentage of completion / Assumptions / Important terms and concepts in chapter 18 / Demonstration problem for review and self-study / Instructions

19

STANDARD COSTS 567

Purpose of chapter / Standard costs / Basic features of a standard cost system / Illustration / Comments about illustration / Variance analysis / Management by exception / Disposition of variances / Factory overhead cost control / Standard overhead rate / Factory overhead variances / Spending variances / Efficiency variance / Volume variance / Performance report / Important terms and concepts in chapter 19 / Demonstration problem for review and self-study / Instructions

20

COST-VOLUME-PROFIT ANALYSIS 593

Purpose of chapter / Cost-volume-profit analysis defined / Contribution margin / The break-even point / The margin of safety / Target profit / Contribution margin analysis / Sales mix / Generalizations on cost-volume-profit analysis / Assumptions / Relevant revenues and costs / Nonfinancial (qualitative) factors in decision making / Important terms and concepts in chapter 20 / Demonstration problem for review and self-study / Instructions

21

CONTRIBUTION APPROACH TO INTERNAL REPORTING 619

Purpose of chapter / Responsibility accounting / Traditional reporting / Controllable costs and expenses / Contribution margin / Contribution margin and responsibility accounting / Variable (direct) costing / The case for variable costing for internal reporting / The case against variable costing for internal reporting / The net income effect in internal reports / Variable costing and external reporting / Import terms and concepts in chapter 21 / Demonstration problems for review and self-study / Instructions

PREFACE

This introduction to accounting is written for the prospective career accountant as well as for potential administrators, for investors, and for those who need to understand the function that accounting performs in providing information useful for economic decision making. As in previous editions, this eighth edition is designed to provide a comprehensive first course in accounting at the college and university level.

This edition retains the blending of financial and managerial accounting of the previous edition but is updated to include the latest relevant pronouncements of authoritative accounting organizations. The basic objective of this text is to introduce the accounting concepts and techniques involved in the communication of relevant financial information in the form of financial statements and to describe the uses of accounting information for managerial decision-making purposes.

Special features in the early chapters that have proven to be highly successful in previous editions are carried forward to this edition. These include the early introduction of the corporate form of business organizations, financial statements, and the theoretical framework underlying financial accounting. Thus the first five chapters present the complete accounting cycle after first discussing the nature of accounting and its theoretical framework.

The following new features have been added to the chapters:

(1) An introductory statement of the purpose of each chapter.
(2) A listing at the end of each chapter of the important terms and concepts discussed in the chapter.
(3) A comprehensive demonstration problem at the end of most chapters that can be used to test the reader's comprehension of the chapter contents. All demonstration problems are followed by complete solutions.

Other significant features of the revision are:

(1) Chapter 2 on financial accounting theory has been considerably expanded over the previous edition. By discussing accounting assumptions, doctrines, and principles, the reader is provided with a conceptual framework of financial accounting.
(2) The coverage of special journals and other procedures used in the processing of repetitive transactions has been moved to the end of the book as an appendix (Appendix A). This provides more flexibility for the instructor in including or excluding this subject matter.
(3) Chapter 6 on cash and marketable securities has been updated to introduce the accounting for marketable equity securities under the provisions of FASB *Statement No. 12.*
(4) The time value of money is introduced much earlier in this edition by including it as an appendix to Chapter 6. Many users may wish to review present value concepts early in the course.
(5) The accounting for receivables and payables has been combined into a single chapter (Chapter 7), and the accounting for payroll and the related liabilities has been included as an appendix to the chapter. The use of a chapter appendix allows the instructor flexibility in the amount of detail he or she wishes to introduce at this point in the course.
(6) The coverage of long-lived assets (Chapter 9) has been updated to include some discussion of nonmonetary transactions consistent with APB *Opinion No. 29.*
(7) Chapter 10 is a completely new chapter that combines the accounting for bond liabilities and investments. This chapter includes material previously covered in separate chapters and contains expanded coverage of the subject matter.
(8) As in the previous edition, two chapters (Chapters 11 and 12) are devoted to stockholders' equity. However, the material has been expanded in Chapter 12 to include an introduction to

the subject of earnings per share. The authors feel that this is desirable given the increased importance attached to the reporting of such information.

(9) The accounting for investments in stocks has been incorporated with the subject of consolidated statements in Chapter 13. The coverage has been expanded significantly and updated to include the latest authoritative pronouncements. For those who choose to exclude coverage of consolidated statements, the accounting for stock investments is presented at the beginning of the chapter and is clearly separated from the consolidations material.

(10) The statement of changes in financial position is discussed in a completely rewritten and vastly expanded chapter (Chapter 15). Both the cash-basis and working-capital basis of preparing the statement are discussed. The pedagogically attractive T-account method is used to explain the preparation of the statement.

(11) Chapter 18 on process costing has been expanded to include interdepartmental transfers from one process to another and to provide more coverage of the production report.

(12) Chapter 19 on standard costs has been expanded to include coverage of flexible budgets, standard factory overhead costs, and factory overhead variances.

(13) The chapter on cost-volume-profit analysis (Chapter 20) has been expanded to include discussion on changes in sales mix of a multiproduct firm and to include more material on relevant revenues and costs for managerial decision-making purposes.

(14) Chapter 22 on capital budgeting is a completely new chapter. The chapter emphasizes the use of the net present value criterion in making capital investment decisions.

Most of the assignment material has been completely rewritten or revised. The short exercises at the end of each chapter have been retained. As in the previous edition, two sets of similar type problems, A series and B series, are provided for each chapter so that instructors may alternate assignments between different classes or different semesters. In addition to the assignment material included in the text, there are additional materials available. These include a student's study guide, which contains objective questions, short exercises, problems, and their solutions for each chapter; working papers with headings and other items already filled in to guide the student's work for all A series problems; practice sets for both merchandising and manufacturing firms; and a checklist of key figures for problems in the text. A solutions manual and an examination booklet are available to instructors.

We would like to express our thanks to Professor David Buehlmann (University of Nebraska at Omaha), Professor Martin Gosman (Boston University), Professor Philip E. Meyer (Boston University), Dr. William N. Schwartz (Arizona State University), Professor John Simon (Northern Illinois University), Dr. Doyle Z. Williams, Dean (University of Southern California), Mrs. Pauline L. Corn (Virginia Polytechnic Institute), Professor E. Dee Hubbard (Brigham Young University), Professor Charles Purdy (University of Minnesota), Professor Michael Sheffey (University of Wisconsin—Parkside), and Professor Robert D. Taylor, Jr. (Virginia Commonwealth University), who reviewed the early manuscript and provided us with many helpful comments and suggestions. We also wish to acknowledge the help of our research assistants, Lynn Thomas and David Larcker of the University of Kansas and John Bullard and Dianna Crowe of Emory University. We also appreciate the support given to us by Ron Ledwith, Accounting Editor, and Barbara Alexander, Production Editor, at Prentice-Hall. Finally, we would like to acknowledge the permission of the American Institute of Certified Public Accountants and the Financial Accounting Standards Board to quote from their publications.

GLENN L. JOHNSON
JAMES A. GENTRY, JR.

ACCOUNTING AS AN INFORMATION SYSTEM

PURPOSE OF CHAPTER In conducting the activities of a business firm, management is constantly involved in evaluating alternative courses of action. Such decisions are based to a considerable extent on data that are financial in nature. Many parties not involved in the management of a business firm are also involved in decisions related to the firm. Examples of such parties are present investors, potential investors, creditors, and the general public.

This chapter discusses the role of accounting as an information system which can be of considerable use in providing financial data for decision-making purposes by those outside the firm. The general-purpose financial statements which are the end product of the financial accounting process are introduced. Later chapters discuss these statements in considerable detail and also discuss the types of data that are especially useful to management for internal decision-making purposes.

INTRODUCTION What might a college student with little knowledge of business matters want to know if he or she inherited 2,000 shares of capital stock in a company called Sight & Sound Corporation? Typical questions might include some of the following:

> What is a share of stock?
> What are the Sight & Sound shares worth?
> In what business is Sight & Sound Corporation engaged?
> Is the company in good financial condition?
> Has it been profitable?
> What is involved in managing a business?
> Should the 2,000 shares of stock be sold or retained?

WHAT IS A SHARE OF STOCK? When a business is organized as a corporation, the resources which enable it to commence operations are acquired through shares of capital stock issued to investors. When Sight & Sound Corporation was organized one year ago it issued 2,500 shares of capital stock for $25,000 cash.

Ownership of shares of capital stock is evidenced by a stock certificate. An illustration of a stock certificate appears on page 2.

As indicated, only one certificate is needed to establish ownership of any number of shares.[1]

---

[1]You might be wondering about the meaning of *par value* shown on the stock certificate of Sight & Sound Corporation. Par value is an arbitrary amount per share a corporation establishes for its stock

Certificate No. _____2_____   _____2,000_____ *Shares*

SIGHT & SOUND CORPORATION

CAPITAL STOCK

THIS CERTIFIES THAT _____(Name of college student)_____ *is the*
owner of _____two thousand_____ *shares at $10 par value of*
the Capital Stock of

SIGHT & SOUND CORPORATION

transferable on the books of the Corporation in person or by duly authorized
attorney upon surrender of this Certificate properly endorsed.

IN WITNESS WHEREOF *the said Corporation has caused this Certificate to be signed*
by its duly authorized officers, and to be sealed with the seal of the Corporation at
_____(Name of city)_____ *, this* ___Second___ *day of* ___January___ *, 19–2*

Although the stockholders are the owners of a corporation, they have no author-ity to transact any corporate business. The authority to conduct corporate business rests with the board of directors, whose members are elected by the stockholders. As a general rule, the board delegates many of the responsibilities associated with managing the operations of the business to the corporate officers who are appointed by it. The appointed officers are often referred to collectively as the management. The board establishes broad policies and, at periodic meetings, re-views the results of management's efforts.

Employees of corporations may also be stockholders, and those employees hold-ing important managerial positions often own a significant number of shares. An employee, if elected, may serve on the board of directors. However, the law generally specifies that board members must be stockholders.

Stockholders may receive a cash return, known as dividends, on their sharehold-ings. Dividend distributions are made by corporations only when so ordered by the board of directors; hence dividends should never be counted on as a certainty. In the year just ended the directors of Sight & Sound Corporation authorized the payment of four quarterly dividends of 20 cents per share. Thus, a stockholder owning 2,000 shares would have received a total of $1,600 (2,000 × $.20 × 4) in dividends for the year.

in its corporate charter and is printed on each stock certificate. It serves to identify the legal or stated capital of a corporation, but it has nothing to do with the market value of the stock. Par value is fully discussed in Chapters 11 and 12.

WHAT ARE THE SIGHT & SOUND SHARES WORTH?   As a general rule, shares of stock are transferable; that is, they may be bought and sold or given away. If a company's stock is listed on a stock exchange, the buying and selling of its shares thereon establishes a market price. The market price of a share of stock will change, often frequently and sometimes significantly, for a number of reasons. Basically, the market price of a share of stock is affected by the earnings prospects of the company, by the prospective dividend payments to stockholders, and by the relative attractiveness of alternative investment opportunities.

The shares of Sight & Sound Corporation are not actively traded; however, a securities dealer has offered to pay $16 a share for the 2,000 shares held by the college student, thus indicating an aggregate market value of $32,000. Incidentally, if the directors continue the existing dividend payments, the dividend yield based on the market value of the investment will amount to 5 per cent per annum ($1,600 annual dividends divided by $32,000 market value, or on a per share basis $.80 ÷ $16).

IN WHAT BUSINESS IS THE CORPORATION ENGAGED?   Sight & Sound Corporation operates a retail store dealing in television and audio equipment. However, in the recent annual report to stockholders, management indicated that consideration is being given to the opening of a service center, which could significantly expand the company's volume of business.

IS THE COMPANY IN GOOD FINANCIAL CONDITION? HAS IT BEEN PROFITABLE?   A stockholder's primary source of information concerning the financial condition and profitability of his or her company is the firm's financial statements. The financial statements of Sight & Sound Corporation for the year just ended are presented on the following pages. Some background comments and definitions are offered at this point to indicate why financial statements are helpful whenever there are questions about financial condition and profitability.

STATEMENT OF FINANCIAL POSITION (BALANCE SHEET)   The *balance sheet* on page 4 *shows the assets of the business, its liabilities, and the owners' equity.* Thus it portrays financial position as of the date stated in the heading of the statement. Observe the *equality* of the total assets ($49,500) and the total equities ($49,500)—hence the name balance sheet. The assets of a business are always *equalled by claims against assets, which accountants refer to as equities.* If the balance sheet fails to "balance," at least one error has been made.

ASSETS   *Assets are future economic benefits, the rights to which are owned or controlled by an organization or individual.* The assets included in a firm's balance sheet are those for which the rights have been acquired by a current or past transaction. Cash, accounts receivable (amounts owed to the business by its customers for sales on open account),[2] merchandise, office supplies, land, buildings, machinery and other equipment, and patents are typical business assets.

[2]Sales on open account refer to sales in which customers are granted credit based on their signatures, rather than by formal promissory notes—credit sales.

Assets may provide future economic benefits for several reasons; for instance:

(1) Because the asset may be used as purchasing power.

Cash is an example. It is valuable because other assets can be acquired with it.

(2) Because the asset is a money claim.

Accounts receivable and United States savings bonds are examples, the holder or claimant being entitled to receive money for them, usually at some specified date.

(3) Because the asset can be sold and thus converted to cash or to a money claim.

Merchandise held for sale by a merchant is an example.

(4) Because the asset offers some potential services, or rights, to the owner.

A building is an example. It provides shelter or a place in which business activities may be conducted. Land, machinery, equipment, patents, and supplies are other examples. Assets of the type described under (4) are acquired by a business with the expectation of earning something from their use.

LIABILITIES

Liabilities are the economic obligations of an organization or individual, such as debts owed to creditors. They arise from a variety of business events such as the borrowing of money or the purchase of goods and services through the use of credit. Accounts payable (amounts owed by the business for inventory purchases on open account—trade credit granted by suppliers), notes payable, salaries and wages payable, taxes payable, and bonds payable are some of the liabilities that may be owed by a business. The "size" and due dates of liabilities must be carefully watched by management because if a business fails to pay its liabilities when they fall due, the business may be thrown into bankruptcy by its creditors.

*Note content of
statement heading:
1. Name of business
2. Name of statement
3. Date*

→**SIGHT & SOUND CORPORATION**
→**Balance Sheet**
→**December 31, 19_1**

Assets			Equities		
Current assets:			Current liabilities:		
Cash	$16,500		Accounts payable	$20,000	
Accounts receivable	11,000		Salaries payable	1,500	$21,500
Merchandise inventory—at cost	12,000	$39,500	Stockholders' equity:		
			Capital stock, 2,500		
Long-term investment:			shares issued and		
Investment in land—			outstanding	$25,000	
at cost		10,000	Retained earnings	3,000	28,000
		$49,500			$49,500

Notes about the financial statements:

For purposes of illustration, the 19_1 stands for the year; however, in actual practice the real year would be reported, such as 1981.

Corporations are subject to income tax, but to keep the illustrative financial statements relatively simple, such taxes are ignored in the early chapters. For the same reason, the dollar amounts in the illustrative statements are small.

Dollar signs are generally used in financial statements, although rarely in any other form or record associated with accounting. In the financial statements it is customary to place a dollar sign beside the first amount in each money column and beside each amount appearing below an underline.

It is customary to list detail figures in an inside column with the total carried to the right on the same line. A final figure is usually double underlined.

OWNER'S EQUITY   *The excess of the assets over the liabilities of a business is the owners' equity.* For instance,

If a business, such as Sight & Sound Corporation, has assets in the amount of	$49,500
And has liabilities of	21,500
Then the owners' equity is	$28,000

Note that total equities equal total liabilities ($21,500) plus owners' equities ($28,000), which equals total assets ($49,500).

Unlike the fixed dollar claims of creditors (liabilities), the equity held by the owners is in the nature of a residual claim or interest. If a corporation goes out of business, the creditors' claims come first. Any assets that remain after the creditors' claims have been satisfied may be distributed to the owners. Thus the total equities of a firm consist of fixed creditor claims (liabilities) and residual owner claims (owners' equity).

The owners' equity in a corporation, called stockholders' equity, may come from the following sources:

From stockholders' investments—Shown in the illustrative balance sheet on page 4 as:	
Capital stock	$25,000
From profitable operations—Shown in the illustrative balance sheet on page 4 as:	
Retained earnings	3,000
Total stockholders' (owners') equity	$28,000

Note that at the beginning of the year the company had no retained earnings because the business was just commencing and had not conducted any profitable operations.

BRIEF APPRAISAL OF COMPANY'S FINANCIAL POSITION   The strong financial position of Sight & Sound Corporation becomes evident from an inspection of its balance sheet. Items:

The current assets (cash and those assets which will be converted to cash in the near future during the normal course of business operations) exceed the current liabilities (those payable in the near future) by a comfortable margin. This is indicated by a current ratio (current assets divided by current liabilities) of 1.8 ($39,500 ÷ $21,500).

The cash balance seems adequate.

The receivables are a source of cash inflow in the near future. The year-end balance ($11,000) does not seem excessive in relation to the sales volume (which was $81,000 for 19_1, as shown by the income statement which follows), especially in view of the fact that the company allows its customers 60 days to pay their accounts. That is, the company's receivables are being turned over (sales divided by average accounts receivable) 14.7 times [$81,000 ÷ ($11,000 ÷ 2)] on the average during the year, which indicates an average collection period of almost 25 days

(365 ÷ 14.7). A large accounts-receivable balance in relation to sales volume might indicate doubtful collectibility.

The inventory is another near-term source of cash, assuming normal sales activity. In relation to the volume of goods sold (see the cost of goods sold from the income statement shown below), the investment in inventory does not appear excessive. The inventory turned over (cost of goods sold divided by average inventory) 8 times [$48,000 ÷ ($12,000 ÷ 2)] on the average during the year, which indicates an average day's supply in inventory of almost 46 days (365 ÷ 8). A large inventory balance in relation to volume of goods sold might indicate "slow-moving" merchandise.

The long-term investment, though probably made for some good business reason such as to acquire a future building site or to participate in rising real estate values, is nevertheless a source of cash if an urgent need for cash arises.

The company has no long-term debt.

INCOME STATEMENT   Most businesses are engaged in a continuing "stream" of operations that are conducted for the purpose of producing *net income* (also called earnings and profit), which *is defined as the excess of revenues over expenses,* with the reverse (expenses exceed revenues) a net loss.[3] The success of a business is judged largely by its profitability, as shown in the income statement below—not only by the amount of net income, but by its trend and by how it compares with the net income of comparable businesses.

Note also the reporting of earnings per share (EPS) in the income statement, which is the amount of net income applicable to each share of capital stock. EPS is a widely quoted figure, since it influences the price of a company's capital stock. For simple capital structures, such as that for Sight & Sound Corporation, EPS is equal to net income divided by the outstanding shares of capital stock ($5,000 ÷ 2,500 = $2.00).

Note the special feature of the heading for an income statement: It indicates a period of time rather than a date

SIGHT & SOUND CORPORATION
Income Statement
For the Year Ended December 31, 19_1

Revenue:		
Sales of merchandise		$81,000
Deduct expenses:		
Cost of goods sold[4]	$48,000	
Salaries expense	18,000	
Rent expense	4,800	
Other expense	5,200	76,000
Net income		$ 5,000
Earnings per share ($5,000 ÷ 2,500)		$ 2.00

Some of the common uses of income statements are:

They may be included in a report to stockholders and used by the stockholders in forming an opinion regarding the progress of the business and the effectiveness of the management group.

[3]This is a simplified definition of net income to introduce the concept. As will be explained subsequently, net income is really equal to revenues minus expenses plus gains and minus losses.

[4]The cost of goods sold for a merchandising firm is the cost to acquire the merchandise or goods sold during the period. It is an expense.

They may be submitted to banks in support of a request for a loan for the banks' use in judging the earnings prospects of the borrower.

They may be used by investors in reaching decisions whether to acquire, to continue to hold, or to dispose of securities issued by the corporation—for example, the corporation's capital stock.

They may be used by management to judge the effectiveness of its past policies and decisions, to detect unfavorable trends and developments, and to provide data upon which to base decisions regarding a wide variety of matters, such as whether to expand production, whether to change advertising policy, whether to introduce a new product, whether to alter selling prices, and whether to merge with another corporation.

For many of the above uses, the balance sheet also will be examined. The balance sheet and the income statement should be thought of as companion statements, each supplementing the other.

REVENUE *Revenue is an inflow of assets in the form of cash, receivables, or other property from customers or clients, which results from sales of merchandise or the rendering of services, or from investments;* for instance, interest may be earned on bonds or on savings deposits. In contrast, revenue does not arise from an inflow of capital funds from stockholders investing in the capital stock of a corporation. Nor does an inflow of borrowed funds qualify as revenue.

Observe that Sight & Sound Corporation has only one kind of revenue: from sales of merchandise.

EXPENSE *Expense is the cost of goods or services used for the purpose of generating revenue.* A business advertises with the expectation of attracting customers, engages employees so that customers may be served, and rents space so that there will be a place to conduct the operations of the business. In all such activities goods or services are utilized for the purpose of generating revenue, and hence expenses are incurred.

Sight & Sound Corporation's expenses for the year just ended amounted to $76,000.

BRIEF APPRAISAL OF THE COMPANY'S PROFITABILITY It is apparent from an examination of the income statement that the management of Sight & Sound Corporation operated the company profitably in the year 19_1. From the merchandising activity $5,000 was earned, as shown by the following schedule, which also sets forth some profit percentages.

Sales of merchandise	$81,000	100%
Cost of goods sold	48,000	59
Gross margin	$33,000	41%
Deduct operating expenses:		
Salaries	$18,000	
Rent	4,800	
Other	5,200	28,000	35
Net income from merchandising activity	$ 5,000	6%

The net income of $5,000 represents approximately an 18% return on the December 31, 19_1 stockholders' equity ($5,000 ÷ $28,000). The return on stockholders' equity shows the rate earned on resources provided by owners (stockholders) and thereby measures the rate of earnings accruing to the owners from their investment in the company.

Whether such profit percentages and the rate of return indicate a truly excellent managerial performance cannot be determined merely by an examination of one set of financial statements. As indicated earlier, the success of a business is judged largely by its earnings—but to "evaluate" the earnings, consideration should be given to their trend and how they compare with the earnings results of comparable businesses. The statements of past years will provide the data needed to determine the trend of earnings. (Earlier statements are not available in this instance because Sight & Sound Corporation is only one year old.) Several organizations publish financial data, classified by industry, which enable anyone interested to make comparisons and thus form an opinion about the relative performance of a particular company.

The analysis of earnings data should not be based solely on absolute amounts. For instance, the relationship between earnings and balance-sheet data is an important consideration. A company with $10,000 earnings and $100,000 of stockholders' equity ($10,000 ÷ $100,000 is a 10% return) has operated more successfully, other things being equal, than a company with larger earnings of $24,000 but stockholders' equity of $300,000 (only an 8% return).

STATEMENT OF RETAINED EARNINGS   The third statement illustrated is the statement of retained earnings. *Retained earnings are that portion of the stockholders' equity attributable to profitable operations, and they equal the aggregate net income minus any net losses and dividends to date.*[5]

Note: This statement also covers a period of time

SIGHT & SOUND CORPORATION
Statement of Retained Earnings
→**For the Year Ended December 31, 19_1**

Retained earnings—beginning of year	$ –0–
Net income for 19_1	5,000
Total	$5,000
Deduct dividends	2,000
Retained earnings—end of year	$3,000

This statement shows the changes that have occurred in the retained earnings during the period covered by the statement.[6] One of the changes is dividends. Dividends are distributions of assets (usually cash) to stockholders as a result of profitable operations. Profitable operations increase assets and retained earnings; therefore, dividends decrease assets and retained earnings. Although dividends reduce retained earnings, they are *not* an expense: they are not paid for the purpose of generating revenue.

[5]This is a simplified definition of retained earnings for purposes of introduction, but as will be explained subsequently, retained earnings really equal accumulated net income minus any net losses and dividends and plus or minus any prior-period adjustments to date.

[6]As previously pointed out, a corporation normally will have a beginning retained earnings balance, but Sight & Sound Corporation has a zero balance because it just began business in 19_1.

Observe that the net income shown in the statement of retained earnings agrees with the net income shown by the income statement and that the year-end retained earnings of $3,000 shown in the statement of retained earnings agree with the amount shown in the balance sheet. Thus the retained earnings statement serves as a connecting link between the income statement and the balance sheet.

The interconnection among the three financial statements can be depicted as follows:

Shown in the income statement (page 6):	
Net income for the period	$5,000⌉
Shown in the statement of retained earnings above:	
Net income for the period	$5,000◄⌋
Less the dividends paid to stockholders	2,000
Retained earnings at the end of the period	$3,000⌉
Shown in the year-end balance sheet (page 4):	
Retained earnings at the end of the period	$3,000◄⌋

Although almost always included in the set of financial statements, it should be pointed out that the presentation of the statement of retained earnings is optional. Also, the statement of retained earnings is sometimes combined with the income statement, especially for larger companies, to present a statement of income and retained earnings.

STATEMENT OF CHANGES IN FINANCIAL POSITION   This financial statement is primarily a *report on financial management, since it discloses how the business firm is being financed and where the financing is being used during an interval of time.* The statement provides information on the overall investing and financing activities of a business enterprise for a period of time. Such information is communicated in the statement by showing the sources and uses of financial resources (assets). That is, the statement reports on the financial activity of the firm by showing all of the significant financial

Note: This statement also covers a period of time

SIGHT & SOUND CORPORATION
Statement of Changes in Financial Position
→**For the Year Ended December 31, 19_1**

Sources of financial resources:			
Cash provided from operations:			
Cash collected from customers		$70,000	
Cash paid for inventory purchases	$40,000		
Salaries paid	16,500		
Rent paid	4,800		
Other expenses paid	5,200	66,500	
Cash provided from operations for period		$ 3,500	
Cash provided from other sources:			
Issuance of capital stock		25,000	
Total financial resources provided for period			$28,500
Uses of financial resources:			
Cash applied:			
Purchase of land		$10,000	
Dividends paid		2,000	
Total financial resources used for period			12,000
Increase in cash for period			$16,500

resources provided during the period and the uses to which they were put, as illustrated on page 9 for Sight & Sound Corporation.[7]

For the year 19_1, the statement shows that the management of Sight & Sound Corporation primarily financed the business by issuing capital stock ($25,000) and, to a lesser extent, by internal financing from normal operating activities ($3,500). Such financing was used to acquire land ($10,000), pay dividends ($2,000), and increase the cash position ($16,500).

Note that the statement expresses the sources and uses of financial resources in terms of cash. The reason for this is that most financing and investing activities affect cash or working capital (current assets minus current liabilities), and therefore the statement format normally expresses most of such activities in terms of either cash or working capital. However, for more complex businesses, there would be changes in financial resources that do not affect cash or working capital (e.g., the acquisition of equipment by issuing long-term notes payable), and such changes would be reported in the statement. In other words, the statement of changes in financial position reports on *all* significant changes in financial position, not just those that affect cash or working capital.

BRIEF APPRAISAL OF THE COMPANY'S FINANCIAL MANAGEMENT By analyzing a company's statements of changes in financial position over several years, it is possible to obtain clues to management strategy in financing the business and how such financing is being used in the business. Such analysis provides an indication of the company's trend toward greater or less financial strength. However, since Sight & Sound Corporation just began business, the analysis of the company's statement of changes in financial position is limited to only one year.

The statement of changes in financial position of Sight & Sound Corporation for 19_1 does indicate that by financing the business primarily from the issuance of capital stock, management has avoided long-term debt financing that could be risky during the time the business is just beginning. Moreover, the avoidance of long-term debt financing means that the management has some flexibility in future financing, since debt financing can be obtained should it be needed. On the other hand, the internal financing from operating activities seems very low and needs to be improved.

With regard to investing activity, by renting the premises occupied by the firm management avoided the large investment necessary to acquire a store during a time when the firm can least afford it. However, management did invest in land, which would seem to indicate that the firm is contemplating building a store in the future. Also, as previously pointed out, the land could be a source of cash if an urgent need arose. In addition to the land purchase, the company paid dividends, which were a relatively small dollar amount, but 40 per cent of earnings ($2,000 dividends ÷ $5,000 earnings).

Overall the company's financial management seems to be adequate. By avoiding

---

[7]The two basic formats for the statement of changes in financial position are the cash basis (format) and the working capital basis (format). The cash basis is used in the illustrative statement for Sight & Sound Corporation because it is easier to understand at this point in your study. However, the working capital basis is the most widely used format. Both formats are discussed in Chapter 15.

debt financing and the building or purchase of a store, management does not seem to be taking undue risk. One might argue that since the company is just beginning, it would have been better to avoid purchasing land and paying dividends and instead reinvest the money in the business to provide a service center.

MANAGING A BUSINESS   To return to the questions that might be raised by the college student who has just inherited stock in Sight & Sound Corporation, if it is management that "runs" the company, what is involved in managing a business? Stated simply, those who manage a business:

> Set goals for the enterprise. This function usually requires extensive and careful planning.
> Control and coordinate the activities of employees as they work to attain the goals established by management.
> Evaluate performance.
> Make decisions.

In pursuing the above activities, management is more or less continually evaluating alternative courses of action. Choosing among alternatives is facilitated by the use of relevant information. Much of the information that is relevant for managerial decision-making purposes is quantitative and is supplied by the company's accounting system. After management has made a decision, the subsequent financial effects of the decision can be determined through the analysis of relevant accounting data. Thus, accounting data help management make decisions and to control the business by feeding back information on the economic results of past and current decisions. An illustration of this process is shown below.

Those involved in management usually acknowledge the value of a good understanding of the accounting process by which data relative to a business are gathered, classified, and set forth in financial reports.

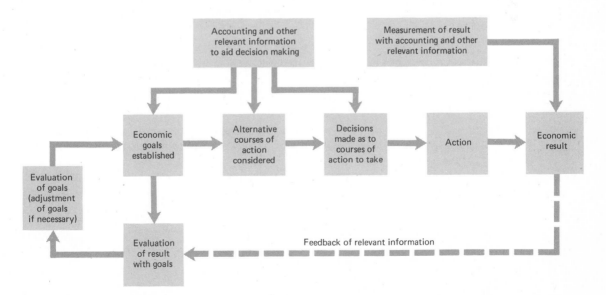

11

SHOULD THE 2,000 SHARES OF STOCK BE SOLD?   By acquiring the shares of stock, the student has become an investor. The student should periodically review his or her holding of "S & S" shares to determine whether a better investment alternative exists.

A number of considerations bear on the question whether the stock should be sold. Some of them are briefly set forth below. It would be up to the student to place his or her own evaluation on the relevance of such considerations.

The student owns 80 per cent of the issued and outstanding shares of capital stock of Sight & Sound Corporation. If the stock is kept, then the student is in a position to control the company by voting the shares at stockholders' meetings and thus electing those he or she favors to the board of directors. The student could even elect himself or herself to the board of directors and, if so desired, could become president of the corporation—if his or her interest, knowledge, and ability suggested such a course of action would be wise. If the student should sell the stock, the opportunity to start at the top would be eliminated; if the student desired to be employed by the company, he or she would probably have to start at the bottom and work up.

The $16 market price of the capital stock is fairly low given its relation to earnings (net income). That is, the stock's price-earnings ratio (market price per share of capital stock divided by earnings per share) is 8, which means the market values every dollar of earnings only 8 times. Consequently, if the company's profits increase as it grows, the stock price is most likely to increase also. If the student sells the stock, he or she may be foregoing the future stock price appreciation.

With regard to management's dividend policy, the company had a payout ratio (dividends per share divided by earnings per share) of 40 per cent ($.80 ÷ $2.00). This is a low to average payout, which would seem to indicate that management's dividend policy is not to distribute a large portion of earnings. Also, as noted earlier, the dividend yield is only 5 per cent. Could a higher yield be obtained if the shares were sold and the proceeds invested elsewhere? A relevant consideration here is that by controlling the board of directors of Sight & Sound Corporation the student can have some influence on the dividend policy. Of course, there must be profitable operations in the first place before there can be any distributions in the form of dividends. But the proportion of earnings to be retained in the business and used for expansion or investment is a matter for the board of directors to decide. As indicated by the illustrative balance sheet of Sight & Sound Corporation, $3,000 of earnings have been retained in the business.

Another relevant consideration concerns the future prospects of the company. In this connection, the following factors seem pertinent:

The market for color television is far from saturated.

Trade publications indicate that, as a result of recent emphasis on research by manufacturing companies, many new products for the home entertainment field are in the final stages of development.

Population of the city in which Sight & Sound Corporation is located is growing at an above-average rate.

As a general rule, it takes several years for a new business to attain a satisfactory profit level. Thus the profit level achieved by the management of Sight & Sound Corporation during its first year of operations can be viewed as a most encouraging sign for the future.

The company has not yet established a service department. Thus an additional source of profit is available for management's consideration.

The company has no long-term debt. Thus long-term debt can probably be counted on as a source should additional financing be required.

Whether or not the stock is sold, the student will continue to face investment decisions. Knowledge of accounting will enable the student to analyze the financial statements of business firms in order to derive useful information for making investment decisions.

ACCOUNTING DEFINED Broadly speaking, *accounting is an economic information system,* or economic information specialization, designed to communicate significant financial and other economic information about organizations in order to permit informed judgments and decisions by users of the information. The information is economic in nature because it involves choice among scarce resources. It deals with how organizations choose to use scarce (limited) and useful productive resources (land, labor, and capital),[8] which have alternative uses, to produce goods and services that satisfy human wants or needs. Since productive resources are scarce, but useful, they command a price (rent for land; wages for labor; and interest, dividends, and profits for capital), as do the resulting goods and services, and information with regard to resources and goods and services are primarily stated in terms of money—financial information.

Accounting as a system, an economic information system, refers to the transformation of an organization's economic data into economic information useful for purposes of financial decision making with regard to that organization. The system is the transformation of input (economic data) into output (economic information). For example, as illustrated by Sight & Sound Corporation, the accounting information system transformed economic data about the firm into financial statements providing information useful for financial decision making.

Information is data useful in choosing from among alternative courses of action—useful for purposes of decision making. It is useful because it reduces the uncertainty of not knowing precisely the consequences of alternative courses of action. Information reduces uncertainty by improving the decision maker's predictions with regard to the consequences of choosing alternative courses of action.

However, information is not costless because it takes time, effort, and resources to generate information. Information has "value" only if its benefits exceed its costs. Consequently, there is a need for information specialists who can provide information at a lower cost and/or higher productivity than can individuals acting on their own behalf.

With the existence of large classes of economic decision makers with similar economic decision problems, and with the need for economic information to aid in solving such problems, accountants or economic information specialists provide such information. Moreover, accountants provide such information based on a specialized body of knowledge or expertise—accounting as an economic information specialization.

The justification for the existence of accounting is that it provides economic

[8]Capital refers to capital goods (e.g., plant, equipment, and materials), which are produced goods that can be used as inputs for further production. Whereas labor and land (including natural resources) are primary factors of production that exist because of nature, capital goods are produced by man and improve the output of land and labor. See Paul A. Samuelson, *Economics,* 9th ed. (New York: McGraw-Hill Book Company, 1973), p. 50.

information useful for purposes of financial decision making. In addition, either directly or indirectly, accounting information with regard to organizations is required by law.

USERS OF ACCOUNTING INFORMATION Accounting information is used by a wide variety of groups concerned about the economic activities of business organizations. Those users who benefit directly from having accounting information about business organizations, because their information needs are directly related to the commitment of personal or financial resources, include the following:

Management at all levels	Present and potential creditors
Present owners (investors)	Suppliers (vendors) of materials, etc.
Potential investors	Employees

Those users with indirect concern about business organizations include the following:

Customers	Financial press and reporting agencies
Representatives of the above users:	Governmental units:
Security analysts and advisors	Securities and Exchange Commission
Credit rating bureaus	Internal Revenue Service
Labor unions	Bureau of the Census
Trade associations	State and local tax agencies
Lawyers	State utility regulation commissions
Economists	General public
Stock exchanges	

Although this book focuses on accounting for business organizations, it should be pointed out that almost all of the above users are also concerned about accounting information with regard to nonbusiness organizations. Churches, hospitals, charitable organizations, social programs, and governmental units cannot operate effectively unless accounting records are maintained and accounting information is provided to interested parties.

INTERNAL AND EXTERNAL USERS The above users of accounting information with regard to the business organization can be conveniently separated into internal and external users. The management of a firm is an internal user and all the others, such as investors, creditors, suppliers, and the general public, are external users of accounting information.

Management uses accounting information inside the business organization to aid in making decisions that directly affect the business organization. Management is an internal user of accounting information for purposes of internal decision making primarily with regard to planning, directing, and controlling the organization.

External users are those outside the business firm who use accounting information to aid in making decisions about their relationship with the business organization, but their decisions do not directly affect the operations of the firm. External users are concerned with business organizations as a source of decision alternatives available to them, such as whether to hold, sell, or buy the capital stock of business firms (investors); loan or not to loan business firms money (creditors); and supply or not to supply materials (vendors). They are concerned with receiving accounting information for evaluating overall firm performance, financial status, and changes in financial status.

MANAGERIAL AND FINANCIAL ACCOUNTING Accounting as an economic information system for organizations provides economic information to those inside the organization (managers or internal users) and to those outside the organization (external users) to aid them in their financial decision making. The internal reporting of economic information useful to managers is called *managerial accounting,* and the external reporting of economic information useful to investors, creditors, governmental agencies, and others outside the organization is called *financial accounting.*

Managerial accounting is internal reporting to managers to aid in formulating long-range plans, in planning and controlling current operations, and in making special, nonroutine decisions. The essence of managerial accounting is the providing of economic information useful in aiding managerial decision making in planning, directing, and controlling the organization's operations. Managerial accounting is discussed more fully later.

Financial accounting is the external reporting of a firm's overall operations, where the primary interest of external users is the review and evaluation of the profitability, financial position, and changes in financial position of the firm as a whole. The form of such external reporting is primarily the financial statements and related notes to the statements. The income statement communicates how well the firm performed for a given period of time, the balance sheet communicates how the firm financially stands at a given point in time, and the statement of changes in financial position provides economic information for the evaluation of the financial management (investing and financing activities) of the firm for a given period of time. Consequently, financial accounting can be viewed as that part of the total economic information system that results in the basic financial statements.

It should also be pointed out that the financial statements are intended for all, not specific, external users. Because external users have different needs and interests, it is impossible for a set of financial statements to meet each external user's special needs; hence, the financial statements are *general-purpose financial statements* intended to serve all external users.

Although the primary purpose of financial accounting is the external reporting of published financial statements and related information, external reporting also includes the reporting of tax returns to taxing agencies (federal, state, and municipal income taxes, payroll taxes, and excise taxes) and the reporting of special reports, depending on the type of business, to certain regulatory agencies (e.g., the Interstate Commerce Commission and state public utility commissions). Such reporting is required by law.

It should also be pointed out that there is not a complete separation between managerial and financial accounting. The primary accounting records are for the preparation of the financial statements, which are directly or indirectly required by law. Much of the accounting information for managerial decision making comes from those records. Moreover, management is responsible for the content of financial accounting statements. Also, management is obviously concerned about the financial statements, since these statements are often used to evaluate management. In addition, external users would probably want to have much of the economic information referred to as managerial accounting, but such information is not provided externally because it would be available to competitors; hence, it is viewed as confidential information. Finally, the term financial accounting is somewhat misleading because all accounting is financial in that it is stated in monetary terms.

Although accounting information is classified by user groups (external users—financial accounting; internal users—managerial accounting), those who pursue a career in accounting are classified by the type of organization for which they work, such as public accounting, private accounting, and governmental accounting. Within each of these organizations, accountants are further classified by the type of accounting specialty they perform. These specialties are further described below under the three organizational headings.

PUBLIC ACCOUNTING With the reliance on financial statements by investors, creditors, and the general public to aid in making informed economic decisions with regard to business enterprises, there exists a need for an independent party to examine or audit financial statements. This need is met by the public accounting profession.

Similar to law and medicine, public accounting is a profession. It has licensing requirements, a comprehensive code of professional ethics, a requirement of a high level of academic study and professional competence, a dedication to public service, and a common body of knowledge. Because of the public interest in audited financial statements, every state recognizes public accounting as a profession and provides a licensing system to enter the public accounting profession. The license is a certified public accounting certificate and allows the holder to practice public accounting as a certified public accountant (CPA). The certificate authenticates that the CPA has passed a rigorous, comprehensive examination and has met experience and education requirements to assure high standards of performance. The examination is prepared by the American Institute of Certified Public Accountants (AICPA), which is the professional organization of the practicing certified public accountant.

Public accountants offer their professional accounting services to the public for a fee much the same as does the lawyer and the physician. Unlike the lawyer and the physician who are primarily responsible to their clients and patients who pay for their services, accountants practicing as public accountants have a unique relationship with their clients in that they are independent of them. Public accountants have a major responsibility to the lending, investing, and general public to provide an impartial review of their clients' financial statements and to report on them favorably or unfavorably to third parties. Public accountants are professionally responsible to third parties who rely on the financial statements "approved" by them even though such parties do not pay their fees and do not have any contractual relationship with them.

Normally, two or more accountants organize an accounting firm in the form of a partnership to operate a public accounting office. Such firms vary in size from the one-office local firm, to the several-office regional firm, to the multihun-

IMPORTANT TERMS AND CONCEPTS IN CHAPTER 1

Statement of financial position (balance sheet)—pp. 3, 4
Dividend yield—p. 3
Equality of total assets and total equities—pp. 3, 4, 5
Assets—p. 3
Accounts receivable—p. 3
Liabilities—p. 4
Accounts payable—p. 4
Owners' equity—p. 5
Total equities equal total liabilities plus owners' equities—pp. 4, 5
Stockholders' equity—pp. 4, 5
Capital stock—pp. 1, 2, 5
Current ratio—p. 5
Receivables turnover—p. 5
Inventory turnover—p. 6
Net income (earnings)—pp. 5, 6
Income statement—p. 5

Earnings per share (EPS)—p. 5
Revenue—p. 6
Cost of goods sold—p. 6
Expense—p. 7
Retained earnings—pp. 5, 8
Statement of retained earnings—p. 8
Dividends—pp. 2, 8
Statement of changes in financial position—pp. 9, 10
Accounting—p. 13
Information system—p. 13
Information—p. 13
Managerial accounting—p. 15
Financial accounting—p. 15
General-purpose financial statements—p. 15
Public accounting—p. 16
Certified public accountant (CPA)—p. 16
Audit or attest function—p. 17
Audit report or opinion—p. 17

DEMONSTRATION PROBLEM FOR REVIEW AND SELF-STUDY   The following data are taken from the accounting records of Clifton Company at December 31, 19_1, the end of the company's first year of operations.

Capital stock	$?
Cash	33,000
Accounts receivable	20,000
Merchandise inventory—at cost	24,000
Land (long-term investment)	20,000
Sales	165,000
Cost of goods sold	90,000
Salaries expense	35,000
Rent expense	9,000
Miscellaneous expense	2,000
Accounts payable	16,000
Salaries payable	500
Dividends	1,500
Retained earnings—beginning of year	–0–

INSTRUCTIONS   Prepare the financial statements listed below for the year 19_1. Note that you will have to determine the amount for capital stock.

(a) Income statement.
(b) Statement of retained earnings.
(c) Statement of financial position (balance sheet).
(d) Statement of changes in financial position.

Note   Attempt to solve the demonstration problem before examining the solution that follows.

Solution:

(a)

CLIFTON COMPANY
Income Statement
For the Year Ended December 31, 19_1

Revenue:		
Sales		$165,000
Deduct expenses:		
Cost of goods sold	$90,000	
Salaries expense	35,000	
Rent expense	9,000	
Miscellaneous expense	2,000	136,000
Net income		$ 29,000

(b)

CLIFTON COMPANY
Statement of Retained Earnings
For the Year Ended December 31, 19_1

Retained earnings—beginning of year	$ –0–
Net income for 19_1	29,000
Total	$29,000
Deduct dividends	1,500
Retained earnings—end of year	$27,500

(c)

CLIFTON COMPANY
Balance Sheet
December 31, 19_1

Assets			Equities		
Current assets:			Current liabilities:		
Cash	$33,000		Accounts payable	$16,000	
Accounts receivable	20,000		Salaries payable	500	$16,500
Merchandise inventory—			Stockholders' equity:		
at cost	24,000	$77,000	Capital stock	$53,000[a]	
Long-term investment:			Retained earnings	27,500	80,500
Land		20,000			$97,000
		$97,000			

[a]$53,000 = $97,000 − $16,500 − $27,500

CLIFTON COMPANY
Statement of Changes in Financial Position
For the Year Ended December 31, 19_1

. . . .

Sources of financial resources:			
Cash provided from operations:			
Cash collected from customers			
($165,000 − $20,000)		$145,000	
Cash paid for inventory purchases			
($24,000 + 90,000 − $16,000)	$98,000		
Salaries paid ($35,000 − $500)	34,500		
Rent paid	9,000		
Other expenses paid	2,000	143,500	
Cash provided from operations for period		$ 1,500	
Cash provided from other sources:			
Issuance of capital stock		53,000	
Total financial resources provided for period			$ 54,500
Uses of financial resources:			
Cash applied:			
Purchase of land		$ 20,000	
Dividends paid		1,500	
Total financial resources used for period			21,500
Increase in cash for period			$ 33,000

Questions

1   What are the four basic financial statements?
2   What are *assets?* What are *liabilities?*
3   What is *owners' equity?* Why is owners' equity a residual claim?
4   What is the basic accounting equation for the statement of financial position?
5   What types of information does the statement of changes in financial position communicate to the user?
6   Why are not *all* asset inflows to the firm classified as revenue?
7   What is the general purpose of an accounting system?
8   What is the distinction between internal users and external users of accounting information?
9   What does the term *general-purpose financial statements* mean?
10 What are the three primary functions of the certified public accountant?
11 Why is public accounting classified as a profession?
12 What are four reasons why assets may provide future economic benefits?
13 What constitutes an indication of "slow-moving" merchandise?
14 Can you state in general equation form the income statement and the statement of retained earnings?

Short exercises

E1-1

You are given below three multiple-choice statements. Select the correct answers and indicate the corresponding letters on a sheet of paper (e.g., 1-a, 2-a, etc.).

(1)   Which of the following is *not* an asset? (a) cash, (b) equipment, (c) capital stock, (d) none of the above.

(2)   If the assets of a business consist of accounts receivable of $8,000 and inventory of $15,000, and if equities consist of capital stock of $4,000 and salaries payable of $6,000, then stockholders' equity is equal to (a) $17,000, (b) $11,000, (c) $5,000, (d) $19,000, (e) none of the above.

(3)   Retained earnings (a) usually equals owners' equity, (b) equals accumulated net income up to the present date, (c) equals accumulated net income minus any net losses, (d) equals accumulated net income minus any net losses minus any dividends and plus or minus any prior-period adjustments, (e) none of the above.

E1-2

You are given three multiple-choice statements. Select the correct answers and indicate the corresponding letter on a separate sheet of paper (e.g., 1-a, 2-a, etc.).

(1)   Which of the following is correct? (a) The market price of a share of stock is usually equal to the earnings per share of the stock. (b) The information referred to as managerial accounting is

usually available to external users. (c) The income statement shows the amount of net income generated over a specific time interval. (d) The statement of retained earnings is a mandatory part of a firm's financial statements. (e) None of the above.

(2) Which of the following is correct with regard to public accountants? (a) Their fees are paid by the state in which they practice. (b) They are independent of their clients. (c) They are not professionally liable to third parties who rely on their information. (d) They must always give an unqualified audit opinion. (e) None of the above.

(3) If one wishes to appraise a company's financial health, one (a) should be concerned only with the balance-sheet ratios, (b) should be concerned only with the EPS, (c) should ignore the auditor's opinion, (d) should be interested in the information gained by analysis of all the financial statements, (e) none of the above.

E1-3

You are given below three multiple-choice statements. Select the correct answers and indicate the corresponding letters on a separate sheet of paper (e.g., 1-a, 2-a, etc.).

(1) Which of the following is *not* an expense? (a) interest, (b) income taxes payable, (c) cost of goods sold, (d) rent, (e) none of the above.

(2) Owners' equity is the sum of (a) capital stock and revenues, (b) assets and liabilities, (c) capital stock and retained earnings, (d) assets and retained earnings, (e) none of the above.

(3) Net income consists of (a) sales minus cost of goods sold, (b) earnings minus total operating expenses, (c) revenues minus the sum of total expenses plus dividends, (d) expenses minus revenues, (e) none of the above.

E1-4

What is wrong with the following income statement?

RIFF CORPORATION

Revenue:		
Sales of merchandise		$25,000
Deduct expenses:		
Cost of goods sold	$20,000	
Salaries expense	4,000	
Rent expense	2,000	26,000
Net income		$ 1,000

E1-5

The following data for the year 19_7 are from the records of Planter Company. Determine the total revenue for the year.

Dividends	$ 12,000
Net income	$ 15,000
Plant and equipment	$250,000
Expenses	$ 30,000

E1-6

Fill in the missing figures in each column (1) through (6).

	(1)	(2)
Retained earnings—beginning of year	$ –0–	$?
Net income	10,000	25,000
Total	$?	$?
Deduct dividends	?	10,000
Retained earnings—end of year	$ 6,000	$ 20,000

		(3)		(4)
Sales of merchandise		$ 50,000		$?
Deduct operating expenses				
Cost of goods sold	$21,000		$75,000	
Salaries	?		10,000	
Rent	6,000		?	
Other	2,000	?	5,000	100,000
Net income		$ 12,000		$ 18,000

	(5)	(6)
Assets		
Cash	$ 10,000	$ 8,000
Accounts receivable	25,000	?
Building	?	20,000
Land	50,000	30,000
Total assets	$100,000	$?
Equities		
Accounts payable	$?	$ 10,000
Salaries payable	15,000	?
Capital stock	45,000	30,000
Retained earnings	20,000	25,000
Total equities	$?	$ 80,000

Problems

A1-1

Prepare the statement of financial position (balance sheet) for Law Corporation. The account balances are correct as of December 31, 19_7.

Cash	$ 4,000
Accounts receivable	13,000
Merchandise inventory—at cost	20,000
Taxes payable	15,000
Retained earnings	10,000
Accounts payable	7,000
Capital stock	5,000

A1-2

Given the following information for Del Company, determine sales and net income for the year ended December 31, 19_3.

Cash	$ 6,000
Rent	3,000
Salaries	4,000
Notes payable	12,000
Merchandise inventory	41,000
Cost of goods sold	33,000
Other expenses	5,000

A1-3
Prepare the income statement, the statement of retained earnings, and the statement of financial position (balance sheet) from the following data of the Paper Company. All data relate to the year ended December 31, 19_5.

Retained earnings—beginning of the year	$ 2,000
Accounts receivable	10,000
Sales of merchandise	80,000
Capital stock	15,000
Rent payable	3,000
Cost of goods sold	50,000
Rent expense	5,000
Merchandise inventory	14,000
Dividends	10,000
Accounts payable	15,000
Repair expense	4,000
Salaries	5,000
Cash	17,000

A1-4
Prepare the 19_2 statement of changes in financial position from the information presented below for Manual Company.

Cash collected from customers	$58,000
Cash paid for inventory purchases	23,000
Salaries paid by cash	10,000
Rent paid by cash	3,000
Other expenses paid by cash	1,000
Purchase of land for cash	5,000
Dividends paid by cash	3,000

A1-5
Although the dollar amounts of the individual accounts are correct, they have not been assembled correctly in the following balance sheet. Prepare a corrected balance sheet.

ECONOMIC COMPANY

Assets			Equities		
Current assets:			Current liabilities:		
Cash	$13,000		Accounts receivable	$ 9,000	
Accounts payable	11,000		Rent payable	2,000	
Merchandise inventory	20,000		Cost of goods sold	17,000	$28,000
Dividends	10,000	$54,000			
Long-term investment:			Stockholders' equity:		
Advertising expense		7,000	Capital stock	$13,000	
			Retained earnings—		
			end of 19_9	16,000	29,000
		$61,000			$57,000

A1-6
Using the following information covering the first year of operations of Omega Corporation, prepare an income statement, statement of retained earnings, and balance sheet for 19_1.

Accounts receivable	$ 40,000
Total assets	260,000
Cash	20,000
Advertising expense	10,000
Sales	150,000

(continued on next page)

Gross margin (sales minus cost of goods sold)	70,000
Accounts payable	?
Capital stock	?
Inventory	40,000
Land	60,000
Dividends	15,000
Salaries	30,000
Patents	20,000
Equipment	?
Owners' equity	200,000
Rent	10,000
Salaries payable	5,000

B1-1

Using the following data, prepare the income statement of Tobacco Company. The data relate to the year ended December 31, 19_4.

Cash	$ 8,000
Sales of merchandise	25,000
Accounts payable	6,000
Dividends	10,000
Cost of goods sold	12,000
Salaries	5,000
Rent	2,000

B1-2

Given the following information for Dole Company, determine the figure for stockholders' equity and for retained earnings. All data relate to the ending account balances on December 31, 19_6.

Cash	$ 5,000
Capital stock	20,000
Accounts payable	8,000
Land	25,000
Patents	15,000
Taxes payable	12,000
Notes payable	10,000
Merchandise inventory	13,000
Building	20,000
Retained earnings	?

B1-3

The following data for the Tape Company relate to the year ended December 31, 19_7. Prepare the income statement, statement of retained earnings, and balance sheet.

Capital stock	$?
Cash	2,000
Accounts receivable	5,500
Merchandise inventory	11,000
Land	5,000
Sales	50,000
Cost of goods sold	31,000
Salaries expense	11,000
Rent expense	4,500
Miscellaneous expense	1,000
Accounts payable	1,500
Salaries payable	250
Dividends paid	750
Retained earnings—beginning of the year	–0–

B1-4   *Prepare the 19_3 statement of changes in financial position from the information presented below for the Riff Corporation.*

Purchase of building for cash	$15,000
Dividends paid by cash	6,000
Cash collected from customers	40,000
Cash paid for inventory purchases	15,000
Expenses paid by cash	4,000

B1-5   *Using the following information covering the first year of operations of Sail Company, prepare an income statement, statement of retained earnings, and balance sheet for 19_7.*

Cash	$ 8,000
Total equities	120,000
Advertising expense	2,000
Rent	?
Building	80,000
Land	15,000
Accounts receivable	?
Net income for 19_7	20,000
Sales	60,000
Dividends	5,000
Cost of goods sold	?
Gross margin (sales minus cost of goods sold)	30,000
Accounts payable	15,000
Capital stock	?
Salaries	6,000
Inventory	10,000

B1-6   *Some mistakes were made in the preparation of the following balance sheet. Prepare a corrected balance sheet. Assume that all account balances are correct.*

STEAM CORPORATION
Balance Sheet
For the Year Ended December 31, 19_3

Assets			Equities		
Current assets:			Current liabilities:		
Cash	$28,000		Accounts payable	$ 20,000	
Accounts receivable	20,000		Rent expense	2,000	
			Cost of goods sold	30,000	$ 52,000
Sales	60,000				
Dividends	10,000	$118,000			
Other assets:			Stockholders' equity:		
Building	$50,000		Capital stock	$100,000	
Land	40,000		Retained earnings—		
			end of 19_3	68,000	168,000
Equipment	50,000	140,000			
		$258,000			$220,000

INTRODUCTION TO FINANCIAL ACCOUNTING THEORY
CHAPTER 2

PURPOSE OF CHAPTER   The preceding chapter illustrated and discussed the general-purpose financial statements which are the end product of the accountant's work. This chapter discusses the nature and role of the "generally accepted accounting principles" which provide the basic theoretical structure of financial accounting. The chapter also introduces the subject of transaction analysis which involves the analysis of business transactions in order to identify their impact on the basic accounting equation and ultimately on the general-purpose financial statements.

ACCOUNTING THEORY   In any field of thought, such as accounting, a theoretical structure is needed to unify the underlying logic or system of reasoning. A theoretical structure provides a frame of reference that gives meaning to and justification for the concepts and procedures identified with a given subject matter area. Thus the manner in which accountants identify, record, classify, and summarize economic data in a form suitable for reporting and interpreting the resulting economic information is given meaning and is explained by financial accounting theory.

   Note, however, that the type of accounting theory that we are concerned with in this book is descriptive financial accounting theory. Such theory explains how economic information is developed and communicated; hence, it provides the framework or structure of existing financial accounting practice. This structure consists of accounting objectives, principles, assumptions, doctrines, and procedures.

ACCOUNTING OBJECTIVES   As discussed in Chapter 1, the basic objective of accounting is to provide useful economic information to aid in making financial decisions. This objective is met in financial accounting by providing general-purpose financial statements that communicate relevant economic information to decision makers.

GENERALLY ACCEPTED ACCOUNTING PRINCIPLES (GAAP)   *Need for principles*   Financial statements provide the means by which management reports on its accountability to stockholders, potential investors, creditors, and the public at large. It is this accountability function that creates the clearest need for accounting principles. The accountant must have some principles or guidelines for a task of such dimensions as that of accounting to outsiders. Unless there exist some generally accepted principles on the nature and measurement of assets, liabilities, revenues, and expenses and on standards of disclosure and reporting, there can be no widespread understanding of and reliance on financial statements. Moreover, financial statements prepared in conformity with generally accepted principles result in statements that can be reasonably compared among firms and among current and prior years' statements. The necessity of some common agreement on accounting principles becomes apparent when we contemplate the chaos that would prevail if each business developed and followed its own accounting principles. Users of financial statements would have to adjust to the peculiarities of each company's accounting principles, and comparability would be nearly impossible.

Meaning of principles   *Accounting principles are general guidelines used in financial accounting practice to serve as a basis for financial reporting.* Because the term principle does not mean a fundamental truth or proposition in accounting, accounting principles are not a body of basic laws similar to those found in the natural sciences. Moreover, as general guides to action, accounting principles do not represent a single detailed set of rules prescribing exactly how each company should record and report its economic activities.

Accounting principles are made by humans and are not rigid. They have evolved from financial accounting practice and are not deduced from basic axioms as in the natural sciences. As problems arose in financial reporting, practices were formulated as solutions and were either rejected, modified, or accepted by the accounting profession. As such practices became widely used by the accounting profession, they were elevated to the status of generally accepted accounting principles (GAAP). As time passed, some accounting principles lost the support of the accounting profession and were eliminated from the status of GAAP. This evolutionary process continues today and is going on continuously.

Authoritative support for principles   The term *principles* is generally modified by the terms generally accepted (that is, generally accepted accounting principles) in order to convey the substantial authoritative support behind them. The most influential support in this country has come from the following authoritative groups:

American Institute of Certified Public Accountants (AICPA): The national professional organization of the practicing certified public accountant. Through its publications and committees the AICPA has been most instrumental in the development of accounting principles. Also, as a professional organization it has the power to implement principles if general agreement is reached among its members with regard to GAAP.

Securities and Exchange Commission (SEC): An agency of the federal government that regulates the financial reporting of publicly held corporations (those whose stock is traded on an organized stock exchange). Such corporations must file with the SEC annual audited financial statements that are acceptable to the Commission. Because the Commission has the authority not to accept the financial statements of publicly held corporations, it has exerted tremendous influence on GAAP.

American Accounting Association (AAA): An academic organization of accounting professors and practicing accountants that encourages and sponsors accounting research. This organization has influenced accounting principles through its scholarly publications.

Accounting principles are the broad guidelines of financial reporting that have been developed and accepted by the accounting profession. They serve as the basis for the independent CPA's audit of financial statements, which adds credibility to the statements by assuring statement users that they have been prepared in conformity with such principles.

Sources of principles Despite the relatively long-time recognition of GAAP by business, courts of law, government, and professional accountants, there does not exist a complete codified list of GAAP. Instead, the most authoritative sources of GAAP are the Statements of the Financial Accounting Standards Board (FASB), the Opinions of the Accounting Principles Board (APB), as modified by the FASB Statements, and the Accounting Research Bulletins of the Committee on Accounting Procedure, as modified by the APB Opinions. The Committee on Accounting Procedure and its successor, the Accounting Principles Board, were established by the AICPA, but they are no longer in existence. The FASB, which replaced the APB, began operating in 1973 as an independent organization to develop and issue Statements of Financial Accounting Standards, which represent expressions of GAAP.

ACCOUNTING ASSUMPTIONS Accounting operates in an economic environment in which uncertainty is an element. Complete or perfect knowledge cannot exist when there is uncertainty; therefore, we must make assumptions when building a theoretical structure for accounting. Assumptions are made to fill the unknowns in knowledge. Then the assumptions plus observable facts are woven together to form the theoretical structure. Thus assumptions are the "givens" that are taken for granted in order that conclusions can be reached despite unavoidable gaps in our knowledge. They are the "building blocks" in the construction of theory. Consequently, to understand accounting and the theory associated therewith, the student must be aware of the following underlying assumptions.

Specific separate-entity assumptions In order to prepare financial statements, the accountant must know the specific unit (entity) to be accounted for. The accountant assumes that the financial statements relate to a specific accounting entity. An accounting entity is a specific unit carrying out economic activity for which an accounting is desired. The accounting entity can be the nation as a whole, the state of Kansas, a business firm, a specific department of a business firm, or a specific person. However, in financial accounting, with its emphasis on external reporting, the specific business firm is considered to be a separate and distinct accounting entity. The accountant identifies, records, classifies, and reports the financial data of business firms separate and distinct from other entities and from the owners, managers, and employees who constitute the firm. In other words, the accountant is accounting for the financial affairs of a specific business firm, not the personal financial transactions of those who make up the firm and not the financial affairs of other business firms or entities.

Going-concern (continuity) assumption Unless there is specific evidence to the contrary, the accountant assumes that the entity will continue in business long enough to complete current plans and fulfill existing commitments. The going-concern assumption removes a liquidation viewpoint from the preparation of the financial statements. In preparing financial statements the accountant ignores the liquidating prices of assets, as well as the resulting losses based on liquidating prices, and ignores the amounts of liabilities payable immediately if the business ceased operations. In the normal situation, financial statements based on liquidating prices would not provide relevant information useful for financial decision making. On the other hand, if the accountant has evidence that the firm will be liquidated, then the going-concern assumption is abandoned and normal financial statements are not prepared.

Money-measuring-unit assumption Accountants assume that the monetary unit, which in the United States is the dollar, is the best measuring unit for purposes of financial reporting. This means that accountants identify, record, classify, report, and interpret only that economic information that is quantifiable in terms of money. Money is the standard unit of measurement in the accounting process.

By using money as the standard measuring unit, accountants are assuming that if business activities cannot be measured in terms of money, they are too subjective to measure and report. The financial statements do not provide a complete picture of the business entity because they omit such qualitative information as the threat of an impending strike, the health of its top executives, the state of its personnel relations, the firm's position on racial discrimination and ecology, the quality of its products relative to competing products, and the like. However, such information is sometimes reported in the notes accompanying the financial statements.

Also, by using money as the basic measuring unit, accountants are assuming that money is a stable measuring unit. Ideally, the dimensions or "size" of whatever is adopted as a unit of measurement should remain constant over time. The distance of an inch or the weight of an ounce or the general purchasing power (the ability to command goods and services in general) of the dollar, to cite three familiar measuring units, should remain constant. In fact, the purchasing power of the dollar varies over time because of changes in the general-price level (average price of all goods and services). During periods of inflation (a rise in the general-price level), the general purchasing power of the dollar decreases, and during periods of deflation (a fall in the general-price level), it increases. Accountants assume that such fluctuations in the general purchasing power of money will be immaterial or inconsequential; hence, in effect, accountants use the dollar as though it were a stable unit of measurement.

During recent years the purchasing power or size of the dollar has declined considerably. Accounting makes no allowance for such a change; it treats all dollars as though they were of equal size. Such accounting could result in misleading information being set forth in the financial statements. For example, assume that a company paid $10,000 for land in 1972 and paid another $10,000 for land in 1977. Assuming that the company continues to hold the land, the balance sheet would report land at $20,000. However, the $20,000 does not represent dollars of current general purchasing power because the purchasing power of the dollar declined approximately 29 per cent during the 1972–1977 period. The company did not make two equal investments in land in terms of general purchasing power invested, since 1972 dollars are not the same as 1977 dollars; yet the two are added together and are reported as if they were the same size.

Some accountants, dissatisfied with the stable-dollar assumption, have advocated that the various-sized dollars shown in the financial statements be converted to current-sized dollars. After conversion, each dollar shown in such modified financial statements would represent the same amount of purchasing power. All of the dollars shown in financial statements would be the "same-size" dollars. More attention will be given to this important matter in a later chapter.

Historical-cost assumption Valuation in accounting is the quantification of, and the changes in, assets and liabilities expressed in terms of the money-measuring unit. In other words, valuation is the assigning of dollar amounts to assets and liabilities. Other than for such assets as cash, marketable securities, and receivables, accountants assume that the cash or cash equivalent to acquire assets (their acquisition cost) is the proper valuation of assets at the time of acquisition and the proper basis for subsequent allocation of cost to expense as the assets expire.[1] For example, when a company buys equipment, the accountant records the equipment at original cost (including costs of putting it in workable condition) and then assigns part of the original (historical) cost to expense each year as the equipment is used. For purposes of balance-sheet reporting, the equipment is reported at historical (original) cost minus that part of the cost that has been assigned to expense. The difference is called the *book amount* (value). Note that the equipment is reported at book amount regardless of its fair market value (selling price currently obtainable in the market).

At the time an asset is acquired, its acquisition cost does represent the fair market value of the assets exchanged, as evidenced by a bargained exchange between an informed buyer and seller. As time passes, however, the fair market value of such assets as land, building, equipment, and inventory is likely to be different from their historical cost. Thus accountants ignore changes in the selling price of such assets and continue to report them on the balance sheet at book amount, which is based on historical cost.

Accountants justify the historical-cost assumption, as well as the rejection of current market values, on the basis of the objectivity of past purchase prices. It is argued that cost is objectively determined in the marketplace by an actual completed transaction representing a bargained exchange between a rational buyer and seller. Moreover, such a cost is verifiable by other accountants. Financial statements based on such objective evidence as historical cost are thought to provide the means for maintaining user confidence in the statements, for holding management accountable for the economic resources entrusted to them by stockholders and creditors, and for reducing the risk of lawsuits charging that the statements are misleading.

It should be pointed out, however, that the use of historical cost for the money measurement of assets is controversial. For example, it can be argued that by using historical cost, accountants are trading relevancy for objectivity, since old purchase prices are not relevant to current financial decisions.

---

[1]The allocation of an asset's cost to expense will be fully explained later.

Fiscal-period (periodicity) assumption   The demand for timely economic information that is useful for financial decision making causes the accountant to choose a convenient accounting (fiscal) period, usually a year, over which to measure net income (reported in the income statement) and the changes in financial position (reported in the statement of changes in financial position) and at the end of which to measure financial position (reported in the balance sheet). In other words, management, investors, creditors, and other interested parties want economic information at frequent points in time, and they especially want to know the firm's periodic economic progress or net income.

The dividing of the economic activity of a business firm into short time periods to provide timely information is an assumption, since business activity does not stop and start as one accounting period ends and another period begins. In effect, it is an assumption that business activity "stops" at periodic intervals to allow the preparation of financial statements—the fiscal-period assumption. Therefore, accounting information associated with fiscal periods, especially net income, should be considered short-run approximations or estimates of a firm's progress and position.

Revenue-recognition assumption   When should revenue be recognized for recording and reporting purposes and thereby be included in the income statement for the fiscal period? Accountants assume that revenue should be recognized during the period in which it is earned, which is the point (date) of sale when goods are delivered or services are rendered to the customer. In other words, revenue is recognized during the period in which the sale of goods or the rendering of services is completed. The income statement includes only those revenues earned during the current period, and it excludes any prior or subsequent period revenue.

The recognition of revenue at a single point in time (the date of sale) is an assumption because the earning of revenue is really an economic process that consists of such activities as selling, financing, purchasing, manufacturing, and distribution. The accountant assumes that the critical event in the recognition of revenue is the point of sale and that such recognition results in providing useful information in the income statement.

Matching assumption   When should expense be recognized for recording and reporting purposes and thereby be included in the income statement? Accountants assume that expense should be recognized during the period in which goods or services are used in the generation of revenue. The expense incurred in generating revenue should be identified (matched) with that revenue and reported in the period in which the revenue is reported. Note that revenue is recognized for the period based on the revenue-recognition assumption, and then expenses are matched with the revenue, not the other way around.

Matching is an assumption because not all expenses can be *directly* matched with the product sold or the services rendered (that is, the resulting revenue). As will be explained in Chapter 4, the impossibility of directly matching all expenses with revenue causes the accountant to do some *indirect* matching in which expense is recognized in the time period incurred.

ACCOUNTING DOCTRINES   Accounting doctrines are normative (should be) attitudes or ideas of the accounting profession as to what ought to represent good accounting practice. They are ethical ideas that reflect the collective judgment of the accounting profession. Accountants believe that adherence to these normative ideas contributes to the usefulness of accounting data. Accounting doctrines include such quality considerations as materiality, consistency, comparability, objectivity, and conservatism.

Materiality   Accountants should report economic items or events only if there is a reasonable expectation that knowledge of them would affect the decisions of reasonable statement users. Materiality refers to the relative importance or significance of an economic item or event. Trivial or insignificant items should not be reported, even if they follow strict accounting theory, because their reporting cost outweighs the usefulness of the resulting information. For example, in theory, pencils should be reported as an asset at cost, with part of the cost assigned to expense as they are used. Based on materiality, in practice, pencils are expensed when they are acquired.

Consistency   Accountants should normally use the same accounting procedures from one period to the next for a particular business firm—consistency of procedures. Accountants should not change accounting procedures from period to period because successive financial statements would not be comparable, manipulation of the financial statements would be possible, and the statements could be misleading in that the effects of changes in procedures could be interpreted as real changes in business conditions or management effectiveness. This is not to say that there cannot be changes in accounting procedures; changes are allowed if they are properly disclosed, but continual changes from year to year are not allowed.

Comparability   Accountants should use similar accounting principles and procedures in preparing the financial statements of different firms, especially firms that are in the same industry. The financial statements of different firms should be based on similar accounting principles and procedures in order to aid statement users in making comparisons among firms for financial decision making. However, this doctrine does not imply strict uniformity in principles and procedures, but rather enough similarity for meaningful comparisons to be made.

Objectivity   The accountant's measurement of economic transactions and events should be unbiased and subject to independent verification by other accountants in order to provide convincing support for the dollar amounts shown in the financial statements. Measurements are objective if several competent accountants making the same measurements would reach substantially the same results based on an examination of the same evidence. The evidence used to support the measurements include legal contracts, bills of sale, canceled checks, employee time cards, physical counts of inventory, and the like. Although it is neither desirable nor possible to remove judgment and opinion from the accounting process, the best evidence in the eyes of the accountant is that which is least influenced by personal opinion and judgment—measurement based on verifiable evidence.

Conservatism   When matters of judgment or opinion are involved, the accountant should proceed with caution and not be too optimistic. Conservatism means that when in doubt about selecting an accounting procedure among several reasonable alternatives, the accountant should select that procedure that is least optimistic with regard to its immediate effect on owners' equity. Although in theory conservatism is not a virtue, it nevertheless plays an important role in existing accounting practice, as will be discussed later.

ACCOUNTING PROCEDURES   Accounting procedures are the specific methods used by accounting in carrying out the general guidelines provided by generally accepted accounting principles (GAAP). Procedures are adopted to apply principles and are the detailed methods, rules, or mechanics used by accountants in their daily work.

It should be pointed out that accounting procedures are diverse. That is to say, there are several acceptable accounting procedures for applying a generally accepted accounting principle. For example, there are several acceptable procedures for the costing of inventory and for assigning the cost of long-lived assets to expense.

Finally, in actual accounting practice GAAP are viewed as including both acceptable general accounting guidelines and acceptable accounting procedures. In other words, accountants often use the terms "principles" and "procedures" more or less interchangeably. Such usage may be the result of carelessness; it also indicates, however, that sometimes it is difficult to sort out and identify the procedural aspect of an accounting principle. In this book GAAP mean acceptable general guidelines and are distinguished from the carrying out of the guidelines by means of specific accounting procedures.

THE ACCOUNTING PROCESS   Accounting is an economic information system, and the theory or framework underlying the existing information system (existing accounting practice) has been described in the preceding pages of this chapter. The system involves the transformation of the economic data of an entity into economic information. The transforming or processing of economic data into economic information is referred to as the *accounting process.* The accounting process is the (1) recording of economic data in the form of transactions (defined and explained below) for the period (including identifying, collecting, analyzing, and measuring the transactions), (2) classifying and summarizing the economic data at the end of the period, and (3) reporting and interpreting the resulting economic information in the form of periodic financial statements.

TRANSACTIONS   The economic events that are recorded in the accounting process are called *transactions.* They are the basic economic data or input into the accounting information system. Transactions are defined as economic events that result in changes to the assets and/or equities of an entity. Transactions are conveniently classified as follows:

External transactions, which are the increases and decreases in the assets and/or equities of a business firm arising from transfers of assets and equities to or from the firm with those outside the firm (external exchanges). Examples include the issuance of capital stock, sales, purchase of merchandise, borrowing money, and buying equipment.

Internal transactions, which are the increases and decreases in the assets and/or equities of a business firm arising from internal asset usage and conversion and internal accounting adjustments. Examples include the assignment of the cost of long-lived assets to expense and the expiration or "using up" of prepaid insurance (insurance premiums paid before the expense is incurred). Internal transactions will be explained more fully later in the text.

THE ACCOUNTING EQUATION   In Chapter 1 the balance sheet (position statement) of Sight & Sound Corporation was illustrated and discussed. It was pointed out (page 3) that the total resources owned by the firm (assets) are equal to the total claims against those resources (equities), or

Assets = Equities

The equality holds because assets and equities are merely two views of the same resources: a listing of the resources owned and a listing of the claims against those resources. Furthermore, since the equity claims indicate the sources of a firm's assets, total sources have to equal total assets and, therefore, total assets have to equal total equities. Finally, total equities consist of liabilities (creditor claims or creditor sources) and owners' equity (owners' residual claims or owners' sources). Owners' equity for a corporation consists of capital stock (stockholders' investment source) and retained earnings (profitable operations source); hence, the basic equation can be expanded as follows:

Assets = Equities
   = Liabilities + Owners' equity
   = Liabilities + Capital stock + Retained earnings

Transactions affect the basic accounting equation because they result in increases and decreases in the assets and equities. Each transaction has a *dual economic effect* (affects at least two items or has two sides) that maintains the equality between total assets and total equities after each transaction. For example, if equipment costing $8,000 is purchased on credit by issuing a note, then both assets (equipment) and liabilities (notes payable) are increased $8,000, and total assets continue to equal total equities. Similarly, if a company invests some idle cash in short-term government securities in the amount of $11,000, then assets increase (marketable securities) and decrease (cash) by $11,000, and the equality of total assets and total equities is maintained by the offsetting increase and decrease in assets.

Because every accounting transaction can be expressed in terms of its effect on the accounting equation, transactions can be analyzed by using the equation. The basic accounting equation facilitates the accounting process because it provides a model for processing economic data in the form of transactions. Moreover, the accounting process of recording, analyzing, and classifying ongoing transactions is done in accordance with financial accounting theory—in conformity with GAAP and their underlying assumptions, objectives, and doctrines.

TRANSACTION ANALYSIS   As implied by the preceding discussion, transaction analysis is the analysis of each transaction to determine how it affects the basic accounting equation, that is, how it affects assets and equities. Whether the system that processes transactions is manual (handwritten), mechanical (accounting machines

and punched-card equipment) or electronic (computerized), the analysis of transactions by means of the basic accounting equation is done by accountants during
the fiscal period and financial statements are prepared at the end of the period.

For purposes of learning about the accounting process and the resulting financial
statements, we now turn to an analysis of the cumulative effect of transactions
on total assets and equities one at a time. This is demonstrated by noting the
effects of the transactions of Sight & Sound Corporation during its first year of
operations (19_1), which resulted in the financial statements illustrated and discussed in Chapter 1, as follows:

19_1 Transactions

(1) Issued capital stock for cash, $25,000.
     Result: The corporation acquired $25,000 cash, which was an asset, and in exchange issued
             capital stock, which resulted in $25,000 of stockholders' equity.

	Assets	= Equities
Before	$ –0–	$ –0–
Changes	+25,000	+25,000
After	$25,000	$25,000

(2) Purchased land as a long-term investment for $10,000 cash.
     Result: The asset cash was decreased $10,000, but the decrease was offset by the new
             asset, land.

	Assets	= Equities
Before	$25,000	$25,000
Changes	–10,000	
	+10,000	
After	$25,000	$25,000

(3) Purchased merchandise on account (on credit, cash not paid), $60,000.
     Result: An asset, merchandise inventory, was acquired, and a liability, called accounts payable,
             was incurred in the amount of $60,000.

	Assets	= Equities
Before	$25,000	$25,000
Changes	+60,000	+60,000
After	$85,000	$85,000

(4a) Made sales of merchandise on account (on credit, cash not received) for $81,000.
     Note: Sales are revenue transactions; revenues *increase* retained earnings, which are part
             of the stockholders' equity.
     Result: An asset, accounts receivable, was acquired, and the revenue increased retained earn-
             ings by $81,000.

	Assets	= Equities
Before	$ 85,000	$ 85,000
Changes	+81,000	+81,000
After	$166,000	$166,000

(4b) The merchandise sold and delivered to the customers from the company's inventory cost the company $48,000.

Note: The cost of the merchandise sold is an expense called cost of goods sold; expenses *decrease* retained earnings, which are part of the stockholders' equity.

Result: The asset merchandise inventory was decreased $48,000, and the expense decreased the retained earnings by $48,000.

	Assets	= Equities
Before	$166,000	$166,000
Changes	−48,000	−48,000
After	$118,000	$118,000

(5) Collected $70,000 from customers who owed money to the company as a result of the sales made on account.

Result: The asset cash was increased $70,000, and the asset accounts receivable was decreased $70,000.

	Assets	= Equities
Before	$118,000	$118,000
Changes	+70,000	
	−70,000	
After	$118,000	$118,000

(6) Paid $40,000 on the amount owing as a result of the merchandise purchases made on account.

Result: The asset cash was decreased $40,000, and the liability accounts payable was decreased $40,000.

	Assets	= Equities
Before	$118,000	$118,000
Changes	−40,000	−40,000
After	$ 78,000	$ 78,000

(7) Paid rent for the year 19_1, $4,800.

Note: This is an expense transaction, rent expense, so retained earnings are reduced.

Result: The asset cash was decreased $4,800, and the expense decreased the retained earnings by $4,800.

	Assets	= Equities
Before	$78,000	$78,000
Changes	−4,800	−4,800
After	$73,200	$73,200

(8) Paid other (miscellaneous) expenses, $5,200.

Result: The asset cash was decreased $5,200, and the expense decreased the retained earnings by $5,200.

	Assets	= Equities
Before	$73,200	$73,200
Changes	−5,200	−5,200
After	$68,000	$68,000

(9) Employees' salaries amount to $1,500 per month, or $18,000 per annum. They are paid monthly on the first business day of the following month. For example, salaries for last January were paid on February 1. Thus salaries for the eleven months January through November have been paid by the disbursement of $16,500 cash, and salaries of $1,500 for December are owed as of December 31.

(a) Note: Salaries are an expense, called salaries expense.

Result: The $16,500 disbursement for salaries reduced the asset cash and the retained earnings.

	Assets	= Equities
Before	$68,000	$68,000
Changes	−16,500	−16,500
After	$51,500	$51,500

(b) Note: Salaries owed are a liability, called salaries payable.

Result: The $1,500 owed for December salaries increased the liabilities and decreased the retained earnings: thus one type of equity (liabilities) was increased and the other type of equity (stockholders' equity) was decreased.

	Assets	= Equities
Before	$51,500	$51,500
Changes		+1,500
		−1,500
After	$51,500	$51,500

Combined result: The expense for salaries for the year amounts to $18,000:

(a)	$16,500	(paid)
(b)	1,500	(owed)
	$18,000	

(10) The board of directors authorized the payment of $2,000 cash dividends.

Note: Dividends reduce the retained earnings but, as indicated earlier, they are not an expense.

Result: The asset cash was decreased $2,000, and the retained earnings were decreased $2,000.

	Assets	= Equities
Before	$51,500	$51,500
Changes	−2,000	−2,000
After	$49,500	$49,500

TRANSACTION WORKSHEET   The increases and decreases resulting from the 19_1 transactions, which have been analyzed in the preceding paragraphs, are noted in the transaction worksheet on page 40. The transaction worksheet is nothing more than the basic accounting equation

Assets = Equities

subdivided for the individual assets and equities, as follows:

Cash + Accounts receivable + Merchandise inventory + Land
= Accounts payable + Salaries payable + Capital stock + Retained earnings.

SIGHT & SOUND CORPORATION
Transaction Worksheet
Year 19_1

	Explanation	Assets				=	Equities						
											Retained Earnings		
		Cash +	Accounts Receivable +	Merchandise Inventory +	Land	=	Accounts Payable +	Salaries Payable +	Capital Stock +	+ Revenues	− Expenses	− Dividends	= Balance
	Beginning balances	-0-	-0-	-0-	-0-		-0-	-0-	-0-				-0-
(1)	Issued capital stock for cash	+25,000							+25,000				
(2)	Purchased land for cash	−10,000			+10,000								
(3)	Purchased merchandise on account			+60,000			+60,000						
(4a)	Sales on account		+81,000							+81,000			
(4b)	Cost of goods sold			−48,000							−48,000		
(5)	Cash receipts from customers	+70,000	−70,000										
(6)	Cash payments on account	−40,000					−40,000						
(7)	Paid rent	− 4,800									− 4,800		
(8)	Paid other expenses	− 5,200									− 5,200		
(9a)	Paid salaries expense	−16,500									−16,500		
(9b)	Liability for December salaries							+1,500			− 1,500		
(10)	Paid dividends	− 2,000										−2,000	
	Ending balances	16,500 +	11,000 +	12,000 +	10,000	=	20,000 +	1,500 +	25,000 +				3,000
		49,500				=	49,500						

FINANCIAL STATEMENTS FOR 19_1   Referring to the transaction worksheet, we can see that the revenues earned and the expenses incurred during the year were listed under Retained Earnings. Revenue and expense items can be thought of as subdivisions of retained earnings. One can, therefore, prepare the income statement for the year ended December 31, 19_1, by summarizing the changes affecting retained earnings caused by revenue and expense transactions. For example, compare the data under Retained Earnings in the transaction worksheet with the income statement on page 6 and the statement of retained earnings on page 8.

Similarly, the ending balances in the transaction worksheet provide the necessary data for the preparation of the balance sheet. Compare the ending balances in the transaction worksheet with the balance sheet on page 4.

Also, the data under the Cash column in the transaction worksheet show the changes in cash. The statement of changes in financial position can be prepared by summarizing these changes, as shown by the statement on page 9.

The agreement of the financial statements with the data accumulated in the transaction worksheet should be readily apparent. For example, the ending balance of the Cash column, $16,500, agrees with the cash balance shown in the balance sheet. Concerning the normal sequence associated with the accounting process, it is probably equally apparent that the data are recorded in accounting forms and records before the financial statements are prepared. In Chapter 1, however, the financial statements were presented first to help answer some of the questions raised by the hypothetical college student. Finally, it should also be apparent that the transaction worksheet is not the normal accounting record for processing economic data, since its use would be feasible in only the smallest of business firms having very few transactions. Instead, the transaction worksheet is used to learn about the accounting process without becoming entangled with the bookkeeping mechanics used in practice to record transactions.

CLASSIFIED BALANCE SHEET   The financial statements of many companies are widely circulated, often as a part of a published (that is, printed and distributed) annual report to stockholders. Stockholders, investors, banks, stockbrokers, investment analysts, and governmental agencies are frequent users of financial statements. Many concerned with business matters review and analyze a considerable number of financial statements in the regular course of their work. Consider the confusion and inconvenience that statement-users might suffer if every business followed its own preference concerning the form and content of financial statements.

To minimize the misunderstanding and annoyance that would be likely to prevail if no uniformity existed, accountants and businessmen have developed some classification and disclosure practices that have become rather widely used. Such practices are designed to aid users in understanding the financial statements, as well as providing more useful information. Their application to the balance sheet will be noted at this time.

The classifications used in a balance sheet depend upon the nature of the business, upon the kinds of assets held and liabilities owed, and upon the type of

business organization adopted. In general, the principal balance sheet categories
are

Assets:

Current assets
Long-term investments
Property, plant, and equipment
Intangible assets
Other assets

Equities:
Liabilities:
  Current
  Long-term
Stockholders' equity (This classification caption is used for corporations. Business operations also
                  may be conducted by an individual proprietorship or a partnership. Captions
                  for such alternative forms of organization will be introduced later.)

Current assets   Cash and other assets, such as temporary investments in securities,
accounts and notes receivable, inventory, supplies, and prepayments that presumably will be converted into cash, or will be used, or will expire during a normal
operating cycle. Such items are viewed as being indicative of short-term debt-paying
ability.

An operating cycle can be described as follows: Business operations consist
of a round of conversions—cash to inventories, to receivables, and back to cash;
the average time required to complete this round is an *operating cycle.* The time
period of an operating cycle depends on the nature of the business.

The current assets are customarily listed in the following order: Cash, short-
term holdings of marketable securities, receivables from customers, other receivables, inventories, supplies, and short-term prepayments. Short-term prepayments
are regarded as current assets because a company with, say, $18,000 of cash
and a $500 rent prepayment for one month is in essentially the same position
as a company with $18,500 of cash but faced with the necessity of immediately
spending $500 for rent.

Long-term investments   Investments other than those properly classifiable as current assets. Examples include investments in the capital stock of other companies
and in land held for resale.

Property, plant, and equipment   Land and depreciable property of a relatively long-
term nature used in the operations of the business and not intended for sale.
Examples are employee parking lots, buildings, machinery, furniture and fixtures,
office equipment, and delivery equipment. Such assets are customarily listed according to their use-life, assets with the longest use-life being listed first and
assets with the shortest use-life being listed last.

Intangible assets   Noncurrent assets lacking physical substance that have future
economic benefits because of the rights they afford the possessor. Examples are
patents, franchises, copyrights, and goodwill.

Other assets   Assets that cannot be reasonably classified in the preceding classifications. An example would be land held as a future building site.

Current liabilities   The debts or obligations that, according to reasonable expectations, are to be satisfied within the operating-cycle period (as described in connection with the discussion of current assets) or one year, whichever is longer. Examples of current liabilities include accounts payable, short-term notes payable, taxes payable, and advances from customers (discussed in Chapter 4). Advances from customers, which are to be earned by the future performance of services or future delivery of merchandise within the operating-cycle period, are properly classifiable as current liabilities, because the earning of such revenue normally requires the utilization of current assets and because they are short-term obligations for future performance or delivery.

The excess of the current assets over the current liabilities is called *working capital,* and the ratio of current assets to current liabilities is called the *current ratio.* Because current assets normally are used to pay the current liabilities, the relationship between current assets and current liabilities is indicative of the ability of the company to meet its short-term financial obligations. Thus a firm with $300,000 in current assets and $100,000 in current liabilities has a current ratio of 3 to 1, which indicates that its current assets could shrink two-thirds and still meet the current liabilities owed, other things being equal. For the purpose of financial analysis, the current ratio of a company should be compared with the current ratios of similar companies, and the trend of the current ratio over several years should be noted. Finally, a current ratio that looks very high may indicate that the company has too much of its money tied up in current assets.

Long-term liabilities   Bonds, mortgages, and other long-term financial obligations not classifiable as current liabilities.

Stockholders' equity   In accounting for the elements of stockholders' equity, the emphasis is placed on the *source:* How much of the stockholders' equity is traceable to

Investments by stockholders, shown as capital stock.[2]
Gifts—such as the gift of a plant to a company to induce it to locate in the donor city, shown as additional paid-in capital.
Earnings, shown as retained earnings.

Definitions and accounting procedures relating to the above balance sheet items will be developed in reasonable depth later in the text.

Alternative form for the balance sheet   A balance sheet customarily is prepared showing the assets at the left and the liabilities and stockholders' equity at the right. Such an arrangement is referred to as the account form.

[2]There are two classes of capital stock, preferred stock and common stock, each of which is reported separately in the balance sheet under stockholders' equity. Capital stock is discussed fully in Chapters 11 and 12.

If space limitations make it desirable, the liabilities and stockholders' equity may be presented below the assets. This arrangement is known as the report form, which is used in the following, more comprehensive illustration of a balance sheet.

HYPOTHETICAL COMPANY
Balance Sheet
December 31, 19_1

Assets:

Current assets:

Cash	$ 18,000	
Temporary investments in marketable securities, at cost		
(market $9,000)	8,000	
Accounts receivable	24,000	
Notes receivable	5,000	
Interest receivable	100	
Inventory, at cost	30,000	
Prepaid rent	500	
Prepaid insurance	400	$ 86,000

Long-term investments:

Land (held for sale)	$ 15,000	
Government bonds	12,000	27,000

Property, plant, and equipment:

Land—Parking lot		$ 25,000	
Buildings	$150,000		
Less accumulated depreciation	30,000	120,000	
Furniture and fixtures	$ 40,000		
Less accumulated depreciation	8,000	32,000	
Delivery equipment	$ 9,000		
Less accumulated depreciation	5,000	4,000	181,000

Intangible assets:

Patents	6,000
	$300,000

Equities:

Current liabilities:

Accounts payable	$ 15,000	
Notes payable	10,000	
Salaries payable	1,500	
Interest payable	300	
Estimated income tax payable	2,800	
Liability for payroll taxes	1,400	
Advances from customers	3,000	
Rent received in advance	1,000	$ 35,000

Long-term liability:

6% bank loan, due in five years	50,000

Stockholders' equity:

Capital stock—authorized, 10,000 shares; issued and			
outstanding, 6,000 shares	$120,000		
Additional paid-in capital	25,000	$145,000	
Retained earnings		70,000	215,000
			$300,000

DISCLOSURE MATTERS Financial statements are not limited to a listing of dollar amounts. They also include as an integral part of the statements the audit report (see page 17), a statement of accounting policies (the specific accounting principles and procedures used to present the financial statements), parenthetical comments, and notes to the financial statements. The latter would include such matters as follows:

> Contingent liabilities.
> Interest rates and maturity dates on long-term liabilities.
> Descriptive features of the company's capital stock.
> Matters concerning any litigation involving the company.
> Changes in accounting methods.
> Any limitation on the availability of retained earnings for dividends (for example, as a condition for a long-term loan, a bank may require that dividends in any year not exceed one-half of that year's net income).

No specific rules can be offered regarding what should be disclosed. No useful purpose would be served by the disclosure of insignificant information; on the other hand, a fair presentation of the financial position, changes in financial position, and results of operations rarely can be achieved by "bare-boned" financial statements. One criterion that has merit, although it does not eliminate the need for the use of judgment on the part of those preparing financial statements for circulation to stockholders, is that any factual information which, if known, could influence an investor's decision to hold or to sell a company's stock should be disclosed.

As a general rule, homework problems included in this book will not include the kind of informative material that would be shown in parenthetical comments or notes to the financial statements.

IMPORTANT TERMS AND CONCEPTS IN CHAPTER 2

Financial accounting theory—p. 28
Accounting objectives—p. 28
Generally accepted accounting principles (GAAP)—pp. 28, 29
American Institute of Certified Public Accountants (AICPA)—p. 29
Securities and Exchange Commission (SEC)—p. 29
Statements of the Financial Accounting Standards Board (FASB)—p. 30
Opinions of the Accounting Principles Board (APB)—p. 30
Accounting assumptions—p. 30
Specific-separate-entity assumption—p. 30
Going-concern assumption—p. 30
Money-measuring-unit assumption—p. 31
General purchasing power—pp. 31, 32
Valuation—p. 32

Historical-cost assumption—p. 32
Fiscal-period (periodicity) assumption—p. 33
Revenue-recognition assumption—p. 33
Earned revenue—p. 33
Matching assumption—p. 33
Incurred expense—p. 33
Direct and indirect matching—p. 33
Accounting doctrines—p. 34
Materiality—p. 34
Consistency—p. 34
Comparability—p. 34
Objectivity—p. 34
Conservatism—p. 35
Accounting procedures—p. 35
The accounting process—p. 35
Transactions—p. 35
External transactions—p. 35
Internal transactions—p. 36

DEMONSTRATION PROBLEM FOR REVIEW AND SELF-STUDY   The results of the 19_3 transactions of Renton Company are summarized below:

(1)   The company was organized and capital stock was issued for cash, $30,000.
(2)   Purchased merchandise for cash, $5,000.
(3a) Made cash sales, $6,000.
(3b) Cost of goods sold for cash, $4,000.
(4)   Purchased merchandise on account, $35,000.
(5)   Paid for advertising expenses, $800.
(6a) Made sales of merchandise on account, $36,000.
(6b) Cost of goods sold on account, $24,000.
(7)   Paid rent for the year, $2,400.
(8)   Cash payments for salaries, $8,000.
(9)   Cash receipts from customers, $31,000.
(10) Cash payments for merchandise purchased on account, $29,000.
(11) At year end securities were acquired as a long-term investment for a cash outlay of $10,000.
(12) At year end the company owed $700 for unpaid salaries.
(13) Paid cash dividends, $1,200.

INSTRUCTIONS

(a)   Prepare a transaction worksheet for the year.
(b)   Prepare the firm's income statement, statement of retained earnings, balance sheet, and statement of changes in financial position for the year.

Note   Attempt to solve the demonstration problem before examining the solution that follows.

Solution:
(a)

RENTON COMPANY
Transaction Worksheet
Year 19_3

Explanation	Cash +	Accounts Receivable +	Merchandise Inventory +	Securities =	Accounts Payable +	Salaries Payable +	Capital Stock +	Retained Earnings +Revenue	−Expenses	−Dividends	=Balance
(1) Issued capital stock for cash	+30,000						+30,000				
(2) Purchased merchandise for cash	− 5,000		+ 5,000								
(3a) Cash sales	+ 6,000							+ 6,000			
(3b) Cost of goods sold			− 4,000						− 4,000		
(4) Purchased merchandise on account			+35,000		+35,000						
(5) Advertising	− 800								− 800		
(6a) Sales on account		+36,000						+36,000			
(6b) Cost of goods sold			−24,000						−24,000		
(7) Rent for the year	− 2,400								− 2,400		
(8) Salaries	− 8,000								− 8,000		
(9) Cash receipts from customers	+31,000	−31,000									
(10) Cash payments for merchandise	−29,000				−29,000						
(11) Long-term investment in securities	−10,000			+10,000							
(12) Liability for salaries						+700			− 700		
(13) Cash dividends	− 1,200									− 1,200	
Ending balances	10,600 +	5,000 +	12,000 +	10,000 =	6,000 +	700 +	30,000 +				900

37,600 = 37,600

(b)

**RENTON COMPANY
Income Statement
For the Year Ended December 31, 19_3**

Revenue:		
Sales		$42,000
Deduct expenses:		
Cost of goods sold	$28,000	
Salaries expense	8,700	
Rent expense	2,400	
Advertising expense	800	39,900
Net income		$ 2,100

**RENTON COMPANY
Statement of Retained Earnings
For the Year Ended December 31, 19_3**

Retained earnings—beginning of year	$ –0–
Net income for 19_3	2,100
Total	$2,100
Deduct dividends	1,200
Retained earnings—end of year	$ 900

**RENTON COMPANY
Balance Sheet
December 31, 19_3**

Assets			Equities		
Current assets:			Current liabilities:		
Cash	$10,600		Accounts payable	$ 6,000	
Accounts receivable	5,000		Salaries payable	700	$ 6,700
Merchandise inventory	12,000	$27,600			
			Stockholders' equity:		
Long-term investment:			Capital stock	$30,000	
Securities		10,000	Retained earnings	900	30,900
		$37,600			$37,600

**RENTON COMPANY
Statement of Changes in Financial Position
For the Year Ended December 31, 19_3**

Sources of financial resources:			
Issuance of capital stock			$30,000
Total financial resources provided for period			$30,000
Uses of financial resources:			
Cash used in operations:			
Cash collected from customers ($6,000 + $31,000)		$37,000	
Cash paid for inventory purchases ($5,000 + $29,000)	$34,000		
Advertising paid	800		
Rent paid	2,400		
Salaries paid	8,000	45,200	
Cash used in operations for period		$ 8,200	
Other cash uses:			
Investment in securities	$10,000		
Dividends paid	1,200	11,200	
Total financial resources used for period			19,400
Increase in cash for period			$10,600

Questions

1 What purpose does accounting theory serve?
2 Why are accounting assumptions necessary for the construction of accounting theory?
3 How does the accountant use accounting principles? What is the origin of generally accepted accounting principles?
4 Does the specific-separate-entity assumption mean that accountants are concerned only with a specific business firm? Explain.
5 Does the balance sheet always show the fair market value of assets? Explain.
6 What disadvantages are inherent in using the dollar as a measuring unit?
7 Why is the fiscal-period assumption necessary?
8 Why is the use of historical cost for the money measurement of assets controversial?
9 What are accounting doctrines?
10 Does the doctrine of consistency mean that a firm's accounting procedures may not be changed?
11 What are business transactions?
12 Why are total assets shown on a balance sheet always equal to total equities?
13 Is it possible to have a business transaction that affects only one account?
14 If a transaction decreases stockholders' equity but does not affect any asset accounts, what change will occur in total liabilities?
15 What are the steps in the accounting process?

Short exercises

E2-1   *You are given below three multiple-choice statements. Select the correct answers and indicate the corresponding letters on a sheet of paper (e.g., 1-d, 2-d, etc.).*

(1) The revenue recognition assumption (a) determines which expenses should be matched against the fiscal-period revenues, (b) recognizes revenue that is not earned by sale of goods or rendering of services, (c) is not really an assumption because the customer usually pays cash at the point of sale, (d) states that the critical event for revenue recognition is the receipt of cash, (e) all of the above, (f) none of the above.

(2) The measure used to account for assets acquired by purchase is (a) cost, (b) market, (c) value, (d) either cost or value, whichever is more historical, (e) none of the above.

(3) Which of the following is correct? (a) Accounting principles are made by humans. (b) The accountant's measurement of economic transactions should be free from bias. (c) There usually is a trade-off between objectivity, usefulness, and feasibility when one applies accounting principles and procedures. (d) The matching assumption is fundamental to accrual accounting. (e) All of the above.

You are given below three multiple-choice statements. Select the correct answers and indicate the corresponding letters on a sheet of paper (e.g., 1-d, 2-d, etc.).

(1) Accounting assumptions are (a) general guidelines used in financial accounting practice, (b) normative attitudes of the accounting profession, (c) detailed methods used by accountants in their daily work, (d) generally accepted doctrines, (e) all of the above, (f) none of the above.

(2) The matching assumption means (a) that similar accounting principles should be used by firms in a particular industry so that their financial statements can be matched, (b) that the use of money as a measuring unit matches the expectations of statement users, (c) that historical cost matches the fair market value at the time of asset purchase, (d) that expenses used to generate revenue are matched during the same fiscal period to determine periodic retained earnings, (e) none of the above.

(3) Which of the following is *incorrect?* (a) The fiscal-period assumption implies that business activity stops at periodic intervals. (b) The consistency doctrine implies that accountants cannot change accounting procedures. (c) The money-measuring-unit assumption implies that money is a stable measuring unit. (d) The going-concern assumption implies that the business will continue long enough to complete current plans. (e) None of the above.

E2-3

The following transactions occurred after Cost Corporation was organized:

Issued capital stock for cash, $15,000
Purchased merchandise on account, $1,500
Purchased land for cash, $4,000
Sales of merchandise on account, $2,500
Cost of goods sold, $1,250
Collected $600 from customers
Paid salaries, $900

If a balance sheet were prepared after the above transactions, what would be the total shown for all the assets? What would be the total equities?

E2-4

(a) If the following information pertains to a tract of land, which dollar amount will appear on the balance sheet?

Fair market value	$180,000
Acquisition cost	25,000

(b) Assume that a firm's fiscal period is one year. Determine the net income from the following:

Rent expense	$ 2,000
Sales on account	10,000
Cash paid to landlord	500
Cash collected from customers	3,000
Cost of goods sold	7,000
Cash paid for merchandise	8,000

E2-5

Describe a transaction that will cause the following effects on the elements of the basic accounting equation:

(a) Increase one asset and decrease another asset.
(b) Increase an asset and increase a liability.

(c) Increase an asset and increase a stockholders' equity account.

(d) Decrease one liability and increase another liability.

(e) Decrease a stockholders' equity account and decrease an asset.

(f) Decrease a liability and decrease an asset.

E2-6 *Show the effect of the following transactions on total assets, total liabilities, and stockholders' equity. Using the format illustrated, prepare your answers by using the following symbols: (I) for increase, (D) for decrease, and (NC) for no change.*

	Total assets	Total liabilities	Stockholders' equity
(a) Purchased a machine for cash			
(b) Obtained a loan from the bank			
(c) Issued capital stock for cash			
(d) Sold merchandise on account			
(e) Recorded cost of goods sold from above sale			
(f) Paid rent expense			
(g) Paid dividends with cash			
(h) Issued bonds for cash			

E2-7 *Analyze the following successive balance sheets to infer what transactions took place (1) during March and (2) during April:*

(1)

BLUE COMPANY
Balance Sheet
March 31, 19_8

Assets		Equities	
Cash	$25,000	Stockholders' equity:	
		Capital stock	$25,000

(2)

BLUE COMPANY
Balance Sheet
April 30, 19_8

Assets		Equities	
Cash	$15,000	Liabilities:	
Building	20,000	Notes payable	$10,000
		Stockholders' equity:	
		Capital stock	25,000
	$35,000		$35,000

Continue Exercise E2-7 by using the following additional balance sheets to determine what Blue Company's transactions were (1) during May and (2) during June:

(1)

BLUE COMPANY
Balance Sheet
May 31, 19_8

Assets			Equities		
Cash	$15,000		Liabilities:		
Inventory	10,000		Accounts payable	$10,000	
Equipment	10,000		Notes payable	20,000	$30,000
Building	20,000	$55,000	Stockholders' equity:		
			Capital stock		25,000
		$55,000			$55,000

(2)

BLUE COMPANY
Balance Sheet
June 30, 19_8

Assets			Equities		
Cash	$ 5,000		Liabilities		
Inventory	10,000		Accounts payable	$10,000	
Equipment	10,000		Notes payable	20,000	$30,000
Building	20,000		Stockholders' equity		
Patent	10,000	$55,000	Capital stock		25,000
		$55,000			$55,000

Problems

You are given below three short cases. Select and briefly explain which accounting doctrine and/ or assumption is violated.

(1) The company president decides to recognize revenue when orders are received by the firm.

(2) Smith offers to buy a tract of land from Jones Company for an amount in excess of the figure listed on the balance sheet. Jones Company decides to increase the balance sheet figure for the land.

(3) Lister Company has changed its balance sheet to reflect liquidating prices on all accounts. The company believes that easier financing will be obtainable for market expansion.

A2-2

The following balance sheet was prepared by the owner *of Racquet Company. Prepare a corrected balance sheet by considering the discussion of accounting theory in Chapter 2.*

RACQUET COMPANY
Balance Sheet
December 31, 19_7

Assets			Equities		
Current assets:			Current liabilities:		
Cash	$ 5,000		Accounts payable	$ 15,000	
Accounts receivable	10,000		Salaries payable	10,000	
Home (cost			Market loss—		
$50,000)—Note 3	40,000		Note 2	40,000	$ 65,000
Inventory (cost					
$10,000)	15,000		Stockholders' equity:		
Pens, pencils,			Litigation loss—		
and tape	200	$ 70,200	Note 4	$115,200	
			Capital stock	40,000	
Noncurrent assets:			Retained earnings	25,000	180,200
Equipment (cost					
$25,000)	$10,000				
Building (cost					
$30,000)	30,000				
Rental property					
(cost $25,000)—					
Note 1	40,000				
Land (cost $10,000)	90,000				
Owner's car—					
Note 3	5,000	175,000			
		$245,200			$245,200

Notes:

1. The owner has title to the rental property.

2. The market loss is the amount of anticipated decline in revenue due to a probable labor strike.

3. None of the owner's property is used for business purposes.

4. The loss is anticipated legal fees for antitrust litigation.

A2-3

Determine the dollar balance of the assets and equities at the end of the period during which the following transactions occurred:

ABC Corporation was organized, and capital stock was issued for $30,000 cash.

Purchased merchandise on account for $1,000.

Paid rent for the period, $1,000.

Sold merchandise on account for $2,300.

The merchandise sold cost ABC Corporation $1,800.

Paid $500 on account for the merchandise purchased above.

Purchased land for $3,000 cash.

Paid salaries, $800.

Sold merchandise for cash, $700.

The merchandise sold cost ABC Corporation $150.

Collected $250 on account from customers.

Paid dividends, $150.

Suggested form for solution:

....

	Assets = Equities

Changes resulting from transactions:
Issuance of capital stock	$ xx	$ xx
Purchase of merchandise on account	xx	xx
Etc.		

A2-4

Use whatever data you need below to prepare the 19_6 income statement for Lab Company.

Cash	$13,000
Cost of goods sold	21,000
Retained earnings—beginning of 19_6	42,000
Retained earnings—end of 19_6	54,000
Accounts payable	16,000
Rent expense	3,000
Advertising expense	5,000
Electricity expense	2,000
Telephone expense	1,000
Dividends	8,000
Sales	?
Capital stock	49,000

A2-5

The transaction worksheet on page 55 relates to White Company. Describe each of the transactions (1) through (10).

A2-6

Law Company had the transactions summarized below during 19_4. At the end of the year the company owed $1,300 for December's rent. The company intends to pay this obligation during 19_5. Assuming that the beginning balance in all accounts is zero, prepare a transaction worksheet.

(1) Issued capital stock for cash, $37,500.

(2) Purchased merchandise on account, $90,000.

(3a) Made sales of merchandise on account, $160,000.

(3b) Cost of goods sold, $72,000.

(4) Purchased land as a long-term investment for $20,000, giving $10,000 cash and a $10,000 mortgage payable.

(5) Collected $100,000 from customers.

(6) Paid rent for 11 months, $14,300.

(7) Paid other expenses, $15,600.

(8) Paid $50,000 of the amount owed for merchandise.

(9) Paid salaries, $27,000.

(10) Paid $2,000 in local taxes for 19_4.

(11) Paid $5,000 in dividends.

A2-7

The results of the 19_5 transactions of Round Company are summarized below. Assume that all beginning account balances are zero.

(1) The company was organized and capital stock issued for cash, $75,000.

(2) Purchased merchandise for cash, $7,500.

Assets = **Equities**

	Cash	+ Accounts Receivable	+ Merchandise Inventory	+ Land	=	Accounts Payable	+ Salaries Payable	+ Capital Stock	+ Revenues	− Expenses	− Dividends
									Retained Earnings		
(1)	+25,000							+25,000			
(2)	−10,000		+10,000								
(3)	+20,000								+20,000		
(4)			−5,000							−5,000	
(5)		+20,000							+20,000		
(6)			−5,000							−5,000	
(7)			+10,000			+10,000					
(8)	−10,000			+10,000							
(9)							+5,000			−5,000	
(10)	−5,000										−5,000

(3a) Made cash sales, $15,000.

(3b) Cost of goods sold for cash, $6,000.

(4) Purchased merchandise on account, $85,000.

(5) Paid advertising expenses, $1,000.

(6a) Made sales of merchandise on account, $90,000.

(6b) Cost of goods sold on account, $60,000.

(7) Paid rent for the year, $4,800.

(8) Cash payments for salaries, $10,000.

(9) Cash receipts from customers, $71,000.

(10) Cash payments for merchandise purchased on account, $31,000.

(11) At year end securities were acquired as a long-term investment for a cash outlay of $15,000.

(12) At year end the company owed $2,100 for *unpaid* salaries.

(13) Paid cash dividends, $3,000.

Required:

(a) Completed transaction worksheet.

(b) The 19_5 income statement, statement of retained earnings, and balance sheet.

A2-8   *Transactions covering the 19_3 operations of Delta Company are listed below. Assume that all beginning account balances are zero.*

(1) Issued capital stock for cash, $25,000.

(2) Purchased merchandise on account, $35,000.

(3) Paid advertising expenses, $250.

(4) Paid rent for 19_3, $1,500.

(5a) Made sales of merchandise:
On account, $40,000.
For cash, $3,500.

(5b) Cost of goods sold, $25,500.

(6) Salaries for 19_3, totaled $10,500:
Paid in cash, $9,750.
Owed at year end, $750.

(7) Other expense for 19_3, total $1,100 of which $950 has been paid.

(8) Cash collections from customers, $35,500.

(9) Cash payments for merchandise purchased on account, $32,000.

(10) At year end the company made long-term investments in land for $15,000 cash.

(11) Paid cash dividends, $1,000.

Required:

(a) Transaction worksheet for 19_3.

(b) Income statement, statement of retained earnings, and balance sheet for 19_3.

A2-9

For each situation presented below, discuss how you would handle the situation based on various accounting assumptions and/or doctrines.

(1) Should items such as tape, pencils, and pens initially be charged to an asset account, or should they be expensed when acquired?

(2) The accounting records for a small business include both the owner's business and personal financial transactions. Does this constitute good accounting practice?

(3) At the beginning of the year a company purchased land, for investment purposes, for $20,000. At year end the current market value of the land is $25,000. Current company financial statements report the land at $25,000 in the balance sheet and show $5,000 land revenue in the income statement. Is such reporting acceptable in current accounting practice?

(4) Why is a company's total cash inventory purchases during the year invariably not equal to its cost of goods sold reported in the income statement?

(5) How would you answer a stockholder of a company who questions how fairly the financial statements represent a company when the statements do not report that the company's president has a serious health problem?

B2-1

On the 19_5 balance sheet of Sold Company the machinery and equipment account had a balance of $20,000.

(a) What accounting *assumptions* should have been applied by the company accountants in the determination of this figure? Explain.

(b) What accounting *doctrines* should have been considered by the company accountants in the determination of this figure? Explain.

B2-2

You are given below three short cases. Select and briefly explain which accounting doctrine and/ or assumption is violated.

(1) Statics Company has decided to list a liability for possible legal action arising from air pollution from company stacks.

(2) The company president decides that expenses should be recognized when cash payments are made.

(3) Tower Company has changed a specific accounting procedure for inventory costing each year for the last five years.

B2-3

Use the following information on the operations of Line Corporation to prepare the statement of retained earnings for 19_4.

Accounts receivable	$32,000
Dividends	6,000
Retained earnings—beginning of 19_4	15,000
Cash	36,000
Rent expense	3,000
Sales	27,000
Inventory	21,000
Cost of goods sold	14,000
Salaries expense	5,000
Salaries payable	2,000
Land	18,000

B2-4   The following transactions related to Boor Corporation. Determine the dollar balance of assets and equities at the end of the period.

(1) Issued capital stock for cash, $37,500.

(2) Purchased merchandise on account, $2,000.

(3) Purchased equipment for cash, $12,500.

(4) Purchased merchandise for cash, $1,500.

(5) Purchased land by giving a mortgage payable, $7,500.

(6) Sales of merchandise on account, $2,500.

(7) Cost of goods sold, $1,750.

(8) Paid for merchandise purchased earlier on account, $2,000.

(9) Paid salaries, $500.

(10) Paid dividends, $300.

Suggested form of solution:

	Assets	Equities
Changes resulting from transactions:		
Issuance of capital stock:	$ xx	$ xx
Etc.		

B2-5   The transaction worksheet on page 59 relates to Black Corporation. Describe each of the transactions (1) through (10).

B2-6   Method Company had the transactions summarized below during 19_7. Assuming that the beginning balance in all accounts is zero, prepare a transaction worksheet.

(1) Issued capital stock for cash, $60,000.

(2) Purchased merchandise on account, $75,000.

(3) Purchased merchandise for cash, $15,000.

(4a) Made sales of merchandise on account, $50,000.

(4b) Cost of goods sold on account, $20,000.

(5a) Made cash sales, $4,000.

(5b) Cost of goods sold for cash, $3,000.

(6) Collected $30,000 from customers.

(7) Paid $41,000 on the amount owed for merchandise.

(8) Paid rent for the year 19_7, $3,000.

(9) Paid salaries for the year 19_7, $17,500.

(10) Other expenses for 19_7 amounted to $1,250, of which $1,050 had been paid and $200 was owed as of December 31, 19_7.

(11) Paid cash dividends, $5,000.

B2-7   Golf Corporation was organized at the beginning of 19_3. Show the increases and decreases resulting from the 19_3 transactions on a transaction worksheet. Prepare the 19_3 financial statements (income statement, statement of retained earnings, and balance sheet).

Assets = **Equities**

	Cash	+ Accounts Receivable	+ Merchandise Inventory	+ Land	=	Accounts Payable	+ Salaries Payable	+ Capital Stock	+	Revenues	− Expenses	− Dividends
										Retained Earnings		
(1)	+50,000							+50,000				
(2)	+50,000									+50,000		
(3)			+30,000			+30,000						
(4)	−10,000											−10,000
(5)	−50,000			+50,000								
(6)			−10,000								−10,000	
(7)			−5,000								−5,000	
(8)							+5,000				−5,000	
(9)		+20,000								+20,000		
(10)	+10,000	−10,000										

(1) Issued capital stock for cash, $100,000.

(2) Salaries for 19_3 total $50,000, of which $30,000 was paid in cash and $20,000 is owed at the end of the year.

(3) Purchased merchandise on account, $130,000.

(4a) Made sales on account, $200,000.

(4b) Cost of goods sold, $60,000.

(5) Paid rent for 19_3, $2,000.

(6) Purchased a building for cash, $50,000.

(7) Paid $10,000 of the amount owed for merchandise.

(8) Collected $150,000 from customers.

(9) Paid other expenses, $14,000.

(10) Paid dividends, $10,000.

(11a) Made cash sales, $50,000.

(11b) Cost of goods sold, $20,000.

B2-8

Puka Company began regular operations as of January 2, 19_2. During the preceding month it had issued capital stock for $70,000, but no other transactions occurred prior to January 2, 19_2. Prepare a transaction worksheet that will provide the information needed for the 19_2 financial statements. Also determine the net income for 19_2, total assets as of December 31, 19_2, and stockholders' equity as of December 31, 19_2.

19_2 transactions

(1) Purchased merchandise on account, $45,000.

(2) Paid rent for 19_2, $2,700.

(3a) Sales for 19_2, $75,000, of which $7,000 were cash sales.

(3b) Cost of goods sold, $43,000.

(4) Salaries for 19_2 totaled $17,000:
   Paid in cash, $16,200.
   Owed at year end, $800.

(5) Paid local taxes, $1,200. (Such taxes are a business expense.)

(6) Collections from customers for sales on account, $60,800.

(7) Cash disbursement for merchandise purchased on account, $40,000.

(8) Paid miscellaneous expense, $1,800.

(9) Purchased land as a long-term investment for $9,000; terms: $3,000 in cash and $6,000 noninterest-bearing note payable due January 31, 19_4.

(10) Paid travel and entertainment expenses, $800.

(11) Paid cash dividends, $3,000.

B2-9

For each situation presented, discuss how you would handle the situation based on various accounting assumptions and/or doctrines.

(1) The corporate president tells you that the dollar valuation of land on the balance sheet is equal to the current fair market value of the land. If the land was purchased a number of years ago, do you believe the president?

(2) For a normal, profitable corporation, are liquidation prices used in preparation of the financial statements?

(3) Preparation of financial statements at frequent points in time requires accountants to make estimates and subjective judgments. How do you reconcile the use of estimates and judgments with the doctrine of objectivity?

(4) The Y Company president has been checking the accounting records and notices that payment has been received from X Company for merchandise not yet sent to X. The president asks you why the receipt of cash from X has not been recorded as revenue. What is your answer?

(5) In 19_1 a certain accounting procedure used by your company was dropped in favor of another acceptable method. In 19_2 management decides to change to a third acceptable procedure. Are such changes in procedures acceptable in current accounting practice?

PROCESSING ECONOMIC DATA

CHAPTER 3

PURPOSE OF CHAPTER   The analysis of business transactions was introduced in the preceding chapter by using the transaction worksheet to organize and classify the impact of transactions on the different elements of the basic accounting equation. The increase–decrease plan discussed in Chapter 2 is applicable to transaction analysis for any business firm, but the transaction worksheet becomes impractical as the volume of transactions increases.

This chapter discusses the use of additional devices to facilitate the recording and organizing of a sizable number of transactions. One of these devices is the account, which serves basically the same purpose as the columns in the transaction worksheet discussed in Chapter 2. The other is the journal, which provides a permanent record of the transactions of the firm recorded in chronological order. They both serve the purpose of accumulating financial data during the accounting period in such a manner that the preparation of financial statements at the end of the period will be facilitated.

THE VALUE OF UNDERSTANDING THE ACCOUNTING PROCESS   As was explained in Chapter 2, the accounting process consists of the (1) recording of economic data in the form of transactions for the period (including identifying, collecting, analyzing, and measuring the transactions), (2) classifying and summarizing the economic data at the end of the period, and (3) reporting and interpreting the resulting economic information in the form of periodic financial statements. Part of the accounting process deals with procedural matters, that is, with record keeping. A career accountant, of course, should be well-versed in procedural matters, not because any significant portion of his or her time will be devoted to keeping records but because others view him or her as an expert and thus expect him or her to have the ability to plan and install record-keeping systems, to evaluate existing systems, and possibly to assume administrative responsibility over such activity. Whether a business is large or small, whether the procedures are simple or complex, and whether manual, machine, or electronic devices are utilized, the task of record keeping, that is, data gathering, is extremely important. Many important decisions are based on the data accumulated in the accounting records of a business.

Whether or not a student intends to become an expert accountant, a knowledge of accounting procedures can be valuable. With such knowledge the student will more easily understand accounting theory. In turn, a good foundation in accounting theory will lead to a better understanding of accounting information, especially that set forth in the form of financial statements.

THE ACCOUNTING SYSTEM   As a general rule, the first accounting work performed for any business involves the development of an accounting system. The accountant studies the nature of the business, determines the types of transactions that probably will occur and the kinds of assets and equities that will result from the expected transactions. The accountant takes cognizance of the needs of those who will make use of accounting data, and plans or selects the necessary forms and records in which the transactions of the business may be recorded. An obvious objective of any accounting system is to provide for each kind of asset and equity a record of the increases and decreases caused by transactions.

In the case of Sight & Sound Corporation for its first year of operations, the record-keeping arrangement should be designed to keep track of the increases and decreases for the following assets and equities:

Assets	Equities
Cash	Accounts payable
Accounts receivable	Salaries payable
Merchandise inventory	Capital stock
Land	Retained earnings

The record maintained for each asset and equity is known as an *account.* If the increases and decreases are correctly processed in the accounting records, the dollar amounts (account balances) needed for the 19_1 financial statements will be available.

Consequently, transactions provide the input (economic data) and the accounting system transforms the input into output (economic information) in the form of financial statements.

THE RECORDING PROCESS   The recording process may be accomplished in a variety of ways, ranging from the use of pen and ink to electronic devices, and the resulting record can be maintained on paper, punched cards, or magnetic tapes, to mention the most commonly used record forms. The transaction worksheet used in Chapter 2 is an acceptable record-keeping device, although it would be cumbersome and impractical for a business of even moderate size when one considers the large number of accounts and the volume of transactions present-day business activity entails.

The point is, the increase-decrease plan illustrated in Chapter 2 is applicable whether accounting records consist of hand- or machine-written entries on paper forms, data punched into cards, or data stored on magnetic tapes. If one has acquired an understanding of the accounting process, such knowledge is effective and useful no matter how modern or how old-fashioned is the accounting system for a particular business enterprise.

THE ACCOUNT   Exposure to the traditional hand-written record-keeping procedures associated with the double-entry method of accounting has the following in its favor:

The knowledge gained by such exposure is transferable to other, more modern record-keeping systems.
Hand-written systems continue to be used by many small businesses.
Most large companies still use some hand-written records in combination with computer records.

The traditional account form set forth below can be used for purposes of demonstrating the basic features of the double-entry method. One such form would be used for each account. Observe that the form has two sides—left and right—with identical columns. Thus increases can be recorded on one side of the form and decreases on the other.

Sheet No.			*Account Title*			Account No.	
DATE	EXPLANATION	REF.	AMOUNT	DATE	EXPLANATION	REF.	AMOUNT

The column headings (*Date, Explanation, Reference,* and *Amount*) shown in the preceding illustration usually do not appear in accounts, but are included in the illustration to indicate the kind of data recorded in each column. Completed accounts will be illustrated later in the chapter.

To simplify illustrations and problem assignments, the account form is often depicted as follows:

Accountants call this abbreviated form a *T-account* because it is shaped like the capital letter T.

THE DEBIT-CREDIT RECORDING PLAN Increases in assets and decreases in equities are recorded on the left side of the account, called the *debit* (abbreviated dr.) *side.* Increases in equities and decreases in assets are recorded on the right side of the account, called the *credit* (abbreviated cr.) *side.* A debit, or debit entry, is the recording of an amount on the left side of an account—debiting the account; a credit, or credit entry, is the recording of an amount on the right side of an account—crediting the account. A debit entry to an account is also sometimes called a *charge* to the account.

Many nonaccountants seem to think that debit means something unfavorable and that credit means something favorable. Also, to some people unacquainted with accounting, debit means an increase and credit a decrease. Neither is the case. The words debit and credit merely refer to the two sides of an account.

The difference between the total debits and the total credits in an account is called the *balance.* If the dollars debited exceed the dollars credited, the amount has a debit balance; if the credits exceed the debits, the account has a credit balance.

When the debit-credit recording plan is followed, asset accounts normally will have debit (left-handed) balances and equity accounts normally will have credit (right-handed) balances. This account balance arrangement, namely, left-side balances for assets and right-side balances for equities, ties in with the customary form of the balance sheet in which the assets are shown on the left side and the equities are shown on the right side.

The increase-decrease-balance plan for accounts outlined above can be restated as follows by the use of T-accounts.

ASSET ACCOUNTS
(They will have debit balances)
. . . .
T-Account

Debit		Credit
Balance	$ xxx	
Increases recorded as debits		Decreases recorded as credits

EQUITY ACCOUNTS
(They will have credit balances)
. . . .
T-Account

Debit	Credit	
	Balance	$ xx
Decreases recorded as debits	Increases recorded as credits	

The application of the recording plan is illustrated in the following asset and equity accounts:

Data for cash account:
  Beginning balance, $1,000
  Cash receipt, $500
  Cash disbursement, $400

	Cash	
Balance	1,000	400
	500	

Data for accounts payable account:
  Beginning balance, $600
  Purchase of merchandise on account, $300
  Payment to reduce accounts payable, $400

	Accounts payable	
400	Balance	600
		300

To repeat, increases in assets and decreases in equities are recorded as debits. And, increases in equities and decreases in assets are recorded as credits.

Assets		Equities	
Debits (increases)	Credits (decreases)	Debits (decreases)	Credits (increases)

Note the relationship of the debit-credit plan to the transaction worksheet discussed in Chapter 2. Instead of columns for each asset and equity in the transaction worksheet, accounts are established for each asset and equity. Also, instead of recording increases and decreases in the individual columns of the transaction worksheet in accordance with the dual economic effect of transactions, the increases and decreases are recorded as debits and credits in each account in accordance with the double-entry system. In effect, each column of the transaction worksheet becomes an account with a left and right side in which transactions are recorded on the left or right side of an account in accordance with the debit-credit plan. This relationship between the transaction worksheet and the debit-credit plan is illustrated below.

Transaction worksheet:

Assets   **Equities**

				Retained earnings		
Cash	+ Accounts receivable	+ ⋯ =	Accounts payable	+ ⋯ +		
				+Revenues	− Expenses	− Dividends
±	±		±			

Debit-credit plan:

Cash		+	Accounts receivable		+ ⋯ =	Accounts payable		+ ⋯ +	Retained earnings	
+ dr.	− cr.		+ dr.	− cr.		− dr.	+ cr.		− dr.	+ cr.

Expenses			Revenues	
+ dr.	− cr.		− dr.	+ cr.

Dividends	
+ dr.	− cr.

REVENUE AND EXPENSE ACCOUNT   As explained earlier, revenues are inflows of assets from the sale of goods or the rendering of services that increase the owners' equity, or, more specifically, that increase the retained earnings of a corporation. Expenses decrease the retained earnings of a corporation and are the cost of services or resources used for the purpose of generating revenue.

The increases and decreases to retained earnings that result from revenue and expense transactions could be recorded in the retained earnings account. However, revenue and expense transactions usually occur in such volume that this recording practice would unduly clutter up the retained earnings account. Furthermore, it would be exceedingly time consuming to extract from the retained earnings account the revenue and expense data therein needed to prepare the income statement. For such reasons, separate accounts are used for each type of revenue and expense.

It may be helpful to think of revenue and expense accounts as "offshoots" or subdivisions of the retained earnings account. By so relating revenue and expense accounts to the retained earnings account, the debit-credit procedure for revenue and expense accounts follows logically:

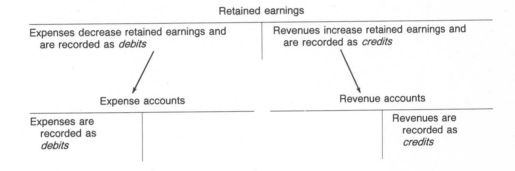

Increases in retained earnings are recorded as credits, revenues increase retained earnings, and, therefore, revenues are recorded as credits in revenue accounts. Similarly, decreases in retained earnings are recorded as debits, expenses decrease retained earnings, and, therefore, expenses are recorded as debits in expense accounts.

DIVIDENDS ACCOUNT   As explained in Chapter 1, dividends are distributions of assets (usually cash) to stockholders as a result of profitable operations. Profitable operations increase assets and retained earnings; therefore, dividends decrease assets and retained earnings. Although dividends reduce retained earnings, they are not an expense: they are not paid for the purpose of generating revenue.

Since dividends reduce retained earnings, they could be recorded in the retained earnings account. However, since they are normally declared (on the declaration date dividends become a legal liability of the corporation) quarterly, the quarterly dividends are accumulated in a separate dividends account. The dividends account is merely a subdivision of retained earnings.

Because decreases in retained earnings are recorded as debits, and because dividends decrease retained earnings, dividends are recorded as debits in the dividends account.

SUMMARY OF DEBIT-CREDIT PLAN The debit-credit plan just explained will result in the following normal account balances:

Debit Balance Accounts	Credit Balance Accounts
Assets	Liabilities
Expenses	Capital stock
Dividends	Retained earnings
	Revenues

Also, the use of the debit (left-hand) and credit (right-hand) sides of the accounts for recording increases and decreases works out as follows:

Debits	Credits
Increases in assets	Decreases in assets
Increases in expenses	Decreases in expenses
Increases in dividends	Decreases in dividends
Decreases in liabilities	Increases in liabilities
Decreases in capital stock	Increases in capital stock
Decreases in retained earnings	Increases in retained earnings
Decreases in revenues	Increases in revenues

or:

Assets	=	Liabilities	+	Capital stock	+	Retained earnings	
+		−		−		−	+
dr.	cr.	dr.	cr.	dr.	cr.	dr.	cr.

Expenses		Revenues	
+	−	−	+
dr.	cr.	dr.	cr.

Dividends	
+	−
dr.	cr.

EQUALITY OF DEBITS AND CREDITS In Chapter 2 it was pointed out that each transaction has a dual economic effect that affects at least two items. Similarly, under the debit-credit plan, every business transaction affects at least two accounts, and each transaction is recorded so that debits equal credits. For each transaction, the dollar amount of the debit (or debits, if more than one account is debited) will equal the dollar amount of the credit (or credits). Moreover, since each transaction results in equal debits and credits, the total of all debit entries is equal to the total of all credit entries. This system of equality of debits and credits for every transaction is called *double-entry accounting.*

RECORDING TRANSACTIONS To illustrate the debiting and crediting of accounts, let us return to the first year's transactions of Sight & Sound Corporation mentioned in Chapter 2, analyze the transactions, and observe the resulting debit and credit entries. For purposes of illustration, the transactions are keyed to the accounts with identifying numbers. Also, italics are used to identify each additional debit and credit when entered in the T-accounts. Accounts debited are shown at the left; accounts credited are shown at the right.

(1) Issued capital stock for cash, $25,000.

Accounts affected	Kind of account	Change in balance	Debit	Credit
Cash	Asset	Increase	25,000	
Capital stock	Stockholders' equity	Increase		25,000

Cash			Capital stock		
(1)	25,000			(1)	*25,000*

(2) Purchased land as a long-term investment for $10,000 cash.

Accounts affected	Kind of account	Change in balance	Debit	Credit
Land	Asset	Increase	10,000	
Cash	Asset	Decrease		10,000

Land			Cash		
(2)	10,000		(1)	25,000	(2)	*10,000*

(3) Purchased merchandise on account, $60,000.

Accounts affected	Kind of account	Change in balance	Debit	Credit
Merchandise inventory	Asset	Increase	60,000	
Accounts payable	Liability	Increase		60,000

Merchandise inventory			Accounts payable		
(3)	60,000			(3)	*60,000*

(4a) Made sales of merchandise on account for $81,000.

Accounts affected	Kind of account	Change in balance	Debit	Credit
Accounts receivable	Asset	Increase	81,000	
Sales	Revenue	Increase		81,000

Accounts receivable			Sales	
(4a)	81,000		(4a)	81,000

(4b) Cost of goods sold, $48,000.

Accounts affected	Kind of account	Change in balance	Debit	Credit
Cost of goods sold	Expense	Increase	48,000	
Merchandise inventory	Asset	Decrease		48,000

Cost of goods sold			Merchandise inventory			
(4b)	48,000		(3)	60,000	(4b)	48,000

(5) Collections from customers, $70,000.

Accounts affected	Kind of account	Change in balance	Debit	Credit
Cash	Asset	Increase	70,000	
Accounts receivable	Asset	Decrease		70,000

Cash			Accounts receivable			
(1)	25,000	(2) 10,000	(4a)	81,000	(5)	70,000
(5)	70,000					

Recording plan restated: increases in assets, expenses, and dividends, and decreases in liabilities and stockholders' equity are recorded as debits; increases in liabilities, stockholders' equity, and revenues and decreases in assets are recorded as credits.

(6) Paid on account, $40,000.

Accounts affected	Kind of account	Change in balance	Debit	Credit
Accounts payable	Liability	Decrease	40,000	
Cash	Asset	Decrease		40,000

Accounts payable			Cash			
(6)	40,000	(3) 60,000	(1)	25,000	(2)	10,000
			(5)	70,000	(6)	40,000

(7) *Paid rent for the year, $4,800.*

Accounts affected	Kind of account	Change in balance	Debit	Credit
Rent expense	Expense	Increase	4,800	
Cash	Asset	Decrease		4,800

Rent expense		Cash			
(7)	4,800	(1)	25,000	(2)	10,000
		(5)	70,000	(6)	40,000
				(7)	*4,800*

(8) *Paid other expenses, $5,200.*

Accounts affected	Kind of account	Change in balance	Debit	Credit
Other expenses	Expense	Increase	5,200	
Cash	Asset	Decrease		5,200

Other expenses		Cash			
(8)	5,200	(1)	25,000	(2)	10,000
		(5)	70,000	(6)	40,000
				(7)	4,800
				(8)	*5,200*

(9a) *Paid employees' salaries for eleven months, $16,500.*

Accounts affected	Kind of account	Change in balance	Debit	Credit
Salaries expense	Expense	Increase	16,500	
Cash	Asset	Decrease		16,500

Salaries expense		Cash			
(9a)	16,500	(1)	25,000	(2)	10,000
		(5)	70,000	(6)	40,000
				(7)	4,800
				(8)	5,200
				(9a)	*16,500*

(9b) *December salaries owed, $1,500.*

Accounts affected	Kind of account	Change in balance	Debit	Credit
Salaries expense	Expense	Increase	1,500	
Salaries payable	Liability	Increase		1,500

Salaries expense		Salaries payable		
(9a)	16,500		(9b)	*1,500*
(9b)	*1,500*			

(10) *Payment of cash dividend, $2,000.*

Accounts affected	Kind of account	Change in balance	Debit	Credit
Dividends	Dividend	Increase	2,000	
Cash	Asset	Decrease		2,000

Dividends			Cash			
(10)	2,000		(1)	25,000	(2)	10,000
			(5)	70,000	(6)	40,000
					(7)	4,800
					(8)	5,200
					(9a)	16,500
					(10)	2,000

The above determination of the debits and credits required to record the 19_1 transactions reveals a basic rule of double-entry accounting: debits must equal credits. The working of this rule is demonstrated by the following summary of the transactions.

Transaction	Increases in assets	Decreases in equities (including increases in expenses)	Debits	Increases in equities (including increases in revenue)	Decreases in assets	Credits
1	X		$ 25,000	X		$ 25,000
2	X		10,000		X	10,000
3	X		60,000	X		60,000
4a	X		81,000	X		81,000
4b		X	48,000		X	48,000
5	X		70,000		X	70,000
6		X	40,000		X	40,000
7		X	4,800		X	4,800
8		X	5,200		X	5,200
9a		X	16,500		X	16,500
9b		X	1,500	X		1,500
10		X	2,000		X	2,000
			$364,000			$364,000

CHART OF ACCOUNTS   In discussing the accounting system earlier in this chapter, it was pointed out that an obvious objective of any accounting system is to provide for each kind of asset and equity a record of the increases and decreases caused by transactions. This record, of course, is the account. Consequently, one of the first steps in the development of an accounting system is the preparation of a chart of accounts. Such a chart lists in a systematic manner the accounts (really account titles) with their identifying numbers that are used by the business firm. The order of the listing is in the following financial-statement order: assets, liabilities, elements of owners' equity, revenues, and expenses.

An appendix to this chapter discusses the chart of accounts, especially its numbering system, and provides a complete illustrative chart of accounts. For purposes of this chapter, a chart of accounts used by Sight & Sound Corporation for the year 19_1 is illustrated below:

Account Number	Account Title	Account Number	Account Title
	Assets:		Assets:
111	Cash	325	Retained earnings
113	Accounts receivable	327	Dividends
115	Merchandise inventory		Revenues:
120	Land	401	Sales
	Liabilities:		Expenses:
211	Accounts payable	501	Cost of goods sold
212	Salaries payable	601	Salaries expense
	Stockholders' equity:	602	Rent expense
321	Capital stock	604	Other expense

ACCOUNT BALANCES   An account balance is the difference between the total debits and the total credits to that account. If the sum of the debit entries to an account exceeds the sum of its credit entries, the account has a debit balance. Conversely, if the sum of the credit entries exceeds the sum of the debit entries, the account has a credit balance. Since asset, expense, and dividend accounts are increased by debits, they normally have debit balances. Similarly, since liability, capital stock, retained earnings, and revenue accounts are increased by credits, they normally have credit balances. For example, observe the following cash account of Sight & Sound Corporation. The data therein agree with that set forth in the T-account on page 72.

CASH

Relevant dates would be entered in this column	This space used when it seems desirable to describe some unusual fea-ture of a transaction	25,000 70,000	Relevant dates would be entered in this column	This space used when it seems desirable to describe some unusual fea-ture of a transaction	10,000 40,000 4,800 5,200 16,500 2,000

The account has a balance because there is a difference between the total debits and the total credits:

Total debits	$95,000
Total credits	$78,500

Because the debits exceed the credits, the account has a debit balance; the balance is $16,500.

ALTERNATIVE ACCOUNT FORM   One disadvantage of the account form just shown above is that there is no convenient way to keep track of and display the current balance of the account. The following account form, widely used in manual accounting systems, overcomes this weakness. The third money column is used as a balance column. To show the use of balance columns, a few of the cash transactions from the previous illustration have been entered in the account.

Account Title		Cash			Account No. 111	
				Debit	Credit	Balance
19_1						
Jan.	2	← For explanation, if needed →		25,000		25,000 Dr.
	3				10,000	15,000 Dr.
	5				4,800	10,200 Dr.

THE LEDGER The accounts, such as the cash account just illustrated above, usually are kept in a loose-leaf binder or a file. The binder or the file, together with the accounts therein, is called a *ledger.* Thus the entire group of accounts is known as the *ledger,* and each account is a separate page in the ledger. The accounts in the ledger usually are arranged in the order in which they will appear in the financial statements.

THE JOURNAL So that the reader could better understand and become thoroughly acquainted with the debit-credit plan, transactions in the form of debits and credits have been made directly to the ledger accounts. Although transactions could be recorded directly in the ledger accounts for very small firms, the volume of transactions for most firms is such that it is more convenient and efficient to record transactions first in a journal and then later transfer the debits and credits to ledger accounts. Thus in recording transactions it is customary to use at least two accounting records: a journal and a ledger.

A *journal* is a book of original entry that contains a record of transactions in their chronological order (that is, in order of date), names the accounts to be debited and credited to record each transaction, and states the debit and credit amounts. The journal is called a *book of original entry* since it is the place for the first recording of each transaction.

JOURNAL ILLUSTRATED The following illustration of a journal, although based on only three transactions of Sight & Sound Corporation, should be sufficient to indicate the clerical process of journalizing.

JOURNAL				(Page 1)
19_1				
Jan.	2	Cash	25,000	
		Capital stock		25,000
		Issued capital stock for cash.		
	3	Land	10,000	
		Cash		10,000
		Purchased land as a long-term investment, for cash.		
	5	Rent expense	4,800	
		Cash		4,800
		Paid rent for the year.		

In connection with the above journal, note the following conventional recording practices:

The year, month, and day of the month are shown with the first journal entry on each page; entries on the same page for subsequent transactions in the same year and month need show only the day of the month.

Always record the debit part of the entry first.

Indent the account credited.

Support each journal entry with a concise explanation of the transaction.

Leave a space between entries.

ADVANTAGES OF THE JOURNAL The journal serves three useful purposes. In the first place, it reduces the possibility of error. If transactions were recorded directly in the ledger, there would be considerable danger of omitting the debit or the credit entry, or of making two debit entries or two credit entries. This danger is reduced to a minimum by use of the journal. In the journal, the debits and credits for each transaction are recorded together, making any such errors more obvious.

In the second place, the journal shows offsetting debit and credit entries for each transaction, and thus provides a complete record of the transaction in one place. Also, the journal provides ample space for an explanation of the transaction.

In the third place, the journal contains a record of transactions in their *chronological* order.

POSTING The debits and credits to the various accounts, as shown by the journal entries, are entered in the accounts by a process called *posting.* Thus posting is the process of transferring data from the journal to the ledger accounts. It is a clerical operation, as can be seen by examining the following posted journal entry and the relevant ledger accounts.

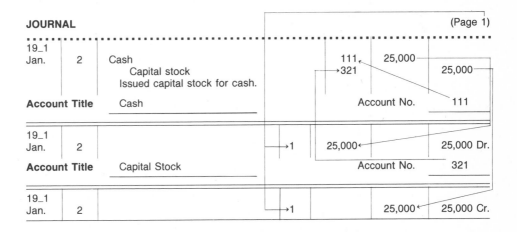

In the journal and ledger account forms, the small column at the left of the money columns is known as the reference column. A number placed in the journal reference column during the posting operation indicates the number of the account in the ledger *to* which the entry was posted. A number placed in the ledger account reference indicates the journal page *from* which the entry was posted.

Recording the journal page number in the ledger and the account number in the journal serves two purposes:

> During the posting operation, it shows how much of the posting has been done. Thus, if the posting work is interrupted, the notations, called *posting references,* indicate where the work was discontinued and where it should be resumed.
>
> After the posting has been completed, the notations serve as cross references between the journal and the ledger. Such cross references can be helpful in the event that errors make it necessary to trace the entries in ledger accounts.

THE TRIAL BALANCE The accounting process being described herein is known as the double-entry method because the recording of each transaction requires debit and credit entries of equal amount. Because the debit and credit entries for each transaction are equal, it follows that the total debit entries in all of the accounts should be equal to the total credit entries. It is equally true that *the total of the debit balances in the accounts should be equal to the total of the credit balances.*

It is customary to check periodically the equality of the debit and credit balances in a ledger by listing and totaling them. Such a list is called a *trial balance.* Many businesses prepare a trial balance at the end of each month. The December 31, 19_1 trial balance of Sight & Sound Corporation, prepared after the 19_1 journal entries had been posted, follows.

SIGHT & SOUND CORPORATION
Trial Balance
December 31, 19_1

	Debit	Credit
Cash	16,500	
Accounts receivable	11,000	
Merchandise inventory	12,000	
Land	10,000	
Accounts payable		20,000
Salaries payable		1,500
Capital stock		25,000
Dividends	2,000	
Sales		81,000
Cost of goods sold	48,000	
Salaries expense	18,000	
Rent expense	4,800	
Other expense	5,200	
	127,500	127,500

USES OF THE TRIAL BALANCE A trial balance is useful in checking the *mathematical* accuracy of the ledger. But it should be understood that a trial balance proves nothing more than the equality of the debit and credit balances. For example, the trial balance will still "balance" even though a transaction was not journalized, or a wrong account was debited or credited in the journal.

A trial balance is also useful to an accountant whenever periodic statements are to be prepared. Although it is possible for the accountant to prepare such statements by working directly from the ledger, it is much easier to use the account balances shown by a trial balance. For example, the above trial balance would provide the information needed for the preparation of the financial statements shown on pages 4, 6, and 8.

COMPOUND JOURNAL ENTRIES Sometimes the recording of a transaction requires more than a single debit and credit. For instance, assume that land which cost $10,000 was sold at cost, and that $6,000 in U.S. Government bonds and $4,000 in cash were received in settlement; the entry to record the transaction would be:

U.S. Government bonds	6,000	
Cash	4,000	
Land		10,000
Sale of land.		

Such entries, having more than one debit and/or more than one credit, are called *compound journal entries.*

IMPORTANT TERMS AND CONCEPTS IN CHAPTER 3

Accounting process—p. 62
Accounting system—p. 63
Account—pp. 63, 64, 73
T-account—p. 64
Debit—p. 64
Charge—p. 64
Credit—p. 64
Debit-credit plan—pp. 64–66, 68
Dividends declared—p. 67
Account balance—pp. 64, 65, 73

Revenues-expenses and debits-credits—pp. 67, 68
Dividends and debits-credits—pp. 67, 68
Double-entry accounting—pp. 69, 72
Chart of accounts—pp. 72, 73
Ledger—p. 74
Journal—pp. 74, 75
Posting—pp. 75, 76
Trial balance—pp. 76, 77
Compound journal entries—p. 77

DEMONSTRATION PROBLEM FOR REVIEW AND SELF-STUDY Air Services, Inc. was organized to perform maintenance and repair services on aircraft. The company has two sources of revenues, one from the sale of parts (sold at twice their cost) and the other from the performance of maintenance and repair services. The company was organized on July 1, 19_4 and uses the following accounts in its ledger:

Account Number	Account Title	Account Number	Account Title
111	Cash	311	Capital stock
112	Accounts receivable	411	Sales of parts
113	Parts inventory	412	Service revenue
114	Shop supplies on hand	511	Cost of parts sold
115	Prepaid insurance	612	Salaries expense
151	Equipment	613	Rent expense
211	Accounts payable		

The July, 19_4 transactions of Air Services, Inc. are listed below.

July   1—Issued $8,000 par value stock for $5,000 cash and equipment valued at $3,000.

2—Paid July rent, $180.

5—Purchased airplane spare parts on account from Curtis Company, $1,817.

7—Purchased shop supplies for $410, cash.

9—Billed Charter Airline $288 for parts and $470 for labor used in making a periodic check on one of its aircraft.

11—Purchased additional airplane parts from Wright Corporation, paying $421 cash.

12—Collected $45 for repair of landing gear on a private plane. No parts were used.

14—Paid the Curtis Company bill.

15—Billed World Air Flights $418 for parts and $614 for labor used in repairing a tail assembly.

15—Paid salaries of $800 for first half of July.

18—Collected $100 for periodic overhaul of a private plane; this amount included $20 for parts.

20—Received $758 from Charter Airline.

20—Signed an agreement with XYZ Company to perform all required labor for maintenance on its company plane.

23—Purchased a one-year fire insurance policy for cash, $30.

25—Received $1,032 from World Air Flights.

26—Billed Charter Airline $310 for parts and $580 for labor used in making a periodic check of one of its aircraft.

27—Purchased airplane parts on account from Curtis Company, $622.

29—Completed rebuilding landing gear on plane belonging to A. Y. Junior. The total bill amounted to $690, of which $200 was for parts. Junior gave his check for the entire bill when he called today for his plane.

30—Purchased shop supplies on account from Modern Supply Co., $84.

31—Paid salaries for last half of July, $825.

31—Billed XYZ Company, pursuant to agreement of July 20, for parts used in maintenance of company plane, $72, and labor of $100.

INSTRUCTIONS

(a)   Journalize the transactions for the month.

(b)   Post the transactions to the ledger accounts.

(c)   Prepare a July 31, 19_4 trial balance.

Note   Attempt to solve the demonstration problem before examining the solution that follows.

(a)

JOURNAL   (Page 1)

19_4					
July	1	Cash	111	5,000	
		Equipment	151	3,000	
		Capital stock	311		8,000
		Issued par value capital stock			
	2	Rent expense	613	180	
		Cash	111		180
		July rent			

July	5	Parts inventory	113	1,817	
		Accounts payable	211		1,817
		Purchase on account from Curtis Company			
	7	Shop supplies on hand	114	410	
		Cash	111		410
		Purchase of shop supplies			
	9	Accounts receivable	112	758	
		Sales of parts	411		288
		Service revenue	412		470
		Billed Charter Airline for parts and labor			
	9	Cost of parts sold	511	144	
		Parts inventory	113		144
		Cost of parts sold			
	11	Parts inventory	113	421	
		Cash	111		421
		Cash purchase of parts			
	12	Cash	111	45	
		Service revenue	412		45
		Repair work on private plane			
	14	Accounts payable	211	1,817	
		Cash	111		1,817
		Paid Curtis Company bill			
	15	Accounts receivable	112	1,032	
		Sales of parts	411		418
		Service revenue	412		614
		Billed World Air Flights for parts and labor			
	15	Cost of parts sold	511	209	
		Parts inventory	113		209
		Cost of parts sold			

JOURNAL   (Page 2)

19_4					
July	15	Salaries expense	612	800	
		Cash	111		800
		Wages for first half of July			
	18	Cash	111	100	
		Sales of parts	411		20
		Service revenue	412		80
		Overhaul of private plane			
	18	Cost of parts sold	511	10	
		Parts inventory	113		10
		Cost of parts sold			
	20	Cash	111	758	
		Accounts receivable	112		758
		Collection from Charter Airline			
		No entry required for signing of agreement with XYZ Company			
	23	Prepaid insurance	115	30	
		Cash	111		30
		One-year fire insurance policy			

(continued on next page)

July	25	Cash	111	1,032	
		Accounts receivable	112		1,032
		Collection from World Air Flights			
	26	Accounts receivable	112	890	
		Sales of parts	411		310
		Service revenue	412		580
		Billed Charter Airline for parts and labor			
	26	Cost of parts sold	511	155	
		Parts inventory	113		155
		Cost of parts sold			
	27	Parts inventory	113	622	
		Accounts payable	211		622
		Purchases on account from Curtis Company			

JOURNAL (Page 3)

19_4						
July	29	Cash	111	690	
		Sales of parts	411		200
		Service revenue	412		490
		Landing gear rebuilt on A. Y. Junior's plane			
	29	Cost of parts sold	511	100	
		Parts inventory	113		100
		Cost of parts sold			
	30	Shop supplies on hand	114	84	
		Accounts payable	211		84
		Purchase on account from Modern Supply Co.			
	31	Salaries expense	612	825	
		Cash	111		825
		Wages for last half of July			
	31	Accounts receivable	112	172	
		Sales of parts	411		72
		Service revenue	412		100
		Billed XYZ Company for parts and labor			
	31	Cost of parts sold (one-half of sales price of $72)	511	36	
		Parts inventory	113		36
		Cost of parts sold			

(b)

Cash 111

19_4						
July	1		1	5,000		5,000 Dr.
	2		1		180	4,820 Dr.
	7		1		410	4,410 Dr.
	11		1		421	3,989 Dr.
	12		1	45		4,034 Dr.
	14		1		1,817	2,217 Dr.
	15		2		800	1,417 Dr.
	18		2	100		1,517 Dr.
	20		2	758		2,275 Dr.
	23		2		30	2,245 Dr.
	25		2	1,032		3,277 Dr.
	29		3	690		3,967 Dr.
	31		3		825	3,142 Dr.

Accounts Receivable   112

19_4						
July	9		1	758		758 Dr.
	15		1	1,032		1,790 Dr.
	20		2		758	1,032 Dr.
	25		2		1,032	—
	26		2	890		890 Dr.
	31		3	172		1,062 Dr.

Parts Inventory   113

19_4						
July	5		1	1,817		1,817 Dr.
	9		1		144	1,673 Dr.
	11		1	421		2,094 Dr.
	15		1		209	1,885 Dr.
	18		2		10	1,875 Dr.
	26		2		155	1,720 Dr.
	27		2	622		2,342 Dr.
	29		3		100	2,242 Dr.
	31		3		36	2,206 Dr.

Shop Supplies on Hand   114

19_4						
July	7		1	410		410 Dr.
	30		3	84		494 Dr.

Prepaid Insurance   115

19_4						
July	23		2	30		30 Dr.

Equipment   151

19_4						
July	1		1	3,000		3,000 Dr.

Accounts Payable   211

19_4						
July	5		1		1,817	1,817 Cr.
	14		1	1,817		—
	27		2		622	622 Cr.
	30		3		84	706 Cr.

Capital Stock   311

19_4						
July	1		1		8,000	8,000 Cr.

Sales of Parts   411

19_4						
July	9		1		288	288 Cr.
	15		1		418	706 Cr.
	18		2		20	726 Cr.
	26		2		310	1,036 Cr.
	29		3		200	1,236 Cr.
	31		3		72	1,308 Cr.

Service Revenue   412

19_4						
July	9		1		470	470 Cr.
	12		1		45	515 Cr.
	15		1		614	1,129 Cr.
	18		2		80	1,209 Cr.
	26		2		580	1,789 Cr.
	29		3		490	2,279 Cr.
	31		3		100	2,379 Cr.

Cost of Parts Sold   511

19_4						
July	9		1	144		144 Dr.
	15		1	209		353 Dr.
	18		2	10		363 Dr.
	26		2	155		518 Dr.
	29		3	100		618 Dr.
	31		3	36		654 Dr.

Salaries Expense   612

19_4						
July	15		2	800		800 Dr.
	31		3	825		1,625 Dr.

Rent Expense   613

19_4						
July	2		1	180		180 Dr.

AIR SERVICES, INC.
Trial Balance
July 31, 19_4

Cash	3,142	
Accounts receivable	1,062	
Parts inventory	2,206	
Shop supplies on hand	494	
Prepaid insurance	30	
Equipment	3,000	
Accounts payable		706
Capital stock		8,000
Sales of parts		1,308
Service revenue		2,379
Cost of parts sold	654	
Salaries expense	1,625	
Rent expense	180	
	12,393	12,393

Questions

1 Are favorable events recorded as debits and are unfavorable events recorded as credits?
2 What is the distinction between a ledger and an account?
3 What is the distinction between a journal and a ledger?
4 Are debits the same as increases and are credits the same as decreases?
5 How are revenues and expenses considered subdivisions of retained earnings?
6 What is the difference between an account balance and a trial balance?
7 What are the advantages of using a journal?
8 What is posting?
9 What are account numbers and how are they used?
10 Which operation is merely a mechanical task, journalizing or posting? Explain.
11 To what rule does the double-entry method of accounting refer?
12 What is the similarity between the visual arrangement of account balances and the customary form of the balance sheet?
13 What does a credit balance in the equipment account indicate?
14 Is it true that the recording of transactions twice, once in a journal and again in the ledger, is a wasteful duplication of information?
15 What transaction results in an increase in a liability and a decrease in an asset?
16 What does a credit balance in the accounts receivable account indicate?

Short exercises

E3-1   *Indicate your knowledge of the debit-credit plan by completing the following with either the word* debits, *or the word* credits.

(a) Increases in dividends are recorded by _____.

(b) Decreases in assets are recorded by _____.

(c) Increases in liabilities are recorded by _____.

(d) Increases in expenses are recorded by _____.

(e) Decreases in revenues are recorded by _____.

(f) Increases in assets are recorded by _____.

(g) Increases in capital stock are recorded by _____.

(h) Decreases in expenses are recorded by _____.

(i) Decreases in liabilities are recorded by _____.

(j) Increases in revenues are recorded by _____.

(k) Decreases in capital stock are recorded by _____.

E3-2 For the following transactions, list the accounts affected; indicate by an X whether the effect is a debit or credit, and indicate by an X whether the effect will increase or decrease the account balance.

Transaction	Account titles	Entry is Debit	Entry is Credit	Effect of entry is Increase	Effect of entry is Decrease
(1) Merchandise is sold for cash	Cash Sales	X	X	X X	
(2) Merchandise is sold for cash and cost of goods sold is recorded					
(3) A building is purchased by partially paying cash and giving a note for the balance					
(4) Purchased merchandise on account					
(5) Made a payment for merchandise purchased on account					
(6) Paid total rent expense for the year					

E3-3 For the following transactions, list the accounts affected; indicate by an X whether the effect is a debit or credit, and indicate by an X whether the effect will increase or decrease the account balance.

Transaction	Account titles	Entry is Debit	Entry is Credit	Effect of entry is Increase	Effect of entry is Decrease
(1) Sold capital stock for cash					
(2) Purchased a building for cash					
(3) Made sales on account and recorded the cost of goods sold					
(4) Made collections on customer accounts					
(5) Paid a cash dividend					
(6) Paid salaries for eleven months and incurred a liability for the month of December					

E3-4 Given the following T-accounts, indicate what transactions occurred to affect the account balances by making journal entries, including concise explanations of the transactions.

Cash				Building		Equipment			
(1)	50,000	(4)	10,000	(2) 30,000		(3) 20,000		(6)	20,000
(6)	20,000	(5)	10,000						

Accounts payable		Mortgage payable		Capital stock	
(5) 10,000	(3) 20,000	(4) 10,000	(2) 30,000		(1) 50,000

E3-5

If the following incorrect *journal entries were recorded, determine whether the affected accounts would be overstated, understated, or correct in relation to the correct entry.*

(1) The purchase of a machine on account (purchase price $3,000) was recorded as a debit to machinery for $3,000 and a credit to cash for $3,000.

(2) The purchase of a building was recorded as a debit to building for $10,000 and a debit to cash for $10,000.

(3) The sale of capital stock was recorded as a debit to capital stock for $5,000 and a credit to cash for $5,000.

(4) The purchase of merchandise on account was recorded as a credit to accounts payable for $20,000 and a credit to merchandise inventory for $20,000.

(5) The sale of merchandise on account was recorded as a credit to sales of $10,000 and a credit to accounts receivable for $10,000.

(6) The payment of rent expense was recorded as a debit to cash of $1,000 and a credit to rent expense for $1,000.

E3-6

Prepare the 19_5 trial balance from the following information for York Corporation:

Capital stock	$10,000
Cash	7,000
Accounts payable	16,000
Retained earnings	?
Building	25,000
Accounts receivable	14,000
Sales	20,000
Cost of goods sold	10,000
Other expense	3,000

E3-7

Apostle Company was organized on March 1, 19_8, for the purpose of leasing and operating an FM radio station. Data in summary form relating to the first month's operations are given below.

Advertising revenue earned for services performed, on account	$42,800

Cash receipts for the month:	
From stockholders for shares of stock	$50,000
From customers representing collections on account	8,200
Total	$58,200

Cash disbursements for the month:	
For salaries	$36,300
For March rent	3,400
For miscellaneous expenses	1,000
For dividends to stockholders	500
Total	$41,200

Equipment costing $10,300 was purchased on account.

Prepare the March 31, 19_8 trial balance.

Problems

A3-1

The transactions listed below are those of Check Company, which was organized on August 1, 19_7.

August   1—Capital stock issued for cash of $6,000.

3—Paid August rent of $100.

4—Finished a job and collected $300.

6—Paid $100 for materials used on above job.

10—A bill delivered to G. Bron in the amount of $700 for work completed today. Bron agreed to pay in 20 days.

14—Paid $80 for materials used on Bron job.

15—Paid wages in the amount of $310.

17—Purchased land as a future building site, paying $1,000.

18—Received $700 from G. Bron for work completed on August 10.

20—A job was finished today; the bill was $700. The customer, B. Slate, promised to pay half of the bill before the end of the month and the balance within 30 days.

21—Paid $80 for materials used on Slate job.

Indicate the accounts to be debited and credited for each of the above transactions. Use the account numbers shown below.

101	Cash	401	Revenue from jobs
103	Accounts receivable	501	Rent expense
131	Land	502	Materials expense
301	Capital stock	503	Wages expense

A3-2

Using the following information, prepare the August 31, 19_3 trial balance of Brewer Corporation. Place the accounts in financial-statement sequence, that is, balance sheet accounts first and ending with income statement accounts.

**December 31, 19_3 Account Balances
(Alphabetical Order)**

Accounts receivable	$ 23,000
Accounts payable	9,000
Advertising expense	1,000
Building	35,000
Capital stock	91,000
Cash	15,000
Cost of goods sold	88,000
Equipment	13,000
Insurance expense	300
Inventory	14,700
Land	9,000
Patents	7,000
Retained earnings	21,200
Salaries expense	27,000
Salaries payable	300
Sales	114,000
Taxes	3,000
Taxes payable	500

86

A3-3   *Journalize the following transactions of Turtle Company:*

19_5

June   1—Received $800 in cash as commissions on sales made today.

   3—Paid office rent for June, $130.

   5—Received a bill from Loco Co. for miscellaneous expenses, $23.

   8—Received $115 rent for the balance of the month of June on land owned by the company.

   9—Paid traveling expenses incurred by employees, $19.

   10—Paid the bill owed to Loco Co. in the amount of $23.

   15—Paid salaries for first half of June, $850.

   16—Received $1,550 in commissions.

   18—Invested $1,000 in municipal bonds.

   21—Paid miscellaneous expenses, $21.

   22—Received a bill for advertising from the *Daily Bugle,* $35.

   26—Paid repair expense in the amount of $36.

   27—Purchased additional land worth $5,000 by issuing capital stock of $2,000 and paying $3,000 in cash.

   29—Paid the bill received on June 22 from the *Daily Bugle.*

   30—Paid salaries for the last half of June, $800.

   30—Paid dividends of $300 to stockholders.

   30—Billed Bilk Co. for $1,800 of commissions earned during June but remaining uncollected as of June 30.

A3-4   *The transactions listed below are those of a newly organized corporation. Journalize the transactions.*

19_4

April   1—Ready-Mix sold capital stock for $6,000 cash.

   1—An agreement was made whereby concrete mixing equipment and facilities were rented on a monthly basis. Rent of $1,020 was paid for April. Ready-Mix assumed responsibility for repairs.

   2—Paid $110 for a newspaper advertisement.

   5—Signed an agreement with Quick-Build, Ltd., to supply its operation with cement.

   15—Billed Quick-Build, Ltd., for supplying cement over the last ten days, $600.

   17—Received a bill for $19 from Doc's Auto Repair for equipment repairs.

   19—Received $600 from Quick-Build, Ltd.

   20—Signed an agreement with Scot's Construction Company to supply it with cement.

   22—Paid miscellaneous expenses, $25.

   25—Paid the bill from Doc's Auto Repair.

   31—Billed Quick-Build, Ltd., $630 and Scot's Construction Company $720 for services performed.

   31—Paid $715 for salaries and wages.

A3-5   *Clipper Company was organized in 19_4. The 19_4 transactions are accumulated by type of transaction. Note that dates have been omitted to lessen work. Assign your own account numbers.*

Issued 1,000 shares of capital stock for cash, $30,000.

Purchased land for $10,000 cash.

Purchased merchandise on account, $130,000.

Made sales of merchandise on account for $200,000.

Cost of goods sold, $121,000.

Collections from customers, $191,000.

Paid on account, $102,000.

Paid rent for ten months, $5,000. Two months of 19_4 rent will be paid in 19_5.

Paid salaries, $24,000. At the end of the year $4,000 additional wages were owed, but will be paid in 19_5.

Paid a cash dividend, $6,000.

Required:

(a) Journalize the transactions. Omit explanations.

(b) Post to ledger accounts.

(c) Take a December 31, 19_4 trial balance.

(d) Prepare the 19_4 financial statements (income statement, statement of retained earnings, and balance sheet).

A3-6

On October 30, 19_5, Bob Miller and Joe Jackson received a charter from the state of Illinois authorizing Tepee Corporation to issue 5,000 shares of stock and to engage in the purchase, sale, and servicing of carts and allied products.

The accountant for the new company plans to use the following accounts in the company's ledger:

Account number	Account title	(*)	Account number	Account Title	(*)
1	Cash	25	70	Sales	5
2	Accounts receivable	10	74	Repair revenue	5
10	Inventory	10	80	Cost of goods sold	5
20	Supplies and parts	5	84	Cost of supplies	
26	Tools and equipment	5		and parts used	5
50	Accounts payable	10	90	Rent expense	5
55	Advertising payable	5	91	Advertising expense	5
56	Wages payable	5	92	Wages expense	5
57	Delivery expense payable	5	93	Delivery expense	5
60	Capital stock	5	94	Salaries expense	5

(*)Suggested number of lines to allow when setting up the ledger accounts.

It will be the company's practice to bill the customer and record sales of merchandise on the day of sale, but in the case of repair work, the billing and recording will be made at month end for the month's work.

19_5

November 1—Tepee Corporation issued 200 shares of stock to Miller upon investment of $10,000 and issued 400 shares of stock to Jackson upon investment of $20,000.

1—A showroom and warehouse-servicing building was rented from the Real Estate Agency for $400 per month. The November rent was paid.

3—Received, per order, 15 carts at an invoice price of $175 each, from Cartage Co.

4—Purchased for cash from Stambo's Inc. tools and light repair equipment for $960.

5—Paid Cartage Co. $2,500 on account and ordered $950 worth of service supplies and parts.

6—Sales for the day totaled two carts. One was sold for $265 cash installed and the other was sold for $285 on credit to R. Striker.

8—Supplies and parts ordered on November 5 were received.

11—Paid balance owed to Cartage Co. and ordered 12 carts.

12—Paid $72 for newspaper advertising for the week ended November 6.

13—Paid employees' wages for the week, $410.

13—Sales for the day: Cash—3 units at $265 each.
Credit—1 unit at $285 to John Fisher.

15—Collection on accounts receivable, $20.

16—Paid $42 for advertising.

17—Received 12 carts ordered on November 11, at an invoice price of $175 each.

20—Paid employees' wages for the week, $320.

20—Sales for the day: Cash—4 units at $265 each.
Credit—1 unit at $285 to Henry Schweppe.
1 unit at $285 to R. J. Noever.

22—Collected $35 on account.

23—Paid newspaper advertising, $81.

25—Paid Cartage Co. $1,320 on account.

26—Paid U-Haul-It Co. $210 for deliveries.

27—Paid employees' wages for the week, $300.

27—Sales for the day: Cash—4 units at $265 each.

29—Purchased repair parts and supplies for $1,250 cash.

30—Received ten carts from Cartage Co. at an invoice price of $195 each. Payment to be on account.

30—Paid $105 for advertising. Additional advertising owed at the end of the month was $66, to be paid next month.

30—Paid salaries of $400.

30—Collected $30 on account.

30—Billed customers $3,511 for repair work completed in November.

30—Supplies and parts used on repair work during November cost $235.

30—As of the end of the month Tepee owed, but did not pay, $120 of wages and $12 of delivery expense. Tepee will pay the amounts due in December.

Required:

(a) Journalize the November transactions.

(b) Post.

(c) Prepare a trial balance.

(d) Prepare the 19_5 financial statements (income statement, statement of retained earnings, and balance sheet). Tepee's fiscal year ends on November 30.

B3-1 *The following accounts and amounts were taken from the 19_4 trial balance of Clock Company. Prepare the trial balance, placing the balance sheet accounts first and ending with the income statement accounts.*

Cash	$ 4,000
Accounts receivable	10,000
Rent expense	1,000
Inventory	9,000
Salaries payable	900
Other expense	2,700
Land	5,000
Salaries expense	10,000
Truck	2,000
Accounts payable	12,000
Cost of goods sold	27,000
Sales	40,000
Dividends	2,000
Retained earnings	9,800
Capital stock	10,000

B3-2   *The transactions listed below are those of Basket Company for June of 19_5.*

June   1—Issued capital stock for cash.

        2—Issued capital stock for a building.

        4—Purchased inventory on account.

        6—Made a sale to Jo Smith on account.

      10—Purchased equipment on account.

      13—Paid dividend with cash.

      15—Recorded cost of goods sold for June 6 sale.

      18—Collected the total owed by Jo Smith.

      20—Paid part of amount owed for inventory purchase.

      25—Issued a note for cash.

Indicate the accounts to be debited and credited for each of the above transactions. Use the account numbers shown below.

101	Cash		400	Note payable
105	Inventory		410	Accounts payable
108	Accounts receivable		500	Capital stock
110	Building		600	Sales
120	Land		700	Cost of goods sold
130	Equipment		800	Dividends

B3-3   *The account balances of Gas Bag Corporation at the beginning of 19_5 are listed below.*

Cash	$3,000
Inventory	3,600
Commissions payable	240
Taxes payable	54
Capital stock	5,600
Retained earnings	710

The inventory consisted of two airplanes costing $1,800 each. Journalize the following January 19_5 transactions:

19_5

January   2—Sold an airplane and collected cash for the sales price, $2,600.

           5—Purchased from Dillow Aircraft Company on account two airplanes costing $2,000 each.

6—Paid the taxes payable.

13—One of the company's salesmen sold the remaining airplane that was on hand at the beginning of the year. He collected $2,600 from the customer. He deducted his 10 per cent commission on this sale and $160 commission owed him from an earlier sale and turned in $2,180 to the company.

15—Delivered one of the airplanes acquired from Dillow Aircraft Company to a customer and collected the sales price of $2,560.

18—Paid the amount owed to Dillow Aircraft Company.

25—Purchased from Dillow Aircraft Company on account four airplanes costing $2,000 each.

31—As of the end of the month, rent owed for January totaled $100. This amount will be paid the next month.

B3-4   *Journalize the following transactions of Faster Sail Makers Company:*

19_1

July   1—Issued capital stock for cash of $25,000.

2—Paid rent for July, $200.

3—Purchased from Supply Company, on account, five sails for $300 each.

7—Sold one sail for $350 cash. (Remember to make the journal entry for cost of goods sold.)

8—Paid $10 as commission to salesman.

9—As a promotional feature the company contributed a sail to the prize-winning ketch Red Witch. The company hopes that use of its product on the Red Witch will give it a reputation for quality sails.

10—Sold a sail for $375 to G. Grimstead on account.

15—Paid $1,500 to Supply Company.

18—Purchased for cash four sails for $300 each.

20—Paid $35 for newspaper advertising.

24—Collected $375 from G. Grimstead.

24—Paid $40 commissions to the salesman.

28—Cash sale of three sails to Jay Lockers for $1,210.

30—Paid $100 cash dividend to stockholders.

B3-5   *The accounts in the ledger of Vance Company with their December 31, 19_3 balances are listed below and at the top of page 92.*

Account number	Account title	Balance
111	Cash	$32,000
113	Accounts receivable	20,000
115	Merchandise inventory	16,000
131	Land (held as an investment)	10,000
152	Delivery truck	—
161	Building	—
211	Accounts payable	20,000
212	Salaries payable	2,000
218	Rent payable	—

Account number	Account title	Balance
311	Capital stock (1,000 shares)	50,000
315	Retained earnings	6,000
319	Dividends	—
411	Sales	—
511	Cost of goods sold	—
512	Salaries expense	—
513	Other expense	—
514	Rent expense	—

In order to reduce the repetition in the recording process (journalizing and posting), yearly totals are given for certain kinds of transactions.

19_4 Transactions

Dates
19_4

January   3—Paid the liability for the December, 19_3 salaries, $2,000.

7—Purchased a delivery truck for cash, $5,000.

13—Issued capital stock for a building, $10,000.

August   11—Paid rent for the first eight months of 19_4, $1,600.

December 31—Purchased merchandise on account, $40,000.

31—Sales on account, $60,000.

31—Cost of goods sold, $36,000.

31—Collections on accounts receivable, $65,000.

31—Payments to creditors, $35,000.

31—Paid other expenses, $4,000.

31—Paid salaries, $12,450.

31—Paid dividends, $1,000.

31—The rent for the last four months of 19_4 will be paid in 19_5.

Required:

(a) Journalize the 19_4 transactions.

(b) Enter the December 31, 19_3 (beginning) balances in the ledger accounts. Allow ten lines for the cash account and four lines for all other accounts.

(c) Post.

(d) Prepare the December 31, 19_4 trial balance.

(e) Prepare the 19_4 financial statements (income statement, statement of retained earnings, and balance sheet).

B3-6

Journalize the October, 19_4 transactions of Krupp Company, post to the ledger accounts, take an October 31, 19_4 trial balance, and prepare the 19_4 financial statements (fiscal year ends on October 31).

The company was organized to perform maintenance and repair services on aircraft. There will be two sources of revenue, one from the sale of parts (parts will be sold at twice their cost) and the other from the performance of maintenance and repair service. The following accounts can be used when recording the October transactions:

Account number	Account title	(*)
111	Cash	(19)
112	Accounts receivable	(9)
113	Parts inventory	(12)
114	Shop supplies on hand	(4)
151	Equipment	(4)
211	Accounts payable	(7)
311	Capital stock	(4)
411	Sales of parts	(10)
412	Service revenue	(10)
510	Cost of parts sold	(10)
512	Wages expense	(5)
513	Rent expense	(4)

(*)Suggested number of lines to allow when setting up the ledger accounts.

October 1—Issued $10,000 par value stock (1,000 shares) for $7,000 cash and equipment valued at $3,000.

2—Paid October rent, $230.

7—Purchased airplane spare parts on account from Seymour Company, $3,592.

7—Purchased shop supplies for $305 cash.

9—Billed Marilyn Airline $266 for parts and $520 for labor used in making a periodic check on one of its aircraft.

12—Purchased additional airplane parts from Shick, Inc., paying $230 in cash.

13—Collected $22 for repair of landing gear on a private plane. No parts were used.

14—Paid the Seymour Company bill.

15—Billed Charter Flights $214 for parts and $308 for labor used in rebuilding a tail assembly.

15—Paid wages of $800 for first half of October.

17—Collected $300 for periodic overhaul of a private plane; this amount included $20 for parts.

18—Received $786 from Marilyn Airline.

20—Signed an agreement with Decca Company to perform all required labor for maintenance on its company plane for $1,200 per quarter, starting today. All parts used will be extra.

25—Received $522 from Charter Flights.

26—Billed Marilyn Airline $310 for parts and $580 for labor used in making a periodic check of one of its aircraft.

28—Purchased airplane parts on account from Seymour Company, $209.

29—Completed rebuilding landing gear on plane belonging to R. M. Buchholz. The total bill amounted to $790 of which $200 was for parts. Buchholz gave her check for the entire bill when she called today for her plane.

30—Purchased shop supplies on account from Supply Co., $42.

31—Paid wages for last half of October, $310.

31—Billed Decca Company, pursuant to agreement of October 20, for parts used in maintenance of company plane, $164.

CHART OF ACCOUNTS
APPENDIX TO CHAPTER 3

CHART OF ACCOUNTS   As a general rule, the first accounting work performed for any business involves the development of an accounting system. The accountant studies the nature of the business, determines the types of transactions that probably will occur, and plans or selects the necessary forms and records in which the transactions of the business may be recorded.

One of the first steps in the development of an accounting system is the preparation of a chart of accounts. Such a chart lists the assets, liabilities, elements of the owners' equity, revenues, and expenses for which a separate record will be maintained.

It is advisable to number the accounts in a systematic manner so that the account numbers indicate classifications and relationships. Numbering systems differ, but the chart of accounts beginning on page 95 illustrates the general principle.

Observe that each account number contains four digits, and that the first digit at the left indicates a main classification, as shown below.

1– – –	Assets and related contra accounts.
2– – –	Liabilities.
3– – –	Stockholders' equity.
4– – –	Sales and related accounts.
5– – –	Purchases and related accounts (for a periodic inventory system).
6– – –	Operating expenses.
7– – –	Other revenue and expense.
8– – –	Income tax.

The second digit indicates a main subclassification, thus:

11– –	Current assets and related contra accounts.
12– –	Long-term investments.
13– –	Property, plant, and equipment and related contra accounts.
14– –	Intangible assets.
21– –	Current liabilities.
24– –	Long-term liabilities.

The third and fourth digits indicate further subclassifications and relationships, thus:

2180	Withholding and F.I.C.A. tax payable.
2181	Federal unemployment tax payable.
2182	State unemployment tax payable.

The third digit, 8, is common to a group of liability accounts for withholding and payroll taxes. The various taxes are differentiated by the fourth digit.

The third and fourth digits in many instances are selected for reasons of consistency, or to show relationships.

As examples of numbers chosen for the sake of consistency, observe the account numbers listed below. The first digit indicates whether the account represents an asset or a liability; the fact that the item is current is indicated by the second digit; the final "30" indicates an account receivable or payable; the final "40" indicates a note receivable or payable.

1130	Accounts receivable.
2130	Accounts payable.
1140	Notes receivable.
2140	Notes payable.

Also observe that contra accounts, representing deductions from related accounts, are numbered with a final "8" or "9":

1130	Accounts receivable.
1139	Allowance for uncollectibles.
1350	Delivery equipment.
1359	Accumulated depreciation—delivery equipment.
4000	Sales.
4008	Sales returns and allowances.
4009	Sales discounts.

As examples of account numbers assigned to show relationships, observe the following:

1191	Prepaid insurance.
6591	Insurance expense.
2155	Salaries payable.
6555	Office salaries.

Illustrative chart of accounts

Current assets

1110	Cash.
1120	Temporary investments.
1130	Accounts receivable.
1139	Allowance for uncollectibles.
1140	Notes receivable.
1154	Interest receivable.
1170	Inventory.
1190	Prepaid rent.
1191	Prepaid insurance.

Long-term investments
1210   Land.
1220   Investments in bonds.

Property, plant, and equipment
1310   Parking lot.
1320   Store fixtures.
1329   Accumulated depreciation—store fixtures.
1350   Delivery equipment.
1359   Accumulated depreciation—delivery equipment.

Intangible assets
1410   Patents.
1420   Goodwill.

Current liabilities
2130   Accounts payable.
2140   Notes payable.
2154   Interest payable.
2155   Salaries payable.
2160   Estimated income tax payable.
2170   Liability for sales taxes.
2180   Withholding and F.I.C.A. tax payable.
2181   Federal unemployment tax payable.
2182   State unemployment tax payable.
2195   Advances from customers.
2196   Rent received in advance.

Long-term liabilities
2410   Mortgage payable.

Stockholders' equity
3510   Capital stock.
3511   Capital in excess of par value.
3610   Retained earnings.
3910   Dividends.

Sales and related accounts
4000   Sales.
4008   Sales returns and allowances.
4009   Sales discounts.

Purchases and related accounts
5170   Purchases.
5178   Purchase returns and allowances.
5179   Purchase discounts.
5200   Transportation in.
5500   Cost of goods sold.

Operating expenses

6001	Store rent.
6002	Advertising.
6029	Depreciation expense—store fixtures.
6059	Depreciation expense—delivery equipment.
6070	Other delivery expense.
6071	Transportation out.
6080	Salesmen's commissions.
6090	Miscellaneous selling expenses.
6501	Office expenses.
6511	Taxes, other than income and payroll.
6549	Bad debts expense.
6555	Office salaries.
6585	Payroll taxes expense.
6591	Insurance expense.

Other revenues and gains

7010	Rent of land.
7054	Interest revenue.

Other expenses and losses

7154	Interest expense.

Income tax

8160	Income tax.

INCOME MEASUREMENT
CHAPTER 4

PURPOSE OF CHAPTER   Of all the amounts reported in a firm's financial statements, net income is probably the most important to the majority of statement users. The basic format of the income statement and the nature of items reported in the statement have already been introduced. However, the purpose of this chapter is to focus on certain key assumptions which are the foundation of income determination under the accrual basis of accounting.

In addition to the recording of transactions during the accounting period, the determination of accrual basis net income also involves the use of end-of-period adjusting entries. This chapter illustrates and discusses the use of adjusting entries to complete the income determination process.

EMPHASIS ON INCOME MEASUREMENT   For many decades accountants regarded the balance sheet as of primary importance and the income statement as of secondary importance—possibly a reflection of the attitude then held by bankers and other grantors of short-term credit. Grantors of credit were concerned with the margin of security for their loans. They were primarily interested in two questions: What assets does the applicant for credit own? What liabilities does he or she already owe? The answers to those questions were found in the balance sheet.

Over the years a shift in emphasis—from the balance sheet to the income statement—has taken place. In part, this shift can be traced to a change in the point of view of credit grantors, their current approach placing more emphasis on the earnings (net income) potential as an indication of debt-paying ability. Another factor has been the increase in the number of investors in corporate securities. Investors and speculators are disposed to measure the attractiveness of securities by the earnings of the issuing company. As net income goes up, security prices tend to increase; as net income goes down, security prices tend to decrease.

With the increasing emphasis on the income statement, the determination and reporting of net income have become the central objectives of the accounting process. As a result, a significant portion of accounting theory is devoted to income measurement, which, as previously noted, is often described as a process of matching revenue and related expense.

NATURE OF NET INCOME   In general terms, net income (also called earnings and profits) is the dollar amount by which a firm has become economically better off during a given period of time. Accountants measure whether or not a firm is better off by the excess of revenues and gains over expenses and losses for a given time period—net income. Such measurement is based on the objective evidence provided by business transactions that occurred during the given time period.

Business firms engage in economic operations to produce income. The operations of a business firm are the primary ongoing economic activities or basic economic processes in which the firm is engaged, such as buying and selling products (merchandising or retailing firm), manufacturing and selling produced products (manufacturing firm), and selling services (service firm). In other words, the operations of a business firm are its normal productive activities, which result in providing goods and services to customers on a regular and recurring basis.

In conducting its operations, the business firm, in effect, is converting inputs into outputs with the expectation that the output will command a price in the market that is greater than the cost of the input. The business firm uses economic resources (inputs) to provide goods and services (outputs) to customers. The assets (normally cash and receivables) received from customers in exchange for the goods and services provided to them during a given time period are called *revenues.* The costs of the economic resources used to provide goods and services (that is, generate revenue) during a given time period are called *expenses.* The excess of revenues from operations over operating expenses over a given time period is called *net operating income.* Since revenues are a measure of a firm's accomplishments and since expenses are a measure of a firm's efforts, net operating income is a measure of a firm's operating performance over a specific period of time.

In addition to its operating activities, a business firm can carry on secondary economic activities that result in nonoperating revenues, expenses, gains, and losses. Examples of nonoperating revenue include interest, dividend, and rent revenues. An example of nonoperating expense is interest expense, which is a financial rather than operating expense. Examples of gains and losses include the gain or loss resulting from the sale of assets not normally held for sale, such as land or equipment, and the gain or loss resulting from the sale of a major segment, such as a division, of a business firm. Note that these nonoperating items are not associated with the providing of the firm's primary goods and services (its operations); however, since nonoperating revenues and gains have a favorable effect and since nonoperating expenses and losses have an unfavorable effect on stockholders' equity via retained earnings, they are included in the determination of net income. Nonoperating items are explained and illustrated later in this chapter.

Net income is the excess of revenues and gains over expenses and losses during a given time period. Conversely, a net loss is the excess of expenses and losses over revenues and gains during a given time period. Since it is the operating activities of a business firm that primarily determine net income, net income is often referred to as the firm's *results of operations* for a period of time. Net income is a measure of the dollar amount by which the firm has economically progressed (become better off) over a period of time.

Net income increases a firm's assets and retained earnings. Assets generated by profitable operations that are retained in the business provide the resources to maintain existing operations, or if profitable enough, to expand operations. Profitable operations provide the assets used to pay dividends to stockholders; hence, profitable operations attract investor financing and normally have an upward effect on stock prices. Also, profitable operations provide the assets to pay creditors or provide the basis for refinancing or obtaining additional credit. Conversely, a firm that continues to have unprofitable operations is not able to attract investor and creditor financing; hence, as assets continue to decline, eventually the business will be unable to survive. The point is that the generation of net income is necessary for the firm to succeed and to survive.

Finally, it should be well understood that a firm's net income for a time period is not the same as its net cash inflow (cash receipts minus cash expenditures) for the same time period. Net income for the period is measured in terms of revenues and expenses instead of in terms of cash receipts and expenditures. The measurement of net income is based on accrual, not cash, accounting, as will be discussed and illustrated in this chapter.

THE ACCOUNTING PERIOD The time period used by accountants for purposes of financial statement reporting is called the *accounting,* or *fiscal, period.* Specifically, the accounting period is the time interval covered by the income statement. The income statement and the statement of changes in financial position cover a specified accounting or fiscal period, and the balance sheet is as of a specific date at the end of the accounting period.

The usual accounting period is 12 consecutive months, called the *fiscal year.* Most businesses' fiscal year is the calendar year ending December 31. There are a number of companies, such as department stores, that use the natural business year in which the end of the fiscal year occurs at the annual low level of business activity. For example, many department stores end their fiscal year on January 31, which is after the Christmas peak activity and the resulting sales returns and clearance sales in January. The fiscal year for the federal government is October 1 to September 30.

The management of most large firms wants financial statements prepared monthly for its own internal use. Publicly owned companies issue quarterly reports to the Securities and Exchange Commission, to the stock exchanges that list their stock, and to their stockholders. These monthly, quarterly, or semiannual financial statements are called *interim statements* (reports) to distinguish them from the annual statements issued for the fiscal year.

FISCAL-PERIOD (PERIODICITY) ASSUMPTION A primary objective of accounting is to provide economic information useful for financial decision making. If that objective is to be fulfilled, accounting information must be timely. Obviously, the accounting information relevant for a particular decision must be available to the decision makers before the deadline for making the decision.

Earnings data are relevant for many business decisions. Income determination would be very easy if the accountant could delay the determination until business operations were discontinued and all assets were converted into cash. The net income for the entire life span of a business would be the excess cash received by the owners, including that received upon liquidation, over their investment in the business. Few estimates or assumptions would be required because there would be relatively no uncertainty.[1] But it obviously would be unsatisfactory to postpone the determination of net income until after liquidation. Management and other users of financial data want such information currently; they want to plan and adapt their courses of action in light of such information. In short, users want timely accounting information.

As was briefly discussed in Chapter 2, the accountant tries to meet this need by assuming that the business operations of a firm can be segmented into time periods. The assumption is that the life span of a business firm can be segmented into short-run time periods in order to provide timely economic information to aid in financial decision making. Such time intervals are accounting periods called *fiscal periods*, and the accountant prepares financial statements at the end of each fiscal period. However, most businesses are engaged in continuous activity that does not stop at the end of each fiscal period. So, in a sense, the fiscal-period assumption implies that business activity "stops" at periodic intervals, which allows the accountant to prepare financial statements and thus provide a report on the firm's progress during the period just ended, on its financial position at the end of the period, and on its change in financial position during the period. In fact, because of the continuous nature of most business activity, accounting information associated with fiscal periods should be viewed as short-run estimates or approximations of progress, financial position, and changes in financial position, but estimates based on the informed judgment of accountants. Thus it should be clearly understood that at any time prior to liquidation, periodic financial measurements are at best informed estimates, especially the periodic measurement of net income, which should be viewed as tentative.

To make the short-run estimates shown in the financial statements as meaningful as possible, the business transactions that provide the basic financial data needed to prepare the statements must be identified with the proper time periods. Yet, because of the continuous nature of business activity, not all business transactions are started and completed in one accounting period; instead, they can overlap two or more accounting periods. Thus there must be a cutoff between periods so that the revenues and expenses associated with the business transactions for 19_8 are kept separate from those of 19_9 and 19_7; otherwise, the net income for each year would be distorted and those who use accounting information for decision making would be misled. To avoid such distortion, the accountant relies on the revenue-recognition and matching assumptions to identify revenues and expenses with the proper time period. The application of these two assumptions reflects the accrual basis of accounting: recognize revenue during the period when earned and recognize expense during the period when incurred in generating that revenue, regardless of the cash flows.

REVENUE-RECOGNITION ASSUMPTION As was briefly discussed in Chapter 2, there is the question of when revenue should be recognized in the accounting records and hence included in the income statement for the fiscal period. There are several

---

[1]There would still be some measurement problems with regard to the time value of money (interest-rate effect) and changes in the general-price level (inflation and deflation).

possibilities. Revenue could be recognized when orders are secured from customers, when the manufacturing process is completed, when the goods are delivered to the customer, or when cash or some other asset is received in payment for the goods sold.

The several events or activities noted in the preceding sentence all contribute to the revenue-earning process. Unless orders are secured, there is no revenue. Unless goods are manufactured or otherwise acquired for resale, there can be no deliveries to customers. If a business fails to generate a cash inflow from customers, it will, in time, cease being a going concern. In short, the earning of revenue is an economic process, since it is based on several coordinated, and often complicated, activities such as selling, financing, purchasing, manufacturing, and distribution. It is difficult, both theoretically and practically, to determine which event or activity is the critical one which, when completed or fulfilled, justifies the recognition of revenue.

For retail, wholesale, and manufacturing businesses, the accountant generally uses the point (date) of sale as the basis for revenue recognition. In essence, the accountant assumes that recognizing revenue at the point of sale will provide a meaningful measurement of the results of management's efforts directed toward the generation of revenue. The following facts support that assumption:

> Generally, by the time the point of sale has been reached, the firm has performed the major economic effort required in the generation of revenue and any remaining expense associated with the sale will be negligible.
>
> At the point of sale the exchange price provides an objective measurement for revenue.
>
> At the point of sale a conversion takes place—one asset is exchanged for another.

Legally, the point of sale occurs when title to the goods passes to the buyer. For expediency, the accountant assumes that passage of title coincides with delivery of the goods to the customer or the customer's agent.

Revenue is earned by service-type businesses as services are performed. In some cases, usually when the rendering of services extends over a fairly long time period and involves more than one accounting period, estimates may be used so that revenue may be recorded and reported during the periods when the work is being performed. Practical considerations may lead to the adoption of a policy of postponing the recognition of any revenue from services until the services are completed; the amount to be charged for the entire service may not be determinable until completion and, as a consequence, the revenue applicable to services rendered during the periods prior to completion may not be determinable.

It should be pointed out that the revenue-recognition assumption is fundamental to accrual accounting. That is, revenue is recognized during the period when earned, regardless of when the cash is collected. The recognition of revenue is not based on when cash is received. Of course, for many transactions the two coincide: Cash is received at the same time the goods are delivered or the services are rendered.

Although the recognition of revenue is normally based on the point of sale, under certain special circumstances accountants may deviate from this revenue-recognition assumption. These exceptions are discussed later in the text.

HOW IS REVENUE MEASURED?   Revenue has been previously defined as an inflow of assets. This leaves unanswered the question of how revenue is measured; that is, what number of dollars and cents should be used when revenue transactions are entered in the company's records and reported in the company's income statement?

In a sense, revenue is measured in the marketplace. The actions of buyers and sellers establish the dollar amounts of revenue transactions. In typical situations this means that the amounts are determined objectively, being a product of bargained transactions and supported by various kinds of evidence such as legal contracts, bills of sale, and checks made out in favor of the seller.

It should be pointed out that the process of revenue measurement also results in measuring, initially, certain assets, namely, those arising from revenue-producing transactions. The revenue figure is used not only as a measure of revenue but also as a measure of the assets received in connection with revenue transactions. This use of the revenue figure follows from the basic equation:

Assets = Equities

The assets most commonly acquired through revenue transactions are cash and accounts and notes receivable. Occasionally securities, or even property, plant, and equipment, are acquired from revenue transactions, in which case they are recorded initially in the company's records at the cash transaction price established for the goods or services sold in exchange by the business. Thus revenue measurement and asset valuation are not completely separate activities. It should be recognized, however, that not all asset balances are traceable to revenue transactions. Many asset balances are the result of purchases by a business. For example, this is typically the case for machinery and equipment and for inventory.

MATCHING ASSUMPTION   The question of when to recognize expense in the accounting records and thereby include it in the income statement for the fiscal period was briefly discussed in Chapter 2. It was pointed out that accountants assume that expense should be recognized during the period in which goods and services are used (expenses incurred) in the generation of revenue. Expenses incurred in the generation of revenue should be identified (matched) with that revenue earned during the same fiscal period. By identifying expenses with the period in which the resulting revenue is earned, expenses are matched with revenue to determine net income for the period.

Matching assumes that there is a direct cause-and-effect relationship between measured effort (expense) and measured accomplishment (revenue) to provide a performance measurement (net income) for a given time period. In reality, it is impossible to associate directly all expenses with revenue. Therefore, accountants implement the matching assumption by making the practical and expedient distinction between direct and indirect expense, which allows the association of expense with revenue in the following two ways:

Direct association with revenue. Those goods and services used that are directly related to the firm's product are expensed when the revenue is earned by the sale of goods or the rendering of services. For example, cost of goods sold for a merchandising firm is expensed during the period when the product is sold; hence, there is a direct matching because both the expense and revenue relate to the same physical product. Similarly, sales commissions would not exist if sales were not made; therefore, they are directly associated with the revenue from sales and should be recorded as expenses in the period in which the sales are reported as revenue.

Indirect association with revenue. Those goods and services used that cannot be directly related to a firm's product are expensed during the period when incurred. That is, these expenses are directly associated with the time period during which revenue is earned; hence, such expenses are *period expenses* associated with overall, not specific, revenue for the period. Examples include selling and administrative salaries, insurance, depreciation, taxes, and advertising—the operating expenses.

HOW IS EXPENSE MEASURED? As defined in Chapter 1, expense is the *cost* of goods and services used in the generation of revenue. Expenses are the goods and services used, and based on the historical-cost assumption expenses are measured at cost. In this respect, cost is defined as the amount paid, in cash or other assets, or the liability incurred to make a future payment, for benefits received or to be received. Goods and services used in the generation of revenue (expenses) are measured at the prices paid for them when acquired—their cost.

RELATION OF COST TO ASSETS AND EXPENSES Cost is not only the measure of expense, but it is also the measure for asset acquisitions. The cost of an asset includes its purchase price and related incidental outlays (so-called *incidental costs*), such as the cost of a title search and legal fees incurred in the acquisition of real estate; transportation, installation, and breaking-in costs incident to the acquisition of machinery; storage, taxes, and other costs incurred in aging certain kinds of inventories, such as wine; and costs incurred in the rehabilitation of a plant purchased in a run-down condition.

A satisfactory net income figure is a primary objective of a business enterprise. In carrying on the numerous and varied activities aimed at generating income, a business spends money for a wide variety of goods and services. Such cost outlays are made in the belief that they will contribute to the profitability of the enterprise (advertising, for example) or because they cannot be avoided without curtailing the activities of the business (taxes, for example). In either case, economic benefits are expected from the cost outlays, or they would not have been made.

If it is known at the time of making a cost outlay that the related economic benefit will not extend beyond the current operating period (as when a year's rent is paid in advance at the beginning of the year), it is customary and expedient to record the transaction as an expense. One could reach the same result by recording the transaction as an asset acquisition, and then later during the period, when the benefit had expired or been consumed, making a transfer of the amount involved from its asset status to an expense account. The recording plan described first is favored because it entails less work. Note, however, that in either case the expense is a period expense that presumably contributes to revenue for the period (indirect association with revenue).

If there is a reasonable expectation at the time of making a cost outlay that the related economic benefits will extend beyond the current accounting period (as when a delivery truck is purchased), it is customary to record the transaction as an asset acquisition. As the benefits expire or are consumed, an appropriate portion of the asset cost is transferred to expense (period expense). Such transfers are made by adjusting entries at the end of an accounting period before the financial statements are prepared.

ADJUSTING ENTRIES   Adjusting entries are entries made at the end of the accounting period to bring the account balances up to date (that is, adjust the account balances) so that financial statements can be prepared. If adjusting entries were omitted or overlooked, the financial statements would be incorrect.

Adjusting entries arise because the continuous nature of business operations means that not all business transactions are started and completed in one accounting period. Transactions that overlap two or more accounting periods are apportioned between accounting periods by end-of-period adjusting entries.

Adjusting entries are fundamental to the accrual basis of accounting, since they provide a cutoff of revenues and expenses as between accounting periods, regardless of cash flows. Adjusting entries will be illustrated later in this chapter and then fully discussed in the next chapter.

ACCRUAL VERSUS CASH ACCOUNTING   The accrual basis of accounting recognizes revenue during the period when earned, regardless of the time of cash receipt, and recognizes the expense incurred in that same time period in generating the revenue, regardless of the time of cash payment, and matches the two to determine net income for the period. Net income under accrual accounting provides a realistic picture of a firm's profitability for a given time period, since both revenue and expense are recognized in the same time period in which the operating activities that caused them occurred.

The cash basis of accounting recognizes revenue when collected in cash and recognizes expense when cash is paid. The problem with cash accounting is that cash receipts and cash disbursements can lead or lag the time period in which the operating activities occurred that give rise to the cash flows. The resulting net cash inflow (outflow) for the period does not provide a measure of operating performance (as does net income), since there is no necessary association between cash receipts as a measure of accomplishment (as is earned revenue) and cash disbursements as a measure of effort (as is incurred expense). As a result, cash accounting is used only by individuals, small businesses, and professional practices (lawyers and physicians) where accounts receivable and payable, inventory, and long-lived assets either do not exist or are immaterial. For most business firms, cash accounting would not be permitted by generally accepted accounting principles.

The illustration on page 106 contrasts the cash basis and the accrual basis of accounting. Note the reasons why the total cash receipts, total cash disbursements, and net cash inflow do not equal the total sales revenue, expense, and net income, respectively, for the year.

Current year

	Amount	Cash receipts	Sales revenue
1. Cash sales made this year	$50,000	$50,000	$50,000
2. Credit sales made this year; cash received this year	60,000	60,000	60,000
3. Credit sales made this year; cash to be received next year	15,000	—	15,000
4. Cash received this year; credit sales made last year	12,000	12,000	—
5. Cash received in advance this year; revenue to be earned next year	5,000	5,000	—
6. Revenue earned this year; cash received in advance in previous years	10,000	—	10,000
Total cash receipts for year		$127,000	
Total revenue for year			$135,000

	Amount	Cash payments	Expense
7. Cash expenses incurred this year	$ 9,000	$ 9,000	$ 9,000
8. Expenses incurred this year on credit; cash paid this year	46,000	46,000	46,000
9. Expenses incurred this year; cash to be paid next year	30,000	—	30,000
10. Cash paid this year; expenses incurred last year	15,000	15,000	—
11. Cash paid this year; expense to be incurred next year	2,000	2,000	—
12. Expense incurred this year; cash paid in previous year	18,000	—	18,000
Total cash paid for year		72,000	
Total expense for year			103,000
Net cash inflow		$ 55,000	
Net income			$ 32,000

ACCRUAL ACCOUNTING APPLIED TO BUSINESS TRANSACTIONS To illustrate further the nature of accrual accounting, the transactions of Sight & Sound Corporation relating to its second year of operations (19_2) will be analyzed. The transactions are keyed to the accounts with identifying numbers, and italics are used to identify each additional debit and credit when entered in the T-accounts. Accounts debited are shown on the left; accounts credited are shown on the right.

19_2 Transactions

(1) Paid the liability for December 19_1 salaries, $1,500.

   Reasoning: Although salaries are expenses, they apply to the period that received the benefit of the services performed by the salaried employees, which may or may not coincide with the period during which the salary payments are made. In this instance, the salaries for December 19_1 were properly treated as a 19_1 expense and the liability therefore was shown in the December 31, 19_1 balance sheet. The payment made in 19_2 merely removed the outstanding liability.

Accounts affected	Kind of account	Change in balance	Debit	Credit
Salaries payable	Liability	Decrease	1,500	
Cash	Asset	Decrease		1,500

Salaries payable				Cash			
(1)	1,500	1/1/_2 Bal.	*1,500*	1/1/_2 Bal.	16,500	(1)	*1,500*

(2)   Purchased a small delivery truck for cash, $4,000. Management believes that the truck will last four years.

  Reasoning: By acquiring the delivery truck, the business has secured the right to some future economic benefits and, since the benefit period extends beyond the current fiscal period, the transaction should be handled as an asset acquisition.

Accounts affected	Kind of account	Change in balance	Debit	Credit
Delivery truck	Asset	Increase	4,000	
Cash	Asset	Decrease		4,000

Delivery truck			Cash			
(2)	*4,000*		1/1/_2 Bal.	16,500	(1)	1,500
					(2)	*4,000*

(3)   Purchased merchandise on account, $60,000.

  Comment: Satisfying inventory needs with only one purchase a year would be most unusual. But since each purchase of merchandise would be handled in the same way, presenting annual data eliminates repetitive transactions.

Accounts affected	Kind of account	Change in balance	Debit	Credit
Merchandise inventory	Asset	Increase	60,000	
Accounts payable	Liability	Increase		60,000

Merchandise inventory			Accounts payable		
1/1/_2 Bal.	12,000			1/1/_2 Bal.	20,000
(3)	*60,000*			(3)	*60,000*

(4a)   Sales on account, $90,000.

  Comment: Here also annual data are given to eliminate repetitive transactions.

Accounts affected	Kind of account	Change in balance	Debit	Credit
Accounts receivable	Asset	Increase	90,000	
Sales	Revenue	Increase		90,000

Accounts receivable			Sales		
1/1_2 Bal.	11,000			(4a)	*90,000*
(4a)	*90,000*				

(4b)   Cost of goods sold, $54,000.

Accounts affected	Kind of account	Change in balance	Debit	Credit
Cost of goods sold	Expense	Increase	54,000	
Merchandise inventory	Asset	Decrease		54,000

Cost of goods sold		Merchandise inventory			
(4b)	*54,000*	1/1/_2 Bal.	12,000	(4b)	*54,000*
		(3)	60,000		

(5)   Collections from customers, $89,000.

Accounts affected	Kind of account	Change in balance	Debit	Credit
Cash	Asset	Increase	89,000	
Accounts receivable	Asset	Decrease		89,000

Cash				Accounts receivable			
1/1/_2 Bal.	16,500	(1)	1,500	1/1/_2 Bal.	11,000	(5)	*89,000*
(5)	*89,000*	(2)	4,000	(4a)	90,000		

(6)   Payments to creditors on account, $55,000.

Accounts affected	Kind of account	Change in balance	Debit	Credit
Accounts payable	Liability	Decrease	55,000	
Cash	Asset	Decrease		55,000

Accounts payable				Cash			
(6)	*55,000*	1/1/_2 Bal.	20,000	1/1/_2 Bal.	16,500	(1)	1,500
		(3)	60,000	(5)	89,000	(2)	4,000
						(6)	*55,000*

(7)   Paid two years' rent in advance, $9,600. At the beginning of 19_2 the company signed a rental agreement covering a two-year period which specified that rent for the two-year period was to be paid in advance.

Reasoning: By making the payment in advance, the company has acquired the right to some future economic benefits, namely, the benefits arising from the use of the rented property for business purposes. Thus the prepaid rent qualifies as an asset acquisition.

Accounts affected	Kind of account	Change in balance	Debit	Credit
Prepaid rent	Asset	Increase	9,600	
Cash	Asset	Decrease		9,600

Prepaid rent			Cash		
(7)	9,600		1/1/_2 Bal.	16,500	(1) 1,500
			(5)	89,000	(2) 4,000
					(6) 55,000
					(7) 9,600

(8) Sold the land owned by the company for $10,200.

Reasoning: The sale of land is a nonoperating transaction because the company is not in the business of selling land. The sale of an asset not normally held for sale is reported *net* of the asset inflow and the related cost to show the resulting gain or loss in the income statement. Because the land cost $10,000 and was sold for $10,200, the result is a $200 gain. (Gains and losses are discussed later in this chapter.)

Accounts affected	Kind of account	Change in balance	Debit	Credit
Cash	Asset	Increase	10,200	
Land	Asset	Decrease		10,000
Gain on sale of land	Gain	Increase		200

Cash				Land		
1/1_2 Bal.	16,500	(1)	1,500	1/1/_2 Bal. 10,000	(8)	10,000
(5)	89,000	(2)	4,000			
(8)	10,200	(6)	55,000			
		(7)	9,600	Gain on sale of land		
					(8)	200

Recording plan restated: Increases in assets, expenses, losses, and dividends and decreases in liabilities and stockholders' equity are recorded as debits. Increases in liabilities, stockholders' equity, revenues, and gains and decreases in assets are recorded as credits.

(9) On October 1, 19_2, $10,000 was invested in 8% bonds. The bonds specify that interest will be paid semiannually on April 1 and October 1.

Reasoning: An asset, bond investment, was acquired at a cost of $10,000 to earn interest revenue.

Accounts affected	Kind of account	Change in balance	Debit	Credit
Bond investment	Asset	Increase	10,000	
Cash	Asset	Decrease		10,000

Bond investment			Cash		
(9)	10,000		1/1/_2 Bal.	16,500	(1) 1,500
			(5)	89,000	(2) 4,000
			(8)	10,200	(6) 55,000
					(7) 9,600
					(9) 10,000

(10) Received $3,000 "cash in advance" from a customer who ordered two custom TV-stereo units. The units were special-ordered by Sight & Sound Corporation with the $1,000-unit expected to be received in late December and the $2,000-unit not expected until January of next year.

Reasoning: Because the articles ordered have not been delivered to the customer, the $3,000 received cannot be considered as revenue. Pending performance, the company has an obligation to its customer, which liability is generally labeled as Advances from Customers.

Accounts affected	Kind of account	Change in balance	Debit	Credit
Cash	Asset	Increase	3,000	
Advances from customers	Liability	Increase		3,000

Cash					Advances from customers		
1/1/_2 Bal.	16,500	(1)	1,500			(10)	*3,000*
(5)	89,000	(2)	4,000				
(8)	10,200	(6)	55,000				
(10)	*3,000*	(7)	9,600				
		(9)	10,000				

(11) Paid other expenses, $5,500.

Accounts affected	Kind of account	Change in balance	Debit	Credit
Other expenses	Expense	Increase	5,500	
Cash	Asset	Decrease		5,500

Other expense			Cash			
(11)	*5,500*		1/1_2 Bal.	16,500	(1)	1,500
			(5)	89,000	(2)	4,000
			(8)	10,200	(6)	55,000
			(10)	3,000	(7)	9,600
					(9)	10,000
					(11)	*5,500*

(12) Paid salaries for the 11 months January through November 19_2, $18,700.

Accounts affected	Kind of account	Change in balance	Debit	Credit
Salaries expense	Expense	Increase	18,700	
Cash	Asset	Decrease		18,700

Salaries expense			Cash			
(12)	*18,700*		1/1/_2 Bal.	16,500	(1)	1,500
			(5)	89,000	(2)	4,000
			(8)	10,200	(6)	55,000
			(10)	3,000	(7)	9,600
					(9)	10,000
					(11)	5,500
					(12)	*18,700*

(13)   The board of directors declared and authorized the payment of $2,000 cash dividends.

      Comment: Remember, dividends reduce retained earnings via the dividend account, but they are not an expense.

Accounts affected	Kind of account	Change in balance	Debit	Credit
Dividends	Dividend	Increase	2,000	
Cash	Asset	Decrease		2,000

Dividends		Cash			
(13) 2,000		1/1/_2 Bal.	16,500	(1)	1,500
		(5)	89,000	(2)	4,000
		(8)	10,200	(6)	55,000
		(10)	3,000	(7)	9,600
				(9)	10,000
				(11)	5,500
				(12)	18,700
				(13)	2,000

(14)   Received the custom TV-stereo that was special-ordered for a customer (see transaction 10). The cost was $750, which was paid in cash, and it was priced to sell for $1,000.

Accounts affected	Kind of account	Change in balance	Debit	Credit
Merchandise inventory	Asset	Increase	750	
Cash	Asset	Decrease		750

Merchandise inventory				Cash			
1/1/_2 Bal.	12,000	(4b)	54,000	1/1/_2 Bal.	16,500	(1)	1,500
(3)	60,000			(5)	89,000	(2)	4,000
(14)	750			(8)	10,200	(6)	55,000
				(10)	3,000	(7)	9,600
						(9)	10,000
						(11)	5,500
						(12)	18,700
						(13)	2,000
						(14)	750

UNADJUSTED TRIAL BALANCE   The entries resulting from the 19_2 transactions that have been analyzed (transaction analysis) in the preceding paragraphs are summarized in the account balances shown in the trial balance on page 112. As previously explained in Chapter 3, the trial balance is a proof of the equality of the debit and credit balances in a ledger. Such a proof is customarily done before using the account balances to prepare the periodic financial statements.

However, the trial balance on page 112 cannot be used to prepare the financial statements because some of the accounts are not up to date for the fiscal year. If the balances were used, there would not be a proper matching of revenue and expense because not all revenues and expenses are included, and the balance sheet would not include all the assets and equities as of the end of the fiscal year.

SIGHT & SOUND CORPORATION
Unadjusted Trial Balance
December 31, 19_2

Cash	11,650	
Accounts receivable	12,000	
Merchandise inventory	18,750	
Prepaid rent	9,600	
Bond investment	10,000	
Delivery truck	4,000	
Accounts payable		25,000
Advances from customers		3,000
Capital stock		25,000
Retained earnings		3,000
Dividends	2,000	
Sales		90,000
Cost of goods sold	54,000	
Salaries expense	18,700	
Other expense	5,500	
Gain from sale of land		200
	146,200	146,200

Adjustments to the year-end balances are needed to bring them up to date. That is why the above trial balance is labeled an unadjusted trial balance; it is before necessary adjusting entries. Such adjusting entries are needed for Sight & Sound Corporation because of the following:

(A-1) No recognition has been given to depreciation on the delivery truck.
   The cost of the truck's services during the period is an expense called depreciation.

(A-2) No recognition has been given to the portion of cash advances that have become earned.
   The $3,000 liability for cash in advance includes the $1,000 TV-stereo unit delivered at the end of December. Revenue of $1,000 needs to be recognized.

(A-3) No recognition has been given to the December salaries.
   As previously noted the company records and pays the monthly salaries on the first business day of the following month. As a consequence, December salaries would not be included among the 19_2 transactions listed in the accounts.

(A-4) No recognition has been given to the fact that one-half of the rent paid in advance is rent expense for 19_2.
   The $9,600 rent payment made by the company at the beginning of 19_2 and recorded as Prepaid Rent covered the two-year period 19_2 and 19_3. Therefore, the rent expense amounts to $4,800 per year.

(A-5) No recognition has been given to the interest revenue earned on the bond investment.
   Although interest on the bond investment will not be received until April 1, 19_3, bonds held for three months earn interest for that period.

REQUIRED ADJUSTMENTS TO YEAR-END BALANCES   To achieve a proper matching of revenue and expense for 19_2, the following adjustments or modifications need to be made to the year-end balances summarized in the unadjusted trial balance:

(A-1) The cost of the services of the delivery truck used in 19_8, called depreciation, must be expensed. Although there are several methods for computing depreciation (as will be discussed in a later chapter), if it is assumed that an equal amount of the asset's total cost should be apportioned to each year's operations (straight-line depreciation), then depreciation is computed and recorded as follows:

Cost of depreciable asset				$4,000
Deduct estimated salvage (amount expected to be recovered at final disposal of asset)				400
Amount subject to depreciation				$3,600
Useful life—4 years				
Depreciation per annum ($3,600 ÷ 4)				$ 900

Accounts affected	Kind of account	Change in balance	Debit	Credit
Depreciation expense	Expense	Increase	900	
Accumulated depreciation	Contra asset	Increase		900

Depreciation expense		Accumulated depreciation	
(A-1) 900			(A-1) 900

Reasoning: As noted, the delivery truck is expected to have a four-year useful life. Because the truck will be used during that period to assist in the business activities carried on to earn revenue, a portion of the cost should be transferred to expense during each accounting period. That is, the cost of the truck's services during the fiscal period is a legitimate expense incurred in the generation of revenue. Such expense is called depreciation and, if it were ignored, net income would be overstated because of the improper matching of revenue and expense.

For purposes of providing more useful information, the accumulated depreciation deduction ($900) is accounted for separately from the original cost of the asset ($4,000) in order to avoid showing only the undepreciated cost ($3,100) in the balance sheet. The accumulated depreciation account, instead of the asset account (delivery truck), is credited in order to report the original cost, the depreciation accumulated to date, and the resulting unexpired cost of the asset in the balance sheet. Accumulated depreciation is called a contra (offset) asset account since it is reported in the balance sheet as a separate deduction from the cost of the related asset; it is contra to or a deduction from the related asset.

Note also that depreciation expense is recognized during each period when incurred even though there is no periodic cash payment. Depreciation is an expense, but not a cash expense. Consistent with accrual accounting, since the asset is used over time, the cost of its services is expensed each period, regardless of the cash flow.

(A-2) Late in December Sight & Sound Corporation delivered to the customer the $1,000 TV-stereo unit, which was paid for in advance earlier in the year. Since delivery discharges the liability (advances from customers), an adjusting entry should be made to reduce the liability and to recognize the revenue earned. In addition, the $750 cost of the unit sold and the reduction of inventory should be recorded in the usual manner.

Accounts affected	Kind of account	Change in balance	Debit	Credit
Advances from customers	Liability	Decrease	1,000	
Sales	Revenue	Increase		1,000
Cost of goods sold	Expense	Increase	750	
Merchandise inventory	Asset	Decrease		750

Advances from customers				Sales	
(A-2a) 1,000	(10) 3,000			(4a)	90,000
				(A-2a)	1,000

Income
Measurement

Cost of goods sold			Merchandise inventory			
(4b)	54,000		1/1/_2 Bal.	12,000	(4b)	54,000
(A-2b)	750		(3)	60,000	(A-2b)	750
			(14)	750		

Reasoning: As previously discussed, at the point of sale there is performance accompanied by the acquisition of an asset. In some circumstances, the asset acquisition may precede the performance, in which case the revenue recognition is postponed until the required performance, whether it be the delivery of merchandise or the rendering of some specified service, has been undertaken.

Such a situation occurred in transaction 10 when the company received $3,000 cash in advance from a customer who ordered two custom TV-stereo units. The mere receipt of the asset in a revenue-type transaction does not justify the recognition of revenue; performance is the essential test for revenue recognition. Pending performance, the company has an obligation to its customer. The cash received in advance creates a liability. Upon delivery of the $1,000 unit in late December, the delivery constitutes the required performance that satisfies that obligation. In the company's records the liability (advances from customers) is reduced $1,000, revenue of $1,000 is recognized, and the remaining liability is $2,000 (= $3,000 − $1,000) pending performance of the delivery of the $2,000 unit.

(A-3) Since December salaries for Sight Sound Corporation are unrecorded, an adjusting entry is needed to record the salaries expense and salaries payable, so that expenses for 19_8 and the year-end liabilities shown in the financial statements are not understated.

Accounts affected	Kind of account	Change in balance	Debit	Credit
Salaries expense	Expense	Increase	1,700	
Salaries payable	Liability	Increase		1,700

Salaries expense			Salaries payable		
(12)	18,700			(A-3)	1,700
(A-3)	1,700				

Reasoning: A business may have incurred an expense, that is, used some economic benefits, before a record thereof was made in the accounting records. At year end, or whenever financial statements are prepared, any such unrecorded, though incurred, expense should be entered in the records. Moreover, such expense should be recorded in the period incurred, regardless of whether paid for or not—accrual accounting.

In the case of Sight & Sound Corporation, employee salaries are paid monthly on the first business day of the following month. At year end the balances shown in the accounting records would not include the expense for December salaries. Such expense would have been incurred, that is, the business would have received the benefit of the employees' services for December, but in the normal course of recording business transactions it is unlikely that the expense for December salaries would have been recorded. Thus an adjusting entry is made for the unrecorded expense and the related liability.

(A-4) One-half of the rent payment made in advance applies to the year 19_2. Therefore, one-half of the prepaid rent balance must be transferred to expense.

Accounts affected	Kind of account	Change in balance	Debit	Credit
Rent expense	Expense	Increase	4,800	
Prepaid rent	Asset	Decrease		4,800

Rent expense			Prepaid rent		
(A-4)	*4,800*		(7)	*9,600*	(A-4)	*4,800*

Reasoning: When the $9,600 payment was made in advance to cover the rent for the years 19_2 and 19_3, the disbursement was properly analyzed as an asset acquisition because the company put itself in a position to benefit from the use of the rented property for a two-year period. By the end of 19_2, however, one-half of the rental benefits had been used. A December 31, 19_2, balance sheet that showed prepaid rent among the assets at $9,600 and an income statement that showed no rent expense for 19_2 would be incorrect. There would be an improper matching of revenue and expense.

(A-5) Interest has been earned on the bond investment from the October 1 date of investment (see transaction 9) to the end of the fiscal period, December 31, 19_2. Such three-month interest amounts to $200, computed and recorded as follows:

Interest = Amount at interest × Rate of interest × Period of time
$200 = $10,000 × .08 × 3/12

Accounts affected	Kind of account	Change in balance	Debit	Credit
Interest receivable	Asset	Increase	200	
Interest revenue	Revenue	Increase		200

Interest receivable			Interest revenue	
(A-5)	*200*			(A-5)	*200*

Reasoning: Revenue may be earned before it is entered in the accounting records. At year end, or whenever financial statements are prepared, any such unrecorded, though earned, revenue should be entered in the records. Otherwise, the financial statements would be in error because revenue for 19_2 and the year-end assets would be understated. Moreover, such revenue should be recorded in the period earned, regardless of whether the cash is received or not—accrual accounting.

In the case of Sight & Sound Corporation, during 19_2 the management sold the land owned by the company for $10,200. On October 1, 19_2, $10,000 of the proceeds were invested in 8% bonds. As long as the bonds are held the company will earn $800 (= $10,000 × .08) interest per year. Since the bonds specify that interest will be paid semiannually on April 1 and October 1, the company will not receive any bond interest until April 1, 19_3. Although not received until 19_3, a portion (one-half in this case) of the six months' interest was earned in 19_2, because interest is earned with the passage of time. April 1 and October 1 are merely the collection dates for the revenue that has been earned during the preceding six months.

During the year, entries are made in the accounting records only when external transactions occur. The first transaction relating to the bond interest would occur on April 1, 19_3, when the interest check for the six-month period October 1, 19_2 to March 31, 19_3, in the amount of $400 (= $10,000 × .08 × ½), is received. Therefore, an adjusting entry would be required at the end of 19_2 so that the 19_2 financial statements based on the accounting records would include interest revenue and the related interest receivable.

ADJUSTED TRIAL BALANCE After all the necessary adjusting entries have been journalized and posted, an adjusted trial balance is prepared. The adjusted trial balance not only provides proof that the ledger is still in balance after making the adjusting entries, but it also provides a convenient form for the preparation of the financial statements.

The adjusted trial balance for Sight & Sound Corporation is illustrated below. It differs from the unadjusted trial balance illustrated on page 112 by the updated balances (inventory, prepaid rent, advances, and salaries) and the new accounts added (interest receivable, accumulated depreciation, salaries payable, interest revenue, rent expense, and depreciation expense) as the result of the adjusting entries.

SIGHT & SOUND CORPORATION
Adjusted Trial Balance
December 31, 19_2

Cash	11,650	
Accounts receivable	12,000	
Interest receivable	200	
Merchandise inventory	18,000	
Prepaid rent	4,800	
Bond investment	10,000	
Delivery truck	4,000	
Accumulated depreciation		900
Accounts payable		25,000
Salaries payable		1,700
Advances from customers		2,000
Capital stock		25,000
Retained earnings		3,000
Dividends	2,000	
Sales		91,000
Cost of goods sold	54,750	
Salaries expense	20,400	
Rent expense	4,800	
Depreciation expense	900	
Other expense	5,500	
Interest revenue		200
Gain from sale of land		200
	149,000	149,000

INCOME STATEMENT The income statement is an accounting report on the results of operations for a business firm during a given period of time. By providing a classified summary report on a firm's revenues and gains and expenses and losses, the income statement shows how much a business has become better off (net income) or worse off (net loss) as the result of its operations during a fiscal period. As a report on a firm's success or failure (economic performance) during a given interval of time, investors, creditors, and management view the income statement as probably the most important financial statement presented.

For purposes of illustration, the income statement for Sight & Sound Corporation is presented on page 117. Note that the statement is for the current and prior years (comparative statements), as is done in actual practice for published statements, to provide a basis for comparison.

SIGHT & SOUND CORPORATION
Income Statement
For the Years Ended December 31, 19_2 and 19_1

	19_2		19_1	
Revenues and gains:				
Sales	$91,000		$81,000	
Interest revenue	200		—	
Gain from sale of land	200	$91,400	—	$81,000
Expenses and losses:				
Cost of goods sold	$54,750		$48,000	
Salaries expense	20,400		18,000	
Rent expense	4,800		4,800	
Depreciation expense	900		—	
Other expense	5,500	86,350	5,200	76,000
Net income		$ 5,050		$ 5,000
Earnings per common share		$ 2.02		$ 2.00

The above income-statement format is called a *single-step format* and is widely used in actual practice. Revenues and gains are grouped in one major category and expenses and losses are grouped in the other major category, and by subtracting the latter from the former (single-step subtraction), net income is shown without any intermediate income amounts.

The other major income-statement format is the *multiple-step format.* Under this format, various groups of data are shown, and after each group an income figure (a "step" difference) is reported in order to show important relationships that exist. Such a format is illustrated below for Sight & Sound Corporation.

SIGHT & SOUND CORPORATION
Income Statement
For the Years Ended December 31, 19_2 and 19_1

	19_2			19_1		
Sales			$91,000			$81,000
Cost of goods sold			54,750			48,000
Gross margin			$36,250			$33,000
Operating expenses:						
Selling expenses:						
Sales salaries	$15,400			$14,500		
Depreciation	900	$16,300		—	$14,500	
General and administrative expenses:						
Salaries	$ 5,000			$ 3,500		
Rent	4,800			4,800		
Other expense	5,500	15,300		5,200	13,500	
Total operating expenses			31,600			28,000
Net operating income			$ 4,650			$ 5,000
Nonoperating items:						
Add: Interest revenue		$ 200				
Gain on sale of land		200	400			
Net income			$ 5,050			$ 5,000
Earnings per common share			$ 2.02			$ 2.00

The above multiple-step income statements show the intermediate income figures of gross margin and net operating income on the way to reporting the "bottom line" net income amounts. The gross margin provides financial information on the average markup on the goods sold, which for Sight & Sound Corporation is 40 per cent for 19_2 ($36,250/$91,000) and is 41 per cent for 19_1 ($33,000/$81,000). Net operating income is reported to show the income from the normal, recurring, and principal economic processes in which the firm is engaged.

Finally, note that the multiple-step format reports the expenses by functional classification: cost of goods sold, selling expenses, and general and administrative expenses. Cost of goods sold is the expense associated with the cost of the product purchased (or manufactured) that was sold during the period. Selling expenses are the amounts incurred during the period in promoting and selling the product. General and administrative expenses are the amounts incurred during the period in the overall administrative function of the business.

NONOPERATING ITEMS   There are certain revenues and expenses that are not associated with the normal operating activities of firms. For example, a merchandising or manufacturing firm may have secondary sources of revenue from bond investment (interest revenue), from capital stock investment (dividend revenue), or from renting facilities (rent revenue), all of which are not related to the normal operating activities of selling goods and services. Similarly, a firm can incur interest expense as a result of borrowing money or having credit extended to it, which is a financing rather than an operating expense.

There are also gains and losses that arise from the sale of noninventory assets. Such gains and losses are nonoperating in that the firm is not in the primary business of selling noninventory assets. Moreover, since they arise from secondary business activities, they are reported *net* in the income statement, rather than reporting both the sale of the asset and its related cost.

Nonoperating revenue, expense, gain, and loss are reported as separate line items in a single-step income statement. They are reported under a separate caption (such as nonoperating items or other revenues and expenses) immediately following net operating income in a multiple-step income statement. Such reporting is illustrated in the income statement for Sight & Sound Corporation.

EXTRAORDINARY ITEMS   Gains and losses that arise from transactions that are *both* unusual in nature and occur infrequently are classified separately in the income statement under an extraordinary items caption.[2] Such separate reporting aids the statement user in evaluating profit performance, since it informs the user that such gains and losses are not normal and will not likely recur in the future.

Examples of extraordinary items include major casualties (such as tornado or earthquake damage that is rare in the area), expropriation of assets by foreign governments, and effects of a prohibition under a newly enacted law or regulation.

[2]Accounting Principles Board, "Reporting the Results of Operations," *Opinion No. 30* (New York: AICPA, June, 1973), paragraphs 19–20.

The reporting of extraordinary items is illustrated below in a partial income statement and assumes 10,000 capital stock shares outstanding:

Income before extraordinary items	$40,000
Extraordinary item:	
Loss from tornado damage	6,000
Net income	$34,000
Earnings per common share:	
Income before extraordinary item	$ 4.00
Extraordinary loss	.60
Net income	$ 3.40

Note the reporting of earnings per share data, which must be shown on the face of the income statement.[3] If extraordinary items exist, then EPS data must be reported for income before extraordinary items and for net income and can be reported (it is optional) for extraordinary items.

IMPORTANT TERMS AND CONCEPTS IN CHAPTER 4

Net income—pp. 98–100

Operations—p. 99

Net operating income—p. 99

Nonoperating items—pp. 99, 118

Accounting (fiscal) period—p. 100

Calendar year—p. 100

Natural business year—p. 100

Interim statements—p. 100

Fiscal-period assumption—pp. 100, 101

Accrual basis of accounting—pp. 101, 105, 106

Revenue-recognition assumption—pp. 101, 102

Revenue measurement—p. 103

Matching assumption—pp. 103, 104

Direct matching—pp. 103, 104

Indirect matching—p. 104

Period expenses—pp. 104, 105

Expense measurement—p. 104

Cost—p. 104

Incidental costs—p. 104

Cost and expense—pp. 104, 105

Cost and assets—pp. 104, 105

Adjusting entries—pp. 105, 112–115

Cash basis of accounting—pp. 105, 106

Unadjusted trial balance—pp. 111, 112

Adjusted trial balance—p. 116

Income statement—p. 116

Comparative statements—p. 116

Single-step format for income statement—p. 117

Multiple-step format for income statement—pp. 117, 118

Extraordinary items—pp. 118, 119

Earnings per share—p. 119

DEMONSTRATION PROBLEM FOR REVIEW AND SELF-STUDY Central Electric Company, which is engaged in inspection and repair work, was organized in 19_1. The company's unadjusted trial balance at the end of 19_8 is presented on page 120.

The building had an expected useful life of 25 years when new, and the equipment an expected life of five years when new. The interest receivable on the notes amounted to $20 as of December 31, 19_8. The insurance coverage was acquired on January 1, 19_7, and the policy covered a three-year term. One-third of the inspection fees received in advance has been earned as of December 31, 19_8. The year-end inventory of electrical supplies amounted to $150.

[3]Accounting Principles Board, "Earnings per Share," *Opinion No. 15* (New York: AICPA, May, 1969), paragraphs 12–13.

CENTRAL ELECTRICAL COMPANY
Trial Balance
December 31, 19_8

Cash	1,100	
Notes receivable	1,000	
Electrical supplies	800	
Prepaid insurance	240	
Land	6,200	
Building	18,800	
Accumulated depeciation—Building		5,264
Equipment	5,000	
Accumulated depreciation—Equipment		1,500
Accounts payable		350
Inspection fees received in advance		1,200
Capital stock (100 shares)		20,000
Retained earnings		3,876
Dividends	1,000	
Repair service revenue		13,250
Inspection fees earned		3,100
Salaries expense	12,500	
Miscellaneous expense	1,900	
	48,540	48,540

INSTRUCTIONS

(a) Prepare the adjusting entries required at December 31, 19_8.

(b) Prepare the firm's income statement for 19_8 in single-step format.

Note Attempt to solve the demonstration problem before examining the solution that follows.

Solution:
(a)

JOURNAL

19_8		Adjusting Entries		
Dec.	31	Depreciation expense—Building	752	
		Accumulated depreciation—Building		752
		Annual depreciation ($18,800 ÷ 25).		
	31	Depreciation expense—Equipment	1,000	
		Accumulated depreciation—Equipment		1,000
		Annual depreciation ($5,000 ÷ 5).		
	31	Interest receivable	20	
		Interest revenue		20
		Interest receivable on notes.		
	31	Insurance expense	120	
		Prepaid insurance		120
		Insurance expired during 19_8. (Allowing for the 19_7 adjustment, the $240 account balance equals two-thirds of the original premium. The premium of $360, divided by 3, gives the annual charge of $120.)		

Income Dec.	31	Inspection fees received in advance		400	
Measurement		Inspection fees earned			400
		Fees received in advance that have been earned.			
	31	Electrical supplies expense		650	
		Electrical supplies			650
		Electrical supplies used ($800 − $150).			

(b)

CENTRAL ELECTRICAL COMPANY
Income Statement
For the Year Ended December 31, 19_8

Revenues:		
Repair service revenue	$13,250	
Inspection fees earned	3,500	
Interest revenue	20	$16,770
Expenses:		
Salaries expense	$12,500	
Depreciation expense—Building	752	
Depreciation expense—Equipment	1,000	
Insurance expense	120	
Electrical supplies expense	650	
Miscellaneous expense	1,900	16,922
Net loss		$ (152)
Loss per common share		$ (1.52)

Questions

1 Why are adjustments needed for accrual accounting?
2 What is the accrual basis of accounting?
3 What is revenue? What is expense?
4 Why does the income statement cover a period of time instead of a specific point in time?
5 Does the process of income measurement depend on the initial measurement of certain assets?
6 How is the cost of acquired assets measured?
7 What is the distinction between the single-step format and the multiple-step format of the income statement?
8 What are nonoperating business activities?
9 What is the distinction between direct matching and indirect matching?
10 Has proper matching been achieved when all external transactions have been correctly recorded?
11 How does depreciation expense differ from other operating expenses?
12 Assets are increased by debits, revenues are assets, and therefore revenues should be increased by debits. Is this statement correct? Discuss.
13 Why should dividends received be recorded as "dividend revenue" rather than "dividend income"?
14 Since net income could be determined by an analysis of the change in retained earnings during a period, why are revenue and expense accounts maintained in the accounting records?
15 What is meant by the following statement? Revenue, expense, and dividend accounts are used to record determinants of income and distributions of income. Discuss.
16 What are extraordinary items? How are these items reported in the financial statements?
17 Revenue is usually recognized at the point of sale. Why is this method of recording revenues an assumption? What facts support this assumption?

Short exercises

E4-1

You are given below three multiple-choice statements. Select the correct answers and indicate the corresponding letters on a sheet of paper (e.g., 1-a, 2-a, etc.).

(1) Which of the following is correct? (a) An example of an extraordinary item is an expropriation of a factory by a foreign government. (b) The earnings per share figure must always be reported on the income statement. (c) Accrual accounting is a natural outgrowth of the revenue-recognition, matching, and fiscal-period assumptions. (d) Adjusting entries are usually made at the end of the fiscal period. (e) All of the above. (f) None of the above.

(2) An example of the receipt of an asset in a revenue-type transaction that creates a liability instead of a revenue would be (a) the receipt of cash by the company for services which go beyond the current accounting period, (b) the payment by the company for a three-year insurance policy, (c) the sale of a product and receipt of cash in the accounting period about to be closed, (d)

(3) the receipt of cash for services performed in the accounting period about to be closed, (e) all of the above, (f) none of the above.

(3) The proper measurement for an asset acquired by purchase would be (a) liquidation price, (b) value, (c) cost, (d) value less incidental costs, (e) all of the above, (f) none of the above.

E4-2

You are given below three multiple-choice statements. Select the correct answers and indicate the corresponding letters on a sheet of paper (e.g., 1-a, 2-a, etc.).

(1) Which of the following is *incorrect?* (a) The adjusted and unadjusted trial balances can have identical figures. (b) The single-step and multiple-step income statements present the same information but in a different format. (c) The failure to record the necessary adjustments will misstate the income for the period. (d) The failure to record the necessary adjustments will misstate the end-of-period balance sheet. (e) All of the above. (f) None of the above.

(2) Which of the following is *correct?* (a) If adjustments are needed, they must be made to insure proper matching. (b) Adjustments are made at the end of the accounting period since it is impractical to record them on a daily or weekly basis. (c) Adjustments are not "triggered" by external business documents. (d) Adjustments may not require an outlay of cash. (e) All of the above. (f) None of the above.

(3) The account "accumulated depreciation" is (a) deducted from its related plant, property, or equipment account listed in the current asset section of the balance sheet, (b) a contra account and will be shown separately on the balance sheet, (c) classified as a liability with a credit balance, (d) adjusted to zero at the end of the period, (e) none of the above.

E4-3

(a) The following is a partial listing of account balances. Determine the total of the current assets.

Cash	$22,000
Land (held for future use)	25,000
Inventory	18,000
Prepaid insurance	500
Salaries payable	3,000
Retained earnings	23,500
Advances from customers	500
Delivery equipment	5,000
Accumulated depreciation—Delivery equipment	800
Accounts receivable	7,500
Rent receivable	700
Temporary investments	5,000

(b) Determine the new total for current assets after giving consideration to the following adjustments. (Remember: Not every adjustment affects current assets.)

Rent receivable of $200

Liability for unpaid salaries of $800

Expired insurance premiums of $100

E4-4

Data taken from a ledger before year-end adjustments have been grouped according to balance-sheet categories, as follows:

Current assets	$ 40,000
Long-term investments	20,000
Property, plant, and equipment	60,000
Intangible assets	20,000
	$140,000

Current liabilities	$ 30,000
Long-term liabilities	30,000
Stockholders' equity	80,000
	$140,000

Adjustments are required for the following:

(a) Depreciation on equipment, $800.

(b) Rent payable, $400.

(c) Interest receivable, $800.

(d) Use of $150 of office supplies (classified as a current asset).

(e) To reduce advances from customers from $600 to $400.

Show the revised totals for the balance-sheet categories after giving consideration to the above adjustments.

E4-5
The income statement prepared by Thermo Company for 19_3 reported net income of $20,000. A variety of accounting mistakes were later discovered.

Required:

(a) For the following transactions, give the *correct* entry in journal form.

    (1) In 19_2 Thermo received $2,000 for services to be performed in 19_3. In 19_3 only one-half of the required work was completed. The 19_3 entry was a debit to advances from customers, $2,000, and a credit to service revenue, $2,000. If it is assumed that the 19_2 entry was correct, what should the 19_3 entry have been?

    (2) Depreciation expense was recorded at $150, but it should have been recorded at $1,500.

    (3) A two-year insurance policy was purchased at the beginning of 19_3 for $1,000. No entry was made during 19_3 for insurance expense.

    (4) The factory supplies account in the ledger has a balance of $2,000. A physical count reveals that only $500 of factory supplies are on hand.

    (5) Rent due in 19_3 was $3,000. No entry and no payment were made.

(b) Compute the correct amount of net income for 19_3.

E4-6
The following data were taken on December 31, 19_3 from the ledger of Garner Company:

Retained earnings, December 31, 19_2	$ 12,000
Sales	240,000
Cost of goods sold	155,000
Salesmen's commissions	20,000
Insurance expense	600
Office salaries	30,000
Dividends	6,000

After giving consideration to the following, since year-end adjusting entries have not been made, prepare the 19_3 income statement by using the **multiple-step** *form.*

The employment agreements with the salesmen specify that the commission payable will amount to 10 per cent of sales.

The $600 insurance expense resulted from the payment of the premium on a one-year policy that went into effect on January 1, 19_3.

The advances from customers account had a balance of $1,000 at year end. The correct balance should be zero.

E4-7 All of the assets and liabilities of Beta Corporation affected by year-end adjustments are shown below.

	December 31, 19_4	
	Before adjustment	After adjustment
Interest receivable	$ 200	$ 600
Prepaid rent	400	200
Prepaid insurance	400	–0–
Accumulated depreciation	600	900
Miscellaneous expenses payable	–0–	350
Subscriptions received in advance	2,000	1,500

Before the year-end adjustments for 19_4 were considered, the net income was computed as $15,000. Determine the net income after giving consideration to the year-end adjustments.

E4-8 The following is a partial listing of balances taken from a ledger:

Government bonds	$ 3,000
Accounts payable	5,000
Retained earnings	11,000
Estimated income tax payable	650
Patents	5,000
Advances from customers	900
Prepaid rent	1,500
Rent received in advance	300
Bank loan due in three years	10,000
Notes payable	3,000

(a) Determine the total of current liabilities.

(b) Determine the **new** total for current liabilities after giving consideration to the following adjustments:

Interest payable of $300 on the bank loan.

Interest payable of $30 on the notes payable.

Expired insurance premiums of $300.

Depreciation expense of $450.

E4-9 Speed Company, publishers of a monthly magazine, began operations on July 1, 19_4, and established the calendar year as the time period to be used in accounting for its operations.

The publication, issued at the end of each month, was available by the copy for 50 cents, through a one-year subscription for $5 or through a two-year subscription for $10. Magazines were sent to subscribers in the month in which subscriptions were received.

All receipts from single-copy sales and from subscriptions were credited to income. The income statement for the six months ended December 31, 19_4, showed Magazine Revenue Earned to be $41,140. Details for single-copy sales and subscriptions are given below.

Month	Single-copy sales	One-year subscriptions	Two-year subscriptions
July	$ 3,540	$ 2,000	$ 700
August	2,890	3,000	1,200
September	1,750	2,400	1,920
October	3,210	3,300	800
November	2,950	2,400	1,800
December	3,560	1,800	1,920
	$17,900	$14,900	$8,340

Compute the correct amount of magazine revenue earned for the six months ended December 31, 19_4.

Problems

A4-1

From the data given, prepare the 19_4 income statement of Davis Company in multiple-step form.

Retained earnings, December 31, 19_3	$ 52,000
Sales	105,000
Cost of goods sold	51,000
Interest revenue	100
Loss on sale of real estate	300
Salaries expense	21,000
Traveling expense	6,300
Advertising expense	700
Dividends received	900
Telephone and telegraph expense	780
Depreciation expense	1,870
Accumulated depreciation	10,300
Insurance expense	150
Unexpired insurance as of December 31, 19_4	800
Other expense	870
Cash receipts for 19_4	99,800
Cash disbursements for 19_4	95,000
Income tax	4,530
Capital stock (1,000 shares)	1,000

A4-2

Given the following information, journalize the necessary adjusting entries. The account balances are correct for December 31, 19_7.

(a) Balances before adjustment:

Prepaid rent	$18,600
Rent expense	–0–

Data

At the beginning of the current year, rent was prepaid for a three-year period.

(b) Balances before adjustment:

Prepaid insurance	$ 900
Insurance expense	–0–

Data

At the beginning of the current year a two-year insurance policy was acquired by payment of a $900 premium.

(c) Balances before adjustment:

Income tax expense	$ 600
Income tax payable	–0–

Data

At year-end there were unpaid taxes of $150 that had not been recorded.

(d) Balances before adjustment:

Delivery expense (includes only rental expense)	$ 240
Truck rent payable	–0–

Data

A delivery truck was rented during the year from Transport Rental Company at the rate of 15 cents a mile. The truck was driven 1,800 miles during December.

(e) Balances before adjustment:

Equipment	$24,000
Depreciation expense	–0–

Data

At the beginning of the year the company purchased equipment that has an expected useful life of 8 years. No salvage or trade-in value is anticipated at the end of the equipment's useful life.

(f) Balances before adjustment:

Interest expense (for 11 months)	$ 2,200
Interest payable	–0–

Data

The company owes $200 for the December interest.

(g) Balances before adjustment:

Advances from customers	$ 1,300

Data

In December, the company shipped $300 of merchandise (cost of $200) to customers in fulfillment of an advance payment.

(h) Balances before adjustment:

Travel advances	$ 500
Travel expense	300

Data

Employees are granted travel advances to cover certain expenses while away on company business. When the employee completes a trip, he reports the amount of the advance used. In this case, half of the travel advances has been used at year-end.

(i) Balances before adjustment:

Office equipment	$10,000
Depreciation expense	–0–

Data

Cost of equipment	$10,000
Salvage	1,000

Useful life: 10 years.

Purchased at the beginning of the current year.

(j) Balances before adjustment:

Bond investment (6% interest rate) $20,000

Interest revenue   –0–

Data

The bond was held for a full 12-month period. No cash interest payment was received during 19_7.

A4-3 *The following income statement is incorrect because it was prepared by a new bookkeeper before year-end adjustments were taken into consideration:*

TYRO COMPANY
Income Statement
For the Year Ended December 31, 19_5

Revenues:		
Sales of service	$50,000	
Interest revenue	400	$50,400
Deduct expenses:		
Salaries expense	$33,000	
Cost of repair parts used	8,000	
Rent expense	600	41,600
Net income		$ 8,800

The assets and liabilities of selected accounts before and after adjustment are listed below.

	December 31, 19_5	
	Before adjustment	After adjustment
Assets:		
Cash	$ 6,000	$ 6,000
Marketable securities	9,000	9,000
Interest receivable	–0–	400
Inventory of repair parts	2,000	2,000
Prepaid rent	2,400	2,200
Equipment	27,000	27,000
Accumulated depreciation	–0–	1,400
Equities:		
Accounts payable	$ 4,000	$ 4,000
Salaries payable	–0–	3,500
Advances from customers	800	700
Capital stock—1,000 shares		

Prepare a corrected income statement in single-step form. Your solution should show net income for 19_5 as $4,200.

A4-4 *The following tentative draft of the condensed income statement of Scotty Company covers the first year of the company's operations:*

SCOTTY COMPANY
Income Statement
For the Year Ended December 31, 19_3

Sales		$200,000
Cost of goods sold		150,000
Gross margin		$ 50,000
Operating expenses:		
Salaries expense	$30,000	
Depreciation expense	8,000	
Interest expense	700	
Other operating expense	16,000	54,700
Net loss		$ (4,700)

You are asked to review the accounting procedures to satisfy the management of the company that those followed are acceptable. You discover that the company has treated all incidental costs associated with the purchase of merchandise and equipment as other operating expense. You also note with approval that the equipment, all of which was acquired at the beginning of the year, is being depreciated over a ten-year period and that no scrap value is anticipated.

The following data have been taken from the company's records:

Capital stock (1,000 shares)	$ 1,000
Merchandise purchased during 19_3—Invoice cost	160,000
Merchandise on hand at year-end (20% of purchases)	32,000
Incidental costs relating to merchandise	2,000
Equipment acquired at beginning of 19_3	80,000
Incidental costs (such as transportation and installation)	3,000
In 19_2, advances received from customers totaled $8,000	
In 19_3, $1,500 of this total has been earned, but has not	
been included in the above sales figure	

Prepare a revised, and improved, draft of the 19_3 condensed income statement, following the multiple-step form.

A4-5

The following data have been taken from McCoy Company's 19_4 unadjusted trial balance:

Cash	$ 4,500
Merchandise inventory	10,500
Advances to salesmen	500
Prepaid rent	1,500
Office supplies	1,000
Equipment	10,000
Accumulated depreciation	1,000
Advances from customers	1,250
Capital stock (1,000 shares)	20,000
Retained earnings	5,750

The retained earnings balance was the result of the following:

Balance, December 31, 19_3	$ 250
Sales	200,000
Cost of goods sold	120,000
Salesmen's commissions	34,500
Office salaries	25,000
Miscellaneous expense	10,000
Dividends	5,000
Balance, per above	$ 5,750

Adjustments are required for the following:

(a) As of December 31, 19_4, a total of $1,250 has been received in advance.

(b) One-half of the $500 advanced on future commissions has been earned by the company's sales-men.

(c) Office salaries owed at year-end amount to $800.

(d) One-fourth of the prepaid rent applies to 19_4.

(e) The unused office supplies amount to $200 at year end.

(f) Unrecorded depreciation for 19_4, $1,000.

(g) Income taxes payable at year end were $2,510.

Required:

The 19_4 financial statements (income statement, statement of retained earnings, and balance sheet).

A4-6

The December 31, 19_4 balances applicable to Holiday Company are as follows:

Cash	$ 5,600
Accounts receivable	5,000
Merchandise inventory	12,000
Prepaid insurance	–0–
Long-term investment in securities	5,000
Equipment	–0–
Accumulated depreciation	–0–
Accounts payable	6,000
Salaries payable	700
Capital stock	20,000
Retained earnings	900

The 19_5 transactions are as follows:

(1) Purchased merchandise on account, $12,000.

(2a) Made sales of merchandise on account, $14,000.

(2b) Cost of goods sold on account, $9,000.

(3) Cash collected on account from customers, $13,000.

(4) Cash payments for merchandise purchased on account, $10,000.

(5) As of January 1, 19_5 purchased equipment for cash, $2,000. The equipment is expected to last for 5 years and have a salvage amount of $1,000.

(6) As of January 1, 19_5 paid $600 cash for a two-year fire insurance policy on the equipment.

(7) Paid advertising expenses, $300.

(8) Paid rent for the year, $800.

(9) Cash payments for salaries:
    For December 31, 19_4 liability, $700.
    For 11 months ended November 30, 19_5, $3,300. (Salaries for 19_5 amount to $300 per month.)

(10) Received $200 dividend revenue from long-term investments.

(11) Paid cash dividends, $400.

Required:

(a) Journalize the 19_5 transactions and adjustments.

(b) Post to ledger (remember to post initial balances).

(c) Prepare the 19_5 single-step income statement, statement of retained earnings, and classified balance sheet.

B4-1

Use what is relevant of the following data to prepare the 19_7 income statement of Chekov Corporation in multiple-step form.

Cash	$ 22,000
Dividends	6,000
Retained earnings, December 31, 19_6	53,000
Sales	200,000
Interest revenue	800
Rent revenue	1,400
Grain on sale of securities	450
Cost of goods sold	121,000
Merchandise inventory, December 31, 19_7	30,000
Wages and salaries	35,000
Rent expense	2,400
Rent payable as of December 31, 19_7	700
Depreciation expense	9,100
Accumulated depreciation	18,200
Miscellaneous expense	9,000
Interest expense	350
Income tax	5,100
Capital stock (1,000 shares)	2,000

B4-2

The following data have been taken from Final Company's 19_6 unadjusted trial balance:

Cash	$ 4,000
Accounts receivable	6,000
Merchandise inventory	10,000
Prepaid rent	4,500
Long-term investment in securities	2,500
Equipment	7,500
Accounts payable	12,000
Advances from customers	1,000
Capital stock	15,000
Retained earnings, December 31, 19_5	4,300
Sales	98,000
Cost of goods sold	54,000
Salaries expense	39,900
Interest expense	1,900

Adjustments are required for the following:

(1) Liability for salaries, $800.

(2) Depreciation on equipment, $3,000.

(3) Interest receivable, $200.

(4) At the beginning of the 19_6 the $1,500 annual rental was prepaid for three years.

(5) Liability for local taxes, $200.

Required:

The December 31, 19_6 classified balance sheet. Remember that you must calculate the net income for 19_6 to determine the figure for December 31, 19_6 retained earnings.

The financial statements below are incorrect for two reasons:

(a) Some of the assets are improperly positioned in the balance sheet.

(b) No provision was made for the following adjustments:

(1) Liability for December salaries, $3,500.

(2) Annual depreciation of building acquired at the beginning of 19_5, $5,200.

(3) Liability for December rent, $800.

(4) Interest receivable, $100.

Required:

Corrected financial statements (income statement, statement of retained earnings, and balance sheet).

MAJOR CORPORATION
Income Statement
For the Year Ended December 31, 19_5

Revenues:		
Sales	$260,000	
Interest revenue	1,000	$261,000
Deduct expenses:		
Cost of goods sold	$168,000	
Salaries expense	43,000	
Rent expense	15,500	226,500
Net income		$ 34,500

MAJOR CORPORATION
Statement of Retained Earnings
For the Year Ended December 31, 19_5

Retained earnings, December 31, 19_4	$36,000
Net income for 19_5	34,500
Total	$70,500
Deduct dividends	7,800
Retained earnings, December 31, 19_5	$62,700

MAJOR CORPORATION
Balance Sheet
December 31, 19_5

Assets:		
Current assets:		
Cash	$ 8,400	
Inventory	30,000	
Accounts receivable	28,000	$ 66,400
Property, plant, and equipment:		
Land (held for future use)	$ 15,000	
Land	7,500	
Building	300,000	322,500
Intangible assets:		
Temporary investment in marketable securities		10,000
		$398,900
Equities:		
Current liabilities:		
Accounts payable		$ 6,200
Stockholders' equity:		
Capital stock (1,000 shares)	$330,000	
Retained earnings	62,700	392,700
		$398,900

B4-4   *The accounting records of Barney Company indicate the following:*

December 31, 19_7 balances:

Cash	$14,000
Accounts receivable	18,000
Prepaid rent	4,800
Service trucks	15,000
Accumulated depreciation	–0–
Salaries payable	2,000
Advances from customers	–0–
Capital stock (1,000 shares)	40,000
Retained earnings	9,800

19_8 transactions:

(1) Sales of service on account, $28,000.

(2) Payment of December 31, 19_7 liability for salaries, $2,000.

(3) Collections from customers, $32,000.

(4) Payment of salaries, $12,000.

(5) Receipt of advances from customers, $400.

(6) Payment for supplies and parts used in the performance of services for customers, $4,000.

(7) Payment of other expenses, $4,000.

(8) Payment of dividend, $1,000.

Adjustments:

(a) Salaries payable as of December 31, 19_8, $1,100.

(b) Rent expense applicable to 19_8, $800.

(c) Depreciation:
     Service trucks were acquired on December 31, 19_7.
     Estimated useful life, 6 years.
     Estimated salvage at end of useful life, $0.

Required:

(a) Journalize the transactions and adjustments.

(b) Post the journal entries to ledger accounts.

(c) Prepare the adjusted trial balance.

B4-5   *The following data are taken from the 19_3 unadjusted trial balance of Jersey Company. An inexperienced bookkeeper has closed the expense, revenue, and dividend accounts before year-end adjusting entries were made.*

Cash	$ 2,000
Merchandise inventory	4,000
Shipping supplies	200
Long-term investment in real estate	20,000
Store building	22,000
Accumulated depreciation	480
Rent received in advance	9,800
Capital stock	30,000
Retained earnings	7,920

The retained earnings balance was the result of the following:

Balance, December 31, 19_2	$ 11,000
Sales	182,000
Rent revenue	5,400
Cost of goods sold	130,480
Salaries expense	41,500
Property taxes expense	6,500
Miscellaneous expense	3,500
Dividends	8,500
Balance, per above	$ 7,920

Journalize the following adjusting entries and prepare the 19_3 statement of retained earnings. (Hint: You must first calculate the net income for the year ended December 31, 19_3 before you calculate the ending balance in retained earnings.)

Additional data

(a) Depreciation expense for 19_3, $240.

(b) A physical count of the shipping supplies on hand as of December 31, 19_3 reveals that the unused supplies cost $100.

(c) Salaries payable as of December 31, 19_3, $700.

(d) During 19_3 the company was able to rent to three tenants parcels of the real estate it owns as a long-term investment. Rent collections from the tenants during 19_3 are detailed below.

From A	$3,000
A's rent is $300 per month. A has paid rent for ten months and owes two month's back rent as of December 31, 19_3, which the company believes is collectible.	
From B	2,400
B's rent is $200 per month and is paid through December 31, 19_3	
From C	–0–
When C signed the rental agreement as of January 1, 19_3, covering a two-year period, C paid the $4,900 annual rental for the two-year period in advance.	
Recorded as rent revenue	5,400

(e) The applicable income tax expense is $3,952.

B4-6

The following income statement is incorrect because it was prepared before year-end adjustments were taken into consideration:

NEED HELP COMPANY
Income Statement
For the Year Ended December 31, 19_3

Revenues:		
Sales of merchandise	$180,000	
Sales of service	30,000	
Interest revenue	600	$210,600
Deduct expenses:		
Cost of goods sold	$105,000	
Cost of repair parts used	9,000	
Salaries expense	75,000	
Miscellaneous expense	3,400	192,400
Net income		$ 18,200

The assets and liabilities before and after adjustments are listed below.

	December 31, 19_3	
	Before adjustment	After adjustment
Assets:		
Cash	$12,000	$12,000
Marketable securities	22,000	22,000
Accounts receivable	6,000	6,000
Interest receivable	–0–	300
Merchandise	18,000	18,000
Inventory of repair parts	2,000	1,700
Prepaid rent	800	–0–
Prepaid insurance	1,500	1,200
Equipment	30,000	30,000
Accumulated depreciation	2,100	4,200
Liabilities:		
Accounts payable	11,300	11,300
Salaries payable	–0–	2,000
Estimated income tax payable	–0–	2,000
Advances from customers (Note 1)	600	900

Note 1 During 19_3, $300 of advances from customers were improperly treated as sales of merchandise. This error was corrected by an adjustment. (Hint: Note that the original entry was a credit to a revenue account and not to a liability account.)

Prepare a corrected income statement in single-step form that should show the net income for 19_3 as $10,700. There are 1,000 shares of capital stock.

COMPLETION OF THE ACCOUNTING CYCLE

PURPOSE OF CHAPTER The process of dividing the financial life of a firm into specific accounting periods creates the need for end-of-period adjusting entries, which were discussed in the preceding chapter. The adjusting entries are an integral part of the accounting cycle, but there are additional steps which are necessary to complete the cycle and prepare the accounting records for recording transactions in the following period.

One purpose of this chapter is to discuss the use of closing entries to update the retained earnings account at the end of each period. This is necessary so that the account will reflect cumulative retained earnings, including the effect of operations and dividends of the current period. Finally, the chapter discusses the use of a worksheet, or working papers, to facilitate the preparation of adjusting entries, financial statements, and closing entries.

SEQUENCE OF ACCOUNTING PROCEDURES The various accounting procedures thus far explained are performed in the sequence shown below.

Transaction analysis—thus determining the effect of transactions on assets and equities.

Journalize—thus providing a chronological record of transactions in books of original entry.

Post—thus classifying and accumulating the results of transactions in the accounts affected.

Prepare an unadjusted trial balance—thus checking on the equality of the debit and credit balances in the ledger and summarizing the data from the ledger.

Journalize and post end-of-period adjustments—thus updating the accounts.

Prepare an adjusted trial balance—thus checking on the equality of the debit and credit balances in the ledger and summarizing the data from the ledger in a convenient form needed for the preparation of the financial statements.

Prepare an income statement—thus reporting on the results of operations for the period.

Prepare a statement of retained earnings—thus accounting for the changes in retained earnings during the period and showing the current balance of the account.

Prepare a balance sheet—thus showing the financial position at the end of the period.

Prepare a statement of changes in financial position—thus reporting on the sources and uses of economic resources for the period. (To be discussed in Chapter 15.)

The additional steps to complete the accounting cycle performed during each accounting (fiscal) period are:

Journalize and post the entries necessary to close the books.

Prepare an after-closing trial balance.

CLOSING ENTRIES We have previously pointed out that revenue and gain and expense and loss accounts are subdivisions of retained earnings used to collect the data needed for income statement preparation and therefore net income determination. Moreover, the net effect of all the revenue and expense transactions for the period is to increase retained earnings (net income) or decrease retained earnings (net loss). We have also previously pointed out that net income has meaning only with regard to a specific time period. Revenue and expense accounts, as well as gain and loss accounts, which provide the classified data needed for income determination, are temporary accounts in that they contain data arising from transactions that occurred during the fiscal period and that fiscal period only.

In order that the revenue and expense accounts provide the data necessary for the preparation of the income statement for one fiscal period only, they must have zero balances at the beginning of each fiscal year. Such zero balances are accomplished by journalizing and posting closing entries at the end of the fiscal year—closing the accounts. Thus closing entries are those entries made at the end of the annual fiscal period to reduce the temporary revenue, expense, gain, and loss accounts to zero and transfer the resulting net income or net loss to the permanent retained earnings account.[1] The closing entries establish zero balances in the revenue and expense accounts so that they will again be ready to collect data needed for income determination for the next fiscal year. Consequently, revenue and expense accounts are called *temporary* or *nominal accounts* since their ending balances are closed and not carried forward to the next fiscal period. In contrast, retained earnings is called a *permanent* or *real account,* as are all balance-sheet accounts, since its ending balance is not closed but is carried forward as the beginning balance for the next fiscal period.

Closing entries are normally made at the end of the accounting year. They are journalized in the normal manner and then immediately posted to the ledger. Since revenue and gain accounts normally have credit balances, and expense and loss accounts normally have debit balances, the former are closed by debiting them and the latter are closed by crediting them at amounts equal to their ending balances. The difference between the closing debits to the revenue and gain accounts and the closing credits to the expense and loss accounts is credited (in the case of net income) or debited (in the case of net loss) to retained earnings.[2]

Since the dividends account is also a temporary account that is a subdivision of retained earnings, it also is closed to retained earnings by debiting retained earnings and crediting dividends. However, because dividends is not an expense account, it is closed by an entry separate from the revenue and expense closing entry.

ILLUSTRATION OF CLOSING ENTRIES   Refer to the December 31, 19_1 balance sheet of Sight & Sound Corporation on page 4. According to the balance sheet, the retained earnings amount to $3,000. However, if you refer to the trial balance for the same date, shown on page 76, you will not find among the data listed thereon a $3,000 balance for retained earnings. This condition is evident from the following columnar comparison of the December 31, 19_1 balance sheet amounts and the trial-balance amounts.

[1]As will be explained, closing entries also include closing the dividends account.

[2]Although unnecessary, a special clearing account called *Income Summary* is often used to facilitate the closing entries. The total of the expenses and losses is debited to Income Summary with offsetting credits to the individual expense and loss accounts in one entry, the total of the revenues and gains is credited to it in a second entry, and a third entry closes the account by transferring its credit or debit balance (net income or loss) to retained earnings.

December 31, 19_1

	Trial balance		Balance sheet	
Cash	16,500		16,500	
Accounts receivable	11,000		11,000	
Merchandise inventory	12,000		12,000	
Land	10,000		10,000	
Accounts payable		20,000		20,000
Salaries payable		1,500		1,500
Capital stock		25,000		25,000
Retained earnings				3,000
Dividends	2,000			
Sales		81,000		
Cost of goods sold	48,000			
Salaries expense	18,000			
Rent expense	4,800			
Other expense	5,200			
	127,500	127,500	49,500	49,500

Because the business began in 19_1 there was no beginning retained earnings balance, and since the trial balance is a list of the account balances as found in the ledger, it follows that the retained earnings ledger account had a zero balance when the trial balance was prepared. The reason for the lack of agreement is that the elements that make up the $3,000 of retained earnings have not been transferred to the retained earnings account. Those elements are found in the following accounts:

The revenue and expense accounts

Revenue:		
Sales—this account has a credit balance		$81,000
Expense:		
Cost of goods sold	$48,000	
Salaries expense	18,000	
Rent expense	4,800	
Other expense	5,200	
The expense accounts have debit balances		76,000
The difference (a net credit) is the net income		$ 5,000

The dividends account

Dividends—this account has a debit balance	2,000
The difference (also a net credit) is the retained earnings resulting from operating the business during 19_1	$ 3,000

These elements are transferred to the retained earnings account by the following journal entries, which are called *closing entries.*

JOURNAL (Page 10)

19_1					
Dec.	31	Sales	401	81,000	
		Cost of goods sold	501		48,000
		Salaries expense	601		18,000
		Rent expense	602		4,800

	Other expense	604		5,200	
	Retained earnings	325		5,000	
	To close the revenue and expense accounts and to transfer the net income to the retained earnings account.				
31	Retained earnings	325	2,000		
	Dividends	327		2,000	
	To close the dividends account and to transfer the dividends to the retained earnings account.				

The account numbers in the Reference column of the journal indicate that the postings have been made. After the above entries have been posted, the retained earnings account will have a credit balance of $3,000, which agrees with the amount shown in the December 31, 19_1 balance sheet. The revenue, expense, and dividends accounts will have zero balances. This condition can be verified by reference to the accounts affected by the closing entries. (The amounts posted from the closing entries are shown in italics.)

Account Title Retained Earnings   Account No. 325

19_1						
Dec.	31		10		*5,000*	5,000 Cr.
	31		10	*2,000*		3,000 Cr.

Account Title Dividends   Account No. 327

19_1						
Dec.	31	(Year-end balance before closing)				2,000 Dr.
	31		10		*2,000*	—

Account Title Sales   Account No. 401

19_1						
Dec.	31	(Year-end balance before closing)				81,000 Cr.
	31		10	*81,000*		—

Account Title Cost of Goods Sold   Account No. 501

19_1						
Dec.	31	(Year-end balance before closing)				48,000 Dr.
	31		10		*48,000*	—

Account Title Salaries Expense   Account No. 601

19_1						
Dec.	31	(Year-end balance before closing)				18,000 Dr.
	31		10		*18,000*	—

Account Title Rent Expense   Account No. 602

19_1						
Dec.	31	(Year-end balance before closing)				4,800 Dr.
	31		10		*4,800*	—

Account Title Other Expense   Account No. 604

19_1						
Dec.	31	(Year-end balance before closing)				5,200 Dr.
	31		10		*5,200*	—

Observe the use of a double rule in the revenue, expense, and dividend accounts to signal the end of an accounting period and that the books have been closed.

Closing the books annually serves to separate, by years, the data accumulated in the accounts relating to revenues, expenses, and dividends. The availability of revenue and expense data by years enables management and investors to make comparisons with earlier years to determine the extent of improvement or deterioration in the current year's operating performance. Since the books are closed annually, the revenue, expense, and dividend accounts start off each new year with zero balances. Closing the books also updates the retained earnings account by transferring thereto the net income (or loss) for the year just ended and the dividends declared for that year.

TRIAL BALANCE AFTER CLOSING After the books are closed, it is advisable to take an *after-closing* trial balance (sometimes called a *post-closing* trial balance) to make sure that the equality of debits and credits in the ledger has not been destroyed through errors made in closing the books. The after-closing trial balance of Sight & Sound Corporation is shown below.

SIGHT & SOUND CORPORATION
After-Closing Trial Balance
December 31, 19_1

Cash	16,500	
Accounts receivable	11,000	
Merchandise inventory	12,000	
Land	10,000	
Accounts payable		20,000
Salaries payable		1,500
Capital stock		25,000
Retained earnings		3,000
	49,500	49,500

Observe that only asset and equity accounts appear in the after-closing trial balance because revenue, expense, and dividend accounts have been closed to retained earnings.

POSSIBLE ADDITIONAL STEPS IN THE ACCOUNTING CYCLE As a general rule, accounting entries are made when business transactions occur. Usually a customer or supplier or employee is a party to the transaction and some sort of business document, such as a check, a sales slip, or an invoice, is issued or received. Such documents serve as evidence in support of business transactions. Their issuance or receipt provides the justification for whatever entry is required to record the changes in the account balances caused by a business transaction. At the end of an accounting period, when it is time to take the trial balance and prepare the financial statements, it is unlikely that any transactions would be unrecorded. The same cannot be said about adjusting entries. They may or may not have been made before the trial balance was prepared. It does not matter whether the adjusting entries are made before or after the trial balance as long as they are made before the account balances are used to prepare the financial statements.

If adjusting entries were made after the trial balance was prepared, another trial balance often is prepared after the adjusting entries have been journalized and posted. Accountants differentiate between the trial balances by calling the first the "unadjusted trial balance" and the second the "adjusted trial balance."

To illustrate such trial balances, let us return to the Sight & Sound Corporation example for 19_2 discussed in the previous chapter. A trial balance prepared after all 19_2 transactions had been journalized and posted would again appear as shown below.

As noted earlier, a proper matching of revenue and expense would not be achieved if the December 31, 19_2 unadjusted trial balance figures were used to prepare the 19_2 financial statements because of five needed adjusting entries. These are reviewed below the following unadjusted trial balance.

SIGHT & SOUND CORPORATION
Unadjusted Trial Balance
December 31, 19_2

Cash	11,650	
Accounts receivable	12,000	
Merchandise inventory	18,750	
Prepaid rent	9,600	
Bond investment	10,000	
Delivery truck	4,000	
Accounts payable		25,000
Advances from customers		3,000
Capital stock		25,000
Retained earnings		3,000
Dividends	2,000	
Sales		90,000
Cost of goods sold	54,000	
Salaries expense	18,700	
Other expense	5,500	200
Gain from sale of land	146,200	146,200

(1) No recognition has been given to depreciation on the delivery truck.

Adjusting entry:

19_2
December 31   Depreciation expense   900
                       Accumulated depreciation   900

(2) No recognition has been given to the portion of cash advances that has become earned.

Adjusting entries:

19_2
December 31   Advances from customers   1,000
                       Sales   1,000
                       Cost of goods sold   750
                            Merchandise inventory   750

(3) No recognition has been given to the December salaries.

Adjusting entry:

19_2
December 31   Salaries expense   1,700
                       Salaries payable   1,700

(4) No recognition has been given to the fact that one-half of the rent paid in advance applies to 19_2.

Adjusting entry:

19_2
December 31   Rent expense   4,800
                          Prepaid rent   4,800

(5)   No recognition has been given to the interest revenue earned on the bond investment.

Adjusting entry:

19_2
December 31   Interest receivable   200
                          Interest revenue   200

To summarize, adjusting entries may be journalized and posted either before or after the trial balance is prepared. The important point is: Consideration must be given to any required adjustments *before* the financial statements are prepared, whether the adjusting entries are recorded before or after the trial balance.

The schedule below shows the relationship between the unadjusted trial balance and the adjusted trial balance.

SIGHT & SOUND CORPORATION
Trial Balances
December 31, 19_2

	Unadjusted trial balance		Adjustments		Adjusted trial balance	
Cash	11,650				11,650	
Accounts receivable	12,000				12,000	
Merchandise inventory	18,750			(2) 750	18,000	
Prepaid rent	9,600			(4) 4,800	4,800	
Bond investment	10,000				10,000	
Delivery truck	4,000				4,000	
Accounts payable		25,000				25,000
Advances from customers		3,000	(2) 1,000			2,000
Capital stock		25,000				25,000
Retained earnings		3,000				3,000
Dividends	2,000				2,000	
Sales		90,000		(2) 1,000		91,000
Cost of goods sold	54,000		(2) 750		54,750	
Salaries expense	18,700		(3) 1,700		20,400	
Other expense	5,500				5,500	
Gain from sale of land		200				200
	146,200	146,200				
Depreciation expense			(1) 900		900	
Accumulated depreciation				(1) 900		900
Salaries payable				(3) 1,700		1,700
Rent expense			(4) 4,800		4,800	
Interest receivable			(5) 200		200	
Interest revenue				(5) 200		200
			9,350	9,350	149,000	149,000

WORKSHEET The worksheet (also called working papers) is a columnar device used by accountants as a convenient and orderly way of organizing the accounting data to be used in the end-of-period preparation of adjusting entries, periodic financial statements, and closing entries. Unlike the formal and permanent records of the journal and the ledger, the worksheet is an informal accounting record prepared in pencil (which facilitates making changes) to aid in avoiding error correction in the formal records and to serve as a preliminary guide or source for the end-of-period work.

The worksheet is optional. If the ledger contains only a few accounts and there are few adjusting entries, the worksheet is not necessary; if the ledger contains numerous accounts or if there are numerous adjustments, the worksheet is very useful. Even though you may never have to prepare a worksheet, you should be generally familiar with the worksheet because it is often used as a way to present data promptly to management for its information or for decision-making purposes.

ILLUSTRATIVE WORKSHEET The account balances of Sight & Sound Corporation at the end of 19_2 and the related adjustments referred to previously will be used to illustrate the preparation of a worksheet. There are so few accounts and adjustments that an experienced accountant probably would not consider it worthwhile to prepare a worksheet, but in a textbook it is desirable to begin with a relatively simple illustration.

The steps in the preparation of a worksheet are stated and illustrated below and on the pages following.

The data in the first six columns of the worksheet coincide with the preceding schedule showing the unadjusted and adjusted trial balances of Sight & Sound Corporation. Note that since the ledger balances are copied into the first two columns of the worksheet, it is unnecessary to prepare a separate trial balance when the worksheet is used.

First step. The account balances before adjustments were entered in the Trial Balance columns; the columns were totaled to determine their equality.

Second step. The required adjustments were entered in the Adjustments columns; the columns were totaled as a check against errors. Observe that the nature of each adjustment is set forth at the bottom of the worksheet, with a key number matching the debit and credit entries in the Adjustments columns with the explanatory material.

Third step. The Adjusted Trial Balance columns were completed by extending and, when necessary, combining the amounts in the Trial Balance and Adjustments columns; the Adjusted Trial Balance columns were totaled to determine their equality.

SIGHT & SOUND CORPORATION
Worksheet
For the Year Ended December 31, 19_2

	Trial Balance (Dr)	Trial Balance (Cr)	Adjustments (Dr)	Adjustments (Cr)	Adjusted Trial Balance (Dr)	Adjusted Trial Balance (Cr)	Income Statement	Retained Earnings Statement	Balance Sheet
Cash	11,650				11,650				
Accounts receivable	12,000				12,000				
Merchandise inventory	18,750			(2) 750	18,000				
Prepaid rent	9,600			(4) 4,800	4,800				
Bond investment	10,000				10,000				
Delivery truck	4,000				4,000				
Accounts payable		25,000				25,000			
Advances from customers		3,000	(2) 1,000			2,000			
Capital stock		25,000				25,000			
Retained earnings		3,000				3,000			
Dividends	2,000				2,000				
Sales		90,000		(2) 1,000		91,000			
Cost of goods sold	54,000		(2) 750		54,750				
Salaries expense	18,700		(3) 1,700		20,400				
Other expense	5,500				5,500				
Gain from sale of land		200				200			
	146,200	146,200							
Depreciation expense			(1) 900		900				
Accumulated depreciation				(1) 900		900			
Salaries payable				(3) 1,700		1,700			
Rent expense			(4) 4,800		4,800				
Interest receivable			(5) 200		200				
Interest revenue				(5) 200		200			
			9,350	9,350	149,000	149,000			

Adjustments

(1) Depreciation for the year.
(2) Advances from customers earned and cost of goods sold recognized.
(3) December salaries.
(4) Rent expense applicable to 19_2.
(5) Interest earned on bond investment.

Fourth step. Each account balance appearing in the Adjusted Trial Balance columns was entered in a column at the right corresponding to the statement in which it should appear. Debit balances were entered in the debit columns; credit balances were entered in credit columns.

SIGHT & SOUND CORPORATION
Worksheet
For the Year Ended December 31, 19_2

	Trial Balance		Adjustments		Adjusted Trial Balance		Income Statement		Retained Earnings Statement		Balance Sheet	
	Dr	Cr	Dr	Cr	Dr	Cr	Dr	Cr	Dr	Cr	Dr	Cr
Cash	11,650				11,650						11,650	
Accounts receivable	12,000				12,000						12,000	
Merchandise inventory	18,750			(2) 750	18,000						18,000	
Prepaid rent	9,600			(4) 4,800	4,800						4,800	
Bond investment	10,000				10,000						10,000	
Delivery truck	4,000				4,000						4,000	
Accounts payable		25,000				25,000						25,000
Advances from customers		3,000	(2) 1,000			2,000						2,000
Capital stock		25,000				25,000						25,000
Retained earnings		3,000				3,000				3,000		
Dividends	2,000				2,000				2,000			
Sales		90,000		(2) 1,000		91,000		91,000				
Cost of goods sold	54,000		(2) 750		54,750		54,750					
Salaries expense	18,700		(3) 1,700		20,400		20,400					
Other expense	5,500				5,500		5,500					
Gain from sale of land		200				200		200				
	146,200	146,200										
Depreciation expense			(1) 900		900		900					
Accumulated depreciation				(1) 900		900						900
Salaries payable				(3) 1,700		1,700						1,700
Rent expense			(4) 4,800		4,800		4,800					
Interest receivable			(5) 200		200						200	
Interest revenue				(5) 200		200		200				
			9,350	9,350	149,000	149,000						

Adjustments

(1) Depreciation for the year.
(2) Advances from customers earned and cost of goods sold recognized.
(3) December salaries.
(4) Rent expense applicable to 19_2.
(5) Interest earned on bond investment.

Fifth step. The net income for the year, amounting to $5,050, was determined as the balance of the Income Statement columns was computed. To facilitate this computation, the items in the two columns were totaled. The $5,050 was entered in the Income Statement debit column as a balancing figure; and, since the net income increases the retained earnings, it was also entered in the Retained Earnings Statement credit column. The Income Statement columns were again totaled and ruled.

SIGHT & SOUND CORPORATION
Worksheet
For the Year Ended December 31, 19_2

Account	Trial Balance Dr	Trial Balance Cr	Adjustments Dr	Adjustments Cr	Adjusted Trial Balance Dr	Adjusted Trial Balance Cr	Income Statement Dr	Income Statement Cr	Retained Earnings Statement Dr	Retained Earnings Statement Cr	Balance Sheet Dr	Balance Sheet Cr
Cash	11,650				11,650						11,650	
Accounts receivable	12,000				12,000						12,000	
Merchandise inventory	18,750			(2) 750 (4) 4,800	18,000						18,000	
Prepaid rent	9,600				4,800						4,800	
Bond investment	10,000				10,000						10,000	
Delivery truck	4,000				4,000						4,000	
Accounts payable		25,000				25,000						25,000
Advances from customers		3,000	(2) 1,000			2,000						2,000
Capital stock		25,000				25,000						25,000
Retained earnings		3,000				3,000				3,000		
Dividends	2,000				2,000				2,000			
Sales		90,000		(2) 1,000		91,000		91,000				
Cost of goods sold	54,000		(2) 750		54,750		54,750					
Salaries expense	18,700		(3) 1,700		20,400		20,400					
Other expense	5,500				5,500		5,500					
Gain from sale of land		200				200		200				
	146,200	146,200										
Depreciation expense			(1) 900		900		900					
Accumulated depreciation				(1) 900		900						900
Salaries payable				(3) 1,700		1,700						1,700
Rent expense			(4) 4,800		4,800		4,800					
Interest receivable			(5) 200		200						200	
Interest revenue				(5) 200		200		200				
			9,350	9,350	149,000	149,000	86,350	91,400				
Net income							5,050			5,050		900
							91,400	91,400				1,700

Adjustments

(1) Depreciation for the year.
(2) Advances from customers earned and cost of goods sold recognized.
(3) December salaries.
(4) Rent expense applicable to 19_2.
(5) Interest earned on bond investment.

Sixth and final step. The retained earnings figure for the end of the year was computed, entered as a balancing figure in the Retained Earnings Statement debit column, and also entered in the Balance Sheet credit column. The two Balance Sheet columns were totaled and found to be in agreement. Lack of agreement would indicate an error somewhere in the worksheet.

SIGHT & SOUND CORPORATION
Worksheet
For the Year Ended December 31, 19_2

	Trial Balance		Adjustments		Adjusted Trial Balance		Income Statement		Retained Earnings Statement		Balance Sheet	
Cash	11,650				11,650						11,650	
Accounts receivable	12,000				12,000						12,000	
Merchandise inventory	18,750			(2) 750	18,000						18,000	
Prepaid rent	9,600			(4) 4,800	4,800						4,800	
Bond investment	10,000				10,000						10,000	
Delivery truck	4,000				4,000						4,000	
Accounts payable		25,000				25,000						25,000
Advances from customers		3,000	(2) 1,000			2,000						2,000
Capital stock		25,000				25,000						25,000
Retained earnings		3,000				3,000				3,000		
Dividends	2,000				2,000				2,000			
Sales		90,000		(2) 1,000		91,000		91,000				
Cost of goods sold	54,000		(2) 750		54,750		54,750					
Salaries expense	18,700		(3) 1,700		20,400		20,400					
Other expense	5,500				5,500		5,500					
Gain from sale of land		200				200		200				
	146,200	146,200										
Depreciation expense			(1) 900		900		900					
Accumulated depreciation				(1) 900		900						900
Salaries payable				(3) 1,700		1,700						1,700
Rent expense			(4) 4,800		4,800		4,800					
Interest receivable			(5) 200		200						200	
Interest revenue				(5) 200		200		200				
			9,350	9,350	149,000	149,000	86,350	91,400				
Net income							5050			5,050		
							91,400	91,400	2,000	8,050		
Retained earnings, Dec. 31, 19_2									6,050			6,050
									8,050	8,050	60,650	60,650

Adjustments
(1) Depreciation for the year.
(2) Advances from customers earned and cost of goods sold recognized.
(3) December salaries.
(4) Rent expense applicable to 19_2.
(5) Interest earned on bond investment.

STATEMENTS PREPARED FROM WORKSHEET The worksheet provides in a convenient form the information required for the financial statements. The income statement from the illustrative worksheet would be in agreement with the one shown previously on page 117 (for both the single-step and multiple-step formats) for the year ended December 31, 19_2. The balance sheet as of December 31, 19_2, and the statement of retained earnings for the year ended December 31, 19_2, obtained from the worksheet are illustrated on page 148. Note that comparative statements (current and prior year statements) are shown as is done in actual practice for published statements in order to provide a basis for comparison.

SIGHT & SOUND CORPORATION
Balance Sheet
December 31, 19_2 and 19_1

Assets:	19_2		19_1	
Current assets:				
Cash	$11,650		$16,500	
Accounts receivable	12,000		11,000	
Interest receivable	200		—	
Merchandise inventory	18,000		12,000	
Prepaid rent	4,800		—	
Total current assets		$46,650		$39,500
Long-term investments:				
Investment in land—at cost	$ —		$10,000	
Bond investment	10,000		—	
Total long-term investments		10,000		10,000
Property, plant, and equipment:				
Delivery truck	$ 4,000		—	
Accumulated depreciation	900		—	
Total property, plant, and equipment		3,100		—
Total assets		$59,750		$49,500
Equities:				
Current liabilities:				
Accounts payable	$25,000		$20,000	
Salaries payable	1,700		1,500	
Advances from customers	2,000		—	
Total current liabilities		$28,700		$21,500
Stockholders' equity:				
Capital stock	$25,000		$25,000	
Retained earnings	6,050		3,000	
Total stockholders' equity		31,050		28,000
Total equities		$59,750		$49,500

SIGHT & SOUND CORPORATION
Statement of Retained Earnings
For the Years Ended December 31, 19_2 and 19_1

	19_2	19_1
Retained earnings beginning of the year	$3,000	—
Add net income	5,000	5,000
	$8,000	$5,000
Deduct dividends	2,000	2,000
Retained earnings end of the year	$6,000	$3,000

ADJUSTING ENTRIES PREPARED FROM WORKSHEET The adjusting entries can be prepared from the data in the Adjustments columns of the worksheet. Refer to the completed worksheet on page 147 for the data used to prepare the adjusting entries. The adjusting entries are identical to those summarized on pages 141 and 142.

CLOSING ENTRIES PREPARED FROM WORKSHEET The closing entries can be prepared from the data in the Income Statement columns and the Retained Earnings Statement columns of the worksheet. Refer to the completed worksheet on page 147 for the data used to prepare the following closing entries.

19_1					
Dec.	31	Sales	401	91,000	
		Interest revenue	701	200	
		Gain from sale of land	702	200	
		Cost of goods sold	501		54,750
		Salaries expense	601		20,400
		Rent expense	602		4,800
		Depreciation expense	603		900
		Other expense	604		5,500
		Retained earnings	325		5,050
		To close the revenue and expense accounts and to transfer the net income to the retained earnings account.			
	31	Retained earnings	325	2,000	
		Dividends	327		2,000
		To close the dividends account and to transfer the dividends to the retained earnings account.			

THE ACCOUNTING CYCLE The fully developed accounting cycle is set forth below. It indicates the sequence in which accounting procedures are customarily performed.

> Transaction analysis.
> Journalize and post entries for all transactions.
> Prepare a trial balance (usually entered directly in the worksheet, if it is prepared).
> Complete the worksheet (optional).
> Journalize and post adjusting entries.
> Prepare financial statements. (When the worksheet is used, the financial statements may be prepared therefrom *before* the adjusting and closing entries are journalized and posted.)
> Journalize and post closing entries.
> Prepare an after-closing trial balance.

These procedures, in total, constitute an accounting cycle. In practice, the complete cycle usually is performed only once a year, because the books ordinarily are not closed more frequently. In some of the illustrations and problems in this text it is assumed, for convenience and simplicity, that the cycle is completed monthly.

If interim financial statements (that is, monthly and quarterly statements) are prepared, such statements can be obtained from a worksheet without making formal monthly and quarterly adjusting and closing entries in the journal and ledger. The latter would be made only at the end of the fiscal year.

FURTHER ANALYSIS OF ADJUSTING ENTRIES As previously explained, transactions provide the basic economic data converted by the accountant to financial information in the form of financial statements. Transactions were defined in Chapter 2 as economic events or occurrences that result in changes to the assets and/or equities of an entity. It was further pointed out that transactions are conveniently classified as external transactions, which arise from exchanges with those outside the firm, and internal transactions, which arise from asset usage and conversion and internal accounting adjustments.

External transactions are recorded as they occur during the accounting period based on the external evidence of sales slips, purchase invoices, checks written and received, and the like. The explicit evidence of external transactions "trigger" their day-to-day recording; hence, the need for making these regular entries easily and obviously comes to the attention of the accountant.

In contrast, the recording of internal transactions is not "triggered" by obvious source documents; hence, they are ignored in the regular day-to-day recording procedures. Instead, they are recorded at the end of the period, after the regular entries are completed, by the accountant making adjusting entries based on a review of the trial balance and prior year's adjusting entries. The mere appearance of some accounts in the trial balance may suggest the necessity for certain adjustments. For instance, depreciable assets suggest adjustments for depreciation; investments in bonds suggest the possibility of earned, but unrecorded, interest revenue; a notes payable account suggests the need for an adjustment for interest payable. Similarly, if any prepayments or advances from customers appear in the trial balance, they should immediately alert the accountant's attention to the possibility that adjustments for cost expirations and revenue earned may be required.

Although an inspection of the trial balance and a review of earlier adjusting entries may suggest the *nature* of the required adjustments, to determine the *amounts* of the adjustments the accountant may need to refer to a variety of business documents or may make physical counts or other suitable quantitative measurements.

PRINCIPAL TYPES OF ADJUSTING ENTRIES As previously discussed, adjusting entries are required whenever transactions overlap two or more accounting periods. Adjusting entries essentially relate to timing differences between revenue earned and receipts and between expenses incurred and payments (cost outlays). With this in mind, we can therefore classify adjusting entries as those required for:

Unrecorded revenues: Unrecorded revenues earned during the current period that are to be collected in a subsequent period.

Unrecorded expenses: Unrecorded expenses incurred during the current period that are to be paid in a subsequent period.

Earned advances from customers: Revenue earned during the current period, the associated cash having been collected in a previous period.

Cost expirations: Expenses incurred during the current period, the associated cash having been paid in a previous period.

Unrecorded revenues Revenue may be earned when goods are delivered or services are rendered during the current period, but because it is not due and therefore not collected, it has not been recorded. At the end of the fiscal period any such unrecorded, though earned, revenue should be entered in the records by means of an adjusting entry debiting a receivable (an asset account) and crediting revenue. Otherwise, the financial statements would be in error because the revenue shown thereon would be understated.

Unrecorded revenue that is earned but not collected is frequently called *accrued revenue.* Examples of accrued revenue are interest and rent revenues. Such revenue is said to accrue (grow or accumulate) since it accumulates day by day and thereby becomes earned as time passes, regardless of the cash inflow. It would be impractical, however, to record such revenue on a daily basis as it accrues.

An adjusting entry for unrecorded interest revenue has been previously illustrated with regard to Sight & Sound Corporation on its bond investment (see pages 115 and 142). Since interest is earned with the passage of time, the three-months' interest on the bond investment is earned, even though uncollected, and should be recorded by the following year-end adjusting entry:

Interest receivable ($10,000 $\times$ .08 $\times$ 3/12)	200	
Interest revenue		200

As another illustration, assume that a company rents a building to a tenant for $2,000 a month and that by December 31, the end of the fiscal year, the December rent has not been received. Since space was made available to the tenant for the month of December, rent revenue for December has been earned, even though uncollected, and should be recorded by the following year-end adjusting entry:

Rent receivable	2,000	
Rent revenue		2,000

Unrecorded expenses An expense may become incurred when goods or services are used during the current period, but because payment is not due and therefore has not been made, the expense has not been recorded. At the end of the fiscal period any such unrecorded, though incurred, expense should be entered in the records by means of an adjusting entry debiting expense and crediting a liability. Otherwise, the financial statements would be in error because the expenses and liabilities shown thereon would be understated.

Unrecorded expense that is incurred but not paid is often called *accrued expense.* Examples of accrued expense are employees' salaries and interest on borrowed money. Such expense is said to accrue (grow or accumulate) since it accumulates day by day and thereby becomes incurred as time passes, regardless of the cash outflow. As with accrued revenue, it would be impractical to record such expense on a daily basis as it accrues.

An adjusting entry for unrecorded salaries expense has been previously illustrated with regard to Sight & Sound Corporation for its December salaries (see pages 114 and 141). Since the employees' services were used during December, expense has been incurred, even though unpaid, and should be recorded by the following year-end adjusting entry:

Salaries expense	1,700	
Salaries payable		1,700

As another illustration, assume that on September 1 a company borrows $3,000 at 7 per cent interest payable one year hence. If the company's fiscal year ends December 31, then the following adjusting entry would be made on December 31 to record the interest expense incurred (the cost of the use of the money for four months), even though not paid, and to record the amount of interest owed at year end:

| Interest expense ($3,000 × .07 × 4/12) | 70 | |
| Interest payable | | 70 |

Earned advances from customers   Sometimes a business will receive cash as an advance payment from a customer for goods to be delivered or services to be rendered in the future. The receipt of such cash advances creates a liability to the firm pending future performance. The recognition of revenue is deferred or delayed to the period in which the goods are delivered or the services rendered in accordance with the revenue-recognition assumption.

As a result of deferring the recognition of revenue, the liability created when the cash advance is received is often referred to as "deferred revenue," "revenue received in advance," or "unearned revenue." However, these terms are misleading because it is cash, not revenue, that is received in advance, and because receipt of the cash gives rise to a liability, not a revenue. Therefore, we will use the term *advances from customers* to refer to the liability for the future delivery of goods and the term *rent* (or subscriptions, etc.) *collected in advance* for the liability to perform future services.

At the time the cash advance is received an entry is made debiting Cash and crediting the liability Advances from Customers. During the subsequent period when the goods are delivered or services are rendered, an end-of-period adjusting entry is made transferring the revenue earned from the liability account to a revenue account: debit Advances from Customers and credit Sales. Of course, if there is partial performance during the period when the cash advance is received, then an adjusting entry would be made at the end of the period to transfer a portion of the liability to revenue.

An adjusting entry transferring the earned portion from the liability account to a revenue account has been previously illustrated with regard to Sight & Sound Corporation (see page 113). The year-end adjusting entry and the accounts affected are reviewed below:

| Advances from customers | 1,000 | |
| Sales | | 1,000 |

	Advances from customers		Sales
Advance collection		3,000	
Adjusting entry	1,000		1,000

As another illustration, assume that a company rents a building to a tenant for $1,000 a month. Further assume that on October 1 the tenant pays $6,000 to the company for six-months' rent paid in advance, which is recorded by debiting Cash and crediting the liability, Rent Collected in Advance. If the company's fiscal year ends December 31, then the following adjusting entry would be made on December 31 to reduce the liability and to reflect the three-months' rent earned:

| Rent collected in advance | | 3,000 | |
| Rent revenue (3 × $1,000) | | | 3,000 |

	Rent collected in advance		Rent revenue
Advance collection		6,000	
Adjusting entry	3,000		3,000

Cost expirations Cost was previously defined as the amount paid, in cash or other assets, or the liability incurred to make a future payment, for economic benefits received or to be received. If a cost outlay is made for goods or services that will benefit more than one period, then it is customary to record the transaction as an asset acquisition—the entire cost is debited to an asset account. As time passes, it is necessary at the end of each period benefited by the cost outlay to transfer, by an adjusting entry, an appropriate portion of the cost from the asset account to an expense account. The underlying rationale is that the expense (expired cost) should be matched with the revenue for each of the periods affected.

Most economic benefits expire through use or with the passage of time. Their expiration converts the cost paid for the benefits from an asset status to an expense or loss status. The expired or consumed portion of the economic benefits from a cost outlay is an expense of the current period, and the remaining unexpired or unused portion is an asset reported in the balance sheet at the end of the current period. The unexpired cost (asset) will become expense (expired cost) in subsequent periods.

The accounting problem is to determine when and by how much such cost expiration occurs and to give recognition thereto in the accounting records and in the financial statements. The accountant attempts to solve this problem by means of estimation by apportioning the cost outlay between cost expiration and cost residue in either of two ways:

By estimating the cost expiration or expense and accepting the remainder as a proper balance for the unexpired cost or asset balance. This is the procedure normally applied to depreciable assets. The cost expiration (depreciation expense) is computed and the remaining balance, the undepreciated cost, is reported as an asset.

By computing the unexpired cost or asset balance and accepting the remainder as the proper estimation of the cost expiration. If the accountant can establish the portion of a cost outlay that is assignable to the future, then, in effect, the cost expiration is established. This procedure is illustrated by the following apportionment of a cost outlay for office supplies:

Office supplies purchased at beginning of period	$3,000
Office supplies on hand at end of period— determined by counting the items on hand with valuation at their cost	600
Office supplies used (expense)	$2,400

To illustrate the adjusting entry necessary for cost expiration, refer to the preceding example of the office supplies. When the office supplies were purchased, the asset, Office Supplies, was debited and Cash was credited for $3,000. At the end of the period the following adjusting entry would be made to apportion cost to expense for matching purposes and to reduce Office Supplies to the cost of supplies on hand at the end of the period:

Supplies expense	2,400	
Office supplies		2,400

	Office supplies		Supplies expense	
Cost outlay	3,000			
Adjusting entry		2,400	2,400	

As another illustration of an adjusting entry for cost expiration, we can refer to the depreciation entry for Sight & Sound Corporation at the end of 19_2 (see page 113). This depreciation entry is a year-end adjusting entry that apportions part of the cost of the delivery truck to expense for the current period (matching) and reduces the amount of the asset to unexpired cost, as shown below:

Depreciation expense [($4,000 − $400) ÷ 4]	900	
Accumulated depreciation		900

Remember that accumulated depreciation is a contra asset account; hence, it is reported in the balance sheet as a separate deduction from the original cost of the delivery truck ($4,000) to show unexpired cost of $3,100 (= $4,000 − $900).

As a final illustration of an adjusting entry for cost expiration, assume that on January 1 a company pays $3,300 for a three-year fire insurance policy on its building. The payment is recorded on January 1 by debiting the asset, Prepaid (or Unexpired) Insurance, and crediting Cash for $3,300. At year end the following adjusting entry would be made to apportion the insurance cost to expense for the current period (matching) and to reduce the cost of prepaid insurance to show the unexpired insurance cost of $2,200 (= $3,300 − $1,100) for balance-sheet reporting purposes as of December 31:

Insurance expense ($3,300 × 12/36)	1,100	
Prepaid insurance		1,100

19XX		Prepaid insurance		Insurance expense	
Jan 1.	Cost outlay	3,300			
Dec. 31	Adjusting entry		1,100	1,100	

IMPORTANT TERMS AND CONCEPTS IN CHAPTER 5

DEMONSTRATION PROBLEM FOR REVIEW AND SELF-STUDY The following trial balance was taken from the books of Portland Company at the close of business for the year 19_6:

PORTLAND COMPANY
Trial Balance
December 31, 19_6

Cash	5,438	
Accounts receivable	12,720	
Inventory	6,500	
Materials and supplies	2,250	
Prepaid insurance	270	
Land	5,000	
Buildings	50,000	
Accumulated depreciation—Buildings		10,000
Equipment	60,000	
Accumulated depreciation—Equipment		32,000
Accounts payable		4,450
Notes payable—5%, due 12/31/_9		16,000
Taxes payable		2,520
Capital stock		60,000
Retained earnings		12,500
Dividends	3,600	
Sales		138,430
Cost of goods sold	82,400	
Selling commissions	6,900	
Delivery expense	2,380	
Salaries expense	33,500	
Property taxes	4,542	
Interest expense	400	
	275,900	275,900

The following information was also obtained from the records maintained by Portland Company.

(1) The building was put into operation on January 1, 19_1, and is expected to have a useful life of 25 years from that date.

(2) The equipment is to be depreciated at 20% per year.

(3) A count of the materials and supplies shows $460 as the cost of those on hand.

(4) The insurance policy was purchased on June 30, 19_5, and expires on June 30, 19_8.

(5) The notes payable bear interest of 5 per cent per year. Interest was last paid on July 1, 19_6.

(6) Salaries payable amount to $110.

(7) Sales commissions payable are $332.

INSTRUCTIONS

(a) Prepare the worksheet for the year ended December 31, 19_6.

(b) Record the closing entries for the year.

Note Attempt to solve the demonstration problem before examining the solution that follows.

Solution:

(a)

PORTLAND COMPANY
Worksheet
For the Year Ended December 31, 19_6

	Trial Balance		Adjustments			Adjusted Trial Balance		Income Statement		Retained Earnings Statement		Balance Sheet	
Cash	5,438					5,438						5,438	
Accounts receivable	12,720					12,720						12,720	
Inventory	6,500					6,500						6,500	
Materials and supplies	2,250			(3)	1,790	460						460	
Prepaid insurance	270			(4)	108	162						162	
Land	5,000					5,000						5,000	
Buildings	50,000					50,000						50,000	
Accumulated depreciation—Buildings		10,000		(1)	2,000		12,000						12,000
Equipment	60,000					60,000						60,000	
Accumulated depreciation—Equipment		32,000		(2)	12,000		44,000						44,000
Accounts payable		4,450					4,450						4,450
Notes payable—5%, due 12/31/_9		16,000					16,000						16,000
Taxes payable		2,520					2,520						2,520
Capital stock		60,000					60,000						60,000
Retained earnings		12,500					12,500				12,500		
Dividends	3,600					3,600				3,600			
Sales		138,430					138,430		138,430				
Cost of goods sold	82,400					82,400		82,400					
Selling commissions	6,900		(7)	332		7,232		7,232					
Delivery expense	2,380					2,380		2,380					
Salaries expense	33,500		(6)	110		33,610		33,610					
Property taxes	4,542					4,542		4,542					
Interest expense	400		(5)	400		800		800					
	275,900	275,900											
Depreciation expense—Buildings			(1)	2,000		2,000		2,000					
Depreciation expense—Equipment			(2)	12,000		12,000		12,000					
Materials and supplies used			(3)	1,790		1,790		1,790					
Insurance expense			(4)	108		108		108					
Interest payable					(5) 400		400						400
Salaries payable					(6) 110		110						110
Sales commissions payable					(7) 332		332						332
			16,740	16,740		290,742	290,742	146,862	138,430				
Net loss									8,432	8,432			
								146,862	146,862	12,032	12,500		
Retained earnings—12/31/_6										468			468
										12,500	12,500	140,280	140,280

Adjustments

(1) Depreciation of buildings.
(2) Depreciation of equipment.
(3) Materials and supplies used.
(4) Insurance expense—(2/5 of $270).

(5) Interest payable—($16,000 × .05 × 1/2).
(6) Salaries payable.
(7) Sales commissions payable.

Closing Entries

19_6					
Dec.	31	Sales		138,430	
		Retained earnings		8,432	
		Cost of goods sold			82,400
		Selling commissions			7,232
		Delivery expense			2,380
		Salaries expense			33,610
		Property taxes			4,542
		Interest expense			800
		Depreciation expense—Buildings			2,000
		Depreciation expense—Equipment			12,000
		Materials and supplies used			1,790
		Insurance expense			108
		To close the revenue and expense accounts and to transfer the net loss to the retained earnings account.			
	31	Retained earnings		3,600	
		Dividends			3,600
		To close the dividends account.			

Questions

1   Give the sequence of procedures in the accounting cycle.
2   When the books have been closed, which kinds of accounts will have zero balances?
3   Is the following statement true or false? ''Closing the books updates the retained earnings account.'' Why?
4   What does one achieve by taking an after-closing trial balance?
5   Does it matter whether adjusting entries are recorded before or after the trial balance has been prepared?
6   What is the worksheet?
7   Is it always desirable to prepare the worksheet before preparing the financial statements?
8   Is it possible to prepare the financial statements by reference only to the completed worksheet?
9   What purpose does closing serve?
10 After the adjusted trial balance heading, the worksheet headings appear in the following order: income statement, statement of retained earnings, and balance sheet. Why?
11 Are the balances of the balance sheet *accounts* in the after-closing trial balance equal to the account balances shown on the balance sheet?
12 Since revenues, expenses, and dividends are all temporary accounts, why is a separate entry made to close dividends?
13 What are the four types of adjusting entries?
14 Why does the receipt of cash as an *advance* payment create a liability?
15 What accounting problem is inherent in the determination of cost-expiration adjustments?
16 Cost expirations are normal adjustments made during the accounting cycle. Through what accounts does the accountant's method of estimation (cost of apportioning) affect the ending balance sheet?

Short exercises

E5-1

You are given below three multiple-choice statements. Select the correct answers and indicate the corresponding letters on a sheet of paper (e.g., 1-d, 2-d, etc.).

(1) The worksheet is (a) a formal and permanent record, (b) a necessary part of the accounting cycle, (c) an optional device used to organize accounting data, (d) seldom useful to the experienced accountant, (e) all of the above, (f) none of the above.

(2) Adjusting entries (a) are triggered by external documents for the interim financial statements, (b) are usually journalized, but this is an optional step in the accounting cycle, (c) only affect the income statement, (d) only affect the statement of changes in financial position, (e) all of the above, (f) none of the above.

(3) The unadjusted trial balance of Kiss Company had a $2,000 balance in the advances from customers account and during the year one-half of the amount was earned. If the adjusting entry is not

made, (a) liabilities would be $1,000 too high, (b) stockholder's equity would be $1,000 too low, (c) assets would be unchanged, (d) net income would be $1,000 too low, (e) all of the above, (f) none of the above.

E5-2   *You are given below three multiple-choice statements. Select the correct answers and indicate the corresponding letters on a sheet of paper (e.g., 1-a, 2-a, etc.).*

(1)   An example of the receipt of an asset in a revenue-type transaction that creates a liability would be (a) the receipt of cash by the company for services not entirely completed in the current accounting period, (b) the payment in cash for a ten-year insurance policy, (c) the sale of a product for cash, (d) the receipt of cash for services performed in the current accounting period, (e) all of the above, (f) none of the above.

(2)   The closing entries are prepared (a) before preparing the financial statements, (b) after the statement preparation, but before the adjusting entries, (c) after the completion of the worksheet, but before the preparation of the financial statements, (d) after the after-closing trial balance, (e) all of the above, (f) none of the above.

(3)   The XYZ company has a $1,000 bond (6 per cent) for investment purposes. The bond was held the entire year, but no interest entry has been made by XYZ. If the correct adjusting entry is not made, (a) net income will be overstated by $60, (b) retained earnings will be understated by $120, (c) assets will be overstated by $60, (d) liabilities will be overstated by $60, (e) all of the above, (f) none of the above.

E5-3   *(a) A company's trial balance is shown below. Prepare journal entries to close the books as of December 31, 19_4.*

TREES INCORPORATED
Trial Balance
December 31, 19_4

Cash	5,050	
Accounts receivable	1,700	
Inventory	1,000	
Land	2,800	
Capital stock		9,000
Dividends	40	
Sales		12,010
Cost of goods sold	6,200	
Store rent expense	800	
Advertising expense	445	
Salaries expense	2,975	
	21,010	21,010

(Remember that after closing entries have been posted the revenue, expense, and dividend accounts should have zero balances.)

(b) The company's trial balance one year later is shown on page 160. This year the company suffered a net loss, that is, the expenses exceeded the revenues. As a result, the retained earnings would be reduced by the amount of the net loss. Prepare closing entries as of December 31, 19_5.

TREES INCORPORATED
Trial Balance
December 31, 19_5

Cash	6,680	
Accounts receivable	975	
Inventory	2,225	
Accounts payable		400
Capital stock		9,000
Retained earnings		680
Sales		6,000
Cost of goods sold	3,500	
Store rent expense	450	
Advertising expense	250	
Salaries expense	2,000	
	16,080	16,080

E5-4

Prepare the December 31, 19_6 after-closing trial balance.

NIGHT COMPANY
Adjusted Trial Balance
December 31, 19_6

Cash	600	
Accounts receivable	800	
Inventory	1,000	
Supplies on hand	200	
Equipment	2,000	
Accumulated depreciation		300
Accounts payable		1,200
Taxes payable		60
Capital stock		2,000
Retained earnings		540
Dividends	80	
Sales		16,400
Cost of goods sold	10,000	
Salaries expense	5,000	
Rent expense	360	
Depreciation expense	100	
Supplies expense	240	
Taxes expense	120	
	20,500	20,500

E5-5

The following accounts and amounts are taken from those shown in the Adjusted Trial Balance columns of the worksheet of Mycenean Corporation. To demonstrate your knowledge of the worksheet, indicate, by the use of the letters A through F shown in the columns, the column or columns in which you would place the amounts listed under "Adjusted Trial Balance." (You are not asked to enter the amounts in the columns. Just write the correct column number beside each account title.)

	Adjusted trial balance	Income statement		Retained earnings statement		Balance sheet	
		A	B	C	D	E	F
Cash	2,800						
Inventory	3,500						
Prepaid insurance	350						
Land	14,000						
Building	70,000						
Accumulated depreciation	7,000						
Accounts payable	4,200						
Salaries payable	2,450						
Capital stock	35,000						
Retained earnings	6,300						
Dividends	1,800						
Sales	262,500						
Cost of goods sold	155,350						
Salaries expense	70,000						
Interest revenue	1,050						
Interest expense	700						

E5-6

Chronkite Company, engaged in inspection and repair work only, has been in business since 19_3. It closes its books on July 31. The company's trial balance at the end of 19_6 was as follows:

CHRONKITE COMPANY
Trial Balance
July 31, 19_6

Cash	4,200	
Notes receivable	2,000	
Electrical supplies	1,600	
Prepaid insurance	480	
Land	12,400	
Building	37,600	
Accumulated depreciation—Building		10,528
Equipment	10,000	
Accumulated depreciation—Equipment		3,000
Accounts payable		700
Inspection fees received in advance		2,400
Capital stock		50,000
Retained earnings	2,248	
Repair service revenue		26,500
Inspection fees earned		6,200
Salaries and wages expense	25,000	
Miscellaneous expense	3,800	
	99,328	99,328

The building had an expected useful life of 50 years when new, and the equipment an expected life of 10 years when new. The interest accrued on the notes receivable amounted to $10 as of July 31, 19_6. The insurance coverage was acquired on August 1, 19_5 and the policy covered a three-year term. The premium for the three-year term was $480. One-third of the inspection fees received in advance has been earned as of July 31, 19_6. The year-end inventory of electrical supplies amounted to $300.

Prepare adjusting entries.

E5-7

The comparative balance sheets of Stamp Company show the following items:

	19_8	19_9
Supplies	$20,000	$35,000
Prepaid insurance	300	1,000
Taxes payable	2,000	1,000

The income statement for 19_9 shows the following items:

Supplies expense	$10,000
Insurance expense	300
Tax expense	3,000

What was the cash paid during 19_9 for (a) supplies, (b) insurance, and (c) taxes?

E5-8

(a) Assume that the Fluid Company records the purchase of a three-year insurance policy as a $3,000 debit to insurance expense and a $3,000 credit to cash. If the policy was purchased at the beginning of the fiscal year, what will be the end-of-year adjustment?

(b) If the original entry was made as a $3,000 debit to prepaid insurance and a $3,000 credit to cash, what will be the end-of-year adjustment?

(c) What caused the difference in the adjusting entries?

Problems

A5-1

Using the trial balance and the data for adjustments given below, prepare the worksheet for Scout Corporation for the month of July.

SCOUT CORPORATION
Trial Balance
June 30, 19_4

Cash	2,356	
Notes receivable	2,600	
Capital stock		2,000
Retained earnings		1,643
Dividends	60	
Fees		2,900
Salaries expense	1,402	
Advertising expense	125	
	6,543	6,543

Data for adjustments:

(a) Interest receivable, $13.

(b) Office rent payable for July, $125.

(c) Liability for advertising expense, $15.

A5-2

Using the following information, prepare the worksheet for the year ended June 30, 19_4.

CRETE CORPORATION
Trial Balance
June 30, 19_4

Cash	2,200	
U.S. Government bonds	2,000	
Inventory	8,500	
Land	2,750	
Building	9,000	
Accumulated depreciation—Building		3,000
Equipment	2,800	
Accumulated depreciation—Equipment		1,200
Taxes payable		200
Capital stock		20,000
Retained earnings (deficit)	3,750	
Sales		30,000
Cost of goods sold	20,000	
Advertising expense	350	
Salaries expense	2,100	
Miscellaneous expense	950	
	54,400	54,400

Depreciation:

(a) Depreciation of building, $210.

(b) Depreciation of equipment, $90.

Accrued amounts as of June 30, 19_4:

(c) Interest receivable, $25.

(d) Salaries payable, $200.

(e) Total taxes payable, $450.

A5-3   *Lawrence Construction Company, engaged in inspection and repair work only, has been in business since 19__. It closes its books on December 31. The company's trial balance at the end of 19_5 was:*

LAWRENCE CONSTRUCTION COMPANY
Trial Balance
December 31, 19_5

Cash	400	
Notes receivable	300	
Electrical supplies	200	
Prepaid insurance	80	
Land	1,000	
Building	16,000	
Accumulated depreciation—Building		2,000
Equipment	3,000	
Accumulated depreciation—Equipment		500
Accounts payable		200
Inspection fees received in advance		600
Capital stock		15,000
Retained earnings		2,100
Dividends	500	
Repair service revenue		5,680
Inspection fees earned		2,000
Salaries and wages expense	5,000	
Miscellaneous expense	1,600	
	28,080	28,080

The building had an expected useful life of 20 years when new, and the equipment an expected life of five years when new. The interest receivable on the notes amounted to $10 as of December 31, 19_5. The insurance coverage was acquired on January 1, 19_4 and the policy covered a two-year term. One-third of the inspection fees received in advance has been earned as of December 31, 19_5. The year-end inventory of electrical supplies amounted to $100.

Prepare adjusting entries and closing entries.

A5-4

The beginning-of-year and end-of-year account balances of Hood Company are listed below.

	19_5	
	January 1	December 31
Cash	$ 4,000	$ 4,550
Accounts receivable	6,000	6,500
Interest receivable	—	50
Inventory	5,000	5,000
Prepaid rent ($50 per month)	300	—
Investment in bonds	—	2,500
Land	2,000	—
Equipment	2,500	2,500
Accumulated depreciation	500	1,000
Accounts payable	1,500	2,500
Salaries payable	250	300
Estimated income tax payable	400	450
Advances from customers	150	—
Capital stock	15,000	15,000
Retained earnings	2,000	2,000
Dividends		1,000
Sales		40,150
Cost of goods sold		25,000
Salaries expense		12,500
Rent expense ($100 per month)		600
Depreciation expense		500
Interest revenue		100
Gain on sale of land		150
Income tax		450

The cash disbursements during 19_5 totaled $41,150, and were for the following purposes:

To suppliers for merchandise purchased on account	$24,500
Investment in bonds	2,500
Payment of 19_4 income tax liability	400
Dividends	1,000
Salaries	12,450
Rent	300
Total cash disbursements	$41,150

During 19_5, $39,500 was collected from customers.

Required:

(a) Present the December 31, 19_5 account balances in trial balance form.

(b) The journal entries for the 19_5 transactions and adjustments (omitting dates) of Hood Company, which will account for all of the changes in the account balances between the beginning of the year and the end of the year. Entries will be required for the following:

Sales of merchandise on account and cost of goods sold.
Purchases of merchandise (all purchases were made on account).

Payments to suppliers of merchandise.

Collections from customers.

The investment in bonds.

The sale of the land.

Payments to settle the $250 liability for salaries and the $400 liability for income taxes.

Payment of dividends.

The 19_5 expenses.

The interest revenue.

A5-5   *Using the following data, prepare the December 31, 19_8 adjusting entries and balance sheet.*

IOLA COMPANY
Unadjusted Trial Balance
December 31, 19_8

Cash	1,750	
Accounts receivable	4,250	
Inventory	6,000	
Supplies	450	
Investment in bonds (long-term)	7,500	
Furniture and fixtures	10,000	
Accumulated depreciation		2,000
Accounts payable		6,970
Service fees received in advance		700
Capital stock		15,000
Retained earnings (deficit)	1,000	
Sales of merchandise		50,000
Revenue from service fees		9,000
Cost of goods sold	32,500	
Salaries and wages	14,000	
Rent expense	6,000	
Advertising expense	550	
Interest revenue		330
	84,000	84,000

Closing entry—December 31, 19_8

Sales of merchandise	50,000	
Revenue from service fees	9,200	
Interest revenue	375	
Cost of goods sold		32,500
Salaries and wages		14,200
Rent expense		6,000
Advertising expense		550
Supplies used		150
Depreciation expense		500
Income tax		1,425
Retained earnings		4,250

To close the revenue and expense accounts and to transfer
the net income to the retained earnings account.

A5-6   *Four Earth Moving Company was formed June 1 to engage in construction projects for municipalities and public utilities. The company planned to use the following chart of accounts:*

Assets

101—Cash

103—Accounts receivable

106—Prepaid rent

110—Equipment

111—Accumulated depreciation—
　　　Equipment

Liabilities

121—Accounts payable
122—Traveling expense payable
124—Salaries and wages payable

Stockholders' equity

130—Capital stock
131—Retained earnings
138—Dividends

Revenue

140—Service revenue

Expenses

145—Salaries and wages expense
146—Repairs expense
147—Supplies expense
148—Traveling expense
149—Depreciation expense—Equipment
150—Rent expense

The transactions for June are set forth below.

19_6

June   1—$50,000 par-value capital stock was issued to the incorporators for cash.

1—Rent was paid for the use of land and building for the next 12 months, $1,200.

2—Equipment with an expected useful life of five years and costing $76,500 was purchased. The company paid $38,000 in cash and agreed to pay the balance within 30 days.

19—Received a bill from Western Sales Corporation for machinery repairs, $93.

21—Paid $57 for supplies which had been used on a large contract.

23—Received a bill from an officer of the company for traveling expense, $210.

28—Paid salaries and wages, $4,500. (The salaries and wages for June 29 and 30 will amount to $83, however they will be paid during July.)

29—Paid a dividend, $150.

30—Completed a contract for Golfan City. The city was billed in full for $8,651 pursuant to the terms of the agreement.

Required:

(a) Journalize transactions and post to ledger accounts. (Plan for five lines in the ledger for each account except cash; allow ten lines for the cash account.)

(b) Prepare the worksheet. (Take depreciation for one-half month.)

(c) Prepare statements.

(d) Make and post journal entries for any necessary adjustments.

(e) Make and post journal entries to close the books.

(f) Take an after-closing trial balance.

B5-1   *Following is the trial balance of Webb Bulldozer Sales Company at the end of operations for the month of April 19_3:*

WEBB BULLDOZER SALES COMPANY
Trial Balance
April 30, 19_3

Cash	3,000	
Inventory	11,000	
Prepaid insurance	150	
Land	9,500	
Building	30,000	
Accumulated depreciation—Building		9,000
Accounts payable		5,000
Capital stock		30,000
Retained earnings		7,300
Dividends	1,500	
Sales		45,500
Cost of tractors sold	26,500	
Advertising expense	1,050	
Miscellaneous expense	1,100	
Salaries and wages expense	13,000	
	96,800	96,800

Salaries and wages payable amount to $200. The building when new had an expected useful life of forty years. Insurance premium (prepaid) at the end of April is $40. Income tax on 19_3 earnings amounts to $800.

Prepare the worksheet covering the year ended April 30, 19_3, and closing entries.

B5-2

The trial balance below was taken from the books of Guppy Company at the close of business for the year 19_8.

GUPPY COMPANY
Trial Balance
June 30, 19_8

Cash	1,087	
Accounts receivable	2,544	
Inventory	1,300	
Materials and supplies	450	
Prepaid insurance	54	
Land	1,000	
Buildings	10,000	
Accumulated depreciation—Buildings		2,000
Equipment	12,000	
Accumulated depreciation—Equipment		6,400
Accounts payable		890
Notes payable—5%, due 12/31/_10		3,200
Taxes payable		506
Capital stock		12,000
Retained earnings		2,500
Dividends	720	
Sales		27,684
Cost of goods sold	16,480	
Selling commissions	1,380	
Delivery expense	476	
Wages and salaries	6,700	
Property taxes	909	
Interest expense	80	
	55,180	55,180

The following information was also obtained from the records maintained by Guppy Company.

(1) The building was put into operation on July 1, 19_2, and is expected to have a useful life of 25 years from that date.

(2) The equipment is to be depreciated at 10% per year.

(3) A count of the materials and supplies shows $55, the cost of those on hand.

(4) The insurance policy was purchased on June 30, 19_8, and expires on June 30, 19_9.

(5) The notes payable bear interest of 5 per cent per year. Interest was last paid on January 1, 19_8.

(6) Wages payable amount to $20.

(7) Sales commissions payable are $66.

Required: Worksheet and closing entries.

B5-3   The trial balance given below was taken from the ledger of Cimmerean Corporation before adjusting entries were posted at the end of operations for 19_5.

CIMMEREAN CORPORATION
Unadjusted Trial Balance
December 31, 19_5

Cash	3,200	
Resale parts	4,500	
Supplies	650	
Service equipment	8,000	
Accumulated depreciation		1,600
Service fees received in advance		1,400
Capital stock		6,000
Retained earnings, December 31, 19_4		1,325
Dividends	375	
Sales of parts		15,000
Service revenue		40,000
Cost of parts sold	9,000	
Salaries expense	37,000	
Rent expense	1,950	
Miscellaneous expense	650	
	65,325	65,325

The following after-closing trial balance was taken from the same ledger after adjusting and closing entries had been posted:

CIMMEREAN CORPORATION
After-Closing Trial Balance
December 31, 19_5

Cash	3,200	
Resale parts	4,500	
Supplies	500	
Prepaid rent	200	
Service equipment	8,000	
Accumulated depreciation		2,600
Service fees received in advance		550
Estimated income tax payable		1,850
Salaries payable		250
Capital stock		6,000
Retained earnings		5,150
	16,400	16,400

Make the closing entries which were entered in the journal of Cimmerean Corporation at the end of 19_5.

B5-4

The after-closing trial balance of Harbour Corporation appears below:

HARBOUR CORPORATION
After-Closing Trial Balance
December 31, 19_6

Cash	1,320	
Rent receivable—Land	260	
Repair supplies on hand	40	
Land	600	
Equipment	1,600	
Accumulated depreciation—Equipment		800
Salaries payable		200
Taxes payable		17
Capital stock		2,400
Retained earnings		403
	3,820	3,820

The corporation closes its books monthly. Journalize the following transactions and all adjustments required for January, 19_7 financial statements:

19_7

January   3—The corporation rents out some of its land as a parking lot for $130 per month. Today the corporation received $520 from the renter covering the four months ending February 28, 19_7.

10—Paid salaries for the month ending January 10, 19_7, $375.

17—Received $800 cash for repair services completed today.

19—Paid $38 for special supplies used on repair work completed January 17.

21—The corporation rented some of its equipment for the next 60 days ending March 20, receiving the $180 rental charge in advance.

31—Additional data required for adjustments:
Depreciation, 9% per annum of cost of equipment.
Taxes payable as of January 31, 19_7, $30.
Salaries payable as of January 31, 19_7, $205.
Repair supplies on hand, $10.
Repair services performed, not billed, $105.

Using the following data, prepare the December 31, 19_5 balance sheet for Sigma Company.

SIGMA COMPANY
Income Statement
For the Year Ended December 31, 19_5

Revenue:	
Sales	$105,000
Rental revenue	10,000
Interest revenue	2,000
Total revenues	$117,000
Deduct expenses:	
Cost of goods sold	$ 50,000
Salaries expense	20,000
Repair expense	5,000
Depreciation expense	10,000
Interest expense	1,000
Insurance expense	1,000
Income tax	3,000
Total expenses	$ 90,000
Net income	$ 27,000

	Trial balance December 31, 19_5		Adjusted trial balance December 31, 19_5	
Cash	80,000		80,000	
Accounts receivable	30,000		30,000	
Prepaid insurance	3,000		?	
Interest receivable	—		?	
Inventory	4,000		4,000	
Bond investment	20,000		20,000	
Building and equipment	100,000		100,000	
Accumulated depreciation		20,000		?
Land	10,000		10,000	
Accounts payable		20,000		20,000
Salaries and wages payable		6,000		?
Interest payable		—		?
Rent received in advance		2,000		?
Advances from customers		5,000		?
Taxes payable		1,000		?
Notes payable		10,000		10,000
Capital stock		100,000		100,000
Retained earnings		48,000		?
Sales		100,000		?
Rental revenue		10,000		?
Interest revenue		—		?
Cost of goods sold	50,000		?	
Salaries expense	18,000		?	
Repair expense	5,000		?	
Depreciation expense	—		?	
Interest expense	—		?	
Insurance expense	2,000		?	
Income tax	—		?	
	322,000	322,000		

Several mistakes were made in completing the following worksheet. The trial balance and the supporting descriptions of the adjusting entries (a through g at the bottom of the working papers) are correct. Prepare a corrected worksheet for Qualye Company.

	Trial Balance		Adjustments		Adjusted Trial Balance		Income Statement		Retained Earnings Statement		Balance Sheet	
Cash	4,000				4,000						4,000	
Corporate bonds	20,000				20,000						20,000	
Inventory	6,000				6,000						6,000	
Expense advances to employees	400			(c) 300	100		100					
Office supplies	500			(d) 350	150						150	
Equipment	7,500			(a) 1,500	6,000						6,000	
Accounts payable		7,000				7,000						7,000
Advances from customers		350						350				
Bank loans (One year loan due 9/1/19_3)		4,500				4,500						4,500
Capital stock		10,000				10,000						10,000
Retained earnings, December 31, 19_1		3,050				3,050				3,050		
Dividends	2,500				2,500		2,500					
Sales		54,500				54,500		54,500				
Cost of goods sold	25,000				25,000		25,000					
Salaries expense	11,000			(b) 2,000	9,000		9,000					
Traveling expense	1,500		(c) 300		1,800		1,800					
Office expense	1,000		(d) 350		1,350		1,350					
	79,400	79,400										
Depreciation expense—Equipment			(a) 1,500		1,500		1,500					
Salaries payable			(b) 2,000			2,000						2,000
Rent expense			(e) 6,000		6,000		6,000					
Rent payable				(e) 6,000		6,000						6,000
Interest expense			(f) 200		200		200					
Interest payable				(f) 200		200						200
Interest receivable			(g) 600		600		600					600
Interest revenue				(g) 600		600						
			10,950	10,950	86,200	86,200	47,850	55,050				
Net income							7,200			7,200		
							55,050	55,050		10,250		
Retained earnings, December 31, 19_2.									10,250			10,250
									10,250	10,250	38,350	38,350

Adjustments

(a) Depreciation for the year—20% rate.
(b) Salaries payable at year-end, $2,000.
(c) Expense advances used as of December 31, 19_2, $300.
(d) Unused office supplies as of December 31, 19_2, $150.

(e) Rent owed as of December 31, 19_2, $6,000.
(f) Interest on bank loans applicable to 19_2, $200.
(g) Interest earned on the corporate bonds, $600.

CASH AND MARKETABLE SECURITIES
CHAPTER 6

PURPOSE OF CHAPTER   This is the first of several chapters devoted to discussion of the assets and equities reported in the balance sheet of a business firm. Traditionally, the most liquid of all assets, cash, is the first asset reported. This chapter discusses the accounting for cash and those investments in marketable securities considered to represent a reserve source of cash. The concept of the time value of money as it pertains to cash flows is introduced in an appendix to the chapter.

Cash

WHAT IS CASH?   The term *cash* is used in accounting to mean coin, currency, bank balances, and other media of exchange such as checks, bank drafts, cashier's checks, and postal money orders. Certain items, such as I.O.U.'s and postage stamps, which are sometimes found with the contents of a cash fund, are not cash. An I.O.U. is a receivable; postage stamps represent a prepayment or a part of office supplies inventory. Generally, any item that a bank will accept as an immediate increase in the bank balance of the depositor can be referred to as cash.

REPORTING CASH BALANCES   Although a firm may have several cash accounts in its ledger, it is considered acceptable to combine the accounts for balance-sheet purposes, describing the combined amount as "Cash on Hand and in Banks," or merely "Cash." This will generally be reported as a current asset because the amount is available for meeting current liabilities.

There may be instances in which cash amounts should not be reported as a current asset. If some of the cash has been set aside for a special purpose or is otherwise restricted and not readily available for disbursement, it should be reported elsewhere in the balance sheet. Examples would be cash amounts designated specifically for the payment of a noncurrent liability and cash in an insolvent bank which has been closed.

CONTROL OF CASH   The very nature of most items of cash is such that careful control must be maintained in order to insure that all cash receipts and disbursements are accounted for. Internal control procedures are used throughout a firm in order to control its operations.

INTERNAL CONTROL   The objectives of a good system of internal control, as it relates to assets, may be summarized as follows:

(1) To safeguard the assets.
(2) To promote reliability in accounting and operating data.

Those two objectives stand a better chance of being achieved if, whenever it is feasible, the custody of assets is entirely separated from the function of recording transactions affecting assets, and if the recording work is divided in such a way that the work of one person is verified by another. An irregularity would then require collusion.

In broad outline, a basic system of internal control with regard to cash must include the following:

(1) Establishment of a definite routine for accounting for cash transactions, with a division of labor that would automatically disclose errors and would require collusion to conceal a misappropriation of cash.
(2) Separation of the handling of cash from the recording function. Persons who handle cash receipts or make disbursements should have no access to the records, and those who record cash transactions should have no access to the cash.
(3) Separation of the activities associated with the disbursing of cash from those associated with the receiving of cash.
(4) Requirement that all cash received be deposited daily in the bank.
(5) Requirement that all disbursements be made by check.

The methods and procedures used to achieve internal control vary greatly in different organizations. The system described below is merely indicative of some of the methods and procedures in use.

CASH RECEIPTS Some cash may be received *over the counter* as the proceeds of cash sales or as collections on account; cash may also come through the mail. Prenumbered invoices may be made out for all cash sales, and in that case it should be the duty of some person to see that the duplicates of cash sales invoices or tickets agree with the record of cash received, and that no invoices are missing and unaccounted for. Prenumbered receipts should be issued for all over-the-counter collections on account; if possible, those receipts should be issued by some person other than the one who receives the cash; and a third employee should compare the duplicates of the receipts with the cash record. All cash received over the counter should be recorded on a cash register, if possible. When this is done, all cash received over the counter should be counted and the total compared with the cash register tape by some person other than the one who collected the cash.

As noted above, the danger of misappropriations of cash is reduced if the system of internal control makes collusion necessary to conceal a theft of cash receipts. As to cash received *through the mail,* a system of internal control can be provided in which the perpetration and concealment of fraud would require the collusion of three people, whose records should be required to agree, as follows:

(1) All remittances received through the mail should go to an employee other than the cashier or bookkeeper for listing on an adding machine; this employee should also obtain the cash register

readings so that his or her tape will include the total receipts for the day. After listing the mail receipts, the employee turns the cash over to the cashier and sends to the bookkeeper any letters or documents relating to the remittances.

(2) The cashier prepares the deposit tickets and deposits the funds. Since all funds received should be deposited daily, the total of the deposit tickets for the day should equal the total of the adding machine tape prepared by the first employee. Some banks issue receipts for deposits; if the bank where a deposit is made does not do so, the cashier should prepare each deposit ticket in duplicate and request the receiving teller at the bank to receipt the duplicate; the cashier should present the bank's receipt or the duplicate deposit slip to the first employee for comparison with his tape.

(3) The bookkeeper records the cash receipts from information shown by the documents accompanying the remittances, cash register tapes, and other papers; the total recorded receipts for the day, as shown by the cash receipts journal, should equal the first employee's tape and the cashier's deposit.

With such a system of internal control, fraud cannot be practiced with the cash receipts and remain undetected without the collusion of three persons. The first employee has no access to the books and cannot falsify the records to conceal a misappropriation; he or she cannot expect to withhold funds received from debtors without detection, because the debtors will receive statements or letters from the credit department and will report their remittances.

If the cashier withholds any cash, the daily deposits will not agree with the first employee's list or with the bookkeeper's record of cash receipts made from the remittance letters and other sources of information. The bookkeeper, having no access to the cash, has no opportunity to misappropriate any of it, and therefore has no incentive to falsify the records unless he or she is participating in a three-party collusion.

CASH DISBURSEMENTS Since all receipts are deposited daily in the bank, all disbursements must be made by check. The person authorized to sign checks should have no authority to make entries in any journal; thus a fraudulent disbursement by check could not be concealed without the collusion of two persons. The collusion of a third person can be made necessary by requiring that all checks shall be signed by one person and countersigned by another.

All checks should be prenumbered. All spoiled, mutilated, or voided checks should be preserved. Some companies even go so far as to require that such checks be recorded in their proper sequence in the cash disbursements record, without entry in the money column, but with a notation that the check is void.

CASH OVER AND SHORT ACCOUNT As a part of the system of internal control, frequent and unannounced cash counts should be made by the internal auditing department. Any unlocated differences between the balance per books and the cash on hand and in bank, whether discovered by the accounting staff or by the internal auditing staff, may be set up in a cash over and short account. If all reasonable efforts fail to disclose the cause of the shortage or overage, the account may be closed at the end of the period along with other revenue and expense accounts.

Cash Over and Short should not be charged with an ascertained defalcation; the loss should be charged to a special account, which should be written off only in the event of failure to collect from the party responsible therefor or from a bonding company.

The cash over and short account is also used to record shortages and overages that result simply from the honest mistakes that inevitably occur when a large number of cash transactions are involved. For example, a retail grocery store uses a cash register that accumulates the total amount of cash that should have been collected from customers during the day. If this amount is $1,500, but the actual cash count at the end of the day shows only $1,495, this is recorded as follows:

Cash	1,495	
Cash over and short	5	
Sales		1,500

If the cash count at the end of the day shows $1,510, the entry would be:

Cash	1,510	
Cash over and short		10
Sales		1,500

At the end of the accounting period a cumulative *debit* balance in the cash over and short account is reported as a miscellaneous *expense*. If the cumulative balance is a *credit*, it is reported as a miscellaneous *revenue*.

PETTY CASH In the discussion of the system of internal control for cash disbursements, the statement was made that all disbursements should be made by check. How is this possible when certain disbursements of small amounts, for carfares and postage, for instance, frequently must be made in cash? Although individual petty disbursements may not actually be made by check, their total can be covered by a check by operating a petty cash fund. The petty cash fund, sometimes called an *imprest fund,* is operated as follows:

(1) Establishment of fund:

A check is drawn for a round amount ($10, $50, or such an amount as will provide for petty disbursements for a reasonable time) and cashed. The cash is held in the office for use in making petty disbursements. The establishment of a fund of $25 is recorded as follows:

Petty cash	25	
Cash		25

(2) Disbursements from fund:

When expenditures are made, receipts or other memoranda are saved to show what the money was spent for. This is essential in order to record properly disbursements from the fund in the accounting records. However, it should be noted that no journal entry is actually recorded at the time a disbursement from the fund takes place, but instead is recorded when the fund is replenished.

(3) Replenishment of fund:

Whenever the petty cash expenditures have nearly exhausted the fund, it is necessary to replenish it. Assume that expenditures from the fund total $24.73 and that cash of $1.20 is on hand at the time the fund is to be replenished. A check for $23.80 ($25.00 — $1.20) will be drawn and the following entry records the facts:

Transportation in	6.20	
Transportation out	7.35	
Advertising expense	8.00	
Office supplies	1.18	
Delivery expense	2.00	
Cash over and short		.93
Cash		23.80

It will be noted that, in the illustration, the only entry in the petty cash account is the one establishing the fund; other entries will be made in this account only if the established amount of the fund is increased or decreased because of a change in the amount of the fund needed. For example, if the fund is to be increased to a total of $50, an additional check for $25 would be drawn and the entry to record the increase would be as follows:

Petty cash	25	
Cash		25

The petty cash account is not debited for replenishments of the fund or credited for petty cash disbursements. The person in charge of the petty cash fund should always have cash or evidence of disbursements equal to the balance of the petty cash account.

As a general rule, all receipts or other memoranda supporting the petty cash disbursements must be presented by the petty cashier to a designated accounting officer for his review and approval. Such supporting memoranda should equal the replenishment check, and, after being marked "cancelled," to prevent their re-use, they are filed as support for the replenishment check. Such memoranda should be prenumbered to insure that they are all accounted for.

The petty cash fund should always be replenished at the end of a period before the financial statements are prepared and the books are closed, so that the effect of expenditures from the petty cash fund will be reflected in the accounts of the period in which the expenditures are made.

OPENING A BANK ACCOUNT   When an account is opened at the bank, the persons authorized to draw checks against the account will be requested to sign cards furnished by the bank, to show the signatures to be used on checks.

These signature cards will be filed by the bank, so that a teller who may be unfamiliar with a depositor's signature can test the authenticity of a check by comparing the depositor's signature on the card with the signature on the check.

If the depositor is a corporation, the bank will request that the directors pass a resolution authorizing certain officers or employees of the corporation to sign checks, and that a copy of this resolution be filed with the bank.

DEPOSITS   Deposits should be accompanied by deposit tickets which describe the items deposited. Deposit tickets are of various forms; an illustration appears on page 177.

MAINTAINING A RECORD OF THE BANK BALANCE Cash receipts and deposits are recorded in the *cash receipts journal,* and disbursements are recorded in the *cash disbursements journal.* At the end of the month, totals are posted from the two journals to the cash account[1] in the ledger, and the resulting balance in this account should show the balance in the bank.

But, during the month, how can one ascertain the balance in the bank? The record may be kept:

(1) On the stubs of the check book, or
(2) In a bank register.

A running record on the check book stub is shown below.

If many checks are drawn, the computation of the bank balance after each deposit and each check is usually regarded as unnecessary. In some cases, unbound checks are used so that carbon copies can be prepared and handed to the book-keeper for his information in recording disbursements. For either of these reasons, it may be expedient to eliminate the running record on the check book stubs and to keep a bank register which will not show the balance after *each* deposit and *each* check, but will show the balance at the end of each day.

Deposit ticket

```
            DEPOSITED WITH
        ILLINOIS NATIONAL BANK
            FOR ACCOUNT OF
_____
_____

CHICAGO, ILLINOIS._____ , 19____
IN RECEIVING ITEMS FOR DEPOSIT OR COLLECTION, THIS BANK ACTS ONLY AS
DEPOSITOR'S COLLECTING AGENT AND ASSUMES NO RESPONSIBILITY BEYOND THE
EXERCISE OF DUE CARE. ALL ITEMS ARE CREDITED SUBJECT TO FINAL PAYMENT.
     PLEASE LIST EACH CHECK SEPARATELY

CURRENCY _____
SILVER _____
    CHECKS AS FOLLOWS:
_____
_____
_____
_____
_____
_____
_____
_____
_____
_____
_____
_____
_____
            TOTAL, $
SEE THAT ALL CHECKS AND DRAFTS ARE ENDORSED
```

Check book stub

```
BALANCE BROUGHT FOWARD   8,503.75

DEPOSIT _____   _____

TOTAL           _____

CHECK NO.    93

DATE  July 17, 19—

PAYEE  J. H. Guthrie    650.00

BALANCE              7,853.75


DEPOSIT  7/17/—    2,300.00

TOTAL            10,153.75

CHECK NO.    94

DATE  July 17, 19—

PAYEE  F. L. Kenyon     400.00

BALANCE CARRIED FOWARD  9,753.75
```

[1]The account title may be the name of a bank, but the account still is a cash account.

The following is an illustration of a bank register:

BANK REGISTER

	First National Bank			First State Bank		
Date	Deposits	Withdrawals	Balance	Deposits	Withdrawals	Balance
19__						
June 30			5,000 00			4,850 00
July 1	3,000 00	2,480 00	5,520 00	2,500 00	3,638 00	3,712 00
2	4,500 00	3,500 00	6,520 00	4,000 00	3,200 00	4,512 00

This record is kept in the following way:

Each day enter, in the Deposits columns of the bank register, the totals of the day's receipts (deposits) recorded in the Cash debit columns of the cash receipts journal.

Similarly, enter, in the Withdrawals columns of the bank register, the daily totals of the disbursements recorded in the Cash credit columns of the cash disbursements journal.

Compute the resulting daily bank balances and enter them in the Balance columns of the bank register.

THE BANK STATEMENT Once a month the bank will render a statement to the depositor and return the checks which it has paid and charged to his account. The statement shows the balance at the beginning of the month, the deposits, the checks paid, other debits and credits during the month, and the balance at the end of the month. A simple illustration of such a statement is shown on page 179.

The symbols on the statement require some explanation:

N.S.F.—(Not sufficient funds)—On June 27 R. M. Walker Company received a check for $63.95 from Wm. Barnes; this check was included in the deposit of June 27. It was returned to The White National Bank because Barnes did not have a sufficient balance in his bank account to cover the check. The White National Bank therefore charged it back to R. M. Walker Company.

When a returned check marked "N.S.F." is received from the bank, an entry should be made crediting Cash and debiting the party from whom the check was received. Such a check should not be regarded as cash, even if it is redeposited, until it has been honored by the drawer's bank, unless the payee's bank gives credit for it at the time it is redeposited.

Col.—On June 27 the bank credited R. M. Walker Company with the proceeds of a note collected by the bank for the company's account, and charged a collection fee of $5.00.

P.S.—(Payment stopped)—If R. M. Walker Company received and deposited with The White National Bank a check from a customer who, for some reasons, stopped payment on the check, the customer's bank would refuse to pay it and would return it to The White National Bank, which would charge it back to the account of R. M. Walker Company.

S.C.—(Service charge)—Banks cannot profitably handle small accounts without making a service charge. The charge may be a fixed amount applicable to all accounts with balances averaging less than a certain minimum amount. Many banks base the service charge on a number of factors, such as the average balance of the account during the month, the number of deposits made, and the number of checks drawn.

When the bank renders the statement, it returns all paid checks to the depositor. Accompanying the statement and the canceled checks there will be *debit memoranda*

Bank statement

STATEMENT OF ACCOUNT WITH

THE WHITE NATIONAL BANK
CHICAGO, ILLINOIS

R. M. Walker Company
135 West State Street
Chicago, Illinois

CHECKS			DEPOSITS	DATE	BALANCES
				May 31, 19 ___	3,500.17
100.00✓			310.00✓	June 1, 19 ___	3,710.17
96.10				June 4, 19 ___	3,614.07
			175.00✓	June 5, 19 ___	3,789.07
75.00	150.50			June 6, 19 ___	3,563.57
			425.50✓	June 8, 19 ___	3,989.07
39.75				June 10, 19 ___	3,949.32
136.50				June 11, 19 ___	3,812.82
			136.75✓	June 12, 19 ___	3,949.57
84.20✓				June 13, 19 ___	3,865.37
164.19			216.80✓	June 15, 19 ___	3,917.98
7.25				June 18, 19 ___	3,910.73
			310.80✓	June 19, 19 ___	4,221.53
39.50				June 20, 19 ___	4,182.03
600.35				June 22, 19 ___	3,581.68
			165.00✓	June 24, 19 ___	3,746.68
13.75	19.50	123.80		June 26, 19 ___	3,589.63
5.00 Col			138.20✓	June 27, 19 ___	3,722.83
76.35				June 29, 19 ___	3,646.48
12.60	63.95 N.S.F.				
109.11				June 30, 19 ___	3,460.82

CC—Certified Check
EC—Error Corrected
DM—Debit Memo

Col—Collection charge
P.S.—Payment stopped
N.S.F.—Not Sufficient Funds
SC—Service Charge

👆 THE LAST AMOUNT
IN THIS COLUMN
IS YOUR BALANCE

PLEASE EXAMINE. IF NO ERRORS ARE REPORTED WITHIN TEN DAYS, THE
ACCOUNT WILL BE CONSIDERED CORRECT.

for all charges to the depositor not represented by checks, such as bank service charges and N.S.F. checks returned by the bank.

RECONCILING THE BANK ACCOUNT The balance shown by the bank statement rarely agrees with the balance shown by the depositor's books. Items may appear on the depositor's books which have not yet been recorded on the bank's books, such as:

Outstanding checks—not presented to and paid by the bank.

Deposits not yet received by the bank—perhaps in transit in the mails.

Negotiable instruments left with the bank and charged to the bank as a deposit, but taken by the bank for collection only and not credited to the depositor until collected.

Similarly, items may appear on the bank's books which have not yet been recorded on the depositor's books, such as:

Service charges.
Charges for collection.
Charges for checks returned N.S.F. Although the bank notifies the depositor immediately of such returned checks, and also of checks returned because payment has been stopped, entries may not be made immediately on the depositor's books.

If a company keeps funds on deposit in several banks, contra errors are sometimes made in the bank accounts on the depositor's books. For instance, checks drawn against one bank account may be recorded as disbursements from another bank, and deposits in one bank may be charged to another bank. Banks may occasionally make errors by charging or crediting one customer with another customer's checks or deposits, particularly if the customers' names are similar. For all these reasons, the bank statement should be reconciled as soon as possible after it has been received.

The reconciliation process is an important element in the internal control system for cash. Not only does it indicate the reasons for differences between the balance reported in the ledger account and the balance in the bank statement, but it may also reveal improper uses of cash. For this reason, the reconciliation should be done by someone other than the person who actually processes cash receipts and disbursements.

A bank reconciliation as of any given date shows the following:

The balance of the bank account according to the depositor's books.
Reconciling items—any charges or credits to the depositor recorded by the bank but not recorded by the depositor.
The correct (adjusted) balance.
The balance of the depositor's account according to the bank's books.
Reconciling items—any charges or credits to the bank recorded by the depositor but not recorded by the bank.
The correct (adjusted) balance.

If the two adjusted balances agree, the bank account is said to be *reconciled.*

Illustration In order to reconcile a bank account, it is necessary to locate all of the reconciling items. This is done by comparing the bank statement with the depositor's books in order to discover those items that have not been recorded by both the bank and the depositor.

In this illustration, we shall reconcile the June bank statement of R. M. Walker Company (page 179) with the data recorded in its books.

The cash account in the ledger appears on page 181.

The posting references have been omitted from the cash account; they would refer to the source record from which the monthly totals of receipts and disbursements were obtained.

The detailed records maintained by R. M. Walker Company show the following cash transactions for June.

JUNE CASH RECEIPTS

	Date	Explanation	Cash Receipts	Deposits
19__				
June	5	Cash sale	175.00	175.00 ✓
	8	Invoice, June 1, less 1%	297.00	
	8	Invoice, May 5	128.50	425.50 ✓
	12	Cash sale	136.75	136.75 ✓
	15	Invoice, June 8, less 1%	148.50	
	15	Cash sale	68.30	216.80 ✓
	19	E. F. Watson note	250.00	
	19	Cash sale	60.80	310.80 ✓
	24	Cash sale	165.00	165.00 ✓
	27	John Smith note	74.25	
	27	Invoice, June 1	63.95	138.20 ✓
	30	Cash sale	60.50	60.50
			1,628.55	1,628.55

JUNE CASH DISBURSEMENTS

	Date	Explanation	Check No.	Amount
19__				
June	1	Cash purchase	131	75.00 ✓
	2	Invoice, May 28	132	150.50 ✓
	3	Store rent for June	133	96.10 ✓
	6	Invoice, June 4	134	136.50 ✓
	9	Scales	135	39.75 ✓
	13	Invoice, June 5	136	164.19 ✓
	16	Invoice, June 6	137	39.50 ✓
	17	Supplies	138	7.25 ✓
	20	Invoice, June 12	139	600.35 ✓
	24	Cash purchase	140	19.50 ✓
	24	Freight on purchases	141	13.75 ✓
	26	Invoice, June 20	142	123.80 ✓
	28	Cash purchase	143	76.35 ✓
	29	Cash purchase	144	12.60 ✓
	29	Invoice, June 17	145	109.11 ✓
	30	C. E. Whitely's salary	146	300.00
				1,964.25

CASH (The White National Bank)   Account No. 101

19__					
May	31	Balance			3,625.97 Dr.
June	30		1,628.55		5,254.52 Dr.
	30			1,964.25	3,290.27 Dr.

Steps in the reconciliation process   The procedure of reconciling the bank account involves the following steps:

(1)   Arrange in numerical order the paid checks returned from the bank.
(2)   Refer to the reconciliation at the close of the preceding month; note the items which were outstanding at that date. The May 31 reconciliation follows.

R. M. WALKER COMPANY
Bank Reconciliation
May 31, 19__

. . . .

Balance, per books		$3,625.97
Balance, per bank statement		$3,500.17
Add deposit not credited by bank		310.00 √
Total		$3,810.17
Deduct outstanding checks:		
129	$100.00 √	
130	84.20 √	184.20
Correct balance		$3,625.97

This reconciliation shows that $310 recorded by the company as a deposit in May had not been credited by the bank at the end of the month, and that checks for $100 and $84.20 were outstanding. Reference to the bank statement on page 179 shows that the deposit was credited by the bank on June 1, and that the checks were paid on June 1 and June 13. These items are now checked (√) on the May 31 reconciliation and on the June 30 bank statement.

(3) See whether the deposits shown by the company's records are in agreement with the entries in the Deposits column of the bank statement. Place check marks in the Deposits column of the company's record of cash receipts and in the Deposits column of the bank statement beside the items which are in agreement.

The unchecked deposits in the company's record represent deposits not recorded by the bank. By reference to the cash receipts record it will be noted that only one of the deposits is unchecked: the June 30 deposit of $60.50. This unchecked item is presumably a deposit in transit; observe that it is added to the balance per bank statement in the bank reconciliation on page 183.

Any unchecked items in the Deposits column of the bank statement would represent credits by the bank not taken up by the depositor. It will be noted that there are no such unchecked items in the Deposits column of the bank statement.

(4) Compare the returned checks (which have been sorted in numerical order) with the entries in the cash disbursements record. Place a check mark in the company's cash disbursements record beside the entry for each check that has been returned by the bank.

Unchecked items are outstanding checks. By reference to page 181 it will be noted that only one item is unchecked: the $300 check drawn on June 30. The bank reconciliation on page 183 shows it as an adjustment of the balance per bank statement.

(5) Examine the bank statement for any items not recorded in the company's books; such items must be included in the bank reconciliation.

Charges by the bank shown by the bank statement that do not appear in the company's cash records are for:

Collection	$ 5.00
N.S.F. check returned	63.95

They are shown in the reconciliation as deductions from the balance per books.

(6) Prepare the reconciliation statement.

R. M. WALKER COMPANY
Bank Reconciliation
June 30, 19__
....

Balance, per books		$3,290.27
Deduct bank's charges not on the books:		
Collection	$ 5.00	
N.S.F. check—Wm. Barnes	63.95	68.95
Correct balance		$3,221.32
Balance, per bank statement		$3,460.82
Add deposit in transit		60.50
Total		$3,521.32
Deduct outstanding checks:		
No. 146		300.00
Correct balance		$3,221.32

CERTIFIED CHECKS An ordinary check is deducted from the drawer's account when the check is presented to the drawer's bank for payment. In contrast, a certified check is deducted from the drawer's account when it is certified by the drawer's bank. The bank, in effect, guarantees that the check will be paid by the bank when presented for payment. Therefore, outstanding certified checks need not be included in the list of outstanding checks in the bank reconciliation.

ADJUSTMENTS AFTER RECONCILIATION If the bank has made charges or credits to the company's account that have not been recorded on the company's books, and if the company recognizes these charges or credits as correct, adjustments should be made to record them on the company's books. This is necessary so that the ledger account for cash will actually report the correct balance on the financial statements.

The following entry records the adjustment to the cash account required by the preceding reconciliation.

Collection expense	$ 5.00	
Accounts receivable (Wm. Barnes)	63.95	
Cash		68.95

PAYROLL BANK ACCOUNT If a company pays a large number of employees by check, it is desirable for it to open a special payroll bank account. At each pay date, a check on the regular bank account is drawn and deposited in the payroll bank account. Individual checks for the employees are then drawn on this special account, which is thus immediately exhausted. If the payroll account and the general account are kept in the same bank, different-colored checks should be used for the two accounts.

This procedure has several advantages. In the first place, the officer authorized to sign checks on the general bank account can be relieved of the work of signing numerous payroll checks; these can be signed by some other employee. In the second place, the general bank account can be reconciled without cluttering the reconciliation statement with all the outstanding payroll checks. And, in the third place, the labor of recording the payroll disbursements is reduced; instead of recording all payroll checks in the cash disbursements journal, check numbers may be entered in a payroll record. Payroll accounting is discussed in detail in an appendix to Chapter 7.

DIVIDEND BANK ACCOUNT   If a company has a large number of stockholders, a special bank account may be used for the payment of dividends. A check for the total amount of the dividend is drawn and deposited in this special bank account. Checks payable to the individual stockholders are drawn on this account.

BANK OVERDRAFTS   A bank overdraft exists when checks written on the account exceed the account balance. An overdraft in a bank account should be shown in the balance sheet as a *liability.* This should be done even if there are balances in other banks that exceed the overdraft; the total of the available balances should be shown on the asset side of the balance sheet and the overdraft should be shown on the liability side.

Marketable securities

CLASSIFICATION OF INVESTMENTS   Business firms frequently purchase corporate stocks and bonds and government securities as investments. Traditionally, these securities were classified as either current assets *(marketable securities)* or noncurrent assets *(long-term investments)* on the balance sheet of the investor. The distinction between these two alternatives depended generally on whether or not the investment could be, within the limits of good management, disposed of to obtain funds for current needs.

INVESTMENTS CLASSIFIED AS CURRENT ASSETS   It has long been recognized as proper to classify investments as current assets if management intends to convert them into cash during the normal operating cycle or one year, whichever is longer (short-term holding period), and if there is a ready market for them either on a securities exchange or elsewhere (highly marketable). Accountants are now leaning toward the opinion that, even though management has no established intention to dispose of the securities in the near future, the securities can be classified as current if they are readily marketable and if they are not being held for purposes of control, for establishing or maintaining good customer or supplier relationships, or for any other reason that would make their disposal inexpedient. Thus such investments are not necessarily temporary investments, but are marketable securities that can be converted into cash without interfering with normal business operations. Such securities consist primarily of marketable equity securities of corporations and marketable debt securities of corporations or governmental units. This distinction between equity and debt securities is based on a Financial Accounting Standards Board statement dealing with the accounting for *marketable equity securities.*[2] The accounting for all investments classified as current assets is discussed in this chapter.

[2]Financial Accounting Standards Board, "Accounting for Certain Marketable Securities," *Statement No. 12* (Stamford, Conn.: FASB, December, 1975).

INVESTMENTS CLASSIFIED AS NONCURRENT ASSETS Investments are sometimes acquired in accordance with a financial policy looking to the accumulation of funds for such purposes as plant expansion or the liquidation of long-term indebtedness. They may represent stock holdings acquired for the purpose of controlling another firm or creating good customer or supplier relationships. Such securities could include noncurrent marketable equity securities or noncurrent debt securities. Discussion of the accounting for investments of this type is deferred until Chapters 10 and 13.

COST OF MARKETABLE SECURITIES The original cost of any current or noncurrent investment in a security includes the purchase price, brokerage fees, taxes, and all other expenditures incident to acquisition.

Assume the purchase of 1,000 shares of Super Company common stock at $25 per share, plus purchase costs totaling $100. The acquisition is recorded as follows:

Marketable equity securities—Super Company common stock	25,100	
Cash		25,100

If the purchaser of stock pays to the seller an amount for dividends already declared, but not yet paid, such amount is not a part of the cost of the stock. Instead, it represents dividends to be received and should be debited to Dividends Receivable.

Investments in interest-bearing securities may take place between interest payment dates, thus requiring that the interest accrued since the last interest payment date be paid to the seller. For example, the acquisition of a $1,000 bond of Super Company at a price of 100 (bond prices are normally quoted as a percentage of face amount) on the date the bond is issued would be recorded as follows:

Marketable debt securities—Super Company bonds	1,000	
Cash		1,000

However, assume that the bond is purchased at a price of 100 at a time when the interest accrued since the last interest payment date is $25. The purchase is recorded by the following entry:

Marketable debt securities—Super Company bonds	1,000	
Interest receivable	25	
Cash		1,025

The $25 interest is not a part of the cost of the bond. It was paid to the seller of the bonds, who may be the issuing corporation, but it will be received by the investor as a part of the interest check at the next interest payment date.

REVENUE FROM MARKETABLE SECURITIES Investments in stocks earn revenue in the form of *cash dividends,* while bonds earn *interest.* Interest accrues and thus is earned with the passage of time, which is not true for dividends. Instead, the investor has a claim for dividends only after they are declared by the issuing corporation. Theoretically, dividends are earned in the period in which they are declared, but as a practical matter they are normally recorded as revenue when received. Assuming that a cash dividend of $1 per share is received on the 1,000 shares of Super Company common stock referred to previously, the receipt of the check is recorded by the following entry:

Cash	1,000	
Dividend revenue		1,000

Note that the above refers to cash dividends. Stock dividends, which are discussed in Chapter 12, are not regarded as revenue.

Interest earned on investments should be recorded in the period *earned,* not when the cash is received. The receipt of $100 interest from a bond investment is recorded as follows, assuming that the entire amount was earned in the current period.

Cash	100	
Interest revenue		100

If the bonds were acquired between interest payment dates, as was the case in the illustration on page 185, only that portion of interest earned since the bonds were acquired is recorded as revenue. For example, assuming that interest of $25 had been paid to the seller, the receipt of the $100 is recorded as shown below:

Cash	100	
Interest receivable		25
Interest revenue ($100 − $25)		75

At the end of the investor's accounting period any interest earned on interest-bearing investments, but not yet received, should be recorded by an adjusting entry.

VALUATION OF MARKETABLE SECURITIES The two most widely used valuation methods for marketable securities are *lower of cost or market* and *cost.* Valuation at "market" is sometimes used.

VALUATION AT LOWER OF COST OR MARKET The lower-of-cost-or-market method is required for the valuation of marketable *equity* securities. The procedure is applied by comparing the aggregate cost of the securities with the aggregate market price of the securities at each balance-sheet date. For example, assume that the following marketable equity securities are held at the balance sheet date.

Security	Cost	Market
Company A stock	$10,000	$11,000
Company B stock	8,000	7,500
Company C stock	12,300	9,400
Totals	$30,300	$27,900

The carrying amount of the securities is written down to the lower market amount by recognizing a loss and establishing a separate *valuation allowance* account. The entry is shown below.

Market loss on securities ($30,300 − $27,900)	2,400	
Allowance to reduce marketable equity securities to market		2,400

This procedure has the effect of reporting the *unrealized* market loss on the firm's income statement. Thus such losses have the same impact on net income for the period as if the securities had been sold at the end-of-period market price.

The entries required to account for the securities in subsequent periods will depend on the relationship between *aggregate* cost and market amounts. For example, assume that the same stocks are held at the end of the following year and the comparison of cost and market reveals the following:

Security	Cost	Market
Company A stock	$10,000	$12,000
Company B stock	8,000	9,900
Company C stock	12,300	9,800
Totals	$30,300	$31,700

In order to report the securities at the lower of cost or market, the balance in the allowance account must be removed. This is done by debiting the account for $2,400 and crediting an income statement account titled Market Gain on Securities. Although the aggregate market price of the securities is in excess of cost, the cost of $30,300 is the *maximum* amount at which the securities can properly be reported in the balance sheet under the lower-of-cost-or-market method. Current accounting practice does *not* sanction the recognition of gains that represent increases in the price of the securities in excess of previously recognized losses. This may be summarized as follows:

First year—$2,400 market loss recognized in full.
Second year—$3,800 total market gain ($31,700 − $27,900).
  $2,400 recognized gain (equal to the loss recognized in the first year).
  $1,400 unrecognized gain. Not recorded in the accounting records.

The lower-of-cost-or-market method is also widely used to account for marketable debt securities. It is usually applied to the aggregate cost and market amounts, just as in the preceding illustration.

Assume that marketable debt securities consist of the following:

Security	Cost	Market
Company D bonds	$50,000	$55,000
Company E bonds	32,000	25,000
Totals	$82,000	$80,000

The market decline is recorded by the following entry.

Market loss on securities ($82,000 − $80,000)   2,000
    Allowance to reduce marketable debt securities to market   2,000

From this point forward there is one important difference between the accounting for debt securities and the previously illustrated procedures for equity securities. Marketable *debt* securities which have been written down to a market amount below cost are *not* written up if the market price should subsequently increase. For example, assume that the debt securities illustrated on page 187 are still on hand at the next balance-sheet date and have a market price of $85,000 at that time. No part of the market recovery of $5,000 ($85,000 − $80,000) is recorded in the accounting records. In effect, the written down valuation amount of $80,000 at the end of the first year becomes an *adjusted cost* amount that is compared with the market price of $85,000 at the end of the second year, with the lower of the two amounts used for financial statement purposes.

VALUATION AT COST   Traditionally, both marketable equity securities and marketable debt securities were frequently reported at cost, even when the market price at the end of the period was below their cost. This treatment was considered acceptable so long as the decline was either immaterial or considered temporary in nature. Even when the market decline is material and not considered to be temporary, the securities are sometimes reported at cost. However, since there is an implied representation that the securities are held as a reserve source of cash, such declines should be disclosed in the firm's financial statements. This can be done by reporting the current market price parenthetically in the balance sheet or in a footnote to the financial statements. For example, marketable debt securities costing $52,500, but having a market price of only $50,000 at the balance-sheet date, would be reported as follows under the cost method.

Current assets:
   Marketable debt securities—at cost (market price, $50,000) $52,500

It should be noted that this procedure reports the decline in the balance sheet, but it does not actually recognize the amount in the accounts. Thus the decline does not have any effect on the firm's income statement for the period.

The procedure just illustrated is not appropriate for marketable *equity* securities, which must be accounted for using the lower-of-cost-or-market method.

VALUATION AT MARKET   It should be noted from the earlier discussion of lower of cost or market that there is a basic inconsistency in the method. Securities may be reported at amounts below cost, but it is not considered acceptable to write the carrying amount up to an amount in excess of the original cost.

This inconsistency is not present if marketable securities are reported on the balance sheet at the current market price at the balance-sheet date, even if this is above the cost of the securities. Although this method is not currently generally accepted accounting practice, a good case can be made for such valuation. It can be determined objectively from quoted market prices, it can be realized without interfering with normal business operations, and it results in the reporting of holding gains and losses on marketable securities in the period in which they occur.

One problem encountered in the use of market valuation for reporting marketable securities is the treatment of any gains recorded at the time the securities are written up to an amount above cost. Traditionally, such *unrealized gains* are not considered appropriate for inclusion in the determination of a firm's periodic income. However, such holding gains could be reported separately from the operating income of the firm.

SALE OF MARKETABLE SECURITIES The gain or loss on the sale of marketable securities is determined by the difference between their cost and the proceeds of the sale. For example, if a security costing $5,000 is sold for $5,600, the sale is recorded as follows:

Cash	5,600	
Marketable equity securities		5,000
Gain on sale of marketable securities		600

If bonds are sold between interest-payment dates, it is necessary first to record the interest accrued since the last interest-payment date before recording the sale, as shown below, assuming accrued interest of $200 on bonds costing $10,000.

Interest receivable	200	
Interest revenue		200

Then the sale of the bonds for $10,500 would be recorded as follows:

Cash	10,500	
Marketable debt securities		10,000
Interest receivable		200
Gain on sale of marketable securities		300

IMPORTANT TERMS AND CONCEPTS IN CHAPTER 6

Cash—p. 172
Internal control—pp. 172–173
Cash over and short—pp. 174–175
Petty cash—pp. 175–176
Bank register—p. 177
Bank statement—pp. 178–179
Bank reconciliation—pp. 179–183
Bank overdraft—p. 184
Marketable securities—p. 184
Cost of marketable securities—p. 185
Valuation of marketable securities—p. 186

Valuation at lower of cost or market—pp. 186–188
Market loss on securities—p. 187
Allowance to reduce marketable equity securities to market—p. 187
Market gain on securities—p. 187
Allowance to reduce marketable debt securities to market—p. 188
Valuation at cost—p. 188
Valuation at market—p. 188
Sale of marketable securities—p. 189

DEMONSTRATION PROBLEM FOR REVIEW AND SELF-STUDY Cascade Company closes its books annually on November 30. The November 30, 19_1 trial balance, prepared before reconciliation of the bank account and the recording of adjusting entries, contains the following amounts:

	Debit	Credit
Cash in bank	$1,669.72	
Marketable equity securities	2,200.00	
Allowance to reduce marketable equity securities to market		$425.00

The following information pertains to the month of November, 19_1:

(1) The bank statement shows a balance of $2,031.55 on November 30, 19_1.

(2) Cash totalling $527.38 has not been deposited in the bank.

(3) An examination of the returned checks reveals that the following have not cleared: No. 197, $13.65; No. 198, $105.09; No. 210, $86.10; No. 213, $303.80; and No. 214, $440.83.

(4) The bank statement shows $40.80 as the amount deducted for a certain check, while the check was made out for $40.08.

(5) During November J. A. Gillis, a customer, stopped payment of his check for $182.64.

(6) The bank collected a noninterest-bearing note for the company's account: face, $155; collection charges, $2.90.

(7) Interest charges on outstanding loans, deducted by the bank, amounted to $20.

(8) The bookkeeper recorded one of Cascade Company's checks in the amount of $321.92 as $312.92; the account was Gordon Supply Company.

(9) A certified check of $134.39, payable to Small Company, is included with the checks returned.

(10) The marketable equity securities consist of the following common stocks:

	Cost	Market price at November 30, 19_1
Dawson Company	$1,600.00	$2,500.00
Ellis Company	600.00	525.00
	$2,200.00	$3,025.00

INSTRUCTIONS

(a) Prepare the firm's bank reconciliation as of November 30, 19_1.

(b) Prepare any journal entries required as of November 30, 19_1 in order to properly report the cash in bank account.

(c) Prepare any journal entries required as of November 30, 19_1 in order to properly report the marketable equity securities.

Note Attempt to solve the demonstration problem before examining the solution that follows.

(a)

CASCADE COMPANY
Bank Reconciliation—Union Banking Company
November 30, 19_1

Balance per books		$1,669.72
Add proceeds of note collected by bank:		
Face amount	$155.00	
Less collection charge	2.90	152.10
Total		$1,821.82
Deduct:		
Error made by bookkeeper in recording check; $321.92		
recorded as $312.92	$ 9.00	
Interest charges	20.00	
J. A. Gillis stopped payment on check	182.64	211.64
Adjusted balance		$1,610.18

Balance per bank		$2,031.55
Add:		
Undeposited cash not credited by bank	$527.38	
Bank error; check for $40.08 deducted as $40.80	.72	528.10
Total		$2,559.65
Deduct outstanding checks:		
No. 197	$ 13.65	
198	105.09	
210	86.10	
213	303.80	
214	440.83	949.47
Adjusted balance		$1,610.18

(b)

JOURNAL (Page 1)

19_1				
Nov.	30	Cash	152.10	
		Bank charges	2.90	
		Notes receivable		155.00
		Note collected by bank.		
	30	Accounts receivable (J. A. Gillis)	182.64	
		Cash		182.64
		Customer stopped payment on check.		
	30	Interest expense	20.00	
		Cash		20.00
		Interest deducted by bank.		
	30	Accounts payable (Gordon Supply Company)	9.00	
		Cash		9.00
		Check of $321.92 recorded as $312.92.		

(c)

19_1				
Nov.	30	Allowance to reduce marketable equity securities to market	425.00	
		Market gain on securities		425.00
		To report securities at the lower of cost or market.		

Questions

1 Which of the following items could properly be classified as *cash?*
   (a) The balance in a bank account.
   (b) Coin and currency on hand.
   (c) Postage stamps on hand.
   (d) Postal money orders.
   (e) Checks received from customers.
   (f) An employee's I.O.U.
2 Outline a basic system for the *internal control* of cash.
3 Describe the procedure for establishing a *petty cash* fund. Why is it necessary that the petty cash fund be replenished at the end of the accounting period?
4 List several items, other than deposits and cancelled checks, that might affect a depositor's bank balance.
5 What is the purpose of a bank reconciliation?
6 List the steps in the bank reconciliation process.
7 What is properly includable in the cost of an investment?
8 What is the difference between an investment that is classifiable as a current asset and one that represents a long-term investment?
9 How does the accounting for income from bond investments differ from the accounting for income from stock investments?
10 How should a bank overdraft be reported in a firm's financial statements?
11 Describe three different valuation methods for marketable securities.
12 What is the difference between a realized gain and an unrealized gain as they pertain to marketable securities?
13 How does the application of the lower-of-cost-or-market method to marketable equity securities differ from the application of the method to marketable debt securities?

Short exercises

E6-1

Listed below are several reconciling items which might appear in a bank reconciliation:

(1) Bank service charges.

(2) Checks written but still outstanding.

(3) Proceeds of a note collected by the bank but not entered on the books.

(4) A deposit in transit.

(5) A check erroneously charged against the account by the bank.

(6) A cancelled check recorded on the books for less than the amount of the check.

(7) A deposit erroneously credited to the account by the bank.

(8) A check deposited in the account but returned due to insufficient funds.

For each item state where it would appear in the reconciliation form by using the letters A, B, C, and D as follows:

A—Add to balance per books.

B—Deduct from balance per books.

C—Add to balance per bank.

D—Deduct from balance per bank.

E6-2   Roberts Company uses a petty cash fund in its operations. The following transactions took place in the order listed:

(1) Established the fund in the amount of $200.

(2) Disbursed $25 from the fund.

(3) Disbursed $15 from the fund.

(4) Replenished the fund by drawing a check for $40.

(5) Reduced the fund to $100.

(6) Disbursed $10 from the fund.

(7) Disbursed $20 from the fund.

(8) Replenished the fund by drawing a check for $30.

(9) Increased the fund to $150.

What is the balance in the petty cash fund immediately after each transaction? What is the balance in the petty cash account in the general ledger immediately after each transaction?

E6-3   The following data pertain to the marketable securities of Cross Company during 19_1, the company's first year of operations:

(1) Purchased 100 shares of A Corporation stock at $15 per share, plus brokerage costs of $40.

(2) Purchased a $1,000 B Corporation bond at face, plus accrued interest of $25.

(3) Received a cash dividend of 40¢ per share on the A Corporation stock.

(4) Sold 50 shares of the A Corporation stock at $17 per share.

(5) Received interest of $35 on the B Corporation bond.

(6) Purchased 100 shares of C Company stock for $2,000.

(7) Received interest of $35 on the B Corporation bond.

(8) Sold 50 shares of the A Corporation stock for $13 per share.

(9) Received a cash dividend of 75¢ per share on the C Company stock.

(10) Interest receivable at year-end on the B Corporation bond amounts to $30.

What is the amount of each of the following for the year?

(a) Bond interest revenue.

(b) Dividend revenue.

(c) Gain or loss on sale of securities.

E6-4   Diffey Company purchased marketable equity securities for $100,000 on January 21, 19_8. The market price of the securities at December 31, 19_8 was $95,000. At December 31, 19_9 the market price had increased to $103,000. Present the entries required at December 31, 19_8 and December 31, 19_9 to properly account for the securities.

E6-5   *Which one of the following transactions results in a debit to the petty cash account? (a) replenishment of the fund; (b) disbursements from the fund; (c) increasing the amount of the fund; (d) decreasing the amount of the fund; (e) none of the above.*

Problems

A6-1   *Information concerning the petty cash fund of New Corporation, which closes its books on November 30, is presented below.*

October 10—A petty cash fund of $200 is established.

October 31—Examination of the fund reveals the following composition:

Currency and coin	$14.25
Receipts for the following disbursements:	
Telephone and telegraph	21.34
Postage expense	30.40
Travel expense	48.14
Entertainment expense	18.76
Office supplies expense	46.76
Miscellaneous expense	20.00

The fund is replenished on this date and the amount is increased to $250.

November 30—The fund consists of the following:

Currency and coin	$90.69
Receipts for the following disbursements:	
Travel expense	67.50
Postage expense	18.11
Office supplies expense	19.94
Entertainment expense	53.76

The fund is not replenished on this date.

Required:

Prepare journal entries to record the above information.

A6-2   *Bullard Corporation opened a bank account with Citizens Trust Company on May 1, 19_1. The bank statement at the top of p. 195 was received at the end of May.*

CITIZENS TRUST COMPANY

Checks		Deposits	Date 19_1	Balance
Balance brought forward				–0–
		5,000.00	May 1	5,000.00
194.34		209.38	May 2	5,015.04
31.73 N.S.F.		122.34	May 3	5,105.65
313.76		306.30	May 4	5,098.19
.75 SC		58.59	May 5	5,156.03
2.02		67.51	May 6	5,221.52
1.50 Col.		108.65	May 9	5,328.67
196.64	83.66	314.92	May 11	5,363.29
90.29		288.37	May 14	5,561.37
106.64		204.89	May 16	5,659.62
157.72		31.59	May 18	5,533.49
81.77	1.25 SC	67.61	May 20	5,518.08
52.35		21.98	May 22	5,487.71
101.36		204.33	May 25	5,590.68
		377.89	May 27	5,968.57
162.06			May 29	5,806.51

A summary of the May cash receipts and disbursements follows.

CASH RECEIPTS

Date		Receipts	Deposits
19_1			
May	1	21.89	
	1	187.49	209.38
	2	122.34	122.34
	3	146.38	
	3	19.97	
	3	139.95	306.30
	4	58.59	58.59
	5	67.51	67.51
	8	84.71	
	8	23.94	108.65
	10	314.92	314.92
	12	198.77	
	12	14.38	
	12	75.22	288.37
	15	204.89	204.89
	17	31.59	31.59
	19	64.52	
	19	3.09	67.61
	21	21.98	21.98
	24	121.70	
	24	82.63	204.33
	26	377.89	377.89
	28	67.87	
	29	9.49	
	30	77.15	154.51
		2,538.86	2,538.86

Date	Check No.	Amount
19_1		
May 1	101	194.34
2	102	313.76
2	103	196.64
3	104	82.52
4	105	83.66
4	106	2.02
6	107	75.26
7	108	90.29
10	109	106.64
11	110	157.72
13	111	93.11
17	112	52.35
18	113	101.36
20	114	81.77
26	115	110.39
27	116	162.06
29	117	42.99
		1,946.88

Required:

(a) A bank reconciliation as of May 31, 19_1. Note: It is necessary to calculate the cash balance per books at May 31, 19_1.

(b) Any necessary journal entries, assuming that the cash journals have been ruled and posted for the month of May.

A6-3

Cedar Corporation maintains a bank account with First Banking Company. The following information pertains to the month of November, 19_1:

(1) The ledger shows a balance of $2,504.58 on November 30, 19_1.

(2) The bank statement shows a balance of $3,141.81 on November 30, 19_1.

(3) Cash totaling $791.07 has been deposited but not yet recorded by the bank.

(4) An examination of the returned checks reveals that the following have not cleared: No. 197, $20.48; No. 198, $157.64; No. 210, $129.15; No. 213, $455.70; and No. 214, $661.24.

(5) The bank statement shows $61.20 as the amount deducted for a certain check, but the check was written for $61.02.

(6) During November Fred Chapman, a customer, stopped payment of his check for $136.98.

(7) The bank collected a noninterest-bearing note for the company's account: face, $200; collection charges, $1.75.

(8) Interest charges on outstanding loans, deducted by the bank, amounted to $30.

(9) The bookkeeper recorded one of Cedar Corporation's checks in the amount of $241.44 as $214.44; the account was Golden Supply Company.

(10) A certified check of $201.58, payable to Box Company, is included with the checks returned.

Required:

(a) A bank reconciliation as of November 30, 19_1.

(b) Any journal entries required as of November 30, 19_1.

A6-4

The following transactions pertain to the marketable equity securities of Zebra Company for the year ended December 31, 19_2.

January 18—Purchased 250 shares of Jones Company common stock at $27 per share, plus brokerage costs of $125.

February 13—Purchased 50 shares of Smith Company common stock at $16 per share, plus brokerage costs of $50.

March 1—Received cash dividend of 50 cents per share on the Jones Company stock.

June 25—Purchased an additional 150 shares of Smith Company common stock at $19 per share, plus brokerage costs of $150.

August 9—Sold 200 shares of the Jones Company common stock at $25 per share.

October 22—Received a cash dividend of $1 per share on the Smith Company stock.

November 27—Sold the 50 shares of Smith Company common stock acquired on February 13 at a price of $22 per share.

Required:

Journal entries to record the transactions for the year.

A6-5

The following information pertains to Allen Company:

(1) The balance per ledger March 31, 19_7, is $1,406.08.

(2) Total receipts for April amount to $4,423.03.

(3) Disbursements for April are $6,210.14.

(4) The bank statement shows a balance of $1,807.09 on April 30, 19_7.

(5) The collection by the bank of a note in the amount of $400 has not been recorded.

(6) Checks outstanding on April 30, 19_7, are: No. 2510, $965.08; No. 2815, $519.62; No. 2903, $408.11; No. 2904, $37.50; No. 2906, $2,003.19; and No. 2907, $993.79. There were no outstanding checks on March 31, 19_7.

(7) A deposit of $1,139.17 has been mailed to the bank but does not appear on the April statement. There were no deposits in transit on March 31, 19_7.

(8) During April the bank charged the account of Allen Company $2,000 for the face amount of a maturing bank loan. This charge has not been recorded on the books.

Required:

The April 30, 19_7 bank reconciliation. Note: It is necessary to calculate the cash balance per books at April 30, 19_7.

A6-6

The following information pertains to the marketable securities of Risk Company on June 30, 19_8, the end of the firm's accounting period. All securities were acquired during the current accounting period.

Investment	Cost	Market
Adams common stock	$ 6,750	$7,025
Bigler bonds	10,500	9,625
Croy common stock	6,875	6,575
Day bonds	4,837	4,662
Early common stock	8,625	8,875

Required:

(a) The entries at year end in order to report the securities at the lower of cost or market.

(b) Presentation of the securities on the balance sheet, assuming that any related accounts are to be shown separately in the balance sheet.

(c) Journal entries to record sale of the following securities during July, 19_8:
   (1) The Adams common stock is sold for $6,950.
   (2) The Croy common stock is sold for $6,700.

B6-1

The following transactions pertain to the petty cash account of Albers Company for the accounting period ending June 30, 19_1:

May 17—A check is drawn to establish a petty cash fund in the amount of $250.

   31—An examination reveals the following composition of the fund, which is replenished on this date:

Currency and coin	$121.05
Receipts for the following disbursements:	
Postage	28.12
Office supplies expense	36.03
Travel expense	20.64
Entertainment expense	44.16

June 30—The following items are found in the fund on this date:

Currency and coin	$77.58
Receipts for the following disbursements:	
Postage	40.25
Office supplies expense	37.65
Telephone and telegraph	14.75
Travel expense	58.80
Miscellaneous expense	20.97

The fund was replenished on June 30 and the amount was reduced to $200.

Required:

Journal entries to record the above information.

B6-2

The following information pertains to the banking activities of Kelly Company with Second National Bank during the month of September, 19_1:

(1) The balance per ledger on September 1, 19_1 is $12,183.89.

(2) Cash receipts for September per the cash journal are $34,226.19; checks during the month total $39,683.51.

(3) The statement from the bank shows a balance of $5,917.48 at the end of the month.

(4) Included in the returned checks is a memo stating that the check of L. Covin has been returned marked N.S.F.; the amount is $165.73.

(5) An examination of the checks reveals that the following are outstanding: No. 1593, $22.88; No. 1812, $82.79; No. 1962, $51.84; No. 2008, $84.52; No. 2009, $3.61; and No. 2010, $21.83.

(6) The bank has deducted from the account, in error, a check of King Inc.; the amount of the check is $140.97.

(7) There is a deposit of $1,575.23 in transit at the end of September.

(8) The bookkeeper made an error in recording a check received on account from R. Morgan; the amount recorded was $90.18; it should have been $901.80.

(9) A debit memo shows that service charges amounted to $6.25.

Required:

(a) A bank reconciliation as of September 30, 19_1.

(b) Any journal entries required as of September 30, 19_1.

B6-3   *The following selected account balances are taken from the books of Benton Company as of February 28, 19_1:*

	Balance	
	Debit	Credit
Cash on hand	$ 200	
Cash in bank—Citizens Bank		$ 150
Cash in bank—First National Bank	1,974	
Cash in bank—Bank of Madison	5,086	
Petty cash	75	
Marketable equity securities—at cost	9,740	
Allowance to reduce marketable equity securities to market		1,740
Investment in marketable debt securities—at cost and face (bonds mature December 31, 19_5)	12,000	

Required:

State how each of the above items would be reported on Benton Company's balance sheet on February 28, 19_1.

B6-4   *Corbett, Inc., had the following transactions pertaining to purchases and sales of marketable securities in 19_1:*

January 10—Bought 60 shares of A stock for $175.00 per share.

February 15—Bought 30 bonds of B, due January 1, 19_3, for 100 plus accrued interest of $300. The bonds have a face value of $1,000 each, with interest payable January 1 and July 1.

19—Bought 1,000 shares of C stock for $8.25 per share, including dividends declared but not yet paid. The dividend is to be 75 cents per share.

March 1—The dividend was received on the C stock.

10—Sold 35 shares of A stock for $182.50 per share.

May 4—Bought 75 shares of D stock for $53.40 per share.

June 1—Sold 30 bonds of B for 98 plus interest of $700.

30—The company's fiscal year ends on June 30. Per share stock quotations, as of June 30 were: A, $168.00; C, $7.50; and D, $50.00.

September 6—Sold 50 shares of D stock for $48.50 per share.

Required:

(a) All entries to record the above transactions.

(b) The presentation of the marketable securities accounts on the balance sheet as of June 30, 19_1.

B6-5   *The following data pertain to the marketable securities of Patterson Company for the year 19_8:*

January 2—Purchased 250 shares of Lucy Company common stock at $18 per share.

February 1—Lucy Company paid a cash dividend of 75 cents per share.

199

February   1—Purchased $10,000 face value 8 per cent bonds of Linda Company for $9,900. Interest is payable February 1 and August 1. The bonds mature February 1, 19_9.

March 24—Purchased an additional 200 shares of Lucy Company common stock for $3,850, including brokerage costs of $100.

May 31—Purchased Lucy Company 6 per cent bonds at face value of $25,000. Interest is payable April 1 and October 1. The bonds mature on October 1, 19_8.

July   3—Sold 150 shares of Lucy Company common stock at $19 per share. These shares were identified as part of the purchase of January 1.

August   1—Received interest on Linda Company bonds.

October   1—Received the principal and interest payment due on the Lucy Company bonds.

November 17—Sold the 100 remaining shares of Lucy Company stock purchased on January 1 for $17 per share.

December 31—The Linda Company bonds have a market price of $9,950.

Required:

Journal entries to record the transactions for the year, including any adjusting entries required at December 31, 19_8. Note: Interest rates are annual rates. Interest should be calculated from last interest payment date to date of transaction.

THE TIME VALUE OF MONEY
APPENDIX TO CHAPTER 6

INTRODUCTION A dollar expected in the future is not equivalent to a dollar receivable today because of the time value of money. A rational person prefers a dollar today to a dollar receivable in the future because a dollar in hand can be invested immediately to earn interest, and to grow to more than one dollar in the future. If a 6 per cent return is available, having $5,000 today would be preferable to receiving $5,000 one year from now. The $5,000 could be invested immediately, would earn $300 interest ($5,000 × .06 × 1), and would amount to $5,300 at the end of one year. With a 6 per cent interest rate, $5,000 today would be preferable to any amount less than $5,300 receivable at the end of one year, ignoring income tax considerations.

Note how the interest calculation in the preceding example converted present-day dollars ($5,000) into equivalent future dollars ($5,300 one year hence). With 6 per cent interest available, the alternative of receiving $5,000 today is equivalent to receiving $5,300 at the end of one year.

Given the fact that money has time value, when deciding which of two amounts is preferable, and the amounts are receivable (or payable) at different dates, it is necessary to make allowance for the time difference. One can accomplish this by comparing the amounts *at the same point in time,* as is shown by the following examples.

Which is the most attractive alternative, assuming that money can earn 6 per cent per annum?

(A) $5,000 today or $5,200 one year hence.
   To make the comparison, state both amounts at their value one year hence:

	Now	One year hence
(a) $5,000 × 1.06 =		$5,300
(b)		$5,200

   Answer: Accept $5,000 now because it will amount to more than $5,200 one year hence.

(B) $5,000 today or $5,400 one year hence.

	Now	One year hence
(a) $5,000 × 1.06 =		$5,300
(b)		$5,400

   Answer: Accept $5,400 one year hence because it is more than $5,000 will amount to when invested at 6% for one year.

(C) $5,000 today or $5,300 one year hence.
   Answer: They are equivalent, assuming, of course, no risk of loss either through investment or while waiting.

The time value of money acknowledges the fact that money has a cost, called interest, just as does land (rent), labor (wages), and owners' risk (profit). Money is in demand and commands a price in the form of interest. If $1,000 is kept in a safety deposit box for one year, the opportunity of investing the money at, say, 6 per cent and earning interest has been foregone. It has cost $60 ($1,000 × .06 × 1) to keep the money idle.

COMPOUND INTEREST   Simple interest is the interest earned on the *original* amount invested (principal); hence the principal and the interest payments remain the same for each interest period. For example, an investment of $2,000 at 6 per cent *simple* interest for two years would earn total interest of $240, as shown below.

	Principal ×	Interest rate	× Time =	Simple interest
End of Year 1	$2,000 ×	.06	× 1 =	$120
End of Year 2	$2,000 ×	.06	× 1 =	120
				$240

Because only the principal earns interest, a rational person would withdraw any simple interest earned and invest it elsewhere so that the invested interest would earn future interest. Otherwise the simple interest previously earned lies idle and does not earn anything in subsequent years. In the example above suppose that the $120 interest earned by the end of year 1 is withdrawn and invested at 6 per cent, which would produce $7.20 more interest, or a total of $247.20 over the two years:

	Simple interest earned on original principal	Simple interest earned on investment of previously earned interest	Total interest earned
End of Year 1	$2,000 × .06 × 1 = $120	—	$120.00
End of Year 2	$2,000 × .06 × 1 = $120	$120 × .06 × 1 = $7.20	127.20
			$247.20

Obviously, financial institutions do not want investors to withdraw interest earned on savings, since earned interest left in savings accounts provides the financial institution with a larger pool of capital that can be used for loans and investments. Consequently, most financial institutions pay compound interest to induce savers to leave earned interest in savings accounts. Compound interest is interest earned on any previously earned interest plus the original principal. Periodically as interest becomes due (either annually, semiannually, quarterly, monthly, or daily), it is added (compounded or converted) to the principal and the larger accumulated amount (called the compound sum, compound amount, or future value) earns interest. In the previous example, the saver would not have to withdraw his $120 interest earned at the end of the first year if the financial institution paid interest at 6 per cent compounded annually.

	Interest per year	Compound interest	Compound sum
End of Year 1	$2,000 × .06 × 1 = $120.00	$120.00	$2,120.00
End of Year 2	$2,120 × .06 × 1 = 127.20	247.20	2,247.20

Where:

$$\frac{\text{Compound sum at}}{\text{end of period}} = \frac{\text{Compound sum at}}{\text{beginning of period}} \times 1 + \text{Interest rate}$$

$2,120.00	=	$2,000.00	×	1.06
2,247.20	=	2,120.00	×	1.06

$$\text{Compound interest} = \frac{\text{Compound sum}}{\text{at end of period}} - \frac{\text{Original}}{\text{principal}}$$

$120.00	=	$2,120.00	−	$2,000.00
247.20	=	2,247.20	−	2,000.00

The determination of the compound sum supplies the answer to the following question: If a certain amount of money is invested today at a given rate of interest, how much will be accumulated at the end of a given number of years? Or, given the dollar amount of the investment today, the interest rate, and the time period, what is the future value (compound sum) of the investment?

Interest tables are available which show the compound sum or future value of $1 at various rates and time periods. An abbreviated table is shown on page 204. To calculate the compound sum of an investment made today, multiply the sum invested by the compound sum of $1 at the given interest rate and time period obtained from compound tables, or

Compound future sum of an investment today $= \dfrac{\text{Present}}{\text{investment}} \times \dfrac{\text{Compound sum of \$1 at given}}{\text{interest rate and time period}}$

today   (available from compound tables)

For example, to calculate the compound sum of $50,000 at 6 per cent interest for five years, multiply $50,000 by 1.3382, which is the compound sum of $1 at 6 per cent for five years according to the table. The compound sum is $66,910. Or

$$S = P(1 + i)^n$$
$$= \$50,000(1.06)^5$$
$$\$66,910 = \$50,000(1.3382)$$

Compound sum (future value) of $1

Periods	1%	2%	3%	4%	5%	6%	7%	8%	9%	10%
	Interest rates									
1	1.0100	1.0200	1.0300	1.0400	1.0500	1.0600	1.0700	1.0800	1.0900	1.1000
2	1.0201	1.0404	1.0609	1.0816	1.1025	1.1236	1.1449	1.1664	1.1881	1.2100
3	1.0303	1.0612	1.0927	1.1249	1.1576	1.1910	1.2250	1.2597	1.2950	1.3310
4	1.0406	1.0824	1.1255	1.1699	1.2155	1.2625	1.3108	1.3605	1.4116	1.4641
5	1.0510	1.1041	1.1593	1.2167	1.2763	1.3382	1.4026	1.4693	1.5386	1.6105
6	1.0615	1.1262	1.1941	1.2653	1.3401	1.4185	1.5007	1.5869	1.6771	1.7716
7	1.0721	1.1487	1.2299	1.3159	1.4071	1.5036	1.6058	1.7138	1.8280	1.9487
8	1.0829	1.1717	1.2668	1.3686	1.4775	1.5938	1.7182	1.8509	1.9926	2.1436
9	1.0937	1.1951	1.3048	1.4233	1.5513	1.6895	1.8385	1.9990	2.1719	2.3579
10	1.1046	1.2190	1.3439	1.4802	1.6289	1.7908	1.9672	2.1589	2.3674	2.5937
11	1.1157	1.2434	1.3842	1.5395	1.7103	1.8983	2.1049	2.3316	2.5804	2.8531
12	1.1268	1.2682	1.4258	1.6010	1.7959	2.0122	2.2522	2.5182	2.8127	3.1384
13	1.1381	1.2936	1.4685	1.6651	1.8856	2.1329	2.4098	2.7196	3.0658	3.4523
14	1.1495	1.3195	1.5126	1.7317	1.9799	2.2609	2.5785	2.9372	3.3417	3.7975
15	1.1610	1.3459	1.5580	1.8009	2.0789	2.3966	2.7590	3.1722	3.6425	4.1772
16	1.1726	1.3728	1.6047	1.8730	2.1829	2.5404	2.9522	3.4259	3.9703	4.5950
17	1.1843	1.4002	1.6528	1.9479	2.2920	2.6928	3.1588	3.7000	4.3276	5.0545
18	1.1961	1.4282	1.7024	2.0258	2.4066	2.8543	3.3799	3.9960	4.7171	5.5599
19	1.2081	1.4568	1.7535	2.1068	2.5270	3.0256	3.6165	4.3157	5.1417	6.1159
20	1.2202	1.4859	1.8061	2.1911	2.6533	3.2071	3.8697	4.6610	5.6044	6.7275
25	1.2824	1.6406	2.0938	2.6658	3.3864	4.2919	5.4274	6.8485	8.6231	10.8347
30	1.3478	1.8114	2.4273	3.2434	4.3219	5.7435	7.6123	10.0627	13.2677	17.4494
35	1.4166	1.9999	2.8139	3.9461	5.5160	7.6861	10.6766	14.7853	20.4140	28.1024
40	1.4889	2.2080	3.2620	4.8010	7.0400	10.2857	14.9745	21.7245	31.4094	45.2593
45	1.5648	2.4379	3.7816	5.8412	8.9850	13.7646	21.0025	31.9204	48.3273	72.8905
50	1.6446	2.6916	4.3839	7.1067	11.4674	18.4202	29.4570	46.9016	74.3575	117.3909

PRESENT VALUE An understanding of compound interest leads to an understanding of present value, because present value is merely the opposite of compounding. With a known future amount, the present value is the dollar amount that would have to be invested today to accumulate the future amount. The unknown to be calculated in compounding is the future amount, while the unknown in present value calculations is the amount of the present investment. Thus, at this point, present value is defined as the equivalent dollar value today of a known future amount, assuming a given interest rate and time period.

An investment of $1,000 at 6 per cent interest for two years grows to a compound amount of $1,123.60 ($1,000 × 1.1236). However, this may be turned around and stated in terms of present value: What is the present value of $1,123.60 due two years hence, if the interest rate is 6 per cent compounded annually? The present value is $1,000, for it would take an investment of $1,000 today to have $1,123.60 at the end of two years at 6 per cent interest compounded annually. Thus a known investment of $1,000 today is equivalent to a future value of $1,123.60; a known future amount of $1,123.60 is equivalent to a present value of $1,000, assuming a 6 per cent interest rate compounded annually for two years.

Assuming a 6 per cent interest rate compounded annually, the illustration on page 205 may provide an insight to the present value concept by showing how present value is the opposite of compounding. Compounding is an accumulation of compound amounts (future values) as time moves forward. Given a future amount, present value is the movement back in time to derive the smaller equivalent dollar amount today of that future amount. In terms of the illustration below, compounding is moving up the hill as time progresses, and present value is moving down the hill as time retrogresses.

The formula for compounding provides the formula for present value, which is used to derive tables showing the present value of $1 at various rates of interest and time periods. An abbreviated present value table of $1 is shown on page 206. Thus, to find the present value of a known future amount, multiply the future amount by the present value of $1 for the appropriate time period and interest rate, or

$$\textit{Present value} = \begin{matrix} \text{Future sum} \\ \text{or compound amount} \end{matrix} \times \begin{matrix} \text{Present value of \$1 at a} \\ \text{given interest rate and} \\ \text{time period (obtained from} \\ \text{present value tables)} \end{matrix}$$

For example, the present value of $3,207.10 at 6 per cent interest compounded annually for 20 years is $1,000 ($3,207.10 × .3118) or

$$P = S(1 + i)^{-n}$$
$$= \$3{,}207.10(1.06)^{-20}$$
$$\$1{,}000 = \$3{,}207.10(.3118)$$

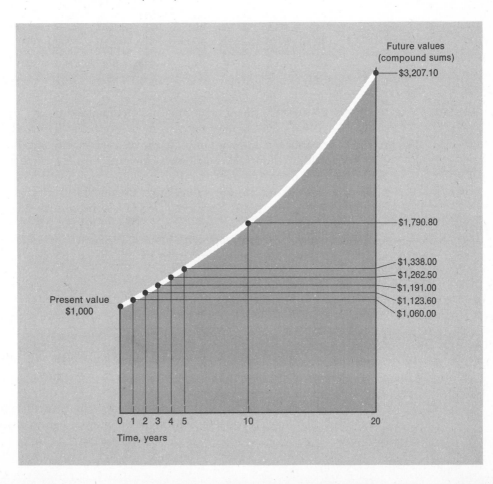

Present value of $1

Interest rates

Periods	1%	2%	3%	4%	5%	6%	7%	8%	9%	10%
1	.9901	.9804	.9709	.9615	.9524	.9434	.9346	.9259	.9174	.9091
2	.9803	.9612	.9426	.9246	.9070	.8900	.8734	.8573	.8417	.8264
3	.9706	.9423	.9151	.8890	.8638	.8396	.8163	.7938	.7722	.7513
4	.9610	.9238	.8885	.8548	.8227	.7921	.7629	.7350	.7084	.6830
5	.9515	.9057	.8626	.8219	.7835	.7473	.7130	.6806	.6499	.6209
6	.9420	.8880	.8375	.7903	.7462	.7050	.6663	.6302	.5963	.5645
7	.9327	.8706	.8131	.7599	.7107	.6651	.6227	.5835	.5470	.5132
8	.9235	.8535	.7894	.7307	.6768	.6274	.5820	.5403	.5019	.4665
9	.9143	.8368	.7664	.7026	.6446	.5919	.5439	.5002	.4604	.4241
10	.9053	.8203	.7441	.6756	.6139	.5584	.5083	.4632	.4224	.3855
11	.8963	.8043	.7224	.6496	.5847	.5268	.4751	.4289	.3875	.3505
12	.8874	.7885	.7014	.6246	.5568	.4970	.4440	.3971	.3555	.3186
13	.8787	.7730	.6810	.6006	.5303	.4688	.4150	.3677	.3262	.2897
14	.8700	.7579	.6611	.5775	.5051	.4423	.3878	.3405	.2992	.2633
15	.8613	.7430	.6419	.5553	.4810	.4173	.3624	.3152	.2745	.2394
16	.8528	.7284	.6232	.5339	.4581	.3936	.3387	.2919	.2519	.2176
17	.8444	.7142	.6050	.5134	.4363	.3714	.3166	.2703	.2311	.1978
18	.8360	.7002	.5874	.4936	.4155	.3503	.2959	.2502	.2120	.1799
19	.8277	.6864	.5703	.4746	.3957	.3305	.2765	.2317	.1945	.1635
20	.8195	.6730	.5537	.4564	.3769	.3118	.2584	.2145	.1784	.1486
25	.7798	.6095	.4776	.3751	.2953	.2330	.1842	.1460	.1160	.0923
30	.7419	.5521	.4120	.3083	.2314	.1741	.1314	.0994	.0754	.0573
35	.7059	.5000	.3554	.2534	.1813	.1301	.0937	.0676	.0490	.0356
40	.6717	.4529	.3066	.2083	.1420	.0972	.0668	.0460	.0318	.0221
45	.6391	.4102	.2644	.1712	.1113	.0727	.0476	.0313	.0207	.0137
50	.6080	.3715	.2281	.1407	.0872	.0543	.0339	.0213	.0134	.0085

PRESENT VALUE OF AN ANNUITY   The previous discussion of compounding and present value has dealt with a single lump-sum cash flow. We have discussed the compound or future amount of a known lump-sum investment today and the present value of a known lump-sum future amount. However, usually there are several cash flows, not one, occurring over the life of a long-term investment or loan.

The compound and present value tables previously illustrated can be used to calculate the future value and present value of a series of cash flows. For example, to find the present value of equal cash flows of $1,000 to be received at the end of each year for three years, with interest at 6 per cent compounded annually, add the present value of a lump sum of $1,000 at the end of each year for three years:

	Cash flow		Present value of $1 at 6% interest		Present value
Year 1	$1,000	×	.9434	=	$ 943.40
Year 2	$1,000	×	.8900	=	890.00
Year 3	$1,000	×	.8396	=	839.60
			2.6730		$2,673.00

The above example shows that the formula for the present value of a series of expected cash flows is equal to the sum of the present values of each individual cash flow:

$$\left.\begin{array}{c} Present\ value \\ of\ a\ series\ of \\ cash\ flows \end{array}\right\} = \left(\begin{array}{cc} \text{Cash flow} & \text{Present value of \$1} \\ \text{end of first} & \times\ \text{at given interest} \\ \text{period} & \text{rate for 1 period} \end{array}\right)$$

$$+$$

$$\left(\begin{array}{cc} \text{Cash flow} & \text{Present value of \$1} \\ \text{end of second} & \times\ \text{at given interest} \\ \text{period} & \text{rate for 2 periods} \end{array}\right)$$

$$+$$

$$\left(\begin{array}{cc} \text{Cash flow} & \text{Present value of \$1} \\ \text{end of third} & \times\ \text{at given interest} \\ \text{period} & \text{rate for 3 periods} \end{array}\right)$$

$$+$$

$$\vdots$$

The computation of the present value of a series of cash flows is simplified if an annuity exists. An annuity is a series of *equal* cash receipts or payments made at *uniform* intervals of time at a *constant* interest rate. For simplicity, the assumption is made that the cash flows of an annuity occur at the *end* of each payment (or receipt) period and that each payment (receipt) period is equal to the compound interest period.

In the previous example, the $1,000 cash inflow is a constant amount that occurs at equal intervals of one year for three years, with interest compounded annually. Hence, an annuity exists. Note that in the example the present value of $1 at the end of each year for three years totals 2.673 (.9434 + .8900 + .8396), and that $1,000 multiplied by 2.673 equals the present value of a series of equal cash flows at equal intervals of time. Thus the present value of an annuity is equal to the constant cash flow each period multiplied by the sum of the present values of $1 for each period. However, the latter summation is available from present value of annuity tables; an abbreviated form appears on page 208.

$$\begin{array}{ccc} \begin{array}{c} Present\ value\ of \\ an\ annuity \end{array} = \begin{array}{c} \text{Constant cash flow} \\ \text{each period} \end{array} \times \begin{array}{c} \text{Present value of an annuity} \\ \text{of \$1 at a given interest} \\ \text{rate and number of periods} \\ \text{(obtained from present value} \\ \text{of annuity tables)} \end{array} \end{array}$$

$$\$2{,}673 \quad = \quad \$1{,}000 \quad \times \quad 2.673$$

Or

$$P_a = R \cdot p_{\overline{n}|i}$$
$$= \$1{,}000\ p_{\overline{3}|.06}$$
$$\$2{,}673 = \$1{,}000\ (2.673)$$

Present value of an annuity of $1

Interest rates

Periods	1%	2%	3%	4%	5%	6%	7%	8%	9%	10%
1	0.9901	0.9804	0.9709	0.9615	0.9524	0.9434	0.9346	0.9259	0.9174	0.9091
2	1.9704	1.9416	1.9135	1.8861	1.8594	1.8334	1.8080	1.7833	1.7591	1.7355
3	2.9410	2.8839	2.8286	2.7751	2.7232	2.6730	2.6243	2.5771	2.5313	2.4869
4	3.9020	3.8077	3.7171	3.6299	3.5460	3.4651	3.3872	3.3121	3.2397	3.1699
5	4.8534	4.7135	4.5797	4.4518	4.3295	4.2124	4.1002	3.9927	3.8897	3.7908
6	5.7955	5.6014	5.4172	5.2421	5.0757	4.9173	4.7665	4.6229	4.4859	4.3553
7	6.7282	6.4720	6.2303	6.0021	5.7864	5.5824	5.3893	5.2064	5.0330	4.8684
8	7.6517	7.3255	7.0197	6.7327	6.4632	6.2098	5.9713	5.7466	5.5348	5.3349
9	8.5660	8.1622	7.7861	7.4353	7.1078	6.8017	6.5152	6.2469	5.9952	5.7590
10	9.4713	8.9826	8.5302	8.1109	7.7217	7.3601	7.0236	6.7101	6.4177	6.1446
11	10.3676	9.7868	9.2526	8.7605	8.3064	7.8867	7.4987	7.1390	6.8052	6.4951
12	11.2551	10.5753	9.9540	9.3851	8.8633	8.3838	7.9427	7.5361	7.1607	6.8137
13	12.1337	11.3484	10.6350	9.9856	9.3936	8.8527	8.3577	7.9038	7.4869	7.1034
14	13.0037	12.1062	11.2961	10.5631	9.8986	9.2950	8.7455	8.2442	7.7862	6.3667
15	13.8651	12.8493	11.9379	11.1184	10.3797	9.7122	9.1079	8.5595	8.0607	7.6061
16	14.7179	13.5777	12.5611	11.6523	10.8378	10.1059	9.4466	8.8514	8.3126	7.8237
17	15.5623	14.2919	13.1661	12.1657	11.2741	10.4773	9.7632	9.1216	8.5436	8.0216
18	16.3983	14.9920	13.7535	12.6593	11.6896	10.8276	10.0591	9.3719	8.7556	8.2014
19	17.2260	15.6785	14.3238	13.1339	12.0853	11.1581	10.3356	9.6036	8.9501	8.3649
20	18.0456	16.3514	14.8775	13.5903	12.4622	11.4699	10.5940	9.8181	9.1285	8.5136
25	22.0232	19.5235	17.4131	15.6221	14.0939	12.7834	11.6536	10.6748	9.8226	9.0770
30	25.8077	22.3965	19.6004	17.2920	15.3725	13.7648	12.4090	11.2578	10.2737	9.4269
35	29.4086	24.9986	21.4872	18.6646	16.3742	14.4982	12.9477	11.6546	10.5668	9.6442
40	32.8347	27.3555	23.1148	19.7928	17.1591	15.0463	13.3317	11.9246	10.7574	9.7791
45	36.0945	29.4902	24.5187	20.7200	17.7741	15.4558	13.6055	12.1084	10.8812	9.8628
50	39.1961	31.4236	25.7298	21.4822	18.2559	15.7619	13.8007	12.2335	10.9617	9.9148

RECEIVABLES AND PAYABLES
CHAPTER 7

PURPOSE OF CHAPTER   A major item in the current assets of most firms is the amount representing claims against customers for sales of goods or services on account. Such amounts are referred to as *accounts receivable* and represent a major source of future cash inflows. This chapter discusses the accounting for such receivables and the related bad debts expense. Receivables arising from other types of transactions are also discussed.

Most firms also acquire goods and services on account, with the resulting liabilities referred to as *accounts payable.* The chapter also discusses accounts payable and other liabilities of a current nature. The proper reporting of receivables and payables in the balance sheet is important because of the use of the balance sheet as a basis for decisions concerning the liquidity of the firm.

Receivables

WHAT ARE RECEIVABLES?   The term receivables describes all amounts resulting from transactions that give a firm some claim to future asset inflows, usually in the form of cash. Examples of such claims are:

(1) Amounts receivable from customers as the result of the sale of goods and services. Such receivables may be represented by accounts receivable or notes receivable. They may result from sales made under an arrangement calling for installment payments.
(2) Amounts receivable from officers and employees.
(3) Amounts receivable from affiliated companies.
(4) Amounts receivable as the result of the sale of assets other than merchandise inventory.
(5) Amounts receivable as the result of money-lending activities.

ACCOUNTS RECEIVABLE   The major source of receivables for most firms is the sale of goods and services to customers on account. The resulting claims are referred to as *trade receivables* and are normally reported in the balance sheet as accounts receivable unless the sale is evidenced by a note, a procedure discussed later in this chapter. The entry to record a credit sale is shown below.

Accounts receivable (Poole Company)	1,000	
Sales		1,000

This entry is recorded at the invoice price of the goods or services sold. However, it is possible that the customer might have been allowed a discount, referred to as a *trade discount,* in determining the invoice price of the item sold.

TRADE DISCOUNTS Customers are frequently allowed deductions, known as trade discounts, from the list price of merchandise. Reasons for allowing such discounts are:

(a) To avoid frequent publication of catalogues; the prices can be changed merely by changing the discount rates.
(b) To allow dealers a deduction from an advertised retail price; this practice is followed, for instance, by publishers whose advertisements state the retail prices of their books, dealers being allowed a discount from the published, or list, price.

Trade discounts may be stated as a single rate or as a series of rates. For instance, assume that the list price is $2,000 and that trade discounts of 30 per cent and 10 per cent are allowed; the sales price is computed as follows:

List price	$2,000
First discount—30% of $2,000	600
Remainder after first discount	$1,400
Second discount—10% of $1,400	140
Sales price	$1,260

Or:

$$(100\% - 30\%, \text{ or } 70\%) - (10\% \text{ of } 70\%, \text{ or } 7\%) = 63\%$$
$$63\% \text{ of } \$2,000 = \$1,260$$

No entries are made in the accounts for trade discounts; entries for sales are made at list price less trade discounts. Thus the entry to record the sale would be:

Accounts receivable	1,260	
Sales		1,260

CASH DISCOUNTS Cash discounts are deductions allowed to customers to induce them to pay their bills within a definite time. Cash discount terms are stated in the following manner: 2/10; n/30 (read, 2% in 10 days; net[1] 30 days). This means that a 2 per cent discount will be allowed if the invoice is paid within 10 days from its date, and that the purchaser, by foregoing the discount, can postpone payment of the invoice until 30 days after its date.

Cash discounts are known as sales discounts to the seller and as purchase discounts to the purchaser.[2] The seller records cash discounts as follows, assuming merchandise having an invoice price of $1,000 is sold under the terms of 2/10; n/30 and is paid for within the discount period:

Accounts receivable	1,000	
Sales		1,000
Cash	980	
Sales discounts	20	
Accounts receivable		1,000

[1]The word "net" is a misnomer because the gross amount of the invoice *(not the net amount)* is payable after ten days.

[2]The accounting for purchase discounts is discussed later in this chapter. See pages 225–226.

Because *sales discounts* reduce the amount received for sales, they are shown in the income statement *contra to sales and not as an expense.*

RETURNS AND ALLOWANCES   Customers, after receiving merchandise sold to them, may return the goods because they are not of the kind or quality ordered, or they may request and receive an allowance on the price. For the selling company such transactions reduce the revenue from sales of merchandise and are recorded as follows, assuming the return of merchandise that was sold for $200 and which has not been paid for:

Sales returns and allowances	200	
Accounts receivable		200

For the purchasing company such transactions reduce the cost of the goods acquired for resale. Accounting for purchase returns and allowances is discussed in the following chapter.

The income statement treatment of the *contra* sales accounts just discussed is illustrated below.

. . . .

Partial income statement		
Sales		$40,560
Deduct:		
Sales returns and allowances	$200	
Sales discounts	640	840
Net sales		$39,720

There is a decided trend in modern accounting practice toward simplifying the income statement by omitting the sales deductions and starting with net sales. This is particularly true in the case of widely circulated statements.

DISCOUNTS ON RETURNED SALES   Assume that a customer buys merchandise for $1,000 subject to a 2 per cent discount and pays the invoice within the discount period with a check for $980. Subsequently, the customer returns one-tenth of the goods, which had been billed at $100 and which were paid for at the net amount of $98. Should the customer receive credit for $100 or $98?

Although this is largely a matter of policy, it would seem that the credit should be $98 if the customer is to be reimbursed in cash, and $100 if the credit is to be traded out. The reasoning may be made clearer if we assume that the entire shipment is returned. Allowing a credit of $1,000 to be repaid in cash would open the way to abuses of the cash discount privilege, whereas allowing a credit of only $980 payable in merchandise would cause the customer to lose the benefit of having paid the bill within the discount period.

FREIGHT PAID AND DISCOUNT TAKEN BY CUSTOMER   It is assumed that a customer buys merchandise amounting to $1,000. The terms specify that the customer is to pay the freight, which amounts to $40, and deduct it in remitting for the merchandise. A 2 per cent discount is also allowed for cash paid within 10 days.

211

Should the 2 per cent discount be based on the $1,000 invoice, or on this amount less the $40 freight?

The discount should be based on the full amount of the invoice, because the customer is paying the freight for the seller and is entitled to a cash discount for the funds so used. The settlement should, therefore, be made as follows:

Invoice		$1,000
Deduct: Freight	$40	
Discount—2% of $1,000	20	60
Net amount of remittance		$ 940

SALES DISCOUNTS ON CUSTOMERS' PARTIAL PAYMENTS Suppose that a customer buys merchandise for $1,000 subject to terms of 2/10; n/30, that the customer is not able to pay the entire invoice, but sends a check for $588 in partial settlement within the ten-day discount period. Since the partial payment was made within the discount period, the seller may, as a matter of policy, allow the discount on the partial payment.

If the discount is granted on partial payments, the amount collected is the net amount, and therefore it is necessary to determine the amount of the gross obligation settled by the partial payment. This can be computed as follows:

$$\$588 \div .98 = \$600$$

In journal form, the collection would be recorded as follows:

Cash	588	
Sales discounts	12	
Accounts receivable		600
To record partial collection of an account receivable within the discount period.		

BAD DEBTS Although business firms selling to customers on account exercise certain procedures to ensure that customer accounts will be paid, it is inevitable that some accounts will ultimately prove to be uncollectible. Two alternative methods used to account for bad debts will now be discussed: the allowance method and the direct write-off method.

ALLOWANCE FOR UNCOLLECTIBLES One method of accounting for bad debts is referred to as the *allowance* method. It is based on the reasoning that since some bad debts are almost certain to occur, the balance sheet of the firm should show the *net* amount that is likely to be collected from the aggregate accounts receivable at the balance-sheet date—the net realizable value of the accounts.

Moreover, the income statement for each period should include all expenses applicable to the period. Losses from uncollectible accounts should, therefore, be deducted in the statement for the period in which they are *incurred*. In what period are bad debts incurred? Bad debts result from selling merchandise to customers who do not pay their accounts; such expenses are, therefore, incurred in the period in which the sales are made. To ensure a proper matching of expense with revenue, bad debts should be matched with the period's sales that caused them. For example, if goods were sold in 19_1 to customers whose accounts were found in 19_2 to be worthless, the expense was incurred in 19_1. The expense was not incurred in 19_2; it was merely discovered in that year.

Thus it is evident that both the balance sheet and the income statement would be incorrect unless recognition were given to the probable losses on accounts receivable.

Assume that a firm has total accounts receivable of $33,000 as of December 31, 19_1, the first year of operations, and it is estimated that $1,000 of this amount will not be collected. The following adjusting entry should be made at the end of 19_1:

Bad debts expense	1,000	
Allowance for uncollectibles		1,000
Estimated loss on uncollectible accounts.		

Bad debts are usually classified as an operating expense in the income statement; however, some accountants advocate reporting them contra to sales, along with sales discounts and returns and allowances.

NATURE OF ALLOWANCE ACCOUNT   The estimated loss from uncollectible accounts cannot be credited to Accounts Receivable because this account should show the gross amount owed by all customers. Therefore, we credit Allowance for Uncollectibles (sometimes called Allowance for Doubtful Accounts), which is a *contra* account to Accounts Receivable. The balances of the two accounts are shown in the balance sheet with the allowance for uncollectibles ($1,000) deducted from the face amount of the accounts receivable ($33,000), which results in the valuation of accounts receivable on the balance sheet at net realizable value ($32,000):

Accounts receivable	$33,000	
Less allowance for uncollectibles	1,000	$32,000

ESTIMATING BAD DEBTS   The adjusting entry to record the estimated bad debts at the end of the accounting period was illustrated above. However, the previous discussion did not deal with the question of how the amount of the entry is determined. The two customary methods of computing the amount of the entry are:

(1)   Increasing the allowance account by a percentage of the credit sales for the period.
(2)   Adjusting the allowance account to the amount of loss estimated by aging the accounts receivable and considering supplementary data.

Percentage of net sales   It was noted previously that bad debts are actually *incurred* in the year the credit sale takes place. Thus they should be recognized in the same period the sale is recorded in order to obtain a proper matching of revenue and expense. Such matching is attainable under the *percentage-of-sales* method of estimating bad debts.

Based upon its own past experience and by adjusting for current business conditions, a firm can determine an estimated percentage relationship between credit sales and bad debts. This percentage estimate can then be applied to actual credit sales at the end of the period to derive the estimated amount of bad debts for the period.

Assume the following data at the end of the current year.

	Debit	Credit
Accounts receivable	$20,000	
Allowance for uncollectibles		$ 315
Sales on account		215,000
Sales returns and allowances on credit sales	1,600	

Assume, further, that experience shows that the allowance account should be credited with a provision for bad debts equal to one-half of 1 per cent of the credit sales for the year less returns and allowances. The provision is computed as follows:

Sales on account	$215,000
Deduct sales returns and allowances	1,600
Net sales	$213,400

Provision $= .005 \times \$213,\!400 = \$1,\!067$

The adjusting entry to record the estimated bad debts is:

Bad debts expense	1,067	
Allowance for uncollectibles		1,067

Note that the credit to the allowance account results in a current addition over and above the balance already in the account based on prior period estimates. Thus the account will now have a *credit* balance of $1,382 ($315 + $1,067).

Use of the percentage-of-sales method requires that the estimated percentage of bad debts be kept up to date. Accounts receivable should be aged at least once a year to ensure that the amount in the allowance account is adequate. If the allowance account balance is too large or too small, the percentage applied to credit sales should be revised accordingly.

Aging accounts receivable   An alternate approach to estimating uncollectible accounts involves determining the net amount at which accounts receivable should be reported in the balance sheet. This is done by analyzing the accounts receivable to see if the balance in the allowance for uncollectibles account is considered sufficient.

After the balance needed in the allowance account has been determined, that amount is compared with its existing balance. The bad debts expense for the period is the difference between the required balance and the existing balance. For example, suppose that management reviewed the accounts receivable, totaling $20,000 (see the preceding illustration), and decided that a $1,500 balance was required in the allowance account. The bad debts expense for the period would be computed as follows:

Balance required in allowance account	$1,500
Existing balance in allowance account	315
Amount to be debited to Bad Debts Expense and credited to Allowance for Uncollectibles	$1,185

It should be noted that when this method is used, the amount of the adjusting entry is affected by the balance already in the allowance account. This was not true in the previous illustration using the percentage-of-sales method.

The preparation of an *aging schedule* is one way of estimating the probable collectibility of the accounts. For example, experience may indicate that an allowance account balance of $4,460, as computed below, would be desirable, considering the age-distribution of $77,000 of accounts receivable.

Age	Accounts receivable balances	Estimated per cent uncollectible	Allowance account requirement
1–30 days old	$32,000	1%	$ 320
31–60 days old	21,000	2	420
61–90 days old	14,000	8	1,120
91 days to 6 months old	8,000	20	1,600
Over 6 months old	2,000	50	1,000
Total accounts receivable	$77,000		
Total allowance account requirement			$4,460

However, supplementary information must also be considered; some accounts which are not old may be of doubtful collectibility, whereas accounts long past due may be collectible.

We may obtain the age-distribution by preparing a schedule of the accounts receivable on columnar paper, with columns headed to indicate various ages, such as *1 to 30 days, 31 to 60 days, 61 to 90 days, 91 days to 6 months,* and *Over 6 months.* The balance of each customer's account is analyzed to determine the age of the component elements, and the aging schedule is completed as shown below:

Accounts Receivable Aging Schedule
November 30, 19___

Name	Total debit balances	1–30 days	31–60 days	61–90 days	91 days to six months	Over six months	Credit balances
J. H. Boyce	775	525		250			
Fred Campbell	1,200		1,200				
G. C. Crane	800				800		
James Dawson	250					250	
Henry Edwards							50
Williams Company	750				750		
Total debit balances	77,000	32,000	21,000	14,000	8,000	2,000	
Total credit balances							175

In addition to being useful in the computation of the allowance account requirements, data by age groups may be used by management to determine whether collections from customers are lagging. Such a trend would be revealed by a shift in the percentage relationships among the age groups, with the older balances making up a larger share of the total receivables than heretofore. Moreover, analysis of the aged receivables by management can aid in determining whether or not credit policy is too stringent and thereby losing business by rejecting acceptable accounts.

WRITING OFF UNCOLLECTIBLE ACCOUNTS   When either of the two methods just discussed is used, an adjusting entry is recorded at the end of each accounting period, resulting in a *credit* to the allowance for uncollectible accounts. Thus the firm begins each accounting period with a credit balance in the allowance account. This account is then used to write off *actual* bad debt losses as they are determined.

Assume that the following account balances are reported after the adjusting entry is posted at the end of the period.

	Debit	Credit
Accounts receivable	$33,000	
Allowance for uncollectibles		$1,000

Let us now assume that it has been found impossible to collect $75 owed by P. K. Lane. This amount should be removed from the accounts receivable by the following journal entry.

Allowance for uncollectibles	75	
Accounts receivable (P. K. Lane)		75
Amount owed by P. K. Lane found to be uncollectible.		

It should be noted that the write-off is charged to the allowance account and not to Bad Debts Expense. If we debited the expense account when the *estimated* loss was recorded and later with *ascertained* losses, a double charge to expense would result.

Also, the *net* accounts receivable reported on the balance sheet are not affected by the write-off. Prior to writing off the worthless account the net amount of the accounts receivable was $32,000 ($33,000 − $1,000). After the write-off the net amount is still $32,000 ($32,925 − $925).

BAD DEBT RECOVERIES   Suppose that an account receivable previously written off is collected. If subsequent developments indicate that the entry writing off the account was in error, the write-off should be reversed. To illustrate, assume that P. K. Lane's account in the amount of $75 had been written off. The reversing entry, at the time of the collection from Lane, will be as follows:

Accounts receivable (P. K. Lane)	75	
Allowance for uncollectibles		75
To reverse entry writing off Lane's account.		

The cash collection will then be recorded by an entry debiting Cash and crediting Accounts Receivable (P. K. Lane).

The proper treatment of partial collections on written-off accounts is somewhat more difficult to determine because it depends upon the probability of further collections. To illustrate, assume that, after Lane's account was written off, he paid $30. If this collection and other facts indicate that the account may be collected in full, the entries should be:

Accounts receivable (P. K. Lane)	75	
Allowance for uncollectibles		75
Cash	30	
Accounts receivable (P. K. Lane)		30

If no more collections are expected, the entries should be:

Accounts receivable (P. K. Lane)	30	
Allowance for uncollectibles		30
Cash	30	
Accounts receivable (P. K. Lane)		30

DIRECT WRITE-OFF OF BAD DEBTS The use of an allowance for uncollectibles account is unique to the allowance method of accounting for bad debt losses. An alternative procedure used by some firms is referred to as the *direct-write-off* method. The latter method has practical advantages and is allowable for income tax purposes, but is theoretically inferior to the allowance method discussed earlier.

The major theoretical deficiency of the direct-write-off method is that it makes no attempt to relate the bad debts expense reported in any period to the credit sales of the period that caused the bad debts. Thus, there is improper matching of revenues and expenses. Also, the direct-write-off method results in an over-statement of the net realizable value of the accounts receivable reported on the balance sheet.

The following entry records the write-off of a $600 bad debt under the direct-write-off method.

Bad debts expense	600	
Accounts receivable (Customer's account)		600

If the entire amount is subsequently recovered in the same accounting period, the following entries record the facts:

Accounts receivable (Customer's account)	600	
Bad debts expense		600
Cash	600	
Accounts receivable (Customer's account)		600

The first entry reinstates the account, and the second entry records the receipt from the customer.

If the recovery occurs in a later accounting period, the following entries are necessary:

Accounts receivable (Customer's account)	600	
Bad debt recoveries		600
Cash	600	
Accounts receivable (Customer's account)		600

Bad Debt Recoveries is a revenue item to be reported on the firm's income statement before extraordinary items.

Under the direct-write-off method, no attempt is made at the end of the accounting period to determine what the appropriate charge to income should be for estimated bad debts. Instead, accounts are written off during the period as they are determined to be worthless, by debiting Bad Debts Expense and crediting

Accounts Receivable. Thus, a basic characteristic of this method is that the allowance for uncollectibles account is not used at all.

CREDIT BALANCES IN CUSTOMERS' ACCOUNTS It is possible that certain customer accounts in the subsidiary accounts receivable ledger may contain credit balances at the balance-sheet date. The balance in the controlling account in the general ledger then represents the net difference between the total of all customers accounts with debit balances and the total of all customers accounts with credit balances.

For example, assume that the accounts receivable ledger shows the following:

Total of customers' accounts with debit balances	$55,000
Total of customers' accounts with credit balances	(1,500)
Balance in the controlling account (net receivables)	$53,500

This information should be shown in the firm's balance sheet by reporting the $55,000 as an asset. The $1,500 should be reported as a *current liability* titled "Credit Balances of Customers' Accounts."

ACCOUNTS RECEIVABLE FROM INSTALLMENT SALES An *installment sale* is a sales arrangement whereby the selling price is collected in periodic installments. Current income tax laws allow the use of the installment method in determining taxable income, but it is allowable for income determination in financial reporting only in exceptional cases. If the installment method is used, the gross margin on installment sales (sales minus cost of installment sales) is taken into income as cash collections are received from the installment customers. Thus, if a customer has paid 60 per cent of the sales price, 60 per cent of the gross margin arising from the installment sale is taken into income and 40 per cent of the gross margin is deferred. In effect, each collection is regarded as including gross margin and a return of cost in the same proportion that these elements are included in the selling price.

For instance, if an item costing $1,200 is sold for $2,000 (gross margin of 40 per cent) payable in 20 equal installments, each collection of $100 ($2,000 ÷ 20) would be regarded as including a $60 (60 per cent of $100) return of cost and $40 (40 per cent of $100) of gross margin. In contrast, under proper accounting for financial statement purposes, the entire gross margin of $800 ($2,000 − $1,200) would be recognized in the year of sale. This is accomplished by reporting the $2,000 as a sale and reporting the $1,200 as a part of cost of goods sold for the year. Adequate provision should be made in the period of sale for estimated subsequent losses resulting from the installment sale.

NOTES RECEIVABLE A note is defined by the Uniform Commercial Code as follows:

A negotiable promissory note within the meaning of this act is an unconditional promise in writing made by one person to another, signed by the maker, engaging to pay on demand or at a fixed or determinable future time a sum certain in money to order or to bearer.

The maker, as signer of the note, is the debtor who is obligated to pay the note at maturity; the payee is the creditor to whom payment is due. The amount of the note is referred to as the *principal* or *face amount*.

MATURITY   Notes may be drawn to mature:

(1) On a date named in the note, thus: "On June 30, 19__, I promise to pay."
(2) On demand, thus: "On demand, I promise to pay."
(3) Upon the expiration of a stated period of time; the time may be stated in several ways, as indicated below.

  (a) Years, thus: "One year after date, I promise to pay."
      Such notes will mature in a subsequent year on the same day of the same month as the date of issue, except that notes issued on February 29, payable in a year having only 28 days in February, will mature on February 28.

  (b) Months, thus: "Three months after date, I promise to pay."
      Such notes will mature in a subsequent month on the same day of the month as the date of issue, except that: (1) notes dated on the 31st of a month and maturing in a month having only 30 days will mature on the 30th of the month; and (2) notes dated on the 29th, 30th, or 31st of a month and maturing in February will mature on the last day of February.

  (c) Days, thus: "Sixty days after date, I promise to pay."
      To determine the maturity date, exclude the first day and include the last. Thus the method of determining the maturity of such notes is illustrated by the following computation of the maturity of a 60-day note dated December 15, 19_2, which would mature on February 13, 19_3:

Remaining days in December (31 − 15)	16
Days in January	31
	47
Days in February (60 − 47)	13 Maturity
	60

INTEREST AND NOTES RECEIVABLE VALUATION   Notes may be either interest-bearing (rate of interest stated in the note) or noninterest-bearing (no stated interest rate). In theory, both types of notes should be reported in the balance sheet at the present value of the future principal and interest payments required by the notes. The Accounting Principles Board took the position that the determination of present value in this case should be based on an appropriate rate of interest that will not necessarily be the same as that stated in the note.[3]

Interest-bearing notes   If a note is interest-bearing and the rate of interest stated in the note reflects the prevailing market rate of interest for similar notes, then the present value of the note to maturity is equal to the principal amount stated in the note, or its face value. This amount can be reported in the balance sheet. For example, a $10,000, one-year, 8 per cent note received in exchange for land having a cost of $10,000 would be recorded as follows (assume that the stated interest rate reflects the prevailing market rate for similar notes):

Notes receivable	10,000	
Land		10,000

[3]Accounting Principles Board, "Interest on Receivables and Payables," *Opinion No. 21* (New York: AICPA, August, 1971).

219

If the note is held to maturity, the amount to be received is the sum of the principal and the interest on the principal amount. As previously discussed in the Appendix to Chapter 6, the interest calculation is made as follows:

$800 = $10,000 × .08

The entry to record receipt of the principal and interest is shown below.

Cash	10,800	
Notes receivable		10,000
Interest revenue		800

Noninterest-bearing notes If a note has no stated rate of interest, then the face value of the note does not equal its present value to maturity. The difference between the present value to maturity and the face value represents a *discount* on the note. In effect, the interest on the note is included in its face value, resulting in a present value below the face value. To report the note in the balance sheet at its face value would overstate the notes receivable.

For example, assume that the seller of the property in the previous example received a $10,000, one-year, noninterest-bearing note in exchange for the land. Since the seller is willing to wait a year before receiving the $10,000, the land is not worth $10,000 because of the time value of money. If the market rate of interest for similar notes is 8 per cent, then the present value of the note can be determined as previously illustrated in the Appendix to Chapter 6. The calculation is shown below, using the present value of $1 to be received one year in the future at a discount rate of 8 per cent, as determined from the table on page 206.

$9,259 = $10,000 × .9259

The sale of the land would be recorded as follows:

Notes receivable	9,259	
Loss on sale of land	741	
Land		10,000

When the note matures, the seller of the land will receive the face amount, or $10,000, and record the following entry:

Cash	10,000	
Notes receivable		9,259
Interest revenue		741

RECORDING TRADE NOTES RECEIVABLE The treatment just illustrated is based on the requirements of APB *Opinion No. 21*. However, the Opinion specifically exempts receivables and payables resulting from "transactions with customers or suppliers in the normal course of business which are due in customary trade terms not exceeding approximately one year."[4] Hence, normal short-term trade receivables and payables are recorded and reported at face value instead of present value, because the difference between the two is usually immaterial as a result of the short time period involved.

[4]*Opinion No. 21*, paragraph 3.

For example, assume that a company sells merchandise to a customer and in exchange receives a $1,000, one-year, noninterest-bearing note. This is normally recorded as follows:

Notes receivable	1,000	
Sales		1,000

The entire $1,000 would be reported as the amount of the note in any balance sheet prepared for the firm prior to the maturity of the note. Theoretically, this is incorrect because this treatment ignores the time value of money and thus the interest element that is inherent in the arrangement.

When the note matures, the seller receives $1,000 and the following entry is recorded:

Cash	1,000	
Notes receivable		1,000

Assume now that the note received from the customer is a $1,000, one-year, interest-bearing note, with a stated rate of interest of 8 per cent. Receipt of the note would be recorded in the same manner as before:

Notes receivable	1,000	
Sales		1,000

At maturity the seller will receive the sum of the face amount of the note, plus the interest on the face amount ($1,000 × .08 × 1 = $80), and the following entry is recorded:

Cash ($1,000 + $80)	1,080	
Notes receivable		1,000
Interest revenue		80

INTEREST CALCULATIONS FOR LESS THAN ONE YEAR The computation of interest for less than one year is based on the simple interest formula expressed as follows:

$$\text{Interest} = \text{Principal} \times \text{Annual rate of interest} \times \text{Fraction of year}$$
$$I \quad = \quad P \quad \times \quad r \quad \times \quad t$$

Note that since interest rates, unless specifically qualified to the contrary, are per annum rates, they must be restated for periods of less than one year.

For a note that is due a specific number of months after the date of the note, the interest calculation is made by determining the interest for a full year and then applying the appropriate fraction for a portion of the year, which assumes 30-day months. Thus the interest on a $10,000, 8 per cent, three-month note dated May 15 would be calculated as follows:

$$\$200 = \$10,000 \times .08 \times 3/12$$

The due date is the appropriate month (August) and the same day as when the note is dated (the fifteenth), or in this case August 15.

If time is expressed in terms of days, the exact number of days is used in the interest computation. However, for interest-computation purposes, especially for accrual purposes, it is commonly assumed that there are 360 days in a year. For example, the interest on a $10,000, 50-day, 8 per cent note dated June 17 is computed as follows:

$111.11 = $10,000 \times .08 \times 50/360$

The maturity date is August 6, as shown below:

Remaining days in June (30 − 17)	13
July	31
August [50 − (13 + 31)]	6 Maturity
	50

Note that by assuming 360 days in a year for interest computations stated in terms of days, time can be saved in computing interest by using the 60-day, 6 per cent rule. If the interest rate is 6 per cent per annum, and if the term of the loan is 60 days, then the interest on any amount can be computed merely by moving the decimal point two places to the left:

$I = P \times .06 \times 60/360 = P \times .01$

END-OF-PERIOD ADJUSTMENTS Any time an interest-bearing note, as well as most noninterest-bearing notes, involves more than a single accounting period, it is necessary that appropriate adjustments be made for accrued interest at the end of the period. To illustrate, assume that the 50-day note referred to in the previous section is dated November 20, 19_1 and that the firm receiving the note closes its books at December 31. Entries applicable to the note are illustrated below.

November 20, 19_1—To record receipt of the note:

Notes receivable	10,000.00	
Sales		10,000.00

December 31, 19_1—To record accrued interest:

Interest receivable ($10,000 × .08 × 41/360)	91.11	
Interest revenue		91.11

Interest is calculated for 41 days based upon the following:

Days in November	30
Less date of note	20
Days remaining in November	10
Days in December	31
Total	41

January 9, 19_1—To record receipt of the principal and interest:

Cash ($10,000.00 + $111.11)	10,111.11	
Notes receivable		10,000.00
Interest receivable		91.11
Interest revenue ($111.11 − $91.11)		20.00

DISHONORED NOTES A note that is not paid by the maker at maturity is said to be dishonored. The holder of the note should transfer the amount due from the maker to Accounts Receivable in order to show, for credit-information purposes, that the note has been dishonored. The total amount due from the maker of the note includes both the principal amount plus any interest on the note. For example, if a $5,000 note on which interest totals $30 is dishonored, the holder of the note would record the following entry:

Accounts receivable	5,030	
Notes receivable		5,000
Interest revenue		30

DISCOUNTING NOTES RECEIVABLE In order to acquire needed cash before the maturity date of a note receivable, a business firm may sell its notes obtained from customers to banks or finance companies. The selling of a note receivable to a financial institution is called *discounting a note receivable.* The firm holding the note receivable endorses the note (signs the back of the note) and delivers it to the financial institution. Since the financial institution expects to collect the *maturity* value (principal plus interest) from the maker of the note at the maturity date, failure of the maker to pay the note results in the endorser's being liable for the payment.

The cash received from the financial institution when the note receivable is discounted is called the *proceeds* and is equal to the maturity value less the discount. The discount is the interest charged by the financial institution to buy the note and is computed by multiplying the *discount rate* (the interest rate required by the financial institution) times the maturity value of the note times the fraction of a year the financial institution will hold the note.

For example, assume that a $2,000, 6 per cent, 90-day note receivable was held for 30 days and then discounted at a rate of 7 per cent. The firm would receive proceeds of $2,006.32, computed as follows:

Principal	$2,000.00
Interest ($2,000 × .06 × 90/360)	30.00
Maturity value	$2,030.00
Less discount ($2,030 × .07 × 60/360)	23.68
Proceeds	$2,006.32

The recording of a note receivable discounted involves a debit to Interest Expense or a credit to Interest Revenue for the difference between the face of the note and the proceeds received. For the example above, the entry would be as follows:

Cash	2,006.32	
Notes receivable		2,000.00
Interest revenue ($2,006.32 − $2,000.00)		6.32

By endorsing the note receivable to a financial institution, the firm becomes contingently liable to pay the note. The contingent nature of the liability is due to the fact that the firm that is discounting the note with the financial institution may or may not have to pay the financial institution when the note matures. If the maker pays the note, then the contingent liability no longer exists. But, if the maker defaults on the payment, the contingent liability becomes a real liability and the firm that discounted the note must pay the financial institution.

For example, assume that the discounted note receivable discussed above was dishonored (not paid at maturity) by the maker. The firm would have to pay the maturity value of the note ($2,030) plus any protest fees,[5] assumed to be $10 in this case, and would record the following entry:

Accounts receivable (maker of the note)	2,040	
Cash ($2,000 + $30 + $10)		2,040

The balance-sheet treatment of the contingent liability on discounted notes is to show on the asset side only the notes receivable held, with a footnote indicating the contingent liability, thus:

Current assets:
Notes receivable (Note D) $10,000
Note D. The Company was contingently liable at December 31, 19_2, in the amount of $2,000 on customers' notes discounted.

CLASSIFICATION OF RECEIVABLES Both accounts and notes receivable are normally shown as *current* assets in the firm's balance sheet and are based on the assumption that they will be converted into cash during the current operating cycle or one year, *whichever is longer.* In the case of installment accounts receivable, it is considered proper to include deferred payments as current assets "if they conform generally to normal trade practices and terms within the business."[6]

Accounts and notes receivable may result from transactions with officers, directors, and stockholders of a firm. When such receivables result from sales transactions in accordance with regular credit terms, they may be reported as current assets. However, they should be reported separately from amounts due from other customers. If they are not likely to be collected with any promptness, they should be reported as a noncurrent asset.

Receivables resulting from cash advances to officers and employees may be classified as current assets if their collection is assured. Very often repayment is at the convenience of the borrower and the receivable represents a noncurrent item.

Accrued receivables such as rent and interest on notes receivable are normally classified as current assets.

Payables

CLASSES OF LIABILITIES Monetary obligations payable by a firm to outsiders are referred to as *liabilities.* However, not all items classified as liabilities represent a claim for a future payment. Liabilities are classified in the balance sheet as follows:

[5]This represents the cost of protesting a dishonored note which involves written notice to each endorser that the note was presented for payment and payment was refused.

[6]Committee on Accounting Procedure, *Accounting Research Bulletin No. 43* (New York: AICPA, 1961), p. 20.

(1) Short-term or current, such as accounts and notes payable.

(2) Long-term or noncurrent, such as bonds and mortgages payable.

Short-term obligations are discussed here, but long-term obligations are discussed in Chapter 10.

CURRENT LIABILITIES   Current liabilities are obligations that must be satisfied from current assets or the creation of other current liabilities within the operating cycle or one year, *whichever is longer.* The amounts of many current liabilities are reasonably certain because of written or implied contracts. Examples are accounts payable, short-term notes payable, cash dividends payable, and accrued liabilities such as rent and interest. For other current liabilities, the amount payable may not be known exactly until the end of the accounting period because it is dependent on operations. Examples are income taxes and sales taxes payable. Finally, there are current liabilities that have to be estimated, since their *exact* amounts, due dates, and payees are not determinable. An example would be the estimated liability under product warranties.

ACCOUNTS PAYABLE   The term *accounts payable* is used in a relatively narrow sense in accounting. It is used to designate amounts owing from the purchase of goods, supplies, and services in the normal course of business. Such liabilities result from the normal trade obligations of the firm and are of a recurring nature. Since a formal debt instrument is not required each time goods are purchased on credit, these liabilities are sometimes referred to as *open* accounts or payables. Each time a liability of this type is created, the accounts payable account is credited. The corresponding debit will be to the appropriate asset or expense account.

RECORDING PURCHASE LIABILITIES   Cash discounts pertaining to merchandise sales were discussed earlier in this chapter. Such discounts also pertain to merchandise acquisitions. The two methods used to record merchandise acquisitions subject to cash discounts are the gross method and the net method.

Gross method.   Under the gross method of recording purchase discounts, the original entry is for the gross invoice amount. For example, assume that goods are purchased at a list price of $1,000 and with terms of 2/10; n/30. The purchase would be recorded as follows:

Merchandise inventory	1,000	
Accounts payable[7]		1,000

If the invoice is paid within the discount period, the payment is recorded as shown below:

Accounts payable	1,000	
Purchase discounts		20
Cash		980

[7]In this and the following entries involving debits or credits to the accounts payable account, the individual customer's account would also be debited or credited.

The foregoing procedure shows the amount of discount *taken*. The accounts do not show the amount of any discount *lost* by failure to pay bills within the discount period.

Net method. An alternative procedure of recording merchandise purchases and the related discounts is to record the purchase at the *net* amount as shown in the following entry:

Merchandise inventory	980	
Accounts payable		980

If payment is made within the discount period, the following entry records settlement of the liability:

Accounts payable	980	
Cash		980

If the bill is paid after the discount period has expired, the following entry is made:

Accounts payable	980	
Discounts lost	20	
Cash		1,000

At the end of each period for which statements are prepared, an adjusting entry debiting Discounts Lost and crediting Accounts Payable should be made for the discount on all invoices for which the discount period has expired.

The method of recording purchases and purchase discounts lost, just described, is commonly known as the "net price" procedure. Many accountants favor the net price procedure for three reasons: (1) it discloses very significant information for management purposes—namely, the amount of discount lost; (2) it records purchases at the price that will secure the goods; and (3) it results in presenting liabilities more nearly in terms of the amounts that will be expended for their settlement; if most invoices are paid before the discount period expires, the recording of purchases and liabilities in terms of gross invoice price tends to overstate the liabilities by the amount of the purchase discounts on unpaid invoices. But, since the net price procedure is unusual, if it is followed the balance sheet should indicate parenthetically that the liability on accounts payable is stated net of available discounts.

There is some difference of opinion regarding the proper position of the discounts lost account in the income statement. Many accountants believe that, as a matter of theory, the net price is the correct measure of cost. Following this theory, they would show the discounts lost in the income statement as an administrative expense, since, presumably, it is the responsibility of the administrative officers to see that obligations of the business are paid within the discount period.

Other accountants believe that cost is equal to the entire amount paid for an item. Under this theory, the balance of the discounts lost account is added to the merchandise inventory.

SHORT-TERM NOTES PAYABLE   Notes payable differ from accounts payable in that the liability is formalized by a written promise to pay. The definition of a negotiable promissory note was presented on page 218. Notes payable result most frequently from cash borrowing activities although in some industries it may be normal practice to require that the purchaser of merchandise give a note to the seller at the time of purchase. Large purchases of long-lived assets may also result in a liability evidenced by a note payable. If notes are payable within the current operating cycle or one year, whichever is longer, they are classified as current liabilities.

As noted earlier in this chapter, trade notes payable are normally reported at their face amount because of their short-term duration. The accounting for such notes will now be illustrated. Assume that a firm purchases merchandise having an invoice price of $5,000 and gives the seller a 6 per cent, 30-day note. The transaction is recorded as follows:

Merchandise inventory	5,000	
Notes payable		5,000

The following entry is recorded when the note matures:

Notes payable	5,000	
Interest expense ($5,000 × .06 × 30/360)	25	
Cash		5,025

Assume now that a firm borrows $10,000 from a bank and gives a 90-day, 7 per cent note. The liability is recorded as follows:

Cash	10,000	
Notes payable		10,000

When the note matures, the total amount to be paid is the principal amount plus interest. Payment is recorded as follows:

Notes payable	10,000	
Interest expense ($10,000 × .07 × 90/360)	175	
Cash		10,175

In the preceding illustration the note stipulated the rate of interest to be paid on the principal amount. The borrower received the total amount of the principal or face of the note at the time the note was given to the lender, repaying this amount plus interest at maturity.

An alternative borrowing arrangement involves the deduction in advance of the interest from the face amount of the note, with the borrower repaying the face amount of the note at maturity. To illustrate, assume that the borrower in the previous example signed a $10,000 noninterest-bearing note maturing 90 days after date. No interest rate is specified in the note, but the bank discounts the face amount of the note in determining the amount of cash to be received by the borrower. If it is assumed that a discount rate of 7 per cent is applied to the face amount of the note, the proceeds can be calculated as shown below:

Face amount of note	$10,000
Less discount ($10,000 × .07 × 90/360)	175
Proceeds received	$ 9,825

The borrower records the transaction as follows:

Cash	9,825	
Discount on notes payable	175	
Notes payable		10,000

When the note matures, the borrower must repay $10,000, which is $175 greater than the proceeds received. This difference represents the interest expense on the note and is recorded as shown below:

Notes payable	10,000	
Interest expense	175	
Discount on notes payable		175
Cash		10,000

It should be obvious that the discounting procedure has the effect of increasing the effective annual rate of interest paid by the borrower (7.12% = $700 ÷ $9,825) when compared with the previous procedure (7% = $700 ÷ $10,000). Although the difference between the amount repaid and the proceeds received is the same ($175), the borrower has the use of $10,000 for the 90-day period in the former example, but in the latter example he or she has the use of only $9,825.

END-OF-PERIOD ADJUSTMENTS In the previous discussion of notes receivable it was stated that whenever the term of a note involves more than one accounting period, appropriate adjustments must be recorded for any accrued interest as a part of the adjusting process at the end of the period. This is also true for notes payable. Accrued interest is recorded by debiting interest expense and crediting interest payable. When the note is subsequently paid, the appropriate charge to interest expense is the total interest on the note, less any accrued interest previously recorded.

For example, assume that the $10,000, 7 per cent, 90-day note given to the bank (illustrated on page 227) was dated December 16, 19_2 and that the borrower's accounting period ends on December 31. The following adjusting entry is required on December 31, 19_2:

Interest expense ($10,000 × .07 × 15/360)	29.17	
Interest payable		29.17

The following entry records payment of the note at maturity on March 16, 19_3:

Notes payable	10,000.00	
Interest payable	29.17	
Interest expense ($175.00 − $29.17)	145.83	
Cash		10,175.00

In the case of the $10,000 noninterest-bearing note discounted by the bank (illustrated on page 227), the following entry would be required at December 31, 19_2, assuming that the note was dated December 16, 19_2:

Interest expense (15/90 × $175)	29.17	
Discount on notes payable		29.17

When the note matures, the maker pays a total of $10,000 and the following entry is recorded:

Notes payable	10,000.00	
Interest expense ($175.00 − $29.17)	145.83	
Discount on notes payable		145.83
Cash		10,000.00

If a balance sheet is prepared for the firm while the note is outstanding, any balance in the discount on notes payable account should be shown as a deduction from the notes payable account in the liabilities section.

OTHER SHORT-TERM LIABILITIES In addition to accounts payable and short-term notes payable, there are other payables reported in the balance sheet as current liabilities because they will have to be paid in cash in the near future.

Cash dividends are recorded as a liability at the time of declaration with a credit to the dividends payable account. Any accrued interest on notes or mortgages normally represents a current liability, even though the principal amount is noncurrent. Under accrual accounting procedures, there may be several other current liabilities, such as rent, taxes, and payrolls. The accounting for payrolls is discussed at length in the appendix to this chapter.

Any cash collected before being earned is a liability because the recipient is obligated to render some service or deliver some product in the future. Examples would include the advance receipt of cash from customers (Advances from Customers) and from rent (Rent Collected in Advance). Such cash advances, sometimes referred to as *deferred revenue,* are usually classified as current liabilities in the balance sheet because they are normally earned within the current operating cycle or one year, whichever is longer.

IMPORTANT TERMS AND CONCEPTS IN CHAPTER 7

Receivables—p. 209
Accounts receivable—p. 209
Trade discounts—p. 210
Cash discounts—p. 210
Returns and allowances—p. 211
Bad debts—p. 212
Allowance for uncollectibles—p. 212
Percentage of net sales method—p. 213
Aging accounts receivable—p. 214
Bad debt write-offs—p. 216
Bad debt recoveries—p. 216
Direct write-off method—p. 217
Installment sales—p. 218

Notes receivable—p. 218
Interest-bearing notes—p. 219
Noninterest-bearing notes—p. 220
Interest calculations—p. 221
Dishonored notes—p. 223
Discounting notes receivable—p. 223
Liabilities—p. 224
Current liabilities—p. 225
Accounts payable—p. 225
Recording purchase liabilities gross—p. 225
Recording purchase liabilities net—p. 226
Notes payable—p. 227

DEMONSTRATION PROBLEM FOR REVIEW AND SELF-STUDY Denton Corporation had the following transactions during October and November of 19_9.

October   18—Sold goods to Dougherty Company for $820, freight charges to be paid by the customer. Terms, 3/10; n/30.

23—Sold goods to Floyd Corporation for $543. Terms, 3/10; n/30.

October 24—Sold goods to Bixler, Inc., for $1,230. Terms, 3/10; n/30.

26—Floyd Corporation returned goods with an invoice price of $100. A credit memo was issued.

27—Received a check from Dougherty Company, accompanied by a paid freight bill for $36.50, in payment of the goods purchased on October 18.

November 2—Received a check from Bixler, Inc., for $800 to apply on account. It is Denton Corporation's policy to allow discounts on customers' partial payments.

9—Received a check from Floyd Corporation for payment in full.

10—Sold goods to Lawrence and Associates, $630. Terms, 3/10; n/30.

12—A noninterest-bearing note receivable for $590 from Mastin Company, a customer, is dishonored and is written off as uncollectible.

18—Received a check from Lawrence and Associates in settlement of the November 10 transaction.

19—Received $300 from Linson Company, a customer whose account had been written off. A notification enclosed stated that the entire amount originally due, $620, is collectible.

20—Lawrence and Associates returned one-fourth of the shipment of November 10. A credit memo was issued.

22—Since the entry for the return by Lawrence and Associates created a credit balance in the account, Denton Corporation issued a check covering the return.

INSTRUCTIONS Prepare two-column journal entries to record the transactions.

Note Attempt to solve the demonstration problem before examining the solution that follows.

JOURNAL (Page 1)

19_1				
Oct.	18	Accounts receivable (Dougherty Company)	820.00	
		Sales		820.00
		Sold goods on terms of 3/10; n/30; f.o.b. destination.		
	23	Accounts receivable (Floyd Corporation)	543.00	
		Sales		543.00
		Sold goods on terms of 3/10; n/30.		
	24	Accounts receivable (Bixler, Inc.)	1,230.00	
		Sales		1,230.00
		Sold goods on terms of 3/10; n/30.		
	26	Sales returns and allowances	100.00	
		Accounts receivable (Floyd Corporation)		100.00
		Goods returned.		
	27	Cash	758.90	
		Freight expense	36.50	
		Sales discounts	24.60	
		Accounts receivable (Dougherty Company)		820.00
		Receipt of payment less freight and discount.		
Nov.	2	Cash	800.00	
		Sales discounts	24.74	
		Accounts receivable (Bixler, Inc.)		824.74
		Receipt of partial payment within discount period (Gross amount paid: $800 ÷ .97 = $824.74).		
	9	Cash	443.00	
		Accounts receivable (Floyd Corporation)		443.00
		Receipt of payment after discount period.		

19_1 Nov.				
	10	Accounts receivable (Lawrence and Associates) Sales Sold goods on terms of 3/10; n/30.	630.00	630.00
	12	Accounts receivable (Mastin Company) Notes receivable Dishonored note.	590.00	590.00
	12	Allowance for uncollectibles Accounts receivable (Mastin Company) To write off uncollectible note.	590.00	590.00
	18	Cash Sales discounts Accounts receivable (Lawrence and Associates) Receipt of payment within discount period.	611.10 18.90	630.00

	19	Accounts receivable (Linson Company)
		    Allowance for uncollectibles
		Notified that account previously written off is now
		    collectible.
			620.00	620.00

	19	Cash Accounts receivable (Linson Company) Receipt of partial payment on reinstated account.	300.00	300.00

	20	Sales returns and allowances
		    Accounts receivable (Lawrence and Associates)
		Customer returned portion of shipment paid for within
		    the discount period ($611.10 ÷ 4).
			152.78	152.78

	22	Accounts receivable (Lawrence and Associates) Cash Check issued to cover return of merchandise.	152.78	152.78

ASSIGNMENT MATERIAL

Questions

1   What amounts are properly includible as accounts receivable in the balance sheet?
2   What are cash discounts? How are cash discounts accounted for in the financial statements?
3   Why should estimated uncollectible accounts be recognized prior to the time they actually prove to be uncollectible?
4   Describe the procedure for writing off an uncollectible account.
5   There are two methods for estimating the adjustment for uncollectible accounts. Name the methods and explain the difference between them.
6   What is an aging schedule? How is it used by the accountant?
7   Describe the procedure for recording bad debt recoveries.
8   What is meant by the installment basis of accounting for installment sales? What is an alternative method of accounting for installment sales?
9   What is a promissory note?
10   When is a note said to be dishonored? How is a customer's dishonored note accounted for?
11   What would be the due date for a 90-day note dated March 20? What would be the due date of the note if it were payable three months after date?
12   Describe the procedure involved in accounting for the discounting of notes receivable.
13   What are current liabilities?
14   What is the difference between notes payable and accounts payable?
15   Explain why a firm that uses notes payable to borrow cash from a bank would prefer to issue an interest-bearing note instead of a noninterest-bearing note.

Short exercises

E7-1

The following accounts pertain to Dean Company for the years 19_2 and 19_3.

. . . .

Accounts receivable

19_2				
January 1	Balance			8,994 Dr.
July 20			600	
December 31		27,000	11,000	
19_3				
May 3			600	
August 26			800	
September 6			150	
December 31		39,113	18,597	

Allowance for uncollectibles

19_2				553 Cr.
January 1	Balance			
July 20		600		
December 31			1,300	
19_3				
May 3		600		
August 26		800		
September 6		150		
December 31			1,100	

Give the following amounts for both 19_2 and 19_3:

(a) Bad debts expense reported on the income statement.

(b) Worthless accounts actually written off.

(c) Net accounts receivable reported on the balance sheet at the end of the year.

E7-2 *From the following selected accounts of Spruce Corporation prepare an income statement in good form for the year ended June 30, 19_8.*

Selling expense	$ 4,000
Cash	8,100
Allowance for uncollectibles (credit balance)	900
Sales	83,000
Accounts receivable	12,400
Accounts payable	13,575
Sales returns and allowances	500
Office expense	3,300
Cost of goods sold	48,000
Merchandise inventory	12,300
Bad debts expense	1,100
Rent expense	2,500
Depreciation expense—Equipment	8,900
Sales discounts	1,400

E7-3 *The ledger of Spring Company, which closes its books on December 31, contained the following balances, before adjustment, on December 31, 19_6: Accounts Receivable, $7,500 debit; Allowance for Uncollectibles, $100 debit. It is estimated that $400 of the accounts will ultimately prove to be uncollectible.*

On January 15, 19_7 the $150 account of Bob Miller is written off as uncollectible. On July 26, 19_7 Miller made a $50 payment on the account and is expected to pay the balance by September 30, 19_7.

Present all entries needed to record the information above.

E7-4

Harris Corporation had the following note transactions during 19_7:

(1) Received a note from customer X in settlement of $800 account receivable.

(2) Received payment of $1,000 plus interest of $10 on a note received in 19_6. One-half of the interest was applicable to 19_6.

(3) Received a note from customer Y in settlement of a $500 account receivable.

(4) The note of customer X matures, with interest of $30. The maker dishonors the note.

(5) Customer Z gives the corporation a $350 note in settlement of an account receivable.

(6) Customer Y pays note plus interest of $15.

(7) Interest earned on the note of customer Z is $18 on December 31, 19_7.

What is the amount to be reported for each of the following in the financial statements prepared at the end of 19_7?

(a) Notes receivable.

(b) Interest receivable.

(c) Interest revenue.

E7-5

Give journal entries to record the proceeds and the payment of notes payable in each of the following cases:

(a) X Company borrows $15,000 and gives its bank a 60-day, 8 per cent note.

(b) X Company signs a $15,000 noninterest-bearing note that will mature in 60 days. The bank applies a discount rate of 8 per cent.

E7-6

The allowance for uncollectibles account of Burns and Company has a credit balance of $500 at the end of the accounting period just prior to recording adjusting entries. The total accounts receivable balance at this time is $44,000. If an aging of the receivables indicates that $1,600 of the receivables will likely prove to be uncollectible, the amount of the adjusting entry to record bad debts expense is (a) $1,100, (b) $2,100, (c) $4,400, (d) $1,600.

E7-7

Which of the following would not normally be classified as a current liability? (a) sales taxes payable, (b) wages payable, (c) mortgage payable, (d) interest payable.

Problems

A7-1

Ranger Company made the following sales during the month of May, 19_3:

Date	List price	Trade discounts	Credit terms	Date of payment
May 3	$800	30%	2/10; n/60	May 10
11	675	20%; 10%	2/10; n/60	May 19
14	350	15%; 10%	n/60	July 10
19	320	20%	2/10; n/30	June 20
31	398	none	3/10; n/60	June 8

Compute the amount required to pay each invoice on the date of payment.

The trial balance of Goth Company contains the following account balances on December 31, 19_3, the end of the firm's accounting period.

	Debit	Credit
Accounts receivable	30,000	
Allowance for uncollectibles		2,000
Sales		200,000
Sales returns and allowances	1,050	
Sales discounts	2,800	

Prepare the adjusting entry at the end of 19_3 under each of the following assumptions:

(a)   It is decided that the balance in the allowance account should be 10 per cent of the total accounts receivable.

(b)   An aging of the receivables indicates that $3,600 will ultimately prove to be uncollectible.

(c)   It is estimated that 1½ per cent of net sales will prove to be uncollectible.

Dyer, Inc. has a balance of $321,159 in its accounts receivable account at January 31, 19_5, the end of the firm's accounting period. An analysis of the receivables balance reveals the following:

Accounts 1–30 days old	$161,139
Accounts 31–60 days old	70,341
Accounts 61–90 days old	45,923
Accounts 91 days to 6 months old	37,934
Accounts over 6 months old	5,822
Accounts with a credit balance	(8,341)
Interest receivable on notes	5,121
Refund due from U.S. Internal Revenue Service	3,220
	$321,159

The company provides for uncollectibles on the basis of the age of the receivables as follows:

1–30 days	1%
31–60 days	5
61–90 days	12
91 days to 6 months	30
Over 6 months	50

Required:

(a)   Computation of the required balance in the allowance for uncollectibles account as of January 31, 19_5.

(b)   The adjusting entry to adjust the allowance account, assuming that the allowance account had a credit balance of $539.61 as of January 31, 19_5.

The following information was taken from the ledger of Bonnet Company on May 31, 19_2, the end of the firm's accounting period. Adjustments have not been recorded for the period.

Accounts receivable	$90,000 debit balance
Allowance for uncollectibles	503 debit balance

An aging of the accounts receivable indicates that accounts totaling $1,200 probably will prove to be uncollectible.

Summary information for the year ending May 31, 19_3 is as follows:

(1) Total sales were $281,000. Eighty per cent of the company's sales were on account.

(2) Uncollectible accounts written off totaled $1,673.

(3) Customers paid $269,000 on their accounts, including $250 that had been written off during the year as uncollectible.

It is estimated that accounts totaling $1,577 on May 31, 19_3, will prove to be uncollectible.

Required:

(a) The adjusting entry for uncollectible accounts as of May 31, 19_2.

(b) Entries to record the data for the year ending May 31, 19_3.

(c) The adjusting entry for uncollectible accounts as of May 31, 19_3.

A7-5

The following T-accounts summarize the debit-credit activity found in the books of East Company during 19_7:

Accounts receivable

1/1 Balance, after deducting		Collections from customers	
credit balances of $1,100	27,400	including overpayments	
Charge sales	317,410	of $700	311,250
Bad debts recovered	220	Write-offs	555
Cash disbursed to customers		Merchandise returns	2,210
for 1/1 credit balances	900	Allowances	810
Goods shipped to cover balance			
of 1/1 credit balances	200		
Subscriptions receivable			
for capital stock	10,500		

Allowance for uncollectibles

Write-offs	555	1/1 Balance	770
		Recoveries	220
		Provision	614

Required:

(a) Calculate the correct balance of the accounts receivable and allowance for uncollectible accounts at December 31, 19_7.

(b) Show how the information pertaining to accounts receivable and the related uncollectibles should be reported in the firm's balance sheet at December 31, 19_7.

(c) What amount should be reported for bad debts expense in the firm's income statement for 19_7?

A7-6

Selected transactions of Deer Company for October 19_3 are listed.

(1) A 6 per cent note in the amount of $2,300 is received from a customer whose account is past due. The note matures in 120 days.

(2) The above note is dishonored at maturity.

(3) Sold goods to Minos Corporation for $400; freight charges to be paid by the customer, who is authorized to deduct the amount of the charges at the time the invoice is paid. Terms, 3/10; n/30.

(4) Cash is received from a customer to cover a $560 account previously written off as uncollectible.

(5) Received a check for $1,940 to apply on account. The terms were 3/10; n/30, and the partial payment was received within the discount period. It is the corporation's policy to allow discounts on customers' partial payments.

(6) A cash refund is paid to a customer who returned one-fourth of the goods purchased under the following terms: Total invoice, $2,400; terms, 3/10; n/30. Customer had paid the invoice within the discount period.

(7) Received a check accompanied by a paid freight bill for $50 which had been deducted, from Minos Corporation within the discount period in payment of the sale in (3) above.

(8) A $73 credit is granted for merchandise returned after expiration of the discount period.

Required:

Journal entries to record the transactions.

A7-7   *The following selected transactions of Fortson, Inc., occurred during 19_5:*

19_5

August 14—Sale of $9,000 to Quality Company. Terms, 3/10; n/30.

27—Receipt of 60-day, 8 per cent note in payment of the August 14 sale to Quality Company.

September 1—Sold merchandise to Alto Corporation for $5,420. Terms, 2/10; n/30. Freight charges are to be paid by the customer and deducted from the remittance.

5—Received a check from Alto Corporation, accompanied by a paid freight bill for $36.50, in payment of the goods purchased on September 1.

18—Sold goods to Arne Corporation, $630. Terms, 3/10; n/30.

21—Arne Corporation returned one-third of the shipment of September 18. A credit memo was issued.

25—Received a check from Arne Corporation for payment in full.

October 3—Paid $330 to First National Bank because a note previously received from Lumber Company and discounted with the bank was dishonored.

7—Sold goods to Arne Corporation, $1100. Terms, 3/10; n/30.

9—The $100 account of Greta Dow was considered uncollectible and was written off.

13—The company received $300 on J. Dyer's $750 amount that had been written off. It is expected that the entire $750 will ultimately be collected.

26—Received principal and interest due on the note of Quality Company.

Required:

Journal entries to record the transactions.

A7-8   *The accounts on p. 238 are taken from the books of Doby Company as of June 30, 19_4, the end of its first year of operations.*

A. Ansley

19_4					
March	3		75.00		75.00
	15			75.00	–0–
April	8		212.00		212.00
	10	Return		40.00	172.00
	12		89.00		261.00
	15			172.00	89.00
May	9		62.00		151.00
	15			62.00	89.00
	20		214.00		303.00

B. Baker

19_3					
Oct.	8		246.00		246.00
19_4					
Feb.	8		317.00		563.00
	12		490.00		1,053.00
March	9			807.00	246.00
April	8		517.00		763.00
May	3			517.00	246.00
	11		203.00		449.00
	15	Return on 5/11 sale		45.00	404.00
June	21		510.00		914.00

C. Cone

19_3					
Sept.	5		95.00		95.00
19_4					
Jan.	15		212.00		307.00
Feb.	3		614.00		921.00
March	1			212.00	709.00
April	10		530.00		1,239.00
	15	Return on 4/10 sale		57.00	1,182.00
June	5	Note, applicable to 4/10 sale		400.00	782.00

D. Douglas

19_4					
April	10		472.00		472.00
	20	Note receivable		200.00	272.00
	29		409.00		681.00
June	10			409.00	272.00
	20		950.00		1,222.00
	28	Partial collection on 6/20 sale		650.00	572.00

E. Evers

19_4					
Jan.	3		1,218.00		1,218.00
April	4			1,218.00	–0–
May	8		550.00		550.00
	15			200.00	350.00
June	10	Return		462.00	CR112.00

The company decided to provide for doubtful accounts as follows:

1–30 days	2%
31–60 days	5%
60–90 days	15%
91 days to 6 months	30%
Over 6 months	50%

There is no balance in the Allowance for Uncollectibles as of June 30, 19_4 prior to adjustment.

Required:

(a) An aging schedule as of June 30, 19_4.

(b) Computation of the required balance in the allowance for uncollectibles account as of June 30, 19_4.

(c) The adjusting journal entry related to the information above as of June 30, 19_4.

B7-1   *The following amounts are taken from the trial balance of Betty Company on December 31, 19_2:*

	Debit	Credit
Accounts receivable	180,000	
Allowance for uncollectibles		800
Sales		300,000
Sales returns and allowances	4,600	
Sales discounts	9,400	

Required:

(a) Assuming that the firm estimates bad debts to be 1 per cent of net sales, prepare the adjusting entry required as of December 31, 19_2.

(b) Assuming that the firm ages the accounts receivable and estimates that $3,300 of the total will ultimately prove to be uncollectible, prepare the adjusting entry required as of December 31, 19_2

(c) The $500 account of customer X proves to be worthless on March 20, 19_3. Prepare the entry to write the account off the books.

B7-2   *The following information pertains to notes received from customers by Venter Company during 19_2:*

Date of note	Face amount	Rate of interest	Time period
(1) March 22, 19_2	$400	6%	90 days
(2) May 5, 19_2	300	7%	2 months
(3) August 26, 19_2	800	4½%	3 months
(4) September 28, 19_2	700	7%	120 days
(5) December 17, 19_2	500	8%	2 months

Determine the due date and the total amount that will have to be paid at maturity for each note.

B7-3   *The following transactions of Lombard Corporation occurred during the month of November, 19_4:*

November   3—Sold goods to Bob Bolling on account, $2,600.
          8—Sold goods to Sam Swallow on account, $1,413.
        11—Sold goods to East and West on account, $1,300.
        14—Issued a credit memo for goods returned by Sam Swallow, $320.
        17—Received a check from Sam Swallow, $650.
        21—Received a check from East and West for $1,300.
        25—Sold goods to Bob Bolling on account, $2,812.
        30—Issued a credit memo for goods returned by Bob Bolling, $521.
        30—Issued a credit memo for goods returned by East and West, $630.

Required:

(a)   Journal entries for the above transactions. Omit explanations.

(b)   A schedule of accounts receivable as of November 30, 19_4.

B7-4   *Below are listed certain selected transactions of Tennis Company for the month of September, 19_2.*

(1)   A collection of $864 was received within the discount period in satisfaction of $900 account receivable.

(2)   A credit of $50 was given for merchandise returned after expiration of the discount period.

(3)   Subsequently the customer in (1) returned one-third of the merchandise and directed that the account be credited.

(4)   A $400 cash loan was granted to an employee.

(5)   The company paid $62 to a customer to eliminate a credit balance in the customer's account.

(6)   Tennis Company paid $150 to a bank because a note previously discounted with the bank had been dishonored. The maker of the note was a customer of Tennis Company.

(7)   The account of a customer in the amount of $630 was considered uncollectible and was written off.

(8)   A request was received from a supplier that the supplier's bill of $25, which has been recorded by a credit to Accounts Payable, be offset against the supplier's account with Tennis Company.

(9)   A customer's 6 per cent, 120-day, $1,000 note held by Tennis Company was dishonored. Accrued interest receivable of $15 on the note was recorded on August 31, 19_2.

(10)   A 9 per cent, 60-day, $1,000 note was collected on its maturity date, September 30, 19_2.

(11)   The company received $250 from the customer whose account was written off in (7). No additional payments on the account are expected.

Tennis Company closes its books annually on August 31.

Required:

Prepare journal entries for the transactions. Omit explanations.

B7-5   *The balances of selected accounts taken from the September 30, 19_6 balance sheet of Diamond Sports Company were as follows:*

Accounts receivable	273,200 Dr.
Allowance for uncollectibles	8,196 Cr.

The following transactions affecting accounts receivable occurred during the year ended September 30, 19_7:

Sales—all on account	$1,311,416
Cash received from customers	1,428,980
The corporation's credit terms were 2/10; n/30; and customers paying $1,005,921 of the above-stated cash took advantage of the discount.	
Cash received included $2,450 recovered in accounts receivable written off as uncollectible	
Accounts written off as uncollectible	9,330
Credit memoranda issued for returned sales and allowances	18,435

An aging of accounts receivable with the estimated percentages uncollectible at September 30, 19_7 is given below:

Age	Amount	Percentage
1–30 days	$85,000	1
31–60 days	15,000	3
61–90 days	5,000	10
91 days–6 months	3,000	20
Over 6 months	All others	50

Required:

Prepare T-accounts for Accounts Receivable, Allowance for Uncollectibles, Sales Discounts, and Bad Debts Expense and show all entries required in the accounts for the year ended September 30, 19_7, including the adjusting entry to record bad debts expense for the year.

B7-6 *The only current liability on the books of Rutherford Company at March 1, 19_7 is accounts payable of $19,600. The following selected information pertains to the operations of the company for the month of March, 19_7:*

(1) Purchased merchandise from Freeman Company on account, $8,425. Terms, 3/10; n/30.

(2) Dividends of $10,000 were declared. The entire amount is to be paid in April, 19_7. (Note: Debit dividends account.)

(3) Lotus Company, a customer, paid $445 in advance for goods to be delivered in June, 19_7.

(4) Additional merchandise was purchased for $4,000. Rutherford Company signed a 9 per cent, 60-day note for the entire amount. The note matures May 15, 19_7.

(5) Supplies were purchased from Perkins Company on account, $640.

(6) A cash payment of $3,880 was made on the purchase in (1) above. The payment was made within the discount period and the appropriate discount was deducted.

(7) The following amounts are owed by Rutherford Company at March 31, 19_7:

Salaries owed to employees	$500
Rent owed for building occupied	750

The company's annual accounting period ends on March 31.

Required:

(a) Journal entries to record the above information including any adjusting entries required at March 31, 19_7.

(b) The Current Liabilities section of the firm's March 31, 19_7 balance sheet.

B7-7   *The following accounts were on the books of Hit Company on February 29, 19_4:*

ACCOUNTS RECEIVABLE SUBSIDIARY LEDGER

D. Daley

19_3					
Oct.	16		1,780.00		1,780.00
Nov.	9		4,920.00		6,700.00
	22			1,780.00	4,920.00
Dec.	3		2,015.00		6,935.00
	16		2,609.00		9,544.00
19_4					
Jan.	6			2,015.00	7,529.00
Feb.	10		595.00		8,124.00
	22	Return on 2/10 sale		63.00	8,061.00

M. Mack

19_3					
Aug.	8		850.00		850.00
Dec.	14	Return		124.00	726.00
19_4					
Jan.	10		485.00		1,211.00
	17		211.00		1,422.00
Feb.	10			485.00	937.00

R. Redding

19_3					
Oct.	17		880.00		880.00
	24			75.00	805.00
Dec.	3		591.00		1,396.00
19_4					
Jan.	17		283.00		1,679.00
Feb.	21	Note		591.00	1,088.00

W. Willis

19_3					
June	8		1,450.00		1,450.00
Sept.	12		314.00		1,764.00
	19			1,250.00	514.00
	28			314.00	200.00
Dec.	4		1,076.00		1,276.00
	6			538.00	738.00
19_4					
Feb.	10		819.00		1,557.00

The company provides for doubtful accounts on the basis of the age of the receivables, as follows:

1–30 days	1%
31–60 days	5%
61–90 days	10%
91 days to 6 months	30%
Over 6 months	40%

There is a balance of $1,312.44 in the allowance for uncollectibles account on February 29, 19_4.

Required:

(a) An aging schedule as of February 29, 19_4.

(b) Computation of the required balance in the allowance for uncollectibles account at February 29, 19_4.

(c) Calculation of the amount of the adjusting entry required to record the bad debts expense for the year.

PAYROLL ACCOUNTING
APPENDIX TO CHAPTER 7

CONTROL PROCEDURES The total amount incurred for labor costs in most business firms is a very significant item in the total of all operating expenses. There are various legal requirements that must be met pertaining to the deduction of certain amounts from employees' wages and the timely payment of such amounts to the proper authorities. In addition to amounts withheld from the employees' earnings, there are also requirements concerning the payment of certain taxes by the employer, with the amount of the taxes determined from the payroll records.

In order to attain adequate internal control over payrolls, it is very important that the three basic functions of record keeping, check preparation, and payment be segregated. The person who actually keeps the records pertaining to rates and hours worked should not be allowed to prepare the checks and distribute them. The check-signing function is obviously a very important element in the internal control system for payrolls. Other internal control procedures should cover the custody of time cards, which normally represent one of the major inputs into the payroll system, and procedures to be used in handling payroll checks for absent employees.

The area of payroll accounting, characterized by a large number of routine recurring transactions, was one of the first areas of accounting to be adapted to processing by computers. Many firms that cannot afford the cost of a computer for processing payrolls utilize outside computer services. The company providing the service supplies forms on which the employer records the data for processing by the computer. However, the fact that the operations are performed by machines does not reduce the need for a strong system of internal control.

GROSS EARNINGS The total amount earned by an employee during a pay period is referred to as *gross earnings.* The amount that is actually paid will be less than the gross earnings because of various deductions made from the earnings by the employer. Some of these deductions are required by law and the employer has no choice but to withhold them. Other deductions are at the option of the employee.

The accounting entry to record the payroll, which will be illustrated later in this chapter, results in a debit to an appropriate expense account for the gross earnings of employees. This is appropriate because the total amount earned by the employees represents a claim against the assets of the firm. Any amounts not paid directly to the employee must ultimately be paid to the appropriate taxing authorities or other payees.

There is no single term used to describe the expense account in which the total payroll is recorded. Wages and Salaries Expense is a title frequently used. In practice, the terms wages and salaries are used interchangeably, although the term *wages* usually refers to the earnings of employees whose rates are quoted on an hourly basis and the term *salaries* describes earnings quoted on a monthly or annual basis.

F.I.C.A. TAXES The Social Security Act of 1935, as amended, provides for federal government disbursements called variously "old age benefits," "old age and survivors' benefits," "old age insurance," and "old age annuities." These payments include monthly benefits to retired workers, supplementary benefits to their wives, husbands, and dependent children, benefits for survivors of deceased wage earners, "disability benefits," and lump-sum payments in some cases.[1]

The funds required for these disbursements are obtained from taxes levied under the Federal Insurance Contributions Act on employers and employees, in amounts based on wage payments for services performed. Certain services are exempt. Payments made to an independent contractor for services are not wages.

The taxes levied on employees are withheld by the employers from wage payments; these tax withholdings, as well as the taxes levied on the employers, are remitted by the employers to the District Director of Internal Revenue for the district in which the principal place of business of the employer is located. At the time of this writing, the rate is 6.13 per cent. It is scheduled for a series of increases that under the present law calls for a rate of 7.45 per cent by the year 2011.

The tax is levied on wages paid to an employee by one employer during a calendar year up to a specified maximum amount. At present the maximum wages subject to the tax in any one year is $22,900. However, if an individual works for two or more employers during a calendar year, each employer is required to pay the tax on wage payments to the employee up to $22,900 and to make similar deductions from the employee's wages. The employee can obtain a refund from the government for deducted taxes on his or her aggregate wages for the year in excess of $22,900. The employers cannot obtain a refund.

Each employer must apply to the Social Security Administration for an "identification number." This number is to be shown on the employer's payroll tax return. Each worker must apply to the Administration for an "account number," often referred to as a social security number; the employer must be informed of the account number of each employee for use in the employer's records and reports.

The law specifies that every employer who withholds taxes must furnish the employee with an annual statement on or before January 31 of the succeeding year which shows the total social security tax withheld. This is one item of information reported to the employee on his or her wage and tax statement which must be prepared for each employee. This statement is referred to as Form W-2 and is illustrated on page 250.

The employer is required to maintain records which show, for each employee the name, address, and social security number; the total compensation due at each pay date; any portion thereof not subject to tax; the period covered by the payment; and the amount of the employee's tax deducted. The employer must also keep copies of all returns and reports filed by the employer with government authorities.

[1]Since 1965 the program has included a tax for health insurance for the aged, commonly referred to as the "Medicare" program.

Illustration In order to illustrate the calculation of F.I.C.A. taxes, assume that an employee has gross earnings of $10,000 during the calendar year. The entire amount is subject to the F.I.C.A. taxes because it is below the maximum of $22,900. The employer is required to withhold $613.00 ($10,000 × 6.13%) from the employee's wages, and the employer must also pay F.I.C.A. taxes of $613.00 on the employee's wages. Thus the employee receives credit for $1,226.00 ($613.00 + $613.00) in his or her account with the Social Security Administration. The portion of the tax paid by the employer is an operating expense.

Assume now that the employee earned $30,000 during the year. The amount withheld from his or her earnings for F.I.C.A. taxes would be $1,403.77 ($22,900 × 6.13%) and the same amount would have to be paid by the employer, resulting in a total credit of $2,807.54 ($1,403.77 + $1,403.77) to the employee's account. Journal entries to record the withholding and payment of the taxes are illustrated later in this appendix.

SELF-EMPLOYED PERSONS The earnings of self-employed persons are not paid by an employer and thus will not have the taxes discussed in the previous section withheld. Since 1950, however, self-employed persons have been covered, with a few exceptions, under the Social Security Act by the payment of a tax on their self-employment income. The self-employment tax is handled in all particulars as an integral part of the payment of the individual's federal income tax. At the time of this writing the F.I.C.A. tax rate for self-employed individuals is 8.10 per cent of the first $22,900 of self-employment income earned in any calendar year.

FEDERAL UNEMPLOYMENT INSURANCE TAXES Taxes are levied against employers (but not against employees) under the Federal Unemployment Tax Act to obtain funds required to meet the provisions of the Social Security Act relative to unemployment insurance, sometimes called *unemployment compensation.* Unemployment compensation payments are not made by the federal government directly to unemployed persons; the funds obtained by the collection of federal unemployment insurance taxes are used to make grants to the various states to assist them in carrying out their own unemployment compensation programs. Laws providing for unemployment compensation payments have been enacted by all the states, the District of Columbia, and Puerto Rico.

The tax is levied on employers who (1) during any calendar quarter in the year or preceding year paid wages of $1,500 or more or (2) on each of 20 days during the calendar year or preceding calendar employed at least one individual, with each such day being in a different calendar week. It is not necessary that the 20 weeks be consecutive. Certain types of employment, such as agricultural and domestic workers, are exempt from the Federal Unemployment Tax Act.

The federal unemployment insurance tax rate is 3.2 per cent.[2] Wages in excess of $6,000 paid to any one individual during the taxable year are not subject to the tax. Although the tax rate is 3.2 per cent, the employer is entitled to a credit for taxes paid to the states, the District of Columbia, and Puerto Rico under their unemployment compensation laws. This credit cannot be more than 90 per

---

[2]Under certain circumstances, this rate may differ, but such exceptions are beyond the scope of the present discussion.

cent of the tax assessed by the federal government at a 3 per cent rate. Because of this provision in the federal law, the states have generally established a 2.7 per cent unemployment compensation tax rate. Since taxable wages are generally (though subject to some minor exceptions) computed in the same manner for both federal and state taxes, the tax rates are usually considered to be as follows:

Federal tax	.5%
State tax	2.7
Total	3.2%

Although the basic rate for most state taxes is 2.7 per cent, the tax actually payable to a state may be computed at a lower—and, in some cases, a higher— rate. Since one of the purposes of state unemployment legislation is to stabilize employment, the state laws contain provisions for merit-rating plans; under these provisions, an employer who establishes a good record for stable employment (thus reducing the claims upon state funds for unemployment compensation) may obtain the benefit of a state tax rate much lower than 2.7 per cent. In order to assure the employer of the enjoyment of the tax saving resulting from the reduced state rate, the federal law provides that an employer paying a state tax at a rate less than 2.7 per cent, as a result of the state's merit-rating plan, may deduct as a credit an amount computed at the 2.7 per cent rate or at the highest rate applicable to any taxpayer in the state, whichever is lower.

The employer must file a federal unemployment tax return with the District Director of Internal Revenue on or before January 31 following the taxable calendar year. To assure the employer of obtaining the credit for state taxes, these taxes should be paid not later than January 31.

The employer's records should contain all information required to support his or her tax return.

STATE UNEMPLOYMENT COMPENSATION TAXES   Stimulated by the enactment of the federal unemployment insurance legislation, all the states, the District of Columbia, and Puerto Rico have passed laws which have, in general, the following principal objectives:

(1)   The payment of compensation, of limited amounts and for limited periods, to unemployed workers.
(2)   The operation of facilities to assist employers in obtaining employees, and to help workers obtain employment.
(3)   The encouragement of employers to stabilize employment; the inducement offered is a reduction in the tax rate, through the operation of merit-rating systems.

Since the laws of the several states differ in many particulars, it is possible here to give only a general discussion. All the states levy a tax on employers; a very few also levy a tax on employees (in most cases, for payment of benefits in nonoccupational disability cases). The list of exempt services in the federal law is rather closely followed in most of the state laws.

In most states the tax is not assessed on salaries in excess of $6,000. In general, the state tax rate is basically 2.7 per cent, but provision is made in some of the laws for increased rates if they are essential to meet disbursement requirements. All state laws include a merit-rating plan of some kind; these plans are intended to effect lower taxes by a reduction of the tax rate or by a credit against taxes for employers who have established (during an experience period, usually of three years) a favorable record of stable employment. The *reserve ratio* plan is typical; in principle it operates as follows:

Assume that an employer's average annual payroll for three years has been $100,000.

Assume, also, that the balance in the state's reserve account with this employer is $5,000; this is the excess of the taxes paid by this employer over the amounts of benefits paid by the state to his former employees.

The reserve ratio ($5,000 ÷ $100,000) is 5%.

The higher the reserve ratio, the lower the tax rate.

Most states require employers to file returns quarterly and to pay the tax by the end of the month following the close of the quarter. Since the amount of taxable wages paid to an individual is usually one of the factors determining the amounts of benefits payable to the employee when he or she is unemployed, employers are required to file information returns showing the amount of compensation paid to each employee during the period.

The states require employers to maintain a compensation record for each employee, showing, among other things, the period of employment, the reason for termination of employment, the cause of lost time, and the amounts of periodical payments of compensation to him or her during the period of employment. The specific requirements of each state are shown in the published regulations.

FEDERAL INCOME TAX WITHHOLDING Employers of one or more employees are required to withhold federal income taxes from the wages of employees, except certain exempt wage payments.

The amount withheld from an employee's wages is affected by his or her income and the number of exemptions ($1,000 each).

An individual is entitled to:

(1) An exemption for himself or herself.

(2) An additional exemption if he or she is over 65 or will become 65 on or before January 1 of the following year.

(3) An additional exemption if he or she is blind.

If the employee is married, he or she can claim any of the above exemptions that his or her spouse could claim if he or she were employed, unless, of course, the spouse is employed and claims the exemptions.

(4) An exemption for each dependent. No additional exemptions are allowed for aged or blind dependents.

A dependent is a person who is closely related to the taxpayer, has a gross income of less than $750 for the year, and received more than one-half of his or her support for the year from the taxpayer.

In order to determine the amount of tax which the employer should withhold from an employee's compensation, the employer must know the number of exemptions claimed by the employee. Therefore, the employee is required to furnish an Employee's Withholding Allowance Certificate to the employer. This is referred to as Form W-4, a copy of which is shown below.

If the employee's exemption status changes during the year, he or she should give the employer an amended certificate. The employee is required to do so if the number of exemptions decreases and is permitted to do so if the number of exemptions increases.

Each employer must file a quarterly combined return for F.I.C.A. taxes and withheld income taxes. Except as noted, the return and taxes are due and payable on or before the last day of the month following the calendar quarter covered by the return. The effect of the following rules is to require that in many instances the taxes be deposited with an authorized commercial bank or a Federal Reserve Bank in advance of the deadline for filing the return. The amount of the taxes determines the frequency of the deposits, but the following rules summarize the basic requirements.

If the total amount of the taxes for the quarter is less than $200, no deposit is required. The taxes are paid with the quarterly return.

If the total is $200 or more at the end of the quarter, the taxes must be deposited by the last day of the first month after the end of the quarter.

If at the end of the first or second month in any quarter the cumulative total of the taxes for the quarter is $200 or more but less than $2,000, the taxes must be deposited within 15 days after the end of the month.

If at the end of any quarter-monthly period[3] the cumulative amount of the taxes for the quarter is $2,000 or more, the amount must be deposited within three banking days after the end of the quarter-monthly period.

On or before January 31 the employer should give each employee a withholding statement, a copy of which is shown on page 250, showing the employee's total wages for the preceding year and the amount of income tax and social security tax withheld therefrom. If an employee's employment is terminated, the employer should give the employee, not later than 30 days after the last wage payment,

Form **W-4** (Rev. May 1977) Department of the Treasury Internal Revenue Service	**Employee's Withholding Allowance Certificate** (Use for Wages Paid After May 31, 1977) This certificate is for income tax withholding purposes only. It will remain in effect until you change it. If you claim exemption from withholding, you will have to file a new certificate on or before April 30 of next year.

Type or print your full name	Your social security number

Home address (number and street or rural route)	Marital Status	☐ Single ☐ Married ☐ Married, but withhold at higher Single rate
City or town, State, and ZIP code		Note: If married, but legally separated, or spouse is a nonresident alien, check the single block.

1 Total number of allowances you are claiming . . . .
2 Additional amount, if any, you want deducted from each pay (if your employer agrees) . . . . $
3 I claim exemption from withholding (see instructions). Enter "Exempt" . . . .

Under the penalties of perjury, I certify that the number of withholding exemptions and allowances claimed on this certificate does not exceed the number to which I am entitled. If claiming exemption from withholding, I certify that I incurred no liability for Federal income tax for last year and that I anticipate that I will incur no liability for Federal income tax for this year.

Signature ▶ _____   Date ▶ _____, 19_____

[3]A quarter-monthly period is the period ending on the 7th, 15th, 22nd, and last day of the month.

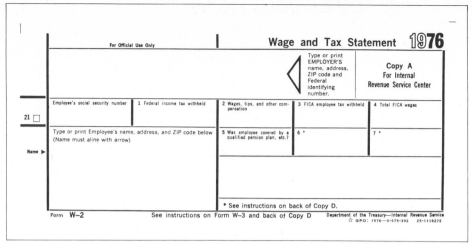

a withholding statement covering the portion of the year during which he or she was employed.

With the return for the last calendar quarter, each employer must file copies of all withholding statements given to employees. These must be accompanied by a listing of the amounts of withheld taxes as shown by the copies of the withholding statements.

OTHER PAYROLL DEDUCTIONS Employers may make other deductions from payrolls, such as the following: deductions for premiums for group hospital insurance, deductions for purchases of government bonds for the employees, and deductions for payment of union dues.

FEDERAL FAIR LABOR STANDARDS ACT The Federal Fair Labor Standards Act establishes a minimum hourly wage rate and maximum hours of work per week for certain classes of employees engaged directly or indirectly in interstate commerce, and provides that payment for overtime hours in excess of 40 hours during any work week shall be at the rate of one and one-half times the regular hourly wage. At the time of this writing the minimum wage rate is $3.10 per hour.

The act also requires that employers subject to it shall maintain a record for each subject employee showing his or her name, address, date of birth (if under 19), occupation, work week, regular rate of pay per hour, basis of wage payment (hourly, weekly, monthly, piecework, and so on), hours worked per day and per work week, daily or weekly wages at his or her regular rate, weekly excess compensation for overtime worked, miscellaneous additions to or deductions from wages, total periodical wage payments, and date of payment.

PAYROLL PROCEDURES The payroll summary on page 251 furnishes information required for the entries in the ledger accounts applicable to wages and payroll deductions. Postings of column totals may be made directly from the payroll summary to the ledger; the debits and credits are shown at the top of p. 251.

Wages expense (If it is desired to debit various accounts for amounts of wages payable for different services, an analysis must be made to obtain the information for this purpose.)   6,530.40

   F.I.C.A. taxes payable   379.35

   Income tax withholding payable   839.80

   Wages payable   5,311.25

One account, "Withholding and F.I.C.A. Taxes Payable," may be used for both the social security and the income tax withholdings, since such withheld amounts are combined and reported, with the employer's share of the F.I.C.A. tax, on the same form to the same agency of the federal government.

The amount shown in the payroll summary for F.I.C.A. withholdings is not exactly 6.13 per cent of the payroll; this is presumably because some of the wage payments represented excesses over $22,900 which therefore were not subject to the social security taxes.

The employer should compute his or her own liability for payroll taxes in the manner shown below.

Total wages	$6,530.40	$6,530.40
Wages (in excess of $22,900) not subject to F.I.C.A. taxes	342.03	
Wages (in excess of $6,000) not subject to unemployment taxes		4,026.09
Wages subject to taxes	$6,188.37	$2,504.31

Taxes:	
F.I.C.A.—6.13% of $6,188.37	$379.35
Federal unemployment—.5% of $2,504.31	12.52
State unemployment—2.7% of $2,504.31	67.62
	$459.49

PAYROLL SUMMARY

For the week ended August 7, 19_6   Date of payment August 9, 19_6

Employee No.	Income Tax Exemptions	Name	Day of Month 1 2 3 4 5 6 7 (Hours Worked)	Total Hours	Hours Over 40	Hourly Wage Rates Regular	Hourly Wage Rates Excess	Wages Regular	Wages Excess	Wages Total	F.I.C.A.	Income Tax	Hospital Insurance	Net	Check No.
35	1	John Jones	7 8 6 8 7 7	43	3	3 95	1 975	169 85	5 93	175 78	10 78	16 70		148 80	5216
36	3	Frank Brown	7 7 7 7 7 7	42	2	4 15	2 075	174 30	4 15	178 45	10 94	11 50		156 51	5217
								6,256 80	273 60	6,530 40	379 35	839 80		5,311 25	

INDIVIDUAL EMPLOYMENT AND COMPENSATION RECORD

Date Employed ____ 8–1–_6 ____
Date of Severance _____
Cause _____

Name ____ John Jones ____
Address ____ 2913 So. Burns Ave., Chicago ____
Phone ____ 229–4631 ____

Employee No. ____ 35 ____
Social Security Acct. No. ____ 325–10–0876 ____
Date of Birth ____ 8–17–38 ____

For Week In 19_6 Ended	Income Tax Exemptions	Lost Time Hours	Lost Time Cause	Hours Worked Total	Hours Worked Over-time	Regular Hourly Rate	Total Wages	F.I.C.A.	Income Tax	Hospital Insurance	Net	Check No.
Aug. 7	1	1	V	43	3	3 95	175 78	10 78	26 80		138 20	5216
14				42	2		169 85	9 94	25 20		134 71	5273

V—Voluntary time off.

The entry to record the expense and the liabilities for these taxes may be recorded as follows:

Payroll taxes expense (separate expense accounts		
may be used if desired)	459.49	
F.I.C.A. taxes payable		379.35
Federal unemployment taxes payable		12.52
State unemployment taxes payable		67.62

Both of the preceding journal entries included a credit to the F.I.C.A. taxes payable account for $379.35. In the first entry, this represented the taxes that the employee must pay; the same amount in the second entry represents the matching contribution required of the employer. Only the latter is charged to the payroll taxes expense account.

All liabilities recorded in the entries would be debited as the payments are made. When the payment of the payroll is recorded, the wages payable account is debited. The various accounts for payroll taxes are debited when the employer remits the amounts to the appropriate taxing authorities.

To meet the requirements of social security laws, it is also desirable to keep individual employment and compensation records. An example of such a record is illustrated on page 251.

WAGE-PAYMENT REPORTS TO EMPLOYEES Many employers make reports to employees of payroll deductions at the time of each wage payment. In fact, a number of states require employers to give employees written statements of deductions with each payment. If wages are paid in cash, the pay envelope may be printed as illustrated below.

THE BROWN COMPANY

Employee's
  name _____

Employee's number _____

Date paid _____ 19 ___

	Hours	Wages
Regular	_____	_____
Overtime	_____	_____
Total	_____	_____

Deductions:

   F.I.C.A. tax . . . . . . _____

   Fed. Inc. tax . . . . . _____

   State Inc. tax . . . . _____

   Insurance . . . . _____

   _____ _____

   _____ _____

    Total deductions . . . . _____

Cash enclosed . . . . _____

If wages are paid by check, a stub may be attached to the check and the data may be shown on the stub, as shown below.

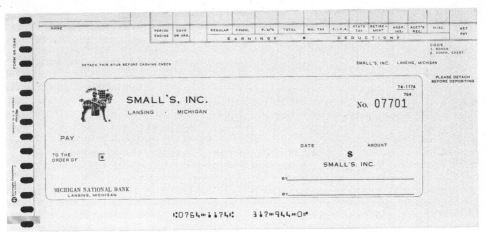

INVENTORY COSTING AND CONTROL

PURPOSE OF CHAPTER The basic procedures associated with the accounting for inventory were introduced in previous chapters, but nothing was said about the way in which the amount of a firm's inventory is determined. This determination is extremely important because of its impact on both the income statement for the accounting period and the balance sheet at the end of the period. This chapter discusses different inventory accounting, costing, and valuation methods and their relationship to the financial statements.

STEPS IN DETERMINING INVENTORY There are three steps involved in the determination of the inventory amount to be reported on a firm's balance sheet at any point in time. These are (1) determining the number of units on hand, (2) determining the cost of the inventory units, and (3) determining the valuation of inventory units at other than cost. The accounting staff of the firm may be involved in the first step, referred to as a *physical inventory*, which normally takes place once a year. The major accounting problems discussed in this chapter, however, are concerned with cost and other valuations of inventories.

CONTENT OF INVENTORY The physical count of the inventory should include all goods to which the company holds title, wherever they may be located, unless the inventory is unsalable because it is obsolete or damaged.

If a business has received a sales order but is holding the goods for future delivery, it is important to determine whether or not title has passed. The mere fact that the goods have been segregated from other merchandise may or may not mean that title has passed to the customer. If title has passed, an entry for the sale should have been made and the goods should be excluded from the inventory; if title has not passed, no sales entry should have been made and the goods should be included in the inventory.

On the other hand, goods that have been ordered but not received by the buyer's inventory date may properly belong in the purchaser's inventory. If the goods are in transit, the general rules concerning passing of title are as follows:

If the goods were shipped f.o.b. destination and have not arrived at the destination, they belong to the seller. F.o.b. destination means "free on board cars (or other means of transportation) at destination." Under these terms the seller bears the transportation charges.

If the goods were shipped f.o.b. shipping point, they belong to the purchaser. F.o.b. shipping point means that the seller delivers the merchandise to the carrier, but the purchaser bears the transportation charges.

If title has passed and the goods are included in the inventory, an entry for the purchase should have been recorded.

A *consignment* is a shipment of merchandise from the owner (called the *consignor*) to another party (called the *consignee*) who attempts to sell the goods as an agent for the consignor. The consignor should not record consignments as sales, and the consignee should not record them as purchases, because there is no change in the ownership of the goods. Because the consignor has not made a sale, no profit should be recognized at the time of making the consignment; no sales entry should be made until a sale is reported by the consignee. Any unsold goods in the hands of the consignee at the end of the accounting period should be included in the consignor's inventory at cost plus consignment expenditures applicable to the unsold goods.

INVENTORY AND INCOME DETERMINATION The importance of accurately determining a firm's inventory is shown in the following illustration, which pertains to the first two years of a company's operations.

	Year 1	Year 2
Beginning inventory	$ -0-	→$3,000
Add: Merchandise acquisitions (purchases)	5,000	6,000
Total merchandise available for sale	$5,000	$9,000
Deduct: Ending Inventory (Balance Sheet)	3,000	5,000
Cost of goods sold (Income Statement)	$2,000	$4,000

It is obvious from the illustration that the amount at which the ending inventory is reported for year 1 will affect not only the balance sheet asset total at year end, but also the net income for the year since the ending inventory is a factor in determining the cost of goods sold. The ending inventory amount for year 1 also affects the income statement of the following year because the year 1 ending inventory becomes the beginning inventory for year 2, thus affecting the calculation of cost of goods sold for the second year. A more detailed illustration of the impact of inventory errors on financial statements is presented later in the chapter.

INVENTORY ACCOUNTING METHODS There are two methods of accounting for inventories and, therefore, cost of goods sold. They are:

Perpetual inventory method.
Periodic inventory method.

The journal entries required to record the acquisition and sale of merchandise will differ in each method. The supporting records needed to account for the inventory will also vary.

PERPETUAL INVENTORY METHOD The basic characteristic of the perpetual inventory method is that it results in a continuous record of the inventory on hand. Changes in the inventory are recorded, as they occur, by debits and credits in the inventory account. Thus, *incoming* merchandise is recorded at cost by a debit to the inventory account. When merchandise is sold or returned to the supplier for some reason, and thus becomes *outgoing* merchandise, the inventory account is credited to record, at cost, the reduction of the asset. The offsetting debit is to Cost of Goods Sold when the merchandise is sold and to Cash or Accounts Payable when the merchandise is returned to the supplier.

Because, under the perpetual method, the cost of all merchandise purchased is debited to the inventory account and the cost of all goods sold or returned is credited to the inventory account, the inventory account balance should indicate the cost of goods on hand at the end of the period, provided that no merchandise has been lost or stolen. At the same time, the cost of goods sold account will contain the amount to be reported on the income statement for the period.

PERPETUAL INVENTORY RECORDS   The use of the *perpetual* inventory method requires the use of detailed subsidiary records for each type of goods in the inventory. These records are used to record, in both quantities and amounts, the purchases, sales, and balance of the inventory on hand at any time. Such a supplementary record is illustrated below.

INVENTORY CARD					
DESCRIPTION		Room Air Conditioners			
DATE	QUANTITIES			DOLLARS		
	PURCHASED	SOLD	BALANCE	DEBIT	CREDIT	BALANCE
19--						
April 1			4			$1,200
3	10		14	$3,000		4,200
18		9	5		$2,700	1,500

As a check on the accuracy of these detailed or subsidiary records, it is advisable and customary to make counts of the physical inventory from time to time. Many concerns count portions of the inventory throughout the year and take a complete inventory annually. Should the physical inventory indicate that there are errors in the perpetual inventory records, then the records must be adjusted to agree with the physical count.

When subsidiary records are maintained their purpose is to provide a record in greater detail than that supplied by a ledger account. Presumably, such details are useful to those managing the business or the subsidiary record would not be maintained. Subsidiary records are not part of the ledger, but the data recorded therein should tie in with the balance shown in the related ledger account. For example, assume that a business carries ten different kinds of merchandise in its inventory and that it maintains in addition to the inventory account in the ledger a subsidiary record which accounts for the changes in the inventory by type of merchandise. Thus there would be an inventory card (subsidiary record) for each kind of merchandise; the total of the balances shown in the inventory cards should be in agreement with the inventory account balance in the general ledger, as illustrated below.

Balances per inventory cards:

Merchandise type 1	$ 100
2	200
3	300
4	400
5	500
6	400
7	300
8	200
9	100
10	1,000
Total per subsidiary record	$3,500
Balance per inventory account in the general ledger	$3,500

PERIODIC INVENTORY METHOD   Under the *periodic* inventory method, no continuous record of the inventory on hand is maintained. Incoming merchandise is recorded in a separate account; the usual account title is "Purchases." Also, no entry for the cost of goods sold is recorded at the time of the sale. Inventory amounts are determined periodically by making a physical count of the merchandise on hand. The accountant then makes use of an adjusting entry to have the accounts show the cost of goods sold for the period and the inventory balance as of the end of the period.

Cost of goods sold   Under the periodic inventory method the cost of goods sold is determined by the computation shown below. The amounts conform to the data used in the inventory card shown on page 256.

Computation		Source of data
Inventory of merchandise at beginning of period		
(4 units at $300)	$1,200	Inventory account
Purchases during period (10 units at $300)	3,000	Purchases account
Cost of merchandise available for sale	$4,200	
Deduct inventory on hand at end of period		(a) For the quantity on
(5 units at $300)	1,500	hand: physical count.
		(b) For the cost information:
		business documents.
Cost of goods sold during period	$2,700	

End-of-period adjusting entry   As indicated by the above cost-of-goods-sold computation, the cost of merchandise that was available for sale equals the total of the following ledger account balances:

Inventory (before adjustment this account balance shows the inventory which was on hand at the beginning of the period)	$1,200
Purchases	3,000
Amount that was available for sale	$4,200

An end-of-period adjusting entry can be used to apportion (regroup or reclassify) the amount that was available for sale, so that the ledger will show the following:

(1)	Ending inventory—Unexpired cost (asset)	$1,500
(2)	Cost of goods sold—Expired cost (expense)	2,700
	Amount that was available for sale	$4,200

The adjusting entry applicable to the data used in the illustration, which would be dated as of April 30, is as follows:

JOURNAL

19—				
Apr.	30	Inventory (ending)	1,500	
		Cost of goods sold	2,700	
		Inventory (beginning)		1,200
		Purchases		3,000
		To adjust the inventory account to show the end-of-period inventory and to place the cost of goods sold in a separate account.		

INVENTORY METHODS CONTRASTED The contrasting features of the two inventory methods can be seen in the following illustration based on the data shown in the Inventory Card.

Beginning inventory—4 units	$1,200
A purchase during the period—10 units	3,000
A sale during the period—9 units:	
Selling price	3,600
Cost of units sold	2,700
Ending inventory—5 units	1,500

Periodic Method			**Perpetual Method**		

Beginning inventory:

Inventory				Inventory		
1,200				1,200		

Purchase:

Purchases	3,000		Inventory	3,000	
Accounts payable		3,000	Accounts payable		3,000

Sale:

Accounts receivable	3,600		Accounts receivable	3,600	
Sales		3,600	Sales		3,600

Adjusting entry under the periodic method—ending inventory determined by physical count:

Inventory	1,500				
Cost of goods sold	2,700				
Inventory		1,200	Cost of goods sold	2,700	
Purchases		3,000	Inventory		2,700

COST OF GOODS AVAILABLE FOR SALE In addition to the invoice price of inventory, there may be other elements of cost incurred to acquire the merchandise. Any additional costs necessary to put the goods into place and condition for sale would be included. Examples are duties, freight, storage, insurance while the goods are being transported or stored, and costs incurred during any aging period. Some of these factors affecting the net cost of merchandise purchases were discussed in the previous chapter. Several elements which might comprise the cost of merchandise acquired for resale are summarized in the following tabulation:

Inventory—beginning of period			$ 7,000
Purchases (Invoice cost of goods purchased)		$30,000	
Add transportation in		1,000	
Total		$31,000	
Deduct:			
Purchase returns and allowances	$700		
Purchase discounts	500	1,200	29,800
Cost of goods available for sale			$36,800

When the *periodic* inventory method is in use, separate accounts are used for the items included in the above tabulation. The debit-credit plan for the separate accounts illustrated is indicated by the following journal entries based on the above data.

Purchases	30,000	
Accounts payable		30,000
Purchases for the period on account.		
Terms, 2/10; n/30.		
Transportation in	1,000	
Cash		1,000
Payment for transportation charges on goods purchased.		
Accounts payable	700	
Purchase returns and allowances[1]		700
Purchase returns (and/or allowances) for the period.		
Accounts payable	25,000	
Purchase discounts		500
Cash		24,500
Payments on accounts within the discount period.		

The end-of-period adjusting entry required to update the inventory account when the *periodic* inventory method is used was previously illustrated on page 258. The entry on p. 260 is basically the same, but it has been expanded to include the additional accounts involving the cost of merchandise acquisitions in the illustration above; it also assumes an ending inventory (determined by physical count) of $10,000.

[1]When a customer returns merchandise previously purchased, the transaction is referred to as *purchase return*. The customer may elect to keep the merchandise with the seller granting a price reduction. The latter arrangement is referred to as a *purchase allowance*. In either instance, if the purchase has not been paid for, the effect of the transaction is to reduce the amount owed to the seller.

Adjusting entry:

Inventory (ending)	10,000	
Cost of goods sold	26,800	
Purchase returns and allowances	700	
Purchase discounts	500	
Inventory (beginning)		7,000
Purchases		30,000
Transportation in		1,000

When the perpetual inventory method is in use, such items are debited and credited to the inventory account, as indicated in the following ledger account.

INVENTORY

Beginning inventory	7,000		7,000 dr.
Purchases	30,000		37,000 dr.
Transportation in	1,000		38,000 dr.
Purchase returns and allowances		700	37,300 dr.
Purchase discounts		500	36,800 dr.
Sales of merchandise		26,800	10,000 dr.

ALLOCATING COST OF GOODS AVAILABLE FOR SALE It should be noted that the cost of goods available for sale is not the same concept as cost of goods sold. In the previous illustration the total cost of all units of inventory on hand at some time during the period is $36,800. However, this includes the cost of units sold during the period, plus the cost of units still on hand at the end of the period. It is necessary that this amount be allocated between the *units sold* and the *units still on hand* in order to determine net income for the period.

This allocation process is the crux of the inventory costing problem and is present whether the perpetual or periodic accounting method is used. In the perpetual method, the allocation takes place during the period as sales are recorded, whereas it is necessary only at the end of the accounting period when the periodic accounting method is used. The process may be shown as follows:

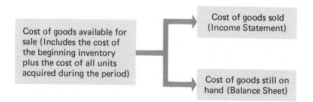

The solution to the allocation problem involves the selection of one of several alternative inventory costing methods.

INVENTORY COST SELECTION It is a readily observable fact that prices change. Therefore, identical goods may be acquired at different costs. Consequently, accountants are faced with the problem of determining which costs apply to the goods that have been sold, and which costs apply to the goods that remain in the inventory.

Several of the more widely used methods of selecting the costs which are to be regarded as applicable to the goods in the inventory are discussed in the following paragraphs.

For purposes of illustration, assume the following facts.

	Units	Unit cost	Total
Beginning inventory	2	$10	$20
First purchase	1	11	11
Second purchase	1	10	10
Third purchase	1	12	12
Fourth purchase	1	13	13
Cost of goods available for sale			$66
Total quantity available for sale	6		
Sold during the period	4		
Ending inventory	2		

SPECIFIC IDENTIFICATION   If the goods on hand can be identified as pertaining to specific purchases, they may be inventoried at the costs shown by the related invoices. Assume, for instance, that the two units in the ending inventory can be identified as having been acquired by the second and fourth purchases; the cost for inventory purposes would be:

Units	Unit cost	Total
1	$10	$10
1	13	13
Ending inventory		$23

Specific identification is not practical where each unit or lot is indistinguishable from another; the bookkeeping would be too costly. Also, the method has the disadvantage of being susceptible to schemes devised to manipulate earnings. A dishonest manager could select low-cost items to include in cost of goods sold, or claim that the low-cost items were sold even though higher-cost items were actually sold, to increase reported net income.

WEIGHTED-AVERAGE METHOD   Under the *weighted-average* method, the cost of the goods available for sale is divided by the total units available for sale. The resulting average unit cost is used for pricing the ending inventory. The computation is illustrated below.

Cost of goods available for sale (beginning inventory cost + cost of purchases)	$66
Total units available for sale (beginning inventory units + units purchased)	6
Average unit cost ($66 ÷ 6)	$11
Ending inventory ($11 × 2)	$22
Cost of goods sold ($11 × 4)	$44

The costs determined by the weighted-average method are affected by purchases early in the period as well as toward the end of the period; therefore, on a rising market, the weighted-average unit cost will be less than current unit cost, and, on a falling market, the weighted-average unit cost will be in excess of the current cost.

FIRST-IN, FIRST-OUT METHOD   This method is based on the assumption that the first goods purchased are the first to be sold, and that the goods which remain are of the last purchases. This method, referred to as the *FIFO* (initial letters of *first-in, first-out*) method, is most commonly used. Applying this method to the facts used for illustrative purposes, the two units in the ending inventory would be regarded as having been acquired by the last two purchases and would be priced as follows:

Units	Unit cost	Total
1	$12	$12
1	13	13
Ending inventory		$25

The assumption that the older stock is usually the first to be disposed of is generally in accordance with good merchandising policy. There are, of course, cases in practice where the assumption does not square with the facts; for instance, the first coal dumped on a dealer's pile will be the last sold.

This method has also been considered desirable because it produces an inventory valuation which is in conformity with price trends; because the inventory is assumed to consist of the most recent purchases and is costed at the most recent costs, the pricing follows the trend of the market.

LAST-IN, FIRST-OUT METHOD   Under this method, referred to as the *LIFO* method, the oldest costs are assumed to be applicable to the goods on hand. In the case assumed here, the two units in the ending inventory would be costed at the unit cost used in costing the two units in the beginning inventory. Thus, the ending inventory would be computed as follows:

Units	Unit cost	Total
2	$10	$20

If the ending inventory had been composed of three units, the third unit would be costed under *LIFO* by using the unit cost applicable to the first purchase. Thus, an ending inventory of three units would total $31 under *LIFO*. Graphically, the beginning and ending inventories under *LIFO* can be shown as follows:

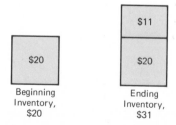

If, one year hence, the ending inventory should again consist of two units, the $11 unit would be dropped, since it was the last one added to the inventory, and the two units would be costed at $10 each for *LIFO* inventory purposes.

PERPETUAL INVENTORY COSTING In each of the four preceding illustrations it was assumed that the costing of the inventory occurred at the end of the accounting period, which is, in fact, what happens when the periodic inventory method is used. However, each of the costing methods can also be used when *perpetual* inventory records are maintained. As noted previously, in the latter case the costing method is applied each time a sale takes place instead of waiting until the end of the accounting period.

In order to illustrate perpetual inventory costing, the same data used on page 261 will be used here. However, it is necessary that the timing of the sales be known. The information is recast below with the four units sold during the period shown in a different manner.

	Units	Unit cost
Beginning inventory	2	$10
First purchase	1	11
First sale	1	
Second purchase	1	10
Third purchase	1	12
Second sale	2	
Third sale	1	
Fourth purchase	1	13

Just as in the previous illustration, the firm begins the period with a total inventory of two units, acquires four additional units during the period, and sells a total of four units during the period, leaving an ending inventory of two units.

SPECIFIC IDENTIFICATION Application of the specific identification method requires that the cost of each sale be determined by identifying the specific purchase price of the units sold. For example, at the time of the first sale, the inventory consisted of two units purchased at a unit cost of $10 and one unit purchased at a cost of $11. If it is assumed that the unit sold is identified as one of the units on hand at the beginning of the period, its cost would be recorded as $10.

WEIGHTED-AVERAGE METHOD Perpetual inventory procedures normally require the use of a moving weighted average because a new average is calculated each time a sale takes place. For example, at the time of the first sale of one unit, the inventory cost consists of the following:

Cost of goods available for sale:		
2 units @ $10 (beginning inventory)	$20.00	
1 unit @ $11 (first purchase)	11.00	$31.00
Total units available for sale		3
Average unit cost ($31.00 ÷ 3)		$10.33 (rounded)

The unit sold at this time is recorded at a cost of $10.33, leaving two units in the inventory at a total cost of $20.67 ($31.00 − $10.33). The cost of the second sale is calculated as follows:

Cost of goods available for sale:

2 units	$20.67	
1 unit @ $10.00 (second purchase)	$10.00	
1 unit @ $12.00 (third purchase)	$12.00	$42.67
Total units available for sale		4
Average unit cost ($42.67 ÷ 4)		$10.67 (rounded)

The cost of the two units sold is $21.34 ($10.67 × 2), and the two units remaining in the inventory at this time are reported at a cost of $21.33 ($42.67 − $21.34).

FIRST-IN, FIRST-OUT METHOD   Use of the *FIFO* method results in a cost of $10.00 being assigned to the first unit sold, since the cost is associated with the beginning inventory. At the time of the second sale the inventory on hand consists of the following costs:

1 unit @ $10.00 (beginning inventory)	$10.00	
1 unit @ $11.00 (first purchase)	11.00	
1 unit @ $10.00 (second purchase)	10.00	
1 unit @ $12.00 (third purchase)	12.00	$43.00

The total cost of the two units sold at this time is $21.00, or the $10.00 cost of the one unit remaining from the beginning inventory plus the $11.00 cost of the unit in the first purchase.

LAST-IN, FIRST-OUT METHOD   Under the *LIFO* method, the cost of the unit in the first sale is $11.00, which is determined by costing out the most recent acquisitions. At the date of the second sale the inventory consists of the following costs:

2 units @ $10.00 (beginning inventory)	$20.00	
1 unit @ $10.00 (second purchase)	10.00	
1 unit @ $12.00 (third purchase)	12.00	$42.00

The cost of the two units in the second sale is $22.00, or the most recent costs recorded in the inventory records ($12.00 + $10.00).

SELECTING A COSTING METHOD   It is obvious from the preceding illustrations that the choice among the various alternative inventory costing methods will have an effect on the amounts reported in a firm's income statement for the cost of goods sold. This, in turn, will affect the gross margin and net income figures. To illustrate the point by a simple, and rather arbitrary, example, let us assume that a company sells one unit of a commodity each year. At the beginning of the first year it purchased one unit for $1 and marked it to sell for $1.50, because a gross margin of $.50 was considered necessary to cover expenses and leave a reasonable net income. Before any sale was made in the first year, the company purchased a second unit for $1.10 and raised its selling price of the commodity to $1.60—a price that will provide for replacing the merchandise and $.50 additional.

Assuming that one unit is subsequently sold for $1.60:

By the *FIFO* method, the cost of goods sold and gross margin would be computed thus:

Sale	$1.60
Cost of unit sold	1.00
Gross margin	$ .60

and the ending inventory would be costed at $1.10.

By the *LIFO* method, the cost of goods sold and gross margin would be computed thus:

Sale	$1.60
Cost of unit sold	1.10
Gross margin	$ .50

and the ending inventory would be costed at $1.00.

Suppose that two separate companies were involved in the above case, one using *FIFO* and the other *LIFO*. Actually, the companies would be in the same position; each would have sold one unit and have one unit remaining in the inventory, but their financial statements would *not* be identical.

Those favoring the *LIFO* method think of the expression "last-in, first-out" as not necessarily referring to an assumption regarding the flow of goods, but rather to an assumption regarding the flow of costs. The advocates of *LIFO* maintain that, during periods of changing costs and selling prices, more meaningful income statements are produced if relatively "current" costs are assigned to cost of sales; this, in their opinion, achieves a better matching of costs and revenues.

The income statement emphasis of the *LIFO* method results in an inventory amount in the balance sheet consisting of the older acquisition costs. Use of the method during a period of rising prices can result in an ending inventory amount that is considerably less than the current cost of the inventory.

In many instances, the income tax effect of the choice is a significant factor in selecting a method. In a period of rising prices, use of the *LIFO* method results in a lower reported taxable income and thus lower income tax payments. Many firms saw the method as a means of reducing income tax payments and increasing the amount of cash available for expansion and other purposes during the mid-1970's, when interest rates on borrowed money reached the highest level in years.

LOWER-OF-COST-OR-MARKET VALUATION   It was stated earlier in the chapter that after determining the cost of the units in a firm's inventory, it is necessary to determine the amount at which the inventory will be reported in the firm's financial statements. Under the *lower-of-cost-or-market* basis for determining the dollar amount of inventories, cost is used except under certain conditions, described later, where market is lower than cost. The term "market," as used here, means current replacement cost.

The lower-of-cost-or-market method is one of the earliest applications of an old rule of accounting conservatism often stated as follows: Anticipate no profit and provide for all possible losses. Thus, if the price for which an item can be purchased declines during the period and if the item is still in the inventory at the end of the period, the decline is reported in the period in which it occurs, not in the period in which the inventory item is sold.

In making the necessary comparisons to see whether market is lower than cost, the accountant may refer to some of the following sources for information regarding market prices: current catalogues or other price lists; recent invoices; market price quotations as published in newspapers or trade journals; specific quotations furnished by suppliers for this purpose; current contracts for the purchase of like goods.

In the use of market prices for purposes of comparison with cost, if prices vary for different quantities, the accountant should use, for inventory purposes, the price for the quantity typically purchased by the business.

APPLICATION OF LOWER-OF-COST-OR-MARKET There are three ways of applying the cost-or-market method:

(1) By comparing the cost and market for each item in the inventory and using the lower figure in each instance.

DETERMINATION OF LOWER OF COST OR MARKET—ITEM-BY-ITEM METHOD

	Quantity	Unit price Cost	Unit price Market	Extension at lower of cost or market
Men's department:				
Suits	200	$40	$37	$ 7,400
Coats	100	31	35	3,100
Ladies' department:				
Dresses	300	10	12	3,000
Coats	80	30	32	2,400
Inventory at lower of cost or market				$15,900

(2) By comparing the total cost and market for major inventory categories and using the lower figure for each category.

DETERMINATION OF LOWER OF COST OR MARKET—CATEGORY METHOD

	Quantity	Unit price Cost	Unit price Market	Extended Cost	Extended Market	Lower of cost or market
Men's department:						
Suits	200	$40	$37	$ 8,000	$ 7,400	
Coats	100	31	35	3,100	3,500	
Total				$11,100	$10,900	$10,900
Ladies' department:						
Dresses	300	10	12	$ 3,000	$ 3,600	
Coats	80	30	32	2,400	2,560	
Total				$ 5,400	$ 6,160	5,400
Inventory at lower of cost or market						$16,300

(3) By comparing the total cost and market for the entire inventory, and using the lower figure.

DETERMINATION OF LOWER OF COST OR MARKET—TOTAL INVENTORY METHOD

	Quantity	Unit price		Extended		Lower of cost or market
		Cost	Market	Cost	Market	
Men's department:						
Suits	200	$40	$37	$ 8,000	$ 7,400	
Coats	100	31	35	3,100	3,500	
Ladies' department:						
Dresses	300	10	12	3,000	3,600	
Coats	80	30	32	2,400	2,560	
Total				$16,500	$17,060	
Inventory at lower of cost or market						$16,500

For many years it was considered imperative to use the item-by-item method; the category and total inventory methods are now regarded as acceptable alternatives. However, the alternative adopted must be used consistently through the years. This consistency requirement applies to inventory methods generally and is not limited to the cost-or-market method.

EFFECT OF LOWER-OF-COST-OR-MARKET ON GROSS MARGIN   Although the lower-of-cost-or-market method is a conservative one and is generally accepted, the application of the rule distorts the gross margin of a period in which lower-than-cost figures are used for inventory-costing purposes.

To illustrate, assume that a company buys goods at a cost of $10,000 and sells one-half of them for $7,500. The gross margin on the goods sold may be determined as follows:

Sales	$7,500
Cost of goods sold (½ of $10,000)	5,000
Gross margin on sales	$2,500

But assume that the inventory valuation of the remaining half at the lower of cost or market is only $4,000. The income statement would usually be prepared in the following manner.

Sales		$7,500
Cost of goods sold:		
Purchases	$10,000	
Less inventory at end of period	4,000	6,000
Gross margin on sales		$1,500

A more comprehensive statement of the facts would be:

Sales		$7,500
Cost of goods sold:		
Purchases	$10,000	
Less inventory—at cost	5,000	5,000
Gross margin on sales		$2,500
Less decline in replacement cost of inventory		1,000
Gross margin less inventory adjustment		$1,500

Of course, to prepare a statement in the latter form illustrated, it would be necessary to compute an aggregate inventory valuation at both cost ($5,000) and the lower of cost or market ($4,000) in order to determine the amount of reduction.

It should also be pointed out that some accountants believe that the lower-of-cost-or-market rule is inconsistent. That is, decreases in replacement cost are given some consideration, but increases in replacement cost are ignored.

NET REALIZABLE VALUE   Merchandise that can no longer be sold at a price in excess of cost because of damage, wear, obsolescence, or any other reason should be reported in the inventory at its net realizable value. Thus the loss on such goods is taken in the period in which the loss developed, not in the period in which the goods are sold.

Net realizable value is the estimated price that will be received for the inventory in the ordinary course of business less the estimated costs of disposal. For example, an item costing $500 is assumed to have an estimated selling price of only $300 because of style changes. Estimated costs to dispose of the item total $50. The appropriate inventory amount for the merchandise is $250 ($300 − $50).

INVENTORY DISCLOSURE MATTERS   The costing method used to price inventories, as well as the valuation method used, should be disclosed either in the balance sheet itself or in comments or footnotes accompanying the balance sheet.

Two examples of such disclosure are presented below:

Inventory, at cost, on a last-in, first-out basis	$123,600
Inventories, on a first-in, first-out basis, at the lower of	
cost or market	$321.400

Many firms follow the alternative of presenting this information in a separate Summary of Significant Accounting Policies which precedes the footnotes to the financial statements or is presented as the first footnote.[2]

In addition to the disclosure requirements above, the Securities and Exchange Commission has recently implemented a requirement that certain replacement cost information be presented for inventories when the reporting firm meets certain criteria.

INVENTORY ERRORS AND NET INCOME   As noted earlier in the chapter, inventory errors affect both the balance sheet and income statement. For example, if the December 31, 19_1 inventory is overstated $5,000, then *both* current assets and the net income before income tax will be overstated $5,000. The effect on the income statement can be seen from the following illustration, in which two income statements are presented. In the first the correct ending inventory, $30,000, is used; in the second the ending inventory is overstated $5,000.

[2]Accounting Principles Board, "Disclosure of Accounting Policies," *Opinion No. 22* (New York: AICPA, April, 1972).

DEUCE COMPANY
Income Statement
For the Year Ended December 31, 19_1

	Correct ending inventory		Incorrect (overstated) ending inventory	
Sales		$100,000		$100,000
Cost of goods sold:				
Beginning inventory, 12/31/19_	$20,000		$20,000	
Purchases	70,000		70,000	
Total	$90,000		$90,000	
Deduct ending inventory, 12/31/19_1	30,000	60,000	35,000	55,000
Gross margin		$ 40,000		$ 45,000
Operating expenses		25,000		25,000
Net income before income tax		$ 15,000		$ 20,000

If it is assumed that the corporate income tax rate is 30 per cent, the effect on net income from the $5,000 ending inventory overstatement is $3,500, thus:

Income Statement—Concluded

Net income before income tax—per above		$ 15,000		$ 20,000
Income tax		4,500		6,000
Net income		$ 10,500		$ 14,000

Because the ending inventory of one year is the beginning inventory of the next year, a misstatement of an inventory will affect two income statements—the statement for the year in which the inventory error occurred, and the statement for the following year. This can be demonstrated by continuing the preceding illustration through 19_2. It is assumed that the correct inventory for December 31, 19_2, is $25,000.

DEUCE COMPANY
Income Statement
For the Year Ended December 31, 19_2

	Correct beginning inventory		Incorrect (overstated) beginning inventory	
Sales		$110,000		$110,000
Cost of goods sold:				
Beginning inventory, 12/31/19_1	$30,000		$ 35,000	
Purchases	65,000		65,000	
Total	$95,000		$100,000	
Deduct ending inventory, 12/31/19_2	25,000	70,000	25,000	75,000
Gross margin		$ 40,000		$ 35,000
Operating expenses		27,000		27,000
Net income before income tax		$ 13,000		$ 8,000
Income tax		3,900		2,400
Net income		$ 9,100		$ 5,600

If the annual net income figures shown above are added to arrive at net income for the two-year period, it will be seen that the net income figure for the two-year period is unaffected by the inventory error.

	Net income computed with		
Year	Correct inventories	An inventory error	Error in net income
19_1	$10,500	$14,000	$3,500 over
19_2	9,100	5,600	3,500 under
Total	$19,600	$19,600	–0–

Although an inventory overstatement causes an overstatement of net income in the first year, it causes an offsetting understatement of net income in the second year. Thus, inventory errors are counterbalancing over a two-year period. The net income is misstated in each of the two years, but it is not misstated in the aggregate.

If the December 31, 19_1 inventory had been understated instead of overstated, the opposite results would have occurred; the 19_1 net income would have been understated and the 19_2 net income would have been overstated.

The above observations are summarized below:

If the *ending* inventory is:	Net income for the period will be:
Overstated	Overstated
Understated	Understated
If the *beginning* inventory is:	Net income for the period will be:
Overstated	Understated
Understated	Overstated

ESTIMATING INVENTORIES It is sometimes convenient to be able to estimate a firm's inventory. Perhaps it is desired to prepare financial statements without taking a physical count or to estimate the cost of an inventory that has been destroyed. Two methods used for such purposes are discussed below.

Gross margin method The gross margin method uses the relationship between net sales and gross margin (profit) to estimate the ending inventory.

To illustrate this method, assume that the goods on hand June 30, 19_2, were destroyed by fire; no physical inventory had been taken since December 31, 19_1. The books showed the following balances at the date of the fire:

	Debit	Credit
Sales		$90,000
Sales returns and allowances	$ 700	
Inventory, December 31, 19_1	20,000	
Purchases	65,000	
Purchase returns and allowances		1,000
Transportation in	800	

Assume, further, that the company's records show that in prior years it made a gross margin of approximately 25 per cent of net sales. Therefore, if it may be assumed that the same rate of gross margin was realized during the six months preceding the fire, the inventory at the date of the fire can be estimated as follows:

Inventory, December 31, 19_1		$20,000
Add net purchases:		
Purchases	$65,000	
Transportation in	800	
Total	$65,800	
Less purchase returns and allowances	1,000	64,800
Total goods available for sale		$84,800
Less estimated cost of goods sold:		
Gross sales	$90,000	
Less sales returns and allowances	700	
Net sales	$89,300	
Less estimated gross margin—25% of $89,300	22,325	66,975
Estimated inventory, June 30, 19_2		$17,825

Retail inventory method   As its name suggests, the retail method of inventory costing is frequently used in department and other retail stores; it is suitable for use by wholesalers also. To apply the retail method, it is necessary to maintain records of:

Purchases (and any returns thereof)—at both cost and selling price.
Sales (and any returns thereof)—at selling price.

With this information it is possible to determine a ratio of cost to selling price, the uses of which are described below:

(1) To prepare an estimate of the inventory for interim financial statements without taking a physical inventory; the procedure is illustrated as follows:

	Cost	Selling price
Inventory at beginning of period	$ 10,000	$ 15,000
Purchases during the period	109,000	188,000
Transportation in	3,000	
Deduct purchase returns	2,000*	3,000*
Totals	$120,000	$200,000

(Ratio of cost to selling price $= \dfrac{\$120,000}{\$200,000} = 60\%$)

Sales		180,000
Estimated inventory at selling price		$ 20,000
Estimated inventory under the retail method of inventory valuation—60% of $20,000 equals	$ 12,000	

*Deduction

(2) To permit costing a physical inventory at marked selling prices and reducing the selling price valuation by applying the ratio of cost to selling price, as follows:

	Cost	Selling price
Determining ratio of cost to selling price:		
Inventory at beginning of period	$ 22,000	$ 40,000
Purchases (none returned)	169,000	260,000
Transportation in	4,000	
Totals	$195,000	$300,000

$$\left(\text{Ratio of cost to selling price} = \frac{\$195,000}{\$300,000} = 65\%\right)$$

Applying cost ratio to ending inventory:	
Physical inventory priced at marked selling prices	$ 50,000
Ratio of cost to selling price—See above	65%
Ending inventory for financial statements	$ 32,500

Using selling prices when compiling the physical inventory reduces the clerical work considerably because it eliminates the work of referring to invoices for cost data and dealing with the problem created by the fact that identical merchandise may have been acquired at several different cost figures and possibly from different suppliers.

IMPORTANT TERMS AND CONCEPTS IN CHAPTER 8

Free on board (f.o.b.)—p. 254

Consignment—p. 255

Perpetual inventory method—p. 255

Periodic inventory method—p. 257

Cost of goods available for sale—p. 259

Cost of goods sold—pp. 256, 260

Inventory costing methods—p. 260

Specific identification—pp. 261, 263

Weighted average—pp. 261, 263

First-in, first-out (FIFO)—pp. 262, 264

Last-in, first-out (LIFO)—pp. 262, 264

Lower-of-cost-or-market—p. 265

Net realizable value—p. 268

Disclosure—p. 268

Inventory errors—p. 268

Gross margin method—p. 270

Retail inventory method—p. 271

DEMONSTRATION PROBLEM FOR REVIEW AND SELF-STUDY Benson Company had an inventory of 500 units at June 1, 19_1. The units had a cost of $150 each. During the month of June the following purchases were made:

Date	Units	Unit cost
June 4	1,500	$155
9	1,000	157
15	2,500	156
26	2,000	160

A periodic inventory was taken on June 30, 19_1; 1,300 units were on hand. On July 1, 19_1 the company opened a bargain basement and began stocking less expensive inventory items, but it continued to carry its regular line of products in its main salesroom. By December 31, 19_1 the inventory on hand in the main salesroom and in the bargain basement was as follows:

	Quantity	Unit price Cost	Unit price Market
Main salesroom:			
Item A	90	$210	$230
Item B	105	100	100
Item C	80	75	95
Item D	70	160	145
Bargain basement:			
Item E	12	155	165
Item F	22	60	70
Item G	35	50	45
Item H	50	120	115

For many years the Company prepared annual financial statements at December 31, but in order to obtain a bank loan, the firm has been requested to prepare financial statements at March 31, 19_4. The records of the Company contain the following information concerning its inventory for the period January 1, 19_4 to March 31, 19_4:

	Cost	Selling price
Inventory, December 31, 19_3	$145,550	$219,000
Purchases	475,000	720,600
Sales		704,600
Transportation in	2,050	
Purchase returns and allowances	3,000	
Sales returns and allowances		4,600
		25,500

INSTRUCTIONS

(a) Calculate the firm's inventory at June 30, 19_1 under each of the following costing methods:
  (1) Weighted-average.
  (2) First-in, first-out.
  (3) Last-in, first-out.
(b) Calculate the firm's inventory at December 31, 19_1. Use the lower-of-cost-or-market method applied to:
  (1) Each item in the inventory.
  (2) The inventory in each department.
  (3) The entire inventory.
(c) Using the retail inventory method, compute the estimated inventory at March 31, 19_4. Carry per cents to two decimal places and round all dollar amounts to the nearest dollar.

Note Attempt to solve the demonstration problem before examining the solution that follows.

(a)

Costing method	Quantity	Unit cost	Total
(1) Weighted-average:			
Beginning inventory	500	$150.00	$ 75,000.00
Purchases: June 4	1,500	155.00	232,500.00
June 9	1,000	157.00	157,000.00
June 15	2,500	156.00	390,000.00
June 26	2,000	160.00	320,000.00
	7,500		$1,174,500.00
Weighted-average cost: $1,174,500.00 ÷ 7,500 = $156.60 per unit.			
Inventory	1,300	$156.60	$ 203,580.00
(2) First-in, first-out:			
June 25 purchase	1,300	$160.00	$ 208,000.00
(3) Last-in, first-out:			
June 1 balance	500	$150.00	$ 75,000.00
June 4 purchase	800	155.00	124,000.00
	1,300		$ 199,000.00

(b)

Item	Quantity	Unit price Cost	Unit price Market	Extended Cost	Extended Market	Lower of cost or market Each item	Lower of cost or market Each department	Lower of cost or market Entire inventory
Main salesroom:								
Item A	90	$210	$230	$18,900	$20,700	$18,900		
Item B	105	100	100	10,500	10,500	10,500		
Item B	80	75	95	6,000	7,600	6,000		
Item D	70	160	145	11,200	10,150	10,150		
Totals—main salesroom				$46,600	$48,950		$46,600	
Bargain basement:								
Item E	12	155	165	$ 1,860	$ 1,980	1,860		
Item F	22	60	70	1,320	1,540	1,320		
Item G	35	50	45	1,750	1,575	1,575		
Item H	50	120	115	6,000	5,750	5,750		
Totals—bargain basement				$10,930	$10,845		10,845	
Grand totals				$57,530	$59,795			$57,530
Inventory						$56,055	$57,445	$57,530

(c)

	Cost	Retail
Inventory, December 31, 19_3	$145,550.00	$219,000.00
Purchases during the period	475,000.00	720,600.00
Transportation in	2,050.00	
Deduct purchase returns and allowances	3,000.00*	4,600.00*
Totals	$619,600.00	935,000.00
(Ratio of cost to retail = $619,600.00 ÷ $935,000.00 = 66.27%)		
Sales		$704,600.00
Deduct sales returns and allowances		25,500.00*
Net sales		$679,100.00
Estimated inventory at selling price		$255,900.00
Estimated inventory at cost ($255,900.00 × 66.27%)	$169,585.00	

* Deduction

Questions

1 Describe two inventory accounting methods.
2 What is the purpose of maintaining detailed subsidiary perpetual inventory records?
3 How is the cost of goods sold determined under the periodic inventory method?
4 What is consignment merchandise? When should the consignor recognize profit on consignment merchandise?
5 What items enter into the determination of cost of goods available for sale?
6 Describe the two most widely used bases for determining the dollar amount at which the inventory is stated.
7 How is inventory costed under each of the following methods?
    (a) Specific identification.
    (b) Weighted-average method.
    (c) First-in, first-out method.
    (d) Last-in, first-out method.
8 How will the choice between the *FIFO* and *LIFO* costing methods affect net income in a period in which all purchases are made at the same per-unit price as the cost of the beginning inventory? What will be the effect in a period of constantly rising prices?
9 Describe the lower of cost or market basis for determining the dollar amount of inventories. What are three ways in which it can be applied?
10 Under what circumstances might the lower-of-cost-or-market rule distort the gross margin?
11 How should obsolete and damaged merchandise be accounted for?
12 Describe the retail inventory method. What are two situations in which it may be used to estimate inventories?

Short exercises

E8-1   *From the following information, taken from the records of Alomar Company, compute the cost of goods available for sale. The company uses the periodic inventory method.*

Sales	$63,000
Cash	21,000
Transportation in	1,800
Accounts payable	20,250
Purchases	82,500
Sales discounts	2,550
Purchase discounts	2,925
Merchandise inventory	24,000
Purchase returns and allowances	2,175
Sales returns and allowances	1,950

E8-2   Smith Corporation had the following transactions pertaining to its inventory during January, 19_3:

January	1	Balance, 100 units at $3 each.
	4	Purchased 100 units at $4 each.
	6	Sold 45 units at $10 each.
	10	Purchased 100 units at $5 each.
	18	Sold 60 units at $12 each.
	25	Sold 50 units at $12 each.

The company uses perpetual inventory procedures. Compute the following under both the first-in, first-out and last-in, first-out costing methods:

(a) Inventory reported on the balance sheet as of January 31, 19_3.
(b) Cost of goods sold for the month.

E8-3   The following data pertain to Lance Corporation for the year ended December 31, 19_3:

Beginning inventory	$12,000
Purchases	44,250
Transportation in	1,800
Purchase returns and allowances	1,575
Purchase discounts	1,050
Cost of goods sold	39,000

How would the information above be reflected in the unadjusted trial balance of the corporation at the end of the year under each of the following assumptions: (a) Periodic inventory procedures are used; (b) Perpetual inventory procedures are used.

E8-4   The following inventory errors were made on the records of Lambert Company during the period 19_1 to 19_5. None of the errors was discovered until early in 19_6.

Date	Ending inventory error
December 31, 19_1	$ 500 understatement
December 31, 19_2	300 overstatement
December 31, 19_3	750 overstatement
December 31, 19_4	800 understatement
December 31, 19_5	1,000 understatement

What is the amount by which the net income for each of the five years is misstated?

E8-5   Harris Company had an inventory of $15,000 on June 1, 19_7. The following data are taken from the records for June:

Sales	$30,000
Sales returns and allowances	1,275
Sales discounts	825
Purchases	37,500
Purchase returns and allowances	450
Purchase discounts	675

In the past, the company's gross margin has averaged 30 per cent of net sales. Compute the estimated inventory on June 30, 19_7.

E8-6

The following information is taken from the records of Lee Company, which uses the periodic inventory method.

Purchases	$60,000
Beginning inventory	10,000
Transportation in	1,000
Ending inventory	13,800
Purchase returns and allowances	1,000
Purchase discounts	1,200

Prepare the end-of-period adjusting entry required by the information above.

E8-7

Max Company uses the perpetual inventory method. The following information pertains to inventory item A for the current year:

Beginning inventory: 5 units @ $3.00
                               4 units @ $3.25

Purchases:
   1/25—10 units @ $3.25
   3/17—15 units @ $3.50
   9/30—12 units @ $4.00

Sales:
   1/15—8 units
   5/5—20 units
   5/29—5 units
   11/3—7 units

Assume that the firm uses the last-in, first-out inventory costing method. The cost of goods sold for the period is (a) $142.75, (b) $137.00, (c) $138.00, (d) $161.00, (e) none of the above.

E8-8

Use the information in E8-7, but assume that the company uses the periodic inventory method. The cost of goods sold for the period is (a) $161.00, (b) $138.00, (c) $137.00, (d) $142.75, (e) none of the above.

Problems

A8-1

Gould Company's beginning inventory and purchases for the month of June 19_3 were as follows:

	Units	Unit cost
June 1 Beginning inventory	1,000	$25
4	2,500	27
9	1,500	29
15	2,000	28
26	500	30

A periodic inventory was taken on June 30, 19_3, and 1,250 units were on hand. Compute the ending inventory under each of the following costing methods:

(a)   Weighted average.

(b)   First-in, first-out.

(c)   Last-in, first-out.

Crowder Company's beginning inventory on January 1, 19_2, consisted of 5,000 units costing $1.25 per unit. Purchases for the six-month period ending June 30, 19_2, were as follows:

	Quantity	Total cost
January 15	3,500	$ 4,200
March 1	4,500	6,075
April 15	2,500	3,200
May 5	4,000	5,200
May 26	2,500	3,375
June 20	3,000	4,200
	20,000	$26,250

The inventory on June 30, 19_2, consisted of 7,000 units. All sales during the period were made at a price of $2.50 per unit.

Assuming the use of the periodic inventory procedure, prepare a partial income statement showing the gross margin on sales, using each of the following costing methods:

(a) Weighted average. (Compute to the nearest cent.)

(b) First-in, first-out.

(c) Last-in, first-out.

The following amounts are found on the books of Bragg Company on January 31, 19_2:

	Cost	Selling price
Inventory, December 31, 19_1	$10,916	$16,500
Purchases	35,625	54,050
Sales		52,845
Transportation in	382	
Purchase returns and allowances	240	350
Sales returns and allowances		2,045

Using the retail inventory method, compute the estimated inventory as of January 31, 19_2. Round per cents to two decimal places and round all dollar amounts to the nearest dollar.

A fire destroyed the entire inventory of Johnson Wholesalers during the night of September 10, 19_1. Although most of the accounting records were destroyed, sufficient information was recovered to compute the following balances:

As of June 30, 19_1, the end of the company's accounting period, the inventory was valued at $18,900. As of September 10, 19_1, selected account balances were as follows:

Purchases	$11,520
Purchase returns and allowances	165
Transportation in	192
Sales	27,650

One of the items recovered from the fire was a copy of a condensed income statement for the preceding year.

JOHNSON WHOLESALERS
Condensed Income Statement
For the Year Ended June 30, 19_1

Sales		$141,000
Cost of goods sold		81,780
Gross margin		$ 59,220
Deduct:		
Selling expenses	$28,800	
Administrative expenses	13,815	42,615
Net income before income taxes		$ 16,605
Income taxes		4,151
Net income		12,454

Compute the cost of the inventory destroyed by the fire. Round amounts to the nearest dollar.

B8-1

Brown Company had a beginning inventory of 100 units of item M-22, costing $1.35 per unit, on April 1, 19_1. During the month the following purchases were made:

	Quantity	Unit cost
April 5	125	$1.45
12	100	1.49
20	90	1.55
24	80	1.60

A count of the inventory on April 30, 19_1 revealed that there were 125 units on hand. Determine the ending inventory by each of the following costing methods:

(a) Weighted-average.

(b) First-in, first-out.

(c) Last-in, first-out.

B8-2

Fuller Company had the following transactions pertaining to an item of inventory during August 19_1:

August   1—Beginning inventory, 50 units at $15 each.

        9—Sold 35 units at $35 each.

     20—Purchased 75 units at $16 each.

     26—Sold 30 units at $38 each.

(a) Compute the August 31, 19_1 inventory using each of the following costing methods. Assume that perpetual inventory procedures are used.

(1) First-in, first-out.

(2) Last-in, first-out.

(b) Assuming the use of the *FIFO* costing method, record the sale of August 26 under each of the following:

(1) Periodic inventory procedures.

(2) Perpetual inventory procedures.

B8-3

The information below is taken from the records of Andrews Corporation for the year 19_1.

Sales	$375,000
Purchases	277,500
Purchase returns and allowances	12,000
Purchase discounts	10,500
Transportation in	1,800
Beginning inventory	37,500
Ending inventory	33,750
Other expenses	70,500

Required:

(a) Compute the following for the year:

    (1) Cost of goods sold.

    (2) Gross margin.

    (3) Net income.

(b) Assuming the use of the lower-of-cost-or-market rule, compute net income when:

    (1) Market value of the ending inventory is $29,550

    (2) Market value of the ending inventory is $35,100

B8-4

Carson Appliance Outlet maintains two departments. On May 31, 19_3 the inventory by departments was as follows:

		Unit price	
	Quantity	Cost	Market
Main salesroom:			
Refrigerators	68	$315	$345
Dryers	79	150	150
Dishwashers	60	115	145
Automatic washers	53	150	135
Bargain basement:			
Refrigerators	28	145	150
Dryers	33	60	55
Dishwashers	20	45	40
Automatic washers	18	80	70

Compute the ending inventory, using the lower of cost or market, applying the method to: (a) Each item in the inventory; (b) The inventory in each department; (c) The entire inventory.

B8-5

The management of Grill Department Store has become concerned about the suspected theft of merchandise from Department X, over which a single clerk has exclusive control. A surprise inventory count in the department on May 15, 19_4, revealed an inventory with a retail value of $21,300.

The company's fiscal period ends on March 31, and its records contain the following information concerning Department X for the period from March 31 to May 15:

	Cost	Selling price
Inventory, March 31, 19_4	$12,600	$18,390
Purchases	9,255	12,330
Sales		8,400
Transportation in	254	
Purchase returns and allowances	293	420

Compute the estimated loss to the company, at cost, due to the employee's theft during the period March 31 to May 15.

The after-closing trial balance of Hood Corporation as of December 31, 19_1 included the following:

Inventory—Product A	$10,800
Inventory—Product B	10,650
Retained earnings	18,000

An audit of the inventory accounts and procedures of the company reveals the following data:

(1) Purchases of 600 units of Product A on November 30, costing $9 each, in transit on December 31, 19_1, were not included in the closing inventory, although the invoice from the vendor had been recorded. The goods were shipped f.o.b. Hood Corporation's plant.

(2) 200 units of Product A were sold to Holly Company and the sale was recorded. Holly Company requested that delivery be postponed until January 15, 19_2. The cost of these goods was included in the Product A inventory on December 31, 19_1, although title had passed to Holly Company.

(3) The inventory records included a purchase of 75 units of Product B at $18 each which were in transit on December 31, 19_1 and not included in the closing inventory. These goods had been shipped f.o.b. shipping point.

(4) Another 75 units of Product B had also been excluded from the ending inventory because they were not on hand when the inventory count was made. These units were shipped to Hooks Wholesalers on consignment, and, as of December 31, 19_1, had not been sold by the consignee.

(5) The company uses the *FIFO* inventory costing method. The accountant had computed the ending inventory by using the following data:

Product A

			Quantity	Price	Total
January	1	Inventory	800	$10	$ 8,000
February	15	Purchase	450	11	4,950
April	1	Purchase	350	12	4,200
	28	Purchase	350	12	4,200
June	5	Purchase	350	11	3,850
August	1	Purchase	600	9	5,400
October	1	Purchase	500	8	4,000
November	30	Purchase	600	9	5,400
		Totals	4,000		$40,000
December	31	Inventory	1,200		

Product B

			Quantity	Price	Total
January	1	Inventory	600	$14	$ 8,400
	20	Purchase	150	15	2,250
March	25	Purchase	180	16	2,880
May	30	Purchase	225	16	3,600
July	15	Purchase	165	17	2,805
September	10	Purchase	135	18	2,430
November	1	Purchase	195	17	3,315
December	15	Purchase	120	19	2,280
		Totals	1,770		$27,960
December	31	Inventory	750		

His computations were as follows:

Product A: 1,200 × $ 9 = $10,800

Product B: 600 × $14 = $ 9,400
                 150 × $15 =   2,250
                 ‾‾‾
                 750          $10,650

Required:

(a) Compute the correct inventory balances as of December 31, 19_1.

(b) Compute the correct retained earnings balance at December 31, 19_1.

LONG-LIVED ASSETS

CHAPTER 9

PURPOSE OF CHAPTER This chapter discusses the accounting for property, plant, and equipment, for natural resources, and for intangibles.[1] Such assets are characterized as having a relatively long life and therefore generating goods and services over several years. Thus such long-lived assets are noncurrent and nonmonetary (i.e., they are not cash and fixed money claims owned).

Property, plant, and equipment are assets of a long-lived nature that are acquired and held for use in the business and are not intended for resale to customers. Such long-lived assets are operational or productive assets because they are used in the operations of a business to produce goods and services over several years.

Natural resources are long-lived assets that are physically consumed and converted into inventory and sold. They are, in effect, a long-term inventory of raw materials to be removed physically from the property.

Whereas property, plant, equipment, and natural resources are tangible long-lived assets that have physical substance, intangible assets have no material and physical substance. Their future service potential is in the *right* their ownership confers.

The accounting problems associated with such long-lived assets can be classified as follows: (1) determining the cost of long-lived assets, (2) allocating the cost of long-lived assets to those periods benefited, and (3) accounting for the disposal of long-lived assets. All of these problems are discussed in this chapter.

COST ALLOCATION Long-lived assets are acquired with the expectation that they will contribute to the revenues of the firm during their life. For most long-lived assets, their useful life is limited and the cost of such assets, less estimated salvage, should be charged off gradually against revenues during the period of their known or estimated useful life. The terminology most commonly used to describe the systematic assignment of asset costs to expense is summarized below.

> Depreciation, which is the systematic assignment of the cost of tangible assets other than natural resources to expense.
> Depletion, which is the systematic assignment of the cost of natural resources to expense.
> Amortization, which is the systematic assignment of the cost of intangible assets to expense.

CLASSIFICATION Long-lived assets may be classified, with respect to their nature and the type of cost assignment to which they are subject, as follows:

---

[1]Such assets are often referred to as *fixed assets,* but such terminology is obsolete and misleading (i.e., they are not really fixed).

(A) Tangible:
    (1) Property, plant, and equipment.
        (a) Subject to depreciation.
            Examples: Buildings, machinery, tools and equipment, delivery equipment, furniture and fixtures.
        (b) Not subject to depreciation.
            Example: Land.
    (2) Natural resources, subject to depletion.
        Examples: Timber tracts, mines, oil wells.
(B) Intangible:
    Examples: Patents, copyrights, franchises, leasehold improvements, trademarks, goodwill.

These classes of long-lived assets will be discussed in greater detail in the balance of the chapter.

PROPERTY, PLANT, AND EQUIPMENT—VALUATION   At acquisition, the valuation of property, plant, and equipment is at *cost,* which is in conformity with the historical-cost assumption. After acquisition, the valuation of property, plant, and equipment (other than land) is at cost less accumulated depreciation—so-called *book* or *carrying amount* (value). Thus property, plant, and equipment are reported in the balance sheet at their book amounts, which represent the portion of their cost to be allocated to expense in future periods. In other words, after acquisition, the cost of property, plant, and equipment (other than land) is periodically expensed so that it is matched with the revenues generated by the assets over their useful lives in accordance with the matching assumption.

Since cost is considered the proper valuation of property, plant, and equipment, it is regarded as an improper accounting practice to write up such assets to current market prices that are above cost to the entity.[2] There is, however, no objection to the disclosure of current market price data as supplementary information.[3]

DETERMINATION OF COST   As a general statement, it can be said that the cost of an asset is measured by, and is equal to, the *cash equivalent of the consideration parted with* when acquiring the asset. As applied to acquisitions of property, plant, and equipment, cost includes all expenditures made in acquiring the asset and putting it into a place and condition in which it can be used as intended in the operating activities of the business. Thus the cost of machinery includes such items as freight and installation costs in addition to its invoice price.

For example, assume that an item of equipment is purchased at a gross invoice price of $2,600. The acquiring firm is entitled to a 5 per cent discount for payment of the purchase price within the discount period and the firm pays $450 for

[2]Accounting Principles Board, "Status of Accounting Research Bulletins," *Opinion No. 6* (New York: AICPA, October, 1965), paragraph 17.

[3]A recent Securities and Exchange Commission requirement makes supplementary replacement-cost data mandatory for corporations that meet certain criteria. The requirement affects the largest industrial corporations and is effective for fiscal years ending on or after December 25, 1976.

installation and $210 for transportation charges. The entry to record the acquisition is shown below.

Equipment		3,130
Cash		3,130
Invoice price	$2,600	
Less 5% discount	130	
Net invoice price	$2,470	
Add: Installation	450	
Transportation	210	
	$3,130	

Separate accounts should be kept for land and buildings, because the buildings are subject to depreciation whereas the land is not. If land and a building thereon are purchased for a lump-sum price, an appraisal may be necessary to provide a basis for dividing the cost between the land and the building. For instance, assume that land and a building are purchased at a lump-sum price of $50,000. An apportionment of the cost on an appraisal basis may be made as follows:

	Appraisal amount	Fraction	Cost apportionment
Land	$15,000	¼	$12,500
Building	45,000	¾	37,500
Total	$60,000		$50,000

The acquisition would be recorded by the following entry:

Land	12,500	
Building	37,500	
Cash		50,000

The procedure shown above is used any time different assets are acquired for a single acquisition price.

LAND   If, in order to obtain a desired building site, it is necessary to acquire land that has an unsuitable building thereon, the land account should be charged with the entire purchase price. Under such circumstances it will be necessary to demolish or remove the unsuitable building. Any costs incurred in this connection should also be charged to the land account, because the costs were incurred to make the site suitable for building purposes. Any amounts received as salvage from the disposal of the building should be credited to the land account.

The cost of land purchased without improvements includes the purchase price, broker's commission, fees for examining and recording title, surveying, draining, clearing (less salvage), and landscaping. Any interest accrued at the date of purchase on mortgages or other encumbrances and paid by the purchaser and any accrued taxes paid by the purchaser are part of the cost of the land. If land and improvements are purchased, the broker's commission and any accrued interest or tax costs should be apportioned between the land and the buildings.

LAND IMPROVEMENTS   Expenditures for land improvements may be charged to the land account if the expenditures result in the addition of costs which are not subject to depreciation. If depreciation must be considered in relation to such expenditures, an account for Land Improvements should be opened. Such an account would be charged with expenditures for fences, water systems, sidewalks, and paving. Special assessments for local improvements which benefit the property may be charged to the land account.

BUILDINGS   When a building has been purchased, any renovating or remodeling costs incurred to put it in a condition suitable for its intended use should be charged to the building account. Any costs for subsequent improvements, in contrast to mere repairs, should also be debited to the building account.

The cost of a building constructed includes the payments to contractors, fees for permits and licenses, architects' fees, superintendents' salaries, and insurance and similar expenditures during the construction period. It is considered permissible to charge the building account with interest costs incurred during the construction period on money borrowed for the payment of construction costs.

ASSETS CONSTRUCTED FOR OWN USE   If a machine or other tangible long-lived asset is constructed by a company for its own use, it should be recorded at cost, and not at some higher price which it might have been necessary to pay if the asset had been purchased from outsiders.

NONCASH ACQUISITION OF ASSETS   It was noted in Chapter 2 that the cost of an asset is measured by the cash or cash equivalent given up in order to acquire the asset. When the acquisition involves only the payment of cash for the asset, the determination of cost is normally straightforward. The procedure for determining cost is not so simple when noncash assets are involved as all or part of the purchase price.

For example, assume that a firm acquires a building by issuing to the previous owner 1,000 shares of the firm's $25 par value common stock. The best measure of the cash equivalent given up to acquire the building is the market price of the stock. If the firm's stock is currently selling for $37 per share, the cost of the asset acquired is recorded as follows:[4]

Building (1,000 × $37)	37,000	
Common stock (1,000 × $25)		25,000
Capital in excess of par value—		
From common stock issuances		12,000

DEPRECIATION   Plant and equipment do not last forever. They either wear out or become obsolete. The wearing out of a depreciable asset is characterized by physical deterioration caused by use or by the action of the elements. The nature of obsolescence is indicated by the following illustrations.

> A company owns a hand machine capable of making 100 articles a day. The business has grown so that 1,000 articles must made each day. Instead of buying nine more hand machines, it may be better to dispose of the one machine owned and buy a power machine capable of making 1,000 units a day. If so, the hand machine is obsolete.

[4]The accounting for stockholders' equity, including the accounts illustrated here, is discussed in detail in Chapters 11 and 12.

The operation of the power machine requires the services of five men. A new automatic machine has been invented. Because of the saving in labor, it may be economical business management to dispose of the recently acquired power machine and purchase the new automatic machine. If so, the power machine is obsolete.

The new automatic machine is capable of producing only one product. The market for this product suddenly ceases. The automatic machine is obsolete.

Whether the usefulness of a plant fixed asset is terminated by physical deterioration or by obsolescence, it is the objective of depreciation accounting to spread the cost of the asset over the years of its usefulness in a systematic and sensible manner. This notion of depreciation is supported by the following definition proposed by the Committee on Terminology of the American Institute of Certified Public Accountants: *"Depreciation accounting* is a system of accounting which aims to distribute the cost or other basic value of tangible capital assets, less salvage (if any), over the estimated useful life of the unit . . . in a systematic and rational manner. It is a process of allocation, not of valuation." It is important to stress the fact that depreciation, in the accounting sense, does not consist of measuring the effects of wear and tear. It is a systematic cost-assignment procedure, determined primarily by the use-life expectancy of assets.

Long-lived assets are, of course, subject to changes in market value, but accountants do not consider it necessary to record such changes, because such assets are not intended for sale. The market values may be up today and down tomorrow; such fluctuations in value may be ignored because the benefit of property, plant, and equipment to a business normally lies in usefulness rather than marketability.

The total depreciation to be charged to expense during the total useful life of an asset is the cost of the asset less any estimated salvage or residual amount to be realized from the asset when it is no longer of any use to the firm. This can be summarized by using the following assumed data for an item of equipment:

Asset cost	$3,900
Less estimated residual or salvage amount	300
Total depreciation	$3,600

In addition to the above data, it is necessary that some estimate of useful life be made. The most widely used depreciation methods state this estimate as a certain number of time periods, usually annual periods. Estimates of useful life may be based on the past experience of a business with assets of the same type, or experience data may be obtained from manufacturers' or trade associations. It will be assumed that the asset referred to above has an estimated useful life of eight years. Three different methods for calculating depreciation expense will now be illustrated using these data: the *straight-line* method, the *sum-of-the-years'-digits* method, and the *declining-balance* method.

Straight-line method   The straight-line method is the simplest of the methods illustrated. It is very widely used because of this and because it is considered to represent a proper pattern of depreciation of charges for many assets. As shown below, the annual depreciation charge is calculated by allocating the amount to be depreciated equally over the number of years in the estimated useful life.

$3,600 \div 8 = $450

The tabulation below shows the accumulation of depreciation over the years.

TABLE OF DEPRECIATION
Straight-line Method

Year	Debit depreciation	Credit accumulated depreciation	Total accumulated depreciation	Carrying amount
				$3,900
1	$ 450	$ 450	$ 450	3,450
2	450	450	900	3,000
3	450	450	1,350	2,550
4	450	450	1,800	2,100
5	450	450	2,250	1,650
6	450	450	2,700	1,200
7	450	450	3,150	750
8	450	450	3,600	300
	$3,600	$3,600		

The annual depreciation *rate* in this case is 12½ per cent ($1.00 \div 8$). For each of the eight years the annual depreciation is recorded as follows:

Depreciation expense	450	
Accumulated depreciation—Equipment		450

Sum-of-the-years'-digits method The sum-of-the-years'-digits method produces a diminishing annual charge to depreciation expense. It is a device for obtaining a larger depreciation charge during the early years of the asset's life than during the later years. Subject to certain limitations, it is acceptable for income tax purposes. The procedure is described below:

Add the numbers representing the periods of life: In the illustration,
$1 + 2 + 3 + 4 + 5 + 6 + 7 + 8 = 36$[5]

Use the sum thus obtained as a denominator.
Use as numerators the same numbers taken in inverse order: Thus, 8/36, 7/36, and so forth.
Multiply the total to be depreciated (cost minus salvage) by the fractions thus produced.

The following tabulation shows the accumulation of depreciation.

TABLE OF DEPRECIATION
Sum-of-the-Years'-Digits Method

Year	Fractions used for computations	Debit depreciation	Credit accumulated depreciation	Total accumulated depreciation	Carrying amount
					$3,900
1	8/36 (of $3,600)	$ 800	$ 800	$ 800	3,100
2	7/36	700	700	1,500	2,400
3	6/36	600	600	2,100	1,800
4	5/36	500	500	2,600	1,300
5	4/36	400	400	3,000	900
6	3/36	300	300	3,300	600
7	2/36	200	200	3,500	400
8	1/36	100	100	3,600	300
		$3,600	$3,600		

[5] The formula for the sum of the digits is $n(n + 1) \div 2$, which in this case is $8(8 + 1) \div 2 = 36$.

Depreciation expense for the first year is recorded as follows:

Depreciation expense	800	
Accumulated depreciation—Equipment		800

It should be noted that in both the straight-line and the sum-of-the-years'-digits methods, the amount being depreciated is net of the estimated residual or salvage amount ($3,900 − $300 = $3,600).

Declining-balance method The declining-balance method is also a device for obtaining larger depreciation expense amounts during the early years of asset life. Under this method a fixed or uniform rate is applied to the undepreciated cost of the asset. More specifically, the depreciation rate is applied at the end of the first period to cost and thereafter to the carrying amount at the beginning of each successive period.

As a practical matter, the rate used is often based on what is permissible for income tax purposes. The law and regulations in effect at the time of this writing permit, for the declining-balance method, the use of a depreciation rate not exceeding twice that acceptable as a straight-line rate. This is called the *double-declining-balance method.* The regulations also provide that estimated salvage need not be taken into account. With an annual rate of 12½ per cent under the straight-line method illustrated on page 288, a rate up to 25 per cent (12½ per cent × 2) is acceptable for the double-declining-balance method. The depreciation charges for each period are shown below and are based on the maximum rate.

TABLE OF DEPRECIATION
Double-Declining-Balance Method
Rate: 25%

Year	Debit depreciation	Credit accumulated depreciation	Total accumulated depreciation	Carrying amount
				$3,900
1 (25% of $3,900)	$975	$975	$ 975	2,925
2 (25% of $2,925)	731	731	1,706	2,194
3 (25% of $2,194)	549	549	2,255	1,645
4 (25% of $1,645)	411	411	2,666	1,234
5 (25% of $1,234)	309	309	2,975	925
6 (25% of $ 925)	231	231	3,206	694
7 (25% of $ 694)	174	174	3,380	520
8 (25% of $ 520)	130	130	3,510	390

Depreciation for the first year is recorded as follows:

Depreciation expense	975	
Accumulated depreciation—Equipment		975

In calculating depreciation for the first year, the estimated salvage amount of $300 was ignored, which is different from the procedure in the preceding methods. However, when the declining-balance method is being used, depreciation should not be continued when the result would be to reduce the carrying amount below the estimated salvage. To reach the estimated salvage amount, the depreciation charge for the last year of useful life would be modified as needed from that shown in the Table of Depreciation.

For example, if it is assumed that the estimated salvage is now $400 for the asset in the previous illustration, the depreciation expense for the eighth year should not reduce the carrying amount of the asset below $3,500 ($3,900 − $400). The carrying amount at the end of the seventh year is $520 as shown in the table on page 289. Although the table shows depreciation expense of $130 for the eighth year, the maximum depreciation to be charged would be $120 ($520 − $400).

Production method   In each of the three preceding depreciation methods, the life of the asset was stated as a certain number of time periods (eight years). The production depreciation method allocates the depreciation deductions among the periods the asset is used in proportion to the use made of the asset each period.

For example, assume that it is estimated that the asset referred to in the previous illustrations will produce 7,200 units of product during its useful life. The depreciation rate is then 50 cents per unit of output ($3,600 ÷ 7,200). If during the first year of service, the asset produced 1,300 units, the entry to record depreciation expense for the year would be:

Depreciation expense (1,300 × $.50)	650	
Accumulated depreciation—Equipment		650

USE OF ACCELERATED DEPRECIATION METHODS   The sum-of-the-years'-digits method and the declining-balance method are referred to as *accelerated depreciation methods* because the pattern of depreciation charges under both methods is such that relatively larger depreciation charges result in the earlier years of asset life than during later years.

The methods are supported conceptually by the reasoning that tangible long-lived assets are normally characterized by decreasing contributions to the firm's revenues and increasing repairs and maintenance. However, the methods are arbitrary because there are many ways to calculate a declining depreciation charge. The methods are very widely used, not for their conceptual merits, but because of income tax considerations. Although total depreciation over the life of an asset will be the same no matter which method is used, the accelerated methods do have the advantage of reducing income tax payments during the earlier years of asset life, thereby making additional cash available to the firm.

DEPRECIATION FOR FRACTIONAL PERIODS   If assets subject to depreciation are acquired during an accounting period, depreciation must be computed and recorded for a fractional period. Since depreciation is an estimate, it seems unnecessary to compute fractional-period depreciation in terms of days. Depreciation is not that precise. As a general rule, fractional-period depreciation is computed in terms of months or fractions of months. This procedure is illustrated below, where it is assumed that the company closes its books annually on December 31.

	Delivery equipment	Office machine
Date asset acquired	March 31	September 17 (treated as Sept. 15 for fractional-period purposes)
Cost of asset	$4,000	$1,200
Depreciation rate per annum	20%	10%
Annual charge for depreciation	$ 800	$ 120
Months asset was in use first year	9	3½ (7 half-months)
Fraction of year	9/12	7/24
Depreciation charge applicable to first accounting period	$ 600	$ 35

IGNORING SALVAGE AMOUNT   Theoretically, the depreciation provisions should be based on cost less salvage, as in the preceding illustrations. As a practical matter, the estimated salvage is often (perhaps usually) ignored and the depreciation provisions are based on total cost. This procedure is probably justified because depreciation allowances are estimates at best; unless estimated salvage amounts are material, they may be ignored.

RECORDING DEPRECIATION   As shown in the preceding illustrations, depreciation is recorded by debiting an expense account and crediting accumulated depreciation, which is a *contra asset* account. Thus the latter account has a credit balance and is deducted in the balance sheet from the related asset account. For example, if the depreciation table shown on page 289 is used for the double-declining-balance method, the asset would be reported as shown below in the firm's balance sheet at the end of the fourth year.

Long-lived assets:		
Equipment	$3,900	
Less accumulated depreciation	2,666	$1,234

The difference between the two amounts is the carrying amount of the asset and it is frequently referred to as the *book amount* (value). The same result would be achieved if depreciation were credited directly to the asset account. However, the method is not desirable for the following reasons. First, if depreciation is credited to the asset account, the cost of the long-lived asset cannot be determined by the account balance. Second, the provision for depreciation is only an estimate. By crediting it to an accumulated depreciation account, the amount of depreciation provided can be shown in the balance sheet, where interested parties can get information on which to base their own opinions as to the adequacy of the provision.

DEPRECIATION VERSUS PROVISION FOR REPLACEMENT   The nature of depreciation accounting is often misunderstood. The misunderstanding arises from a tendency to assume that depreciation entries somehow produce funds for the replacement of depreciable assets; this false assumption may have been caused by a misunderstanding of the expression "provision for depreciation" frequently used by accountants.

Depreciation entries merely charge operations, during a series of periods, with the cost of an asset previously acquired. Depreciation entries as such in no way affect the cash account. If it is desired to provide a fund for the replacement of depreciable assets, cash may be set aside in a special bank account or invested in securities to be held until money is required for replacement purposes. The creation of such a replacement fund is very unusual, because management usually believes that the cash can be more profitably used to finance regular business operations.

DEPRECIATION REVISIONS The accuracy of the estimates used in the calculation of periodic depreciation amounts will obviously not be known until the asset is retired from service. However, after an asset has been in use for some time, additional information or experience may indicate that the depreciation deductions previously recorded are either too large or too small. Such a condition may be the result of a change in the estimated useful life of the asset or in the estimated salvage amount. In any event, it would not be proper to continue with the existing depreciation program under such circumstances unless, of course, the amount involved is so small that it can be ignored on practical grounds.

When a change is warranted, it is accomplished by spreading the undepreciated amount over the remaining useful life of the asset by revised depreciation provisions without changing the current balance in the accumulated depreciation account.[6] For example, assume the following data pertaining to the depreciation of an asset during the first six years of an estimated life of ten years.

Asset cost	$9,000
Estimated salvage	–0–
Estimated useful life—10 years.	
Depreciation entries to date:	
Year 1	$ 900
2	900
3	900
4	900
5	900
6	900
Accumulated depreciation at the end of 6th year	$5,400

At the beginning of the seventh year it is estimated that the asset will probably last six more years (revised useful life = 12 years). Calculation of the straight-line depreciation deduction for the seventh and subsequent years is as follows:

Undepreciated cost:		
Cost	$9,000	
Accumulated depreciation	5,400	$3,600
Revised remaining useful life—6 years.		
Revised annual depreciation provision ($3,600 ÷ 6)		$ 600

[6]Accounting Principles Board, "Accounting Changes," *Opinion No. 20* (New York: AICPA, August, 1971), paragraphs 31–32.

The entry to record depreciation for the seventh and subsequent years is shown below.

Depreciation expense	600	
Accumulated depreciation		600

The additional information available at this time indicates that the depreciation amounts recorded in each of the six preceding years was excessive given a total useful life of 12 years. The effect of the procedure just illustrated is to record smaller depreciation amounts in each of the years remaining in the asset life in order to compensate for the excess depreciation of previous years. If the earlier depreciation amounts had been too small (for example, if the revised estimate of useful life is eight years), the same procedures would be used, but the subsequent provisions for depreciation will be larger than the annual amounts for the preceding years.

EXPENDITURES DURING ASSET LIFE An expenditure is the payment, or the incurring of an obligation to make a future payment, for a benefit received. There are two major types of expenditures which may take place during the life of a long-lived asset.

> Those that should be *capitalized*—recorded by increasing the book amount of the assets. In most cases, this is done by a debit to the asset account; in some cases, it is done by a debit to the accumulated depreciation account.
> Those that should be *expensed*—recorded by charges to appropriate expense accounts.

A careful distinction must be made between capitalizing and expensing if a correct accounting for long-lived assets and for net income is to be maintained. If an expenditure that should be capitalized is charged to an expense account, the book amount of some asset is understated, and the owners' equity and the net income for the current period also are understated. On the other hand, if an expenditure that should be expensed is charged to an asset account, the book amount of the asset is overstated and the owners' equity and the net income for the current period also are overstated.

In general, expenditures that are capitalized are those undertaken to make some asset more valuable for its intended use or to extend its useful life. However, it is not always easy to determine whether a given expenditure should be capitalized or expensed. The proper treatment of some of the more common types of expenditures is indicated on page 294.

DISPOSAL OF DEPRECIABLE ASSETS If a depreciable asset is disposed of during the year and it is the accounting policy to record depreciation for fractional periods, an entry is required to debit depreciation and to credit accumulated depreciation for depreciation from the date of the last preceding depreciation provision to the date of disposal. For example, assume that an item of equipment costing $10,000 and having no salvage amount is being depreciated over a ten-year life by the straight-line method. The asset was acquired on January 2, 19_4 and depreciation was last recorded on December 31, 19_7. If the asset is sold on

	Expendi-tures Expensed	Expenditures Capitalized	
		Book Amount of Assets Increased by Debits to	
Explanation	Debit Expense Accounts	Asset Account	Accumulated Depreciation Account
Acquisition cost:			
A company purchased three second-hand machines; charge the asset account		$3,000	
Expenditures to make good depreciation which took place prior to acquisition:			
Before the machines were put into use, they were thoroughly overhauled. This was a capital expenditure		400	
Installation cost:			
This is a capital expenditure		50	
Betterment:			
Additional accessories were purchased for use with the machines; this expenditure is chargeable to the asset account		75	
Ordinary repair:			
At the end of the first month of operations, a repair bill was paid; this was a revenue expenditure or expense	$18		
Extraordinary repair:			
After three years of use, the machines were again thoroughly reconditioned at a cost of $400. Such reconditioning had not been anticipated when the useful life of the machines was established. This was capitalized because it made good some of the depreciation subsequent to acquisition and thus extended the useful life of the asset; it is customarily recorded by a charge to the accumulated depreciation account			$400
Reinstallation expense:			

The first cost of installing machinery in a factory is a proper charge to the asset account. If machinery is rearranged in the factory for the purpose of improving the routing or otherwise reducing the time and cost of production, a question arises with respect to the proper treatment of the reinstallation expense. Presumably, the cost of one installation will already have been charged to the machinery account. Theoretically, therefore, the cost, or the undepreciated remainder of the cost, of the first installation should be removed from the accounts (by crediting the fixed asset with the original cost and debiting the accumulated depreciation account with the accumulated depreciation thereon), and the reinstallation cost should be capitalized by charge to the machinery account.

April 1, 19_8, the following entry is required to record depreciation expense on the asset for 19_8:

Depreciation expense [($10,000 ÷ 10) × 3/12]	250	
Accumulated depreciation—Equipment		250

It is necessary that the entry above be recorded before the sale of the asset is recorded. Otherwise, the book amount of the asset would not be correctly stated at the time of disposal, resulting in a misstatement of any gain or loss on the sale.

To record the disposal of a depreciable asset, it is necessary that both the original cost and all accumulated depreciation on the asset be removed from the accounting records. This is accomplished by an entry debiting cash for any cash received, debiting the accumulated depreciation account for all prior amounts provided for the asset, and crediting the asset account for the cost. Any gain or loss on the disposal is recorded as a debit or credit in the entry.

In the illustrations that follow it is assumed that any required entries for fractional-period depreciation have been made, after which the asset has total accumulated depreciation of $2,200.

(1) *Selling price equal to book amount:*
Assume that, at the date of disposal of a machine, the asset and accumulated depreciation accounts had the following balances:

	Debit	Credit
Machinery	$2,500	
Accumulated depreciation—Machinery		$2,200

The asset had a book amount of $300 and was sold for $300. The entry to record the sale is:

Cash	300	
Accumulated depreciation—Machinery	2,200	
Machinery		2,500
To record the sale of machinery, relieving the accounts of the cost and accumulated depreciation.		

(2) *Selling price less than book amount:*
Assume that the accounts had the following balances:

	Debit	Credit
Machinery	$2,500	
Accumulated depreciation—Machinery		$1,760

The asset had a book amount of $740 and was sold for $400; hence there was a loss of $340. The entry to record the sale is:

Cash	400	
Loss on disposal of machinery	340	
Accumulated depreciation—Machinery	1,760	
Machinery		2,500
To record the sale of machinery.		

(3) *Selling price more than book amount:*
Assume that the accounts had balances as below:

	Debit	Credit
Machinery	$2,500	
Accumulated depreciation—Machinery		$2,200

The asset had a book amount of $300 and was sold for $500; hence there was a gain of $200. The entry to record the sale of the machine at a gain of $200 is:

Cash	500	
Accumulated depreciation—Machinery	2,200	
Machinery		2,500
Gain on disposal of machinery		200
To record the sale of machinery.		

TRADE-INS AND EXCHANGES OF PRODUCTIVE ASSETS The preceding paragraphs dealt with disposals of depreciable assets by sale. However, it is not uncommon for a business to dispose of depreciable assets by trading them in on new assets. Thus a productive asset can be acquired by trading in an old asset and paying cash (often referred to as *boot*) for the difference between the amount allowed on the trade-in by the seller and the current cash price of the new asset. In addition, a productive asset can be acquired in exchange for another asset with no cash involved (an exchange of noncash assets).

Consistent with the accounting for the acquisition of assets at the cash or cash equivalent paid (acquisition cost), a productive asset acquired in exchange for another productive asset should be accounted for at the fair market value (selling price currently obtainable in the market) of the productive asset given in exchange. That is, the fair market value of the productive asset exchanged represents the cost of the acquired asset. Also, since the fair market value of the asset exchanged will seldom be equal to the book amount (value) of the asset exchanged, a gain or loss on the disposed asset should be recognized in accounting for the exchange.

In actual accounting practice the accounting for productive assets acquired through exchanges, including trade-ins, depends on whether the productive assets exchanged are similar (e.g., a truck exchanged for another truck) or dissimilar (e.g., a truck exchanged for machinery).[7] If there is an exchange of dissimilar productive assets, the acquired asset is accounted for at the fair market value of the asset exchanged, plus any cash paid, and any gain or loss on the exchanged asset is recognized in accounting for the exchange. If there is an exchange of similar productive assets, the acquired asset is recorded at an amount equal to the book amount (value) of the asset exchanged plus any cash paid in the exchange, not to exceed the fair market value of the asset received. The rationale for such accounting treatment is that a mere exchange of similar productive assets is not the culmination of an earning process, since the company's economic position has not really changed and therefore full gains should not be recognized for such exchanges.[8] However, losses on the exchange of similar productive assets are recognized when the fair market value of the asset acquired is less than the sum of the book amount (value) of the exchanged asset plus any cash paid.

The accounting for exchanges of productive assets is illustrated on page 297, where it is assumed that Case A is an exchange of productive assets and Cases B and C are trade-in transactions.

[7]Accounting Principles Board, "Accounting for Nonmonetary Transactions," *Opinion No. 29* (New York: AICPA, May, 1973), paragraphs 18–22.

[8]Although not discussed here, partial gains are recognized on an exchange of similar assets by the recipient of boot.

Data	Case A	Case B	Case C
Asset exchanged:			
Cost	$5,000	$5,000	$5,000
Accumulated depreciation	3,000	3,000	3,000
Book amount (value)	$2,000	$2,000	$2,000
Fair market value	2,200	2,100	1,800
Cash paid (boot)	—	3,700	4,100
Fair market value of asset			
acquired	2,200	5,800	5,900
Entries:			
Exchange of dissimilar assets:			
Asset account (new)	2,200	5,800	5,900
Accumulated depreciation	3,000	3,000	3,000
Loss on disposal of old asset	—	—	200[b]
Asset account (old)	5,000	5,000	5,000
Cash	—	3,700	4,100
Gain on disposal of old asset	200	100[a]	—
Exchange of similar assets:			
Asset account (new)	2,000[c]	5,700[d]	5,900[e]
Accumulated depreciation	3,000	3,000	3,000
Loss on disposal of old asset	—	—	200
Asset account (old)	5,000	5,000	5,000
Cash	—	3,700	4,100

[a]$100 = $2,100 − $2,000

[b]$200 = $1,800 − $2,000

[c]$2,000 = $5,000 − $3,000

[d]$5,700 = ($5,000 − $3,000) + $3,700

[e]Recorded at the fair market value of the asset acquired $(5,900) because the sum ($6,100) of the book amount of the asset exchanged ($2,000) plus the cash paid ($4,100) is greater than the fair market value.

Note that the above accounting treatment of exchanges of similar productive assets shows that the recording of the acquired assets is not at their cash equivalent cost or fair market value. Instead, the acquired assets, under exchanges of similar assets, are recorded generally at the book amount (value) of the asset exchanged plus any boot. But the book amount of the asset exchanged is not a relevant measure of the consideration given in exchange. For example, in Case A (similar assets exchanged) the acquired asset is recorded at the book amount of the asset exchanged ($2,000), which, in effect, has been reduced by the $200 gain unrecognized on the exchange.

Finally, it should be pointed out that for income tax purposes no gain or loss is recognized when an asset is traded in on another similar asset. Thus in the above illustration of the accounting for trade-ins (Cases B and C) for similar assets, Case B is the same as the tax method, but Case C is not, since the asset acquired would be recorded at $6,100 with the $200 loss not recognized.

UNIT AND GROUP BASES OF DEPRECIATION ACCOUNTING   In the discussion thus far it has been assumed that the accountant, in his attempts to compute and account for depreciation, approaches the problem by considering each asset as a separate unit. Thus the estimated useful life or depreciation rate selected is one believed to be specifically applicable to the unit of property being depreciated. Accumulated depreciation is related to each unit and, if an asset is retired, the accumulated depreciation related to that particular asset is removed from the accounts when the cost of the asset is removed. It is not uncommon for gains and losses on disposals to arise under this general plan of depreciation accounting.

In contrast, depreciation may be computed on a *group* basis. Under such a plan, each asset group is depreciated on the basis of an average useful life representative of the entire group. Justification for the use of a group basis does not exist unless a business owns a relatively large number of assets that can be identified as belonging to a class. Examples of acceptable asset classes include hotel furniture, telephone poles, and typewriters.

Under this plan, accumulated depreciation is not associated with individual assets. When assets are disposed of or retired, the cost less salvage is charged against the accumulated depreciation account, and no loss or gain is recognized. This procedure is based on a presumption, which should be supported by past experience, that any underdepreciation on assets retired early will be offset by overprovisions of depreciation on assets which prove to have a longer life than estimated.

NATURAL RESOURCES—VALUATION   Natural resources, such as timber tracts, mines, and oil wells, should be carried in the asset accounts at cost. Such assets are sometimes called *wasting assets.* As the resource is converted, a portion of its cost is removed from the asset account and assigned to an inventory account as part of the cost of the product obtained from the natural resource, thereby reducing the book amount of the natural resource. Such cost transfers give recognition to *depletion.*

Development expenditures, such as those made for the removal of surface earth for strip-mining operations, which do not result in the acquisition of separate tangible assets, may be charged to the wasting asset account. Depreciable assets acquired for use in the conversion of a wasting asset should be recorded in separate accounts; they should be depreciated in amounts proportionate to the depletion, if the assets will render service throughout the entire life of the wasting asset; they should be depreciated over a shorter period if their useful lives will expire before the wasting asset is completely depleted.

DEPLETION   To compute per-unit depletion, the cost of the wasting asset is divided by the estimated number of units (tons, barrels, thousand feet, and so forth) in the asset. To compute the depletion for any period, then, the unit rate is multiplied by the number of units converted during the period.

To illustrate, assume that $90,000 was paid for a mine which was estimated to contain 300,000 tons of available deposit. The unit depletion is $90,000 ÷ 300,000, or $.30. If 60,000 tons are mined during a given year, the depletion is $.30 × 60,000, or $18,000, and is recorded as follows:

Inventory	18,000	
Accumulated depletion		18,000

For purposes of income determination, the amount thus entered in the inventory account is transferred to expense via cost of goods sold as the resources are sold. If some of the units converted are unsold at year end, the depletion related to such units should remain in the inventory account.

The credit balance in an accumulated depletion account should be deducted in the balance sheet from the asset being depleted.

INTANGIBLE ASSETS Certain assets are of considerable benefit to a firm even though they do not have physical substance. Such assets are referred to as *intangible assets* and their contribution to the revenues of the firm results from certain rights they afford their owner. Intangible assets may be purchased by a firm or they may be developed within the firm.

AMORTIZATION OF INTANGIBLE ASSETS At one time certain intangible assets were considered to have unlimited life and such assets were reported at cost for an indefinite period, with no attempt being made to allocate their cost over a specified number of accounting periods. However, current treatment requires that all intangible assets be amortized by systematic charges to income.[9] Under no circumstances is the amortization period to exceed 40 years.[10]

Many intangible assets are subject to amortization because their lives are limited by law, regulation, contract, or the nature of the asset. Examples are patents, copyrights, franchises for limited periods, leaseholds, and leasehold improvements. It should be understood that the period fixed by law, regulation, or contract is the maximum period of life, and that the usefulness of such assets may cease prior to the expiration of that period; in such instances, the shorter useful life should be the period on which the amortization is based. If the original estimate of useful life is subsequently regarded as incorrect, the same procedure as those discussed on pages 292–293 concerning depreciable assets would be used to amortize the remaining book amount over the years remaining in the revised estimate of useful life.

Although they do not have physical substance, most intangible assets are *identifiable* in that they may be acquired individually. However, they may also be acquired as part of a group of assets or even as part of an entire firm. Several examples of identifiable intangible assets are discussed in the following paragraphs.

PATENTS If a patent is acquired by purchase, its cost is the purchase price. If it is obtained by the inventor, its cost is the total of the outlays for experiments and costs of constructing working models and obtaining the patent, including drawings, attorney's fees, and filing costs. Because a patent has no proven value until it has stood the test of an infringement suit, the cost of a successful suit may be charged to the patents account. If the suit is unsuccessful, and the patient is thereby proved to be valueless, the cost of the suit and the cost of the patent should be written off.

A patent is issued for 17 years, and its cost should be amortized over that period, unless it was acquired after the expiration of a portion of the 17-year

---

[9]Research and development costs are no longer capitalized and amortized. They are now expensed as incurred (with some exceptions) per Financial Accounting Standards Board, "Accounting for Research and Development Costs," *Statement No. 2* (Stamford, Conn.: FASB, October, 1974), paragraphs 12, 13.

[10]Accounting Principles Board, "Intangible Assets," *Opinion No. 17* (New York: AICPA, August, 1970), paragraph 29.

period, in which case it should be written off over its remaining life. If there is a probability that the patented device or the product of the device will become obsolete before the expiration of the patent, conservatism would suggest writing off the patent during a period shorter than its legal life.

Even though a patent may give its owner a monopoly which enables him or her to develop the business to a point where, after the expiration of the patent, competitors will find it extremely difficult to enter the field and overcome the handicap, the patent should be amortized.

Assuming that the total patent amortization for a given year is $3,500, the following entry is recorded:

Patents expense	3,500	
Patents		3,500

An accumulated patent amortization account could be used, but the normal practice is to credit the periodic amortization of intangible assets directly to the asset account.

COPYRIGHT

A copyright gives its owner the exclusive right to produce and sell reading matter and works of art. The fee for obtaining a copyright is only a nominal amount, too small to justify an accounting procedure of capitalization and amortization. Costs sufficient in amount to justify such an accounting procedure may be incurred, however, when copyrights are purchased.

For many years copyrights were issued for 28 years with a possibility of renewal for an additional 28 years. Recently, the legal life was changed to cover the life of the author plus 50 years.[11] However, the active market for many publications is much shorter, and it usually is regarded as advisable to write off copyright costs over a much shorter period.

FRANCHISES

A franchise arrangement allows the party receiving the franchise certain exclusive rights, such as the right to market a product under a specific name or within a specific geographical area. Certain payments are normally required in order to obtain the franchise. Such payments represent the cost of the franchise and should be amortized over the legal or economic life of the franchise, whichever is shorter.

LEASEHOLDS

A lease is a contract that grants the lessee the right to possess and use the leased property for a specified period. The personal-property right conveyed by the lease is referred to as a *leasehold.* Many leases have characteristics that are in substance very similar to a purchase transaction and are referred to as *capital leases.* They involve rather complex accounting procedures which are beyond the scope of this discussion.

Leases that do not have these characteristics are essentially rental agreements, perhaps for a rather lengthy period, and are referred to as *operating leases.* If the lease arrangement requires an advance payment for future periods by the lessee, the payment should be debited to an asset account such as Prepaid Rent—Leased Building (or Leasehold) and then amortized over the period covered by the advance payment.

[11]Copyright Act of 1976, effective January 1, 1978.

LEASEHOLD IMPROVEMENTS   Leases of real estate for long periods frequently provide that the lessee (the party who acquired the right to occupy the property) shall pay the cost of any alterations or improvements which he or she may desire, such as new fronts, partitions, and built-in shelving. Such alterations and improvements become a part of the real estate and revert to the owner of the real estate at the expiration of the lease; all that the lessee obtains by the expenditure is the intangible right to benefit by the improvements during the life of the lease. The lessee should therefore charge such expenditures to a leasehold improvements account; the cost should be amortized over the life of the lease or the expected useful life of the improvements, whichever is shorter, by journal entries debiting Amortization—Leasehold Improvements and crediting Leasehold Improvements.

GOODWILL   The following statement, intended to indicate the nature of goodwill, is quoted from a court decision:

> "When an individual or a firm or a corporation has gone on for an unbroken series of years conducting a particular business, and has been so scrupulous in fulfilling every obligation, so careful in maintaining the standard of the goods dealt in, so absolutely fair and honest in all business dealings that customers of the concern have become convinced that their experience in the future will be as satisfactory as it has been in the past, while such customers' good report of their own experience tends continually to bring new customers to the concern, there has been produced an element of value quite as important as—in some cases, perhaps, far more important than—the plant or machinery with which the business is carried on. That it is property is abundantly settled by authority, and, indeed, is not disputed. That in some cases it may be very valuable property is manifest. The individual who has created it by years of hard work and fair business dealing usually experiences no difficulty in finding men willing to pay him for it if he be willing to sell it to them."

This quotation is interesting because it indicates some of the ways in which goodwill may be created. However, it does not adequately indicate the nature of goodwill for two reasons.

In the first place, it implies that goodwill is produced only by satisfactory customer relations; but because goodwill is dependent upon earnings, and because many things other than customer satisfaction contribute to earnings, there are many sources of goodwill. Some of these sources are: location; manufacturing efficiency; satisfactory relations between the employees and the management, which contribute to earnings through effective employee service and the reduction of losses from labor turnover; adequate sources of capital and a credit standing which is reflected in low money costs; advertising; monopolistic privileges; and, in general, good business management.

In the second place, in placing the emphasis on customer relations, the quotation fails to put the emphasis where it really belongs: on the relation between earnings and assets. A company may be scrupulous, fair, and honest, and its good repute may tend continually to attract new customers, and yet the company may have no goodwill. The existence of goodwill depends upon the amount of the earnings.

The meanings of three terms, as used in the following discussion of goodwill, are stated as follows:

Investment—The assets of a business exclusive of any goodwill.
Basic rate of income—The rate of net income on the investment which, for the particular industry,

may be agreed upon by the purchaser and seller as the rate which a new enterprise entering the field might reasonably be expected to earn.

Excess earnings—The amount by which the earnings of a business exceed earnings on the investment at the basic rate of income.

Goodwill may be defined as the value of the excess earnings. Let us assume the following conditions:

	Company A	Company B
Investment	$100,000	$100,000
Basic rate of income	10%	10%
Net income earned	$ 10,000	$ 15,000
Income on investment at basic rate	10,000	10,000
Excess earnings	$ —	$ 5,000

The excess earnings of Company B indicate that it has a goodwill; Company A apparently has no goodwill because it has no excess earnings.

METHODS OF COMPUTING GOODWILL The price to be paid for goodwill in connection with the sale of a business may be an amount arbitrarily agreed upon by the purchaser and seller, without formal computation. On the other hand, it may be computed on the basis of past or anticipated earnings of the business. When the purchaser of a business pays a price for goodwill, he or she is not paying for the excess earnings of the past, but for probable excess earnings of the future. The accomplishments of the past, however, may furnish the best available evidence of the probable accomplishments in the future. But when past earnings data are used as a basis for an estimation of future excess earnings, all extraneous and nonoperating gains and losses should be excluded. Also, allowance should be made for anticipated changes in revenue and expense, such as higher wage rates, because of their impact on future earnings.

These goodwill valuation bases are illustrated below.

(1) Some multiple of the average past annual earnings, after adjustment for unusual and nonrecurring items and anticipated changes affecting future revenue and expense. For instance, assume that the average adjusted earnings for five years prior to the sale of the business have been $10,000, and that the valuation of goodwill is at twice the average earnings; the goodwill valuation will be $20,000. The price so computed is said to be "two years' purchase" of the average annual earnings.

   This method is illogical because it fails to give recognition to the fact that goodwill is dependent upon the existence of excess earnings. Recognition is given to this fact in the two following bases of goodwill valuation.

(2) Some multiple of the average past earnings, as adjusted, in excess of a return at an agreed rate on the average investment. For instance, assume average annual earnings for five years of $10,000, an average investment of $100,000, and an agreement to pay three years' purchase of the average earnings in excess of 8 per cent on the average investment. The goodwill computation would be:

Average earnings, as adjusted	$10,000
Less 8% on average investment	8,000
Excess	$ 2,000
Multiply by number of years' purchase	3
Goodwill	$ 6,000

(3) THe capitalized amount of excess earnings. For instance, assuming the same facts as in (2) with respect to average income and investment, and assuming an agreement to compute goodwill by capitalizing, at 10 per cent, the average annual adjusted earnings in excess of 8 per cent on the average investment, we would compute the goodwill as follows:

Average earnings, as adjusted	$10,000
Less 8% on average investment	8,000
Excess to be capitalized	$ 2,000
Capitalized amount	$2,000 ÷ .10 = $20,000

RECORDING GOODWILL Goodwill can properly appear in the accounting records *only* when it is specifically paid for. For example, assume that a company, using the third method discussed above, acquires on January 2, 19_8, another company for a price that is $20,000 in excess of the net tangible assets of the purchased firm. The purchaser records a $20,000 debit to Goodwill. As noted earlier in the chapter, this amount must be amortized over a period not exceeding 40 years. If it is assumed that ten years is considered a reasonable estimate of the economic life of the goodwill, the following entry records the amortization at December 31, 19_8:

Amortization of goodwill	2,000	
Goodwill		2,000

The management of a firm may believe that the company has created goodwill internally by advertising expenditures or otherwise and may wish to recognize this by a debit to the goodwill account. However, such treatment is not acceptable because of the practical impossibility of identifying specific expenditures of this type as representing the cost of goodwill.

ORGANIZATION COSTS AND DEFERRED CHARGES The organization of a corporation involves expenditures for attorneys' fees, the fee paid to the state at the time of incorporation, and other costs.

Organization costs have sometimes been regarded as a sheer loss, to be written off as soon as possible. Such an attitude is illogical. The very existence of a corporation is dependent upon the incurring of organization costs; they benefit the business during its entire existence. Management is entirely justified, from the standpoint of acceptable accounting principles, in regarding such costs as an intangible asset to be amortized according to the provisions of APB *Opinion No. 17.*

Organization costs are sometimes reported in the balance sheet under a completely separate asset caption such as Deferred Charges. Deferred charges are actually long-term prepayments such as bond-issue costs and machinery-rearrangement costs.

IMPORTANT TERMS AND CONCEPTS IN CHAPTER 9

Depreciation—pp. 283, 286
Depletion—pp. 283, 298
Amortization—pp. 283, 299
Tangible assets—p. 284
Intangible assets—pp. 284, 299
Valuation—p. 284
Straight-line method—p. 287
Sum-of-the-years'-digits method—p. 288 .
Double-declining-balance method—p. 289

Production method—p. 290
Accelerated depreciation—p. 290
Fractional period depreciation—p. 290
Depreciation revisions—p. 292
Capital expenditures—p. 293
Disposal of assets—p. 293
Trade-ins and exchanges—p. 296
Wasting assets—p. 298
Goodwill—p. 301

DEMONSTRATION PROBLEM FOR REVIEW AND SELF-STUDY   Mission Coal Company began operations in 19_5. The following information pertains to the long-lived asset transactions of the Company during the first year of operations:

January 5—Purchased a new building costing $100,000 and having an estimated useful life of 50 years.

January 17—Took delivery on machinery costing $75,000 and having an estimated useful life of ten years.

February 2—Acquired four trucks costing $5,000 each and having an estimated useful life of four. years.

March 3—Acquired property containing coal reserves for a total of $500,000. It was estimated that the reserves amounted to 75,000 tons of coal and that the land would have a value of $10,000 after removal of the coal.

  Additional expenditures were $80,000 for development costs and $150,000 for equipment. The equipment will be abandoned when the reserves are depleted. Production during 19_5 totaled 12,000 tons of coal.

July 27—One of the machines acquired on January 17, having an original cost of $8,000 and a fair market value of $7,400, is traded for a new asset with a fair market value of $10,000. Cash equal to the difference between the fair market values is paid.

November 11—One of the trucks acquired on February 2 is sold for $3,600 cash.

Early in 19_6 the Company completed a deal for the acquisition of Dixon Coal Company. Condensed financial statement information for Dixon Coal Company for the past three years is presented below.

	December 31,		
	19_3	19_4	19_5
Tangible assets	$500,000	$518,000	$525,000
Total assets	$500,000	$518,000	$525,000
Liabilities	$ 48,000	$ 54,000	$ 65,000
Common stock	300,000	300,000	300,000
Retained earnings	152,000	164,000	160,000
Total liabilities and stockholders' equity	$500,000	$518,000	$525,000
Net income	$ 42,000	$ 54,000	$ 56,000

The terms of the acquisition call for the computation of goodwill by capitalizing, at 10 per cent, the average annual earnings in excess of 7 per cent on the average investment for the past three years.

INSTRUCTIONS

(a) Calculate the depreciation applicable to the building, machinery, and trucks for the year ending December 31, 19_5. Assume that the firm uses the unit basis of depreciation accounting, uses the straight-line method of computing depreciation, and computes fractional period depreciation to the nearest month. Round all calculations to the nearest dollar.

(b) Prepare all journal entries required to account for the firm's coal reserves, including any end-of-year adjustments.

(c) Calculate the amount to be paid for goodwill upon the acquisition of Dixon Coal Company.

Note: Attempt to solve the demonstration problem before examining the solution that follows.

(a)

Building (annual rate 2%):
  Depreciation:
    $100,000 × 2% $2,000

Machinery (annual rate 10%):
  Depreciation:
    Machinery used from January 17 to December 31
      ($75,000 − $8,000 × 10% × 11/12) $6,142
    Machine traded July 27 ($8,000 × 10% × 6/12)   400
    Machine acquired July 27 ($10,000* × 10% × 5/12)   417
  Total $6,959

*Basis of new machine:
  Book amount of asset traded:
    Cost $8,000
    Less accumulated depreciation   400
                                     $7,600

  Add cash paid:
    Fair market value of new asset $10,000
    Less fair market value of old asset   7,400 $ 2,600
  Total $10,200

However, basis of new asset may not exceed its fair market value ($10,000)

Trucks (annual rate 25%):
  Depreciation:
    Trucks used from February 8 to December 31
      ($20,000 − $5,000 × 25% × 11/12) $3,438
    Trucks sold November 11 ($5,000 × 25% × 9/12)   938
  Total $4,376

(b)

19_6					
Jan.	1	Coal property		500,000	
		Cash			500,000
		Purchased coal property.			
	1	Coal property		80,000	
		Cash			80,000
		Development costs.			
	1	Equipment		150,000	
		Cash			150,000
		Purchased equipment.			
Dec.	31	Coal inventory		91,200	
		Accumulated depletion			91,200
		Production for the year (12,000 tons @ $7.60 per ton).			

Depletion per ton:

Cost of coal property	$500,000	
Less portion applicable to land	10,000	
Applicable to coal reserves	$490,000	
Add development costs	80,000	
Total cost	$570,000	

$570,000 ÷ 75,000 = $7.60 per ton

	31	Depreciation expense—Equipment	24,000	
		Accumulated depreciation—Equipment		24,000
		Depreciation for the year based on the rate of coal extraction (12,000/75,000 × $150,000).		

(c)

Computation of earnings at 7 per cent of average investment:

Investment, December 31:

19_3	$500,000	
19_4	518,000	
19_5	525,000	$1,543,000
Average investment ($1,543,000 ÷ 3)		$ 514,333
Agreed rate on average investment		7%
Earnings at 7 per cent of average investment		$ 36,003

Average annual earnings for the last three years:

Net income:

19_3	$ 42,000	
19_4	54,000	
19_5	56,000	$ 152,000
Average earnings ($152,000 ÷ 3)		$ 50,667
Excess earnings ($50,667 − $36,003)		$ 14,664
Capitalized value of excess earnings ($14,664 ÷ 10)		$ 146,640

Questions

1 Define the following terms:
   (a) Depreciation.
   (b) Depletion.
   (c) Amortization.
2 Describe a classification system for long-lived assets.
3 How is the cost of an asset determined?
4 How should expenditures for land improvements be treated?
5 What is the difference between depreciation and obsolescence?
6 What is the relationship between depreciation and the replacement of assets?
7 Distinguish between the unit and group bases of depreciation accounting.
8 Describe the proper procedure to account for depreciation revisions.
9 What rule should be followed in determining the period over which intangible assets should be amortized?
10 What rules are followed in accounting for exhanges of productive assets?
11 What is the relationship between goodwill and the earnings of a firm?
12 Describe three ways in which goodwill may be computed.

Short exercises

E9-1

Murphy Company acquired an asset on January 1, 19_1 at a cost of $10,000. The asset has an estimated useful life of ten years and an estimated salvage value of $2,000. Compute the depreciation for each of the first two years: Assume the following depreciation methods: (a) straight-line; (b) sum-of-the-years'-digits; and (c) declining-balance at twice the straight-line rate. Round all amounts to the nearest dollar.

E9-2

Loomis Corporation purchased a machine on January 1, 19_1 at a cost of $9,700. The estimated life was ten years and the estimated salvage value was $700. On January 1, 19_4 it was estimated that the remaining life of the machine was four years. The asset was sold for $500 cash on January 1, 19_7.

   Compute the following by using the straight-line method:

   (a) Depreciation for 19_1.

   (b) Depreciation for 19_4.

   (c) Gain or loss on disposal of the machine.

E9-3

Meyer Company acquired a building having an estimated life of 50 years and zero salvage value on July 1, 19_1 at a cost of $75,000. On January 1, 19_2 a new wing costing $39,800 was added to the building. On January 1, 19_3 the entire building was painted at a cost of $5,500. Show how the building account and its related accumulated depreciation account would appear for the period July 1, 19_1 to December 31, 19_3. Assume that the firm closes its books on December 31.

E9-4

Through December 31, 19_3 accumulated depreciation of $14,000 has been recorded on a machine having an original cost of $21,000. Record the disposal of the asset on that date under each of the following assumptions:

(a) The asset is sold for $10,000 cash.

(b) The asset is junked, and there are no proceeds.

(c) The asset, which has a fair market value of $6,000, is traded for a similar asset. The fair market value of the new asset is $9,500. Boot of $3,500 is paid.

(d) The conditions are the same as in part (c) except that the income tax rule is to be followed.

E9-5

The following asset accounts were originally debited on January 1, 19_1 for the amounts shown. All amounts represent cash payments.

Patents (the patent is expected to have value during its entire legal life, 12 years of which had expired when purchased)	$ 2,500
Leasehold improvements (the improvements have a ten-year life. The lease expires on December 31, 19_5)	3,000
Goodwill (it was decided at the time of purchase that the goodwill should be amortized over five years)	$10,000
Organization costs	1,500

At what amount should each of the items be reported on the balance sheet at December 31, 19_3?

Problems

A9-1

Selected information concerning long-lived asset acquisitions of Thomas Corporation during 19_5, its first year of operations, is presented below.

January 17—Occupied a new building costing $80,000 and having an estimated life of 50 years. Took delivery on machinery costing $55,000 and having an estimated useful life of 10 years.

February 8—Acquired four trucks costing $1,500 each and having an estimated life of 4 years.

July 27—A machine acquired on January 17 and having an original cost of $6,000 is traded for a new machine. The new machine is recorded at a cost of $8,000 and is expected to have a 10-year life.

November 11—One of the trucks is sold for $800 cash.

Assuming that the company uses the unit basis of depreciation accounting and the straight-line method of computing depreciation, determine the depreciation applicable to the building, machinery, and trucks for the year ending December 31, 19_5. Round amounts to the nearest dollar.

A9-2

In 19_1, Beman Coal Company paid $8,000,000 for property which was estimated to contain 800,000 tons of coal. It was estimated that the land would have a value of $200,000 after depletion of the coal reserves.

The following quantities were mined during the first three years:

19_1	34,000 tons
19_2	67,000 tons
19_3	55,000 tons

Early in 19_4, adjoining property containing an estimated 80,000 tons of coal was purchased for $968,000. It was estimated this additional property would have a value of $20,000 after the coal had been removed. In 19_4, 45,000 tons of coal were mined.
Compute the depletion charges for each of the four years.

A9-3

The following data pertain to certain equipment belonging to Young Company.

Asset	Date acquired	Cost	Estimated useful life	Estimated salvage
A	July 1, 19_1	$5,000	6 years	–0–
B	January 1, 19_2	6,000	4 years	$ 600
C	May 1, 19_3	7,600	4 years	1,000

Information concerning the disposal of the assets during the year 19_5 is given below.

Asset	Date traded	Fair market value of new asset	Cash paid	Fair market value of old asset
A	January 1, 19_5	$4,200	$2,000	$2,200
B	October 1, 19_5	5,175	4,575	600
C	December 31, 19_5	6,000	3,575	2,425

All assets are being depreciated by the straight-lined method.

Required:

(a) The entry to record the trade of Asset A, assuming similar assets and that the income tax method is followed.

(b) The entry to record the trade of Asset B, assuming similar assets.

(c) The entry to record the trade of Asset C, assuming the equipment is traded for a truck.

A9-4

Condensed financial statement information for Ryder Corporation for the past three years is presented below.

	December 31,		
	19_1	19_2	19_3
Tangible assets	$350,000	$475,000	$600,000
Total assets	$350,000	$475,000	$600,000
Liabilities	$ 36,000	$ 45,000	$ 90,000
Common stock	$245,000	$245,000	$245,000
Retained earnings	$ 69,000	$185,000	$265,000
Total liabilities and stockholders' equity	$350,000	$475,000	$600,000
Net income	$ 35,000	$ 50,000	$ 55,000

The company has been sold and the sales agreement calls for the computation of goodwill by capitalizing, at 10 per cent, the average annual earnings in excess of 7 per cent on the average investment for the past three years.

Compute the amount to be paid for the goodwill.

A9-5 Atlantic Corporation acquired a machine on January 1, 19_1, at an invoice price of $23,000. Additional amounts were paid for transportation, $310, and installation, $490. It was estimated that the machine would have a useful life of 8 years and no salvage value. The company used the declining-balance method at twice the straight-line rate to compute depreciation.

On January 1, 19_3, the company reexamined its estimates of useful lives and salvage values, and decided that the remaining life of this machine was 4 years from that date, and that it had a salvage value of $700.

On January 1, 19_6, $5,500 was paid for a major overhaul of the machine, and it was estimated that the overhaul would result in a total useful life of 7 years and a salvage value of $3,500 for the asset.

Required:

(a) The entry to record annual depreciation on December 31, 19_6.

(b) Computation of the gain or loss on disposal if the asset is sold for $4,200 on July 1, 19_7.

B9-1 Goldman Company acquired land, on which a building was located, for $155,000. In order to construct a new plant on the site, the existing building was demolished. Demolition costs totaled $5,700, and materials from the old building were sold for $2,300. The following costs were incurred during construction of the new building:

Contract price paid to contractor	$535,000
Fees paid to architect	3,770
Real estate taxes (Building, $1,500; Land, $1,050)	2,550
Grading costs to prepare site for new building	5,350
Building permit	355
Landscaping	3,900
Surfacing of parking lot	5,000
Installation of outside lighting for parking lot	2,200
Construction of fence around parking lot	1,700
Interest on money borrowed for payments to contractor	1,750

Record the information above in appropriate general ledger accounts.

B9-2 Austin Company acquired the following assets on January 1, 19_3:

	A	B	C
Cost	$27,000	$15,000	$21,000
Scrap value	$ 3,000	None	1,000
Estimated life	6 years	10 years	5 years

Compute the depreciation to be recorded for each asset for the years ending December 31, 19_3 and 19_4, under each of the following depreciation methods:

(a) Straight-line.

(b) Sum-of-the-years'-digits.

(c) Declining balance at twice the straight-line rate.

Round all amounts to the nearest dollar.

Ryan Corporation made the following equipment acquisitions and dispositions.

Date acquired	Cost	Estimated scrap value	Estimated useful life	Depreciation method	Disposal Date	Details
(a) 7/1/_1	$2,750	$750	5 years	Straight-line	12/31/_2	Traded in on (b)
(b) 12/31/_2	$500 plus trade in	$300	8 years	Declining balance— (25%)	1/3/_5	Sold for $700
(c) 1/2/_2	$3,600	–0–	5 years	Sum-of-the-years'-digits	10/1/_4	Traded in on (d)
(d) 10/1/_4	$875 plus trade in	$175	4 years	Straight-line	12/31/_8	Sold as scrap for $100

Required:

(a) Entries to record the purchases of the assets.

(b) Entries to record the depreciation for each asset at the end of each of the first two accounting periods, assuming the company is on a calendar-year basis.

(c) Entries to record the disposals of the assets under the income tax rule. At December 31, 19_2, asset A had a fair market value of $2,000 and asset B had a fair market value of $2,500. At October 1, 19_4, asset C had a fair market value of $1,000 and asset D had a fair market value of $1,875.

Warsham Oil Company acquired property containing oil reserves for a total of $850,000 on January 1, 19_6. It was estimated that the reserves amounted to 85,000 barrels of oil and that the land would have a value of $25,000 after removal of the oil.

Additional expenditures were made of $55,000 for development costs and $275,000 for equipment. The equipment will be abandoned when the reserves are depleted.

Production during the first year was 15,550 barrels of oil.

Prepare journal entries to record the above information.

Smith Company purchased a machine for $25,000 on July 1, 19_1. It was estimated at that time that the useful life would be 10 years and salvage value would be $750. Transportation charges of $355 were paid to have the asset delivered and $785 was invested in a special foundation.

On January 1, 19_6, Smith Company paid $3,035 for a major overhaul of the machine. It was then estimated that the remaining life after the overhaul would be 8 years and that the asset would be worthless at the end of that time.

Required:

Journal entries for the following, assuming the straight-line method is used to depreciate the asset:

(a) Purchase of the asset on July 1, 19_1.

(b) The adjustment for depreciation expense on December 31, 19_1, and December 31, 19_2.

(c) The adjustment for depreciation expense on December 31, 19_6.

(d) The sale of the asset on July 1, 19_7, for $2,270 cash.

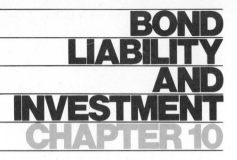

BOND LIABILITY AND INVESTMENT
CHAPTER 10

PURPOSE OF CHAPTER   Bonds represent a long-term liability to the company issuing them and an investment to the lenders acquiring them. Since the accounting for bonds is similar for both the borrower (company issuing the bonds) and the lender (bond investor), we will discuss the accounting for both the bond issuer and investor. Thus the purpose of this chapter is to explain (1) the nature of long-term financing and investing, (2) the nature and characteristics of bonds, and (3) the measurement, recording, and reporting of long-term bonds payable and bond investment.

LONG-TERM FINANCING   One of the most important functions of financial management is the financing or obtaining of funds necessary to operate a business. When a business finds it necessary or desirable to raise additional funds, it may borrow them on a short-term note payable, on a long-term note payable, on a long-term mortgage note payable, or on bonds, or it may issue additional capital stock (discussed in Chapters 11 and 12). It usually is regarded as sound financial management to borrow on short-term notes only if the funds are needed for current operations and if the current operations presumably will produce the cash with which to repay the loan. If the funds are to be used for long-term purposes, such as the acquisition of plant and equipment or the construction of a new plant, the funds usually should be obtained by long-term borrowing (issuing long-term notes or bonds) or by issuing additional capital stock.

Long-term borrowing versus stock issues   Long-term borrowing in the form of long-term notes or bonds has certain advantages over stock issues:

> Unlike stockholders, lenders have no vote; therefore, the existing stockholders do not have to share the management with lenders.
> Since interest is at a fixed rate, a company may be able to earn a higher return on the borrowed funds than the rate of interest it pays, which benefits the existing stockholders. The use of borrowed money to increase the return to stockholders is called *trading on the equity* or *leverage*.
> Since interest is tax deductible, whereas dividends to stockholders are not, this reduces the net cost (after taxes) of borrowing funds.

On the other hand, dividends are usually paid only when a company is profitable, while interest on debt is a legal obligation and must be paid when due regardless of whether the borrowing company is profitable or not. Similarly, capital stock does not mature, while long-term borrowing has a definite maturity date on which the borrowing company is legally bound to repay the debt. Thus if interest and maturity payments are not made when due, the lender may institute foreclosure proceedings and the borrowing company may lose some of its property, plant, and equipment, which are essential to its operations. The borrowing company may even be forced into liquidation with a consequent loss that may leave a very small equity, if any at all, for the stockholders. Finally, unlike capital stock, the long-term borrowing agreement may subject the borrowing company to various covenants for the protection of the lender (such as restrictions on additional debt, working capital, dividends, etc.).

Mortgage notes and bonds   If funds are needed for long-term purposes, such as plant and equipment additions, the borrowing will usually be obtained by issuing long-term mortgage notes payable or bonds payable. The incurring of such long-term debt allows time for the increased earnings to be obtained from the new acquisitions to be used in repaying the debt. Moreover, it is presumed that such debt would not be incurred unless it is expected that the rate of return to be earned by investing the borrowed funds will be higher than the rate of interest paid; hence, it is long-term financing to increase the earnings available to stockholders.

If the desired long-term funds can be borrowed from one lender, the borrower may issue a note and a mortgage (a long-term mortgage note payable). The note specifies the terms of the obligation (date, maturity, interest rate, and so forth) and the mortgage is a document that pledges certain property (land, buildings, and other long-lived assets) as security for the loan.[1] If the borrower (or mortgagor) should default, the mortgage gives the lender (or mortgagee) the right to take possession of the mortgaged property. Mortgage notes payable are usually issued by small businesses, such as single proprietorships, partnerships, or small corporations.

Although a large corporation may issue mortgage notes, usually the amount of money needed is so large that it is impossible to obtain the funds from one lender; hence, an issue of bonds may be offered to the public. By issuing bonds the corporation, in effect, splits the loan into a large number of small investing units, usually of $1,000 each, and thereby enables more than one lender (or bond investor) to participate in the loan. Because long-term borrowings by corporations are usually represented by bonds, this chapter will deal largely with bonds. However, except as indicated above, long-term mortgage notes are essentially of the same nature as secured bonds. Therefore, what is said about secured bonds generally applies also to long-term mortgage notes.

LONG-TERM INVESTMENTS   A corporation (or an individual) may acquire the capital stock (discussed in Chapter 13) or bonds of another company to be held as a long-term investment. Bonds are acquired as a long-term investment because they provide a specified rate of interest, maturity amount, and maturity date, and

---

[1]A mortgage originally was a conveyance of property from a debtor to a creditor, subject to the proviso that if the debtor met the obligation, the conveyance would be nullified. In most states the form of the mortgage has been changed to give it the status of a lien instead of a conveyance or transfer of title.

because, as debt instruments, they provide a prior claim over stockholders in the event of liquidation. Thus bonds provide investors with a fixed return that must be legally paid periodically regardless of the issuing company's earnings and regardless of the price of the bonds.

Bonds may be acquired at the date of their issuance or at later dates during the life of the bonds. Since the bonds of most large corporations are listed on organized securities exchanges, they may be acquired through any brokerage house that is a member of an exchange. In addition, brokerage firms provide for the buying and selling of unlisted bonds in the so-called over-the-counter market.

NATURE OF BONDS A bond is a certificate promising to pay the principal of and interest on a loan. The principal of the bond, also called its *face, par,* or *maturity amount* (value), is the dollar amount payable by the borrower at the maturity or due date specified on the bond certificate. The face amount of a bond is usually $1,000, but it can be at other denominations, such as $100, $10,000, or $100,000. For example, a bond issue with a total face amount of $500,000 could consist of 500 bonds with a face amount of $1,000 each.

In addition to the face amount payable upon maturity, the issuing company makes periodic interest payments, usually semiannually, throughout the life of the bonds. The interest payments are based on the contractual interest rate of a bond, called its *nominal, stated,* or *coupon* rate, which is expressed as an annual rate. For bonds with interest payable semiannually, the face amount multiplied by one-half the annual nominal rate is equal to the total interest paid by the issuing company every six months. For example, a 7 per cent, $500,000 bond issue pays interest of $17,500 (= $500,000 × .07 × 1/2) semiannually.

From the viewpoint of the issuing company, the bonds are a long-term liability. To the lenders acquiring the bonds, the bonds are an investment. The terms of the agreement between the borrower (company issuing the bonds) and lenders (investors) are specified in a bond contract, called a *bond indenture.* This contract is normally held by a trustee (such as a bank or trust company), selected by the borrower, who acts as an independent third party to protect the interests of the bondholders, as well as the borrower, in making sure that the provisions of the bond indenture are fulfilled. In addition, if property is pledged as security for the bonds, a deed of trust is used to convey the pledged property to the trustee as agent for the bondholders.

The board of directors and stockholders of a company usually must give formal approval before bonds can be issued. Once approved, the borrowing company can issue bonds to the public, to an underwriter (such as an investment banker or syndicate) who in turn markets the bonds to the public, or to a financial institution (such as an insurance company). Usually the entire bond issue will be given to an underwriter at a specified price, who then markets the bonds to the general public at a slightly higher price.

CLASSES OF BONDS Although it is impossible to discuss all the different kinds of bonds that have been devised for use in corporate financing, some of the more common forms of bonds can be classified according to their basic characteristics as follows:

Bond classification as to their underlying security:

Secured bonds. These are bonds secured by a mortgage (mortgage bonds) or a pledge of specific assets as a guarantee of repayment. Although secured bonds differ as to the nature of the property that is pledged, three classes of secured bonds in common use are:

Real estate mortgage bonds, secured by mortgages on land or on land and buildings.

Chattel mortgage bonds, secured by mortgages on tangible personal property, such as machinery and equipment of various kinds.

Collateral trust bonds, secured by a pledge of stocks, bonds, or other negotiable instruments.

It should also be pointed out that bonds may be secured by first, second, or even third mortgages on the same property. If the obligations are not met and foreclosure ensues, the proceeds from the disposal of the mortgaged property must go first to the satisfaction of the first-mortgage bondholders, any residue to the satisfaction of the second-mortgage bondholders, and so on.

Unsecured bonds, usually called *debentures*. These are bonds not secured by the pledge of any specific property; hence, their marketability depends on the general credit of the borrower.

Bond classification as to the nature of maturity:

Ordinary bonds. These are bonds with principal or maturity amount payable in full at a single fixed maturity date in the future. They mature all at one time. Ordinary bonds are also referred to as *straight* or *term bonds*.

Serial bonds. These are bonds with principal or maturity amount payable in installments at specified future dates. They mature on a series of stated installments.

Bond classification as to early retirement:

Callable bonds. These are bonds with a call privilege, stated in terms of issuance, that gives the issuing company the right to retire, before maturity, specified bonds or bonds determined by lot at its option. (The call privilege may be made applicable to the entire issue.)

Convertible bonds. These are bonds that give the bondholder the right to exchange them for the issuing company's securities, usually common stock, at the option of the bondholder.

Bond classification as to the evidence of ownership:

Registered bonds. These are bonds in which the names and addresses of the owners of the bonds are kept on file (registered) with the issuing company or its fiscal agent; interest is paid by check mailed to the registered owners.

Coupons bonds. These are nonregistered bonds with attached printed coupons; hence, they are transferable by delivery, without endorsement, and interest is collected by clipping coupons and presenting them to a bank for deposit or collection.

BOND PRICES Bonds are bought and sold on organized security exchanges and on a less formal exchange called the *over-the-counter market*. The board prices used in such trading are quoted as a percentage of their face or par amount, which is usually $1,000. A bond quoted at 97 would have a market price of $970 (= $1,000 × .97), one quoted at 102 would be priced at $1,020 (= $1,000 × 1.02), and one quoted at 100 (or par) would be priced at $1,000 (= $1,000 × 1.00). Thus a bondholder can sell a bond at the going market price by merely placing a telephone call to a broker and thereby convert the bond investment into cash.

Although it is common to speak about a newly issued bond as being "sold" by the borrowing company, the bond is *not* an asset, similar to merchandise, that is sold by a corporation. Instead, a corporation *issues* bonds to lenders for cash in exchange for the promise to pay periodic interest and principal upon maturity. To the bondholders, on the other hand, the bonds are an asset (investment) and can be sold in the bond market; however, such a sale has no cash effect on the corporation originally issuing the bonds. Thus when bonds are originally issued by a company, the transaction is between the issuing company (or the company's underwriter) and lenders (investors). However, the large volume of daily transactions in bonds does not usually involve original bond issues; instead, it involves the purchase and sale of bonds from one investor to another investor, normally acting through a broker.

The market price of a bond is determined by the current market rate of interest for bonds of a similar risk and maturity. Since the market rate of interest varies from day to day depending on the demand for and the supply of money, the fixed contractual interest rate printed on the bond certificates (the nominal, coupon, or stated rate) will not likely be the same as the current market rate of interest existing at the time the bonds are issued, which is called the *effective interest rate* or *yield*.

If the fixed nominal interest rate on bonds is less than the effective interest rate, the bonds would have to be issued at a price below face (at a discount) in order to attract lenders who could earn the effective rate on comparable alternative investments. If the nominal rate is greater than the effective rate, the bonds would have to be issued at a price above face (at a premium), since the issuing company would not be willing to pay interest at a rate higher than the current market rate of interest. Of course, if the nominal rate is the same as the effective rate, the bonds would be issued at a price equal to the face amount (issued at par). Thus, in effect, bond prices bring the nominal interest rate, which cannot be changed, in line with the current market interest rate.

BOND ISSUE AUTHORIZATION After the board of directors and the stockholders have approved a bond issue, the deed of trust is drawn and the bonds are printed. The deed of trust states the amount of bonds that can be issued or the bonds authorized. Although there is no need for a formal entry in the books for bond authorization, a memorandum notation may be made indicating the amount of bonds authorized, and the balance sheet should disclose the total authorization. Also, in anticipation of future financial requirements greater than present needs, a company may issue only a portion of the total bonds authorized.

BONDS ISSUED AND ACQUIRED AT PAR If bonds are issued at their face amount, or at par, this means that lenders are willing to invest in the bonds at the contractual interest rate (the nominal, stated, or coupon rate) stated on the bonds. In other words, the fixed nominal rate is equal to the market rate of interest at the time of issuance.

To illustrate the recording of a bond issuance and acquisition at par, assume that Topeka Corporation authorized 600, $1,000 face amount, 7 per cent, four-year bonds.[2] Each $1,000 bond is dated January 1, 19_1, which is the date from which interest is computed, interest is payable semiannually on June 30 and December 31, and the bonds mature December 31, 19_4. If Topeka Corporation issued $500,000 of the bonds on January 1, 19_1, and if Lawrence Corporation

---

[2]Although most bond issues have a maturity of 20 to 30 years, we are using a short four-year maturity to facilitate the illustrations.

acquired all the bonds, then the following entries would be made on the books of each company as follows:

Topeka Corporation (Bond issuer)			Lawrence Corporation (Bond investor)		
January 1, 19_1:					
Cash	500,000		Bond investment	500,000	
Bonds payable		500,000	Cash		500,000
Issuance of 7%, 4-year bonds at par.			Acquisition of 7%, 4-year bonds of Topeka Corporation at par.		

After issuance of the bonds, Topeka Corporation must pay interest at 3½ per cent (one-half of the 7 per cent annual rate) of face every six months (on June 30 and December 31) until the bonds mature. For the year 19_1, the following entries would be made to record the bond interest paid and received:

Topeka Corporation (Bond issuer)			Lawrence Corporation (Bond investor)		
June 30, 19_1:					
Bond interest expense	17,500		Cash	17,500	
Cash ($500,000 × 3½%)		17,500	Bond interest revenue		17,500
Paid semiannual interest on $500,000 face amount, 7%, 4-year bonds.			Receipt of semiannual interest on $500,000 face amount, 7%, 4-year Topeka Corporation bonds.		
December 31, 19_1:					
(Same entry as above)			(Same entry as above)		

If it is assumed that both companies' annual fiscal period ends December 31, 19_1, the financial statements of the two companies would report the following with regard to the bonds:

Topeka Corporation (Bond issuer)		Lawrence Corporation (Bond investor)	
Income statement:			
Bond interest expense	$35,000[a]	Bond interest revenue	$35,000[a]
Balance sheet:			
Long-term liabilities:		Long-term investments:	
Bonds payable, 7%, due December 31, 19_4; authorized $600,000; unissued $100,000; issued and outstanding at maturity amount	$500,000	Bond investment in 7%, 4-year bonds of Topeka Corporation, due December 31, 19_4, at cost	$500,000

[a]$35,000 = $17,500 + $17,500

Note the facts about authorized, unissued, and issued bonds shown in the balance sheet for Topeka Corporation. The amount of unissued bonds should be disclosed in the balance sheet to show the potential indebtedness available to the firm without further authorization or pledge of additional assets. Furthermore, bondholders have a right to know that $100,000 of additional bonds can be issued under the same trust deed that secures their bonds.

Finally, upon maturity of the bonds, and after making the last interest entry, Topeka Corporation would make an entry to retire the bond liability and Lawrence Corporation would make an entry for the receipt of the loan repayment, shown as follows:

Topeka Corporation (Bond issuer)			Lawrence Corporation (Bond investor)		
December 31, 19_4:					
Bonds payable	500,000		Cash	500,000	
Cash		500,000	Bond investment		500,000
To retire 7%, 4-year, $500,000 face bonds at maturity date.			Collection of maturity amount on Topeka Corporation bonds retired at maturity date		

BONDS ISSUED AND ACQUIRED AT A DISCOUNT   If bonds are issued at a price below par, at a discount, this means that the current market rate of interest for comparable bonds (the effective rate) is greater than the fixed nominal interest rate stated on the bonds. In such a situation, lenders are unwilling to invest in the bonds at par, since they would earn interest at the lower nominal rate, when they could invest in comparable alternative investments and earn at the higher current market rate. Lenders would only be willing to invest in the bonds at a price below par in order to earn interest at the current market rate. Also, since the issuing company receives an amount less than par, the company is, in effect, paying interest at the going market rate, which it must do if it wishes to borrow money by issuing bonds.

To illustrate the recording of a bond issuance and acquisition at a discount, assume the same data as in the preceding illustration except that the bonds were issued by Topeka Corporation to Lawrence Corporation at a price of $483,168, which is a $16,832 (= $500,000 − $483,168) discount. Assume that the bonds were issued at a discount because the effective rate at time of issuance was 8 per cent, which was higher than the 7 per cent nominal rate stated on the bonds. Thus the following entries would have been made at the time of issuance and acquisition:

Topeka Corporation
(Bond issuer)

Lawrence Corporation
(Bond investor)

January 1, 19_1:

Cash	483,168	
Bond discount	16,832	
Bonds payable		500,000

Issuance of 7%, 4-year,
$500,000 face bonds
at a $16,832 discount
based on an 8%
effective rate.

Bond investment	483,168	
Cash		483,168

Acquisition of 7%, 4-year,
$500,000 face bonds of
Topeka Corporation at a
$16,832 discount based
on an 8% effective rate.

Note that in the above entry, from the bond issuer's viewpoint, the discount is recorded in a separate account, Bond Discount, which is a contra-liability account because it is reported in the balance sheet as a direct deduction from bonds payable. Bond discount is reported contra to bonds payable because it represents additional bond interest expense that will be paid as part of the face amount of the bonds at maturity. Note, however, that from the bond investor's viewpoint, no separate bond discount account is established. This is done purely by convention, since a bond discount account could be established.

Bond discount amortization To the bond issuer, bond discount represents an increase of bond interest expense over the life of the bonds. Since the bond issuer receives an amount less than the face amount (par) at time of issuance but pays interest on the higher face amount, the issuer incurs interest expense over the life of the bonds that is greater than the nominal interest paid, by the amount of the bond discount. Thus the total interest expense over the life of the bonds is equal to the sum of the regular semiannual interest payments and bond discount.

Similarly, since the bond investor pays an amount less than the face amount at time of acquisition but receives interest on the higher face amount, the investor earns interest revenue over the life of the bonds that is greater than the nominal interest received, by the amount of the bond discount. Thus the total interest revenue of bonds acquired at a discount, held to maturity, and collected at their face amount is equal to the total semiannual interest receipts plus bond discount.

To account for this additional interest represented by bond discount, the discount is amortized (apportioned) to each interest period as an increase in interest expense (bond issuer) or interest revenue (bond investor) over the life of the bonds. That is, bond discount amortization means that part of the discount is transferred to Bond Interest Expense (bond issuer) or Bond Interest Revenue (bond investor) each interest period from the date of issuance or acquisition to the maturity date. There are two acceptable accounting methods for amortizing bond discount: the straight-line method, which we will now discuss, and the effective-interest method, which will be discussed later.

Under the straight-line method, bond discount is allocated to each interest period in equal dollar amounts. For example, in the preceding illustration there would be eight semiannual interest dates during the four-year life of the bonds. Thus the $16,832 bond discount would be amortized each six-month period to Bond Interest Expense or Bond Interest Revenue in equal dollar amounts of $2,104 (= $16,832 ÷ 8). The entries to record bond interest for both companies for the year 19_1 would be as follows:

Topeka Corporation (Bond issuer)			Lawrence Corporation (Bond investor)		
June 30, 19_1:					
Bond interest expense	19,604[a]		Cash	17,500[c]	
Bond discount		2,104[b]	Bond investment	2,104[b]	
Cash		17,500[c]	Bond interest revenue		19,604[a]

Topeka Corporation:
Paid semiannual interest on $500,000 face amount, 7%, 4-year bonds and amortized $16,832 bond discount for 6 months.

Lawrence Corporation:
Receipt of semiannual interest on Topeka Corporation bonds and amortization of $16,832 bond discount for 6 months.

[a]$19,604 = $17,500 + $2,104
[b]$2,104 = $16,832 ÷ 8
[c]$17,500 = $500,000 × 3½%

December 31, 19_1:
(Same entry as above)   (Same entry as above)

Note that from the bond issuer's viewpoint, the bond discount amortization increases Bond Interest Expense and decreases Bond Discount by $2,104 each interest payment period. From the bond investor's viewpoint, the bond discount amortization increases Bond Investment, since there is no separate bond discount account, and Bond Interest Revenue by $2,104 each interest receipt period.

At the end of the annual fiscal period, December 31, 19_1, the financial statements of the two companies would report the following with regard to the bonds:

Topeka Corporation (Bond issuer)			Lawrence Corporation (Bond investor)	
Income statement:				
Bond interest expense		$ 39,208[a]	Bond interest revenue	$ 39,208[a]
Balance sheet:				
Long-term liabilities:			Long-term investments:	
Bonds payable, 7%, due December 31, 19_4; authorized $600,000; unissued $100,000; issued and outstanding at maturity amount	$500,000		Bond investment in 7%, 4-year, $500,000 face bonds of Topeka Corporation due December 31, 19_4 at amortized cost based on 8% effective rate	$487,376
Less bond discount (based on 8% effective rate)	12,624[b]	$487,376		

[a]$39,208 = $19,604 + $19,604
[b]$12,624 = $16,832 − $2,104 − $2,104

From the bond issuer's viewpoint, bond discount is reported in the balance sheet as a direct deduction from bonds payable at face to show the valuation of the liability (its so-called *carrying amount*), which at December 31, 19_1 was $487,376. Each year bond discount will decrease $4,208 (= $2,104 + $2,104) and the carrying amount (face amount minus unamortized bond discount) will increase each year by $4,208. At the maturity date of the bonds, the bond discount will be zero (fully amortized) and the carrying amount of the liability will be at its maturity amount, or $500,000.

From the bond investor's viewpoint, bond investment is reported in the balance sheet at its carrying amount (cost plus amortized bond discount), which at December 31, 19_1 was $487,376. Each year bond investment increases $4,208, the amount of the annual bond discount amortization, until by the maturity date the balance of the bond investment account is equal to the maturity amount, or $500,000.

The discount amortization process is illustrated in the following interest and discount amortization schedule:

**Schedule of Bond Interest and Discount Amortization
Under the Straight-Line Method**

Semiannual period	Interest expense (revenue)	Interest paid (received)	Bond discount amortization	Unamortized bond discount	Carrying amount of bonds
1/1/_1				$16,832	$483,168
6/30/_1	$ 19,604[a]	$ 17,500[b]	$ 2,104[c]	14,728[d]	485,272[e]
12/31/_1	19,604	17,500	2,104	12,624	487,376
6/30/_2	19,604	17,500	2,104	10,520	489,480
12/31/_2	19,604	17,500	2,104	8,416	491,584
6/30/_3	19,604	17,500	2,104	6,312	493,688
12/31/_3	19,604	17,500	2,104	4,208	495,792
6/30/_4	19,604	17,500	2,104	2,104	497,896
12/31/_4	19,604	17,500	2,104	-0-	500,000
	$156,832	$140,000	$16,832		

[a]$19,604 = $17,500 + $2,104
[b]$17,500 = $500,000 × 3½%
[c]$2,104 = $16,832 ÷ 8
[d]$14,728 = $16,832 − $2,104
[e]$485,272 = $483,168 + $2,104

Entries for periodic interest and discount amortization can be taken directly from the schedule for both the bond issuer and bond investor. Also, the schedule shows:

that under straight-line amortization the bond interest expense (revenue) is the same amount ($19,604) each six-month period;

that the total interest expense (revenue) for the life of the bonds ($156,832) equals the semiannual cash disbursements (receipts) for interest ($140,000) plus the bond discount ($16,832);

that the balance in the bond discount account is reduced to zero by the time the bonds mature;

that by the time of maturity the carrying amount is equal to the face or maturity amount of the bonds.

Thus the amortization of the discount gradually brings the carrying amount of the bonds up to their face or maturity amount, spreading the discount over the period between issuance (acquisition) and maturity as an addition to bond interest expense (revenue).

BONDS ISSUED AND ACQUIRED AT A PREMIUM If the fixed nominal interest rate for a given bond issue is higher than the market rate for bonds of a similar nature, then the bonds would be issued at a price above par, at a premium, because of the attractive nominal interest rate. The borrower would not be willing to issue the bonds at par, since this would result in paying interest at a rate greater than the going market rate of interest for comparable bonds. The borrower would issue the bonds at a premium and thereby would incur interest expense at the market rate of interest (the effective rate), which is lower than the nominal rate. Similarly, by paying a premium to acquire the bonds, the bond investor would earn interest revenue at the market rate of interest.

To illustrate the recording of a bond issuance and acquisition at a premium, assume the same data as in the preceding illustration except that the bonds were issued by Topeka Corporation to Lawrence Corporation at a price of $517,549, which is a $17,549 (= $517,549 − $500,000) premium. Assume that the bonds were issued at a premium because the effective rate at time of issuance was 6 per cent, which was lower than the 7 per cent nominal rate stated on the bonds. Thus the following entries would have been made at the time of issuance and acquisition:

Topeka Corporation (Bond issuer)			Lawrence Corporation (Bond investor)		
January 1, 19_1:					
Cash	517,549		Bond investment	517,549	
Bond premium		17,549	Cash		517,549
Bonds payable		500,000	Acquisition of 7%,		
Issuance of 7%,			4-year, $500,000 face		
4-year, $500,000 face			bonds of Topeka		
bonds at a $17,549			Corporation at a		
premium based on a			$17,549 premium		
6% effective rate.			based on a 6% effec-		
			tive rate.		

Note that in the above entry, from the bond issuer's viewpoint, the premium is recorded in a separate account, Bond Premium, which is an adjunct-liability account in that it is reported in the balance sheet as a direct addition to bonds payable. Bond premium is reported as an adjunct to bonds payable because it will not be repaid at maturity and therefore represents reduced interest expense.

Bond premium amortization To the bond issuer, bond premium represents reduced interest expense over the life of the bonds. Since the bond issuer receives an amount greater than the face amount (par) at time of issuance but pays interest on the lower face amount, the issuer incurs interest expense over the life of the bonds that is less than the nominal interest paid, by the amount of the bond premium. Thus the total interest expense over the life of the bonds is equal to the regular semiannual interest payments minus the bond premium.

Similarly, since the bond investor pays an amount greater than the face amount at time of acquisition but receives interest on the lower face amount, the investor earns interest revenue over the life of the bonds that is less than the nominal interest received, by the amount of the bond premium. Thus the total interest revenue of bonds acquired at a premium, held to maturity, and collected at their face amount is equal to the total semiannual interest receipts minus the bond premium paid at acquisition and not recovered at maturity.

To account for this reduced interest represented by bond premium, the premium is amortized to each interest period as a decrease in interest expense (bond issuer) or interest revenue (bond investor) over the life of the bonds. Referring to the preceding illustration, we see that the $17,549 bond premium would be amortized, under the straight-line method, in equal dollar amounts of $2,194 (= $17,549 ÷ 8). Thus the entries to record bond interest for both Topeka Corporation and Lawrence Corporation for the year 19_1 would be as follows:

Topeka Corporation
(Bond issuer)

June 30, 19_1:
Bond interest expense	15,306[a]	
Bond premium	2,194[b]	
Cash		17,500[c]

Paid semiannual interest on $500,000 face amount, 7%, 4-year bonds and amortized $17,549 bond premium for 6 months.

Lawrence Corporation
(Bond investor)

Cash	17,500[c]	
Bond investment		2,194[b]
Bond interest revenue		15,306[a]

Receipt of semiannual interest on Topeka Corporation bonds and amortization of $17,549 bond premium for 6 months.

[a]$15,306 = $17,500 − $2,194
[b]$2,194 = $17,549 ÷ 8
[c]$17,500 = $500,000 × 3½%

December 31, 19_1:
(Same entry as above)   (Same entry as above)

Note that from the bond issuer's viewpoint, the bond premium amortization reduces Bond Interest Expense and Bond Premium by $2,194 each interest payment period. From the bond investor's viewpoint, the bond premium amortization reduces Bond Investment, since by convention there is no separate bond premium account established, and Bond Interest Revenue by $2,194 each interest receipt period.

At the end of the annual fiscal period, December 31, 19_1, the financial statements of the two companies would report the following with regard to the bonds:

Topeka Corporation (Bond issuer)		Lawrence Corporation (Bond investor)	
Income statement:			
Bond interest expense	$ 30,612[a]	Bond interest revenue	$ 30,612[a]
Balance sheet:			
Long-term liabilities:		Long-term investments:	
Bonds payable, 7%,		Bond investment in	
due December 31, 19_4;		7%, 4-year, $500,000	
authorized $600,000;		face bonds of Topeka	
unissued $100,000;		Corporation due De-	
issued and out-		cember 31, 19_4 at	
standing at ma-		amortized cost based	
turity amount	$500,000	on 6% effective rate	$513,161
Add bond premium			
(based on 6%			
effective rate)	13,161[b] $513,161		

[a]$30,612 = $15,306 + $15,306
[b]$13,161 = $17,549 − $2,194 − $2,194

From the bond issuer's viewpoint, bond premium is reported in the balance sheet as a direct addition to bonds payable at face to show the liability at its carrying amount (face amount plus unamortized bond premium), which at December 31, 19_1 was $513,161. Each year bond premium will decrease $4,388 (= $2,194 + $2,194) and the carrying amount will decrease each year by $4,388. At the maturity date of the bonds the bond premium will be fully amortized and the carrying amount of the liability will be at its maturity amount, or $500,000.

From the bond investor's viewpoint, bond investment is reported in the balance sheet at its carrying amount (cost minus amortized bond premium), which at December 31, 19_1 was $513,161. Each year bond investment decreases $4,388, the amount of the annual bond premium amortization, until by the maturity date the balance of the bond investment account is equal to the maturity amount, or $500,000.

The premium amortization process is illustrated in the following interest and premium amortization schedule:

Schedule of Bond Interest and Premium Amortization
Under the Straight-Line Method

Semiannual period	Interest paid (received)	Interest expense (revenue)	Bond premium amortization	Unamortized bond premium	Carrying amount of bonds
1/1/_1				$17,549	$517,549
6/30/_1	$ 17,500[a]	$ 15,306[b]	$ 2,194[c]	15,355[d]	515,355[e]
12/31/_1	17,500	15,306	2,194	13,161	513,161
6/30/_2	17,500	15,306	2,194	10,967	510,967
12/31/_2	17,500	15,306	2,194	8,773	508,773
6/30/_3	17,500	15,306	2,194	6,579	506,579
12/31/_3	17,500	15,306	2,194	4,385	504,385
6/30/_4	17,500	15,306	2,194	2,191	502,191
12/31/_4	17,500	15,309[f]	2,191[g]	–0–	500,000
	$140,000	$122,451	$17,549		

[a]$17,500 = $500,000 \times 3\frac{1}{2}\%$

[b]$15,306 = $17,500 - $2,194$

[c]$2,194 = $17,549 \div 8$

[d]$15,355 = $17,549 - $2,194$

[e]$515,355 = $517,549 - $2,194$

[f]Rounded up $3

[g]Rounded down $3

Note that the amortization of the premium gradually brings the carrying amount of the bonds down to their face or maturity amount, spreading the premium over the period between issuance (acquisition) and maturity as a reduction to bond interest expense (revenue).

BOND ISSUANCES AND ACQUISITIONS BETWEEN INTEREST DATES Most bonds provide for the payment of interest semiannually. The interest-payment dates are printed on the bonds; for example, June 30 and December 31, March 1 and September 1, or June 1 and December 1.

Although bonds may be issued on an interest date, as has been assumed in the foregoing illustrations, very often market factors may cause the bonds to be issued between interest dates. Since the full amount of nominal interest is paid every six months regardless of whether or not the bonds were issued between interest dates, the lender (bond investor) is usually required to pay for the interest that has accrued from the last interest date to the issuance date, in addition to the bond price. Of course, such payment for accrued interest is returned to the lender as part of the first six-month interest payment. The result is that the issuing company incurs interest expense only for the number of months the bonds were outstanding and the lender earns interest revenue only for the number of months the bonds were held.

In accounting for bonds issued between interest dates, Bond Interest Payable is credited with the accrued interest from the previous interest-payment date to the date of issuance. Also, any discount or premium on bonds issued subsequent to the date of the bonds should be amortized over the period between the date of issuance (rather than the date of bonds) and the date of maturity—the remaining period outstanding.

Similarly, in accounting for bonds acquired between interest dates, Bond Interest Receivable is debited with the accrued interest from the last interest date to the date of acquisition. Any bond premium or discount on bonds acquired between interest dates is amortized over the period from the date of acquisition to the maturity date.

To illustrate the accounting for a bond issuance and acquisition between interest dates, let us refer to the preceding example in which bonds were issued and acquired at $517,549 on January 1, 19_1, except now we will assume that the transaction took place on March 1, 19_1. Topeka Corporation would receive and Lawrence Corporation would pay cash on March 1, 19_1 consisting of the market price of the bonds ($517,549) plus two months (January and February) accrued interest ($500,000 $\times$ 3½% $\times$ 2/6 = $5,833.33), or a total of $523,382.33. The following entries would be made by both companies:

Topeka Corporation (Bond issuer)			Lawrence Corporation (Bond investor)		
March 1, 19_1:					
Cash	523,382.33		Bond investment	517,549.00	
Bond premium		17,549.00	Bond interest		
Bonds payable		500,000.00	receivable	5,833.33	
Bond interest			Cash		523,382.33
payable		5,833.33	Acquisition of 7%,		
Issuance of 7%,			4-year, $500,000		
4-year, $500,000			face bonds of		
face bonds at 6%			Topeka Corpora-		
effective rate plus			tion at 6% effec-		
2 months accrued			tive rate plus 2		
interest.			months accrued		
			interest.		

The bond premium is amortized over the remaining period outstanding, or 46 [= (4 $\times$ 12) − 2] months, which results in straight-line amortization of $381.50 (= $17,549 ÷ 46) per month. Thus at the first interest date four months of bond premium would be amortized, as shown by the following entries for both companies:

Topeka Corporation (Bond issuer)			Lawrence Corporation (Bond investor)		

June 30, 19_1:

Topeka Corporation			Lawrence Corporation		
Bond interest			Cash	17,500.00[d]	
expense	10,140.67[a]		Bond investment		1,526.00[b]
Bond premium	1,526.00[b]		Bond interest		
Bond interest			receivable		5,833.33[c]
payable		5,833.33[c]	Bond interest		
Cash		17,500.00[d]	revenue		10,140.67[a]
Paid semiannual in- terest on $500,000 face amount, 7%, 4-year bonds and amortized $17,549 bond premium for 4 months.			Receipt of semiannual interest on Topeka Corporation bonds and amortization of $17,549 bond premium for 4 months.		

[a]$10,140.67 = $17,500.00 − $1,526.00 − 5,833.33

[b]$1,526.00 = $381.50 × 4

[c]$5,833.33 = $500,000 × 3½% × 2/6

[d]$17,500.00 = $500,000 × 3½%

Note that the bond interest expense (revenue) shown in the above entries consists of four months' nominal interest ($500,000 × 3½ % × 4/6 = $11,666.67) minus four months' bond premium amortization ($1,526.00) for a total of $10,140.67 interest expense (revenue) incurred (earned) for four months.

YEAR-END ADJUSTMENTS FOR ACCRUED INTEREST If an interest date coincides with the close of the issuing (acquiring) company's fiscal year, as has been assumed in the foregoing illustrations, then no year-end adjustment for bond interest expense (revenue) is needed. If, however, an interest date does not correspond with the end of a fiscal year, an adjusting entry is needed at year end for the interest accrued and for the amortization of any bond premium or discount from the last interest date to the end of the fiscal year. Such an adjusting entry brings the bond accounts up to date so that they may be properly reported in the financial statements.

To illustrate year-end adjusting entries for bond interest, assume that the bonds issued by Topeka Corporation and acquired by Lawrence Corporation at $517,549 were issued on April 1, 19_1, the date of the bonds, and pay interest semiannually on April 1 and October 1. At December 31, 19_1, the end of the fiscal year for both companies, the following entries would be made for three months' (October, November, and December) accrued interest and bond premium amortization:

Topeka Corporation
(Bond issuer)

Lawrence Corporation
(Bond investor)

December 31, 19_1:

Bond interest expense	7,653[a]		Bond interest receivable	8,750[c]	
Bond premium	1,097[b]		Bond investment		1,097[b]
Bond interest payable		8,750[c]	Bond interest revenue		7,653[a]

To accrue interest for 3 months on $500,000 face amount, 7%, 4-year bonds and amortize $17,549 bond premium for 3 months.

To accrue interest for 3 months on Topeka Corporation bonds and to amortize $17,549 bond premium for 3 months.

[a]$7,653 = $8,750 − $1,097

[b]$1,097 = ($17,549 ÷ 8)(3/6)

[c]$8,750 = $500,000 × 3½% × 3/6

RETIREMENT OF BONDS   Bonds may be retired:

(1) In total at maturity:
   (a) By payment from the company's general funds, or from the proceeds of a refunding operation in which new securities are issued.
   (b) Through the operation of a sinking fund.

(2) In installments:
   (a) Bonds may be issued payable in installments; these are called *serial bonds*.
   (b) A call privilege, stated in the terms of issuance, may give the company the right to retire, before maturity, specified bonds or bonds determined by lot. (The call privilege may be made applicable to the entire issue.)
   (c) Bonds may be retired periodically through the operation of a sinking fund.

SERIAL BONDS

As an illustration of serial bonds, assume that $100,000 is borrowed; nothing is to be paid off during the first five years; at the end of the sixth year and each year thereafter, $20,000 is to be paid, so that the bonds will be retired serially by the end of the tenth year. Each retirement is recorded by a debit to Bonds Payable and a credit to Cash from the bond issuer viewpoint and a debit to Cash and a credit to Bond Investment from the bond investor viewpoint.

Amortization of premium or discount on serial bonds   Premium or discount on serial bonds may be amortized by the "bonds outstanding" method. The following illustration of the procedure is based on the facts assumed in the preceding paragraph, with the further assumption that the bonds were issued at a discount of $4,000.

To compute the fractions of total, the amounts of bonds outstanding each year were divided by the $800,000 total. To determine the discount amortizations, the $4,000 discount was multiplied by the fractions of total.

SCHEDULE OF DISCOUNT AMORTIZATION
Bonds Outstanding Method

During year	Bonds outstanding	Fraction of total	Discount amortization
1	$100,000	10/80 (100,000/800,000)	$ 500 (10/80 of $4,000)
2	100,000	10/80	500
3	100,000	10/80	500
4	100,000	10/80	500
5	100,000	10/80	500
6	100,000	10/80	500
7	80,000	8/80	400
8	60,000	6/80	300
9	40,000	4/80	200
10	20,000	2/80	100
	$800,000	80/80	$4,000

SINKING FUNDS If bonds are to be retired at maturity or periodically through the operation of a sinking fund, the borrowing company agrees, as one of the terms of the bond agreement, to make periodic deposits with a sinking fund trustee, who may or may not also be the trustee under the mortgage. When deposits are made with the trustee, the company debits Sinking Fund and credits Cash. The trustee generally invests such deposits in securities; any interest or dividend revenue therefrom increases the fund (debit Sinking Fund and credit Interest and Dividend Revenue from Sinking Fund).

In recent years there has been an increasing tendency to use a sinking fund procedure for the periodic retirement of bonds through the exercise of a call privilege. The sinking fund trustee may call the bonds by lot, or in accordance with any other arrangement set forth in the indenture. Usually the call price is above face—with the call premium declining as the maturity date approaches. Any gain or loss on retirement, after any unamortized issuance discount or premium applicable to the retired bonds has been written off, should be recorded on the company's books as shown below. It is assumed that the retirement premium was $500, that $100,000 of bonds were outstanding, and that the unamortized bond premium as of the retirement date was $2,000; thus 10 per cent of the bonds were being retired.

Bond issuer			Bond investor		
Bonds payable	10,000		Cash	10,500	
Bond premium	200		Bond investment		10,200
Loss on bond retirement	300		Gain on sale of		
Sinking fund		10,500	bond investment		300

Note that from the bond issuer's viewpoint any loss on bond retirement is equal to the excess of reacquisition price over the carrying amount of the bonds and any gain would be the excess of carrying amount over reacquisition price. Any gain or loss on debt extinguishment must be reported in the income statement as an extraordinary item, except when the reacquisition satisfies current or future sinking fund requirements (as in the above illustration) and the gain or loss is reported as a separate line item.[3]

[3]Financial Accounting Standards Board, "Reporting Gains and Losses from Extinguishment of Debt," *Statement of Financial Accounting Standards No. 4* (Stamford, Conn.: FASB, March, 1975), paragraph 8.

CONVERTIBLE BONDS Bonds sometimes contain a provision entitling their holders to convert the bonds into other securities of the issuing company, such as capital stock. When such a conversion is made, consideration must be given to the terms of the conversion as set forth in the bond indenture. Such terms will indicate the kind and quantity of securities to be received in exchange and the disposition to be accorded accrued interest on the bonds if the conversion occurs between interest dates. At the time of conversion, any unamortized premium or discount on the converted bonds should be removed from the accounts.

Assume that $10,000 of bonds are converted into 200 shares of no-par common stock; that the stock has a stated value of $40 per share; that there is unamortized discount of $300 applicable to the converted bonds at the conversion date; and that there is no accrued interest. The entries for the conversion are:

Bond issuer			Bond investor		
Bonds payable	10,000		Investment in common		
Bond discount		300	stock	9,700	
Common stock		8,000	Bond investment		9,700
Capital in excess of					
stated value-common					
stock		1,700			

The credit to the capital-in-excess account is based on the concept that because the cancelation of the liability on the bonds constitutes payment for the stock, the amount at which the liability is carried in the accounts is the amount received for the stock. The excess of the amount thus received over the stated value of the stock is a proper credit to paid-in capital.[4]

BOND RESTRICTIONS ON DIVIDENDS As a protection to bondholders, the borrowing company may agree to certain limitations on the payment of dividends. For instance, the borrowing company may agree that dividends shall not reduce the working capital or the stockholders' equity below the amounts existing at the date of issuance of the bonds. Such restrictions should be shown in balance sheet footnotes, or parenthetically in the balance sheet, thus:

Stockholders' equity:		
Capital stock	$100,000	
Retained earnings (of which $40,000 is not available for dividends because of restrictions in the bond indenture)	65,000	$165,000

EFFECTIVE-INTEREST AMORTIZATION Although the straight-line method of bond premium or discount amortization is widely used in actual accounting practice, it is acceptable only if it does not produce results materially different from those produced under the effective-interest method.[5] Since in many cases bond premium or discount is not a material amount, the simpler straight-line method is used for convenience. However, the straight-line method is not conceptually sound.

[4]Paid-in capital is discussed in Chapter 11.

[5]Accounting Principles Board, "Interest on Receivables and Payables, *Opinion No. 21* (New York: AICPA, August, 1971), Paragraph 15.

Bonds are issued, bought, and sold on the basis of effective-interest rates to maturity. In fact, the price of a bond is equal to the present value (discussed in the appendix to Chapter 6) of the future interest payments plus the present value of the future maturity (face) amount, where the present value is based on the effective rate at the time of issuance or acquisition. Thus interest expense and revenue should be based on effective rates consistent with bond prices, not straight-line averages, and bonds should be reported in the balance sheet at present value, not approximations of present value resulting from straight-line amortization. In other words, effective-interest amortization is a theoretically sound method for measuring true bond interest expense (revenue) and the true present value of bonds.

Under the effective-interest method, the effective rate at time of issuance (acquisition) is multiplied by the present value of the bonds at the beginning of the interest payment (receipt) period to determine the bond interest expense (revenue) for the period. The difference between the periodic interest expense (revenue) and the periodic nominal interest paid (received) is equal to the amount of periodic bond premium or discount amortization.

To illustrate effective-interest amortization, again assume that Topeka Corporation issued on January 1, 19_1 (the date of the bonds), $500,000 face, 7 per cent, four-year bonds paying interest semiannually on June 30 and December 31 to Lawrence Corporation. The price of the bonds was $483,168, which reflected the 8 per cent effective rate at issuance.[6] The entries to record bond interest for both companies for the year 19_1, under the effective-interest method, would be as follows:

Topeka Corporation (Bond issuer)			Lawrence Corporation (Bond investor)		
June 30, 19_1:			Cash	17,500.00c	
Bond interest			Bond investment	1,826.72b	
expense	19,326.72a		Bond interest		
Bond discount		1,826.72b	revenue		19,326.72a
Cash		17,500.00c	Receipt of semi-		
Paid semiannual			annual interest		
interest on			on Topeka Corpo-		
$500,000 face			ration bonds and		
amount, 7%, 4-year			amortization of		
bonds and amortized			$16,832 bond		
$16,832 bond			discount for 6		
discount for 6			months.		
months.					

a$19,326.72 = ($483,168)(.08 × 1/2) = $483,168 × .04
b$1,826.72 = $19,326.72 − $17,500.00
c$17,500.00 = $500,000 × 3½%

---

[6]Price of bonds = Present value of $17,500 interest payments to be paid each 6 months for 4 years + Present value of $500,000 maturity amount to be paid at end of 4 years

$$P = (\$500{,}000)(3\tfrac{1}{2}\%)p_{\overline{8}|.04} + (\$500{,}000)(1.04)^{-8}$$
$$= (\$17{,}500)(6.732745) + (\$500{,}000)(.730690)$$
$$= \$483{,}168$$

Topeka Corporation
(Bond issuer)

Lawrence Corporation
(Bond investor)

December 31, 19_1:

Bond interest		
expense	19,399.79ᵃ	
Bond discount		1,899.79ᵇ
Cash		17,500.00
Paid semiannual		
interest on . . .		

Cash	17,500.00	
Bond investment	1,899.79ᵇ	
Bond interest		
revenue		19,399.79ᵃ
Receipt of semi-		
annual interest . . .		

ᵃ$19,399.79 = ($483,168 + $1,826.72)(.04)
ᵇ$1,899.79 = $19,399.79 − $17,500.00

The discount amortization process under the effective-interest method is illustrated in the following schedule:

Schedule of Bond Interest and Discount Amortization under the Effective-Interest Method

Semiannual period	Interest expense (revenue)	Interest paid (received)	Bond discount amortization	Unamortized bond discount	Carrying amount (present value) of bonds
1/1/_1				$16,832.00	$483,168.00
6/30/_1	$ 19,326.72ᵃ	$ 17,500.00ᵇ	$ 1,826.72ᶜ	15,005.28ᵈ	484,994.72ᵉ
12/31/_1	19,399.79	17,500.00	1,899.79	13,105.49	486,894.51
6/30/_2	19,475.78	17,500.00	1,975.78	11,129.71	488,870.29
12/31/_2	19,554.81	17,500.00	2,054.81	9,074.90	490,925.10
6/30/_3	19,637.00	17,500.00	2,137.00	6,937.90	493,062.10
12/31/_3	19,722.48	17,500.00	2,222.48	4,715.42	495,284.58
6/30/_4	19,811.38	17,500.00	2,311.38	2,404.04	497,595.96
12/31/_4	19,904.04ᶠ	17,500.00	2,404.04	–0–	500,000.00
	$156,832.00	$140,000.00	$16,832.00		

ᵃ$19,326.72 = $483,168 × .04
ᵇ$17,500.00 = $500,000 × 3½%
ᶜ$1,826.72 = $19,326.72 − $17,500.00
ᵈ$15,005.28 = $16,832.00 − $1,826.72
ᵉ$484,994.72 = $483,168.00 + $1,826.72
ᶠRounded up 20¢

Note that the bond interest expense (revenue) is not a constant amount each period, as it is under straight-line amortization (see page 321), but changes each period. The reason for this is that under the effective-interest method a constant rate (effective rate at issuance or acquisition) is applied to a changing carrying amount. In the case of a bond discount, the carrying amount of the bonds increases each period as the result of the amortization of the bond discount as the bonds approach maturity; hence, bond interest expense (revenue) increases each period. The total interest expense or revenue ($156,832) is equal to the total interest paid or received ($140,000) plus the total bond discount amortization ($16,832), as under the straight-line method, but the interest expense or revenue per period is different from that under the straight-line method.

If the bonds were issued (acquired) when the effective rate was 6 per cent, then the price of the bonds would have been $517,549.[7] The amortization of the bond premium under the effective-interest method would decrease the carrying amount of the bonds each period as they approached maturity; hence, bond interest expense (revenue) would decrease each period and not remain constant per period as under the straight-line method. Of course, total interest expense or revenue ($122,451) would be equal to the total interest paid or received ($140,000) minus the total bond premium amortization ($17,549), as under the straight-line method (see page 325), but the interest expense or revenue per period is different from that under the straight-line method.[8]

IMPORTANT TERMS AND CONCEPTS IN CHAPTER 10

DEMONSTRATION PROBLEM FOR REVIEW AND SELF-STUDY Clark Company is authorized to issue ten-year, 9 per cent bonds having a face amount of $100,000. The bonds are dated April 1, 19_1 and pay interest semiannually on April 1 and October 1. Bonds having a face amount of $50,000 are issued to Winder Company on June 1, 19_1 at a price of 97½ plus accrued interest. The remaining bonds were issued to Monroe Company on October 1, 19_1 at a price of 101.

INSTRUCTIONS Assume that all three companies close their books annually on December 31 and use the straight-line method to account for bond premium and discount. Prepare journal entries for the following:

$$
\begin{aligned}
^7P &= (\$500,000)(3\tfrac{1}{2}\%)p_{\overline{8}|.03} + (\$500,000)(1.03)^{-8} \\
&= (\$17,500)(7.019692) + (\$500,000)(.789409) \\
&= \$122,844.61 + \$394,704.50 \\
&= \$517,549
\end{aligned}
$$

[8]The preceding discussion is meant to be an introduction to the effective-interest method and its relationship to the present value of bonds. For a complete discussion, see Glenn L. Johnson and James A. Gentry, Jr., *Finney and Miller's Principles of Accounting: Intermediate* (Englewood Cliffs, N.J.: Prentice-Hall, Inc., 1974), Chapter 7.

(a) To account for the bonds on the books of Clark Company for the period June 1, 19_1 to April 1, 19_2.

(b) To account for the bonds on the books of Winder Company for the period June 1, 19_1 to April 1, 19_2.

(c) To account for the bonds on the books of Monroe Company for the period October 1, 19_1 to April 1, 19_2.

Round all computations to the nearest dollar.

Note Attempt to solve the demonstration problem before examining the solution that follows.

(a)

19_1					
June	1	Cash		49,500[a]	
		Bond discount		1,250[b]	
		Bonds payable			50,000
		Bond interest payable			750
		Issuance of $50,000 face amount of bonds at 97½ plus accrued interest.			
		(a) $50,000 × 97½%	$48,750		
		2 months accrued interest ($50,000 × 9% × 2/12)	750		
			$49,500		
		(b) Face amount	$50,000		
		Less issuance price	48,750		
			$ 1,250		
October	1	Bond interest expense ($50,000 × 9% × 4/12)		1,500	
		Bond interest payable ($50,000 × 9% × 2/12)		750	
		Cash ($50,000 × 9% × 6/12)			2,250
		Payment of 6 months' interest.			
	1	Bond interest expense ($11 × 4)		44	
		Bond discount			44
		Amortization of 4 months' discount.			
		Total life of bonds	120 months		
		Less time elapsed before issuance at a discount	2 months		
		Amortization period	118 months		
		Monthly amortization ($1,250 ÷ 118)	$11 (rounded)		
		Note: This entry could be combined with the entry to record the payment of interest on October 1.			
	1	Cash ($50,000 × 101%)		50,500	
		Bonds payable			50,000
		Bond premium			500
		Issuance of $50,000 face amount of bonds at 101.			
December	31	Bond interest expense ($100,000 × 9% × 3/12)		2,250	
		Bond interest payable			2,250
		Accrued interest for October–December.			

December 31	Bond interest expense ($11 × 3)		33	
	Bond discount			33
	Amortization of 3 months' discount.			
31	Bond premium ($4 × 3)		12	
	Bond interest expense			12
	Amortization of 3 months' premium.			
	Total life of bonds	120 months		
	Less time elapsed before			
	issuance at a premium	6 months		
	Amortization period	114 months		
	Monthly amortization			
	($500 ÷ 114)	$4 (rounded)		
19_2				
April 1	Bond interest expense		2,250	
	Bond interest payable		2,250	
	Cash			4,500
	Payment of 6 months' interest.			
1	Bond interest expense		33	
	Bond discount			33
	Amortization of 3 months' discount.			
1	Bond premium		12	
	Bond interest expense			12
	Amortization of 3 months' premium.			

(b)

19_1				
June 1	Bond investment		48,750	
	Bond interest receivable		750	
	Cash			49,500
	Acquisition of $50,000 face amount of bonds at 97½			
	plus 2 months' accrued interest.			
October 1	Cash		2,250	
	Bond interest revenue ($50,000 × 9% × 4/12)			1,500
	Bond interest receivable ($50,000 × 9% × 2/12)			750
	Receipt of 6 months' interest.			
1	Bond investment		44	
	Bond interest revenue			44
	Amortization of 4 months' discount.			
	Note: This entry could be combined with the entry to			
	record receipt of the interest on October 1.			
December 31	Bond interest receivable ($50,000 × 9% × 3/12)		1,125	
	Bond interest revenue			1,125
	Accrued interest for October–December.			
31	Bond investment		33	
	Bond interest revenue			33
	Amortization of 3 months' discount.			
19_2				
April 1	Cash		2,250	
	Bond interest revenue ($50,000 × 9% × 3/12)			1,125
	Bond interest receivable ($50,000 × 9% × 3/12)			1,125
	Receipt of 6 months' interest.			
1	Bond investment		33	
	Bond interest revenue			33
	Amortization of 3 months' discount.			

(c)

19_1				
October	1	Bond investment	50,500	
		Cash		50,500
		Acquisition of $50,000 face amount of bonds at 101.		
December	31	Bond interest receivable ($50,000 × 9% × 3/12)	1,125	
		Bond interest revenue		1,125
		Accrued interest for October–December.		
	31	Bond interest revenue	12	
		Bond investment		12
		Amortization of 3 months' premium.		
19_2				
April	1	Cash ($50,000 × 9% × 6/12)	2,250	
		Bond interest revenue ($50,000 × 9% × 3/12)		1,125
		Bond interest receivable ($50,000 × 9% × 3/12)		1,125
		Receipt of 6 months' interest.		
	1	Bond interest revenue	12	
		Bond investment		12
		Amortization of 3 months' premium.		

Questions

1 What are the advantages of issuing bonds as compared to issuing stock for purposes of long-term financing?

2 Why are bonds acquired as long-term investments?

3 How does the accounting for revenue from bond investments differ from the accounting for revenue from stock investments?

4 What is a bond? Why is the accounting for the bond issuer and bond investor conceptually the same?

5 What is the difference between the nominal interest rate and the effective interest rate?

6 Why is a bond issued at par? At a discount? At a premium?

7 Why is it necessary to amortize bond premium or discount?

8 If an investor purchased a bond at a discount, what equation would determine the interest revenue received by the investor over the life of the bond? What would be the equation if the investor purchased the bond at a premium?

9 What is the distinction between straight-line and effective-interest amortization?

10 How is the present value (discounted amount) of a bond determined?

11 What methods can be utilized to retire a bond issue?

12 If bonds are issued at par, does this imply that the face amount of the bonds is equal to the maturity amount of the bonds?

13 Does the fact that a bond will be redeemed at par at some future maturity date insure that its market price will move closer to par each year of its life?

14 If you bought a ten-year bond for 110 and sold it after eight years for 100, assuming straight-line amortization, did you incur a loss of $100? Explain.

Short exercises

E10-1

You are given three multiple-choice statements. Select the correct answers and indicate the corresponding letters on a sheet of paper (e.g., 1-a, 2-a, etc.).

(1) The true periodic interest revenue on a bond purchased at a premium is at a rate (a) lower than the nominal interest rate, (b) higher than the nominal interest rate, (c) the same as the nominal interest rate, (d) either higher or lower than the nominal interest rate depending on the method of amortization used, (e) none of the above.

(2) On February 1, 19_4 Z Company purchased three $1,000, 6 per cent bonds. The bonds were dated November 1, 19_3 and are four-year bonds with interest paid on May 1 and November 1. Which of the following entries reflect the purchase of the bonds on February 1, 19_4 at 104½?

(a) Investment in bonds   3,135
    Cash   3,135

(b)	Investment in bonds	3,090	
	Interest receivable	45	
	Cash		3,090
	Interest revenue		45
(c)	Investment in bonds	3,135	
	Cash		3,090
	Interest revenue		45
(d)	Investment in bonds	3,000	
	Bond premium	135	
	Cash		3,135
(e)	None of the above		

(3) The account "Unamortized Bond Discount" appears (a) on the income statement as an addition to interest expense, (b) on the income statement either as additional revenue or expense depending on whether one is the issuer or purchaser of a bond, (c) on the balance sheet as a liability, (d) on the balance sheet of the issuer as a contra account directly below the associated bonds payable account, (e) none of the above.

E10-2   *You are given below three multiple-choice statements. Select the correct answers and indicate the corresponding letters on a sheet of paper (e.g., 1-d, 2-d, etc.).*

(1) Which of the following is *correct?* (a) The market value of a bond purchased at a discount will tend to decrease to par as the maturity date approaches. (b) The carrying amount of a bond is gradually increased to par by amortizing the associated bond premium. (c) Bond investment valuation is based on the lower-of-cost-or-market rule. (d) The total interest revenue over the life of a bond equals the total interest payments plus the original bond discount. (e) All of the above. (f) None of the above.

(2) The straight-line amortization method (a) results in an increasing periodic interest expense (revenue), (b) results in a periodic interest expense (revenue) that is equal to the nominal interest rate multiplied by the discounted amount of the bond at the end of the period, (c) results in a constant periodic interest expense (revenue) and therefore an increasing bond premium or discount amortization, (d) of bond discount causes an overstatement of the periodic interest expense (revenue) in the early life of the bond, (e) all of the above, (f) none of the above.

(3) The effective-interest amortization method (a) results in an increasing periodic interest expense (revenue) when the bond was issued at a discount, (b) causes the discounted amount of the bond originally issued at a premium to decrease as the maturity date approaches, (c) results in periodic interest expense (revenue) equal to the constant effective-interest rate multiplied by the discounted amount of the bonds at the beginning of the period, (d) results in a bond premium or discount amortization equal to the difference between the periodic interest expense (revenue) and the nominal interest rate multiplied by the face amount of the bonds, (e) all of the above, (f) none of the above.

E10-3   *Engineering Company is authorized to issue $10,000 of 6 per cent, ten-year bonds dated January 1, 19_1. Interest is payable January 1 and July 1. Compute the total amount of cash received at the time of sale in each of the following cases:*

(a) The bonds are issued at 100 on January 1, 19_1.

(b) The bonds are issued at 105 on April 1, 19_1.

(c) The bonds are issued at 97 on May 1, 19_1.

(d) The bonds are issued at 100 on October 1, 19_1.

Plant Company, which closes its books on December 31, purchased ten $1,000, 6 per cent, ten-year bonds of Phone Company on January 1, 19_3 as a long-term investment. The bonds are dated January 1, 19_3, and interest is payable on January 1 and July 1.

If it is assumed that the company uses straight-line amortization, present all entries pertaining to the bonds in 19_3 under the two following situations:

(a) The bonds were purchased at 103.

(b) The bonds were purchased at 91.

Corporations A and B each issued a ten-year, $10,000 bond during 19_6. Data pertaining to the issues are given below.

Corporation	Date of bonds	Date of issue	Interest rate	Interest payment dates	Selling price
A	January 1, 19_6	January 1, 19_6	6%	1/1; 7/1	101
B	March 1, 19_6	March 1, 19_6	4½%	3/1; 9/1	97

The corporations close their books on December 31 and use the straight-line method of amortization. For each corporation, compute the following for 19_6:

(a) Interest paid.

(b) Interest expense.

(c) Interest payable at the end of the year.

One hundred $1,000 bonds, 6 per cent nominal interest, semiannual interest payments, and a ten-year life should be issued for $86,411 to yield an 8 per cent effective-interest rate. Determine the amount of interest expense (revenue) and bond discount amortization for each period of the first five years. Assume that the straight-line amortization method is used.

Complete the following bond discount amortization table for the first three years of a bond issue:

Semiannual period	Interest expense (revenue)	Interest paid (received)	Bond discount amortization	Unamortized bond discount	Carrying amount (present value) of bonds
0				$13,589	$86,411
1					
2					
3					
4					
5					
6	3,000	3,555	555	10,562	89,438

The bond has a ten-year life and was issued to yield 8 per cent. The interest is payable in semiannual installments. Assume that the bonds were issued at the beginning of the first semiannual period. The effective-interest amortization method should be used to complete the schedule.

Problems

Rack Company issued $200,000 of 10 per cent bonds at 95 on January 1, 19_3. The bonds mature in ten years and pay interest on January 1 and July 1. The bonds were purchased by Coat Company on January 1, 19_3. Assume that both companies use the straight-line amortization method.

(a) Prepare the journal entry to record the bond issue by Rack Company.

(b) Prepare the journal entry to record the bond purchase by Coat Company.

(c) Prepare the journal entries for Rack Company on July 1, 19_3, December 31, 19_3, and January 1, 19_4. Assume that the accounting period for Rack Company ends on December 31.

(d) Prepare the journal entries for Coat Company on July 1, 19_3, December 31, 19_3, and January 1, 19_4. Assume that the accounting period for Coat Company ends on December 31.

(e) What unamortized bond discount should be reported in the December 31, 19_4 financial statements for Rack Company?

A10-2

On January 1, 19_7 Miller Corporation issued $100,000 of 8 per cent bonds at 104. The bonds are dated January 1, 19_7 and mature in five years. Coupons are dated January 1 and July 1.

(a) Prepare the journal entry to record the issuance of the bonds.

(b) Prepare the journal entry to record the purchase of the bonds by investor.

(c) Prepare a schedule of bond interest expense (revenue), interest paid (received), bond premium amortization, the amount of unamortized bond premium, and the carrying amount of the bonds over the five-year period. Use the straight-line method of amortization.

A10-3

Sun Corporation, which closes its books annually on December 31, issued 10 per cent, ten-year debenture bonds having a face amount of $100,000 on January 1, 19_3 for $80,000. Interest is payable on January 1 and July 1.

Moon Corporation, which closes its books annually on December 31, purchased all the bonds of Sun Corporation on January 1, 19_3. Both companies use the straight-line method of amortization.

Required:

(a) All entries required by Sun Corporation for the year ending December 31, 19_3.

(b) All entries required by Moon Corporation for the year ending December 31, 19_3.

(c) The entry required by Sun Corporation to retire the bonds at maturity.

A10-4

President Company is authorized to issue $200,000 of ten-year, 6 per cent bonds dated April 1, 19_5. Interest is payable on April 1 and October 1. The entire issue is acquired by John Company from President Company on July 1, 19_5 at 98 plus accrued interest. Both corporations close their books on December 31 and both use the straight-line amortization method.

Required:

(a) All entries for President Company for 19_5 (omit explanations).

(b) All entries for John Company for 19_5 (omit explanations).

(c) Present the balance sheet section of President Company relating to the long-term liabilities as of the end of 19_5.

(d) Present the balance sheet section of John Company relating to the long-term investment as of the end of 19_5.

A10-5

Texas Company issues $10,000 of 6 per cent bonds dated January 1, 19_1, due January 1, 19_5. Interest will be paid on January 1 and July 1. Cost Company purchases the bonds on April 1, 19_1 at 104½ plus accrued interest. Assume that both companies use straight-line amortization.

Required:

(a) All entries for Texas Company for 19_1 (omit explanations).

(b) All entries for Cost Company for 19_1 (omit explanations).

(c) If the bonds contained a callable feature, such that they can be retired at any time for the call price of 105 plus accrued interest, prepare the Texas Company entry for the retirement of all bonds on April 1, 19_3.

(d) Prepare the Cost Company entry on April 1, 19_3 for bond retirement.

A10-6

The December 31, 19_6 balance sheet of Memory Corporation reports bonds payable at $97,336. The 6 per cent bonds were originally issued to yield an effective interest of 7 per cent and a face amount of $100,000. Interest was to be paid on January 1 and July 1.

What entry should be made on July 1, 19_7 to retire the bonds at 102? Assume that Memory Corporation uses the effective-interest amortization method.

A10-7

Kappa Company issued 6 per cent, three-year bonds having a face amount of $100,000 on January 1, 19_5 for $102,750 (effective-interest rate 5 per cent). Interest is payable on January 1 and July 1.

Sigma Company purchased all the bonds issued by Kappa Company on January 1, 19_5. Both corporations close their books on December 31 and both use the effective-interest amortization method.

Required:

(a) Prepare a schedule showing the bond interest expense (revenue), interest paid (received), bond premium amortization, the amount of unamortized bond premium, and the discounted amount of the bonds over the three-year period. You may round your figures to the nearest dollar.

(b) All entries required by Kappa Company for the year ended December 31, *19_6.*

(c) All entries required by Sigma Company for the year ended December 31, *19_6.*

B10-1

James Corporation is authorized to issue $50,000 in 8 per cent debentures. The bonds are dated September 1, 19_2 and mature in four years. Interest is to be paid on March 1 and September 1.

(a) Prepare the journal entry of James Corporation if the bonds are issued at 93 on September 1, 19_2.

(b) Prepare the journal entry of James Corporation if the bonds are issued at 93 plus accrued interest on October 1, 19_2.

(c) Prepare the journal entry of James Corporation if the bonds are issued at 103 plus accrued interest on October 1, 19_2.

(d) Prepare the journal entry of the investor if the bonds are purchased at 103 plus accrued interest on October 1, 19_2.

(e) If the bonds are issued at 105 on October 1, 19_2, what will be the interest expense (revenue) per interest period (other than the first period)? Assume the straight-line amortization method.

B10-2

The following data are a partial December 31, 19_6 balance sheet for Taco Corporation:

Long-term liabilities:
  Bonds payable, 6%, due December 31, 19_8;
    authorized $150,000; unissued $50,000;
    issued and outstanding at maturity amount $100,000
  Add bond premium (based on 5% effective
    rate)   1,793 $101,793

Assume that the bonds were issued on January 1, 19_5 and pay interest on January 1 and July 1.

Required:

(a) Using the straight-line method, complete a schedule of bond interest and premium amortization. You may round your figures to the nearest dollar.

(b) Prepare the journal entry to record the retirement of the bonds on December 31, 19_8.

B10-3

On September 1, 19_6 Jay Company issued $20,000 of 8 per cent, ten-year life, convertible bonds that pay interest on April 1 and October 1. The bonds were purchased by Hawk Company on September 1, 19_6 for $23,000 plus accrued interest. The bonds contain a provision whereby a $1,000 bond can be converted into 20 shares of Jay Company common stock. Jay Company common stock has a par value of $30 per share. Assume that both companies use straight-line amortization methods and end their fiscal year on December 31.

(a) Prepare all journal entries necessary for Jay Company during 19_6.

(b) Prepare all journal entries necessary for Hawk Company during 19_6.

(c) Assume that Hawk Company converts all of the Jay Company bonds into Jay Company common stock on April 1, 19_7. Prepare the necessary journal entry for Hawk Company.

(d) Assuming that the conversion in part (c) has occurred, prepare the necessary journal entries for Jay Company.

B10-4

Missouri Corporation is authorized to issue $80,000 of ten-year, 12 per cent bonds dated March 1, 19_3. Interest is payable on March 1 and September 1. The entire issue is acquired by Louis Company from Missouri Corporation on June 1, 19_3 at 96 plus accrued interest. The fiscal year for both firms ends on December 31. Assume straight-line amortization.

Required:

(a) Prepare all entries for Missouri Corporation for 19_3.

(b) Prepare all entries for Louis Company for 19_3.

(c) Compute the carrying amount of the bonds on December 31, 19_3.

(d) Present the balance sheet section of Missouri Corporation relating to the long-term liabilities as of December 31, 19_3.

(e) Present the balance sheet section of Louis Company relating to the long-term investments as of December 31, 19_3.

B10-5

Pot Company issues $70,000 of 6 per cent bonds dated March 1, 19_2 and due March 1, 19_6 (life of four years) on May 1, 19_2 to Clay Corporation. Interest will be paid on March 1 and September 1. The market price of the bonds on May 1, 19_2 was 104⅗ plus accrued interest. Both companies use the straight-line method of amortization and close their books on December 31.

Required:

(a) All entries for Pot Company for 19_2 (omit explanations).

(b) All entries for Clay Corporation for 19_2 (omit explanations).

(c) If the entire investment in Pot Company bonds were sold by Clay Corporation on February 1, 19_4 for 104 plus accrued interest, what would be the journal entry for Clay Corporation?

(d) If the bonds are retired by Pot Company on September 1, 19_5 at 101 plus accrued interest, what would be the journal entry for Pot Company?

B10-6 *Cup Company is authorized to issue $300,000 of five-year, 6 per cent bonds dated January 1, 19_8. Interest is payable on January 1 and July 1. The bonds were issued for $287,525 (effective yield of 7 per cent).*

Saucer Company purchases the entire issue on January 1, 19_8. Both companies close their books on December 31 and both use the effective-interest method of amortization.

(a) Present all entries required by Cup Company for 19_8.

(b) Present all entries required by Saucer Company for 19_8.

(c) Assuming that Cup Company retires the bond issue on January 1, 19_13, what entry is required by Saucer Company?

B10-7 *Refer to problem B10-6 and assume that the bonds were issued to obtain an effective yield of 4 per cent (market price of bonds $326,963).*

(a) Present all entries required by Cup Company for 19_8. Use the effective-interest method of amortization.

(b) Present all entries required by Saucer Company for 19_8. Use the straight-line method of amortization.

STOCKHOLDERS' EQUITY
CHAPTER 11

PURPOSE OF CHAPTER The total stockholders' equity of a corporation may consist of equity from different sources. The two major sources of equity are represented by paid-in capital, or amounts paid to the corporation by shareholders in stock transactions, and retained earnings. One of the major objectives in accounting for stockholders' equity is to clearly indicate the various sources.

Paid-in capital may come from more than a single class of stockholders; and, if so, this should be indicated in the financial statements. In many instances, the different classes of stock have different legal rights as to dividend payments and the right to receive payment in the event of liquidation of the firm.

This chapter discusses the nature of the various elements of stockholders' equity, as well as the various rights of different classes of capital stock. The chapter also illustrates the manner in which the various elements are recorded and reported in the firm's balance sheet.

THE CORPORATION Probably the most famous definition of the corporation is the one given in 1819 by Chief Justice Marshall in the Dartmouth College case decision, in which he described a corporation as "an artificial being, invisible, intangible, and existing only in contemplation of law."

This definition emphasizes the basic characteristic of the corporation—its separate legal entity. It is not a group of separate persons, as is the case with a partnership; it is itself a legal "person." It can make contracts in its own name; it can sue and be sued, even by its own stockholders; and it can own real estate. Within the limits of its charter, it can perform any business act which could be performed by a natural person.

Because a corporation is a legal entity, a stockholder usually is not liable for its debts unless his shares have a par value and were issued at a discount, and even under such circumstances he is liable only for the amount of the discount. Stockholders of certain classes of corporations, such as banks organized under the laws of some of the states, may have a personal liability in an amount not in excess of the par value of their shares. Although relief from personal liability is an advantage to the stockholders, it sometimes operates to the disadvantage of the corporation by limiting its borrowing power: banks sometimes refuse to lend money to a corporation unless stockholders of means endorse the notes.

The separate legal entity of a corporation gives it a continuity of life. A partnership is dissolved by the death, insanity, insolvency, or withdrawal of a partner. A corporation can be dissolved only by agreement of the stockholders, by forfeiture of the charter to the state, by judicial decree, or by the expiration of the period stated in the charter. A charter may give a corporation an unlimited life; if the life is limited by the charter, a renewal usually can be obtained.

Continuity of corporate life, notwithstanding changes in ownership, is brought about by the issuance of transferable shares. Transferability of interest gives a stockholder several advantages not enjoyed by a partner. (1) A partner cannot withdraw from a partnership or sell his interest without the consent of the other partners; if he undertakes to do so without their consent, he renders himself liable to a suit for damages. Unless there is an agreement among the stockholders to the contrary, a stockholder may sell his stock to any willing purchaser whenever he desires to do so; the consent of the other stockholders is not required. (2) If a partner dies, his heirs have a right to be paid the amount of his capital interest, but they have no right to enter the business as partners without the consent of the other partners. If a stockholder dies, his stock passes to his heirs, who thus acquire an interest in the business. (3) A stockholder can pledge his stock as collateral to a loan; a partner cannot easily pledge his partnership interest. Therefore, a stockholder is in a better position than is a partner to borrow needed funds.

These characteristics of the corporation make it an attractive form of business organization even for small enterprises. In large businesses, in which the capital requirements make it necessary to obtain funds from many investors, the adoption of the corporate form is virtually imperative.

On the other hand, the corporation has certain disadvantages, the chief of which are mentioned below.

Corporations are required to pay income taxes, and the stockholders are required to pay income taxes on dividends received in excess of an amount stated by the Internal Revenue Code. This "double taxation" has induced a number of small corporations to reorganize as partnerships.

The state requires the payment of a fee at the time the corporation is organized and may impose an annual franchise tax for the privilege of continuing operations. Numerous reports, not required of partnerships, must be submitted to the state of incorporation and to other states where business is transacted.

A corporation has a right to conduct only the kind of business authorized in its charter; to engage in other lines of business, it must obtain an amendment of its charter.

Each state regards corporations organized in other states as *foreign* corporations. If a corporation desires to do business in states other than the one from which it obtained its charter, it may be required to obtain licenses from those states and pay a license fee to each of them. Failure to obtain such licenses may result in losses of far greater amount than the fees. For instance, a state may refuse unlicensed foreign corporations the privilege of bringing actions in its courts, and heavy losses may be incurred because of the inability to enforce claims by actions at law.

Restrictions of various kinds are placed upon corporations by the states. In some states a corporation cannot own the stock of another corporation; in some states, it cannot own its own stock; in some states, its liabilities cannot exceed a certain percentage of its capital stock. Also, corporations frequently are prohibited from owning more real estate than they require for business uses.

ORGANIZATION OF A CORPORATION The organization of most corporations is governed by the laws of the respective states.[1] The procedure differs in the various states and normally the services of an attorney should be used to be certain that the applicable laws are complied with.

In general the following steps are involved:

(1) An application, signed by a required number of incorporators, is filed with a designated state officer. The application states, among other things:
   (a) The name of the corporation.
   (b) The nature of the business which it is desired to conduct.
   (c) The amount of the authorized capital stock, and the number of shares into which it is to be divided.
   (d) The names and addresses of the original subscribers to the stock.
   (e) The assets paid into the corporation by those original subscribers.
(2) If the application is approved, a charter (which is often the approved application itself) is received from the state officer with whom the application was originally filed. This charter evidences the fact that the corporation has been organized and is authorized to conduct business.
(3) A meeting of the incorporators (or stockholders) is held for the purpose (among other things) of electing directors.
(4) A meeting of the directors is held, and officers are elected.
(5) Capital stock certificates are issued.

CORPORATE MANAGEMENT If a business is organized as a corporation, the stockholders are its owners, but they have no authority to transact its business. The stockholders elect directors, to whom the general management of the business is committed. In most states a person cannot serve as a director of a corporation unless he is one of its stockholders.

Although the directors are charged with responsibility for the general management of the business, their duties are to a considerable extent supervisory, since most of the work of management is performed by officers elected by them. The officers usually include a president, a vice-president, a controller, a secretary, and a treasurer. Sometimes one individual holds more than one office; for instance, one person may be secretary and treasurer. On the other hand, there may be several vice-presidents (vice-president—sales; vice-president—production, vice-president—finance; etc.), an assistant secretary, and an assistant treasurer. The president usually is the ranking officer, but in some corporations there is an officer called the "chairman of the board," whose rank is superior to that of the president. The secretary is the official custodian of the corporate records and seal. The treasurer is the chief financial officer and the chief accounting officer is generally known as the controller.

TRANSFER AGENT AND REGISTRAR Large corporations, particularly those whose stock is listed on a stock exchange, may (either by requirement of the stock exchange or voluntarily) engage a transfer agent and a registrar to perform the duties incident to the issuance and transfer of shares and the keeping of records showing the names and addresses of stockholders and the number of shares owned by each stockholder. A bank or trust company usually is engaged to perform the duties

---

[1]The federal government charters firms such as national banks and certain quasi-governmental corporations.

of transfer agent. Another bank or trust company is engaged to perform the duties of registrar.

The employment of a transfer agent and a registrar serves as a safeguard to the stockholders. When certificates are to be transferred, they are delivered to the transfer agent, who cancels the old certificates, signs the new certificates, and passes them to the registrar, who also signs them. Records of the stockholders are kept by the transfer agent. The registrar's chief function is to act as a control against any possible overissuance of stock, and for this purpose the registrar maintains a record showing the aggregate number of shares outstanding.

MINUTE BOOK   A record of all the actions taken by the stockholders and directors at their meetings is kept in a minute book.[2] This book does not contain debit and credit entries; it contains a record of events written in narrative form, or in the form of resolutions.

The minute book contains information which may be required by the company's accountant for purposes of making entries in the accounting records, and by the public accountants when they audit the company's accounts. For instance, reference to the minutes may be necessary to validate the stated value of no-par stock, the amounts of officers' salaries, the valuations assigned to noncash assets acquired for stock, and liabilities for dividends.

The minute book usually contains a copy of the company's by-laws. The rights and duties of the stockholders, directors, and officers are in general governed by the state corporation law; in many particulars, however, they are stipulated by the corporation's own by-laws. The by-laws contain other stipulations with respect to the management of the corporation, such as the dates on which the regular meetings of the stockholders and directors shall be held, the formalities to be complied with in calling special meetings, and any transactions (such as the issuance of new stock with special privileges) that require the approval of the stockholders. The by-laws are usually passed by the stockholders, but in some states they may be passed or amended by the board of directors.

ELEMENTS OF STOCKHOLDERS' EQUITY   Corporate accounts need not differ from the accounts of other types of business organization except in the manner of displaying the elements of the owners' equity. In accounting for the elements of stockholders' equity of a corporation, the emphasis is placed on *source:* how much of the stockholders' equity is traceable to:

Investments by stockholders.
Gifts—such as the gift of a plant to a company to induce it to locate in the donor city.
Earnings.

Accounting for these matters is discussed on the following pages.

CAPITAL STOCK   Stockholder investments in a corporation are represented by shares of capital stock and are commonly referred to as *paid-in capital.* The two principal classes of stock are common and preferred. Capital stock may have a par value or be without par value.

---

[2]Separate minutes are kept by the stockholders and the directors, but it is common practice to file them in a single minute book.

PAR VALUE STOCK The *par value* of a share of stock is a purely arbitrary amount and is in no way related to the market value of the stock. Par value per share can be any amount the organizers wish it to be. Three possibilities for a corporation organized with an authorized capital of $100,000 are:

Par value per share		Number of shares		Total authorized capital
$1,000	×	100	=	$100,000
100	×	1,000	=	100,000
10	×	10,000	=	100,000

The primary accounting significance of par value is that it determines the amount credited to the capital stock account upon issuance of the stock. It may also have implications for the determination of legal capital, a concept discussed in greater detail in the next chapter.

At one time all states required that stock have a par value. This led to abuses by some promoters who found the public unable to resist buying stock at an amount below its par value. For many people there is an inevitable attraction about a $100 par value share of stock being offered for $50, even though the par value is completely unrelated to market value. Under the laws of some states, if par value stock was issued for an amount below par (that is, at a discount), the corporation's creditors could hold the stockholder liable for the difference in the event the firm should later encounter financial difficulty. However, such laws were ineffective in preventing abuses, particularly when stock was issued for noncash assets. The sale of stock at a price below par value is no longer legal.

NO-PAR STOCK The abuses of par value led, in 1912, to the enactment of the first American law permitting the issuance of stock without par value, called *no-par* stock, by the State of New York. It was felt that the no-par designation might result in a closer inspection of the assets and earnings of a corporation by prospective investors. Another advantage of no-par stock was that it eliminated the potential liability for the issuance discount.

AUTHORIZED STOCK The kind of stock, its basic features, and the number of shares authorized are recorded directly in the ledger, as follows:

COMMON STOCK

Date		(Authorized issue, 10,000 shares of $10 par value.)				

The number of shares authorized is usually in excess of the number of shares to be issued at the time the corporation is organized, thus allowing for future issues.

RECORDING THE ISSUANCE OF PAR VALUE SHARES   In the case of *par value* stock, the stock account is always credited with the par value of shares issued, regardless of the issuance price of the shares.

Using the preceding stock authorization data, if 5,000 shares of common stock are issued at par, the entry for the issuance is:

Cash	50,000	
Common stock		50,000
Issuance of 5,000 authorized shares at their par value of $10.		

When this entry is posted, the common stock account will appear as follows:

COMMON STOCK

Date		(Authorized issue, 10,000 shares of $10 par value.)		50,000	50,000 Cr.

If stock is issued for more than par value, the excess may be credited to a "premium on common stock" account, or preferably to an account called Capital in Excess of Par Value—From Stock Issuances (with the class of stock included in the title). The entry below illustrates a case where 4,000 shares of $10 par value common stock are issued for $11 per share.

Cash	44,000	
Common stock		40,000
Capital in excess of par value—From common stock issuances		4,000
Issuance of 4,000 authorized shares at a premium of $1 per share		

Stock may be issued at a premium at the time of the organization of the corporation. Stock premiums are probably more common, however, when additional shares are issued at a subsequent date. For instance, assume that a company with 1,000 outstanding shares of capital stock with a total par value of $100,000 has been successful in its operations and has accumulated, over several years, retained earnings of $50,000, thus giving the stock a book value of $150 per share [($100,000 + $50,000) ÷ 1,000 shares].[3] It might not be fair to the old stockholders to allow new stockholders to acquire stock at par. Moreover, because of the book value of the outstanding stock and the company's earnings record and prospects, its stock might be so attractive that investors would willingly pay a premium to obtain it.

STOCK PREMIUM IN THE BALANCE SHEET   The balance of the account credited with stock premiums should be shown in the Stockholders' Equity section of the balance sheet in the manner illustrated below:

Stockholders' equity:		
Common stock—$10 par value; authorized, 10,000 shares; issued,		
9,000 shares	$90,000	
Capital in excess of par value—From common stock issuances	4,000	$94,000
Retained earnings		25,000

[3]The concept of book value is discussed further in the following chapter.

RECORDING THE ISSUANCE OF NO-PAR STOCK The methods just described for recording issuances of par value stock can be used for recording issuances of no-par stock. But, in the absence of a par, this question arises: At what amount should the shares be recorded in the capital stock accounts? The answer depends on the law of the state of incorporation and on any resolution which the directors, with the permission of the law, may have passed.

The laws of some states require that the entire amount received for no-par stock shall (like the par of par value shares) be regarded as stated, or legal, capital, not to be impaired by distributions to stockholders; if a corporation is organized in a state with such a law, the entire amount received for its no-par stock should be credited to a capital stock account.

Some states allow a corporation's directors to establish a stated value for the company's no-par shares. If the directors elect to take no action establishing a stated value, the entire proceeds of the issuance of no-par shares should be credited to a capital stock account. However, when a stated value has been established, that amount should be credited to a capital stock account for each share issued.

The amount established as the stated value may be less than that received for such shares. What account should be credited for the proceeds in excess of the stated value? A paid-in surplus account has been used for this purpose, but the American Institute of Certified Public Accountants has recommended the discontinuance of the term "surplus" in the title of any account showing an element of the stockholders' equity. Compliance with the recommendation is rapidly increasing. In line with the recommendation, the excess over stated value could be credited to the account Capital in Excess of Stated Value—From Stock Issuances.

BASIS OF ILLUSTRATIONS In the following illustrations of entries recording the issuance of no-par stock, it is assumed that the corporation is authorized to issue 1,000 shares of no-par value common stock. The authorization is recorded by a memorandum notation in the common stock account, in the manner previously illustrated.

Entire proceeds regarded as stated capital In this illustration it is assumed that the corporation was organized in a state which requires that the entire proceeds of the issuance of shares be regarded as stated capital, and that all of the authorized shares were issued at $60 per share. The entry to record the issuance is:

Cash	60,000	
Common stock		60,000
Issuance of 1,000 authorized shares at $60 per share.		

Board of directors establish stated capital It is again assumed that all of the authorized stock was issued for $60,000, that the laws of the state of incorporation permitted the company to credit Common Stock with an amount less than the total issuance proceeds, and that the directors established a $50 stated value for the shares. The entry to record the issuance is:

Cash	60,000	
Common stock		50,000
Capital in excess of stated value—From common stock issuances		10,000
Issuance of 1,000 shares at $60 per share. Stated value of $50 per share established by the directors.		

PAID-IN CAPITAL IN THE BALANCE SHEET   If only a portion of the proceeds of no-par stock is credited to a capital stock account, the facts may be shown in the balance sheet as follows:

Stockholders' equity:
Common stock—No par value; authorized and issued, 1,000
   shares at stated value $50,000
Capital in excess of stated value—From common stock
   issuances   10,000 $60,000
Retained earnings   15,000

STOCK SUBSCRIPTIONS   Corporations sometimes issue stock using a procedure involving stock subscriptions. Under this arrangement, the subscriber agrees to purchase a specified number of shares at an agreed price. The agreement may allow payment for the stock to be made in installments. Thus there may be some interval between the date when stock subscriptions are received and the date when the cash is received and the stock is issued. The illustrations that follow show the accounts which are used to record the subscriptions and subsequent payments by the subscribers.

Par value stock   Assume that a corporation has been authorized to issue 1,000 shares of $100 par value common stock. Subscriptions for 750 shares at $110 per share are recorded as follows:

Subscriptions receivable	82,500	
Common stock subscribed		75,000
Capital in excess of par value—From common stock issuances		7,500
Subscriptions for 750 authorized shares at $110 per share.		

When payment is received the following entries are made:

Cash	82,500	
Subscriptions receivable		82,500
Collection of subscriptions in full.		
Common stock subscribed	75,000	
Common stock		75,000
Issuance of 750 shares after full payment of subscriptions.		

No-par stock   Assume the same facts as in the previous illustration except that the stock has no par value. Subscriptions for 750 shares at $110 per share are recorded as follows:

Subscriptions receivable	82,500	
Common stock subscribed		82,500
Subscriptions for 750 authorized shares at $110 per share.		

It should be noted that the total amount to be paid by the subscribers is credited to the common stock subscribed account.

When the subscriptions are collected, the following entries are made:

Cash	82,500	
Subscriptions receivable		82,500
Collection of subscriptions in full.		
Common stock subscribed	82,500	
Common stock		82,500
Issuance of 750 shares after full payment of subscriptions.		

If the no-par stock had a stated value of $50 per share, only the stated value of the stock subscribed would be credited to the common stock subscribed account, as shown below:

Subscriptions receivable	82,500	
Common stock subscribed		37,500
Capital in excess of stated value—From common stock		
issuances		45,000
Subscriptions for 750 shares at $110 per share. Stated value of		
$50 per share established by the directors.		

UNCOLLECTED BALANCES OF SUBSCRIPTIONS FOR CAPITAL STOCK If it is expected that uncollected balances of stock subscriptions will be collected in the near future, they may be shown in the balance sheet under the Current Assets caption, but they should be distinctively labeled and not combined with accounts receivable from customers.

If there is no immediate intention to call on the subscribers for the uncollected balances arising from their stock subscriptions, the receivables may still be shown on the asset side of the balance sheet, but not under the Current Assets caption.

The common stock subscribed account would be reported as part of stockholders' equity if a balance sheet was prepared before the stock was issued.

STOCK ISSUED FOR PROPERTY When capital stock is issued for property other than cash, a valuation problem may arise. If 1,000 shares of $25 par value stock are issued for a piece of property, it does not follow that $25,000, the aggregate par value of the shares issued, is the proper amount to use in recording the transaction, since it does not reflect the fair market value of the stock or the property. In accounting, the property should be recorded initially at cost. The problem is, how is cost measured when shares of stock are issued to make payment?

Under such circumstances, cost may be estimated by reference to current market prices. For example, suppose that the stock being issued for property is actively purchased and sold by investors through an established stock exchange. If recent stock transactions indicate a current price of $80 per share, it would be reasonable to deduce that property acquired for 1,000 shares of stock "cost" the corporation $80,000. As an alternative, the accountant might use, as an indication of the price being paid for the property, the per-share amount at which stock of the same class was issued recently for cash.

If there are no data available regarding the current value of the shares issued, the accountant will look for evidence indicative of the current value of the property acquired. Perhaps there have been recent cash sales of identical or similar property. In some instances the appraisal amount of the property may be relevant.

To summarize, the accountant will settle on a figure for accounting purposes by using the current value of the shares issued or the current value of the asset acquired, whichever is the better indicator under the circumstances of the amount "paid" for the property.

Three illustrations follow.

Data

A corporation acquires land for 1,000 shares of $50 par value common stock.
The common stock is actively traded on a national stock exchange; recent transactions were completed at $65 per share.
There is no recent information regarding the value of the land.

Entry

Land (1,000 × $65)	65,000	
Common stock		50,000
Capital in excess of par value—From common stock issuances		15,000
Acquisition of land for 1,000 shares of common stock.		

Data

A corporation acquires a patent in exchange for 1,000 shares of no-par common stock, no stated value.
The common stock is not listed on any stock exchange.
Several days ago, 1,500 shares were issued for $10 per share.
There is only meager information regarding the current value of the patent.

Entry

Patent (1,000 × $10)	10,000	
Common stock		10,000
Acquisition of patent for 1,000 shares of common stock.		

Data

A corporation acquires land in exchange for 500 shares of common stock having a stated value of $20 per share.
No shares have been issued for five years and there is no established market for the outstanding shares.
During recent weeks similar plots of land have been sold to other businesses for $12,500, cash.

Entry

Land	12,500	
Common stock		10,000
Capital in excess of stated value—From common stock issuances		2,500
Acquisition of land for 500 shares of common stock.		

It should be mentioned that the law allows the directors of a corporation to set a valuation for accounting purposes on property acquired by the issuance of shares of stock. If the directors have exercised their prerogative in this matter, the accountant will record the property at the valuation ordered by the board of directors.

CLASSES OF STOCK Shares of stock entitle their holders to four basic rights, namely:

(1) To share in the management; that is, to vote at the stockholders' meetings.
(2) To share in the earnings; that is, to receive dividends when they are declared by the directors.
(3) To share in the distribution of the assets of the corporation if it is dissolved.
(4) To subscribe to any additional issues of stock of the class held. This is known as the *pre-emptive right*.

If there is only one class of stock, these four fundamental rights are enjoyed proportionately, share and share alike, by all stockholders, and this basic class of stock is called *common stock.*

If there are two or more classes of stock, one class may enjoy more than its proportionate share of some right, or may have some right curtailed. Stock that has certain preferences over the basic issue (common stock) is called *preferred stock.* Thus preferred stock may enjoy special preferences in the matter of dividends or in the distribution of assets in liquidation; on the other hand, the preferred stockholders may have no right to vote, or may have a right to vote only under certain conditions, such as the failure of the corporation to pay preferred dividends for a stated period of time.

STOCK PREFERRED AS TO DIVIDENDS Stock which is preferred as to dividends entitles its holders to a dividend at a stipulated rate on par, or to a stipulated amount per share in the case of no-par stock, before any dividend is paid on the common stock. Stockholders have no right to dividends unless the directors declare them. Directors may decline to declare dividends on preferred as well as common stock on the ground that the funds are needed in the business; the stockholders then have no recourse except to elect a board that will pay dividends, or to bring action in the courts in the hope of proving that the retention of the funds is not justifiable.

Cumulative and noncumulative stock Stock which is preferred as to dividends may be:

(a) *Cumulative,* in which case all dividends in arrears (dividends not paid in previous year or years) on preferred stock must be paid before dividends can be paid on the common stock.

To illustrate, assume $100,000 par value of 6% cumulative preferred stock, $100,000 par value of common stock, and retained earnings of $30,000; no dividends have been paid on the preferred stock for four years—three prior years and the current year. Since the preferred stock is cumulative, the preferred stockholders are entitled to dividends of $24,000 ($100,000 × .06 × 4) before any dividends can be paid to the common stockholders. Note, however, that dividends in arrears are not liabilities, since the liability is incurred only when dividends are declared by the board of directors.

(b) *Noncumulative,* in which case dividends omitted in any year are lost forever.

Noncumulative preferred stock is not a desirable investment because of the danger that dividends may be lost. This is particularly true if the preferred stock is nonvoting, or if the voting power of the common stock exceeds that of the preferred stock and the directors are elected by the common stockholders.

Participating and nonparticipating stock Stock which is preferred as to dividends may be:

(a) *Fully participating,* or entitled to dividends at as high a rate as the dividends paid on the common stock.

To illustrate, assume $100,000 par value of 6% fully participating preferred stock, $200,000 par value of common stock, and retained earnings of $27,000.

The preferred stock is entitled to a 6% dividend, or $6,000.

A 6% dividend (or $12,000) may then be paid to the common stockholders without any additional dividend payment being made to the preferred stockholders.

But if a 9% dividend ($18,000) instead of a 6% dividend is paid to the common stockholders, an extra 3% must be paid to the preferred stockholders.

(b) *Partially participating*, or entitled to participate with the common stock, but only to a limited degree. For instance, the preferred may carry a 6% preference rate, with a right to participate to a total of 8%.

(c) *Nonparticipating*, or entitled to receive its stipulated preferred dividend but no more, regardless of the rate paid on the common stock.

Rights under various conditions of preference   If the preferred stock is noncumulative and nonparticipating, its holders have a right to only the stipulated rate of return, regardless of the earnings; and if a dividend is not paid in one year, the right to it is forever lost. On the other hand, if the stock is participating and cumulative, the preferred stockholders will receive as high a rate of dividend as the common stockholders receive, and the preferred dividend for every year must be paid before anything can be paid to the common stockholders.

If a corporation is successful, and its preferred stock is nonparticipating, the common stockholders may receive larger dividends than those paid to the preferred stockholders. As a consequence, the common stock may have a much higher market value than the preferred stock.

STOCK PREFERRED AS TO ASSETS   In the event of dissolution and liquidation, stock that is preferred as to assets is entitled to payment in full (the par value of par stock or a stated liquidation value for no-par stock) before any distribution is made on the common stock.

To illustrate, assume $100,000 par value of preferred stock, $100,000 par value of common stock, and assets of only $150,000 after all liabilities are paid. If the preferred stock is preferred as to assets, $100,000 should be paid to the preferred stockholders and only $50,000 to the common stockholders. If the preferred stock is not preferred as to assets, the assets should be divided between the common and the preferred stockholders in the ratio of the par value of the two classes of stock—that is, equally in this case.

The preference as to assets may extend only to the par of the stock, or the preferred stockholders may have a right to receive par and all dividends in arrears. Just what the preferred stockholders' rights are must be determined in each case by reference to the stock certificate or the charter.

The fact that stock is preferred as to dividends does not make it preferred as to assets also, nor is stock which is preferred as to assets necessarily preferred as to dividends also.

CONVERTIBLE PREFERRED STOCK   Preferred stock may be convertible into shares of common stock of the issuing corporation. If it is, the conversion ratio will be stated in the certificate. The ratio may change with the passage of time. Sometimes the terms specified give the corporation the right to call (redeem) the entire issue at a predetermined price per share.

The principal appeal of convertible preferred is the conversion feature, which enables the holder to switch to common shares whenever such an action would be to the stockholder's advantage. For example, a good earnings record and bright prospects of the corporation together with a high common stock dividend rate may well make the holding of common shares more lucrative than the retention of the convertible preferred with its fixed dividend rate.

Whenever conversion occurs, the amount of stockholders' equity identifiable with the preferred should be transferred from the preferred stock and related capital-in-excess accounts, if any, to the common stock and related capital-in-excess accounts. To illustrate, assume that one-fourth of the following preferred shares, or 5,000 shares, are converted into 12,500 shares of common stock with a stated value of $5 per share.

Outstanding convertible preferred before conversion:

Convertible preferred stock—$1 cumulative, nonparticipating; $10 stated value; authorized and issued, 20,000 shares; callable at $20 per share	$200,000
Capital in excess of stated value—From convertible preferred stock issuances	100,000

The accounting entry for the conversion will need to transfer one-fourth of the balance in the preferred stock account out of that account. Apparently the preferred stock was issued for more than its stated value, so one-fourth of the capital-in-excess account balance should also be transferred. In effect, $75,000 (¼ of $300,000) of the stockholders' equity must be transferred from preferred stock accounts to common stock accounts.

Entry for conversion:

Convertible preferred stock (one-fourth of $200,000)	50,000	
Capital in excess of stated value—From convertible preferred stock issuances (one-fourth of $100,000)	25,000	
Common stock (12,500 shares at $5)		62,500
Capital in excess of stated value—From common stock issuances [($50,000 + $25,000) − $62,500]		12,500
Conversion of 5,000 shares of $10 stated value convertible preferred for 12,500 shares of $5 stated value common.		

Now assume that the remaining outstanding convertible preferred shares, which number 15,000, are called by the corporation at the $20 per-share call price.

Entry for call of convertible preferred:

Convertible preferred stock ($200,000 − $50,000)	150,000	
Capital in excess of stated value—From convertible preferred stock issuances ($100,000 − $25,000)	75,000	
Retained earnings [$300,000 − ($150,000 + $75,000)]	75,000	
Cash ($20 × 15,000)		300,000
Call of 15,000 shares of convertible preferred at the $20 per-share call price.		

Observe that the amount by which the cash payment exceeded the paid-in capital identified with the convertible preferred stock was charged to Retained Earnings. In essence, a portion of the corporation's retained earnings was distributed to the convertible preferred shareholders.

If the cash payment had been less than the paid-in capital identified with the called preferred stock, the difference would have been credited to a special paid-in capital account, as follows (where it is assumed that the call price is $12 per share):

Convertible preferred stock		150,000
Capital in excess of stated value—From convertible preferred		
stock issuances		75,000
Cash (15,000 × $12)	180,000	
Paid-in capital—From call of preferred shares	45,000	
Call of 15,000 shares of convertible preferred at the $12		
per-share call price.		

REASONS FOR CLASSES OF STOCK Different classes of stock with differing rights have been devised to meet the desires of management and to make the shares sufficiently attractive to investors.

One reason for issuing preferred stock might be to obtain control of a corporation. Assume that the prospective buyers of a going concern have the opportunity to purchase the business for $500,000, but have only $250,000 available. They decide to organize a corporation to acquire the business. If they obtain a charter which authorizes the corporation to issue only common stock, they would not have control, because outsiders could purchase half of the stock and have equal voting rights with them. They decide to issue $250,000 par value of common stock, which they purchase, giving them complete control of the voting stock of the firm, and $250,000 par value of nonvoting preferred stock.

Another reason for issuing preferred stock is to obtain *financial leverage*. This involves the use of funds bearing a limited return to finance a portion of the firm's assets. For example, if money can be obtained at a cost of 6 per cent per year and invested to earn 10 per cent per year, the difference, which is favorable in this case, has the effect of increasing the rate of return to the common stockholders.

Using the above example, assume that the firm is expected to earn $50,000 per year and that the buyers are able to sell $250,000 of 6 per cent cumulative preferred stock. The effect of the sale of preferred stock on the rate of return earned by the common stockholders is shown below.

	Sale of common stock only	Sale of preferred and common stock
Net income	$ 50,000	$ 50,000
Less:		
Preferred dividend ($250,000 × 6%)	–0–	15,000
Net income to common stockholders	$50,000	$35,000
Investment of common stockholders	$500,000	$250,000
Rate of return to common stockholders	10%	14%

In this case, the common stockholders increase the rate of return on their investment by using some preferred stock financing. The proceeds of the preferred stock issue are invested to earn 10 per cent, but only 6 per cent has to be paid to the preferred stockholders.

ACCOUNTING FOR VARIOUS CLASSES OF STOCK The methods of recording the issuance of preferred stock are the same as for common stock. If several classes of stock are issued, the account title for each class should clearly indicate its nature. If there are two classes of stock, the amounts thereof should be shown separately in the balance sheet, and the special rights of the preferred stock should be described briefly. The balance sheet presentation of the facts may, therefore, be as follows:

Stockholders' equity:
  Capital stock:

Preferred, 6% participating, cumulative; par value, $100; authorized and issued, 1,000 shares		$100,000	
Common, no par value; stated value, $10; authorized and issued, 10,000 shares		100,000	$200,000
Capital in excess of par or stated value—From stock issuances:			
Preferred stock	$ 2,000		
Common stock	10,000	12,000	$212,000
Retained earnings			75,000
Total			$287,000

IMPORTANT TERMS AND CONCEPTS IN CHAPTER 11

Corporation—p. 344
Stockholders' equity—p. 347
Capital stock—p. 347
Paid-in capital—p. 347
Par value stock—p. 348
No-par stock—p. 348
Capital in excess of par value—p. 349
Capital in excess of stated value—p. 350
Stock subscriptions—p. 351

Noncash issuance of stock—p. 352
Pre-emptive right—p. 353
Common stock—p. 354
Preferred stock—p. 354
Cumulative stock—p. 354
Participating stock—p. 354
Convertible preferred stock—p. 355
Leverage—p. 357

DEMONSTRATION PROBLEM FOR REVIEW AND SELF-STUDY Albert Alvis, Benny Baker, and Clyde Coats organized Sunset Corporation on January 2, 19_1, with authorized capital of 10,000 shares of $100 par value common stock and 1,000 shares of $50 par value, 8 per cent cumulative, convertible preferred stock. The following information pertains to the stock transactions of the firm during the first year of operation.

On January 2, the organizers subscribed to common stock at $105 per share as follows: Alvis, 1,000 shares; Baker, 1,200 shares; and Coats, 900 shares.

On January 2, 500 shares of preferred stock were sold for cash at $60 per share.

On January 10, Alvis transferred land having a value of $30,000 and a building valued at $60,000 to the corporation in partial payment of his subscription.

On January 12, 500 shares of common stock were sold to Danny Davis for cash at $110 per share.

Edward Earnest transferred a patent to the corporation on January 14, receiving in exchange 1,000 shares of common stock. Virtually nothing is known about the value of the patent.

A local attorney rendered a bill on January 23 for legal fees incurred in the organization of the firm. The attorney accepted 50 shares of stock in full payment and the certificate was issued.

On January 31, the balance was collected on all subscriptions and stock certificates were issued.

On June 30 one-half of the annual dividend on the preferred stock was declared and paid. (Note: The accounting for dividends is discussed in detail in the following chapter. Record this transaction by debiting Retained Earnings and by crediting Cash.)

On July 2 one-half of the preferred stock outstanding was converted into 100 shares of common stock.

No additional dividends were paid during the first year of operation.

INSTRUCTIONS

(a) Prepare journal entries to record the transactions for the year.

(b) Assuming that a dividend of $5,000 is declared on December 31, 19_2 and that no other dividends are declared during the year, calculate the total dividends to be paid to each class of stock.

Note Attempt to solve the demonstration problem before examining the solution that follows.

(a)

JOURNAL   (Page 1)

19_1				
Jan.	2	Subscriptions receivable	325,500	
		Common stock subscribed		310,000
		Capital in excess of par value—From common		
		stock issuances		15,500
		Subscriptions for 3,100 shares at a premium of $5 per share.		
	2	Cash	30,000	
		Preferred stock		25,000
		Capital in excess of par value—From		
		preferred stock issuances		5,000
		Sold 500 shares at $60 per share.		
	10	Building	60,000	
		Land	30,000	
		Subscriptions receivable		90,000
		Partial collection of subscription from Albert Alvis.		
	12	Cash	55,000	
		Common stock		50,000
		Capital in excess of par value—From common		
		stock issuances		5,000
		Issuance of 500 shares at a premium of $10 per share.		
	14	Patent	110,000	
		Common stock		100,000
		Capital in excess of par value—From common		
		stock issuances		10,000
		Issuance of 1,000 shares for patent. Recent market value, $110 per share.		
	23	Organization costs	5,500	
		Common stock		5,000
		Capital in excess of par value—From common		
		stock issuances		500
		Issuance of 500 shares in payment of attorney's fees. Recent market value, $110 per share.		

Jan.	31	Cash		235,500	
		Subscriptions receivable			235,500
		Collection of subscriptions in full.			
	31	Common stock subscribed		310,000	
		Common stock			310,000
		Issuance of 3,100 shares after full payment of			
		subscriptions.			
June	30	Retained earnings		1,000	
		Cash			1,000
		Paid preferred stock dividend of $2 per			
		share.			
July	2	Preferred stock ($25,000 × ½)		12,500	
		Capital in excess of par value—From			
		preferred stock issuances ($5,000 × ½)		2,500	
		Common stock ($100 × 100 shares)			10,000
		Capital in excess of par value—From			
		common stock issuances			5,000
		Conversion of 250 shares of preferred stock			
		into 100 shares of common stock.			

(b)

	Preferred dividends	Common dividends
Payment for last half of 19_1:		
250 shares × $2 per share	$ 500	
Payment for 19_2:		
250 shares × $4 per share	1,000	
Balance to common shareholders:		
$5,000 − ($500 + $1,000)		$3,500
Totals	$1,500	$3,500

ASSIGNMENT MATERIAL

Questions

1 Describe the basic characteristics of a corporation.
2 Outline the steps involved in the organization of a corporation.
3 Discuss the significance of the par value of a share of stock.
4 Illustrate the procedure involved in recording the sale of par value stock at a price in excess of par value.
5 Describe two ways in which the sale of no-par stock may be recorded.
6 What is the relationship between the common stock account and the common stock subscribed account?
7 What is the proper balance sheet treatment of the subscriptions receivable and common stock subscribed accounts?
8 Describe the nature of the problem which may arise when capital stock is issued for property other than cash. How does the accountant solve this problem?
9 List the four basic rights of stockholders.
10 Describe the following features of preferred stock;
   (a) Preferred as to dividends.
   (b) Cumulative preferred stock.
   (c) Participating preferred stock.
   (d) Convertible preferred stock.
   (e) Preferred as to assets.
11 What is the general rule to be followed in accounting for the conversion of preferred stock into common stock?

Short exercises

E11-1
Clayton Company is authorized to issue 20,000 shares of $10 par value common stock. Present the Stockholders' Equity section of the firm's balance sheet immediately after each of the following unrelated transactions:

(a) The sale of 10,000 shares for cash at $12 per share.

(b) The entire issue is subscribed at $20 per share, and half of the subscribers pay their accounts in full. Stock is issued only to those subscribers who have paid the total subscription price.

(c) The entire issue is sold for cash at $11 per share.

E11-2
Present the Stockholders' Equity section of the balance sheet after each of the transactions in Exercise 1, assuming that the Clayton Company stock is no-par stock.

E11-3 The following transactions pertain to the sale of no-par common stock, having a stated value of $20 per share, by Butler Company. Stock is issued only to those subscribers who have paid the total subscription price.

(1) Received subscriptions for 4,000 shares at $21 per share.

(2) Received payment of one-half of the amount owed by all subscribers.

(3) Subscribers for 2,000 shares paid their accounts in full.

(4) Received subscriptions for 6,000 shares at $25 per share.

Present entries to record the information above. Omit explanations.

E11-4 Dalton Corporation has 1,000 shares of $100 par value preferred stock outstanding. The stock was originally issued at a price of $108 per share. Present entries to record the following on August 1, 19_4:

(a) Conversion of 500 of the preferred shares into 4,000 shares of the company's $10 par value common stock.

(b) Call of the remaining shares by the company at a price of $112 per share. The retained earnings balance is $200,000 on August 1, 19_4.

E11-5 On May 1, 19_8, the date of organization, Fayette Company acquired a tract of land in exchange for 500 shares of its $10 par value common stock. The best information available indicated the land was worth $12,000 at the time. A second tract was acquired on October 1, 19_8, in exchange for 1,000 shares of stock. The corporation had sold 750 shares of stock on September 24, 19_8, for $20 per share.

Assuming that there were no other transactions during the period, prepare a balance sheet for the company as of September 30, 19_8.

Problems

A11-1 North Corporation was organized on January 1, 19_2, with its authorized capital consisting of 5,000 shares of common stock. All of the 5,000 shares were sold for $27 per share on January 15, 19_2.

Show the journal entry to record the sale of the stock under each of the following assumptions:

(a) Authorization had been obtained for 5,000 shares of no-par stock, and the company was organized in a state in which the laws require that the entire amount received for no-par shares shall be legal capital.

(b) Authorization had been obtained for 5,000 shares of no-par stock. The company was organized in a state in which the laws require that a stated value be assigned to no-par stock. The directors have voted to assign a stated value of $25 per share.

(c) Authorization has been obtained for 5,000 shares of $20 par value stock.

A11-2 Lee Corporation was organized on May 1, 19_4, with authorized capital as follows:

10,000 shares of 5% cumulative preferred stock, $100 par value.

75,000 shares of common stock, $50 par value.

During the month of May, 19_4, the following transactions occurred:

May   3—Sold 1,500 shares of preferred stock for cash at $103 per share.

12—Sold 5,000 shares of common stock for cash at $55 per share.

17—Received subscriptions for 2,500 shares of common stock at $62 per share. Stock is issued only to those subscribers who have paid the total subscription price.

27—Subscribers to 2,000 shares paid their subscriptions in full and the stock certificates were issued.

31—Subscribers to the remaining 500 shares paid half of the balance owed.

Required:

(a)   Journal entries to record the stock transactions.

(b)   A balance sheet as of May 31, 19_4, assuming that the transactions above are the only ones for the month.

A11-3

Monaco Corporation was organized early in January, 19_7. Authorization was obtained to issue 20,000 shares of $10 par value common stock. The following transactions took place during the month of January:

January 10—Subscriptions were received for 5,000 shares at $10 per share.

13—The subscriptions received January 10 were collected in full and stock certificates were issued.

20—Subscriptions were received for 3,000 shares at $12 per share.

23—The subscriptions received January 20 were collected in full and stock certificates were issued.

26—Subscriptions were taken for 2,000 shares at $14 per share.

30—Subscriptions received January 26 for 500 shares were collected in full and $4,500 cash was received from other subscribers of that date.

Required:

(a)   Journal entries for the stock transactions.

(b)   Postings to the following general ledger accounts:
Subscriptions Receivable
Common Stock
Common Stock Subscribed
Capital in Excess of Par Value—From Common Stock Issuances

(c)   The Stockholders' Equity section of the January 31, 19_7 balance sheet.

A11-4

The stockholders' equity of Arnold Company consists of $250,000 of $10 par value common stock, all of which was sold for cash at $10 per share. The management of the firm is considering the following alternatives for obtaining additional financing of $100,000:

(a)   Sale of $10 par value common stock at par.

(b)   Sale of 8 per cent cumulative preferred stock at par.

Required:

(a)   Computation of the rate of return to common stockholders under each alternative, assuming an annual income of $42,000.

(b)   The same computations, assuming an income of $15,000 annually.

A11-5

The charter of Davidson Corporation authorized 100,000 shares of no-par common stock and 75,000 shares of $100 par value, 6 per cent cumulative preferred stock. The following stock transactions have taken place since the date of organization:

March 1, 19_2—Sold 40,000 shares of common stock at $12 per share.

August 1, 19_2—Sold 5,000 shares of preferred stock at $106 per share.

December 31, 19_2—Sold 15,000 shares of common stock at $18 per share.

Required:

(a) Journal entries to record the stock transactions.

(b) Preparation of the Stockholders' Equity section of the firm's balance sheet as of December 31, 19_2, assuming retained earnings of $64,000.

(c) The entry to record the calling of all the preferred stock at $112 per share on December 31, 19_4, assuming a retained earnings balance of $165,000.

A11-6

Smitty Smith, John Jones, and Ben Brown organized Rabun Corporation on January 1, 19_4, with authorized capital of 50,000 shares of $10 par value common stock.

On January 1, the organizers subscribed to stock at $15 per share as follows: Smith, 10,000 shares; Jones, 12,000 shares; and Brown, 5,000 shares.

On January 20, Henry Hill purchased 5,000 shares of common stock for cash at a price of $15 per share.

Mary Moore transferred land to the corporation on January 30, receiving in exchange 3,000 shares of common stock. No appraisal amount is available for the land.

On January 31, the balance was collected on all subscriptions and stock certificates were issued. No other transactions occurred this month.

Required:

(a) Journal entries for the January transactions.

(b) Postings of the transactions to ledger accounts.

(c) A classified balance sheet as of January 31, 19_1.

B11-1

Plum Corporation has an authorized capital of 10,000 shares of common stock. The entire issue is to be sold at $25 per share.

Required:

The entry to record the sale of the stock under each of the following assumptions:

(a) The par value of the stock is $25 per share.

(b) The par value of the stock is $5 per share.

(c) The stock has no par value.

(d) The stock is no-par stock with a stated value of $12.50 per share.

(e) The par value of the stock is $1 per share.

B11-2

Martin Corporation was organized on October 1, 19_2, and was authorized to issue 150,000 shares of $5 par value common stock. The company issued the following stock during the month of October:

October   2—Forty thousand shares for cash at $5 per share.
          14—Twenty thousand shares in exchange for land valued at $25,000, a building worth $75,000, and $25,000 cash.
          26—Thirty thousand shares for cash at $6 per share.

Prepare the Stockholders' Equity section of Martin Corporation's balance sheet as of October 31, 19_2. Assume earnings of $32,100 for the month and no dividend payments.

B11-3

Midway Corporation was authorized to issue 25,000 shares each of the following classes of stock:

Eight per cent preferred stock, $100 par value.

Common stock, $10 stated value.

The following transactions occurred during the month of November 19_3:

November   2—Two thousand shares of common stock were issued for cash at $10 per share.
          8—Five hundred shares of preferred stock were issued for $100 per share.
          12—Twenty-five shares of preferred stock were issued to an attorney for services rendered in organizing the corporation. The attorney purchased an additional 50 shares for $103 per share.
          15—Ten thousand shares of common stock were issued at $12 per share.
          16—Nine hundred shares of common stock were issued in exchange for a tract of land.

Show the journal entries to record the above information.

B11-4

Cocoa Corporation was organized on July 1, 19_8, with authorized capital of 25,000 shares of no-par common stock. In order to comply with state laws, a stated value of $25 per share has been assigned to the stock.

   The following transactions occurred during the month of July, 19_8:

July 15—Three thousand shares were issued at $27 per share.
    20—One thousand shares were issued at $31 per share.
    24—Paid legal fees of $2,500 incurred in organizing the firm.
    27—Received subscriptions for 4,000 shares at $29. The subscribers paid for 20 per cent of their subscriptions.

Required:

(a)   Journal entries for the transactions.

(b)   The Stockholders' Equity section of the firm's balance sheet as of July 31, 19_8, assuming no retained earnings.

B11-5

Polk Company was organized on January 1, 19_4, with an authorized capital consisting of 10,000 shares of $75 par value, 8 per cent preferred stock and 15,000 shares of $50 par value common stock. The preferred stock is convertible into common stock at any time at the rate of 2 shares of preferred for 3 shares of common.

   The company issued 3,000 shares of preferred stock for cash at $81 on January 10, 19_4. On the same date, 5,000 shares of common stock were issued at a price of $62 per share. One-third of the preferred shares was converted on July 31, 19_7, the end of the company's accounting period. All dividends had been paid on the preferred stock.

Required:

(a) Appropriate stockholders' equity ledger accounts for the company just prior to conversion, assuming a retained earnings balance of $116,000.

(b) The journal entry to record conversion of the preferred shares.

(c) The journal entry required on August 1, 19_7, assuming that the remaining shares of the preferred stock are called at a price of $95 per share.

B11-6

The following information is taken from the ledger of Hunter Company as of December 31, 19_7. The firm's books have been closed for the year.

Cash	$105,530
Accounts receivable	54,872
Land (Cost, $15,000)	46,000
Building	350,000
Common stock subscriptions receivable	20,000
Organization costs	6,500
Capital in excess of par value—From preferred stock issuances	28,000
Common stock	200,000
Bonds payable	100,000
Preferred stock	100,000
Bond discount	8,000
Allowance for uncollectibles	1,800
Accumulated depreciation—Building	40,000
Retained earnings	?
Capital in excess of par value—From common stock issuances	86,400
Inventory	57,400
Accounts payable	35,224
Common stock subscribed	16,000
Bond interest payable	3,000

The company is authorized to issue 5,000 shares of 6 per cent cumulative preferred stock and 10,000 shares of $25 par value common stock. As of December 31, 19_7, 1,000 shares of preferred stock and 8,000 shares of common stock have been issued. An additional 640 shares of common stock have been subscribed.

Prepare a classified balance sheet as of December 31, 19_7, following proper accounting practices.

STOCKHOLDERS' EQUITY (CONCLUDED)

CHAPTER 12

PURPOSE OF CHAPTER   Dividend distributions to shareholders may take the form of cash or they may be in the form of additional shares of stock. In addition to dividend declarations, there are other transactions that may affect the balance of stockholder accounts other than the capital stock accounts. One purpose of this chapter is to discuss the accounting for such transactions and the proper method of reporting them in the financial statements.

In recent years there has been an increasing emphasis on the reporting of the amount of net income available to each share of common stock outstanding. This measure is referred to as earnings per share and is now required as a part of the presentation of an income statement. The chapter also discusses the calculation and presentation of earnings per share data.

TERMINOLOGY   The following terms, some of which were referred to in the previous chapter, are used in reference to capital stock:

Par value   This is a nominal value, printed on the certificate. For instance, if a corporation is authorized to issue $100,000 of capital stock, represented by 1,000 shares, the par value of each share is $100. When a dividend rate is stated in connection with par value stock, such as 6% preferred stock with a $25 par value, the rate is applied to the par value.

Book value (amount)   To determine the book value of a share of stock of a certain class, divide the stockholders' equity applicable to the class by the number of shares of the class outstanding.

For instance, if a corporation has 1,000 shares of common stock (and no preferred stock) outstanding, and its balance sheet shows:

Capital stock	$100,000	
Retained earnings	30,000	
Total		$130,000

the book value of each share is $130,000 ÷ 1,000, or $130.

If there is preferred stock outstanding, the preferred stockholders' interest in the retained earnings will depend upon whether the stock is participating, and also upon whether the preferred stock is cumulative and whether there are preferred dividends in arrears. Certain of these situations will be discussed later in this chapter.

Generally, book value is a poor indicator of what a share of stock is worth. Unless all of the corporation's assets are stated in the accounts at their present value, the stockholders' equity, being the remainder after subtracting the liabilities from the assets (Assets − Liabilities = Stockholders' Equity), will not indicate the value of the company's outstanding capital stock.

Market value   This is the price at which a share of stock can be sold. It depends partly on the book value of the stock and partly on the corporation's earnings record and the prospects of future earnings and dividends.

Liquidation value   This is the amount which a stockholder will be entitled to receive if the corporation goes out of business, disposes of its assets, pays its liabilities, and distributes the balance among its stockholders. If common stock only is outstanding, its liquidation value will depend only on the amount available for distribution to the stockholders after the realization of the assets and the payment of liabilities and liquidation expenses. If common and preferred stocks are outstanding, the liquidation values of both classes will also depend upon whether the preferred stock is preferred as to assets and whether the preferred stockholders are entitled to any dividends in arrears.

Redemption value   Corporations sometimes issue preferred stock with a right to redeem it. The redemption or call price may be stated in terms such as: *par, par and dividends in arrears,* or *par and a premium of $5 per share.*

Stated (legal) capital   Among the advantages of the corporate form of business organization is that of limited liability: the stockholders are not personally liable for the debts of the corporation. Since the law gives stockholders this protection, it is only fair that creditors should be given some assurance that the corporation will not make payments to its stockholders, either as dividends or for the acquisition or retirement of stock, which will reduce the stockholders' equity below a stipulated amount.

Originally the corporation laws placed restrictions only on dividends. More recently it has been recognized that the protection of creditors is inadequate unless, in addition to a restriction on dividends, there is a restriction on the amount which can be paid to stockholders for the acquisition or retirement of their stock.

For the reasons indicated above, a definition of stated capital has been included in the laws of many states. Unfortunately, the concepts of stated capital are not uniform in all states. In some, the stated capital includes the total amount received for par or no-par shares issued, including any amount credited to an account other than Capital Stock. In other states, the stated capital is measured by the par value of par shares or, with respect to no-par shares, the amount per share which the directors elect to credit to a capital stock account. In some states, the amount which the directors elect to establish as stated capital per share cannot be less than a minimum fixed by law.

LEGALITY OF DIVIDENDS   Under what conditions does a company have a legal right to declare a dividend? It is difficult to state general rules; they would be subject to exceptions because the laws of the various states differ in their regulations. In general, but subject to restrictions mentioned below, it may be said that a corporation has a right to pay a dividend if it has retained earnings that were produced by either operations or extraneous transactions, but dividends must not reduce the stockholders' equity below the amount of the stated or legal capital.

The opinion has sometimes been expressed that dividends should be paid only from funds generated by the retention of earnings. This may be incorrect, depending on the law of the state of incorporation. It probably would be better to say that stockholders should have a right to assume that dividends come from funds generated from retained earnings, and that, if they come from any other source, disclosure should be made to the stockholders. There have been instances in which a corporation has charged dividends to an account that was credited with the excess of the issuance proceeds of stock over the par or stated value thereof, thus merely giving back to the stockholders a portion of their investment but giving the impression that they are receiving dividends out of earnings.

DIVIDEND RESTRICTIONS   Dividend restrictions may result from:

(A)   *Contracts:*
   (1)   With creditors.
      Bond indentures may place a limitation on the amount of dividends that can be paid while the bonds are outstanding.
   (2)   With preferred stockholders.
      If, under the terms of issuance, the preferred stock of a company is to be retired (periodically or otherwise) out of funds provided by earnings, the charter provisions for the retirement of the preferred stock may place a limitation on dividends to the holders of common stock while any of the preferred stock is outstanding.

Such restrictions are intended to safeguard the bondholders or preferred stockholders by preventing an impairment of working capital. If part of the funds produced by operations were used for the retirement of bonds or stock and, in addition, dividends were paid to the full amount of the net income, the working capital might be depleted to the point where operations would be hampered and the corporation's financial condition weakened.

(B)   *Law:*
      Mention has previously been made of the fact that many state statutes prescribe that the total of dividends and disbursements for the acquisition of a company's own shares must not impair the stated capital. As a result, a portion of the retained earnings equal to the cost of the stock acquired becomes unavailable for dividend charges.
(C)   *Voluntary action by the directors:*
   (1)   To indicate that dividends will be limited in order to permit the accumulation of funds for general purposes or for some specific purpose, such as the acquisition of additional equipment.
   (2)   To indicate the existence of a contingency that might result in a loss, but a loss so problematical and so impossible of reasonable estimate that a charge therefor against current earnings or retained earnings at this time would be unwarranted.

In the past, dividend restrictions such as those mentioned above frequently were recorded by journal entries making transfers from the retained earnings account to "restricted" or "appropriated" retained earnings accounts, which were shown in the Stockholders' Equity section of the balance sheet. No charges could properly be made against such accounts except to restore all or portions of their balances to the retained earnings account.

More recently it has come to be recognized that better disclosure can be made: By parenthetical comments in the balance sheet, such as:

Retained earnings (of which $15,000 is not available for dividend
  charges because of restrictions in the bond indenture) $90,000

Or by footnotes below the balance sheet totals, such as:

Note—The company is defendant in a suit alleging patent infringement. The company's management and counsel are of the opinion that the allegation is unwarranted.

Footnotes and notes accompanying the financial statements are regarded by accountants as being part of the statements.

A balance sheet procedure for showing a dividend restriction resulting from the purchase of a company's own stock is shown on page 380.

FINANCIAL POLICY WITH RESPECT TO DIVIDENDS   In making their decisions with respect to the amounts of dividend payments, directors give consideration not only to the amount legally available for the payment of dividends but also to matters of financial policy. A dividend payment may be undesirable because the available cash is inadequate; but, if there is only a temporary shortage of cash, the directors may consider it advisable to borrow money for dividend purposes in order to maintain a continuity of dividend payments. Even when adequate cash is available, the directors may consider it advisable to pay no dividends, or to pay dividends of only limited amounts, in order to conserve the funds for expansion of the business.

SIGNIFICANT DATES APPLICABLE TO DIVIDENDS, AND RELATED ENTRIES   For corporations with only a few stockholders and with infrequent transfers of shares, it may be practicable to declare and pay a dividend on the same day. But for large corporations with many stockholders and frequent transfers of shares, such a procedure would be impracticable. Under such conditions there are three significant dates applicable to dividends: the date of declaration, the date of record, and the date of payment.

Date of declaration   On the date when the dividend is declared, and a liability therefore created, the following entry is made:

Dividends (contra to retained earnings)   100,000
    Dividends payable   100,000
  To record the declaration of a dividend.

Date of record   The directors' resolution authorizing the payment of a dividend states a date as of which the corporation, by an examination of its stock records, will determine the "stockholders of record." For instance, a dividend may be declared on January 5, payable on January 30 to stockholders of record on January 20. If stock is purchased after the dividend declaration date but in time to have the change in ownership recorded by the date of record, the *purchaser* obtains the right to the dividend. When there is no longer sufficient time to record the change in ownership before the date of record, the stock is sold "ex-dividend"— that is, the *seller* is entitled to the dividend.

No entry need be made by the company on the date of record.

Date of payment A period of time is usually required between the date of record and the date of payment because of the work involved in the determination of the stockholders of record and the preparation of the dividend checks. When the checks are mailed, thus removing the liability, the following entry is made:

Dividends payable	100,000	
Cash		100,000
Payment, to stockholders of record on January 20, of dividend declared on January 5.		

UNPAID DECLARED DIVIDENDS After a dividend has been legally declared and notice of the declaration has been given to the stockholders, by publication or otherwise, the unpaid dividend ranks as a liability and should be shown as such in the balance sheet, usually under the Current Liabilities caption. The directors may rescind the declaration of a dividend, but they can do so only if no notice of the declaration has been given to the shareholders.

DIVIDENDS IN ARREARS ON PREFERRED STOCK Since even a preferred stockholder has no right to a dividend until it is declared, preferred dividends do not accrue; no entry for them should be made until the date of declaration when they become a legal liability of the company.

But if dividends on cumulative preferred stock are in arrears, these arrearages must be paid before dividends are paid to the common stockholders. The amount of the cumulative dividends in arrears should, therefore, be shown in the balance sheet. This is usually done in a footnote below the balance sheet totals, thus:

Note: Cumulative dividends on preferred stock were in arrears on (the balance sheet date) in the amount of $12,000.

PREFERRED DIVIDENDS AND THE CALCULATION OF BOOK VALUES (AMOUNTS) It was noted earlier that when preferred stock is outstanding, the preferred stockholders' interest in retained earnings will affect the calculation of book values. Assume that a corporation has the following stockholders' equity:

8% cumulative preferred stock (1,000 shares, $50 par)	$ 50,000
Common stock (10,000 shares, $25 par)	250,000
Retained earnings	200,000
Total stockholders' equity	$500,000

The first step in the calculation of book values for the two classes of stock is to determine the portion of the stockholders' equity applicable to the preferred stock. The calculation is affected by the specific features of the stock. This amount divided by the number of preferred shares outstanding will give the book value per share.[1]

If it is assumed that the preferred stockholders in the illustration above have been paid all dividends to which they are entitled, the book values for each class of stock are calculated as follows:

Preferred stock ($50,000 ÷ 1,000 shares)	$50.00
Common stock [($500,000 − $50,000) ÷ 10,000 shares]	45.00

As indicated by the calculations, the total stockholders' equity applicable to the common stock is the residual amount after allocating the proper portion to the preferred stock.

Assume now that the preferred stockholders have not been paid the dividend for the current year. The portion of the total stockholders' equity allocated to the cumulative preferred stock is increased by the amount of the dividend, and the book amounts are calculated as follows:

Preferred stock [($50,000 + $4,000) ÷ 1,000 shares]	$54.00
Common stock [($500,000 − $54,000) ÷ 10,000 shares]	44.60

SIGNIFICANCE OF BOOK VALUE Simply stated, the book value of a share of stock measures the underlying net assets per share, based on the amounts recorded in the accounting records for assets and liabilities; and this is obviously a direct result of the accounting procedures followed by the firm. Alternative choices among alternative accounting methods (i.e., straight-line depreciation versus accelerated depreciation) will affect the amounts at which the net assets of the firm will be reported and will thus affect book values.

Only by coincidence will the book value per share of stock be the same as its par value. The arbitrary nature of the latter amount was discussed in the previous chapter. It is also erroneous to assume that there is a direct relationship between book value and the market price of a share of stock. Book value may be one factor affecting the market price, but market prices are influenced by many factors which simply cannot be quantified. The fact that a stock is selling at a price below its book value does not necessarily indicate a bargain price.

Finally, it should be pointed out that book value does not measure the amount to be received by stockholders in the event of liquidation of the firm. This is especially true whenever the liquidation results from the financial difficulty of the firm. Under such circumstances, the stockholder may realize considerably less than book value because of losses incurred in the liquidation process.

CASH DIVIDENDS AND RETAINED EARNINGS One prerequisite to any dividend payment is that sufficient cash be available. Some stockholders may equate the amount of retained earnings reported on the balance sheet with cash. However, there is no direct relationship between the amounts. Retained earnings are a part of the stockholders' equity in the assets of the firm, and cash is only one of many

---

[1]Most references to book value are for common stock only. However, calculations will be shown here for both classes of stock.

forms the assets may take. A business firm may sometimes find itself with sufficient retained earnings to legally declare a dividend, but with such other demands for cash that the dividend is impractical.

For example, assume that a corporation has the following balance sheet:

Cash	$100,000	Common stock	$ 50,000
		Retained earnings	50,000
	$100,000		$100,000

If the firm purchases a building for $95,000 cash, the balance sheet will be:

Cash	$ 5,000	Common stock	$ 50,000
Building	95,000	Retained earnings	50,000
	$100,000		$100,000

Retained earnings are still $50,000, but only $5,000 is available for dividends.

STOCK DIVIDENDS Dividends are sometimes paid in capital stock instead of in cash. Usually the dividend distribution is in common stock to holders of common stock.

To illustrate, assume that a company has 10,000 authorized shares of common stock of $10 par value, of which 6,000 shares are outstanding; also assume that a 10 per cent stock dividend (600 shares) is declared and immediately issued. The Committee on Accounting Procedure of the American Institute of Certified Public Accountants has taken the position that, when the shares issued as a dividend are less than about 20 per cent of the shares previously outstanding, an amount equal to the fair value of the shares issued should be capitalized by a transfer from retained earnings. The primary reason given for this position by the committee was that many shareholders view stock dividends as distributions of earnings in the amount of the fair value of the additional shares received. In practice, fair value is generally considered to be best measured by the current market price of the stock.

Assuming that the shares issued in this illustration have a market price of $12 each, the entry to record the distribution of the stock dividend is:

Stock dividends (to be closed to Retained Earnings)	7,200	
Common stock (600 × $10)		6,000
Capital in excess of par value—From stock dividends		1,200
Issuance of a 10% dividend: 600 shares of $10 par value stock having a fair value of $12 each.		

Assume that the stock was without par value and that it had been given a stated value of $7.50 per share; the entry would be:

Stock dividends (to be closed to Retained Earnings)	7,200	
Common stock (600 × $7.50)		4,500
Capital in excess of stated value—From stock dividends		2,700
Issuance of a 10% dividend: 600 shares of no-par stock (stated value, $7.50 per share) having a fair value of $12 each.		

STOCK SPLITS A stock split should be distinguished from a stock dividend. A stock split occurs when a corporation, after obtaining the required approval of its board of directors and stockholders, issues additional shares based on some multiple of the outstanding shares held by existing stockholders prior to the split. For example, after a 2-for-1 stock split, every stockholder would hold twice as many shares.

The increase in the number of shares is accompanied by a proportionate reduction in the par or stated value of the class of stock being split. To expand on the above example of a 2-for-1 stock split, assume that the stock being split had a stated value of $10 per share. The stated value would be changed to $5 per share. Consequently, a stock split does not cause any changes in the dollar balances of the stockholders' equity accounts. To illustrate:

Account balances *before* stock split:

Stockholders' equity:		
Common stock, $10 stated value: 100,000 shares issued and out-standing	$1,000,000	
Capital in excess of stated value—From stock issuances	200,000	$1,200,000
Retained earnings		600,000
		$1,800,000

Account balances *after* a 2-for-1 stock split; stated value reduced by one-half, to $5 per share:

Stockholders' equity:		
Common stock, $5 stated value: 200,000 shares issued and outstanding	$1,000,000	
Capital in excess of stated value—From stock issuances	200,000	$1,200,000
Retained earnings		600,000
		$1,800,000

No debit-credit entry need be made in the accounts for a stock split. Of course, the title of the common stock account should be revised to indicate the new stated value. Also, the company's records should show the new number of shares outstanding. Such revisions can be made by suitable notations in the ledger and supporting records, or the following journal entry can be made to accomplish the same purpose:

Common stock, $10 stated value	1,000,000	
Common stock, $5 stated value		1,000,000
Reduction in stated value and increase in outstanding shares from 100,000 to 200,000 as a result of a 2-for-1 stock split.		

Since a stock split does not result in any changes in account balances or changes in the proportionate holdings of the individual stockholders (if a stockholder owned 5 per cent of the outstanding shares before a stock split he or she would continue to own 5 per cent of the outstanding shares after a stock split), why does a corporation split its stock? The reasons relate to such matters as the level of market price of the company's stock and the extent of distribution of stock ownership desired by the company's management. To elaborate, suppose that a company's stock has a market price of $300 per share. If the company made a 5-for-1 stock split, the market price should drop to about one-fifth of its former price, or $60 per share. Experience indicates that the new price level will attract additional investors. The commission charged by stockbrokers for the purchase of shares of stock is less per share for a round lot of 100 shares than for an odd lot of less than 100 shares. The actions of investors support the following generalization: Investors are more inclined to purchase 100 shares of $60 stock than 20 shares of $300 stock.

The following list of questions and answers should help differentiate stock dividends and stock splits.

	Stock dividends	Stock splits
Will the action:		
Change the number of shares outstanding?	Yes	Yes
Change the per cent of stock ownership among the company's stockholders?	No	No
Alter the par or stated value of the capital stock?	No	Yes
Result in income to the stockholders?	No	No
Alter the retained earnings balance?	Yes (reduce it)	No
Alter the capital stock account balance?	Yes (increase it)	No
Change the dollar balance of the Stockholders' Equity section of the balance sheet?	No	No

RETAINED EARNINGS APPROPRIATIONS   Corporations sometimes report their total retained earnings in several different retained earnings accounts in the balance sheet. These additional accounts, referred to as *appropriations of retained earnings,* result from transfers of a portion of the balance in the retained earnings account. In some instances, the reason for the transfer may be to meet a legal requirement. For example, the issuance of a $100,000 long-term bond issue may require that the firm restrict the retained earnings balance that can be used as a basis for dividends in an amount equal to the face amount of the bonds. This is accomplished by the following entry:

Retained earnings	100,000	
Retained earnings appropriated for		
bond retirement		100,000

Other appropriations of retained earnings may occur voluntarily as management attempts to convey to stockholders information pertaining to the amount of retained earnings that should be viewed as available as a basis for dividends. For example, retained earnings may be used as the major source of financing for a large expansion of the firm's physical plant. If this is the intent of management, the following entry may be recorded as the result of action by the board of directors:

Retained earnings	500,000	
Retained earnings appropriated for		
plant expansion		500,000

Several important points should be noted concerning an appropriation of retained earnings. Although the appropriation does reduce the amount of retained earnings that should be viewed as available as a basis for dividend declarations, it does not change either the total retained earnings or the total stockholders' equity of the firm. Also, the appropriation does not guarantee the accumulation of cash to be used for the reason for which retained earnings are appropriated. This will be accomplished only as management designates cash by depositing it in a separate account to be used solely for that purpose.

When the purpose for which the appropriation was made is no longer present, the appropriated amount should be transferred back into the retained earnings account. Thus when the bond issued referred to above has been paid, the following entry should be recorded:

Retained earnings appropriated for		
bond retirement	100,000	
Retained earnings		100,000

The proper balance sheet presentation of retained earnings when there are appropriation accounts on the books is illustrated below:

Retained earnings:		
Appropriated for bond retirement	$100,000	
Appropriated for plant expansion	500,000	$600,000
Unappropriated		300,000
Total retained earnings		$900,000

RETAINED EARNINGS ADJUSTMENTS Almost all items of profit and loss recognized during an accounting period should be reported in the income statement for that period. The exceptions to this rule are items referred to as *prior-period adjustments,* which are reported in the financial statements as adjustments to the retained earnings balance at the beginning of the period.

A recent pronouncement of the Financial Accounting Standards Board defines prior-period adjustments in such a manner that very few items can be so classified.[2] An example is the correction of an error in the financial statements of a prior period.

To illustrate the financial statement presentation of a prior-period adjustment, assume that a firm discovered in 19_7 that it had understated depreciation expense for 19_6 by $20,000 because of an error in calculating the annual charge. This is recorded by the following entry:

Prior-period adjustment—Correction		
of 19_6 depreciation expense	20,000	
Accumulated depreciation		20,000

The prior-period adjustment account is closed to Retained Earnings at the end of the period. Financial statement presentation of this information is shown in the following section.

STATEMENT OF RETAINED EARNINGS The statement of retained earnings was introduced in Chapter 2. It is usually included as a part of the financial statements in corporation annual reports to stockholders, although it is often combined with the income

[2]Financial Accounting Standards Board, "Prior-Period Adjustments," *Statement No. 16* (Stamford, Conn.: FASB, June, 1977).

statement in a form referred to as a *statement of income and retained earnings*. A comparative statement of retained earnings which includes the prior-period adjustment referred to previously is presented below.

CLARKSTON COMPANY
Statement of Retained Earnings
For the Year Ended December 31, 19_7

Retained earnings at beginning of year:	
As previously reported	$175,000
Deduct prior-period adjustment for additional 19_6 depreciation	20,000
As restated	$155,000
Add net income	100,000
	$255,000
Deduct cash dividends on common stock:	
$1.50 per share	75,000
Retained earnings at end of year	$180,000

TREASURY STOCK   *Treasury stock* is a corporation's own stock which has been issued, reacquired, and not canceled in accordance with a formal procedure specified by law. It will be noted that there are three important elements in this definition:

(1) Treasury stock must be the company's own stock; holdings of the stocks of other companies are not treasury stock.
(2) The stock must have been issued.
(3) The stock, although reacquired, must not have been canceled. Cancellation of stock is brought about by a procedure prescribed by law, and places the stock in the status of unissued, or sometimes even unauthorized, shares.

TREASURY STOCK IS NOT AN ASSET   Although treasury shares may have a ready marketability and may again become outstanding, it seems obvious that treasury stock, like unissued stock, is not an asset but is merely a possible source of additional funds.

Although treasury stock has been shown in balance sheets as an asset (sometimes even combined with securities which *are* assets, under some title such as "Government Bonds and Other Securities"), accountants now generally recognize that the acquisition of treasury stock causes a reduction in the stockholders' equity.

TREASURY STOCK IN THE BALANCE SHEET   Since the acquisition of treasury stock causes a reduction of the stockholders' equity to the extent of the cost of the stock, the cost should be shown as a deduction in the Stockholders' Equity section of the balance sheet. There are several ways of showing the deduction; the method illustrated on page 378 is generally regarded as acceptable provided the corporation was organized in a state where the holding of treasury stock does not impose a restriction on dividends. (Balance sheet presentations when dividend restrictions exist are shown later.) The illustration is based on the following facts with respect to the capital stock:

The authorized issue is 1,000 shares of $100 par value common.
All the authorized stock has been issued.
The corporation has reacquired 100 shares at a cost of $12,000.

The distinction between "issued" and "outstanding" should be noted. All of the 1,000 shares have been issued, and are so shown. The number of outstanding shares is not stated directly in the balance sheet, but can be easily determined; there are 900 outstanding, the difference between the issued shares and the treasury shares.

Stockholders' equity:		
Common stock—$100 par value; authorized and issued,		
1,000 shares, of which 100 shares are in the treasury	$100,000	
Retained earnings	25,000	
Total	$125,000	
Deduct cost of treasury stock	12,000	$113,000

Incidentally, corporations do not pay dividends on treasury stock. Continuing with the above illustration, should the board of directors authorize the payment of a cash dividend of $1 per share, the dividend payment would amount to $900 ($1 × 900 shares outstanding).

If a company originally issued its stock at more than par or stated value, the facts may be shown in the balance sheet in this manner:

Stockholders' equity:			
Common stock—$100 par value; authorized and			
issued, 1,000 shares, of which 100 shares are			
in the treasury	$100,000		
Capital in excess of par value—From common			
stock issuances	10,000	$110,000	
Retained earnings		25,000	
Total		$135,000	
Deduct cost of treasury stock		12,000	$123,000

If treasury stock is acquired by donation, there is no cost to deduct; the facts may be shown as follows:

Stockholders' equity:		
Common stock—$100 par value; authorized and issued,		
1,000 shares, of which 100 shares, acquired by dona-		
tion, are in the treasury	$100,000	
Retained earnings	25,000	$125,000

RECORDING TREASURY STOCK ACQUISITIONS   As indicated above, the cost of treasury stock may properly be shown in the balance sheet as a deduction in the Stockholders' Equity section. To provide the information for this balance sheet presentation, it is considered proper to debit the treasury stock account with the *cost* of the stock acquired. If this procedure is adopted, an acquisition of treasury stock is recorded as follows:

Treasury stock	12,000	
Cash		12,000
To record the acquisition of 100 shares of $100 par value		
stock at a cost of $12,000.		

An entry of this nature should be made regardless of whether the shares have a par value or are without par value, and regardless of the amount which was received for the shares when they were issued. The treasury stock account title should indicate the nature of the stock if there is more than one class of issued stock. If the company has only one class of stock, the account title may be merely Treasury Stock; otherwise, it might be Treasury Stock—Preferred, or Treasury Stock—Common, or Treasury Stock—Common—No Par Value.

As noted, stockholders sometimes donate shares to the company; this may be done because the company needs working capital and the stockholders do not wish to invest additional funds; they, therefore, donate portions of their stock, which possibly can be used to obtain additional funds. Since donated shares are acquired without cost, no debit and credit entries are made to record the acquisition. A memorandum notation is made in the treasury stock account, as shown below:

TREASURY STOCK

Date		50 shares donated				

DISPOSAL OF TREASURY SHARES   When acquired treasury stock is disposed of, the treasury stock account should be credited with the acquisition price. Entries under various conditions are shown below.

Disposal at cost   Assume that the treasury stock acquired for $12,000 is disposed of for $12,000; the entry is:

Cash	12,000	
Treasury stock		12,000

Disposal at a price in excess of cost   Assume that the shares were sold for $13,500; the entry is:

Cash	13,500	
Treasury stock		12,000
Capital in excess of par value—From treasury stock		
transactions		1,500

Disposal at a price less than cost   The method of recording disposals of treasury stock at a price less than the original cost depends on the law of the state of incorporation and the stockholders' equity accounts on the company's books. Assume that shares acquired for $12,000 are reissued for only $11,500. If treasury stock of the same class had previously been disposed of at more than cost, the entry for the present disposal might be:

Cash	11,500	
Capital in excess of par value—From treasury stock		
transactions	500	
Treasury stock		12,000

In the absence of any such applicable capital in excess accounts, the charge should be made to Retained Earnings, thus:

Cash	11,500	
Retained earnings	500	
Treasury stock		12,000

Disposal of donated shares The entire proceeds from the disposal of donated treasury stock should be credited to Capital in Excess of Par Value—From Treasury Stock Transactions. For example, if donated treasury shares are reissued at a total price of $12,000, the following entry would be recorded:

Cash	12,000	
Capital in excess of par value—From treasury stock transactions		12,000

DIVIDEND RESTRICTIONS RESULTING FROM TREASURY STOCK ACQUISITIONS Assume that a company has issued capital stock of $100,000 par value and has retained earnings of $25,000, but that it is holding treasury stock which it acquired at a cost of $12,000. Assume also that the law of the state of incorporation provides that dividend payments and treasury stock acquisitions, together, must not impair the stated capital—which, in this illustration, is assumed to be par value of the issued shares, including the treasury shares. In effect, this means that a $12,000 portion of the retained earnings is restricted[3] so long as the treasury stock is retained, and that, so long as this restriction exists, dividends and disbursements for additional treasury stock acquisitions must not, together, exceed the $13,000 unrestricted retained earnings. The balance sheet should be prepared in such a way as to disclose this restriction. The following Stockholders' Equity section of the balance sheet illustrates a method of making the disclosure.

Stockholders' equity:		
Common stock—$100 par value; authorized and issued,		
1,000 shares, of which 100 shares are in the treasury		$100,000
Retained earnings:		
Not available for dividend charges—Equal to cost of treasury stock	$12,000	
Unrestricted	13,000	25,000
Total		$125,000
Deduct cost of treasury stock		12,000
Stockholders' equity		$113,000

REPORTING STOCKHOLDERS' EQUITY BY SOURCES Stockholders' equity accounts are generally presented in the balance sheet so as to show the major sources of the equity. Basically there are two sources:

Paid-in capital. This includes all amounts invested in the corporation by the stockholders in exchange for shares of stock.

Retained earnings. The portion of the earnings of the firm which has been kept within the firm. This would be the sum of all earnings since organization, reduced by losses and dividends, and plus or minus any prior-period adjustments.

[3]The state laws differ with respect to the effect of a treasury stock acquisition on retained earnings. In at least one state, the retained earnings are reduced; more commonly, they are merely restricted.

The following illustration shows the balance sheet treatment of various matters affecting the stockholders' equity.

Stockholders' equity:
  Capital stock:
    Preferred stock—6% cumulative, participating;
    par value, $100; authorized and issued,
     1,000 shares $100,000
    Common stock—No par value; stated value,
    $10; authorized and issued, 10,000 shares,
     of which 500 shares are in the treasury   100,000 $200,000

Capital in excess of par or stated value:			
From preferred stock issuances	$ 5,000		
From common stock issuances	27,000		
From treasury stock transactions	2,000		
From stock dividends	3,000	37,000	$237,000
Retained earnings:			
Not available for dividend charges—Equal to cost of treasury stock		$ 7,500	
Unrestricted		132,000	139,500
Total			$376,500
Deduct cost of treasury stock			7,500
Total Stockholders' equity			$369,000

Instead of detailing the four elements of Capital in Excess of Par or Stated Value, a balance sheet will usually show merely:

Capital in excess of par or stated value   37,000

However, a separate ledger account is used for each element in order to classify the source of each item.

CHARGES TO CAPITAL IN EXCESS ACCOUNTS Accounts such as those shown in the foregoing illustrative Stockholders' Equity section under the caption "Capital in excess of par or stated value" should never be charged with asset write-downs and losses that normally would be charged to income or retained earnings. Following are two illustrations of the application of the rule. If the allowance for uncollectible accounts is inadequate, it should not be increased by an offsetting debit to such an account; nor should such an account be charged with write-downs of long-lived assets or write-offs of goodwill.

DONATED CAPITAL Donated capital results from gifts of assets to a corporation. A common example was mentioned earlier, namely, the gift of a plant to induce a business to locate in the donor city.

    Donated assets are recorded at their estimated value, with the credit to Donated Capital. The donated capital account is shown in the balance sheet under the Stockholders' Equity caption. It is usually listed separately just above retained earnings.

APPRAISAL INCREMENTS Prior to 1940, it was not an uncommon practice for companies to write up their long-lived assets to appraised values. The offsetting credit was shown as an element of the stockholders' equity. Various account titles were given to the credit-balance account; those most appropriate clearly indicated the source of the credit balance and that the amount represented an unrealized increment.

As noted in Chapter 10, the writing up of long-lived assets to appraised values is now regarded by the accounting profession as an improper practice. It follows that a credit balance denoting an unrealized increment from the writing up of long-lived assets is not a proper element of stockholders' equity.

There is an instance when an unrealized loss is recognized in the balance sheet under the stockholders' equity section. This occurs in the accounting for investments in noncurrent marketable equity securities under the lower-of-cost-or-market method, which is required per FASB *Statement No. 12.*[4] Consequently, at the end of the accounting period an adjusting entry is made to write down the aggregate cost of the portfolio to its aggregate market value, and the unrealized loss is reported in the balance sheet as follows:

Stockholders' equity:

Unrealized loss on investment in noncurrent
marketable equity securities   ($10,000)

EARNINGS PER SHARE   Earnings per share (EPS) is the amount of net income (earnings) applicable to each share of common stock outstanding. Since common stock prices are quoted, and therefore stock is bought and sold, on a per-share basis, it is useful to calculate earnings on a per-share basis also. Such EPS data are used by investors and financial analysts in evaluating the past performance of a company and as indicators of a company's future performance to aid in making investment decisions. Thus EPS data are probably the most widely quoted and used of all accounting statistics. Because of the importance of EPS data, they must be reported on the face of the income statement and they must be calculated in a standardized manner, as provided by APB *Opinion No. 15.*[5]

Simple capital structure   If a firm has a simple capital structure, which consists of only common stock or common stock and nonconvertible preferred stock, then the calculation of EPS is as follows:

$$EPS = \frac{\text{Net income} - \text{Dividends on nonconvertible preferred stock}}{\text{Weighted-average number of common shares outstanding}}$$

Since the preferred stockholders' claims to dividends take precedence over the common stockholders' claims, preferred dividends are subtracted from net income

[4]Financial Accounting Standards Board, "Accounting for Certain Marketable Securities," *Statement No. 12* (Stamford, Conn.: FASB, December 1975), paragraph 11.

[5]Accounting Principles Board, "Earnings per Share," *Opinion No. 15* (New York: AICPA, May, 1969). The Financial Accounting Standards Board has since suspended the requirement for nonpublic enterprises. See Financial Accounting Standards Board, "Suspension of the Reporting of Earnings per Share and Segment Information by Nonpublic Enterprises," *Statement of Financial Accounting Standards No. 21* (Stamford, Conn.: FASB, April, 1978).

in computing the EPS numerator (income available to common stockholders). The denominator is the number of common shares weighted by the time they were outstanding during the period. This weighting is done to reflect additional shares issued during the period, since the proceeds from the issuance would not have been available during the whole period to generate earnings. For example, if a company issued 6,000 common shares on March 1, then such shares would be outstanding ten months and the 6,000 shares would be equivalent to 5,000 (= 6,000 × $^{10}/_{12}$) shares for a full year. Of course, if there were no changes in the number of common shares outstanding during the period, then the denominator in the EPS calculation would simply be the number of common shares outstanding at year end.

As pointed out and illustrated in Chapter 4, if a firm has extraordinary items, then EPS data must be presented on the face of the income statement for both income before extraordinary items and net income and is optional for extraordinary items per *Opinion No. 15*.

To illustrate the calculation and reporting of EPS under a simple capital structure, assume the following data for a company for 19_8:

Common stock shares:	
Shares 1/1/_8	6,000
Shares issued 4/1/_8	4,000
Shares issued 9/1/_8	3,000
Nonconvertible preferred stock, dividend	
rate $3.00 per share, shares outstanding	
for year	1,000
Income before extraordinary item	$80,000
Extraordinary loss	$ 4,000
Net income	$76,000

The weighted-average number of common shares during 19_8 would be 10,000, calculated as follows:

6,000 × 12/12 of a year = 6,000	or alternatively	6,000 × 3/12 = 1,500
4,000 × 9/12 of a year = 3,000		10,000 × 5/12 = 4,167
3,000 × 4/12 of a year = 1,000		13,000 × 4/12 = 4,333
10,000		10,000

Given the 10,000 weighted-average number of common shares, the EPS data would be presented at the bottom of the income statement as illustrated below:

.
.
.

Income before extraordinary item	$80,000
Extraordinary loss	(4,000)
Net income	$76,000
Earnings per common share:	
Income before extraordinary item	$ 7.70[a]
Extraordinary loss	(.40)[b]
Net income	$ 7.30[c]

[a]$7.70 = ($80,000 − $3,000 preferred dividends) ÷ 10,000

[b]$ .40 = $4,000 ÷ 10,000

[c]$7.30 = ($76,000 − $3,000) ÷ 10,000

Complex capital structure For purposes of computing EPS, a corporation is viewed as having a complex capital structure if it has such securities as convertible preferred stock, convertible bonds, stock warrants, or stock options outstanding. Since convertible preferred stock and convertible bonds may be exchanged by their owners for common stock, and since stock options and stock warrants give their holders the right to buy common shares at a predetermined price, the corporation has a commitment to issue shares of common stock at the discretion of the owners of these securities. If such securities were converted (convertible preferred stock or bonds) or exercised (stock options or warrants), the issuing corporation's earnings would be spread over more shares of common stock and earnings per share would be diluted (reduced). Thus convertible preferred stock, convertible bonds, stock options, and stock warrants are potentially dilutive securities. Consequently, for complex capital structures, APB *Opinion No. 15* requires that the potential dilution from these securities be reflected in EPS data, and in many cases it requires the presentation of two EPS figures: *primary* EPS and *fully diluted* EPS.

Potentially dilutive securities that are equivalent to, but not in actual form, common stock because they derive their value primarily from the related common stock, rather than from the interest or dividends they pay, are called *common stock equivalents.* In other words, the attractiveness of common stock equivalents lies in their potential right to share in the future earnings of a corporation; hence, their market value generally reflects the market value of their related common stock. Since common stock equivalents are viewed as being nearly the same as common stock, APB *Opinion No. 15* requires that they be included in computing primary EPS. Consequently, primary EPS is based on the weighted-average number of common shares outstanding plus common stock equivalents.

Not all potentially dilutive securities are considered to be common stock equivalents. *Opinion No. 15* specifies a test to determine whether or not a convertible security appears to be held for its conversion rights and therefore qualifies as a common stock equivalent.[6] Stock options and stock warrants are considered to be common stock equivalents, since the only reason for holding them is the right to acquire common stock at a specified price. Potentially dilutive securities that do not qualify as common stock equivalents are used in computing fully diluted EPS. Consequently, fully diluted EPS is based on the weighted-average number of common shares outstanding plus common stock equivalents and plus all potentially dilutive securities to show maximum potential dilution.

For example, assume the same basic data as in the previous illustration (see page 383) plus the following additional data:

Two thousand shares of convertible preferred stock, $2.00 dividend rate, convertible into common stock at the rate of four shares of common stock for each share of convertible preferred, and qualifies as a common stock equivalent

Five hundred shares of convertible preferred, $2.50 dividend rate, convertible into common stock at the rate of three shares of common stock for each share of convertible preferred, and does not qualify as a common stock equivalent

[6]Convertible securities are common stock equivalents per *Opinion No. 15* if their cash yield (interest or dividend per share divided by current market price at time of issuance) is less than two-thirds the bank prime rate (rate charged by banks to their borrowers with the very best credit rating).

The primary and fully diluted EPS would be reported at the bottom of the income statement as follows:

> .
> .
> .

Earnings per common share:
  Primary:
    Earnings before extraordinary item $4.21[a]
    Extraordinary loss   (.22)[b]
    Net income $3.99[c]

  Fully diluted:
    Earnings before extraordinary item $3.95[d]
    Extraordinary loss   (.21)[e]
    Net income $3.74[f]

[a] $4.21 = [\$80,000 - (\$3 \times 1,000) - (\$2.50 \times 500)] \div [10,000 + (2,000 \times 4)]$
[b] $.22 = \$4,000 \div 18,000$
[c] $3.99 = (\$76,000 - \$3,000 - \$1,250) \div 18,000$
[d] $3.95 = (\$80,000 - \$3,000) \div [10,000 + (2,000 \times 4) + (500 \times 3)]$
[e] $.21 = \$4,000 \div 19,500$
[f] $3.74 = (\$76,000 - \$3,000) \div 19,500$

IMPORTANT TERMS AND CONCEPTS IN CHAPTER 12

Par value—p. 367
Book value (amount)—pp. 367, 371
Market value—p. 368
Liquidation value—p. 368
Redemption value—p. 368
Stated (legal) capital—p. 368
Legality of dividends—p. 368
Dividend restrictions—p. 369
Declared dividends—p. 370
Preferred dividends in arrears—p. 371
Cash dividends and retained earnings—p. 372
Stock dividends—p. 373
Stock splits—p. 374

Retained earnings appropriations—p. 375
Prior-period adjustments—p. 376
Treasury stock—p. 377
Donated capital—p. 381
Unrealized capital—p. 382
Earnings per share—p. 382
Simple capital structure—p. 382
Complex capital structure—p. 384
Potentially dilutive securities—p. 384
Common stock equivalents—p. 384
Primary EPS—p. 384
Fully diluted EPS—p. 384

DEMONSTRATION PROBLEM FOR REVIEW AND SELF-STUDY

Fisher Company was organized on January 2, 19_1, with authorized capital of 10,000 shares of no-par common stock. A stated value of $10 per share was assigned to the stock. The following selected transactions occurred in the order listed over a period of several years:

(1) Issued 2,000 shares of stock at $10 per share.
(2) Issued 2,000 shares of stock at $12 per share.
(3) Acquired 500 shares of treasury stock at $14 per share.
(4) Paid a cash dividend of $1 per share.
(5) Sold 300 shares of treasury stock at $15 per share.
(6) Paid a cash dividend of $1 per share.
(7) Sold 200 shares of treasury stock at $19 per share.
(8) Paid a 10 per cent stock dividend. Fair value of the stock at the time was $19 per share.

(9) Paid a cash dividend of $1.25 per share.
(10) Split the stock 2-for-1.
(11) Paid a cash dividend of $1 per share.
(12) Paid a 5 per cent stock dividend. Fair value of the stock at this time was $11 per share.
(13) Acquired 1,000 shares of treasury stock at $15 per share.
(14) Sold 300 shares of treasury stock at $16 per share.

INSTRUCTIONS

(a) Prepare journal entries to record the transactions. Omit explanations.
(b) Prepare the Stockholders' Equity section of the balance sheet as of December 31, 19_8, the end of the period covered by the above transactions. Retained earnings on this date totaled $67,000. The company was organized in a state where treasury stock acquisitions must not impair stated capital.

Note Attempt to solve the demonstration problem before examining the solution that follows.

(a)

JOURNAL (Page 1)

(1)	Cash	20,000	
	Common stock		20,000
(2)	Cash	24,000	
	Common stock		20,000
	Capital in excess of stated value—From common stock issuances		4,000
(3)	Treasury stock	7,000	
	Cash		7,000
(4)	Dividends	3,500	
	Cash		3,500
	[(4,000 shares issued − 500 treasury shares) × $1.00]		
(5)	Cash	4,500	
	Treasury stock		4,200
	Capital in excess of stated value—From treasury stock transactions		300
(6)	Dividends	3,800	
	Cash		3,800
	[(4,000 shares issued − 200 treasury shares) × $1.00]		
(7)	Cash	3,800	
	Treasury stock		2,800
	Capital in excess of stated value—From treasury stock transactions		1,000
(8)	Stock dividends	7,600	
	Common stock		4,000
	Capital in excess of stated value—From stock dividends		3,600
	(4,000 shares × 10% = 400 shares)		
(9)	Dividends	5,500	
	Cash		5,500
	(4,400 shares × $1.25)		

(10)	No entry required. The following entry may be made: Common stock, $10 stated value	44,000	
	Common stock, $5 stated value		44,000
(11)	Dividends	8,800	
	Cash		8,800
	(8,800 shares × $1.00)		
(12)	Stock dividends	4,840	
	Common stock		2,200
	Capital in excess of stated value—From stock		
	dividends		2,640
	(8,800 shares × 5% = 440 shares)		
(13)	Treasury stock	15,000	
	Cash		15,000
(14)	Cash	4,800	
	Treasury stock		4,500
	Capital in excess of stated value—From treasury		
	stock transactions		300

(b)

FISHER COMPANY
Partial Balance Sheet
December 31, 19_8

Stockholders' equity:			
Common stock—No-par; stated value, $5; authorized 20,000 shares; issued 9,240 shares of which 700 shares are in the treasury		$46,200	
Capital in excess of stated value:			
From common stock issuances	$4,000		
From treasury stock transactions	1,600		
From stock dividends	6,240	11,840	$ 58,040
Retained earnings:			
Not available for dividend charges—Equal to cost of treasury stock		$10,500	
Unrestricted		56,500	67,000
Total			$125,040
Deduct cost of treasury stock			10,500
Total stockholders' equity			$114,540

Questions

1 How is the book value of a share of stock determined? Why is book value generally a poor indicator of the worth of a share of stock?

2 What are two ways in which state laws define stated capital? What is the significance of stated capital?

3 Generally, when may a corporation legally declare a dividend?

4 Discuss three situations in which dividends may be restricted.

5 What factors influence a corporation's dividend policy?

6 What are three significant dates pertaining to dividends? Show by example the entries, if any, which are required on each date.

7 Describe the proper accounting treatment of a stock dividend.

8 What is the difference between a stock split and a stock dividend?

9 Why might a corporation wish to effect a stock split?

10 Define treasury stock. How should treasury stock be reported in the financial statements?

11 What are the two major sources of stockholders' equity?

12 How are prior-period adjustments accounted for?

13 Define a common stock equivalent.

14 What is the distinction between a simple capital structure and a complex capital structure?

Short exercises

E12-1

The stockholders' equity of Oliver Corporation consists of the following on December 31, 19_8:

Preferred stock (5%, $100 par)	$25,000
Common stock ($25 par)	40,000
Capital in excess of par—From common stock issuances	8,000
Retained earnings	10,000
Total	$83,000

Dividends were last paid on the preferred stock for the year ended December 31, 19_5. Compute the book value per share of the preferred and common stock, assuming: (a) that the preferred stock is noncumulative; (b) that the preferred stock is cumulative.

E12-2

Darby Company has 4,000 shares of 6%, $50 par value preferred stock and 15,000 shares of no-par value common stock outstanding. Present entries for the following dividend transactions which took place during 19_5. Omit explanations.

(1) Paid the annual cash dividend on the preferred stock. The dividend was declared on December 15, 19_4. The firm's accounting period ends on December 31.
(2) Declared a cash dividend of $1 per share on the common stock.
(3) Paid the common stock dividend.
(4) Declared and issued a 10 per cent stock dividend on the common stock. The fair value of the stock issued is $15 per share.

E12-3   *The stockholders' equity of Bethel Corporation consists of the following:*

Common stock ($10 par)	$ 60,000	
Capital in excess of par—From common stock issuances	25,000	
Retained earnings	100,000	$185,000

Present the Stockholders' Equity section of the firm's balance sheet after the declaration and issuance of a 10 per cent stock dividend. The fair value of the common stock is $12 per share.

E12-4   *Using the data in Exercise 3, present the Stockholders' Equity section after a 4-for-1 stock split rather than a 10 per cent stock dividend.*

E12-5   *Bennett Corporation acquired 1,000 shares of its own $25 par value common stock at a total cost of $27,000. Journalize the following reissuances of the stock: (a) 200 shares at $30 per share; (b) 200 shares at $39 per share; (c) 250 shares at $26 per share.*

E12-6   *Capital Company had the following capital structure during 19_8:*

Common stock, $10 par value:	
Shares outstanding at January 1	10,000
Shares issued July 1	10,000
Shares issued November 1	6,000
8% preferred stock, $100 par value:	
Shares outstanding entire year	3,000

The preferred stock is cumulative and nonconvertible. Calculate any earnings per-share amounts required to be reported in the firm's income statement for 19_8. Assume net income of $80,000.

E12-7   *Assume that in addition to the stock outstanding in E12-6, Capital Company also had outstanding during the entire year 1,000 shares of $100 par value preferred stock with a 6% dividend rate. This stock is convertible into the common stock of Capital Company at the rate of one share of preferred stock for two shares of common stock and is considered to be a common stock equivalent. Calculate any earnings per share amounts to be reported in the firm's income statement for 19_8.*

Problems

A12-1   *Hellam Corporation has authorized capital of 100,000 shares of $10 par value common stock. There were 50,000 shares outstanding on October, 1, 19_3, all having been sold at a price of $12 per share.*
          The following transactions took place during the month of October:

October 3—Acquired 5,000 shares of treasury stock at $18 per share.
10—Sold 2,000 shares of treasury stock for $21 per share.
12—Received 3,000 shares of the company's stock as a donation.
18—Sold the donated treasury stock for $18 per share.
26—Sold 3,000 shares of treasury stock for $14 per share.

Prepare journal entries to record the transactions.

A12-2

Midland Company acquired 1,000 shares of its no-par common stock on August 2, 19_2, at a price of $25 per share. The stock has a stated value of $20 per share. Of the 50,000 shares authorized, 25,000 shares were originally sold for $23 per share.

The treasury stock, which was recorded at cost, was disposed of as follows:

September 3, 19_2	300 shares for $25 per share.
December 12, 19_2	300 shares for $28 per share.
January 8, 19_3	400 shares for $23 per share.

Required:

(a) Journal entries to record the acquisition and subsequent sale of the treasury stock.

(b) The Stockholders' Equity section of the company's balance sheet as of December 31, 19_2, assuming a retained earnings balance of $75,000. The company was organized in a state where treasury stock acquisitions must not impair stated capital.

A12-3

James Corporation was organized on January 2, 19_2 with an authorized capital of 5,000 shares of 6 per cent, $100 par value cumulative preferred stock and 25,000 shares of $50 par value common stock.

As of December 31, 19_6, the company had issued the following stock:

January 2, 19_2	12,500 shares of common at $50 per share.
January 11, 19_2	2,500 shares of preferred at $106 per share.
January 3, 19_4	1,250 shares of common issued as a stock dividend.
January 3, 19_4	6,250 shares of common at $56 per share.

During the period from January 1, 19_2, to December 31, 19_6, the corporation reported earnings and paid cash dividends as follows:

	Net income or (loss)	Preferred dividends	Common dividends
For Year Ended:			
December 31, 19_2	$ 25,000	$10,000	
December 31, 19_3	75,000	10,000	
December 31, 19_4	150,000	25,000	$15,000
December 31, 19_5	(90,000)	15,000	50,000
December 31, 19_6	107,500		

Compute the book value per share for each class of stock as of December 31, 19_6.

A12-4

The outstanding stock of Evans Corporation on December 31, 19_5, consists of 10,000 shares of $25 par value common stock and 5,000 shares of $50 par value, 8 per cent preferred stock. Cash dividends totaling $60,000 are to be paid on stock outstanding on this date.

Compute the allocation of the total dividends between the common and preferred stock under each of the following assumptions:

(a) The preferred stock is cumulative and dividends have been paid to December 31, 19_4.

(b) The preferred stock is cumulative and dividends have been paid to December 31, 19_3.

(c) The preferred stock is noncumulative and dividends have been paid to December 31, 19_3.

(d) The preferred stock is cumulative and fully participating. Preferred stock dividends have been paid to December 31, 19_4.

A12-5

Palmer Corporation, whose accounting period ends on December 31, has an authorized capital of 8,000 shares of $40 par value common stock. On August 31, 19_6, the following account balances were taken from the firm's ledger:

Common stock	$200,000
Capital in excess of par value—From common stock issuances	50,000
Retained earnings	100,000

The company had net income of $1,000 per month throughout the period covered by the following dividend transactions:

On September 20, 19_6, the directors declared a dividend of $.75 per share, to be paid in cash on October 10, 19_6, to stockholders of record on September 28, 19_6.

A 10 per cent stock dividend was issued on July 10, 19_7. Fair value of the shares was $50 per share.

Another cash dividend of $.40 per share was declared by the directors on September 20, 19_7, to be paid on October 10, to stockholders of record on September 28. One-half of the dividend was to be charged to Capital in Excess of Par Value—From Common Stock Issuances, which was permissible under the laws of the state in which the company was incorporated.

Show the journal entries to record the dividend transactions and the related closing entries on December 31, 19_6, and December 31, 19_7.

A12-6

The December 31, 19_7 balance sheet of Crucible Corporation presented the Stockholders' Equity section as follows:

Stockholders' equity:	
Capital stock:	
7% cumulative preferred—3,000 shares authorized; 1,000 shares issued; par value, $100	$190,000
No-par common—20,000 shares issued; 3,000 shares held in treasury; 25,000 shares authorized; stated value, $20	334,000
Retained earnings:	
Capital in excess of par value—From common stock issuances	70,000
Operating income (see Note A)	186,000
	$780,000

Note A: In view of a planned future purchase to reduce the number of preferred shares outstanding, the directors have designated $50,000 of accumulated earnings as not available for dividend purposes.

The common stock has been issued at various dates. Collections from shares issued have been: 10,000 shares at $22 per share, and 10,000 shares at $25 each.

The 3,000 shares of common stock held in the treasury were purchased recently at $22 per share. The company is organized in a state where treasury stock acquisitions must not impair the stated capital.

The preferred stock was issued on January 1, 19_5. To date no dividends have been declared on this stock.

Prepare the Stockholders' Equity section of the balance sheet in a more acceptable form.

A12-7 Letson Corporation was organized early in 19_3. During 19_6 the company had the following capital structure:

Preferred stock, 7%, cumulative, nonconvertible, $50 par value:	
Shares outstanding during the entire year	10,000
Common stock, $100 par value:	
Shares outstanding at January 1	50,000
Additional shares issued April 1	10,000
Additional shares issued September 1	24,000

During the year the firm reported net income of $220,000, including an extraordinary gain of $20,000. There are no dividends in arrears on the preferred stock.

Required:

(a) Calculate the weighted-average number of common shares outstanding during the year.

(b) Calculate the earnings per common share for the year and show how the earnings per share information should be reported in the firm's income statement.

B12-1 Hanover Corporation had 1,000 shares of 5 per cent cumulative $50 par value preferred stock and 10,000 shares of $25 par value common stock outstanding on July 1, 19_6. The following transactions took place during the month of July:

July 2—Declared a cash dividend of $1.75 per share on the preferred stock.
     5—Declared a 5 per cent stock dividend on the common stock. Fair value at the time was $26 per share.
   13—Acquired 500 shares of common stock for $12,500.
   20—Sold 200 shares of treasury stock at $27 per share.
   22—Sold 200 shares of treasury stock for $7,500.
   31—Paid the cash dividend declared on July 2.

Show the journal entries required to record the transactions.

B12-2 Fairfax Company has 2,000 shares of $50 par value, 8 per cent preferred stock and 8,000 shares of $50 par value common stock outstanding. The company paid dividends during a three-year period as follows:

19_2	$ 5,000
19_3	16,000
19_4	50,000

Compute the total dividends paid to each class of stock for the three-year period under each of the following assumptions:

(a) The preferred stock is noncumulative and nonparticipating.

(b) The preferred stock is cumulative and nonparticipating.

(c) The preferred stock is cumulative and fully participating.

B12-3 The following information pertains to Camden Corporation as of December 31, 19_4:

Preferred stock—6% cumulative; par value, $100; 1,500 shares authorized	$150,000
Common stock—Par value, $10; 20,000 shares authorized	200,000
Retained earnings	40,000
Capital in excess of par value—From treasury stock transactions	10,000
Donated capital	20,000
Capital in excess of par value—From common stock issuances	15,000

Dividends have been paid on the preferred stock through December 31, 19_2.

Required:

(a) The Stockholders' Equity section of the balance sheet as of December 31, 19_4.

(b) Computation of book value per share for each class of stock as of December 31, 19_4.

B12-4 Neville Company had a retained earnings balance of $59,000 on January 1, 19_4. At this date the firm had outstanding 5,000 shares of $100 par value, 8 per cent, cumulative preferred stock on which dividends had been paid to December 31, 19_3. During 19_4 the firm reported net income of $25,000 and paid total dividends of $13,000. In 19_5 the firm had net income of $14,000 and paid total dividends of $10,000. The firm's outstanding common stock consisted of 100,000 shares of $10 par value stock during the entire period.

In late 19_5 the firm became aware of the fact that depreciation expense for 19_4 had been overstated by $12,000 as a result of recording depreciation on assets which had previously been fully depreciated but which were still in use. This was considered to be a material error and was corrected as a part of the adjusting process at the end of 19_5.

Required:

(a) Prepare the December 31, 19_5 entry to record the correction of the error in depreciation expense. Ignore income taxes.

(b) Prepare the firm's Statement of Retained Earnings for the year ended December 31, 19_5.

(c) Calculate the book value per share for the preferred and common stock at December 31, 19_5. All preferred stock outstanding had been sold at a price of $102 per share. Total capital in excess of par value for the common stock was $23,000.

B12-5 Wilfert Company was organized on January 1, 19_1, with authorized capital of 10,000 shares of no-par common stock. A stated value of $10 per share was assigned to the stock. The following selected transactions occurred in the order listed over a period of several years:

(1) Issued 2,000 shares of stock at $10 per share.
(2) Issued 2,000 shares of stock at $12 per share.
(3) Acquired 500 shares of treasury stock at $14 per share.
(4) Paid a cash dividend of $2 per share.
(5) Sold 300 shares of treasury stock at $12 per share.
(6) Paid a cash dividend of $1 per share.
(7) Sold 200 shares of treasury stock at $19 per share.
(8) Paid a 10 per cent stock dividend. Fair value of the stock at the time was $19 per share.
(9) Paid a cash dividend of $1.25 per share.
(10) Split the stock 2-for-1.
(11) Paid a cash dividend of $1 per share.
(12) Paid a 10 per cent stock dividend. Fair value of the stock at this time was $11 per share.
(13) Acquired 1,000 shares of treasury stock at $15 per share.
(14) Sold 300 shares of treasury stock at $20 per share.

Required:

(a) Journal entries to record the transactions. Omit explanations.

(b) The Stockholders' Equity section of the balance sheet as of December 31, 19_8, the end of the period covered by the above transactions. Retained earnings on this date totaled $97,000. The company was organized in a state where treasury stock acquisitions must not impair stated capital.

B12-6

On March 31, 19_9, the ledger accounts of Meriden Company had the following balances:

Cash	$ 9,485
Accounts receivable	28,543
Land	23,000
Building	150,000
Treasury stock—Preferred	8,800
Treasury stock—Common	5,700
Organization costs	2,980
Capital in excess of par value—From common stock issuances	12,260
Common stock subscribed	10,000
Subscriptions receivable—Common	8,000
Common stock	90,000
Dividends payable—Common	1,700
Preferred stock	60,000
Subscriptions receivable—Preferred	12,500
Preferred stock subscribed	20,000
Allowance for uncollectibles	1,200
Accumulated depreciation—Building	15,000
Retained earnings	33,868
Capital in excess of par value—From treasury stock transactions	5,800
Merchandise inventory	16,500
Accounts payable	15,680

The company was authorized to issue 1,000 shares of 5 per cent cumulative participating preferred stock with a par value of $100, and 3,000 shares of $50 par value common stock. It has issued 600 shares of preferred and 1,800 shares of common. Shares subscribed for but not issued consist of 200 shares of preferred and 200 shares of common, and the subscriptions are due in the near future. The company holds 80 shares of preferred and 100 shares of common in the treasury. The company is organized in a state where treasury stock acquisitions must not impair the stated capital.

Required

Prepare a classified balance sheet for the company as of March 31, 19_9.

B12-7

Hoyle Corporation was authorized to issue 500,000 shares of $5 par value common stock and 100,000 shares of $25 par value, 8 per cent cumulative, convertible preferred stock. The preferred stock is convertible into common stock of the company at the rate of ten shares of common stock for each share of preferred. The preferred stock does not qualify as a common stock equivalent.

At January 1, 19_6 the stockholders' equity of the firm consisted of the following:

Preferred stock, 10,000 shares	$ 250,000
Common stock, 200,000 shares	1,000,000
Capital in excess of par value—From preferred stock issuances	30,000
Capital in excess of par value—From common stock issuances	200,000
Retained earnings	750,000
Total	$2,230,000

Dividends have been paid on the preferred stock through 19_5.

On July 1, 19_6 the firm sold an additional 50,000 shares of common stock at par value. Net income reported for the year was $75,000, two-thirds of which was paid as dividends.

Required:

(a) Calculate the book value per share of the common and preferred stock outstanding at December 31, 19_6.

(b) Calculate all earnings per share amounts to be reported in the firm's income statement for 19_6.

PURPOSE OF CHAPTER   There are many reasons why a business firm acquires the equity or debt securities of another corporation. Some of these were discussed in Chapter 6 which dealt with the accounting for certain marketable equity securities and Chapter 10 which discussed long-term investments in bonds. This chapter is devoted primarily to discussion of investments in equity securities that are acquired as long-term investments, frequently for the purpose of acquiring a controlling interest in another firm. In most instances in which one company owns a controlling interest in another, consolidated financial statements are prepared for the affiliated companies. This chapter also discusses the procedures involved in the preparation of such statements.

ACQUISITION OF STOCK   The stock of another company may be acquired by purchase. The purchaser is referred to as the *investor* and the company whose stock is acquired is referred to as the *investee.* The investor may purchase the stock of a previously existing company, or the stock may be that of a new company organized by the investor. A second way in which the investor may acquire the investee's stock is through an exchange of the investor's stock for that of the investee. This normally occurs when the purpose is to acquire a controlling interest (over 50 per cent of the outstanding voting stock) in the investee and is discussed later in the chapter.

RECORDING THE PURCHASE OF STOCK   As noted in Chapter 6, the cost of any purchased stock investment includes the purchase price, brokerage, taxes, and all other expenditures incident to the acquisition. For example, if Anson Company purchases for cash on January 2, 19_1 25 per cent of Bison Company's 20,000 shares of common stock at a price of $25 per share, plus purchase costs totaling $3,000, the following entry would be recorded:

Investment in Bison Company		
common stock [(5,000 × $25) + $3,000]	128,000	
Cash		128,000
Purchase of 5,000 shares of Bison		
Company common stock at $25 per share.		

ACCOUNTING FOR STOCK INVESTMENTS SUBSEQUENT TO ACQUISITION   The preceding entry to record the initial acquisition of a stock investment is the same no matter what portion of the investee's stock is acquired. However, the accounting for the investment after acquisition depends on the extent to which the investor can influence the operating and financial policies of the investee and will require the use of either the cost method or the equity method.

COST METHOD Traditionally, most long-term stock investments were carried at cost except when there was evidence of a permanent major decline in their price. Under the *cost* method, the amount at which the investment is reported is not affected by changes in the owners' equity of the investee. Dividends of the investee are recorded as revenue by the investor.

To illustrate, assume that Bison Company earns $100,000 in 19_1 and declares a dividend of $20,000, or $1 per share. The following entry is recorded by Anson Company:

Cash (5,000 × $1)	5,000	
Dividend revenue		5,000
Dividend of $1 per share on Bison Company common stock.		

The 19_1 financial statements of Anson Company will report the following information related to the investment:

In the balance sheet:
  Investments:
    Investment in Bison Company common stock, at cost (market $130,000) $128,000
In the income statement:
    Dividend revenue $ 5,000

EQUITY METHOD The major difference between the *equity* method of accounting for stock investments and the cost method is that the former gives recognition to the fact that the earnings of the investee company increase the net assets that underlie the stock investment and that investee losses and dividends decrease the net assets. In order to reflect these changes in the records of the investor, the investment account balance is debited or credited for the investor's share of the investee's earnings, losses, and dividends.

Anson Company would record the following entries in 19_1 to account for its investment in Bison Company under the equity method:

Investment in Bison Company common stock ($100,000 × 25%)	25,000	
Investment revenue		25,000
Investor's proportionate share of investee's reported net income.		
Cash ($20,000 × 25%)	25,000	
Investment in Bison Company common stock		5,000
Investor's proportionate share of investee's dividend.		

The financial statements of Anson Company for 19_1 will report the following information related to the investment:

In the balance sheet:
  Investments:
    Investment in Bison Company common stock, equity method
    (cost $128,000; market $130,000) $148,000
In the income statement:
    Investment revenue $ 25,000

It should be noted that the amounts reported in the financial statements are not the same as under the cost method. The investment account balance reported in the balance sheet no longer reports the original cost of the investment. The $148,000 balance includes the portion of the increase in the investee's net assets applicable to the stock held by the investor [($100,000 − $20,000) × 25%].

The income statement now reports as revenue the entire portion of the earnings of the investee applicable to the investor's stock ($100,000 × 25%), not just the portion paid out as dividends. It should be apparent from the preceding illustration that to the extent the investor is able to control the dividend policy of the investee, the dividend revenue of the investor can also be controlled. This possibility is not present when the equity method is used.

USE OF THE COST AND EQUITY METHODS For many years the choice between the cost and equity methods was a rather arbitrary decision left to the investor. However, this is no longer true as the result of the Accounting Principles Board's *Opinion No. 18*.[1] The Board has set forth guidelines to be used in determining whether the cost or equity method is appropriate in a given situation. The primary consideration in the determination is the degree of control exercised by the investor over the investee, which includes the concept of significant influence over the operating and financial policies of the investee. When such significant influence is present, the equity method must be used.

The Board concluded that "an investment (direct or indirect) of 20 per cent or more of the voting stock of an investee should lead to a presumption that in the absence of evidence to the contrary an investor has the ability to exercise significant influence over an investee."[2] The Board went on to state that the ability to exercise significant influence may be indicated by (1) representation on the board of directors, (2) participation in policy-making processes, (3) material intercompany transactions, (4) interchange of managerial personnel, and (5) technological dependency.[3]

MARKET-VALUE METHOD In addition to the cost and equity methods, Accounting Principles Board *Opinion No. 18* also discussed the market-value method. The basic characteristics of the method are: (1) Dividends received on the stock investment are treated as revenue by the investor. (2) Changes in the market price of the stock investment are treated as revenues or losses by the investor. The method is used only in special situations.

LOWER-OF-COST-OR-MARKET METHOD The application of the lower-of-cost-or-market method to marketable equity securities classified as current assets was discussed in Chapter 6. The method is also used to account for marketable equity securities classified as noncurrent assets (Investments) in a firm's balance sheet when the investment is accounted for by the cost method. This treatment is required by

---

[1]Accounting Principles Board, "The Equity Method of Accounting for Investments in Common Stock," *Opinion No. 18* (New York: AICPA, March, 1971).

[2]Ibid., paragraph 17.

[3]Ibid.

the provisions of the Financial Accounting Standards Board's *Statement No. 12*.[4]

The method is applied to noncurrent marketable equity securities just as it is applied to current marketable equity securities—by calculating the aggregate cost and the aggregate market price of the entire portfolio at the balance sheet date. However, declines below market, and subsequent recoveries, are recorded in a valuation account which is reported as a part of stockholders' equity, not as an income statement item to be considered in determining net income.

To illustrate, assume that Anson Company, in addition to its 25 per cent investment in Bison Company, has the following long-term investments acquired during 19_1:

Investment	Cost	Market price at December 31, 19_1
10% interest in Chester Company common stock	$100,000	$115,000
15% interest in Dykes Company common stock	85,000	60,000
Totals	$185,000	$175,000

Since there is an aggregate excess of cost of the portfolio over market at December 31, the difference of $10,000 is recorded as follows:

Net unrealized loss on noncurrent marketable equity securities	10,000	
Allowance for excess of cost of marketable equity securities over market		10,000

The net unrealized loss account would be reported in the company's balance sheet as a deduction in the stockholders' equity section following retained earnings. The allowance account balance is deducted in arriving at the amount reported for long-term investments.

In subsequent periods the entry to record any reductions in the amount of the required balance in the valuation allowance for noncurrent marketable equity securities would be just the reverse of the entry above and would have no effect on the firm's income.

We may summarize the requirements of accounting for long-term stock investments as follows:

Ownership interest	Method
(1) Less than a controlling interest:	
(a) Less than 20% of the outstanding voting stock, with no evidence of significant influence	Lower-of-cost-or-market
(b) 20% to 50% of the outstanding voting stock and significant influence presumed	Equity
(2) Controlling interest presumed when over 50% of the outstanding voting stock is owned	Equity with consolidated statements required

---

[4]Financial Accounting Standards Board, "Accounting for the Cost of Certain Marketable Securities," *Statement of Financial Accounting Standards No. 12* (Stamford, Conn.: December, 1975).

It is obvious from the above that use of the cost method is limited primarily to investments that either do not qualify as equity securities or that are considered to be nonmarketable.

PARENT-SUBSIDIARY RELATIONSHIP None of the investor-investee relationships discussed previously involved a controlling interest in the investee by the investor. Although significant influence may be exercised with a stock investment of 50 per cent or less, a controlling interest is present only when the investor owns over 50 per cent of the outstanding voting stock of the investee. In this situation, the investor is referred to as the *parent company* and the investee is referred to as the *subsidiary company.*

There are several reasons why the acquisition of a controlling interest may be desirable for the investor. For instance, the use of subsidiaries to conduct particular segments of a business may result in lower income taxes than if the operations were combined and carried on by a single corporation. Or, the use of subsidiaries may improve management effectiveness if the operations of a business are widely diversified; for example, a grocery chain may operate a bakery and one or more canning plants, or a fruit company may own banana plantations and ocean-going freight ships; under such circumstances, a separate corporation for each kind of business activity can have directors and officers having specialized knowledge of the particular operations. Or, it may be prudent to limit the risks of a hazardous venture by making its liabilities a claim against only the assets of a single company instead of those of the entire organization. Or, part of the operations may be subject to governmental regulations; for instance, an automobile finance company may organize a subsidiary to insure the cars that are security for its receivables.

CONSOLIDATED FINANCIAL STATEMENTS The parent-subsidiary relationship involves two different legal entities. However, for financial reporting purposes, they are considered a single economic entity, under unified management and control. Separate financial statements may be prepared for each firm, but consolidated financial statements are considered preferable. "There is a presumption that consolidated statements are more meaningful than separate statements and that they are usually necessary for a fair presentation when one of the companies in the group directly or indirectly has a controlling financial interest in the other companies."[5]

If there are limitations that make it impossible for the parent company to control the subsidiary, even though over 50 per cent of the voting stock is owned, consolidated statements would not be appropriate. For example, many foreign subsidiary's are located in countries in which political and economic factors preclude the parent company from exercising control.

PURCHASE VERSUS POOLING OF INTERESTS A firm may acquire a controlling interest in the voting stock of another corporation either by organizing a new corporation or by acquiring the stock of a previously existing firm. In either case, the acquisition

[5]Committee on Accounting Procedure, "Consolidated Financial Statements," *Accounting Research Bulletin No. 51* (New York: AICPA, August, 1959), paragraph 1.

is accounted for in one of two ways: Certain acquisitions must be accounted for as purchases while others must be accounted for as poolings of interests.

The two methods are not alternatives in a given situation, since the choice is determined by the attendant circumstances. The treatment as a purchase or a pooling of interests is determined by applying criteria stated in the Accounting Principles Board's *Opinion No. 16*.[6] If all of the criteria are met by the attendant circumstances of the acquisition, it must be accounted for as a pooling of interests. If any one of the criteria is not met, the purchase treatment must be applied.

The nature of the criteria is such that the acquisition of the subsidiary's stock in exchange for cash, noncash assets, or debt will be treated as a purchase, while an acquisition achieved by issuing additional stock of the parent company will generally be treated as a pooling of interests.

ACQUISITION TREATED AS A PURCHASE   The basic characteristic of the purchase treatment is that one company is considered to have acquired another company. The parent has acquired all or a portion of the net assets (stockholders' equity) of the subsidiary by purchase of the latter's stock. Since acquisitions of purchased assets are recorded at cost, the price paid for the subsidiary's stock is the amount debited to the investment account. However, this amount will not necessarily be the same as the book value of the stock acquired. In fact, for a previously existing investee company, the two would be the same only by coincidence. The treatment of any difference between the price paid for the subsidiary's stock and its book value will be discussed later in this chapter.

After the acquisition of the subsidiary's stock treated as a purchase, the balance sheet of the parent will contain an additional asset that represents the cost of the subsidiary stock. From a legal viewpoint, the parent owns the stock of its subsidiary. It does not own the subsidiary's assets and it is not legally responsible for the subsidiary's liabilities.

However, the separate balance sheet of the parent does not reflect the fact that the parent has economic control over the assets of the subsidiary. Through stock ownership parent company management controls the subsidiary. The purpose of the consolidated balance sheet is to report the financial position of the economic entity under unified management and control. It accomplishes this purpose by reporting in a single statement all assets owned or controlled by the parent and the liabilities which represent claims against those assets.

PURCHASE OF WHOLLY OWNED SUBSIDIARY   In order to illustrate the preparation of a consolidated balance sheet for a parent and purchased subsidiary at the date of acquisition, assume that Company P and Company S have prepared the following balance sheets as of December 31, 19_1:

[6]Accounting Principles Board, "Business Combinations," *Opinion No. 16* (New York: AICPA, August, 1970), par. 45–48.

	Company P	Company S
Assets:		
Cash	$ 74,000	$ 31,000
Accounts receivable (net)	5,000	15,000
Merchandise inventory	11,000	24,000
Plant and equipment (net)	60,000	30,000
	$150,000	$100,000
Equities:		
Accounts payable	$ 25,000	$ 35,000
Common stock	75,000	50,000
Retained earnings	50,000	15,000
	$150,000	$100,000

PURCHASE OF SUBSIDIARY STOCK AT BOOK VALUE   It will first be assumed that the parent acquires for $65,000 cash all of the common stock of Company S on December 31, 19_1. The price paid is exactly equal to the book value of the stock acquired and is paid to the former shareholders of Company S who are no longer involved as owners. Company P records the acquisition of the stock as follows:

Investment in stock of Company S	65,000	
Cash		65,000
Purchase for cash of 100% interest in common stock of Company S.		

The preparation of a consolidated balance sheet for the two companies immediately after the stock acquisition is illustrated on page 403. A working paper is normally utilized to facilitate the preparation of the consolidated statement. The information in the first two columns of the working paper is taken from the separate balance sheets of the two companies immediately after the stock acquisition by Company P. The balance sheet of Company S is unaffected by the transaction between Company P and the former stockholders of Company S. The balance sheet of Company P now contains an additional asset Investment in Stock of Company S, while the cash balance of the parent company has been reduced by the $65,000 paid for the Company S stock.

The eliminations columns of the working papers are used to eliminate certain items properly reported in the separate balance sheets of the two companies, but they would be improper in a consolidated balance sheet. For example, the parent's asset account Investment in Stock of Company S reports the interest of the parent in the net assets (stockholders' equity) of the subsidiary. However, the consolidated balance sheet will include the individual assets and liabilities of the subsidiary. This would result in a double counting of the subsidiary's net assets if the parent's investment account is not eliminated. The other half of the elimination entry is to remove the stockholders' equity accounts of the subsidiary, since the total amount of $65,000 is considered to have been purchased by the parent.

Purchase treatment.
Wholly owned subsidiary.
Cost of subsidiary stock equals book value.

COMPANY P AND SUBSIDIARY
Consolidated Balance Sheet Working Papers
(Date of Acquisition)

	Company P	Company S	Eliminations		Consolidated
Assets:					
Cash	9,000	31,000			40,000
Accounts receivable (net)	5,000	15,000			20,000
Merchandise inventory	11,000	24,000			35,000
Plant and equipment (net)	60,000	30,000			90,000
Investment in stock of Company S (100%)	65,000		(a) 65,000		
	150,000	100,000			185,000
Equities:					
Accounts payable	25,000	35,000			60,000
Capital stock:					
Company P	75,000				75,000
Company S		50,000	(a) 50,000		
Retained earnings:					
Company P	50,000				50,000
Company S		15,000	(a) 15,000		
	150,000	100,000	65,000	65,000	185,000

Eliminations:
*Book value of subsidiary's stock at date of acquisition.

It should be emphasized that the elimination is solely for the purpose of preparing the consolidated balance sheet and is recorded only in the working papers. It has absolutely no effect on the individual account balances in either the parent or subsidiary books. Once the elimination is entered in the working papers, the consolidated balance sheet information is obtained by horizontally summing each line. The final column presents the information needed to prepare the consolidated balance sheet.

PURCHASE PRICE IN EXCESS OF BOOK VALUE As noted earlier, the amount paid by the parent for the subsidiary's stock will in most cases be different from the book value of the stock acquired. The treatment of this difference will now be illustrated by assuming that Company P pays $70,000 cash for all of the common stock of Company S, or $5,000 more than the book value of the stock acquired.

In the absence of accounting errors on the books of Company S, there are two reasons why the investor may be willing to pay an amount in excess of the book value of the stock acquired. It is possible that certain subsidiary assets have a fair market value at the date of acquisition of the stock that is greater than the amounts at which they are recorded in the accounting records. Another reason is that the parent may anticipate advantages to be realized as the result of operating the companies as a single economic entity. In this case, the parent is willing to pay for an intangible asset that cannot be identified.

The preparation of a consolidated balance sheet at the date of the stock acquisition requires that the $5,000 excess paid for the stock be accounted for in the statement. As shown in the working papers on page 404, the elimination of the parent's investment account balance against the stockholders' equity accounts of the subsidiary results in a debit to an account that appears only in the consolidated balance sheet. The account title used here is Excess of Cost of Subsidiary Stock over Book Value. This is frequently titled Goodwill in consolidated balance sheets.

403

Purchase treatment.
Wholly owned subsidiary.
Cost of subsidiary stock exceeds book value.

COMPANY P AND SUBSIDIARY
Consolidated Balance Sheet Working Papers
(Date of Acquisition)

	Company P	Company S	Eliminations		Consolidated
Assets:					
Cash	4,000	31,000			35,000
Accounts receivable (net)	5,000	15,000			20,000
Merchandise inventory	11,000	24,000			35,000
Plant and equipment (net)	60,000	30,000			90,000
Investment in stock of Company S (100%)	70,000			(a) 70,000	
Excess of cost of subsidiary stock over book value			(a) 5,000		5,000
	150,000	100,000			185,000
Equities:					
Accounts payable	25,000	35,000			60,000
Capital stock:					
Company P	75,000				75,000
Company S		50,000	(a) 50,000		
Retained earnings:					
Company P	50,000				50,000
Company S		15,000	(a) 15,000		
	150,000	100,000	70,000	70,000	185,000

Eliminations:
ªBook value of subsidiary's stock at date of acquisition.

The treatment of the $5,000 in the working papers is based on the assumption that there is no significant difference between the book amounts and the market prices of the subsidiary's assets at December 31, 19_1. If it were assumed that the excess was paid because the plant and equipment of the subsidiary had a market price $5,000 greater than their book amount at the date of purchase, the amount reported for plant and equipment would be increased by $5,000 in the consolidated balance sheet and the excess account would not be used.

ACQUISITION TREATED AS POOLING OF INTERESTS The rationale for treating the acquisition of the subsidiary's stock as a pooling of interests is that there is simply a combining of ownership interests resulting from the exchange of shares in one company for ownership shares of another company. The parent company acquires its interest in the subsidiary by issuing additional shares of parent company stock to the former stockholders of the subsidiary, who are now stockholders in the parent company.

Since the transaction is not considered to be a purchase of an ownership interest in the subsidiary, it is meaningless to consider the market prices of the subsidiary's assets at the date of the stock acquisition. In exchange for its additional stock issued, the parent is considered to have acquired an investment in the subsidiary equal to the book value of the subsidiary stock now owned by the parent. This amount is debited to the parent's investment account.[7] Since there is no basis for recognizing the market prices of subsidiary assets, the preparation of the consolidated balance sheet results in the combining of the assets and liabilities of the parent and subsidiary by using the book amounts reported in their separate records.

[7]In certain instances, the acquisition may qualify for pooling of interests treatment if some cash is involved in the transaction with investee shareholders. However, the Accounting Principles Board criteria previously referred to are such that most poolings of interests involve a stock-for-stock exchange only.

The December 31, 19_1 balance sheets of Company P and Company S previously shown on page 402 will be used to illustrate the stock acquisition and preparation of a consolidated balance sheet under the pooling of interests treatment. The stockholders' equity of both companies is shown below.

	Company P	Company S
Common stock, $1 par	$ 75,000	
Common stock, $5 par		$50,000
Retained earnings	50,000	15,000
	$125,000	$65,000

Company S acquires all 10,000 shares of the subsidiary's stock in a 1-for-1 stock exchange. The former shareholders of Company S will now own 10,000 shares of Company P stock. The parent accounts for the stock acquisition as follows:

Investment in stock of Company S (100%)	65,000	
Common stock (10,000 × $1)		10,000
Additional paid-in capital from pooling of interests ($65,000 − $10,000)		55,000
Acquisition of 100% interest in Company S.		

Obviously, the entry above does not have the same effect on the accounts of the parent as would the purchase of the subsidiary's stock for cash. At the same time, it has absolutely no effect on the accounts of the subsidiary. Balance sheets for the two companies after the stock acquisition are presented below.

	Company P	Company S
Assets:		
Cash	$ 74,000	$ 31,000
Accounts receivable (net)	5,000	15,000
Merchandise inventory	11,000	24,000
Plant and equipment (net)	60,000	30,000
Investment in stock of Company S (100%)	65,000	
	$215,000	$100,000
Equities:		
Accounts payable	$ 25,000	$ 35,000
Common stock	85,000	50,000
Additional paid-in capital from pooling of interests	55,000	
Retained earnings	50,000	15,000
	$215,000	$100,000

Working papers for the preparation of a consolidated balance sheet as of the date of acquisition are illustrated on page 406. The investment account of the parent is eliminated against the common stock account of the subsidiary, all of which is owned by the parent. The difference between the credit to the parent's investment account ($65,000) and the debit to the common stock account of the subsidiary ($50,000) is debited to Additional Paid-in Capital from Pooling of Interests because the credit to this account was a part of the original debit to the investment account.

The major differences between the consolidated balance sheet prepared in this case and the comparable statement from the purchase illustration are found in the stockholders' equity section. The consolidated balance sheet is prepared by first eliminating the intercompany investment account as shown in the working papers. The remaining items are combined by using the book amounts at which they are reported in the separate records of the parent and subsidiary. This is based on the reasoning that since the parent did not acquire the subsidiary in a purchase transaction, there is no basis for any change in the previously recorded amounts.

Pooling of interests treatment
Wholly owned subsidiary.

COMPANY P AND SUBSIDIARY
Consolidated Balance Sheet Working Papers
(Date of Acquisition)

	Company P	Company S	Eliminations	Consolidated
Assets:				
Cash	74,000	31,000		105,000
Accounts receivable (net)	5,000	15,000		20,000
Merchandise inventory	11,000	24,000		35,000
Plant and equipment (net)	60,000	30,000		90,000
Investment in stock of Company S (100%)	65,000		(a) 65,000	
	215,000	100,000		250,000
Equities:				
Accounts payable	25,000	35,000		60,000
Common stock	85,000	50,000	(a) 50,000	85,000
Additional paid-in capital from pooling of interests	55,000		(a) 15,000	40,000
Retained earnings	50,000	15,000		65,000
	215,000	100,000	65,000 65,000	250,000

Eliminations:
ᵃEliminate parent's investment account and related stockholder's equity.

The consolidated balance sheets resulting from each acquisition treatment are presented on page 407 along with an explanation of each difference.

CONSOLIDATED STATEMENTS AFTER ACQUISITION At the date of acquisition the only consolidated statement to be prepared is the balance sheet. The consolidated income statement and statement of retained earnings can be prepared only after the affiliated companies have operated as an economic entity. An important consideration in the preparation of consolidated statements after acquisition is the elimination of intercompany transactions in the consolidation process. For example, the consolidated income statement should include revenues, expenses, gains, and losses resulting from transactions between the economic entity and outsiders. Thus the sale of merchandise by one of the affiliated companies to another does not produce revenue for the consolidated entity since the merchandise does not leave the affiliated companies. Separate balance sheets prepared after acquisition might contain intercompany receivables and payables. However, these must be eliminated from the consolidated balance sheet since they do not represent amounts receivable from or payable to parties outside the affiliated companies.

ACQUISITION TREATED AS A PURCHASE In order to illustrate the preparation of consolidated financial statements at the end of the first year after acquisition, it will be assumed that Company P acquired 100 per cent of the stock of Company S at December 31, 19_1, paying cash of $70,000.

COMPANY P AND SUBSIDIARY
Comparison of Consolidated Balance Sheets Under
Purchase and Pooling of Interests

	Purchase	Pooling of interests	Explanation of difference
Assets:			
Cash	$ 35,000	$105,000	No cash required to acquire subsidiary in pooling of interests.
Accounts receivable (net)	20,000	20,000	None.
Merchandise inventory	35,000	35,000	None.
Plant and equipment (net)	90,000	90,000	None.
Excess of cost of subsidiary stock over book value	5,000		No such difference exists in the acquisition by pooling of interests.
	$185,000	$250,000	
Equities:			
Accounts payable	$ 60,000	$ 60,000	None.
Common stock	75,000	85,000	Parent company issued additional shares to acquire the subsidiary in a pooling treatment.
Additional paid-in capital from pooling of interests		40,000	Represents the difference between the par value of the subsidiary stock acquired and the par value of the additional parent company stock issued ($10,000). In effect, the additional parent company stock has replaced the subsidiary stock in the hands of former subsidiary shareholders.
Retained earnings	50,000	65,000	Under the purchase treatment, the retained earnings of the subsidiary at acquisition is eliminated since it represents an element of the net assets purchased.
	$185,000	$250,000	

At the date of acquisition the balance sheets of the two companies were as follows:

	Company P	Company S
Assets:		
Cash	$ 74,000	$ 31,000
Accounts receivable (net)	5,000	15,000
Merchandise inventory	11,000	24,000
Plant and equipment (net)	60,000	30,000
	$150,000	$100,000
Equities:		
Accounts payable	$ 25,000	$ 35,000
Common stock	75,000	50,000
Retained earnings	50,000	15,000
	$150,000	$100,000

The parent paid $5,000 more for its investment in the subsidiary than the book value of the stock acquired. This difference is assumed to be attributable to the plant and equipment of the subsidiary. Although carried at a book amount of $30,000 on the subsidiary's balance sheet, they are assumed to have a current market price of $35,000. The plant and equipment of the subsidiary are estimated to have a ten-year remaining life at the date of acquisition.

Separate financial statements of the two companies for the year ended December 31, 19_2 are presented in the first two columns of the working papers on page 408. The following observations should be made: The parent accounts for its investment in the subsidiary by the equity method. Therefore, the following entry is recorded by Company P at the end of 19_2 to report its share of Company S earnings for the year:

Investment in Company S common stock (100%)	8,000	
Investment revenue		8,000
Subsidiary's net income.		

The subsidiary reported net income of $8,000 for the year (second column in working papers below), all of which is applicable to the stock held by the parent. The subsidiary statements also indicate that Company S paid dividends of $1,000 during 19_2, all of which would have been paid to Company P.

This would have been recorded as follows by Company P:

Cash	1,000	
Investment in Company S common stock		1,000
Subsidiary's dividends.		

There is one additional entry that would have been recorded by Company P during 19_2 as a result of the stock investment. This is necessary because under

Purchase treatment.
Wholly owned subsidiary.

COMPANY P AND SUBSIDIARY
Consolidated Working Papers
For the Year Ended December 31, 19_2

	Company P	Company S	Eliminations		Consolidated
Income Statement:					
Sales	189,000	117,000			306,000
Cost of goods sold	146,000	89,000	(a)	500	235,500
Gross margin	43,000	28,000			70,500
Expenses	30,000	20,000			50,000
Net income from operations	13,000	8,000			20,500
Investment revenue	7,500		(a) 7,500		
Net income	20,500	8,000	8,000		20,500
Statement of Retained Earnings:					
Retained earnings—beginning of year	50,000	15,000	(a) 15,000		50,000
Net income—per above	20,500	8,000	8,000		20,500
Total	70,500	23,000			70,500
Dividends:					
Company P	10,000				10,000
Company S		1,000		(a) 1,000	
Retained earnings—end of year	60,500	22,000	23,000	1,000	60,500
Balance sheet:					
Assets:					
Cash	20,000	3,000			23,000
Accounts receivable (net)	28,000	17,000			45,000
Notes receivable—Company S	5,000			(b) 5,000	
Inventory	19,000	36,000			55,000
Plant and equipment (net)	60,000	30,000	(a) 4,500		94,500
Investment in Company S common					
stock	76,500			(a) 76,500	
	208,500	86,000			217,500
Equities:					
Accounts payable	73,000	9,000			82,000
Notes payable—Company P		5,000	(b) 5,000		
Capital stock:					
Company P	75,000				75,000
Company S		50,000	(a) 50,000		
Retained earnings—per above	60,500	22,000	23,000	1,000	60,500
	208,500	86,000	82,500	82,500	217,500

Eliminations:
ªEliminate intercompany investment, revenue, and dividends and allocate excess of cost of subsidiary stock over book value to expenses and assets.
ᵇEliminate intercompany receivable and payable.

the purchase treatment the higher amount attributed to the plant and equipment of the subsidiary in determining the amount the parent paid for its stock investment (current market price, $35,000, versus net book amount, $30,000) is not reflected in the separate accounts of the subsidiary. Therefore, the $8,000 net income of the subsidiary was determined by using the amount at which the plant and equipment are recorded in the Company S books and not the higher price reflected in the amount Company P paid for its stock.

If it is assumed that the plant and equipment have a remaining estimated life of ten years from the date of the stock acquisition, the following entry is recorded by Company P to write off the portion of the $5,000 difference attributable to the current year:

Investment revenue	500	
Investment in Company S common stock		500
To write off current year's portion of		
excess of cost of subsidiary stock over		
book value		

The three preceding entries recorded by the parent company result in the following amounts in the separate statements of the parent for 19_2:

Investment revenue:		
Parent's share of subsidiary net income (100%)		$ 8,000
Less write off of portion of excess of		
cost over book value of stock		500
Balance per parent's income statement		$ 7,500
Investment in Company S common stock:		
Original cost		$70,000
Add parent's share of 19_2 net income		
reported by subsidiary (100%)		8,000
		$78,000
Deduct:		
Parent's share of subsidiary's dividends	$1,000	
Write off of portion of excess of cost over		
book value of subsidiary's stock	500	1,500
Balance per parent's balance sheet		$76,500

In order to complete the preparation of consolidated financial statements, the following eliminations must be recorded in the working papers:

(a) Intercompany stockholding. The balance in the parent's investment account at December 31, 19_2 is $76,500, as calculated in the preceding paragraph. The entry to eliminate the investment account balance also accomplishes the following:

(1) Elimination of the subsidiary's stockholders' equity at the beginning of the year.

(2) Elimination of the investment revenue recorded by the parent and the dividends paid by the subsidiary during the current year. These represent intercompany transactions and should not be reported in the consolidated statements.

(3) Recognition in the consolidated income statement of the portion of the excess of the cost of the subsidiary stock over book value attributable to the current year as an item of expense. From a consolidated viewpoint, the plant and equipment used during the year had a cost $5,000 greater than the amounts reported on the separate records of the companies. In the working papers $500, or one-tenth of this amount, has been debited to Cost of Goods Sold based on the assumption that the plant and equipment of Company S are used in

the manufacturing process and that most of the units produced this period were sold by the end of the period. A theoretical refinement would be to allocate the $500 to Cost of Goods Sold and the inventory on hand at the end of the period.

(4) Allocation of the remaining portion of the excess ($5,000 − $500) to the plant and equipment assets in the consolidated balance sheet. This recognizes in the consolidated balance sheet the restatement of certain asset amounts which may be required by the purchase treatment.

(b) Intercompany receivables and payables. It is assumed that Company P loaned $5,000 to Company S on December 31, 19_2. Since the transaction did not involve any party outside the affiliated companies, it must be eliminated. Failure to do so would overstate both the assets and liabilities in the consolidated balance sheet.

Once these two eliminations have been recorded, the information for consolidated financial statements to be prepared at the end of 19_2 can be obtained from the final column in the working papers.

ACQUISITION TREATED AS A POOLING OF INTERESTS Using the same two companies whose December 31, 19_1 balance sheets are shown on page 407, we can now assume that the parent company acquired a 100 per cent interest in the subsidiary on December 31, 19_1 by issuing 10,000 shares of its $1 par value common stock in exchange for the 10,000 shares of $5 par value common stock of the subsidiary. We can also still assume that the parent uses the equity method to account for its investment.

The first two entries illustrated at the top of page 408 for the purchase treatment would still be recorded by the parent during 19_2. The first entry records the parent's share of the subsidiary's net income and the second entry records the dividends received by the parent from the subsidiary. The entry on page 409 would not be recorded because under the pooling of interests treatment, there is no new accounting basis established for any of the subsidiary's assets.

Separate financial statements for Company P and Company S at December 31, 19_2 are shown in the first two columns of the working papers on page 411. For reasons explained earlier in the chapter, certain amounts reported in the statements of the parent company are different because of the use of the pooling of interests method. The following account balances are derived as indicated:

Investment revenue:	
Parent's share of subsidiary net income (100%)	$ 8,000
Balance per parent's income statement	$ 8,000
Investment in Company S common stock:	
Original cost	$65,000
Add parent's share of 19_2 net income	
reported by subsidiary (100%)	8,000
	$73,000
Deduct parent's share of subsidiary's dividends	1,000
Balance per parent's balance sheet	$72,000

If it is assumed that all transactions for both companies are the same for 19_2 in this case as they were under the purchase method, the cash balance of the parent at December 31, 19_2 will be $70,000 greater because no cash was paid to acquire the subsidiary stock. All amounts reported in the subsidiary's statements for 19_2 are identical to the previous illustration because the parent's method of accounting for the stock of the subsidiary has no effect at all on the subsidiary's books.

The working papers for consolidated financial statements are completed by recording the following eliminations:

(a) Intercompany stockholding. The balance in the parent's investment account at December 31, 19_2 is $72,000 as calculated above. The entry to eliminate the investment account also accomplishes the following:

    (1) Elimination of the related stockholders' equity accounts. Under the purchase method, the beginning retained earnings balance of the subsidiary was debited (see page 408) since it was considered to have been purchased by the parent. In this case, however, the debit is to the additional paid-in capital from pooling of interests account because the implicit assumption in the pooling of interests method is that there is simply a substitution of the parent company stock for that of the subsidiary.

    (2) Elimination of the intercompany investment revenue recorded by the parent and the intercompany dividends paid by the subsidiary.

(b) Intercompany receivables and payables. From a consolidated viewpoint, the loan of $5,000 by Company P to Company S does not represent an asset or a liability.

Pooling treatment.
Wholly owned subsidiary.

COMPANY P AND SUBSIDIARY
Consolidated Working Papers
For the Year Ended December 31, 19_2

	Company P	Company S	Eliminations		Consolidated
Income Statement:					
Sales	189,000	117,000			306,000
Cost of goods sold	146,000	89,000			235,000
Gross margin	43,000	28,000			71,000
Expenses	30,000	20,000			50,000
Net income from operations	13,000	8,000			21,000
Investment revenue	8,000		(a) 8,000		
Net income	21,000	8,000	8,000		21,000
Statement of Retained Earnings:					
Retained earnings—beginning of year	50,000	15,000			65,000
Net income—per above	21,000	8,000	8,000		21,000
Total	71,000	23,000			86,000
Dividends:					
Company P	10,000				10,000
Company S		1,000		(a) 1,000	
Retained earnings—end of year	61,000	22,000	8,000	1,000	76,000
Balance Sheet:					
Assets:					
Cash	90,000	3,000			93,000
Accounts receivable (net)	28,000	17,000			45,000
Notes receivable—Company S	5,000			(b) 5,000	
Inventory	19,000	36,000			55,000
Plant and equipment (net)	60,000	30,000			90,000
Investment in Company S common stock	72,000			(a) 72,000	
	274,000	86,000			283,000
Equities:					
Accounts payable	73,000	9,000			82,000
Notes payable—Company P		5,000	(b) 5,000		
Capital stock:					
Company P	85,000				85,000
Company S		50,000	(a) 50,000		
Additional paid-in capital from pooling of interests	55,000		(a) 15,000		40,000
Retained earnings—per above	61,000	22,000	8,000	1,000	76,000
	274,000	86,000	78,000	78,000	283,000

Eliminations:
ªEliminate intercompany investment, revenue, and dividends.
ᵇEliminate intercompany receivable and payable.

MINORITY INTEREST When the parent company owns less than a 100 per cent interest in the subsidiary, the ownership interest of the minority shareholders is referred to as the *minority interest* and must be accounted for in consolidated financial statements. It cannot be eliminated because it does not represent an intercompany investment.

To illustrate, assume that Company P organized Company S December 31, 19_1 and that the subsidiary sold 50,000 shares of $1 par value common stock. Stock sales were made at the par value as follows:

Purchased by Company P (45,000 shares or 90%)	$45,000
Purchased by minority shareholders (5,000 shares or 10%)	5,000
Total	$50,000

It is further assumed that the subsidiary completes the following transactions on the date the subsidiary is organized. Inventory costing $30,000 is purchased, with $22,000 of the amount paid in cash. Land is purchased for a cash price of $15,000.

The balance sheet of the subsidiary, after these transactions, is shown below:

COMPANY S
Balance Sheet
December 31, 19_1

Assets		Equities	
Cash	$13,000	Accounts payable	$ 8,000
Merchandise inventory	30,000		
Land	15,000	Stockholders' equity:	
		Capital stock	50,000
	$58,000		$58,000

Consolidated financial statements should be prepared in this case because the parent obviously has a controlling interest in the subsidiary, even with the presence of the minority interest. The consolidated balance sheet working papers at the date of acquisition are shown at the top of page 413. Assumed balance sheet data for Company P are shown in the first column. The single elimination entry is to eliminate the parent's investment account against the portion of the subsidiary's stockholders' equity applicable to the ownership interest of the parent ($50,000 × 90%). The remainder of the subsidiary's stockholders' equity represents the minority interest and is reported as a separate item in the consolidated balance sheet.

Preparation of consolidated financial statements after the date of acquisition requires that the minority shareholders' interest be accounted for in each of the statements. Working papers for the year ended December 31, 19_2, are presented at the bottom of page 413.

The fact that the parent company owns only 90 per cent of the subsidiary's stock affects the separate statements of the parent as follows:

(a) Investment revenue. The subsidiary reported a net income of $8,000 for the year. However, the parent records only 90 per cent of this amount, or $7,200, as investment revenue.

(b) Investment in Company S common stock. The investment account is debited for $7,200, the parent's share of the subsidiary's net income for the year, and it is credited for 90 per cent of the dividends paid by the subsidiary during the year, or $900 ($1,000 × 90%).

Purchase treatment.
90 per cent owned subsidiary.

COMPANY P AND SUBSIDIARY
Consolidated Balance Sheet Working Papers
(Date of Acquisition)

	Company P	Company S	Eliminations	Minority interest	Consolidated
Assets:					
Cash	35,000	13,000			48,000
Accounts receivable—net	25,000				25,000
Inventory	65,000	30,000			95,000
Investment in Company S common stock (90%)	45,000		(a) 45,000		
Land		15,000			15,000
	170,000	58,000			183,000
Equities:					
Accounts payable	27,000	8,000			35,000
Capital stock:					
Company P	100,000				100,000
Company S		50,000	(a) 45,000	5,000	
Retained earnings	43,000				43,000
Minority interest				5,000	5,000
	170,000	58,000	45,000	45,000	183,000

Elimination:
ªEliminate parent's investment account and related stockholders' equity of subsidiary.

Purchase treatment.
90 per cent owned subsidiary.

COMPANY P AND SUBSIDIARY
Consolidated Working Papers
For the Year Ended December 31, 19_2

	Company P	Company S	Eliminations	Minority interest	Consolidated
Income Statement:					
Sales	189,000	117,000			286,000
Cost of goods sold	146,000	89,000			215,000
Gross margin	43,000	28,000			71,000
Expenses	30,000	20,000			50,000
Net income from operations	13,000	8,000			21,000
Investment revenue	7,200		(a) 7,200		
Minority interest—10% of $8,000				800	800
Net income	20,200	8,000	7,200	800	20,200
Statement of Retained Earnings:					
Retained earnings—beginning of year	43,000				43,000
Net income—per above	20,200	8,000	7,200	800	20,200
Total	63,200	8,000			63,200
Dividends:					
Company P	6,000				6,000
Company S		1,000	(a) 900	100	
Retained earnings—end of year	57,200	7,000	7,200	900	57,200
Balance Sheet:					
Assets:					
Cash	30,000	18,000			48,000
Accounts receivable (net)	33,000	2,000			35,000
Inventory	69,000	36,000			105,000
Investment in Company S common stock (90%)	51,300		(a) 51,300		
Land		15,000			15,000
	183,300	71,000			203,000
Equities:					
Accounts payable	26,100	14,000			40,100
Capital stock:					
Company P	100,000				100,000
Company S		50,000	(a) 45,000	5,000	
Retained earnings—per above	57,200	7,000	7,200	900 700	57,200
Minority interest				5,700	5,700
	183,300	71,000	52,200	52,200	203,000

Elimination:
ªEliminate intercompany investment, revenue, and dividends.

The elimination recorded in the working papers eliminates the investment account of the parent along with the portion of the beginning stockholders' equity of the subsidiary applicable to the 90 per cent ownership interest held by the parent. It also eliminates the intercompany investment revenue ($8,000 × 90%) and dividends ($1,000 × 90%) recorded by the parent during the year.

The accounting for the minority interest in the consolidated working papers may be summarized as follows:

Income Statement:

Ninety per cent of the net income of the subsidiary is included in consolidated net income. This is proper since the firms operated during the year as an economic entity. The remaining 10 per cent, or $800, which is not a part of consolidated net income, represents the interest of the minority shareholders in the net income reported by the subsidiary and increases their interest in Company S.

Statement of Retained Earnings:

The portion of the dividends paid to the minority shareholders, or $100, has the effect of reducing the equity represented by their 10 per cent interest in the subsidiary and is deducted from their share of the net income reported by the subsidiary, which is brought forward from the Income Statement section of the working papers. If the subsidiary had retained earnings at the beginning of the year, as would be the case in consolidated working papers for the following year, 10 per cent of any such balance would also represent an item to be included in calculating the minority interest.

Balance Sheet:

The difference between the minority interest in subsidiary net income ($800) and the dividends paid to the minority shareholders ($100) is brought forward from the Statement of Retained Earnings section of the working papers. When added to the portion of the subsidiary's common stock account applicable to the minority interest ($5,000), this gives a minority interest of $5,700 to be reported in the consolidated balance sheet at December 31, 19_2.

INTERCOMPANY SALES AND PROFITS IN INVENTORY Assume that one of the affiliated companies makes sales to the other company at a profit. From the selling company's standpoint, the profit is made at the time of sale; but from the consolidated standpoint, profits are made only by sales to outsiders. Therefore, if, at the end of the period, any intercompany-sold goods remain in the purchasing company's inventory, any intercompany profit thereon must be eliminated in the preparation of consolidated statements. The elimination affects the balance sheet valuation of the inventory and the sales and cost of goods sold shown in the income statement. To illustrate, assume that we are preparing consolidated statements of Company P and its subsidiary Company S for the year 19_1; the parent company made sales of $18,000 to the subsidiary during the year, the merchandise sold cost the parent $14,000, and the merchandise remained in the year-end inventory of the subsidiary. Thus the year-end inventory of Company S contained intercompany profit of $4,000 which, from a consolidated point of view, was unrealized profit and which, therefore, should be eliminated from the consolidated financial statements.

The above sales would result in the following account balances:

	In the financial statements of	
	Parent	Subsidiary
Sales	$18,000	
Cost of goods sold	14,000	
Inventory		$18,000

The required elimination is indicated below:

	In the financial statements of			
	Parent	Subsidiary	Elimination	Consolidated
Sales	18,000		18,000	
Cost of goods sold	14,000		14,000	
Inventory		18,000	4,000	14,000

Observe that, as a consequence of the above elimination, the intercompany sales and related cost of goods sold are excluded from the consolidated income statement and that the inventory acquired by an intercompany transaction is reduced to the amount it cost the company making the intercompany sale, or $14,000.

In the example, the intercompany sale was made by the parent. The need to eliminate intercompany sales and any unrealized profits therefrom also exists when a subsidiary has made sales to its parent or to another subsidiary of the parent.

SUBSEQUENT REALIZATION OF INTERCOMPANY PROFIT To show the subsequent realization of intercompany profit, we shall continue the foregoing illustration through 19_2. During 19_2 the merchandise acquired from the parent in 19_1 was sold to outsiders for $20,000, which was $2,000 above the cost to the subsidiary but $6,000 above the cost to the parent. The consolidated income statement for 19_2 should include the following:

Sales	$20,000
Cost of goods sold	14,000
Gross margin	$ 6,000

The cost of goods sold was determined as follows:

Cost paid by subsidiary when it purchased the goods from its parent	$18,000
Less intercompany profit element therein	4,000
Cost to parent	$14,000

Thus, the income in 19_2 would include the $4,000 of profit associated with last year's intercompany sales, which was not included in last year's consolidated income statement because the merchandise had not been sold to outsiders.

LIMITATIONS OF USEFULNESS OF CONSOLIDATED STATEMENTS Consolidated statements were devised for the purpose of giving interested parties an overall view of the financial position and operating results of a group of affiliated companies without requiring them to examine the statements of all of the related companies and to attempt to piece them together into a composite picture. For this purpose, consolidated statements are quite useful; but they do not serve all of the purposes for which individual company statements may be used or required. Creditors of the parent and subsidiary companies can obtain little information of value to them because consolidated statements do not detail the assets, liabilities, revenues, and expenses of the several companies.

There are also limitations to the usefulness of consolidated statements as a source of information to the parent company's stockholders. Because the balance sheet does not show the financial position of the parent as a separate legal entity, it does not disclose such facts as the ratio of subsidiary stock investments to total assets or stockholders' equity and the parent's working capital. The consolidated retained earnings statement does not show the retained earnings of the parent, which is generally the legal limit for dividends to be paid to parent company stockholders. The consolidated net income presumably includes an undisclosed amount of subsidiary earnings, which are not available for parent company dividends until transferred to the parent by subsidiary dividends.

It is customary to show as finished goods inventory in the consolidated balance sheet the total finished goods inventories of all companies and to combine the other inventories in a similar manner. However, if intercompany sales are made and finished goods of one company become raw materials of another company, such an inventory classification may be misleading and give a false impression of the liquidity of the inventories.

Ratio analyses based on consolidated data may result in misleading impressions. Such ratios are composites; the good and bad features of individual companies are not disclosed by them. For instance, assume the following facts about working capital.

	Current assets	Current liabilities	Working capital ratio
Company P	$60,000	$20,000	3.0
Company S	30,000	25,000	1.2
Consolidated	$90,000	$45,000	2.0

The precarious working capital position of the subsidiary is not disclosed; and, if the consolidated working capital were assumed to be that of the parent, the assumption is unwarranted.

IMPORTANT TERMS AND CONCEPTS IN CHAPTER 13

Investor—p. 396
Investee—p. 396
Controlling interest—p. 396
Cost method—p. 397
Equity method—p. 397
Significant influence—p. 398

Market-value method—p. 398
Lower-of-cost-or-market method—p. 398
Parent-subsidiary relationship—p. 400
Consolidated financial statements—p. 400
Purchase of controlling interest—p. 400
Pooling of interests—p. 400

DEMONSTRATION PROBLEM FOR REVIEW AND SELF-STUDY   Brinson Company acquired 90 per cent of the common stock of Hardy Company on December 31, 19_6, paying $75,000 cash. At the date of the investment the records of Hardy Company indicated a total stockholders' equity of $86,400, consisting of common stock of $60,000 and retained earnings of $26,400. The excess of the book value of the stock acquired over the price paid is attributable to an overvaluation of the land account on the books of Hardy Company. The amount of the excess is $2,760 [($86,400 × 90%) − $75,000].

During the year ended December 31, 19_7 Hardy Company purchased merchandise from Brinson Company for $152,000. This merchandise had cost Brinson Company $128,000. The December 31, 19_7 inventory of the subsidiary included one-fourth of the merchandise purchased from the parent during the year.

Trial balances of the two companies at December 31, 19_7 are presented below.

BRINSON COMPANY AND HARDY COMPANY
Trial Balances
December 31, 19_7

	Brinson Company	Hardy Company
Debits:		
Cash	32,400	14,500
Accounts receivable—net	51,600	33,100
Inventories, December 31, 19_7	72,500	37,400
Prepaid expenses	3,800	1,800
Investment in Hardy Company	105,420	
Land	22,400	25,400
Buildings	103,600	39,100
Equipment	180,700	61,400
Cost of goods sold	416,200	218,300
Expenses	219,700	97,900
Dividends paid	35,000	10,000
	1,243,320	538,900
Credits:		
Accumulated depreciation—buildings	17,900	10,600
Accumulated depreciation—equipment	72,900	24,200
Accounts payable	138,000	57,700
Common stock	200,000	60,000
Retained earnings, December 31, 19_6	64,800	26,400
Sales	710,300	360,000
Investment revenue	39,420	
	1,243,320	538,900

INSTRUCTIONS

(a) Prepare consolidated working papers for the year ended December 31, 19_7.

(b) Prepare a consolidated income statement and a consolidated statement of retained earnings for the year ended December 31, 19_7 and a consolidated balance sheet as of December 31, 19_7.

Note Attempt to solve the demonstration problem before examining the solution that follows.

(a)

BRINSON COMPANY AND SUBSIDIARY
Consolidated Working Papers
For the Year Ended December 31, 19_7

	Brinson Company	Hardy Company	Adjustments and eliminations		Minority interest	Consolidated
Income Statement:						
Sales	710,300	360,000	(c) 152,000			918,300
Cost of goods sold	416,200	218,300	(d) 6,000	(c) 152,000		488,500
Gross margin	294,100	141,700				429,800
Expenses	219,700	97,900				317,600
Net income from operations	74,400	43,800				112,200
Investment revenue—90% of $43,800	39,420		(b) 39,420			
Minority interest—10% of $43,800					4,380	4,380
Net income	113,820	43,800	197,420	152,000	4,380	107,820
Statement of Retained Earnings:						
Retained earnings—beginning of year	64,800	26,400	(b) 23,760		2,640	64,800
Net income—per above	113,820	43,800	197,420	152,000	4,380	107,820
Total	178,620	70,200				172,620
Dividends:						
Brinson Company	35,000					35,000
Hardy Corporation		10,000		(b) 9,000	1,000*	
Retained earnings—end of year	143,620	60,200	221,180	161,000	6,020	137,620
Balance Sheet:						
Assets:						
Cash	32,400	14,500				46,900
Accounts receivable—net	51,600	33,100				84,700
Inventories	72,500	37,400		(d) 6,000		103,900
Prepaid expenses	3,800	1,800				5,600
Investment in Hardy Company	105,420		(a) 2,760	(b) 108,180		
Land	22,400	25,400		(a) 2,760		45,040
Buildings	103,600	39,100				142,700
Accumulated depreciation—buildings	17,900*	10,600*				28,500*
Equipment	180,700	61,400				242,100
Accumulated depreciation—equipment	72,900*	24,200*				97,100*
	481,620	177,900				545,340
Equities:						
Accounts payable	138,000	57,700				195,700
Capital stock:						
Brinson Company	200,000					200,000
Hardy Company		60,000	(b) 54,000		6,000	
Retained earnings—per above	143,620	60,200	221,180	161,000	6,020	137,620
Minority interest					12,020	12,020
	481,620	177,900	277,940	277,940		545,340

*Deduction.
Adjustments and Eliminations:
ªAssignment of excess of book value over cost to the land account.
ᵇIntercompany stockholding.
ᶜIntercompany sales.
ᵈIntercompany profit in inventories.

BRINSON COMPANY AND SUBSIDIARY
Consolidated Income Statement
For the Year Ended December 31, 19_7

Sales	$918,300
Cost of goods sold	488,500
Gross margin	$429,800
Expenses	317,600
Net income before deducting minority interest	$112,200
Deduct minority interest	4,380
Net income	$107,820

BRINSON COMPANY AND SUBSIDIARY
Consolidated Statement of Retained Earnings
For the Year Ended December 31, 19_7

Retained earnings, December 31, 19_6	$ 64,800
Net income	107,820
Total	$172,620
Deduct dividends	35,000
Retained earnings, December 31, 19_	$137,620

BRINSON COMPANY AND SUBSIDIARY
Consolidated Balance Sheet
December 31, 19_7

Assets:

Current assets:			
Cash		$ 46,900	
Accounts receivable—net		84,700	
Inventories		103,900	
Prepaid expenses		5,600	$241,100
Property, plant, and equipment:			
Land		$ 45,040	
Buildings	$142,700		
Less accumulated depreciation	28,500	114,200	
Equipment	$242,100		
Less accumulated depreciation	97,100	145,000	304,240
			$545,340

Equities:

Current liabilities:			
Accounts payable			$195,700
Minority interest			12,020
Stockholders' equity:			
Capital stock		$200,000	
Retained earnings		137,620	337,620
			$545,340

Questions

1 Describe the difference between the cost and equity methods of accounting for stock investments.
2 Under what circumstances must the equity method be used to account for stock investments?
3 What are the basic characteristics of the market-value method of accounting for stock investments?
4 How is the lower-of-cost-or-market method applied to noncurrent marketable equity securities?
5 Discuss the role of the concept of "significant influence" in determining the choice between the cost and equity methods of accounting for stock investments.
6 What is a subsidiary company?
7 What are some reasons why subsidiaries may be created or acquired?
8 What is the purpose of consolidated statements?
9 Describe the difference between the purchase treatment and pooling-of-interests treatment of a stock acquisition.
10 What is the purpose of the elimination of the parent's investment in the subsidiary when consolidated statements are prepared?
11 List some reasons why a parent company may be willing to pay more than book value for the subsidiary stock acquired.
12 Why is a consolidated balance sheet the only consolidated statement that can be prepared as of the date of the parent's acquisition of the subsidiary?
13 When a parent pays more than book value for the subsidiary stock, and the difference is attributable to the plant and equipment of the subsidiary, what is the ultimate disposition of the excess paid in consolidated statements?
14 Define the term "minority interest" and describe how it is reported in a consolidated balance sheet.
15 Does the presence of a minority interest have any effect on the preparation of a consolidated income statement? If it does, describe the effect.
16 Why are the inventories of affiliated companies reduced in consolidated statements by the amount of any intercompany profit therein?
17 Discuss the limitations of consolidated statements.

Short exercises

E13-1

Action Company purchased the following common stocks for the prices indicated:

5% of the stock of Bluff Company	$15,000
25% of the stock of Cruse Company	55,000
80% of the stock of Dillon Company	60,000

Prepare the entry needed to record each stock acquisition on the books of Action Company.

E13-2   On January 2, 19_5 Axel Company acquired 8,000 of the 10,000 outstanding shares of Belton Company common stock at a price of $15 per share. Additional costs associated with the acquisition totaled $2,500. During 19_5 Belton Company reported earnings of $76,000 and paid cash dividends of $20,000. The following year Belton had a net loss of $25,000 and paid cash dividends of $10,000.

Calculate the balance in Axel Company's investment account at the end of 19_6 under the equity method of accounting for the investment.

E13-3   Assume the same facts as E13-2, except that Axel Company purchased only 1,000 of the Belton shares at $15 per share plus additional costs of $500. Prepare the journal entries to account for the investment on Axel's records for 19_5 and 19_6. The cost method is used in this case. Assume the dividends were declared on December 31 of each year.

E13-4   Melton Corporation's noncurrent stock investments at December 31, 19_4 consist of the following:

Stock	Cost	Market price December 31
5% interest in Nelson Company common stock	$28,000	$25,000
12% interest in Olson Company common stock	51,000	57,000
15% interest in Porter Company common stock	43,000	30,000

The investments are presently recorded at cost. Prepare the journal entry necessary to report the above information in the firm's 19_4 financial statements.

E13-5   Assume that Melton Corporation (see E13-4) still holds the same noncurrent stock investments at the end of 19_5 and that the market prices at that time are: Nelson stock, $29,000; Olson stock, $55,000; and Porter stock, $31,000. Prepare any journal entry required on Melton's books at December 31, 19_5 and show the presentation of the investments in the balance sheet at that date.

E13-6   Balance sheet information of Dexter Company at December 31, 19_3 is shown below.

Assets		Equities	
Cash	$ 45,000	Accounts payable	$ 75,000
Accounts receivable (net)	121,000	Bonds payable	100,000
Merchandise inventory	95,000	Common stock	200,000
Land	70,000	Retained earnings	256,000
Plant and equipment (net)	300,000		
	$631,000		$631,000

On this date Elson Company acquired all of the stock of Dexter, paying cash in an amount equal to the book value of the stock acquired.

Prepare, in journal entry form, the eliminating entry required in working papers to prepare a consolidated balance sheet at December 31, 19_3.

E13-7   Assume that Elson Company (see E13-6) acquired all of the Dexter stock for a total cash price of $460,000 and that any excess of cost of the stock over its book value is attributed to the land owned by Dexter. What amounts would be reported in the December 31, 19_3 consolidated balance sheet for the following items in the Dexter Company balance sheet? Land, Common Stock, and Retained Earnings.

E13-8   The December 31, 19_2 balance sheets of Parent Company and Subsidiary Company show the following assets:

	Parent company	Subsidiary company
Current assets:		
Cash	$ 50,000	$ 37,000
Accounts receivable—Customers	112,500	75,000
Allowance for uncollectibles	(2,250)	(1,250)
Advances to Subsidiary Company	10,000	—
Inventory	187,500	125,000
Prepaid expenses	2,250	1,250
	$ 360,000	$237,000
Long-term investments:		
Investment in Subsidiary Company	$ 375,000	—
Property, plant, and equipment:		
Land	$ 125,000	$ 62,500
Buildings	375,000	250,000
Accumulated depreciation	(175,000)	(75,000)
Equipment	187,500	150,000
Accumulated depreciation	(85,000)	(50,000)
	$ 427,500	$337,500
Total assets	$1,162,500	$574,500

Parent Company owns 80 per cent of the common stock of Subsidiary Company. The stock was acquired at book value and is accounted for by the equity method. All of the inventory of Subsidiary Company was purchased from Parent Company. The inventory cost Parent Company $105,000.

The chief accountant of Parent Company must prepare a consolidated balance sheet. Determine the asset total to be reported in the consolidated balance sheet.

E13-9   The Stockholders' Equity sections of the December 31, 19_4 balance sheets of Jones Company and its wholly owned subsidiary, Smith Company, are presented below.

	Jones company	Smith company
Stockholders' equity:		
Capital stock	$200,000	$100,000
Retained earnings	60,000	25,000

As of December 31, 19_4, Smith Company was indebted to Jones Company for $10,000.

Show the Stockholders' Equity section of the December 31, 19_4 consolidated balance sheet under each of the following conditions:

(a) Jones Company purchased its interest in Smith Company several years after Smith Company was organized and when Smith Company's retained earnings amounted to $10,000.

(b) Jones Company acquired its interest in Smith Company by a pooling-of-interests transaction and when Smith Company's retained earnings amounted to $5,000.

E13-10 *From the following selected data, prepare a consolidated income statement for the year ended December 31, 19_4.*

	Prime company	Sub company
Sales, including $22,500 of sales by Prime Company to its wholly owned subsidiary, Sub Company	$720,000	$352,500
Cost of goods sold	420,000	217,500
Operating expenses	255,000	105,000
Dividends declared	15,000	10,000
Investment revenue—From Sub Company	30,000	
Intercompany profit in ending inventory		–0–

Problems

Note In the following problem assignments, working papers are required only when specifically called for.

A13-1 *Reel Company purchased for $10,000 cash 5,000 shares of the common stock of Stinson Company on January 3, 19_5. The following selected transactions occurred during the following three years:*

(1) Stinson paid a cash dividend of $4,000 on December 31, 19_5.

(2) Stinson reported net income of $15,000 for 19_5.

(3) Reel sold 1,000 shares of the Stinson stock at $5.00 per share on January 2, 19_6.

(4) Stinson reported a net loss of $6,000 for 19_6.

(5) Stinson paid a total dividend of $10,000 on December 31, 19_6.

(6) Reel sold 500 shares of the Stinson stock at $4.00 per share on January 3, 19_7.

(7) Stinson reported a net income of $20,000 for 19_7.

Required:

Calculate the balance in Reel's investment account at the end of the three-year period under each of the following assumptions:

(a) Stinson had a total of 100,000 shares of common stock outstanding during the period and Reel uses the cost method to account for the investment.

(b) Stinson had a total of 5,000 shares of common stock outstanding during the period and Reel uses the equity method to account for the investment.

A13-2 *Drace Company was involved in the following transactions during the year 19_3. All securities acquired are considered to be noncurrent assets.*

(1) Purchased 10 per cent of the outstanding common shares of Eustis Company, paying a total of $6,300.

(2) Paid cash of $15,000 for 5 per cent of the common stock of Folkston Company.

(3) Sold one-half of the Eustis Company shares for $3,550.

(4) Acquired 40 per cent of the common stock of Galvin Company, paying cash of $28,000.

(5) Purchased 90 per cent of the common stock of Halper Company for $180,000.

(6) Received the following cash dividends on the stocks at December 31.

Eustis Company	$ 500
Folkston Company	1,600
Galvin Company	3,000
Halper Company	12,500

Required:

(a) Prepare journal entries to record the transactions for the year.

(b) Assuming the following year-end amounts, prepare any adjusting entries required to properly report the investments at the end of the year.

Stock	Market price at December 31
Eustis Company	$ 3,050
Folkston Company	17,500
Galvin Company	34,000
Halper Company	166,000

(c) Show the proper balance sheet presentation of the investments at December 31, 19_3.

A13-3

The adjusted trial balances of a parent and its 100 per cent owned subsidiary are presented below. The investment was acquired at book value.

Adjusted Trial Balances
June 30, 19_4

	Bull company		Bear company	
Cash	46,500		34,125	
Accounts receivable	36,000		48,600	
Advances to subsidiary	15,000		—	
Inventory	39,000		49,950 .	
Investment in Bear Company	187,050		—	
Property, plant, and equipment—net of accumulated depreciation of $30,500 (combined)	111,710		75,000	
Accounts payable		40,890		12,375
Advances from parent				15,000
Capital stock		300,000		112,500
Retained earnings, June 30, 19_3		72,410		67,500
Dividends	21,000		6,750	
Sales		525,000		348,000
Cost of goods sold	330,000		206,250	
Expenses	159,090		134,700	
Investment revenue—From Bear Company		7,050		—
	945,350	945,350	555,375	555,375

The advances are noninterest-bearing. Intercompany sales were $52,500. However, there was no intercompany profit in the inventories.

Prepare consolidated financial statements for the year ended June 30, 19_4.

A13-4

The Stockholders' Equity sections of the December 31, 19_7 balance sheets of High Company and its subsidiary, Point Corporation, are presented below.

	High company	Point corporation
Stockholders' equity:		
Capital stock	$600,000	$200,000
Retained earnings	156,000	48,600

High Company acquired 95 per cent of the capital stock of Point Corporation on December 31, 19_4, for $209,970, when the total stockholders' equity of Point Corporation was $212,600.

Required:

Determine the amounts at which the following items would be shown in the December 31, 19_7 consolidated balance sheet. Show all pertinent computations.

(1) Difference between the cost of the subsidiary stock and the book value thereof.

(2) Minority interest.

(3) Consolidated retained earnings.

A13-5

The condensed balance sheets of Sam Corporation and Steve Company appeared as follows on June 30, 19_8:

	Sam corporation	Steve company
Assets:		
Cash	$ 55,500	$12,600
Accounts receivable—net	108,900	15,900
Inventory	151,500	24,300
Property, plant, and equipment—net of accumulated depreciation	182,100	43,350
Investment in Steve Company	74,250	—
	$572,250	$96,150
Equities:		
Accounts payable	$ 39,450	$13,650
Bonds payable—Due December 31, 19_9	150,000	
Capital stock	300,000	75,000
Retained earnings	82,800	7,500
	$572,250	$96,150

The investment in Steve Company represents the cost of 90 per cent of the capital stock of Steve Company acquired by Sam Corporation on June 30, 19_8.

Included in the accounts payable of Sam Corporation is $1,800 due to Steve Company.

Required:

(a) Prepare the June 30, 19_8 consolidated balance sheet.

(b) Assume that the following data relate to the year ended June 30, 19_9:

	Sam corporation	Steve company
Net income	$30,000	$15,000
Dividends paid	7,500	–0–

Compute the consolidated retained earnings as of June 30, 19_9.

(c) As an alternative, assume that Steve Company also paid a dividend, as indicated by the following revised data which relate to the year ended June 30, 19_9:

	Sam corporation	Steve company
Net income	$30,000	$15,000
Dividends paid	7,500	3,500

Compute the consolidated retained earnings as of June 30, 19_9.

A13-6

Balance sheet information for Farnsworth Company and Gaston Company at December 31, 19_3 is shown below:

	Farnsworth company	Gaston company
Assets:		
Cash	$ 47,640	$ 9,105
Accounts receivable	62,500	35,960
Allowance for uncollectibles	(1,800)	(1,000)
Inventories	62,800	41,640
Land	50,000	15,640
Buildings	68,450	39,250
Accumulated depreciation— Buildings	(21,600)	(14,160)
Fixtures and equipment	74,500	32,640
Accumulated depreciation— Fixtures and Equipment	(31,200)	(18,500)
	$311,290	$140,575
Equities:		
Accounts payable	$ 83,670	$ 17,340
Wages payable	4,290	
Common stock, $10 par	150,000	
Common stock, $25 par		100,000
Retained earnings	73,330	23,235
	$311,290	$140,575

On January 2, 19_4 Farnsworth Company acquired all of the stock of Gaston Company by issuing one share of Farnsworth stock for every two shares of Gaston Company stock. The acquisition is to be accounted for as a pooling-of-interests.

Required:

(a) Prepare the balance sheet of Farnsworth Company immediately after the acquisition of the Gaston Company stock.

(b) Prepare a consolidated balance sheet for the parent and subsidiary as of January 2, 19_4.

Maxwell Company purchased 90 per cent of the stock of Niven Company on July 1, 19_3, the date on which the subsidiary began operations, for $45,000 cash. The subsidiary issued stock with a total par value of $50,000 on this date.

The following trial balance information was taken from the records of the affiliated companies on June 30, 19_8, five years after acquisition of the stock by Maxwell Company.

	Maxwell company	Niven company
Debits:		
Cash	23,820	9,905
Accounts receivable	31,250	17,580
Allowance for uncollectibles	(900)	(500)
Inventories, June 30, 19_8	31,400	20,820
Investment in Niven Company	59,913	—
Land	25,000	7,820
Buildings	34,225	19,625
Accumulated depreciation—Buildings	(10,800)	(7,080)
Fixtures and equipment	37,250	16,320
Accumulated depreciation—Fixtures and equipment	(15,600)	(9,250)
Cost of goods sold	224,487	110,280
Selling expenses	36,230	15,650
Administrative expenses	40,710	21,400
Dividends	15,000	5,000
	531,985	227,570
Credits:		
Accounts payable	41,880	8,670
Wages payable	2,100	—
Capital stock	125,000	50,000
Retained earnings, June 30, 19_7	16,330	11,200
Sales	337,342	157,700
Investment revenue—From Niven Company	9,333	—
	531,985	227,570

During the year ended June 30, 19_8 Maxwell Company sold Niven Company merchandise at a sales price of $91,250. The inventories of Niven Company included intercompany profits in the following amounts:

June 30, 19_7	$2,050
June 30, 19_8	1,100

Required:

Using what is needed of the data above, prepare the following:

(a) Calculation of the consolidated retained earnings at June 30, 19_7, the beginning of the current year.

(b) A consolidated income statement for the year ended June 30, 19_8.

Kyle Company had the following transactions pertaining to investments in noncurrent securities during 19_4:

(1) Acquired 100 per cent of the common stock of Lamison Company for $150,000.

(2) Purchased 75 per cent of the common stock of Maxton Company for $90,000.

(3) Acquired 100 per cent of the common stock of Neville Company in a pooling-of-interests transaction. Kyle Company issued 5,000 shares of its $10 par value common stock in exchange for the 5,000 shares of $25 par value common stock of Neville Company. At the date of the stock acquisition the retained earnings balance of Neville Company was $46,000.

(4) Paid cash of $55,000 for 25 per cent of the common stock of Oakton Company.

(5) Paid cash of $80,000 for 15 per cent of the common stock of Pelzer Company.

During the year the investee companies had total net income and dividend payments as shown below. All dividends were paid on December 31.

	Net income	Dividends
Lamison Company	$35,000	$ 5,000
Maxton Company	26,000	6,000
Neville Company	82,000	20,000
Oakton Company	44,000	None
Pelzer Company	12,000	5,000

Required:

(a) Prepare journal entries for Kyle Company to account for the acquisition, earnings, and dividends of the investee companies. Assume that Kyle Company uses a separate account for each stock investment.

(b) Assume that Kyle Company uses a single investments account to record all of the investments above. Calculate the balance in the account at December 31, 19_4.

B13-2

The following condensed balance sheets were prepared from the records of Eastern Company and Western Company at December 31, 19_7:

	Eastern company	Western company
Assets:		
Current assets	$120,600	$ 10,100
Property, plant, and equipment—net	134,500	122,400
	$255,100	$132,500
Equities:		
Current liabilities	$ 16,800	$ 18,200
Bonds payable	50,000	
Common stock, $5 par	150,000	100,000
Retained earnings	38,300	14,300
	$255,100	$132,500

On this date Eastern Company acquired 100 per cent of the stock of Western Company by issuing one share of Eastern Company stock for each share of Western Company stock in a pooling-of-interests transaction.

Required:

(a) Prepare the journal entry necessary to record the acquisition on the books of Eastern Company.

(b) Prepare a consolidated balance sheet as of December 31, 19_7.

B13-3 The condensed balance sheets of Lewis Corporation and Roth Company on December 31, 19_8, are presented below.

	Lewis corporation	Roth company
Assets:		
Current assets	$ 30,900	$ 15,150
Investment in Roth Company	154,305	—
Property, plant, and equipment—net	201,750	183,600
	$386,955	$198,750
Equities:		
Current liabilities	$ 70,200	$ 27,300
Capital stock	225,000	150,000
Retained earnings	91,755	21,450
	$386,955	$198,750

On December 31, 19_3 Lewis Corporation acquired 90 per cent of the capital stock of Roth Company at a cost of $175,500. On this date the balances of the retained earnings accounts of the two companies were:

Lewis Corporation	$73,350
Roth Company	45,000

Required:

(a) The amount of minority interest which would be included in the December 31, 19_8 consolidated balance sheet.

(b) The Stockholders' Equity section of the December 31, 19_8 consolidated balance sheet.

B13-4 The condensed balance sheets of Clifton Corporation and Bolton Company appeared as follows on December 31, 19_2.

	Clifton corporation	Bolton company
Assets:		
Current assets	$150,000	$ 75,000
Investment in Bolton Company	165,000	—
Property, plant, and equipment—net of accumulated depreciation	300,000	165,000
	$615,000	$240,000
Equities:		
Current liabilities	$ 90,000	$ 45,000
Long-term liabilities	60,000	30,000
Stockholders' equity:		
Capital stock	300,000	150,000
Retained earnings	165,000	15,000
	$615,000	$240,000

Clifton Corporation organized Bolton Company one year ago and holds all of the outstanding capital stock of the subsidiary.

Required:

(a) Prepare the December 31, 19_2 consolidated balance sheet.

(b) Assume that the following data relate to the next year, which ends December 31, 19_3.

	Clifton corporation	Bolton company
Net income	$37,500	$15,000
Dividends paid	15,000	7,500

Compute the consolidated retained earnings as of December 31, 19_3.

(c) As an alternative to (b), assume that during 19_3 Clifton Corporation made intercompany sales to Bolton Company of $7,500, on which there was $750 of intercompany profit, and that the goods are included in the December 31, 19_3 inventory of Bolton Company. Compute the consolidated retained earnings as of December 31, 19_3.

B13-5

The trial balances presented below were taken from the records of Grogan Company and its subsidiary, Haskell Company, as of the end of their fiscal year ending April 30, 19_8.

	Grogan company	Haskell company
Debits:		
Cash	145,200	27,900
Accounts receivable—net	149,550	33,300
Inventory, April 30, 19_8	174,600	16,200
Investment in Haskell Company	103,800	—
Equipment	258,150	88,050
Cost of goods sold	441,750	101,400
Operating expenses	135,900	39,900
Dividends	30,000	15,000
	1,438,950	321,750
Credits:		
Accounts payable	131,550	27,300
Accumulated depreciation—Equipment	197,400	8,400
Capital stock	450,000	75,000
Retained earnings, April 30, 19_7	39,450	—
Sales	564,750	211,050
Investment revenue—From Haskell Company	55,800	—
	1,438,950	321,750

Grogan Company acquired 80 per cent of the capital stock of Haskell Company on May 1, 19_7, the date of organization of the latter company.

During the year ended April 30, 19_8, Haskell Company purchased merchandise from Grogan Company at a billed price of $127,500, which was the cost of this merchandise to Grogan. On April 30, 19_8, Haskell Company had not paid for $12,300 of the billed price of this merchandise.

Required:

Prepare consolidated working papers for Grogan Company and Haskell Company for the year ended April 30, 19_8.

The June 30, 19_8 balance sheet information of Johnstown Company and Kelly Corporation are presented below.

	Johnstown company	Kelly corporation
Assets:		
Cash	$ 42,600	$ 10,200
Accounts receivable—net of allowance for uncollectibles	69,150	15,300
Advance to Kelly Corporation	37,500	—
Inventory	125,250	27,750
Prepaid expenses	9,600	3,900
Investment in Kelly Corporation	54,450	—
Land	22,500	9,600
Buildings—net of accumulated depreciation	162,900	30,150
Furniture and equipment—net of accumulated depreciation	208,350	18,450
	$732,300	$115,350
Equities:		
Accounts payable	$ 28,350	$ 21,300
Income tax payable	93,600	6,450
Advance from Johnstown Company	—	37,500
Capital stock	450,000	37,500
Retained earnings	160,350	12,600
	$732,300	$115,350

Johnstown Company acquired its 90 per cent interest in Kelly Corporation on July 1, 19_4, for $45,000 on which date the balance of retained earnings of Kelly Corporation was $2,100. On this date there was evidence that the land owned by Kelly Corporation was worth more than its book value. All stock of Kelly Corporation has been outstanding since July 1, 19_4.

On June 30, 19_8, the inventory of Kelly Corporation included merchandise purchased from Johnstown Company for $9,600, which was $2,700 above cost to Johnstown Company.

Required:

(a) The Assets portion of the consolidated balance sheet as of June 30, 19_8.

(b) The Equities portion of the consolidated balance sheet as of June 30, 19_8.

OTHER FORMS OF BUSINESS ORGANIZATIONS
CHAPTER 14

PURPOSE OF CHAPTER Previous chapters have assumed the corporate form of business organization. However, two other widely used forms of business organization are individual proprietorships and partnerships. It is only in the accounting for owners' equity that the records of the individual proprietorship and the partnership necessarily differ from those of a corporation. This chapter discusses the nature of proprietorships and partnerships and the accounting problems that are unique to these organizations.

Individual proprietorships

CAPITAL AND DRAWING ACCOUNTS In place of the capital stock, retained earnings, and dividends accounts kept by a corporation, the books of an individual proprietorship include a capital account and a drawing account.

The capital account is credited with the proprietor's original investment and with any additional investments; it is credited with the net income or debited with the net loss for the period.

A drawing account is generally kept in addition to the capital account, although all changes in a proprietor's equity could be, and sometimes are, recorded in his capital account.

When a drawing account is kept, it is debited with:

(a) Withdrawals of cash or other business assets.

   When a proprietor takes merchandise for his own use, it is customary to charge him for it at cost. Debiting the proprietor at sales price and crediting the sales account would be illogical; a withdrawal of merchandise is not a sale. The debit to the proprietor's drawing account is offset by a credit to Purchases or Inventory, depending on the inventory method in use.

(b) Disbursements of business cash for the personal benefit of the proprietor—as, for instance, a payment for fuel used in heating his home.

(c) Collections of business accounts receivable where the proprietor personally retains the cash collected.

When the books are closed at the end of the period, the balance of the drawing account is transferred to the capital account. Thus owner withdrawals of assets reduce owners' equity and are not expenses because they are not incurred to generate revenue.

Typical entries in both kinds of accounts are shown here:

JAMES WHITE, CAPITAL

19__					
Jan.	1	Investment		7,500	7,500 Cr.
Feb.	15	Additional investment		1,500	9,000 Cr.

JAMES WHITE, DRAWINGS

19__					
Mar.	25		900		900 Dr.
July	8		400		1,300 Dr.
Sept.	5		750		2,050 Dr.
Dec.	17		600		2,650 Dr.

WORKING PAPERS AND FINANCIAL STATEMENTS Working papers used to facilitate the preparation of financial statements for a corporation were illustrated in Chapter 5. The only difference between the corporate working papers and those for an individual proprietorship is that the latter does not require columns for the retained earnings statement. It is a common practice to use only Income Statement columns and Balance Sheet columns to complete the proprietorship working papers, although separate Statement of Owner's Equity columns could be used. In this case, the working papers would be headed as follows:

JAMES WHITE
Working Papers
For the Year Ended December 31, 19__

Account Title	Trial Balance	Adjustments	Adjusted Trial Balance	Income Statement	Statement of Owner's Equity	Balance Sheet

The arrangement of data in the income statement of an individual proprietorship does not differ from that of a corporation in the same line of business. An income statement for an individual proprietorship is shown below.

JAMES WHITE
Income Statement
For the Year Ended December 31, 19__

Sales		$48,000
Sales returns and allowances		1,000
Net sales		$47,000
Cost of goods sold	$30,500	
Operating expenses	12,000	42,500
Net income		$ 4,500

Note that no income tax expense is shown in this income statement. In contrast to a corporation, a business conducted as an individual proprietorship is not regarded as a separate entity for the purpose of income taxation. In his individual tax return, the proprietor reports his taxable income or his loss from his business and all other sources. Since graduated rates are applied to the total, the tax on his business income is affected by matters outside the business. Therefore, an income statement showing taxes that would be assessed on business income without consideration of the tax-rate effect of other income and losses might be very misleading.

Instead of the statement of retained earnings prepared for a corporation, a statement of the owner's equity is prepared.

JAMES WHITE
Statement of Owner's Equity
For the Year Ended December 31, 19__

Owner's equity, January 1, 19__		$ 7,500
Add:		
Additional investment	$1,500	
Net income for the year	4,500	6,000
Total		$13,500
Deduct withdrawals		2,650
Owner's equity, December 31, 19__		$10,850←

The investment at the beginning of the year and the additional investment during the year were determined from the capital account.

The balance sheets of an individual proprietorship and a corporation do not necessarily differ except in the owners' equity section. The balance sheet of an individual proprietorship shows the owner's equity in one amount, whereas the balance sheet of a corporation shows the capital stock and retained earnings.

JAMES WHITE
Balance Sheet
December 31, 19__

Assets		Equities	
Current assets:		Current liabilities:	
Cash	$ 3,850	Accounts payable	$ 6,000
Accounts receivable	9,000	Notes payable	2,000
Notes receivable	2,000	Total current liabilities	$ 8,000
Merchandise inventory	4,000		
		Owner's equity:	
		James White, capital	10,850←
	$18,850		$18,850

CLOSING THE BOOKS The procedure of closing the revenue and expense accounts is the same for an individual proprietorship as for a corporation except that the net income or net loss, as the case may be, is transferred to the proprietor's capital account instead of to a retained earnings account. A retained earnings account will not be found in the books of proprietorships or partnerships.

The closing of the revenue and expense accounts is illustrated by the following entry which is based on the data shown in the income statement of James White on page 433.

Sales	48,000	
Sales returns and allowances		1,000
Cost of goods sold		30,500
Operating expenses		12,000
James White, capital		4,500
To close the revenue and expense accounts and transfer the net income to the proprietor's capital account.		

To complete the closing procedure, the balance of the drawing account is transferred to the capital account by the following entry:

James White, capital	2,650	
James White, drawings		2,650
To close the drawing account.		

Partnerships

NATURE OF A PARTNERSHIP "A partnership," as defined by the Uniform Partnership Act, "is an association of two or more persons to carry on, as co-owners, a business for profit."

The partnership and the corporation are the two most common forms of organization by which two or more persons can join in a business enterprise. The partnership form is usually found among comparatively small businesses requiring no more capital than can be contributed by a few partners; or in professional practices, such as law, medicine, and accounting, in which the relations of the firm to its clientele should involve a personal responsibility.

The partnership relation is created by a contract. The contract may be oral, but it is much better to have it in writing, because partners have been known to forget the features of oral agreements which prove ultimately to be to their disadvantage. A partnership contract is sometimes called *the partnership agreement* and sometimes *the articles of partnership*. Some of the more important matters that should be covered by the partnership contract are listed below.

(1) The names of the partners and the name of the partnership.
(2) The date when the contract becomes effective.
(3) The nature of the business.
(4) The place where operations are to be conducted.
(5) The amount of capital to be contributed by each partner and the assets to be invested and the valuations to be placed on them.
(6) The rights and duties of the partners.
(7) The dates when the books are to be closed and the profits ascertained and divided.
(8) The portion of the net income to be allowed to each partner.
(9) The drawings to be allowed each partner and the penalties, if any, to be imposed because of excess withdrawals.
(10) The length of time during which the partnership is to continue.
(11) The conditions under which a partner may withdraw or may be compelled to withdraw; the bases for the determination of his equity in the event of withdrawal; and agreements regarding the payment of his equity in full or in installments.
(12) Procedures in the event of the death of a partner.
(13) Provision for arbitration in the event of disputes.
(14) The rights and duties of the partners in the event of dissolution.

Some of the significant characteristics of the partnership form of business organization are briefly discussed on the following page. For a comprehensive treatment of these matters, a text on the law of partnerships should be consulted.

No separate legal entity Although the accountant treats a partnership as a separate entity for accounting purposes, it has no *legal* status as an entity. The assets are owned, and the liabilities are owed, by the partners collectively. However, this common-law concept of the partnership has been somewhat modified by the Uniform Partnership Act, which, for instance, enables a partnership to hold real and personal property in its own name. The Uniform Partnership Act has not been adopted by all of the states.

Mutual agency Each partner is an agent for all of the other partners in matters coming within the scope of partnership activities. Therefore, outsiders have a right to assume that the partnership is bound by the acts of any partner relative to its affairs.

Unlimited liability Usually each partner is individually liable for all of the debts of a partnership incurred during his membership in the firm; he may assume a liability for debts incurred before his admission to the partnership; and, unless proper notice of withdrawal is given to the public, he may be liable for partnership debts incurred after his retirement. If a partner pays partnership debts from his personal assets, he is entitled to reimbursement from the other partners.

Limited partnerships are permissible in some states. A limited partner has no personal liability to creditors, but he must maintain his investment at an amount at least equal to that contributed at the time of organization. There must be at least one general partner who is liable to creditors for debts which cannot be paid from firm assets.

Limited right to dispose of interest A partner has a legal right to assign his partnership interest to another person, although he may be subject to a suit for damages for any loss incurred by his partners as a consequence of such an assignment. But he cannot compel the other partners to accept the assignee as a partner.

Division of income Partnership income may be divided among the partners in any manner to which they agree. Consequently, the division of income is more flexible in a partnership than in a corporation.

Withdrawal of assets Because the stockholders of a corporation generally have no personal liability for corporate debts, the law places limitations on the amounts of dividend payments or other asset distributions which may be made to corporate stockholders. There are no similar legal restrictions on partners' withdrawals of cash or other assets; however, the partners may make agreements among themselves placing limitations on the amounts which they may withdraw.

Limited life Unless the partnership agreement provides otherwise, the death or retirement of an old partner or the addition of a new partner automatically dissolves the old partnership. If this is not the intention of the partners, the partnership agreement should specify clearly what effect such events will have on the continued existence of the partnership.

PARTNERSHIP VERSUS A CORPORATION In choosing between the corporate or partnership form of business, most of the advantages are usually with the corporation. These include limited liability, ease of raising large sums of capital via stock ownership, and unlimited life. The corporation also has a tax advantage over the partnership in those cases where partners have high personal income tax rates in excess of corporate tax rates. Obviously, the reverse is true when partners are in low personal income tax brackets.

The partnership is usually found in small businesses where the partnership advantages of ease and minimum cost of formation, ease of asset withdrawals by partners, and flexibility of the division of net income are more important than raising large sums of capital.

CAPITAL AND DRAWING ACCOUNTS The capital and drawing accounts of a partnership are similar to those of an individual proprietorship. The following accounts are illustrative:

D. E. SNYDER, CAPITAL

19__					
Jan.	1	Investment		9,000	9,000 Cr.
June	1	Additional investment		1,000	10,000 Cr.

D. E. SNYDER, DRAWINGS

19__					
Apr.	15		200		200 Dr.
Oct.	20		800		1,000 Dr.

J. O. LONG, CAPITAL

19__					
Jan.	1	Investment		15,000	15,000 Cr.
July	1	Additional investment		4,000	19,000 Cr.

J. O. LONG, DRAWINGS

19__					
Mar.	10		500		500 Dr.
Nov.	5		700		1,200 Dr.

LOAN ACCOUNTS A partnership may be in need of funds, which a partner is able to supply but which he is willing to provide for a short time only. In such instances the credit to the partner may be recorded in a loan account. Such loans should not be shown in the balance sheet as part of the partners' equity; they should be shown among the liabilities, but clearly distinguished from liabilities to outsiders.

On the other hand, a partner may wish to make a temporary withdrawal of funds in the form of a loan. A loan receivable account will then appear on the partnership books. Such a loan should be shown separately from receivables from outsiders in the balance sheet.

OPENING THE BOOKS If all original capital contributions of the partners are in the form of cash, the entry to open the books creates no problems. The cash account is debited and each partner's capital account is credited. For example, the original investments of Snyder and Long, illustrated in the accounts above, would be recorded as follows, assuming that cash was the only asset invested.

Cash ($9,000 + $15,000)	24,000	
D. E. Snyder, capital		9,000
J. O. Long, capital		15,000
To record original investments.		

If noncash assets are invested, it is extremely important that they be recorded at their *fair values* at the date of the investment. Assume, for instance, that a partner invests land and a building which he is carrying on his books at $40,000, which was the cost to him less depreciation. At the date when he invests this property in the partnership, it is worth $50,000. If the property were recorded on the partnership books at $40,000 and later sold for $50,000, all of the partners would share in the gain; this would not be fair to the partner who invested the property and who should have received a $50,000 credit for it.

If any liabilities of a partner are assumed by the partnership, they should, of course, be credited to liability accounts, and the partner's capital account should be credited with the net investment; that is, the difference between the assets and the liabilities.

To illustrate, it will now be assumed that Snyder and Long organize a partnership by contributing the assets and liabilities of proprietorships they previously owned individually. The original investments would be recorded as follows:

Cash	15,000	
Accounts receivable	8,000	
Inventory	12,000	
Accounts payable		26,000
D. E. Snyder, capital		9,000
To record initial investment of partner.		
Cash	5,000	
Land	22,000	
Accounts payable		12,000
J. O. Long, capital		15,000
To record initial investment of partner.		

Goodwill   If a partner's investment consists of a going business, it may be equitable to give the partner a capital credit for the goodwill of the business. A business may have goodwill if it has exceptionally good earnings. The valuation of the goodwill is a matter of agreement among the partners, and should be based on the probable future amount of earnings attributable to the business brought in by the partner. The amount, if any, agreed upon should be debited to a goodwill account, with an offsetting credit to the partner's capital account.

THE PROFIT AND LOSS RATIO   The ratio in which partners divide their net income or net loss is called the *profit and loss ratio.* If partners make no agreement regarding the division of income and losses, the law assumes an agreement to divide them equally. If partners make an agreement regarding the division of income, without any mention of losses, the agreed method for the division of income applies also to the division of losses.

WORKING PAPERS AND STATEMENTS   The working papers of a partnership contain capital columns for each partner in place of columns for retained earnings, as shown on page 439. The information in the capital columns is used to prepare the Statement of Partners' Capitals, which will be illustrated later.

SNYDER AND LONG
Working Papers
For the Year Ended December 31, 19__

Account Title	Trial Balance	Adjustments	Adjusted Trial Balance	Income Statement	Snyder, Capital	Long, Capital	Balance Sheet

Income statement The income statement of a partnership is similar to that of an individual proprietorship or a corporation in the same line of business. Frequently, the income statement will show the allocation of the net income to the partners in an additional section at the bottom of the statement. This is illustrated below. It is assumed that the partners share profits and losses equally.

SNYDER AND LONG
Income Statement
For the Year Ended December 31, 19__

Sales			$90,000
Sales discounts			200
Net sales			$89,800
Cost of goods sold		$54,300	
Operating expenses		27,500	81,800
Net income			$ 8,000
Allocation of net income:			
To D. E. Snyder—50%		$ 4,000	
To J. O. Long—50%		4,000	$ 8,000

This statement does not show any deduction for income taxes. A partnership, as such, does not ordinarily pay any federal income tax, but it is required to file an information return showing the results of its operations and each partner's share of the net income or net loss. Each partner is subject to income tax on his or her share of the partnership net income.

Statement of partners' capitals In order to prepare the following statement, it was necessary to refer to the capital accounts to determine the investments at the beginning of the year and the additional investments during the year.

SNYDER AND LONG
Statement of Partners' Capitals
For the Year Ended December 31, 19__

	D. E. Snyder	J. O. Long	Total
Investments, January 1, 19__	$ 9,000	$15,000	$24,000
Add:			
Additional investments	1,000	4,000	5,000
Net income for the year	4,000	4,000	8,000
Totals	$14,000	$23,000	$37,000
Deduct withdrawals	1,000	1,200	2,200
Balances, December 31, 19__	$13,000	$21,800	$34,800

Balance sheet The balance sheet of a partnership usually shows the capital of each partner, with a reference to the statement of partners' capitals, where details can be found.

SNYDER AND LONG
Balance Sheet
December 31, 19__

Assets			Equities		
Current assets:			Current liabilities:		
Cash	$14,800		Accounts payable		$ 3,000
Accounts receivable	18,000		Partners' equity:		
Merchandise inventory	5,000		D. E. Snyder, capital	$13,000	
			J. O. Long, capital	21,800	34,800
	$37,800				$37,800

CLOSING THE BOOKS Closing entries for a partnership are shown below. The data agree with the financial statements of Snyder and Long.

Sales	90,000	
Sales discounts		200
Cost of goods sold		54,300
Operating expenses		27,500
D. E. Snyder, capital		4,000
J. O. Long, capital		4,000
To close the revenue and expense accounts and transfer the net income to the partners' capital accounts.		
D. E. Snyder, capital	1,000	
D. E. Snyder, drawings		1,000
To close the drawings account.		
J. O. Long, capital	1,200	
J. O. Long, drawings		1,200
To close the drawings account.		

ALLOCATION OF EARNINGS AND LOSSES Some of the factors which may be given consideration in the determination of an equitable division of partnership earnings are:

The relative amounts of capital provided by the partners.
The relative values of the services rendered by the partners.
    These may differ because of differences in business ability and/or in time devoted to partnership affairs.
Various matters, such as seniority, business contacts, earnings potential of a going business contributed by a partner, and the degree of risk-taking. The degree of risk-taking depends on the dangers of loss and the relative amounts of the partners' capitals, as well as their outside assets to which the firm creditors may have recourse for the payment of partnership debts.

Various methods of dividing partnership earnings and losses are shown below.

BASIS OF ILLUSTRATIONS Let us assume, for example, that the capital accounts of two partners appear as follows:

J. L. LANE, CAPITAL

19_1					
Jan.	1			10,000	10,000 Cr.
June	1		500		9,500 Cr.
Aug.	1			2,000	11,500 Cr.
Nov.	1		1,500		10,000 Cr.

D. K. BURTON, CAPITAL

19_1					
Jan.	1			20,000	20,000 Cr.
Apr.	1		1,000		19,000 Cr.
July	1			2,000	21,000 Cr.
Dec.	1		2,000		19,000 Cr.

The debits in the capital accounts record withdrawals in excess of the agreed monthly drawing amounts. Drawings equal to the agreed monthly amounts are debited to the drawings accounts. In the absence of any agreement about the amounts of withdrawals, all drawings should be debited to the drawings accounts.

The amount of net income for the year is $12,000.

(1) Divisions in a fractional ratio. The equal division of the net income to Snyder and Long previously illustrated is an example of a division in a fractional ratio. Partners, after consideration of the determinants of an equitable division of earnings, may agree to any fractional ratio.

(2) Divisions in a capital ratio. If the capital investments are the major source of income and the other determinants of an equitable division of earnings are not pertinent, the net income may be divided in a capital ratio. Two illustrations are given below.

Division in ratio of capitals at beginning of period The capital accounts above show the following balances on January 1:

J. L. Lane	$10,000
D. K. Burton	20,000

The net income division on this basis is shown below:

Partner	Capitals at beginning	Fraction	Income amount
Lane	$10,000	$\frac{1}{3}$	$ 4,000
Burton	20,000	$\frac{2}{3}$	8,000
Total	$30,000		$12,000

Division in ratio of capitals at end of period As an inducement for partners to refrain from making withdrawals of substantial amounts during the period for which income is being divided, and to encourage them to invest additional capital as needed, it may be preferable to divide the net income in the ratio of the capitals at the end of the period, thus:

Partner	Capitals at end	Fraction	Income amount
Lane	$10,000	$\frac{10}{29}$	$ 4,138
Burton	19,000	$\frac{19}{29}$	7,862
Total	$29,000		$12,000

(3) Interest on capitals; remainder in fractional ratio. Suppose that the partners agree that *some* consideration should be given to capital investments, but that consideration should also be given to other determinants of an equitable division of the net income. Therefore, they agree to divide a portion of the net income in the capital ratio by allowing 6% interest on the capitals, and to divide the remainder in some other fractional ratio—say, equally. The interest may be computed on the capitals at the beginning or at the end of the year, as agreed; in the following tabulation, the interest is computed on opening capitals.

	J. L. Lane	D. K. Burton	Total
Interest on opening capitals:			
6% on $10,000	$ 600		
6% on $20,000		$1,200	
Total			$ 1,800
Remainder equally	5,100	5,100	10,200
Totals	$5,700	$6,300	$12,000

(4) Salaries to partners, and remainder in a fractional ratio. Partners may agree to make a partial division of the net income in the form of salaries in order to give recognition to the difference in the value of their services. The remaining net income may be divided equally or in any other ratio to which the partners agree. One illustration will be sufficient: salaries and an equal division of the remainder.

Assume that Lane is allowed a salary of $3,600 a year and Burton is allowed a salary of $4,800. The following distribution will be made:

	J. L. Lane	D. K. Burton	Total
Salaries:	$3,600	$4,800	$ 8,400
Remainder equally	1,800	1,800	3,600
Totals	$5,400	$6,600	$12,000

(5) Salaries, interest, and remainder in a fractional ratio. Assume that Lane and Burton agree to make the following income division:

Salaries:
Lane $3,600
Burton 4,800
Interest on capitals—6% on January 1 balances.
Remainder equally.

	J. L. Lane	D. K. Burton	Total
Salaries:	$3,600	$4,800	$ 8,400
Interest on opening capitals:			
Lane—6% of $10,000	600		
Burton—6% of $20,000		1,200	
Total			1,800
Remainder equally	900	900	1,800
Totals	$5,100	$6,900	$12,000

Interest on partners' capitals and salaries to partners are not expenses but are divisions of net income; therefore, they do not enter into the computation of the net income shown by the income statement, but are shown in the statement of partners' capitals.

SALARIES AND INTEREST IN EXCESS OF NET INCOME   The salaries and interest in the preceding illustration totaled $10,200. Suppose that the net income had been only $9,000; how should it have been divided? Such a situation does not void the provisions of the partnership agreement. Therefore, the partners must be allowed the salaries and interest agreed upon. After this has been done the total credits allowed the partners will be greater than the net income. Because the partners agreed to an equal division of any income after salaries and interest, the $1,200 balance, which is negative in this case ($9,000 minus $10,200), is divided equally between Lane and Burton. This is illustrated below.

	J. L. Lane	D. K. Burton	Total
Credits:			
Salaries	$3,600	$4,800	$ 8,400
Interest on capitals	600	1,200	1,800
Total credits	$4,200	$6,000	$10,200
Less debit for remainder	600	600	1,200
Distribution of net income	$3,600	$5,400	$ 9,000

ADMISSION OF A NEW PARTNER   In some instances, new partners may be admitted to the partnership without making any cash contribution to the firm. In most cases, however, a new partner acquires an interest in the firm in one of the following ways:

(1)   The new partner *purchases* all or part of the interest of one or more old partners and makes his or her payment directly to them. The partnership does not receive any assets from the new partner; thus total assets do not change.

(2)   The new partner *invests* assets in the partnership, thus increasing the assets of the firm.

PURCHASE OF INTEREST OF OLD PARTNER   The only effect the purchase of the interest of an old partner by a new partner has on the firm's books is the transfer of the interest purchased from the capital account of the selling partner to the capital account of the purchasing partner. For example, assume that Akin and Booker presently have capital balances of $10,000 each in the AB Company. Cale offers Akin $10,000 for Akin's interest and Akin agrees to sell for this price. Booker agrees to the admission of Cale to the firm. The only entry required on the partnership books to record the admission of the new partner is as follows:

Akin, capital	10,000	
Cale, capital		10,000

If the price agreed upon by Akin and Cale had been 15,000, the entry to record the admission of Cale to the firm would have been the same as above because the price represents an amount paid by the new partner to the old partner, not to the partnership. The new partner now has the same capital investment in the firm as that previously held by the old partner.

LIQUIDATION OF A PARTNERSHIP   A partnership is liquidated when the business is discontinued or the assets (or net assets) are transferred to other parties. The balance sheet of a partnership about to liquidate appears below.

A AND B
Balance Sheet
October 31, 19___

Assets			Equities	
Cash		$ 5,000	Accounts payable	$ 9,000
Accounts receivable	$25,000		A, capital	30,000
Less allowance for			B, capital	20,000
uncollectibles	1,000	24,000		
Inventory		30,000		
		$59,000		$59,000

DISPOSAL OF ASSETS   Assume that X desires to acquire the business of A and B, and that the partners sell their inventory and accounts receivable to X for $52,000. A and B retain the $5,000 of cash shown in the foregoing balance sheet and are to pay the $9,000 of accounts payable. The sale of the inventory and receivables will be recorded as follows:

Receivable from X	52,000	
Loss on sale of business [($24,000 + $30,000) − $52,000]	2,000	
Allowance for uncollectibles	1,000	
Inventory		30,000
Accounts receivable		25,000
To record the sale of the assets to X.		
Cash	52,000	
Receivable from X		52,000
To record collection for assets sold.		

DIVISION OF THE GAIN OR LOSS   Any gain or loss on the disposal of the assets should always be divided between the partners *before* any cash distribution is made to them, because the amounts of cash to which the partners are entitled cannot be determined until their shares of the gain or loss have been credited or charged to them. The gain or loss should be divided between the partners in their profit and loss ratio. Assuming that A and B share earnings equally, the $2,000 loss on the sale of the assets to X will be divided by the following entry:

A, capital	1,000	
B, capital	1,000	
Loss on sale of business		2,000

DISTRIBUTION OF CASH After the disposal of the inventory and the receivables, the collection of the cash, and the division of the loss between the partners, the balance sheet of the firm is as shown below.

A AND B
Balance Sheet
November 3, 19___

Assets		Equities	
Cash	$57,000	Accounts payable	$ 9,000
		A, capital	29,000
		B, capital	19,000
	$57,000		$57,000

The distribution of cash should be made in the following order:

(1) In payment of liabilities to outside creditors:

Accounts payable	9,000	
Cash		9,000

(2) In payment of partners' capitals:

A, capital	29,000	
B, capital	19,000	
Cash		48,000

PARTNER WITH A DEBIT BALANCE It sometimes happens that a partner has a debit balance in his or her capital account as a result of operating losses, drawings, and losses on the disposal of assets during liquidation. Two illustrative cases are presented.

Case 1. Assume that, after the sale of all assets and the payment of liabilities, the trial balance of a partnership shows the following balances:

Cash	20,000	
M, capital	5,000	
N, capital		25,000
	25,000	25,000

The entire cash balance should be paid to N; this payment would reduce N's capital credit to $5,000. N has a right to collect $5,000 from M.

Case 2. In this case it is assumed that, after the sale of all assets and the payment of all liabilities, a partnership's trial balance appears as follows:

Cash	20,000	
R, capital	5,000	
S, capital		15,000
T, capital		10,000
	25,000	25,000

The profit-and-loss-sharing arrangement was as follows: R, 20%; S, 40%; T, 40%. R should pay $5,000 cash into the partnership to make good the debit balance in R's capital account; if R does so, there will be $25,000 cash on hand, which will be sufficient to pay S and T in full.

But suppose that it is desired to distribute the $20,000 of cash on hand to S and T before it is known whether or not R will be able to pay in the $5,000. In determining how to divide the cash between S and T, we should remember that, if R fails to pay in the $5,000, this loss will have to be borne by S and T in their profit and loss ratio. In the past, S and T each had a 40 per cent share in the net income or net loss; that is to say, their shares were equal. Therefore, if R should fail to pay in the $5,000, S and T would share the loss equally. Accordingly, they should be paid amounts that will reduce their capital balances to $2,500 each, thus leaving each of these partners with a capital balance sufficient to absorb his share of the loss if R fails to pay in the $5,000. The entry to record the payment is:

S, capital	12,500	
T, capital	7,500	
Cash		20,000
To record the distribution of cash to S and T.		

The resulting trial balance will be:

R, capital	5,000	
S, capital		2,500
T, capital		2,500
	5,000	5,000

INCORPORATION OF A PARTNERSHIP Partners may decide to organize a corporation to take over the operation of the partnership. In such a case, the partnership books may be retained for use by the corporation or the partnership books may be closed and new books opened for the corporation.

Assume that the December 31, 19__ after-closing trial balance of the Able and Baker partnership appears as follows:

ABLE AND BAKER
After-Closing Trial Balance
December 31, 19__

Cash	200	
Accounts receivable	2,100	
Allowance for uncollectibles		200
Merchandise inventory	5,900	
Land	12,000	
Building	22,500	
Accumulated depreciation		6,500
Accounts payable		1,000
Notes payable		600
Able, capital		16,000
Baker, capital		18,400
	42,700	42,700

On this date the partners decide to incorporate with an authorized capital of 5,000 shares of $10 par value common stock, of which 3,700 shares will be issued to the partners for their present interests.

Partnership books retained As a preliminary step it may be necessary to adjust certain accounts on the partnership books in order to reflect the amounts agreed upon for the purpose of transfer to the corporation. The net effect of such adjustments is carried to the partners' capital accounts in the profit and loss ratio.

Assume that Able and Baker agree that the assets of the partnership should be taken over by the corporation at the following amounts:

Cash	$ 200
Accounts receivable—net	1,800
Merchandise inventory	5,900
Land	14,200
Building	16,500

The following entries are required to give effect to the above agreement.

Land	2,200	
Accumulated depreciation [(22,500 − 6,500) − 16,500]	500	
Allowance for uncollectibles		100
Capital adjustment account		2,600
Adjustment of accounts prior to incorporation.		
Capital adjustment account	2,600	
Able, capital		1,300
Baker, capital		1,300
Division of the net result of asset adjustments made prior to incorporation.		

To make the change from the partnership form of organization to the corporate form, the partners' capital accounts are debited to close them, and a capital stock account is credited for the shares issued to the partners. If the sum of the partners' capital account balances exceeds the par or stated value of the shares issued to the partners in exchange for the net assets of the partnership, a paid-in capital account will be credited.

The entry for the issuance of the shares to Able and Baker is:

Able, capital (16,000 + 1,300)	17,300	
Baker, capital (18,400 + 1,300)	19,700	
Common stock ($10 × 3,700)		37,000
Issuance of 3,700 shares of stock to Able and Baker.		

New books opened for the corporation If the partnership books are to be closed and new books opened for the corporation, the following entries should be recorded:

(1) Adjusting entries to bring the account balances into conformity with agreed-upon transfer values.
(2) Entries to record the effect of the adjustments on the partners' capital accounts.
(3) Entries to close the asset and liability accounts taken over by the corporation and to record the capital stock received in exchange.
(4) Entries to distribute the capital stock of the corporation to the partners, which entries will close the partners' capital accounts.

Individual proprietorship—p. 432
Drawing accounts—p. 432
Working papers—p. 433
Partnerships—p. 435
Loan accounts—p. 437

Profit and loss ratio—p. 438
Allocation of profit and loss—p. 440
Admission of a new partner—p. 443
Liquidation of a partnership—p. 444
Incorporation of a partnership—p. 446

DEMONSTRATION PROBLEM FOR REVIEW AND SELF-STUDY F. R. Todd began operating a business as a sole proprietorship in March, 19_1. The firm's adjusted trial balance at December 31, 19_2 is presented below:

F. R. TODD
Adjusted Trial Balance
December 31, 19_2

Cash	10,700	
Accounts receivable—net	17,690	
Merchandise inventory, December 31, 19_2	17,316	
Building	50,000	
Accumulated depreciation—Building		1,360
Accounts payable		5,124
Notes payable		3,000
F. R. Todd, capital		75,000
F. R. Todd, drawings	9,400	
Sales		162,000
Cost of goods sold	122,200	
Operating expenses	19,628	
Interest revenue		450
	246,934	246,934

Todd made an additional capital investment of $15,000 on May 10, 19_2.

Early in 19_3 Todd and Len Lang formed the Todd and Lang partnership. The partnership's adjusted trial balance at December 31, 19_8 is presented below.

TODD AND LANG
Adjusted Trial Balance
December 31, 19_8

Cash	10,590	
Accounts receivable—net	17,385	
Merchandise inventory, December 31, 19_8	42,565	
Equipment	99,000	
Accumulated depreciation—Equipment		35,400
Accounts payable		60,450
Notes payable		5,000
Loans payable (Len Lang)		7,000
F. R. Todd, capital		40,000
Len Lang, capital		28,000
F. R. Todd, drawings	5,200	
Len Lang, drawings	5,900	
Sales		298,910
Sales returns and allowances	3,625	
Cost of goods sold	269,515	
Selling expenses	17,150	
Office expenses	3,830	
	474,760	474,760

The partners share profits and losses equally. The only changes in the partners' capital accounts during 19_8 were additional investments of $10,000 by Lang on May 15 and of $5,000 by Todd on October 1. The loan owed by the partnership to Lang is due on July 1, 19_9.

INSTRUCTIONS

(a) Prepare a statement of owner's equity for the F. R. Todd proprietorship for the year ended December 31, 19_2.

(b) Prepare a balance sheet for the F. R. Todd proprietorship as of December 31, 19_2.

(c) Prepare the December 31, 19_2 closing entries for the F. R. Todd proprietorship.

(d) Prepare a statement of partners' capitals for the Todd and Lang partnership for the year ended December 31, 19_8.

(e) Prepare a balance sheet for the Todd and Lang partnership as of December 31, 19_8.

Note Attempt to solve the demonstration problem before examining the solution that follows.

(a)

F. R. TODD
Statement of Owner's Equity
For the Year Ended December 31, 19_2

Balance, December 31, 19_1			$ 60,000
Add:			
Additional investment		$ 15,000	
Net income for the year		20,622	35,622
Total			$ 95,622
Deduct withdrawals			9,400
Balance, December 31, 19_2			$ 86,222

Computation of net income:			
Sales		$162,000	
Interest revenue		450	$162,450
Deduct:			
Cost of goods sold		$122,200	
Operating expenses		19,628	141,828
Net income			$ 20,622

(b)

F. R. TODD
Balance Sheet
December 31, 19_2

Assets			Equities		
Current assets:			Current liabilities:		
Cash	$ 10,700		Accounts payable	$ 5,124	
Accounts receivable	17,690		Notes payable	3,000	$ 8,124
Merchandise inventory	17,316	$ 45,706	Proprietor's equity:		
			F. R. Todd, capital		86,222
Long-lived assets:					
Building	$ 50,000				
Less accumulated depreciation	1,360	48,640			
		$ 94,346			$ 94,346

449

(c)

JOURNAL

19_2			
Dec. 31	Sales	162,000	
	Interest revenue	450	
	Cost of goods sold		122,200
	Operating expenses		19,628
	F. R. Todd, capital		20,622
	To close the revenue and expense accounts and transfer the net income to the proprietor's capital account.		
31	F. R. Todd, capital	9,400	
	F. R. Todd, drawings		9,400
	To close the drawings account.		

(d)

TODD AND LANG
Statement of Partners' Capitals
For the Year Ended December 31, 19_8

	F. R. Todd	Len Lang	Total
Balances, December 31, 19_7	$ 35,000	$ 18,000	$ 53,000
Add:			
Additional investments	5,000	10,000	15,000
Net income for the year	2,395	2,395	4,790
Totals	$ 42,395	$ 30,395	$ 72,790
Deduct withdrawals	5,200	5,900	11,100
Balances, December 31, 19_8	$ 37,195	$ 24,495	$ 61,690

Computation of net income:

Net sales ($298,910 − $3,625)		$295,285
Deduct:		
Cost of goods sold	$269,515	
Selling expenses	17,150	
Office expenses	3,830	290,495
Net income		$ 4,790

(e)

TODD AND LANG
Balance Sheet
December 31, 19_8

Assets			Equities		
Current assets:			Current liabilities:		
Cash	$10,590		Accounts payable	$60,450	
Accounts receivable	17,385		Notes payable	5,000	
Merchandise inventory	42,565	$ 70,540	Loans payable—Len		
Long-lived assets:			Lang	7,000	$ 72,450
Equipment	$99,000		Partners' equity:		
Less accumulated			F. R. Todd, capital	$37,195	
depreciation	35,400	63,600	Len Lang, capital	24,495	61,690
		$134,140			$134,140

ASSIGNMENT MATERIAL

Questions

1 Name the three principal forms of business organization.
2 Describe the use of a drawings account on the books of a proprietorship or a partnership.
3 What information is reported in a statement of proprietor's capital?
4 Define a partnership. How is a partnership created?
5 How does the legal status of a partnership differ from that of a corporation?
6 What is the profit and loss ratio? How is the ratio determined?
7 Describe the closing procedure for the books of a partnership.
8 List several factors that may be considered in the division of partnership earnings.
9 How are gains and losses resulting from the liquidation of a partnership divided among the partners? Why should such gains and losses be divided before cash payments are made to the partners?
10 How does a debit balance in the capital account of a partner affect the liquidation of a partnership?
11 Describe two alternatives which may be used to account for the incorporation of a partnership.
12 What is meant by the unlimited liability characteristic of a partnership?
13 Briefly describe two methods by which a new partner may be admitted to a partnership.

Short exercises

E14-1

Present the equity section of the balance sheet immediately after the organization of the following business firms:

(a) Toby T. begins operation as an individual proprietor by transferring assets totaling $100,000 to the proprietorship.

(b) Toby T. and Doby D. form a partnership by investing $60,000 and $40,000, respectively.

(c) Toby T. and Doby D. organize a corporation, with each of the organizers acquiring $50,000 of common stock at par.

E14-2

Jim Jones and Sam Smith formed a partnership on January 1, 19_7, investing $45,000 and $15,000, respectively. They agreed to share profits and losses in a 60:40 ratio. On July 30, 19_7 the partners each withdrew $10,000 from the firm. Smith invested an additional $15,000 on August 15, 19_7. Assuming that the first year's profit is $10,000, present the partners' capital and drawings accounts after the books have been closed.

E14-3

Using the data in E14-2, prepare a statement of partners' capitals for the year ended December 31, 19_7.

E14-4   The partnership agreement of *Winston Hall* and *Leroy Small* states that profits will be divided as follows: (a) salaries of $5,000 each; (b) interest at 5 per cent on beginning capital balances; and (c) remainder to be shared equally. Hall and Small had capital balances on January 1, 19_9 of $14,000 and $17,000, respectively. Compute the allocation of (a) a $20,000 profit for the year and (b) an $8,550 profit for the year.

E14-5   *Davis, Edison,* and *Fulcher,* who share profits and losses in a 4:2:2 ratio, are in the process of liquidating their partnership. Present journal entries for the distribution of cash. Assume the following trial balance data:

Cash	$30,000	
Accounts payable		$ 6,000
Davis, capital		18,000
Edison, capital		15,000
Fulcher, capital	9,000	
	$39,000	$39,000

Fulcher is personally insolvent and unable to pay any portion of his debit balance to the partnership.

Problems

A14-1   The following information is taken from the adjusted trial balance of *Amos Brown,* an individual proprietor, as of June 30, 19_5.

Accounts payable	$38,430
Accumulated depreciation—Equipment	7,700
Cash	11,905
Equipment	40,500
General expenses	3,845
Merchandise inventory, June 30, 19_5	10,640
Accounts receivable—net	15,700
Cost of goods sold	50,840
Sales	74,820
Sales returns and allowances	2,760
Selling expenses	9,960
Amos Brown, capital	42,800
Amos Brown, drawings	17,600

The only change in the proprietor's capital account during the year was an additional investment of $6,500 on March 15.

Required:

(a)   An income statement for the year ended June 30, 19_5.

(b)   A statement of proprietor's capital for the year ended June 30, 19_5.

(c)   A balance sheet as of June 30, 19_5.

A14-2

The December 31, 19_8 adjusted trial balance of Freeman and Turner, a partnership, is presented below.

FREEMAN AND TURNER
Adjusted Trial Balance
December 31, 19_8
....

Cash	10,590	
Accounts receivable—net	17,385	
Merchandise inventory, December 31, 19_8	42,565	
Equipment	94,000	
Accumulated depreciation—Equipment		35,400
Accounts payable		60,450
Notes payable		5,000
Loans payable (T. Turner)		7,000
J. Freeman, capital		37,500
T. Turner, capital		25,500
J. Freeman, drawings	5,200	
T. Turner, drawings	5,900	
Sales		298,910
Sales returns and allowances	3,625	
Cost of goods sold	269,515	
Selling expenses	17,150	
Office expenses	3,830	
	474,760	474,760

Partnership profits and losses are shared equally. The only changes in the partners' capital accounts during the year were additional investments of 7,500 by Turner on May 15 and of 2,500 by Freeman on October 1.

The loan is to be repaid to T. Turner on July 1, 19_9.

Required:

(a) A statement of partners' capitals for the year.

(b) A balance sheet as of December 31, 19_8.

A14-3

Garland and Frye, who share profits and losses equally, decide to liquidate their partnership on May 1, 19_9. Certain assets of the business are sold to Pine Corporation on the following basis:

Merchandise inventory	$50,000
Land	7,200
Accounts receivable	77,000

Garland and Frye are to keep the cash and pay all debts.

GARLAND AND FRYE
After-Closing Trial Balance
May 1, 19_9
....

Cash	6,000	
Accounts receivable	84,000	
Merchandise inventory	40,000	
Land	8,000	
Accounts payable		14,000
Loans payable (F. Frye)		20,000
G. Garland, capital		70,000
F. Frye, capital		34,000
	138,000	138,000

Required:

Entries to close the books of the partnership, assuming that cash is received from Pine Corporation and that all cash is distributed.

A14-4

The capital accounts of Jordan, Knight, and Lanier for the year 19_1 are presented below. The accounts show investments and drawings in excess of agreed amounts for the year.

H. J. JORDAN, CAPITAL

19_1						
Jan.	1	Balance				28,500 Cr.
Mar.	31			8,500		20,000 Cr.

I. J. KNIGHT, CAPITAL

19_1						
Jan.	1	Balance				48,000 Cr.
May	15				6,000	42,000 Cr.
Aug.	31			1,200		43,200 Cr.
Sept.	30			1,800		45,000 Cr.

J. K. LANIER, CAPITAL

19_1						
Jan.	1	Balance				38,500 Cr.
Sept.	4				3,500	35,000 Cr.

Net income for the year was $19,400.

Required:

Computation of each partner's share of the income under each of the following arrangements.

(a) The first $7,200 is to be divided equally, the remainder 1:2:1.

(b) Each partner is to be allowed a salary of $6,000, the remainder divided equally.

(c) The net income is to be divided in the ratio of partners' capitals at year end.

(d) Salaries are to be allowed as follows: Jordan, $8,400; Knight, $6,000; and Lanier, $6,800; the remainder to be divided equally.

(e) Interest at 8% is to be allowed on capitals at the beginning of the year, salaries of $3,600 each are to be paid and the remainder divided 3:2:1.

A14-5.

Deegan and Sylvia have been operating as a partnership for some time, sharing profits and losses in a 40:60 ratio. On July 1, 19_3, they decide to incorporate as Bozo Corporation. The after-closing trial balance of the partnership on that date appears on the next page.

DEEGAN AND SYLVIA
After-Closing Trial Balance
July 1, 19_3

. . . .

Cash	3,846	
Accounts receivable	17,154	
Allowance for uncollectibles		900
Merchandise inventory	10,000	
Furniture and fixtures	8,800	
Accumulated depreciation—Furniture and fixtures		1,980
Land	30,000	
Goodwill	10,000	
Accounts payable		16,500
Notes payable		12,400
D. Deegan, capital		30,020
S. Sylvia, capital		18,000
	79,800	79,800

An examination of the assets reveals that the merchandise inventory is worth only $9,500. The land is appraised at a current value of $35,000. It is decided that the goodwill is not to be carried forward to the corporation.

A new set of books is to be opened for Bozo Corporation, which has an authorized capital of 10,000 shares of $10 par value common stock.

Required:

All entries to close the partnership books.

A14-6

D. E. Myers has been operating his business as a sole proprietor for some time. The following information is taken from his ledger as of March 31, 19_2.

Cash	$10,000
Accounts receivable—net	28,000
Merchandise inventory	70,000
Patent	14,000
Accounts payable	58,000
Notes payable (due July 1, 19_3)	20,000
D. E. Myers, capital	44,000

On March 31, 19_2, it was agreed that W. G. Parker would join Myers in a partnership. Parker was to invest the following:

Goodwill	$14,000
Land	6,000
Building	50,000

The building had an estimated useful life of 50 years as of March 31, 19_2.

The partnership was also to assume Parker's accounts payable of $6,000, giving Parker beginning capital of $64,000.

It was also agreed that certain assets of Myers would be recorded on the partnership books at the following amounts: accounts receivable, $26,000; merchandise inventory, $71,000; and patent, $5,000. The patent is to be amortized over a 10-year period. A new set of books is to be opened for the partnership.

During its first year of operations, the partnership earned a net income of $77,500, which was divided equally. Each partner withdrew $15,000 in cash, leaving a cash balance of $25,000 in the partnership bank account as of March 31, 19_3. Changes other than in cash were as follows:

$ 8,000 increase in inventory

38,000 increase in accounts receivable

12,000 increase in accounts payable

N. R. Herzog joined the partnership on March 31, 19_3, under the following terms:

Partnership Inventory is to be valued at	$ 90,000
Herzog is to invest cash of	100,000

Required:

(a) Entries to record the formation of the partnership on March 31, 19_2.

(b) Entries to record the admission of Herzog to the partnership on March 31, 19_3.

(c) The balance sheet of the Myers, Parker, and Herzog partnership on March 31, 19_3.

B14-1

Jan Owens began operations as an individual proprietor on March 3, 19_1. The following selected transactions took place between then and December 31, 19_1:

March   3—Invested cash of $20,000 and a building having a value of $35,000.

June 10—Invested an additional $5,000 cash.

August 31—Withdrew $2,000 cash and inventory having a selling price of $1,500. The inventory cost $1,200.

November 15—Proprietorship cash was used to pay $2,800 of medical expenses incurred by Owens.

December 20—Withdrew $1,400 cash.

Required:

(a) Journal entries to record the transactions.

(b) Postings to Owen's capital and drawings accounts.

B14-2

The December 31, 19_2 adjusted trial balance of Clyde Smallwood, an individual proprietor, is presented below:

CLYDE SMALLWOOD
Adjusted Trial Balance
December 31, 19_2

Cash	8,086	
Accounts receivable—net	12,022	
Merchandise inventory, December 31, 19_2	14,492	
Building	40,000	
Accumulated depreciation—Building		1,267
Accounts payable		6,833
Notes payable		2,500
Clyde Smallwood, capital		60,000
Clyde Smallwood, drawings	25,364	
Sales		181,450
Cost of goods sold	136,800	
Operating expenses	16,336	
Interest revenue		1,050
	253,100	253,100

Required:

(a) A statement of proprietor's capital for the year ended December 31, 19_2, assuming an additional investment of $22,000 by Smallwood on May 10, 19_2.

(b) A balance sheet as of December 31, 19_2.

(c) Closing entries.

B14-3

F. A. Rose and O. U. Thomas decide to form the Farout partnership by combining the operations of their individual proprietorships as of July 1, 19_7.

The after-closing trial balances of the proprietorships on this date are presented below.

F. A. ROSE
After-Closing Trial Balance
July 1, 19_7

Cash	10,000	
Accounts receivable	14,320	
Allowance for uncollectibles		1,025
Merchandise inventory	15,760	
Accounts payable		6,380
Notes payable		15,000
F. A. Rose, capital		17,675
	40,080	40,080

O. U. THOMAS
After-Closing Trial Balance
July 1, 19_7

Cash	2,005	
Merchandise inventory	10,420	
Land	12,000	
Building	30,000	
Accumulated depreciation—Building		18,500
Accounts payable		4,940
O. U. Thomas, capital		30,985
	54,425	54,425

An analysis of the assets of the proprietorships reveals that Rose's accounts receivable have a net value of $11,800. His inventory is to be valued at $16,450 and Thomas' at $8,620. The building and land have values of $22,500 and $16,500, respectively.

Required:

(a) Journal entries on the partnership books to record the investments of Rose and Thomas. The accounts receivable and building are to be recorded at their net values.

(b) A balance sheet for the partnership as of July 1, 19_7, immediately after organization.

B14-4

Stone, Wall, and Wu are in the process of liquidating their partnership. All assets have been sold except the equipment, but no cash has yet been paid to the partners during the liquidation process.

A trial balance taken on March 1, 19_2, is presented below.

STONE, WALL, AND WU
Trial Balance
March 1, 19_2

Cash	50,000	
Equipment	125,000	
Accumulated depreciation—Equipment		35,000
Accounts payable		38,000
Stone, capital		48,000
Wall, capital		34,000
Wu, capital		20,000
	175,000	175,000

Required:

Computation of the cash distribution under each of the following assumptions:

(a) The equipment is sold for $105,000.

(b) The equipment is sold for $45,000.

(c) The equipment is sold for $15,000.

B14-5

Heath, Franklin, and Hawkins decide to liquidate their partnership on January 1, 19_6. The after-closing trial balance of the firm as of that date is presented below.

HEATH, FRANKLIN, AND HAWKINS
After-Closing Trial Balance
January 1, 19_6

Cash	8,000	
Accounts receivable	37,000	
Allowance for uncollectibles		3,000
Merchandise inventory	45,000	
Equipment	50,000	
Accumulated depreciation—Equipment		24,000
Accounts payable		43,000
Heath, capital		30,000
Franklin, capital		15,000
Hawkins, capital		25,000
	140,000	140,000

The partners share profits and losses as follows: Heath, 40%; Franklin, 30%; and Hawkins, 30%.

On January 1, 19_6, the assets were sold for the following cash amounts: accounts receivable, $29,000; inventory, $42,000; and equipment, $15,000.

Required:

All entries to record liquidation of the partnership.

B14-6

JoAnn Jones and Rex Roper formed a partnership on January 1, 19_3. The capital and drawing accounts of the partners appeared as follows at the end of the first year of operation prior to closing the books.

JOANN JONES, CAPITAL

19_3					
Jan.	1			12,500	12,500 Cr.
June	1		5,000		7,500 Cr.
Dec.	31			10,000	17,500 Cr.

JOANN JONES, DRAWINGS

19_3					
June	30		3,000		3,000 Dr.
Dec.	31		3,000		6,000 Dr.

REX ROPER, CAPITAL

19_3					
Jan.	1			18,000	18,000 Cr.
July	1			10,000	28,000 Cr.

REX ROPER, DRAWINGS

19_3					
June	30		4,000		4,000 Dr.
Dec.	31		4,000		8,000 Dr.

The net income for the year was $20,225. According to the partnership agreement, net income is to be divided as follows:

(1) Salaries of $6,000 to Jones and $8,000 to Roper.

(2) Interest at the rate of 7 per cent on beginning capital balances.

(3) Remainder divided equally.

Required:

(a) Computation of each partner's share of net income for the year.

(b) Posting of all closing entries to the partners' capital and drawing accounts.

B14-7   The income statement of the WOW partnership showed a net income of $25,000 for the year ended December 31, 19_4.

Wilson's capital account balance was $22,000 during the entire year. Oliver's capital account had a balance of $16,000 on December 31, 19_4. This included an investment of $5,000 made on August 1, 19_4. Welch's ending capital balance was $10,000. His capital account had been debited for a withdrawal of $2,000 on June 30, 19_4.

Required:

(a) Schedules showing the division of net income under each of the following arrangements:

(1) Oliver is to be allowed a salary of $6,000. The remainder is to be divided: Wilson, 40%; Oliver, 20%; and Welch, 40%.

(2) A salary of $5,000 is to be allowed each partner. Interest at 6 per cent is to be allowed on beginning capitals. The remainder is to be divided in a 2:1:1 ratio.

(3) Wilson is to be allowed interest at 8 per cent on his beginning capital. The remainder is to be divided in a 2:4:4 ratio.

(b) Schedules showing the division of net income under each of the arrangements in part (a), assuming a net loss of $5,000 for the year.

STATEMENT OF CHANGES IN FINANCIAL POSITION
CHAPTER 15

PURPOSE OF CHAPTER   In addition to the income statement and the balance sheet, a third basic statement that *must* be presented for purposes of external reporting is the statement of changes in financial position (SCFP).[1] This chapter discusses the rationale for the SCFP, its underlying flow concept, and the analytical techniques for its preparation.

RATIONALE FOR THE SCFP   The balance sheet reports on the financial position of a firm as of a given date; hence, it is a stock, not a flow or change, statement showing dollar amounts of assets and equities at a specific point in time. In contrast, the income statement is a flow or change statement reporting on the revenue inflows, the expense outflows, and the resulting increase in net assets (net income) arising from profitable operations over a specified period of time. Also, the optional, but usually presented, statement of retained earnings is a flow or change statement reporting the causes of the change in retained earnings during a specified period. However, none of these statements reports on all the significant changes in assets and equities and the *causes* of these changes. Thus the SCFP is a flow or change statement designed to provide such information.

The SCFP is a flow or change statement that reports on a firm's financing and investing activities during a specified period of time that caused the changes in a firm's assets and equities. It reports on resource inflows, resource outflows, and the net increase (or decrease) in resources during a specified period. These resource inflows and outflows reflect the causes of the changes in assets, liabilities, and stockholders' equity. Thus the SCFP is similar to a statement of financial management in that it explains where the firm received its financing and to what use such financing was put during the period. For example, the SCFP provides information on the internal financing of cash or working capital from operations, how acquisitions of new plant and equipment were financed, what the proceeds were from a capital stock or bond issue and how they were used, how much debt or preferred stock was converted into common stock, what the proceeds were from the sale of long-lived assets, and the like.

UNDERLYING FLOW CONCEPT   APB *Opinion No. 19* states that the SCFP "should be based on a broad concept embracing all changes in financial position."[2] This is referred to as the *all-resources concept.* The concept is interpreted to mean that all significant changes in assets, liabilities, and owners' equity, regardless of whether cash or

[1]Accounting Principles Board, "Reporting Changes in Financial Position," *Opinion No. 19* (New York: AICPA, March, 1971), paragraph 7.

[2]*Opinion No. 19,* paragraph 8.

other elements of working capital are affected, should be reported in the SCFP. Since assets and equities increase and decrease as resources (also called funds) are generated and used, the all-resources concept means that all significant inflows and outflows of resources are to be reported in the statement.

Most changes in assets and equities affect cash or working capital (current assets minus current liabilities). For example, if bonds or capital stock are issued, the inflow of resources (a source) is measurable in terms of cash received or the increase in working capital (since cash is an element of working capital). Similarly, if equipment or land is acquired, the outflow of resources (a use) is measurable in terms of cash paid or the decrease in working capital. However, there are also some significant changes in assets and equities that do not affect cash or working capital, such as direct exchanges, that must be reported in the SCFP. For example, if machinery is acquired by issuing a long-term note payable, there is no use of cash or working capital. Under the all-resources concept, the issuance of the note would be reported as a source of resources and the acquisition of the machinery would be reported as a use of resources in the SCFP.

Thus the SCFP reports the sources and uses of resources, where the resource changes are in terms of (1) sources and uses of cash or working capital and (2) direct exchanges not affecting cash or working capital. A company has the option of explaining most of the changes in resources in terms of cash (the cash basis or format) or working capital (the working capital basis or format), but regardless of which one is used, financing and investing activities not affecting cash or working capital must also be reported—the all-resources concept.[3]

The general formats of the SCFP under the cash basis and the working capital basis are as follows:

Cash basis

Sources of financial resources:
  Cash sources
  Financial resources provided, not affecting cash
Uses of financial resources:
  Cash uses
  Financial resources applied, not affecting cash
Increase (decrease) in cash for period

Working capital basis

Sources of financial resources:
  Working capital sources
  Financial resources provided, not affecting working capital
Uses of financial resources:
  Working capital uses
  Financial resources applied, not affecting working capital
Increase (decrease) in working capital for period
Schedule of working capital changes

SCFP—CASH BASIS The cash basis SCFP reports all the significant changes in assets, liabilities, and owners' equity during a specified period of time by expressing these changes in terms of (1) sources and uses of cash, and (2) exchanges that did not affect cash. The primary sources and uses under the cash basis are as follows:

---

[3]Although most companies use the working capital basis (by far the most widely used) or the cash basis, *Opinion No. 19* (paragraph 11) also allows the use of cash and temporary investments combined or of all quick assets (cash plus temporary investments plus accounts receivable) to express most of the changes in financial position.

Cash basis

Sources of financial resources:
    Cash sources:
        Cash provided from operations
        Sale of long-lived assets (investments, land, plant, and equipment)
        Issuance of long-term notes payable or bonds
        Issuance of capital stock (preferred or common stock)
        Sale of treasury stock
    Financial resources provided, not affecting cash:
        Direct exchange transactions
Uses of financial resources:
    Cash uses:
        Purchase of long-lived assets
        Retirement of capital stock
        Acquisition of treasury stock
        Payment of dividends on capital stock
    Financial resources used, not affecting cash:
        Direct exchange transactions

It should be apparent from the above that the cash basis SCFP is *not* a simple summary of cash receipts and cash disbursements. That is, the SCFP is not prepared from the entries in the cash account; it is prepared from an analysis summarizing the changes in assets and equities in order to explain the causes of the changes. For example, note that in the above sources and uses of cash, the cause of each source and use is explained. Also, the SCFP emphasizes the cash provided from operations, which is not directly apparent from a summary of cash receipts and disbursements. Finally, the SCFP reports on significant changes in assets and equities that do not affect cash and would therefore not appear in a summary of cash receipts and disbursements.

With the exception of cash provided from operations, the above sources and uses of cash need no further explanation, since they are obvious. In contrast, cash provided from operations is not so obvious and needs further explanation. Cash provided from operations is the excess of revenues generating cash over expenses using cash. Thus it represents the cash actually made available to management from operations for use in the business and for distributions (dividends)—the internal financing of the business.

SCFP—WORKING CAPITAL BASIS   The working capital basis SCFP reports all the significant changes in assets, liabilities, and stockholders' equity during a specified period of time by expressing these changes in terms of (1) sources and uses of working capital and (2) sources and uses that did not affect working capital. Since under the working capital basis most of the changes in assets and equities are expressed in terms of sources and uses of working capital, the concept of working capital must be clearly understood.

Working capital is the excess of current assets over current liabilities. It consists of positive current assets (such as cash, temporary investments, accounts receivable, inventories, and short-term prepayments) and negative current liabilities (accounts payable, short-term notes payable, accrued liabilities, and advances from customers), with the positive difference, working capital, representing a "pool" or "fund" of liquid resources. That is, current assets are constantly being converted into cash during operations, the cash is used to pay the current liabilities that provide needed short-term financing, and the excess of current assets over current liabilities can be viewed as a "pool" of short-term liquid resources available to management at any given time.

Under the working capital basis, any transaction that increases the amount of working capital is reported in the SCFP as a source of working capital. Any transaction that decreases the amount of working capital is reported in the SCFP as a use of working capital. Note that the amount of working capital, or the working capital "pool," must change as the result of a transaction to qualify as a source or use of working capital. Such changes in the amount of working capital occur when the transaction results in a change in *both* a working capital account (a current asset or a current liability account) and a nonworking capital account (a noncurrent asset, a noncurrent liability, or a stockholders' equity account). Specifically, a transaction that involves a debit to a working capital account and a credit to a nonworking capital account represents a source of working capital. A transaction that involves a debit to a nonworking capital account and a credit to a working capital account represents a use of working capital. By referring to the noncurrent accounts and determining what caused the change in them, we shall at the same time ascertain the causes of the change in the amount of working capital.

The primary sources and uses of financial resources under the working capital basis are as follows:

Working capital basis

    Sources of financial resources:
        Working capital sources:
            Working capital provided from operations
            Sale of long-lived assets
            Issuance of long-term notes payable or bonds
            Issuance of capital stock
            Sale of treasury stock
        Financial resources provided, not affecting working capital:
            Direct exchange transactions
    Uses of financial resources:
        Working capital uses:
            Purchase of long-lived assets
            Retirement of capital stock
            Acquisition of treasury stock
            Declaration of dividends on capital stock
       Financial resources used, not affecting working capital:
            Direct exchange transactions

Working capital provided from operations is the excess of the inflow of working capital from sales (cash and accounts receivable increased) over the expenses using working capital (cash paid, inventory reduced, and current liabilities incurred); hence, there is a net increase in the amount of working capital, or a source of working capital. The sale of long-lived assets, such as investments, land, plant, and equipment, increases working capital by the cash inflow, and the decrease in the noncurrent asset explains the cause of the source of working capital. The issuance of long-term notes, bonds, or common stock increases working capital by the cash received, and the increase in the noncurrent liability or capital stock explains the cause of the source of working capital. The sale of treasury stock increases working capital by the cash received and the decline in the noncurrent treasury stock, which increases stockholders' equity, explains the cause of the source of working capital.

The use of cash reduces working capital and the increase in the noncurrent asset (long-lived asset acquired) explains the cause of the use of working capital. The use of cash reduces working capital, and the decrease in the noncurrent capital stock explains the cause of the use of working capital. The use of cash reduces working capital and the increase in the noncurrent treasury stock, which reduces stockholders' equity, explains the cause of the use of working capital. Finally, the increase in the current dividends payable reduces working capital, and the reduction of the noncurrent retained earnings explains the cause of the use of working capital.

Also note the two main differences between the sources and uses of working capital and the sources and uses of cash: working capital, instead of cash, provided from operations and dividends declared, instead of paid.

Changes within working capital Changes within the working capital "pool" are *not* reported as sources and uses of working capital in the SCFP. Such changes affect the internal content or composition of working capital, but they do not change the amount of working capital. Such changes arise from transactions that affect current asset and/or current liability accounts only (that is, debits and credits to working capital accounts only) and therefore do not affect the amount of working capital. For example, the payment of accounts payable reduces both cash (a current asset) and accounts payable (a current liability) and the effect on the amount of working capital is zero. Other examples of changes within working capital include the purchase of inventory, the purchase of short-term marketable securities, the collection of accounts receivable, and the write-off of an uncollectible receivable.

Because changes within working capital are not reported in a working capital basis SCFP, there could be significant changes in individual current assets and current liabilities during the period that could be overlooked in analyzing the SCFP. For this reason, a separate schedule of the increase or decrease in each current asset and current liability must be presented to accompany a working capital basis SCFP in order to present a complete picture of the changes in financial position.[4] Such a schedule is not presented with a cash basis SCFP, since, as will be explained, the net changes in current assets and current liabilities are reported in the body of the cash basis SCFP as adjustments of net income to report cash provided from operations.

A schedule of the changes in the internal content of working capital is illustrated on page 465 and is based on the comparative balance sheets of Sight & Sound Corporation, which are reproduced from Chapter 5, page 148.

---

[4]*Opinion No. 19,* paragraph 12.

SIGHT & SOUND CORPORATION
Schedule of Working Capital Changes
December 31, 19_8 and 19_7

	December 31 balances		Working capital increase (decrease)
	19_8	19_7	
Current assets:			
Cash	$11,650	$16,500	$(4,850)
Accounts receivable	12,000	11,000	1,000
Interest receivable	200	—	200
Merchandise inventory	18,000	12,000	6,000
Prepaid rent	4,800	—	4,800
Total current assets	$46,650	$39,500	
Current liabilities:			
Accounts payable	$25,000	$20,000	(5,000)
Salaries payable	1,700	1,500	(200)
Advances from customers	2,000	—	(2,000)
Total current liabilities	$28,700	$21,500	
Working capital	$17,950	$18,000	
Decrease in working capital			$ (50)

FLOW FROM OPERATIONS An important source of resources reported in the SCFP is the flow from operations, which is normally reported as the first item in the statement. It represents the liquid resource inflow from the primary economic activity conducted by the firm on a continuing basis (its business operations), which is available to management for use in the business or for distribution (dividends). Thus it indicates how much the company is financing itself internally from operations.

Under the cash basis, the flow from operations is measured in terms of cash—cash provided from operations. It is equal to the excess of cash inflows associated with revenues over the cash outflows associated with expenses during the fiscal period, or the net amount of cash generated by operations. It is the ultimate expression of the flow from operations because it represents the actual cash made available to management from operations.

Under the working capital basis, the flow from operations is measured in terms of working capital—working capital provided from operations. It is equal to the excess of revenues providing working capital over the expenses using working capital, or the net liquid asset inflow provided from operations. In other words, working capital provided from operations reflects the increase in net liquid assets resulting from the operating process: Inventory is purchased on credit, the inventory is converted into a larger amount of receivables, the receivables are collected, the resulting cash is used to pay the current liabilities, and the cycle begins again. The operating process generates additional working capital.

It should be pointed out that the flow from operations could be negative. For example, if expenses using cash exceeded revenues providing cash, then "Cash used in operations" would be reported in the cash basis SCFP. Similarly, if expenses using working capital exceeded revenues providing working capital, then "Working capital used in operations" would be reported in the working capital basis SCFP.

Because net income is based on accrual accounting, neither cash nor working capital provided from operations is the same as net income. Both cash and working capital provided from operations differ from net income because there are some expenses (such as depreciation, amortization of intangibles, and amortization of discount on bonds payable) and nonoperating losses (such as loss on sale of equipment) that are subtracted in arriving at net income but that do not use (decrease) either cash or working capital. Also, there are nonoperating gains (such as gain on sale of land) that are added in arriving at net income but that do not generate (increase) either cash or working capital. Consequently, net income can be converted into working capital provided from operations by adding these nonworking capital (noncash) expenses and losses to net income and subtracting nonworking capital (noncash) gains from net income.

In addition to the noncash expenses, losses, and gains, cash provided from operations also differs from net income because of the leads and lags in cash flows in relation to the operational activities that cause the cash flows: sales on credit from prior and current periods, cash advances from customers from prior and current periods, expenses incurred on credit in prior and current periods, and prepayments in prior and current periods.[5] These differences in cash and income flows are reflected in the net increases or decreases in current assets and current liabilities (other than cash, short-term marketable securities, and nontrade receivables and payables). Consequently, net income can be converted into cash provided from operations by adjusting it for the net increases or decreases in current assets and liabilities, as well as adjusting it for the noncash expenses, losses, and gains.

The foregoing discussion of converting net income into cash and working capital provided from operations can be summarized as follows:

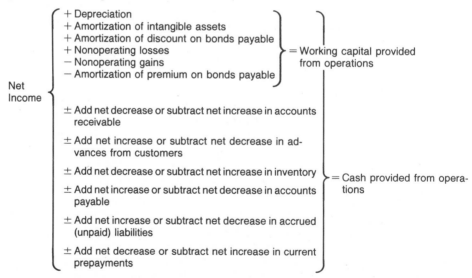

Using the above relationships, we can determine cash or working capital provided from operations for Sight & Sound Corporation for the year ended December 31, 19_2, as shown on page 467. Note that net income, noncash expense (depreciation), and noncash gain (gain on sale of land) are obtained from the income statement (page 471). The net increases and decreases in current assets and current

[5]Refer to the illustration on page 106 that shows the differences between cash and income flows.

liabilities are obtained from the comparative balance sheets (see page 470) by subtracting the beginning balances on the 19_1 balance sheet from the ending balances on the 19_2 balance sheet.

Cash provided from operations:

Net income		$5,050
Add (deduct) items not using or generating cash:		
Depreciation	$ 900	
Gain on sale of land	(200)	
Increase in accounts receivable	(1,000)	
Increase in interest receivable	(200)	
Increase in merchandise inventory	(6,000)	
Increase in accounts payable	5,000	
Increase in prepaid rent	(4,800)	
Increase in salaries payable	200	
Increase in advances from customers	2,000	(4,100)
Cash provided from operations for period		$ 950

Or:

Working capital provided from operations:

Net income		$5,050
Add (deduct) items not using or generating working capital:		
Depreciation	$ 900	
Gain on sale of land	(200)	700
Working capital provided from operations for period		$5,750

It should be pointed out that the general practice is to report in the SCFP the cash or working capital provided from operations in terms of net income plus and minus noncash or nonworking capital items, as shown above. Alternatively, cash or working capital provided from operations could be reported in terms of revenue generating cash (or working capital) less expenses using cash (or working capital).

DIRECT EXCHANGE TRANSACTIONS As previously pointed out, the SCFP reports all significant changes in assets and equities, regardless of whether cash or working capital is affected. The SCFP is not simply a narrow statement reporting only the changes in working capital or cash. Thus there are transactions that significantly change assets and equities but that do not affect cash or working capital. These transactions are to be reported in the SCFP. Such transactions may be conveniently referred to as *direct exchanges.*

Examples of direct exchanges are long-lived assets (such as land, equipment, and intangibles) acquired by issuing capital stock, by issuing long-term notes or bonds payable, by exchanging shares of stock in another company (long-term investment), or by exchanging another long-lived asset. Other examples include bonds or preferred stock converted into common stock and long-term debt settled by issuing capital stock. Note that in all these direct exchanges no cash or working capital would be affected.

For purposes of reporting in the SCFP, a direct exchange transaction is viewed as if it consisted of two economic activities: a financing activity and an investing activity. For example, assume that equipment with a fair value of $20,000 was acquired by a company in exchange for common stock issued by the company. The transaction would be viewed as consisting of a financing activity, the issuance of common stock to generate $20,000 in resources (a source), and an investing activity, the use of $20,000 to acquire or invest in equipment. Thus the direct exchange transaction would be reported in the SCFP as follows:

Financial resources provided, not affecting cash:
  Issuance of common stock to acquire equipment $20,000

Financial resources applied, not affecting cash:
  Acquisition of equipment by issuing common stock $20,000

Note, as illustrated above, that direct exchange transactions reported in the SCFP increase *both* sources and uses and therefore do not affect the reported net increase (decrease) in cash or working capital. However, the main point is that such "in and out" reporting results in the inclusion of direct exchanges in the SCFP and therefore the reporting of all significant changes in assets and equities.[6]

PREPARING THE SCFP The balance sheet, income statement, and statement of retained earnings are prepared directly from a firm's accounts. The accounts, however, do not directly provide the needed data to prepare the SCFP. Instead, the SCFP is derived analytically from the accounts by analyzing the transactions, in summary form, that affected the asset, liability, and stockholders' equity accounts during the year. Thus the SCFP can be prepared from working papers that contain the beginning and ending balances of the asset and equity accounts (obtained from comparative balance sheets) and in which the year's transactions can be reconstructed, in summary form, to explain the causes of the changes in assets and equities.

The T-account method will be used to prepare the SCFP.[7] Under this method, T-accounts are set up for assets and equities and serve as the working papers for the preparation of the SCFP. Beginning balances (from last year's balance sheet) are posted to the asset T-accounts as debits and posted to the equity accounts as credits. Ending balances (from the current year's balance sheet) are posted to the asset T-accounts as credits and posted to the equity T-accounts as debits. Transactions that were made during the current period are reconstructed, in summary form, by analyzing the T-accounts in light of the basic data provided by the comparative balance sheets, income statement, statement of retained earnings, and other accounting records concerning certain transactions. These reconstructed entries are posted to the T-accounts and explain the increases and decreases in the T-accounts. Such explanations serve as the basis for the SCFP because they explain how assets and equities changed during the current period. This follows from the fact that each balance-sheet account can be viewed as follows:

[6]Stock splits, stock (not cash) dividends, and appropriations of retained earnings are not considered significant exchange transactions and are not reported in the SCFP.

[7]The T-account method was developed by Professor William J. Vatter. A modified version of Vatter's T-account method is presented here.

$$\text{Beginning balance of account} + \text{Increase in account} - \text{Decrease in account} = \text{Ending balance of account}$$

$$\text{Beginning balance of account} + \text{Increase in account} - \text{Ending balance in account} + \text{Decrease in account}$$

Asset account				Equity account			
Beginning balance	X	Ending balance	X	Ending balance	X	Beginning balance	X
Increase	X	Decrease	X	Decrease	X	Increase	X
	X		X		X		X

Note that for asset T-accounts the beginning balances and increases are debits, but for equity T-accounts the beginning balances and increases are credits. Note also that given the beginning and ending balance (from comparative balance sheets) and knowledge of the increase (decrease) in the T-account, the decrease (increase) can be deduced because the two sides of the T-account must be equal.

The change in each T-account, which is equal to the difference between its ending and beginning balances, is to be explained. Each change will be explained when entries are made to the T-account that bring it into balance (total debits equal total credits). Thus these entries are essentially analytical entries that explain the changes in the T-accounts by reconstructing the original entries in summary form. When these entries affect cash (or working capital) and cash (working capital) from operations, the effect is isolated and labeled in master T-accounts for the two and serve as the data base for the preparation of the formal SCFP.

The procedure   The steps in the T-account method are as follows:

(1) Decide whether a cash or working capital basis (format) is to be used.
  (a) If a cash basis is used, set up a large T-account for cash and post to it the beginning (labeled "B") and ending (labeled "E") balances from the cash account on the comparative balance sheets.
  (b) If a working capital basis is used, set up a large T-account for working capital and post beginning (B) and ending (E) working capital balances to the T-account. These two balances are obtained from a constructed schedule of working capital changes (see page 465).
(2) Set up a large T-account for cash (or working capital) from operations. This is the only T-account that does not have any beginning or ending balances posted to it, since it includes only the current period's net income and income adjustments to derive cash (working capital) provided from operations.
(3) Set up small T-accounts for each asset and equity account, other than cash (cash basis) or current assets and current liabilities (working capital basis), and post beginning and ending balances from the comparative balance sheets to the T-accounts. Note that under the working capital basis, T-accounts are not set up for current assets and current liabilities.
(4) Reconstruct the transactions that occurred during the period and make entries summarizing these transactions in the T-accounts until the accounts (other than the two large T-accounts) are in balance. Number the entries for locating errors.
  (a) Make the first entry in the T-accounts by debiting the cash (or working capital) from operations T-account and crediting the retained earnings T-account for net income (or income before extraordinary items, if extraordinary items exist). The opposite would be done for a net loss.
  (b) If the reconstructed transaction affects cash (or working capital), make the entry to the cash (working capital) T-account and label its cause.

(c) If the reconstructed transaction affects cash (working capital) from operations, make the entry to the cash (working capital) from operations T-account and label its cause.

(d) For direct exchange transactions, make an "in and out" entry in the cash (working capital) T-account, in addition to entries in the accounts affected by the exchange.

(e) If a cash basis is used, close out the current asset and current liability T-accounts (other than cash and nontrade receivables and payables) and transfer their net increases or decreases to the cash from operations T-account. These entries adjust net income to reflect cash provided from operations.

(5) When all the T-accounts are in balance, except for the two large T-accounts, close the cash (working capital) from operations T-account by transferring its ending balance to the cash (working capital) T-account. This amount represents cash (working capital) from operations and brings the cash (working capital) T-account into balance.

(6) Prepare the formal SCFP from the cash (working capital) T-account. The labeled debits are the sources and the labeled credits are the uses of financial resources. The details for reporting the cash (working capital) provided from operations are obtained from the labeled entries in the cash (working capital) from operations T-account.

Illustration To illustrate the preparation of the SCFP using the T-account method, we will prepare the statement for Sight & Sound Corporation for the year ended 19_2. Sight & Sound Corporation's comparative balance sheets, income statements, and statements of retained earnings for the years 19_2 and 19_1 will serve as

SIGHT & SOUND CORPORATION
Balance Sheet
December 31, 19_2 and 19_1

	19_2		19_1	
Assets:				
Current assets:				
Cash	$11,650		$16,500	
Accounts receivable	12,000		11,000	
Interest receivable	200		—	
Merchandise inventory	18,000		12,000	
Prepaid rent	4,800		—	
Total current assets		$46,650		$39,500
Long-term investments:				
Investment in land—at cost	$ —		$10,000	
Bond investment	10,000		—	
Total long-term investments		$10,000		$10,000
Property, plant, and equipment:				
Delivery truck	$ 4,000		—	
Accumulated depreciation	900		—	
Total property, plant and equipment		3,100		—
Total assets		$59,750		$49,500
Equities:				
Current liabilities:				
Accounts payable	$25,000		$20,000	
Salaries payable	1,700		1,500	
Advances from customers	2,000		—	
Total current liabilities		$28,700		$21,500
Stockholders' equity:				
Common stock	$25,000		$25,000	
Retained earnings	6,050		3,000	
Total stockholders' equity		31,050		28,000
Total equities		$59,750		$49,500

SIGHT & SOUND CORPORATION
Statement of Retained Earnings
For the Years Ended December 31, 19_2 and 19_1

	19_2	19_1
Retained earnings beginning of the year	$3,000	—
Add net income	5,050	5,000
	$8,050	$5,000
Deduct dividends	2,000	2,000
Retained earnings end of the year	$6,050	$3,000

our data base and are reproduced on pages 470 and 471 from Chapters 4 and 5.[8]

The T-account working papers are illustrated on pages 472–73 (cash basis) and 473 (working capital basis). To explain the numbered entries to the T-accounts, we will illustrate the entries (beginning on page 472) in general journal form for *both* the cash basis and working capital basis and then we will analyze each entry. Note, however, that the general journal entries are made for explanatory purposes, since the entries would normally be made in the T-account working papers only and would never be entered in the formal journal and ledger.

SIGHT & SOUND CORPORATION
Income Statement
For the Years Ended December 31, 19_2 and 19_1

	19_2			19_1		
Sales			$91,000			$81,000
Cost of goods sold			54,750			48,000
Gross margin			$36,250			$33,000
Operating expenses:						
Selling expenses:						
Sales salaries	$15,400			$14,500		
Depreciation	900	$16,300		—	$14,500	
General and adminis-						
trative expenses:						
Administrative						
salaries	$ 5,000			$ 3,500		
Rent	4,800			4,800		
Other expense	5,500	15,300		5,200	13,500	
Total operating						
expenses			31,600			28,000
Net operating income			$ 4,650			$ 5,000
Nonoperating items:						
Add: Interest revenue		$ 200				
Gain on sale of						
land		200	400			
Net income			$ 5,050			$ 5,000
Earnings per common						
share			$ 2.02			$ 2.00

[8]The 19_2 transactions for Sight & Sound Corporation are discussed in Chapter 4.

	Summary original entry	T-Account entry, cash basis	T-Account entry, working capital basis
(1) Entry:			
Income summary	5,050	—	—
Cash from operations	—	5,050	—
Working capital from operations	—	—	5,050
Retained earnings	5,050	5,050	5,050

Analysis: To avoid the detail of revenues generating cash (or working capital) and expenses using cash (working capital), accountants use a shortcut by starting with the net income (or income before extraordinary items, if extraordinary items exist) reported in the income statement and adjusting it to reflect cash (working capital) provided from operations. The credit to Retained Earnings repeats the original entry, since it reflects the closing process whereby net income increased retained earnings.

Cash

(Sources)		(Uses)	
Beginning balance	16,500	Ending balance	11,650
(3) Sale of land	10,200	(4) Investment in bonds	10,000
(a) Cash from operations	950	(5) Purchase of delivery truck	4,000
		(6) Dividends	2,000
	27,650		27,650

Cash from operations

(Net income and noncash additions to net income)		(Noncash deductions from net income)	
(1) Net income	5,050	(3) Gain on sale of land	200
(2) Depreciation	900	(7) Increase in accounts receivable	1,000
(10) Increase in accounts payable	5,000	(8) Increase in interest receivable	200
(12) Increase in salaries payable	200	(9) Increase in inventory	6,000
(13) Increase in advances from customers	2,000	(11) Increase in prepaid rent	4,800
		(a) Balance	950
	13,150		13,150

Accounts receivable

B	11,000	E	12,000
(7)	1,000		
	12,000		12,000

Interest receivable

B	—	E	200
(8)	200		
	200		200

Inventory

B	12,000	E	18,000
(9)	6,000		
	18,000		18,000

Prepaid rent

B	—	E	4,800
(11)	4,800		
	4,800		4,800

Investment in land

B	10,000	E	—
		(3)	10,000
	10,000		10,000

Bond investment

B	—	E	10,000
(4)	10,000		
	10,000		10,000

Delivery truck

B	—	E	4,000
(5)	4,000		
	4,000		4,000

Accumulated depreciation-truck

E	900	B	—
		(2)	900
	900		900

Accounts payable

E	25,000	B	20,000
		(10)	5,000
	25,000		25,000

Salaries payable

E	1,700	B	1,500
		(12)	200
	1,700		1,700

Advances from customer

E	2,000	B	—
		(13)	2,000
	2,000		2,000

Common stock

E	25,000	B	25,000

Retained earnings

E	6,050	B	3,000
	2,000	(1)	5,050
	8,050		8,050

Working capital

(Sources)		(Uses)	
Beginning balance	18,000	Ending balance	17,950
(3) Sale of land	10,200	(4) Investment in bonds	10,000
(a) Working capital from operations	5,750	(5) Purchase of delivery truck	4,000
		(6) Dividends declared and paid	2,000
	33,950		33,950

Working capital from operations

(Net income and nonworking capital additions to net income)		(Nonworking capital deductions from net income)	
(1) Net income	5,050	(3) Gain from sale of land	200
(2) Depreciation	900	(a) Balance	5,750
	5,950		5,950

Investment in land

B	10,000	E	—
		(3)	10,000
	10,000		10,000

Bond investment

B	—	E	10,000
(4)	10,000		
	10,000		10,000

Delivery truck

B	—	E	4,000
(5)	4,000		
	4,000		4,000

Accumulated depreciation-truck

E	900	B	—
		(2)	900
	900		900

Common stock

E	25,000	B	25,000

Retained earnings

E	6,050	B	3,000
(6)	2,000	(1)	5,050
	8,050		8,050

(2) Entry:	Summary original entry		T-Account entry, cash basis		T-Account entry, working capital basis	
Depreciation expense	900		—		—	
Cash from operations	—			900	—	
Working capital from operations	—		—		900	
Accumulated depreciation		900		900		900

Analysis: Depreciation expense, obtained from the income statement, is debited to Cash (Working Capital) from Operations as an adjustment to net income that was previously debited to Cash (Working Capital) from Operations in entry 1. In terms of cash (working capital) flow, net income is too low by $900 and is, in effect, adjusted (added to net income) by debiting Cash (Working Capital) from Operations. Although depreciation is a legitimate expense for the income statement, as a cost allocation it does not require an outlay of cash. The cash outlay occurred when the truck was originally acquired, not when it was depreciated. In other words, depreciation is a noncash (nonworking capital) adjustment to net income to derive cash (working capital) from operations. The credit to Accumulated Depreciation repeats the original entry, since it reflects the increase in accumulated depreciation by the amount of periodic depreciation.

(3) Entry:	Summary original entry		T-Account entry, cash basis		T-Account entry, working capital basis	
Cash	10,200		10,200		—	
Working capital	—		—		10,200	
Land		10,000		10,000		10,000
Gain on sale of land		200	—		—	
Cash from operations	—			200	—	
Working capital from operations	—		—			200

Analysis: Because this transaction generated cash (and therefore working capital) of $10,200, Cash (Working Capital) is debited to reflect this source. Note, however, that the $200 gain from the sale of land is not a source of cash (working capital), since it has no effect on cash (working capital). In terms of cash (working capital) flow, net income is too high by the $200 gain and is, in effect, adjusted (subtracted from net income) by crediting Cash (Working Capital) from Operations. The credit to Land merely repeats the original entry to reflect the land disposal. The data source for this entry is obtained from company records, although it can be deduced given the gain on sale of land from the income statement and the decrease in the investment in land T-account.

(4) Entry:	Summary original entry		T-Account entry, cash basis		T-Account entry, working capital basis	
Bond investment	10,000		10,000		10,000	
Cash		10,000		10,000		—
Working capital		—		—		10,000

Analysis: The investment in bonds was a use of cash (and therefore a use of working capital); hence, Cash (Working Capital) is credited to reflect this use. The debit to Bond Investment repeats the original entry to reflect the increase in bond investment. The data source for this entry is obtained from company records, although it can be deduced given the increase in the bond investment T-account.

	Summary original entry		T-Account entry, cash basis		T-Account entry, working capital basis
(5) Entry:					
Delivery truck	4,000		4,000		4,000
Cash		4,000		4,000	—
Working capital		—		—	4,000

Analysis: The purchase of a delivery truck was a use of cash (and therefore a use of working capital); hence, Cash (Working Capital) is credited to reflect this use. The debit to Delivery Truck repeats the original entry to reflect the increase in assets. The data source for this entry is obtained from company records, although it can be deduced from the increase in the delivery truck T-account.

	Summary original entry		T-Account entry, cash basis		T-Account entry, working capital basis
(6) Entry:					
Retained earnings	2,000		2,000		2,000
Cash		2,000		2,000	—
Working capital		—		—	2,000

Analysis: The declaration and payment of dividends was a use of cash (and therefore a use of working capital); hence, Cash (Working Capital) is credited to reflect this use. The debit to Retained Earnings summarizes the original reduction of retained earnings via the dividend account. The data source for this entry is provided by company records, although the entry can be deduced from the change in retained earnings, obtained from the statement of retained earnings, and the change in any dividends payable, obtained from comparative balance sheets.

	Summary original entry		T-Account entry, cash basis		T-Account entry, working capital basis
(7) Entry:					
Accounts receivable	—		1,000		—
Cash from operations		—		1,000	—

Analysis: Under a cash basis, the net increases and decreases in current assets and current liabilities (as determined by the difference between beginning and ending balances in their T-accounts obtained from comparative balance sheets) are debited and credited to the cash from operations T-account in order to adjust net income to reflect cash provided from operations. In this particular instance, Accounts Receivable is debited to reflect its summary increase (from $11,000 to $12,000) and Cash from Operations is credited to adjust net income to reflect cash collected from customers. That is, the increase in accounts receivable means that the company sold more than it collected from sales during the period. The cash receipts from sales were less than the net sales (and therefore net income) by the amount of the increase in accounts receivable ($1,000), and the amount of the increase should therefore be subtracted from net income (credit Cash from Operations) to reflect the cash receipts from sales in determining cash provided from operations. The opposite would be true if accounts receivable decreased.

	Summary original entry	T-Account entry, cash basis	T-Account entry, working capital basis
(8) Entry:			
Interest receivable	—	200	—
Cash from operations	—	200	—

Analysis: Under a cash basis, Interest Receivable is debited to reflect its summary increase (from zero to $200) and Cash from Operations is credited to adjust net income to reflect cash provided from operations. That is, the increase in interest receivable means that interest revenue (and therefore net income) is greater than the cash received from interest by the amount of the increase ($200) in the receivable. Thus the amount of the increase should be subtracted from net income (credit Cash from Operations) in determining cash provided from operations. The opposite would be true if interest receivable decreased.

	Summary original entry	T-Account entry, cash basis	T-Account entry, working capital basis
(9) Entry:			
Merchandise inventory	—	6,000	—
Cash from operations	—	6,000	—

Analysis: Under a cash basis, Merchandise Inventory is debited to reflect its summary increase (from $12,000 to $18,000) and Cash from Operations is credited to adjust net income to reflect cash provided from operations. That is, the increase in inventory means that the company purchased more inventory than it sold during the period. The total purchases of inventory were larger than the cost of goods sold (and therefore net income) by the amount of the increase ($6,000) in inventory, and the amount of the increase should therefore be subtracted from net income (credit Cash from Operations) to reflect the inventory purchased in determining cash provided from operations. Of course, the opposite would be true if inventory decreased. Note, however, that the inventory adjustment merely adjusts net income to reflect inventory purchased, and when combined with the adjustment for accounts payable (explained next), the net income is adjusted to reflect cash paid for merchandise inventory.

	Summary original entry	T-Account entry, cash basis	T-Account entry, working capital basis
(10) Entry:			
Cash from operations	—	5,000	—
Accounts payable	—	5,000	—

Analysis: Under a cash basis, Accounts Payable is credited to reflect its summary increase (from $20,000 to $25,000) and Cash from Operations is debited to adjust net income to reflect cash provided from operations. That is, the increase in accounts payable means that the company bought more merchandise than it paid for during the period. The cash disbursements for merchandise were smaller than the total merchandise purchased, and hence net income would be larger (because of the inventory adjustment discussed above), by the amount of the increase ($5,000) in accounts payable. The amount of the increase should therefore be added to net income (debit Cash from Operations) to reflect the cash paid for merchandise inventory in determining cash provided from operations. The opposite would be true if accounts payable decreased. Note, however, that the adjustment of net income to reflect cash paid for inventory requires two adjustments: the adjustment for the change in inventory (entry 9) and the adjustment for the change in accounts payable (entry 10).

	Summary original entry	T-Account entry, cash basis	T-Account entry, working capital basis
(11) Entry:			
Prepaid rent	—	4,800	—
Cash from operations	—	4,800	—

Analysis: Under a cash basis, Prepaid Rent is debited to reflect its summary increase (from zero to $4,800) and Cash from Operations is credited to adjust net income to reflect cash provided from operations. That is, the increase in prepaid rent means that more cash was spent for the prepayment than was recognized as rent expense. In terms of cash, net income would be too high by the amount of the increase ($4,800) in the prepayment, and the amount of the increase should therefore be subtracted from net income (credit Cash from Operations) in determining cash provided from operations. The opposite would be true if prepayments decreased.

	Summary original entry	T-Account entry, cash basis	T-Account entry, working capital basis
(12) Entry:			
Cash from operations	—	200	—
Salaries payable	—	200	—

Analysis: Under a cash basis, Salaries Payable is credited to reflect its summary increase (from $1,500 to $1,700) and Cash from Operations is debited to adjust net income to reflect cash provided from operations. That is, the increase in salaries payable means that an expense was incurred (salaries expense), which reduced net income, for which no cash was paid. In terms of cash, net income would be too low by the amount of the increase ($200) in the accrued liability, and the amount of the increase should therefore be added to net income (debit Cash from Operations) in determining cash provided from operations. The opposite would be true if an accrued liability decreased.

	Summary original entry	T-Account entry, cash basis	T-Account entry, working capital basis
(13) Entry:			
Cash from operations	—	2,000	—
Advances from customers	—	2,000	—

Analysis: Under a cash basis, Advances from Customers (a current liability) is credited to reflect its summary increase (from zero to $2,000) and Cash from Operations is debited to adjust net income to reflect cash provided from operations. That is, the increase in advances from customers means that the cash inflow from the advances was not included in revenues (and therefore net income) because it was not earned. Thus cash receipts were greater than net income by the amount of the increase ($2,000) in advances from customers, and the amount of the increase should therefore be added to net income (debit Cash from Operations) in determining cash provided from customers. The opposite would be true if advances decreased.

	Summary original entry	T-Account entry, cash basis	T-Account entry, working capital basis
(a) Entry:			
Cash	—	950	—
Working capital	—	—	5,750
Cash from operations	—	950	—
Working capital from operations	—	—	5,750

Analysis: After entry 13, all the T-accounts under the cash basis are in balance except for the cash from operations T-account and the cash T-account. Similarly, after entry 6, all the T-accounts under the working capital basis are in balance except for the working capital from operations T-account and the working capital T-account. Thus the final entry (entry a) closes the cash (working capital) from operations T-account by transferring its ending balance to the cash (working capital) T-account, which puts the latter in balance. For example, under the cash basis, the ending balance in the cash from operations T-account is a $950 debit balance; hence, the account is closed by crediting it $950 and debiting the cash T-account for $950, which represents a cash source—cash provided from operations. Similarly, under the working capital basis, the working capital from operations T-account has a $5,750 debit balance, which is transferred to the working capital T-account (debit Working Capital and credit Working from Operations for $5,750) and represents a working capital source—working capital provided from operations. After this final entry, all T-account changes have been explained and the change in cash (working capital) has also been explained.

The formal SCFP for Sight & Sound Corporation can now be prepared from the labeled entries from the cash (working capital) T-account. The labeled debits to the cash (working capital) T-account are sources of cash (working capital) and the labeled credits are uses of cash (working capital).

The formal SCFP normally begins by reporting cash (working capital) provided from operations by showing net income plus and minus noncash (nonworking capital) items. The details for the noncash (nonworking capital) adjustments to net income are obtained from the labeled entries in the cash (working capital) from operations T-account. Noncash (nonworking capital) additions to net income are debits and noncash (nonworking capital) deductions from net income are credits in the cash (working capital) from operations T-account.

The formal SCFP for Sight & Sound Corporation is illustrated below, under the cash basis, and on page 480, under the working capital basis.

IMPORTANT TERMS AND CONCEPTS IN CHAPTER 15

Rationale for SCFP—p. 460

All resources concept—pp. 460, 461

Working capital—pp. 461, 462

Sources and uses—pp. 461–464

Direct exchanges—pp. 461, 467, 468

Cash basis—pp. 461, 462

Cash from operations—pp. 462, 465–467

Working capital basis—pp. 462–464

Working capital from operations—pp. 463, 465–467

Changes within working capital—pp. 464, 465

Net income does not equal flow from operations—pp. 465, 466

Noncash (nonworking capital) expenses, losses, and gains—pp. 466, 467

Net increases in current assets and current liabilities—pp. 466, 467, 475–477

SCFP is derived analytically—p. 468

T-Account method—pp. 468, 469

Steps in T-account method—pp. 469, 470

SIGHT & SOUND CORPORATION
Statement of Changes in Financial Position—Cash Basis
For the Year Ended December 31, 19_2

Sources of financial resources:			
Cash provided from operations:			
Net income		$ 5,050	
Add (deduct) items not using or generating cash:			
Depreciation	$ 900		
Gain on sale of land	(200)		
Increase in accounts payable	5,000		
Increase in salaries payable	200		
Increase in advances from customers	2,000		
Increase in accounts receivable	(1,000)		
Increase in interest receivable	(200)		
Increase in merchandise inventory	(6,000)		
Increase in prepaid rent	(4,800)	(4,100)	
Cash provided from operations for period		$ 950	
Cash provided from other sources:			
Sale of land		10,200	
Total financial resources provided for period			$11,150
Uses of financial resources:			
Cash applied:			
Investment in bonds		$10,000	
Purchase of delivery truck		4,000	
Dividends on common stock		2,000	
Total financial resources used for period			16,000
Decrease in cash for period			$ (4,850)

SIGHT & SOUND CORPORATION
Statement of Changes in Financial Position—Working Capital Basis
For the Year Ended December 31, 19_2

Sources of financial resources:			
Working capital provided from operations:			
Net income		$ 5,050	
Add (deduct) items not using or generating working capital:			
Depreciation	$900		
Gain on sale of land	(200)	700	
Working capital provided from operations		$ 5,750	
Working capital provided from other sources:			
Sale of land		10,200	
Total financial resources provided for period			$15,950
Uses of financial resources:			
Working capital applied:			
Investment in bonds		$10,000	
Purchase delivery truck		4,000	
Dividends on common stock		2,000	
Total financial resources used for period			16,000
Decrease in working capital for period			$ (50)

SIGHT & SOUND CORPORATION
Schedule of Working Capital Changes
December 31, 19_2 and 19_1

	December 31 balances		Working capital increase (decrease)
	19_2	19_1	
Current assets:			
Cash	$11,650	$16,500	$(4,850)
Accounts receivable	12,000	11,000	1,000
Interest receivable	200	—	200
Merchandise inventory	18,000	12,000	6,000
Prepaid rent	4,800	—	4,800
Total current assets	$46,650	$39,500	
Current liabilities:			
Accounts payable	$25,000	$20,000	$(5,000)
Salaries payable	1,700	1,500	(200)
Advances from customers	2,000	—	(2,000)
Total current liabilities	$28,700	$21,500	
Working capital	$17,950	$18,000	
Decrease in working capital			$ (50)

Questions

1 What is the objective of the statement of changes in financial position?
2 If you were given comparative balance sheet data, would it be possible to prepare a statement of changes in financial position?
3 What is the difference between net income and working capital provided from operations?
4 What is the difference between net income and cash provided from operations?
5 Do internal accounting adjustments (e.g., depreciation, amortization, etc.) affect cash or working capital?
6 Why is working capital viewed as a "pool" of liquid financial resources?
7 What information can the reader gain from the statement of changes of financial position, which is not found on the balance sheet?
8 What information can the reader gain from the statement of changes of financial position, which is not found on the income statement?
9 How can the cash from operations be less than the net income plus depreciation?
10 Why is a financial-resource-flow (funds flow) concept necessary to prepare the statement of changes in financial position?
11 How would an accountant report a conversion of preferred stock into common stock on the statement of changes of financial position?
12 A company declares a cash dividend in 19_1, payable in 19_2. Will this action have any effect on the statement of changes in financial position (working capital basis) for 19_1? For 19_2?
13 Why is the income statement generally a poor indicator of current cash flows of a firm?
14 What does the fund flow from operations represent?
15 Why is the cash basis SCFP not a simple summary of cash receipts and cash disbursements?
16 "In and out" reporting results in the inclusion of direct exchange transactions in the SCFP. All significant changes in assets and equities are therefore reported. Considering the above comments, what is the correct SCFP presentation for distribution of a stock dividend?

Short exercises

E15-1   *You are given below three multiple-choice statements. Select the correct answers and indicate the corresponding letters on a sheet of paper (e.g., 1-d, 2-d, etc.).*

(1) Which of the following is incorrect? (a) The amortization of goodwill will not affect working capital. (b) The charge for depreciation does not involve any utilization of working capital. (c) Working capital provided from operations can be equal to net income. (d) A machine having a historical cost of $10,000, accumulated depreciation of $4,000, and sold for $7,000 would be a $6,000 source of working capital. (e) None of the above.

(2) A statement of changes in financial position would disclose the amortization of bond discount as (a) a use, (b) both a source and a use, (c) noncash (nonworking capital) addition to net

income in the determination of financial resources provided from operations, (d) a source, (e) none of the above.

(3) A statement of changes in financial position would disclose which of the following as deductions from net income to determine financial resources provided from operations? (a) depreciation, (b) loss on sale of equipment, (c) bond discount amortization, (d) all of the above, (e) none of the above.

E15-2

You are given below three multiple-choice statements. Select the correct answers and indicate the corresponding letters on a sheet of paper (e.g., 1-a, 2-a, etc.).

(1) The T-account method (a) is a necessary part of company records, (b) is the only way to prepare the statement of changes in financial position, (c) is merely an aid in the preparation of the statement of changes in financial position, (d) does not reconstruct the transactions made during the period, (e) none of the above.

(2) The statement of changes in financial position (a) does not replace the other basic financial statements, (b) provides financial information that may not be found on other financial statements, (c) should disclose all significant changes in financial position arising from external transactions, (d) all of the above, (e) none of the above.

(3) Which of the following is incorrect? (a) Internal accounting transactions are excluded in the statement. (b) All significant changes in financial resources affect either cash and/or working capital. (c) A bond ($1,000 face) sold at 95 is a $950 source of working capital. (d) Cash paid for merchandise is equal to purchases plus the decrease in accounts payable. (e) All of the above. (f) None of the above.

E15-3

The comparative balance sheet of Will Corporation is presented below:

WILL CORPORATION
Comparative Balance Sheet
December 31, 19_4 and 19_3

	December 31,	
	19_4	19_3
Assets:		
Cash	$ 16,000	$ 13,000
Accounts receivable	16,100	19,100
Allowance for uncollectibles	(430)	(750)
Merchandise inventory	17,300	13,700
Land	35,000	20,000
Equipment	45,000	43,000
Accumulated depreciation—Equipment	(8,400)	(7,800)
	$120,570	$100,250
Equities:		
Accounts payable	$ 20,000	$ 16,000
Salaries payable	1,600	4,300
Mortgage payable	15,000	10,000
Common stock	64,000	60,000
Retained earnings	19,970	9,950
	$120,570	$100,250

Prepare a schedule of working capital changes for 19_4.

E15-4 *An analysis of noncurrent accounts of Horngren Corporation reveals the following changes during the year ended March 31, 19_8:*

  Long-term investments—Increased $2,500 as the result of an additional purchase for cash.

  Land—Decreased $8,000 as the result of a sale. No gain was realized by the corporation.

  Plant—Increased $12,000 as the result of a purchase. Cash of $4,000 was paid and a note due in four years was given for the balance.

  Accumulated depreciation—plant—Increased $3,000 by recording depreciation for the year.

  Patents—Decreased $5,000 by amortization charged against income.

  Notes payable—Increased $8,000 by purchase of equipment.

  Common stock—Increased $7,000 by stock dividend.

  Retained earnings—Decreased $9,000 from the net loss from operations and the stock dividend.

Required:

(a) What was the working capital provided by operations?

(b) Compute the total increase or decrease in working capital.

E15-5 *For the transactions and adjustments listed below, determine the effect on (a) working capital and (b) cash. Answer by indicating either increase, decrease, or no effect.*

  (1) Write-off of an uncollectible amount.

  (2) Purchase of a two-year insurance policy for cash.

  (3) Issuance of common stock for cash.

  (4) Issuance of common stock for land.

  (5) Declaration of cash dividend.

  (6) Payment of cash dividend previously declared.

  (7) Recording of annual depreciation charges.

  (8) Sale of machinery for cash.

  (9) Conversion of convertible bonds into common stock.

  (10) Amortization of discount on bonds.

  (11) Adjustment for insurance expense at year end.

  (12) Adjustment for estimated bad debts at year end.

E15-6 *The income statement of Frigate Company is presented below:*

FRIGATE COMPANY
Income Statement
For the Year Ended December 31, 19_3

Revenue:		
Net sales		$40,000
Deduct expenses:		
Cost of goods sold	$20,000	
Rent	2,000	
Depreciation	3,000	
Salaries	8,000	33,000
Net income		$ 7,000

Required:

(a) What is the working capital provided from operations?

(b) What is the cash provided from operations? Assume that accounts receivable decreased $3,000, salaries payable increased $500, inventory increased $5,000, accounts payable remained the same, and prepaid rent decreased $2,000.

E15-7

Selected account balances from the ledger of Lee, Inc. are presented below:

Account	Balance March 31,	
	19_7	19_6
Accounts receivable	$35,000	$42,000
Merchandise inventory	26,800	27,000
Prepaid rent	290	300
Prepaid insurance	540	500
Accounts payable	13,800	13,000
Interest payable	1,250	900
Sales	96,000	
Cost of goods sold	77,000	
Rent expense	440	
Insurance expense	710	
Interest expense	890	

Required:

Computation of the following for the year ended December 31, 19_7.

(a) Cash collected from customers.

(b) Purchases of merchandise inventory.

(c) Cash payments for insurance premiums.

(d) Cash payments for rent.

(e) Cash payments for interest.

(f) Cash payments for merchandise inventory. (*Hint:* Start with purchases from (b) above.)

E15-8

For transactions (1) through (10), select the lettered answer that describes the transaction's effect on working capital.

(A) The transaction results in a use of financial resources which is a decrease in working capital.

(B) The transaction results in a source of financial resources which is an increase in working capital.

(C) The transaction involves two noncurrent accounts that will have no effect on working capital.

(D) The transaction involves two current accounts that will have no effect on working capital.

(E) None of the above.

(1) The collection of a ten-day note receivable.

(2) The declaration of a cash dividend.

(3) The issuance of long-term bonds for land.

(4) The purchase of machinery for cash.

(5) The amortization of bond premium.

(6) The payment of a dividend previously declared.

(7) The issuance of a stock dividend.

(8) The write-off of a bad debt.

(9) The purchase of treasury stock.

(10) The sale of a plant for less than book value.

E15-9 *The balance sheets of Check Company for years 19_3 and 19_4 are as follows:*

	19_4	19_3
Cash	$156,250	$ 50,000
Land	37,500	12,500
Buildings	62,500	62,500
Equipment	737,500	625,000
Accumulated depreciation	(225,000)	(125,000)
	$768,750	$625,000
Bonds payable	$312,500	$250,000
Common stock, $100 par value	337,500	312,500
Retained earnings	118,750	62,500
	$768,750	$625,000

Additional information: Cash dividends of $93,750 were charged to Retained Earnings in 19_4, and net income accounted for the remaining change in Retained Earnings. Additional land was acquired during the year by the issuance of common stock.

Required:

Prepare T-account working papers used in the preparation of the statement of changes in financial position (cash basis).

Problems

A15-1 *Bluff Corporation's income statement for the year ended September 30, 19_8, is presented below:*

BLUFF CORPORATION
Income Statement
For the Year Ended September 30, 19_8

Net sales		$130,000
Cost of goods sold		90,500
Gross margin		$ 39,500
Expenses:		
Salaries	$18,100	
Rent	6,000	
Insurance	800	
Office expense	3,860	28,760
Net income		$ 10,740

Comparative balance sheet data for September 30, 19_7 and 19_8 are presented below:

	September 30,	
	19_8	19_7
Assets:		
Cash	$ 19,680	$17,300
Accounts receivable	22,200	25,640
Merchandise inventory	42,862	27,842
Land	19,000	21,000
	$103,742	$91,782
Equities:		
Accounts payable	$ 7,000	$16,390
Salaries payable	840	630
Common stock	70,000	60,000
Retained earnings	25,902	14,762
	$103,742	$91,782

All accounts payable are for merchandise purchases.
What is the cash provided from operations?

A15-2

The comparative balance sheets for Red Company for December 31, 19_8 and 19_9 are below.

	December 31,		
	19_9	19_8	Change
Working capital	$329,420	$250,600	$78,820
Property, plant, and equipment	94,800	114,800	(20,000)
Accumulated depreciation	(22,960)	(17,220)	(5,740)
	$401,260	$348,180	$53,080
Bonds payable	$160,000	$100,000	$60,000
Bond discount	(7,600)	—	(7,600)
Common stock, $100 par value	140,000	140,000	—
Capital in excess of par	42,000	42,000	—
Retained earnings	66,860	66,180	680
	$401,260	$348,180	$53,080

Additional information: During the year equipment that cost $20,000 and that had a book value of $13,000 was sold for $10,000. On June 30 all of the outstanding bonds payable were called at 103. New ten-year bonds with face value of $160,000 were issued at 95. Cash dividends of $14,000 were paid during the year.

Required:

Prepare T-account working papers used in the preparation of the statement of changes in financial position—working capital basis. Note: Remember to take amortization of bond discount for one-half year.

A15-3

Yellow Tavern Company's after-closing trial balances as of December 31, 19_5 and 19_6 are presented below:

YELLOW TAVERN COMPANY
After-Closing Trial Balances
December 31, 19_6 and 19_5

	December 31,			
	19_6		19_5	
	Debit	Credit	Debit	Credit
Cash	26,250		14,850	
Accounts receivable	16,550		16,140	
Merchandise inventory	24,900		19,800	
Investment in securities	10,000		9,000	
Land	12,500		7,500	
Buildings	63,000		60,000	
Accumulated depreciation—Buildings		11,900		9,750
Equipment	14,000		12,500	
Accumulated depreciation—Equipment		4,100		3,450
Accounts payable		9,500		11,060
Mortgage payable		12,785		17,730
Common stock		100,000		85,000
Capital in excess of par		10,000		8,000
Retained earnings		18,915		4,800
	167,200	167,200	139,790	139,790

All accounts payable are for merchandise purchases. No dividends were declared.
The corporation's income statement for the year ended December 31, 19_6 shows the following:

YELLOW TAVERN COMPANY
Income Statement
For the Year Ended December 31, 19_6

Sales		$209,715
Expenses:		
Cost of goods sold	$160,000	
Depreciation expense—Buildings	2,150	
Depreciation expense—Equipment	650	
Selling expense	22,500	
General expense	9,500	
Interest expense	800	195,600
Net income		$ 14,115

Required:

Prepare the statement of changes in financial position (cash basis).

Staple Company's financial statements are presented below:

STAPLE COMPANY
Income Statement
For the Year Ended December 31, 19_4

Sales		$71,752
Expenses:		
Cost of goods sold	$47,500	
Salaries	6,015	
Rent	3,600	
Insurance	800	
Advertising	2,600	
Office	1,000	
Interest	750	
Depreciation—Building	2,625	
Depreciation—Equipment	550	65,440
Net income		$ 6,312

STAPLE COMPANY
Comparative Balance Sheet
December 31, 19_4 and 19_3

	December 31, 19_4	December 31, 19_3
Cash	$ 8,800	$ 6,600
Accounts receivable	21,350	18,850
Merchandise inventory	22,300	21,200
Prepaid insurance	720	800
Land	10,000	9,000
Buildings	55,000	50,000
Accumulated depreciation—Buildings	(15,125)	(12,500)
Equipment	6,000	5,000
Accumulated depreciation—Equipment	(3,050)	(2,500)
	$105,995	$ 96,450
Accounts payable	$ 21,700	$ 19,767
Interest payable	600	500
Long-term notes payable	—	8,000
Bonds payable	20,000	15,000
Capital stock	46,200	42,000
Retained earnings	17,495	11,183
	$105,995	$ 96,450

Required:

Prepare the statement of changes in financial position—cash basis.

From the following financial statements relating to Blegen Corporation prepare: (a) schedule of working capital and (b) statement of changes in financial position—working capital basis. When information on the causes of the changes in noncurrent accounts is lacking, use your best judgment regarding the probable causes.

BLEGEN CORPORATION
Comparative Balance Sheet
August 31, 19_3 and 19_2

	August 31,	
	19_3	19_2
Assets:		
Cash	$14,600	$13,560
Accounts receivable	11,500	11,810
Merchandise inventory	31,810	31,510
Prepaid insurance	300	300
Long-term investments	8,000	22,000
Land	30,000	9,000
	$96,210	$88,180
Equities:		
Accounts payable	$ 9,610	$ 8,730
Current installment due on bonds payable	4,000	4,000
Bonds payable	5,000	9,000
Capital stock	72,000	60,000
Retained earnings	5,600	6,450
	$96,210	$88,180

BLEGEN CORPORATION
Statement of Retained Earnings
For the Year Ended August 31, 19_3

Balance, August 31, 19_2		$ 6,450
Add:		
Net income[a]		5,730
Total		$12,180
Deduct:		
Stock dividend	$5,000	
Cash dividend	1,580	6,580
Balance, August 31, 19_3		$ 5,600

[a]Includes gain on sale of long-term investments, $300.

Comparative balance sheets of Antietam Company are presented below:

ANTIETAM COMPANY
Comparative Balance Sheet
December 31, 19_8 and 19_7

	December 31,	
	19_8	19_7
Assets:		
Cash	$ 20,000	$ 27,500
Marketable securities	26,200	7,000
Accounts receivable	14,000	13,500
Merchandise inventory	6,000	13,300
Land	15,000	20,000
Buildings	60,000	40,000
Accumulated depreciation—Buildings	(29,600)	(27,600)
Equipment	50,000	30,000
Accumulated depreciation—Equipment	(28,900)	(16,700)
	$132,700	$107,000
Equities:		
Accounts payable	$ 26,790	$ 25,300
Mortgage payable (due December 1, 19_9)	23,000	27,000
Common stock ($100 par)	50,000	30,000
Retained earnings	32,910	24,700
	$132,700	$107,000

All accounts payable are for merchandise purchases. During 19_8, 200 shares of common stock were issued for a new building. The firm's income statement for the year ended December 31, 19_8, shows the following:

ANTIETAM COMPANY
Income Statement
For the Year Ended December 31, 19_8

Net sales		$135,750
Cost of goods sold		85,000
Gross margin		$ 50,750
Operating expenses:		
Salaries expense	$16,650	
Advertising expense	6,700	
Depreciation expense—Buildings	2,000	
Depreciation expense—Equipment	12,200	
Taxes expense	2,500	
Office expense	1,440	
Interest expense	1,050	42,540
Net income		$ 8,210

Required:

Prepare a statement of changes in financial position—cash basis for the year ended December 31, 19_8. (Hint: Do not treat the change in marketable securities as an adjustment of net income.)

Financial statements of Forest Corporation are presented below:

FOREST CORPORATION
Income Statement
For the Year Ended December 31, 19_7

Net sales		$81,971
Cost of goods sold		52,731
Gross margin		$29,240
Expenses:		
Salaries	$7,015	
Rent	4,100	
Depreciation—Building	1,425	
Depreciation—Equipment	650	
Insurance	700	
Advertising	2,100	
Office expense	500	
Interest expense	1,450	17,940
Net income		$11,300

FOREST CORPORATION
Comparative Balance Sheet
December 31, 19_7 and 19_6

	December 31,	
	19_7	19_6
Assets:		
Cash	$ 7,800	$ 7,100
Accounts receivable	24,350	17,850
Merchandise inventory	21,400	20,800
Prepaid insurance	620	600
Land	11,000	8,000
Buildings	56,300	55,000
Accumulated depreciation—Buildings	(16,425)	(15,000)
Equipment	9,000	4,000
Accumulated depreciation—Equipment	(4,050)	(3,500)
	$109,995	$94,850
Equities:		
Accounts payable	$ 22,760	$22,255
Notes payable (nontrade)		9,000
Interest payable	540	400
Bonds payable	21,000	16,000
Capital stock	48,200	41,000
Retained earnings	17,495	6,195
	$109,995	$94,850

What is the cash provided from operations?

B15-2

Following is the comparative balance sheet of January, Inc.:

JANUARY, INC.
Comparative Balance Sheet
December 31, 19_4 and 19_3

	December 31,	
	19_4	19_3
Assets:		
Cash	$ 2,000	$ 4,000
Accounts receivable	9,000	6,750
Land	3,600	2,500
Trademarks	450	400
	$15,050	$13,650
Equities:		
Accounts payable	$ 3,800	$ 3,200
Common stock	9,500	9,000
Retained earnings	1,750	1,450
	$15,050	$13,650

Asset acquisition for cash during the year included land for $600 and trademarks for $50. Stock was issued at par for $500 in exchange for land. Net income for the year was $300.

Required:

(a) A schedule of working capital.

(b) A statement of changes in financial position using a working capital basis.

B15-3

Following are comparative balance sheet data of Klopper Company:

	June 30,	
	19_5	19_4
Debits:		
Cash	$ 800	$ 1,500
Accounts receivable	3,150	2,480
Merchandise inventory	11,300	8,200
Land	4,500	3,300
Goodwill	800	1,600
	$20,550	$17,080
Credits:		
Accounts payable	$ 2,010	$ 1,730
Allowance for uncollectibles	200	110
Bonds payable	1,500	3,000
Capital stock	13,600	11,600
Retained earnings	3,240	640
	$20,550	$17,080

Some of the information regarding the noncurrent accounts is given.

Net income for the year amounted to $3,230.

Dividends were paid totaling $630.

Goodwill was amortized to the extent of $800.

Land was purchased for $1,200.

One-half of the bonds outstanding at the beginning of the year were retired at face.

Prepare:

(a) A schedule of working capital.

(b) A statement of changes in financial position using a working capital basis.

B15-4   *The following information is taken from the general ledger of Sherman, Inc.:*

	December 31,	
	19_5	19_4
Debits:		
Cash	$ 2,800	$ 5,600
Marketable securities	12,700	9,000
Accounts receivable	26,800	22,200
Prepaid rent	2,900	—
Machinery	25,000	25,000
Goodwill	6,000	8,000
	$76,200	$69,800
Credits:		
Accumulated depreciation—Machinery	$18,500	$15,300
Salaries payable	1,300	1,260
Taxes payable	575	510
Common stock	40,000	30,000
Capital in excess of par	4,000	3,000
Retained earnings	11,825	19,730
	$76,200	$69,800

The company's income statement for the year ended December 31, 19_5 is presented below:

SHERMAN, INC.
Income Statement
For the Year Ended December 31, 19_5

Service revenue		$77,396
Expenses:		
Depreciation	$ 3,200	
Rent	15,000	
Salaries	29,600	
Taxes	4,894	
Advertising	19,800	
Utilities	2,692	
Amortization of goodwill	2,000	
Office expense	8,015	85,201
Net loss		$ (7,805)

Required:

Prepare a statement of charges in financial position using the cash basis. (Hint: Do not treat the change in marketable securities as an adjustment of net income.)

B15-5

The change in working capital and various balance sheet accounts of Illinois Company for December 31, 19_8 are as follows:

	Debit	Credit
Working capital	$30,000	
Investments		$15,000
Land	3,000	
Building	25,000	
Machinery	5,000	
Accumulated depreciation—Building	2,000	
Accumulated depreciation—Machinery	1,000	
Bonds payable		30,000
Bond discount	1,500	
Common stock		10,000
Capital in excess of par—Common stock		2,500
Retained earnings		10,000
	$67,500	$67,500

Additional information:

(1) The net income for the year was $20,000.

(2) A cash dividend of $4,000 was distributed to the common stockholders. A stock dividend of 600 shares of $10 par common stock was distributed. Present market price is $10 per share.

(3) The investments were sold at a loss of $2,000.

(4) An old building was sold for $32,000. The historical cost was $50,000 and accumulated depreciation was $20,000. A new building was purchased during the year.

(5) A fully depreciated machine was junked. Historical cost was $10,000. A new machine was purchased for $15,000.

(6) Bonds were issued on December 30, 19_8.

Required:

Prepare a statement of changes in financial position using the working capital basis. Do not prepare a schedule of working capital changes.

B15-6

From the following data and the information provided by the statement below, prepare a schedule of working capital and a statement of changes in financial position using a working capital basis:

Bonds of $200,000 face value were issued at 98 at the beginning of 19_4.
Depreciation and amortization were charged to operations during the year as follows:

By credit to accumulated depreciation accounts:	
Buildings	$12,000
Equipment	13,000
By credit to the asset accounts:	
Containers	$10,000
Patents	4,000
By credit to Discount on Bonds:	
Discount on bonds	$ 400

During the year equipment which cost $20,000 was sold for its book amount, $12,000.
Land that cost $8,000 was sold for $8,600 and an additional parcel was purchased for $18,000.
Investments were sold at their original cost.

ELMER COMPANY
Comparative Balance Sheet
December 31, 19_4 and 19_3

	December 31,	
	19_4	19_3
Assets:		
Cash	$ 14,300	$ 13,000
Accounts receivable	63,200	59,400
Allowance for uncollectibles	(3,000)	(2,400)
Inventory	76,040	76,600
Advances to salesmen	2,000	1,500
Prepaid insurance	500	600
Land	140,000	130,000
Buildings	310,000	220,000
Accumulated depreciation—Buildings	(32,000)	(20,000)
Equipment	220,000	200,000
Accumulated depreciation—Equipment	(27,000)	(22,000)
Containers—less depreciation	44,000	50,000
Patents—less amortization	56,000	60,000
Long-term investments	—	50,000
	$864,040	$816,700
Equities:		
Accounts payable	$ 28,000	$ 71,000
Notes payable	10,000	54,000
Bank loans	—	40,000
Bonds payable—19_8	600,000	400,000
Discount on bonds	(3,600)	—
Capital stock	200,000	200,000
Retained earnings	29,640	51,700
	$864,040	$816,700

Analysis of retained earnings:	
Balance, December 31, 19_3	$51,700
Add:	
Net income—19_4	7,940
Total	$59,640
Deduct:	
Dividends paid	30,000
Balance, December 31, 19_4	$29,640

BASIC CONCEPTS ASSOCIATED WITH MANUFACTURING OPERATIONS
CHAPTER 16

PURPOSE OF CHAPTER   In preceding chapters we have dealt with accounting as applied to firms that buy and sell merchandise (merchandising firms) or provide services (service firms). Manufacturing is another major area of business activity. Manufacturing firms not only buy goods and sell products, but they also engage in the manufacturing (production) process of converting raw materials into finished products. Although the accounting principles and procedures we have previously discussed for merchandising firms are also applicable to manufacturing firms, the manufacturing process requires some additional concepts in order to account for manufacturing firms. These concepts have primarily to do with the measurement, control, and reporting of factory production costs. Consequently, the purpose of this chapter is to acquaint you with some basic concepts of cost accounting for manufacturing operations.

COST OBJECTIVES   Although cost is defined broadly as the money measurement of resources used (foregone or sacrificed) to achieve a specific purpose (objective), the noun cost is usually modified by an adjective (e.g., product cost, direct cost, variable cost, etc.) to make its meaning less ambiguous. Which cost concept is relevant depends on the purpose to be served by the cost information—its cost objective.

A cost objective is the purpose for which costs are measured. In accounting for a manufacturing firm, two fundamental purposes of cost information are:

(1) Product costing.

   The concern here is primarily with gathering and recording financial data for the purpose of preparing financial statements for those outside the firm. That is, product costing is used to determine cost of goods sold (via the cost of goods manufactured) for the income statement and to determine inventory costs for the balance sheet. Also, in product costing, historical costs normally are used and manufacturing costs are kept separate from costs incurred in connection with selling and administrative activity.

(2) Planning and control.

   The aim here is primarily to provide relevant information to management for decision-making purposes. For such purposes the distinction between relevant and irrelevant costs, as well as between variable and fixed costs, is especially useful. These and other cost classifications are discussed in this chapter.

MANUFACTURING COSTS   A merchandising concern buys its goods ready for resale. A manufacturing concern also buys goods, but the goods purchased are raw materials which are not ready for resale. To change the raw materials to finished goods (fully completed goods as to manufacturing) ready for sale requires expenditures for labor and for a great variety of other manufacturing costs. Therefore, provision must be made for accounts in which to record such costs.

The accountant usually views manufacturing costs as consisting of three classes: direct materials (often called raw materials), direct labor, and manufacturing (factory) overhead.

Direct materials are all raw materials that are directly traceable to the finished goods. Those raw materials that enter into and become part of the finished product are obviously direct materials, for they are directly identifiable with the finished goods. Supplies used in the operation of the factory are not classified as direct materials because they do not become part of, nor are they traceable to, the finished product; factory supplies such as glue and screws are classified as indirect materials.

Direct labor is all factory labor that is directly identifiable with the finished product; normally it is that factory labor that converts the direct materials into finished goods. The nature of direct labor can best be understood by contrast with indirect labor. Employees who work on the product with tools, or who operate machines in the process of production, are direct laborers; but superintendents and foremen, who supervise the production process, and janitors and engineers, whose services are incidental to the process of production, are indirect laborers.

Manufacturing (factory) overhead is all factory costs that are not directly traceable to the finished product; hence it includes all manufacturing costs other than direct materials and direct labor. The term *factory overhead cost* is synonymous with indirect manufacturing costs. Examples of manufacturing overhead are indirect labor, indirect materials (e.g., factory supplies), depreciation of the factory buildings and equipment, the power used in production, taxes and expired insurance on the assets used in manufacture, and repairs and upkeep of the factory.

The sum of the direct material and direct labor costs is called *prime cost*. The sum of the prime cost and the indirect cost (factory overhead) is called *full* or *absorption cost*. In other words, full cost is the absorption of all manufacturing cost into units of product.

SELLING AND ADMINISTRATIVE EXPENSES A manufacturing business can incur selling and general and administrative expenses. Such operating expenses must not be commingled with the manufacturing costs. They are not part of the cost of manufacturing a product. As indicated by the illustration on page 498, they are shown in the income statement below gross margin as they are for a merchandising concern.

Financial statements

Statement of cost of goods manufactured Whereas a merchandising firm acquires inventory for resale, a manufacturing firm transforms raw materials through the production process into finished goods ready for sale. The cost of the goods fully completed during the fiscal period is called the cost of goods manufactured.

If all units of product were both started and completed during the period, the cost of goods completed is simply the sum of the costs of direct materials, direct labor, and manufacturing (factory) overhead used to carry on the manufacturing process. Accountants refer to them as "utilized" costs. However, if some goods are only partially completed—called goods (work) in process—at the end of the period, their cost is deducted from the total production costs for the period to determine the cost of the units completed. Similarly, there may have been partially completed goods in process at the beginning of the current period. Any prior period's manufacturing costs applicable to such partially finished goods are added to the current period's production cost to determine the total cost of goods completed in the current period. Therefore, the cost of fully completed goods during a time period (the cost of goods manufactured) is calculated as follows:

$$\begin{pmatrix} \text{Cost of} \\ \text{goods} \\ \text{manufactured} \end{pmatrix} = \underbrace{\begin{pmatrix} \text{Direct} \\ \text{material} \\ \text{cost} \end{pmatrix} + \begin{pmatrix} \text{Direct} \\ \text{labor} \\ \text{cost} \end{pmatrix} + \begin{pmatrix} \text{Factory} \\ \text{overhead} \\ \text{cost} \end{pmatrix}}_{\substack{\text{Production costs utilized} \\ \text{during the current period}}} + \begin{pmatrix} \text{Cost of} \\ \text{beginning} \\ \text{goods in} \\ \text{process} \end{pmatrix} - \begin{pmatrix} \text{Cost of} \\ \text{ending} \\ \text{goods in} \\ \text{process} \end{pmatrix}$$

The above equation is formalized by the statement of cost of goods manufactured, as shown below.

ABC COMPANY
Statement of Cost of Goods Manufactured
For the Year Ended December 31, 19_2

Direct material cost	$ 895,750
Direct labor cost	662,550
Factory overhead cost	441,700
Production cost utilized during period	$2,000,000
Add beginning goods in process, December 31, 19_1	215,250
Total production cost	$2,215,250
Deduct ending goods in process, December 31, 19_2	120,000
Cost of goods manufactured	$2,095,250

ABC COMPANY
Income Statement
For the Year Ended December 31, 19_2

Net sales		$2,955,000
Deduct cost of goods sold:		
Beginning finished goods inventory,		
December 31, 19_1	$ 200,000	
Cost of goods manufactured	2,095,250	
Goods available for sale	$2,295,250	
Deduct ending finished goods inventory,		
December 31, 19_2	170,000	2,125,250
Gross margin		$ 829,750
Operating expenses:		
Selling expense	$ 390,100	
General and administrative expense	259,400	649,500
Net income		$ 180,250
Earnings per common share		$ 1.80

Income statement The income statements of manufacturing companies do not necessarily differ from those of merchandising companies except in one particular: in determining the cost of goods sold, manufacturing companies use the cost of goods manufactured while merchandising companies use the cost of goods purchased, as shown below:

Manufacturing firm

$$\begin{pmatrix} \text{Cost of} \\ \text{goods} \\ \text{sold} \end{pmatrix} = \begin{pmatrix} \text{Cost of} \\ \text{beginning} \\ \text{finished goods} \\ \text{inventory} \end{pmatrix} + \begin{pmatrix} \text{Cost of} \\ \text{goods} \\ \text{manufactured} \end{pmatrix} - \begin{pmatrix} \text{Cost of} \\ \text{ending} \\ \text{finished goods} \\ \text{inventory} \end{pmatrix}$$

Merchandising firm

$$\begin{pmatrix} \text{Cost of} \\ \text{goods} \\ \text{sold} \end{pmatrix} = \begin{pmatrix} \text{Cost of} \\ \text{beginning} \\ \text{merchandise} \\ \text{inventory} \end{pmatrix} + \begin{pmatrix} \text{Cost of} \\ \text{merchandise} \\ \text{purchased} \end{pmatrix} - \begin{pmatrix} \text{Cost of} \\ \text{ending} \\ \text{merchandise} \\ \text{inventory} \end{pmatrix}$$

The equation for the manufacturing firm is formalized in the income statement, as shown on page 498.

Balance sheet The balance sheet of a merchandising firm shows only one merchandise inventory account, and it shows property, plant, and equipment associated with selling and administrative functions only. In contrast, the balance sheet of a manufacturing firm shows three inventory amounts (finished goods, goods in process, and raw materials) and property, plant, and equipment associated with both manufacturing and the selling and administrative functions. A balance sheet for a manufacturing firm follows.

ABC COMPANY
Balance Sheet
December 31, 19_2

. . . .

Assets:			
Current assets:			
Cash		$ 240,000	
Accounts receivable	$ 400,000		
Less allowance for uncollectibles	10,000	390,000	
Inventories:			
Finished goods	$ 170,000		
Goods in process	120,000		
Materials	90,000	380,000	
Prepaid insurance		3,000	$1,013,000
Property, plant, and equipment:			
Land		$ 100,000	
Plant and equipment	$1,350,000		
Less accumulated depreciation	387,500	962,500	1,062,500
			$2,075,500
Equities:			
Current liabilities:			
Accounts payable		$ 228,000	
Salaries and wages payable		67,750	$ 295,750
Stockholders' equity:			
Capital stock		$1,000,000	
Retained earnings		779,750	1,779,750
			$2,075,500

PRODUCT COST Note, in the preceding statement of cost of goods manufactured, that the direct materials, direct labor, and manufacturing overhead costs were not charged directly to expense. During the manufacturing process the services associated with direct labor and factory overhead are utilized in converting direct materials into finished goods. Such conversion increases future economic benefits, in that goods fully or partially completed are worth more than basic raw materials. The increase in future economic benefits justifies the accountant's treatment of direct material, direct labor, and factory overhead costs as assets, not expenses, when the associated services are utilized in production.

The costs of factors used (costs utilized) in manufacturing are called *product costs*. The costs shown in the cost of goods manufactured statement on page 498 are all product costs. Product costs are assets in the form of goods in process or finished goods inventories. When finished goods are sold, the related product costs are treated as expense via cost of goods sold in order to match revenue and expense. The distinction between cost incurred and cost utilized is set forth in the illustration that follows.

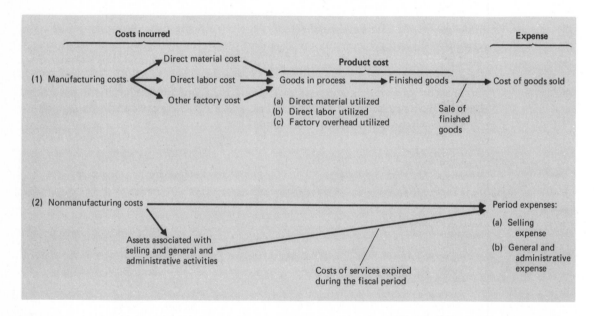

During an accounting period, factory costs incurred probably will not equal product costs because of the time lag between cost incurrence and cost utilization. The cost of raw materials purchased is a factory cost incurred, but it is not a product cost until the raw materials are used in production. The purchase of factory equipment is a factory cost incurred, but not a product cost. When the services of the equipment are utilized in production, then the cost of these services (depreciation) is treated as a product cost via factory overhead cost. On the other hand, there is no time lag between incurrence and utilization in the case of direct labor; therefore, the accountant treats direct labor cost incurred as a product cost immediately.

The statement of cost of goods manufactured, shown on page 498, includes only those costs which are product costs. The income statement, shown on page

498, shows those product costs that have become expense via cost of goods sold. To summarize the distinctions made in the preceding paragraphs:

The items shown in the statement of cost of goods manufactured (page 498) are product costs: the manufacturing costs utilized in production.

The product costs which have reached the status of expense are reported in the income statement (page 498) as cost of goods sold.

The total of the manufacturing costs incurred during a fiscal period is not shown in the traditional financial statements.

The data from the preceding statements plus the manufacturing costs incurred are tied together in the illustration below.

The determination of product cost is generally easier for a merchandising concern than for a manufacturing concern. The accountant for a merchandising concern determines product cost by ascertaining costs of merchandise purchased ready for sale—usually a fairly simple matter. Conceptually, transportation, storage, handling, and like charges are product costs because they can be traced to or associated with the merchandise acquired for sale. If such incidental outlays are not included as part of inventory cost, it is because the amounts involved are insignificant and, therefore, are immediately assigned to expense, for practical reasons.

In contrast, to determine the product costs of a manufacturing company can be a most complex matter. First, it must be decided which of the many and varied costs incurred can be traced to or associated with the manufacturing activity. For example, is some part of the salary of the company's president a manufacturing cost and hence a product cost? Is some part of the cost of operating the personnel department a product cost? If so, how is the share determined? In short, to classify costs and expenses by such broad categories as manufacturing, selling, and general and administrative, though a necessary task since selling expenses and general and administrative expenses are not product costs, may not be an easy task. Many activities carried on by a business can be said to contribute in some measure to more than one of the three categories noted above. These costs must be distrib-

ASSETS

Manufacturing costs incurred		Manufacturing costs utilized	Product cost	Cost of goods manufactured	Cost of finished goods	Cost of goods sold (expense)
Raw materials purchased	$950,000	Raw materials used	$ 895,750			
Direct labor cost	662,550	Direct labor cost	662,550			
Other factory costs	900,000	Factory overhead cost	441,700			
(e.g. factory plant		Production cost utilized				
and equipment acquired		during current period	$2,000,000 ──→	$2,000,000		
and factory prepayments)		Add cost of beginning goods				
		in process inventory		215,250		
		Total production cost		$2,215,250		
		Deduct cost of ending goods				
		in process inventory		120,000		
		Cost of goods manufactured		$2,095,250 ──→	$2,095,250	
		Add cost of beginning finished				
		goods inventory			200,000	
		Goods available for sale (included				
		in product costs until sold)			$2,295,250	
		Deduct cost of ending finished				
		goods inventory			170,000	
					$2,125,250 ──→	$2,125,250

uted if the cost of goods manufactured is to be shown. Such cost distributions require judgment and practical considerations. As a result, the amounts reported in the financial statements for inventories and for cost of goods sold should be recognized as approximations.

PRODUCTION AND SERVICE DEPARTMENTS   Most manufacturing companies are divided into production departments and service departments. In a production department, work is done directly on the products manufactured. The segmentation of the factory into production departments usually is based on (1) types of products produced (Department 1 produces ball-point pens and Department 2 produces pencils); (2) kinds of manufacturing processes used (preparation department, assembly department, and finishing department); or (3) product components (one department produces the barrels and another department produces the caps for ball-point pens).

In contrast to production departments, service departments provide services that aid other departments of the firm. Although the service departments do not provide direct work on the products manufactured, they provide services necessary for the producing departments to function properly. Examples of service departments include the maintenance department, the personnel department, and the company cafeteria.

Each production and service department is a *cost center*—an area of operating activity for which responsibility can be assigned for the work performed and the costs incurred. The assignment of costs to departments may improve the operating performance of a business because it facilitates the fixing of responsibility for various functions. Thus to treat the department as a cost center is useful for both planning and control purposes, as discussed in Chapter 21 dealing with responsibility accounting.

Departments are also useful for purposes of income determination and product costing. As products pass through production departments, they must have departmental costs assigned to them to provide the data necessary for preparation of financial statements. Also, departmental costs may show whether a company's product pricing policy is in line with its costs.

FACTORY OVERHEAD ALLOCATION TO DEPARTMENTS   Generally it is not difficult to assign direct material and direct labor costs to departments and to products. Problems do arise when the indirect factory overhead costs are assigned to departments and thus to products. Because factory overhead costs are not readily identifiable with departments, they are allocated (prorated) to the departments by an averaging process:

$$\text{Allocation rate} = \frac{\text{Total of one item of overhead cost to be allocated}}{\text{Allocation base}}$$

$$\begin{matrix} \text{Overhead cost allocated} \\ \text{to a department} \end{matrix} = \begin{matrix} \text{Allocation} \\ \text{rate} \end{matrix} \times \begin{matrix} \text{Amount of allocation base} \\ \text{in the department} \end{matrix}$$

The allocation plan should be based on a logical relationship between the cost to be allocated and some measure (base) that, hopefully, is indicative of benefits received or to be received by each production and service department. Possible allocation bases for certain items of manufacturing overhead are shown in the distribution schedule on page 503. For example, in the distribution schedule the

ABC COMPANY
Manufacturing Overhead Distribution Schedule
For the Year Ended December 31, 19_2

Item	Total Amount	Production Departments			Service Department— Maintenance	Basis of Distribution
		Dept. A	Dept. B	Dept. C		
Primary allocation:						
Indirect labor	$153,250	$ 81,250	$ 36,000	$ 36,000	$ —	Payroll data
Heat, light, and power	30,000	11,000	7,000	8,000	4,000	Cubic space
Machinery repairs and maintenance	67,950	—	—	—	67,950	Direct
Depreciation:						
Building	32,000	12,000	8,000	10,000	2,000	Floor space used
Machinery and equipment	60,000	20,000	14,000	18,000	8,000	Time used
Insurance premiums expired	8,500	4,100	2,200	1,400	800	Insurable value of assets
Property taxes	12,000	6,000	3,000	2,000	1,000	Assessed valuation
Factory supplies used	42,000	14,000	14,000	14,000	—	Equally among production departments
Miscellaneous factory costs	36,000	9,000	9,000	9,000	9,000	Equally
Total manufacturing overhead	$441,700	$157,350	$ 93,200	$ 98,400	$92,750	
Secondary allocation:						
Distribution of service department cost to production departments	—	37,650	23,000	32,100	92,750*	Hours worked for production departments
Total distributed to production departments	$441,700	$195,000	$116,200	$130,500		

*Deduction.

factory depreciation on machinery and equipment is allocated (assuming that each department shares the same machinery and equipment) according to the time the machinery and equipment is used in each department, as shown below with regard to Department A.

$$Allocation\ rate = \frac{Total\ depreciation\ cost\ of\ machinery\ and\ equipment}{Total\ time\ machinery\ and\ equipment\ used}$$

$$\$3\ per\ hour = \frac{\$60,000}{20,000\ hours}$$

$$\begin{matrix} Depreciation\ cost \\ allocated \\ to\ Department\ A \end{matrix} = \begin{matrix} Allocation \\ rate \end{matrix} \times \begin{matrix} Actual\ length\ of\ time\ the\ machinery\ and \\ equipment\ are\ used\ in\ Department\ A \end{matrix}$$

$$\$20,000\ (rounded) = \$3 \times 6666\ hours$$

Once the factory overhead costs have been allocated to the production departments (primary allocation), the service department costs are allocated to the production departments (secondary allocation). This secondary allocation is necessary because no products are produced by service departments and, therefore, service department costs cannot be *directly* assigned to products. Because products are manufactured by the production departments, all manufacturing costs (both production and service department costs) are assigned to the production departments. In other words, service department costs are *indirect* costs of the product (factory overhead) and are allocated on the basis of benefits received by the production departments from the service departments. The total cost of each service department is related to a base, such as hours worked for the production departments, and the resulting rate is used to allocate the service department cost to the production departments (see illustration above allocating the maintenance cost to the production departments).

ALLOCATION OF ACTUAL FACTORY OVERHEAD TO PRODUCTS After the service department costs have been allocated to the production departments, the actual factory overhead costs are totaled for each production department. In the preceding illustration the departmental totals were:

Department	Actual factory overhead
A	$195,000
B	116,200
C	130,500

These costs must, in turn, be assigned to the products which pass through the departments.

Assume that 3,250 units of product were manufactured in Department A during 19_2. Returning to the illustration, the actual factory overhead cost per unit for that department is $60 ($195,000 ÷ 3,250 units).

APPLYING FACTORY OVERHEAD COST TO PRODUCTS Because it takes time to accumulate and allocate factory overhead following the procedures just described, accurate data about departmental costs and product unit cost would not be available promptly. Such delay would, in turn, delay the preparation of financial statements, whether prepared monthly, quarterly, or annually, because product unit cost data are needed to determine the cost of goods sold and the goods in process and finished goods inventories. To overcome such delay, accountants may use an approximation method involving factory overhead rates based on planned (budgeted) factory overhead. The determination of such an overhead rate is illustrated below. It relates to Department A of ABC Company.

$$Overhead\ rate = \frac{Budgeted\ factory\ overhead}{Budgeted\ direct\ labor\ hours}$$

$$\$4 = \frac{\$200,000}{50,000\ (hours)}$$

The denominator, or application base, used in the computation of the rate is some type of business activity that is logically related to factory overhead. The base used in the example, direct labor hours, is suitable if it is reasonable to believe, in the given circumstances, that a change in the number of direct labor hours used in the production process would be accompanied by a similar change in factory overhead.

The amounts used in the determination of the factory overhead rate are based on some concept of expected business activity. For the determination of such expected amounts, reliance on expected annual activity for the coming year would be acceptable.

To illustrate the use of overhead rates, assume that 49,000 direct labor hours were used in Department A during the year following the establishment of the

$4 overhead rate. The overhead applied to products manufactured in the department would amount to $196,000 ($4 × 49,000 hours). If 3,250 units of product were produced in Department A, the applied factory overhead cost per unit would be $60.31 ($196,000 ÷ 3,250).

At the $4 application rate, $196,000 of factory overhead would be applied to the production of Department A and unit cost data would be available without delay. Should it develop that the *actual* factory overhead for the year differed from the amount applied, which would be the usual case, an adjustment for the difference would be required. Such disposition of the underapplied or overapplied factory overhead cost is discussed in Chapter 19.

To further illustrate applied factory overhead cost, assume that the following data pertain to two different products manufactured in Department A:

Product #1—25,000 actual direct labor hours used, 2,000 units produced
Product #2—24,000 actual direct labor hours used, 1,250 units produced

Assuming a $4 applied factory overhead rate per direct labor hours, the factory overhead cost *applied* to the products manufactured in Department A is as follows:

	Total amount	Per unit
Product #1:		
Total applied overhead ($4 × 25,000)	$100,000	
Applied overhead per unit ($100,000 ÷ 2,000)		$50.00
Product #2:		
Total applied overhead ($4 × 24,000)	96,000	
Applied overhead per unit ($96,000 ÷ 1,250)		76.80
Total applied overhead ($4 × 49,000) Department A	$196,000	

Referring to the preceding discussion, the $4 overhead rate is called an *applied* overhead rate and the $196,000 estimated factory overhead cost is called *applied* factory overhead cost. In accounting jargon, the term "applied factory overhead cost" generally refers to *estimated* factory overhead cost, *not* actual factory overhead cost, allocated to products.

VARIABLE AND FIXED COSTS AND EXPENSES   *Variable cost* is that part of total cost that varies in direct proportion to changes in *production* volume, assuming a relevant production volume range. As production volume changes, total variable cost changes proportionately so that the variable cost per unit produced remains constant. Stated in other words, variable cost per unit does not change with changes in production volume. For example, suppose that production is at 10,000 units when total variable cost is $30,000. A 10 per cent increase in volume (10% of 10,000) to 11,000 units causes total variable cost to change proportionately (10% of $30,000) to $33,000; however, note that at both the 10,000 and 11,000 volume levels the variable cost per unit remains constant at $3 ($30,000 ÷ 10,000 units and $33,000 ÷ 11,000 units). Thus, total variable cost and variable cost per unit are graphed as follows:

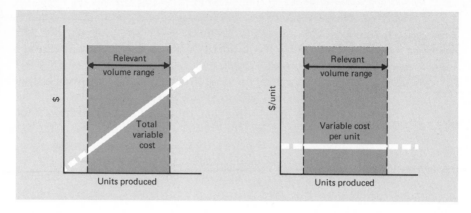

The proportionate change in total variable cost with changes in production volume is assumed only over a company's normal operating range of volume—the relevant range. At unusually high and low production volume levels, total variable costs may not change proportionately. For example, direct labor is normally a variable cost, but at an extremely high level of production volume the addition of more workers may not increase production volume proportionately because of the crowded working conditions. Also, even over the relevant volume range the concept of proportionate changes in total variable cost is an approximation that holds only on the average.

Variable expense is that part of total expense that varies in direct proportion to changes in *sales* volume, assuming a relevant sales volume range. Whereas variable *cost* varies with changes in production volume, variable *expense* varies with changes in sales volume. Sales volume can be measured either in dollars or in quantities (units) sold.

Graphically, variable expense looks the same as variable cost (see above) except that the horizontal axis is stated in terms of sales volume (not units produced).

Fixed cost is that part of total cost that remains constant as *production* volume changes, assuming a relevant production volume range and a short-run time period. Fixed costs include such costs as the salaries of factory executives, straight-line depreciation on factory plant and equipment, and factory rent on a long-term lease.

Given a long enough time period, all costs are variable; hence, fixed costs exist only in the short run. For example, factory rent cost is fixed only for the term of the lease. Straight-line depreciation is fixed only for the useful life of the factory equipment. The salary of a factory executive is fixed until his or her contract expires or possibly until top management takes an action changing it.

The short run is a period of time that is not long enough to permit a company to increase production volume by acquiring additional capacity. Capacity is the company's upper limit of output brought about by existing plant and equipment, management, and financing. Over the short run, a company operates with given capacity because capacity can be changed only over a long period of time; therefore, the costs related to capacity normally are fixed costs in the short run. Thus short-run increases in production volume result in increased variable costs with fixed costs remaining constant.

With a constant total fixed cost, the greater the production volume the smaller the fixed cost per unit of volume. The total fixed cost is spread over more units as production volume increases and fixed cost per unit decreases. If factory depreciation is $10,000 annually, then with production of 5,000 units the fixed cost per unit is $2 ($10,000 ÷ 5,000); with 8,000 units, fixed cost per unit is $1.25 ($10,000 ÷ 8,000); and with 10,000 units it is $1 per unit. Consequently, total fixed cost and fixed cost per unit are graphed as shown below.

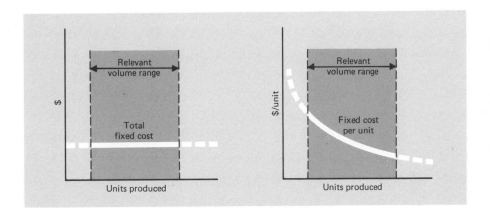

Besides assuming a short-run time period, the concept of fixed cost also assumes a normal operating range of volume (the relevant range). Over the relevant range, changes in production volume have no effect on fixed costs because capacity usually is not affected. However, at extreme production volume levels, total fixed cost may not remain constant. An extreme increase in output may necessitate changes in plant and equipment and cause changes in total fixed costs.

Fixed expense is that part of total expense that remains constant as *sales* volume changes, assuming a relevant sales volume range and a short-run time period. Fixed period expenses include the annual salaries of administrative and sales executives and the straight-line depreciation on the salesmen's cars and on office equipment. Graphically, fixed expense looks the same as fixed cost (see above), except that the horizontal axis is stated in terms of units sold (not units produced).

RELEVANT COSTS AND EXPENSES When costs and expenses are used for decision making, it is important to exclude those costs and expenses that are not relevant to the particular decision at hand. A cost or an expense is relevant if it is *different* under the given alternatives and if it is a *future* cost or expense. For example, if factory depreciation remains constant no matter whether a new product line is added or not, then depreciation is irrelevant to the decision to add the new product. Similarly, a cost that has already occurred cannot be revoked and has no effect on a particular decision today, except possibly for tax purposes. For example, the fact that a company paid $100,000 for factory equipment five years ago is irrelevant to the decision to buy new equipment today.

The concept of relevant costs and expenses is explained more fully in Chapter 21.

SUMMARY OF COST AND EXPENSE CLASSIFICATIONS The cost and expense concepts previously discussed are summarized below.

I. Function
    (1) Manufacturing costs
    (2) Selling expenses
    (3) General and administrative expenses

II. Traceability
    (1) Direct costs
       (a) Direct materials
       (b) Direct labor
    (2) Indirect costs
       (a) Factory overhead cost

III. Timing of recognition of expense
    (1) Product cost
    (2) Period expense

IV. Departmental costs
    (1) Production department costs
    (2) Service department costs

V. Volume changes
    (1) Production volume
       (a) Variable cost
       (b) Fixed cost
    (2) Sales volume
       (a) Variable expense
       (b) Fixed expense

VI. Decision making
    (1) Relevant costs and expenses
    (2) Irrelevant costs and expenses

IMPORTANT TERMS AND CONCEPTS IN CHAPTER 16

Ending materials inventory	$ 50,000
Equipment	1,000,000
General and administrative expenses	61,000
Income taxes payable	52,000
Ending goods in process inventory	100,000
Retained earnings	270,000
Net sales	700,000
Accounts receivable	300,000
Labor utilized	206,000
Common stock	800,000
Beginning goods in process inventory	49,000
Selling expenses	134,000
Ending finished goods inventory	60,000
Allowance for uncollectibles	55,000
Factory overhead utilized	150,000
Beginning finished goods inventory	40,000
Accumulated depreciation	400,000
Accounts payable	28,000
Materials utilized	35,000
Cash	95,000

INSTRUCTIONS Given the above data, prepare (a) a statement of cost of goods manufactured, (b) an income statement, and (c) a balance sheet. Note: Attempt to solve this demonstration problem before examining the solution that follows.

Solution:
(a)

MAURER COMPANY
Statement of Cost of Goods Manufactured
For the Year Ended December 31, 19_3

Direct materials cost	$ 35,000
Direct labor cost	206,000
Factory overhead cost	150,000
Production cost utilized during period	$391,000
Add beginning goods in process	49,000
Total production cost	$440,000
Deduct ending goods in process	100,000
Cost of goods manufactured	$340,000

(b)

MAURER COMPANY
Income Statement
For the Year Ended December 31, 19_3

Net sales		$700,000
Cost of goods sold:		
Beginning finished goods inventory	$ 40,000	
Cost of goods manufactured	340,000	
Goods available for sale	$380,000	
Deduct ending finished goods inventory	60,000	320,000
Gross margin		$380,000
Operating expenses:		
Selling expense	$134,000	
General and administrative expense	61,000	195,000
Net income before taxes		$185,000
Income taxes		52,000
Net income after taxes		$133,000

(c)

MAURER COMPANY
Balance Sheet
December 31, 19_3

Assets:		
Current assets:		
Cash		$ 95,000
Accounts receivable	$ 300,000	
Less allowance for uncollectibles	55,000	245,000
Inventories:		
Finished goods	$ 60,000	
Goods in process	100,000	
Materials	50,000	210,000
Property, plant, and equipment:		
Equipment	$1,000,000	
Less accumulated depreciation	400,000	600,000
Total assets		$1,150,000
Equities:		
Current liabilities:		
Accounts payable	$ 28,000	
Income taxes payable	52,000	$ 80,000
Stockholders' equity:		
Common stock	$ 800,000	
Retained earnings	270,000	1,070,000
Total equities		$1,150,000

ASSIGNMENT MATERIAL

Questions

1. What is wrong with a narrow definition of cost?
2. What is the difference between the balance sheet of a merchandising firm and the balance sheet of a manufacturing firm?
3. What is the difference between the income statement of a merchandising firm and the income statement of a manufacturing firm?
4. Why do accountants make the distinction between product costs and period expenses?
5. How can depreciation be an expense to a merchandising firm and a cost (asset) to a manufacturing firm?
6. Why is it necessary to allocate service department costs to production departments? Is such allocation useful for decision making?
7. Other than labor costs, why do manufacturing costs incurred tend to differ from manufacturing costs utilized? Why do labor costs incurred normally equal labor costs utilized?
8. How should the accountant select a base for allocating factory overhead cost to departments? to products?
9. What is the difference between variable cost and variable expense? between fixed cost and fixed expense? Why is the distinction between cost and expense important?
10. What is the concept of the short-run time period and why is it important?
11. What are the two ways in which the term "relevant" is used in this chapter?
12. Would the calculation of cost of goods sold by a merchandising firm illustrated in this chapter be performed primarily by a firm utilizing the perpetual inventory method or the periodic inventory method?

Short exercises

E16-1 *Classify the following items as either (a) direct materials cost, (b) direct labor cost, (c) manufacturing overhead cost, or (d) selling and administrative expense, by writing the appropriate letter in the space provided.*

___c___ 0. Factory foreman's salary

_____ 1. Depreciation on office equipment

_____ 2. Salary of janitor who cleans the factory building

_____ 3. Metal used in production

_____ 4. Salaries of factory machine operators

_____ 5. Salesmen's commissions

_____ 6. Glue, nails, screws, and bolts used in production

_____ 7. Freight charges on products sold

511

_____ 8. Overtime premium on factory wages

_____ 9. Employer's F.I.C.A. taxes on factory workers

E16-2 *What is wrong with the following statement of cost of goods manufactured?*

BALDERSON COMPANY
Statement of Cost of Goods Manufactured
December 31, 19_6

Direct materials cost	$ 200,000
Direct labor cost	400,000
Manufacturing overhead cost	300,000
Production cost utilized during period	$ 900,000
Add beginning finished goods, December 31, 19_5	700,000
Total production cost	$1,600,000
Deduct ending finished goods, December 31, 19_6	600,000
Cost of goods manufactured	$1,000,000

E16-3 *Denault Company uses an applied factory overhead rate based on budgeted machine hours. It was estimated at the beginning of the year that total factory overhead cost and machine hours would be $700,000 and 100,000, respectively, for the current fiscal year. If 25,000, 20,000, 15,000, and 55,000 machine hours were used in the company's four production departments during the year, what was the applied factory overhead for each department? If 15,000 units of the 25,000 units of product produced in Department #1 were sold, what was the applied factory overhead cost allocated to ending inventory and to the units sold for Department #1?*

E16-4 *V-Reeble Company produced 250,000 units and sold 200,000 units of a product during the current year (no beginning inventory). The total cost to produce the product was $2,550,000, which included total fixed costs of $1,500,000.*

(a) What was the variable cost per unit? Show all your work.

(b) What was the total variable *expense* for the year?

(c) What was the fixed cost per unit?

(d) What was the total fixed *expense* for the year?

(e) What was the difference between variable cost per unit and variable expense per unit? between fixed cost per unit and fixed expense per unit?

E16-5 *You are given below three multiple-choice statements. Select the correct answers and indicate the corresponding letters on a sheet of paper (e.g., 1-a, 2-a, etc.).*

(1) The major distinction between a manufacturing firm and a merchandising firm is that (a) the former deals in wholesale goods and the latter in retail goods, (b) the former transforms raw materials into finished goods before they are sold and the latter does not, (c) the former sells raw materials and the latter sells finished goods, (d) the former only manufactures goods and the latter only sells goods, (e) none of the above.

(2) Wages paid to factory supervisors should be classified as (a) direct labor, (b) direct materials, (c) manufacturing overhead, (d) administrative expenses, (e) none of the above.

(3) Full or absorption cost is equivalent to (a) prime cost, (b) the sum of direct materials and direct labor, (c) factory overhead, (d) the sum of prime costs and variable manufacturing overhead, (e) none of the above.

You are given below three multiple-choice statements. Select the correct answers and indicate the corresponding letters on a sheet of paper (e.g., 1-a, 2-a, etc.).

(1) For a given period the cost of goods manufactured is equal to the cost of goods sold if (a) there are no beginning and ending inventories of finished goods, (b) there are no beginning and ending inventories of raw materials, (c) the beginning and ending inventories of goods in process are equal, (d) none of the above.

(2) All manufacturing costs may be classified as (a) supplies, indirect labor, or factory overhead; (b) direct materials, direct labor, or indirect labor; (c) raw materials, goods in process, or finished goods; (d) direct materials, direct labor, or factory overhead; (e) none of the above.

(3) The proper sequence for allocating manufacturing overhead is (a) to the product and then to the cost center; (b) to the production department and then to the service department; (c) to the cost center, from service departments to production departments, and then to the product; (d) to the product and then to the service departments, if necessary; (e) none of the above.

Problems

A16-1

The data below pertain to Panton Company for the fiscal year ended December 31, 19_2. Note that the data are not in any particular sequence, but are all mixed up. You are asked to prepare a cost of goods manufactured statement and an income statement. In the preparation of the income statement, show the component parts of the cost of goods sold section.

Selling expenses	$100,000
Beginning goods in process inventory	250,000
Ending finished goods inventory	600,000
Direct material cost	150,000
General and administrative expenses	80,000
Ending goods in process inventory	200,000
Factory overhead cost	180,000
Beginning finished goods inventory	500,000
Direct labor cost	200,000
Net sales	600,000
10,000 shares of common stock were outstanding for the entire year	

A16-2

You are given cost data below that are used in calculating cost of goods manufactured. However, some cost data are missing, as indicated by the question marks. You are to solve for the missing data and in so doing to show all your calculations, not just the final answers. Note that the three sets of costs given below (see columns a, b, and c) are unrelated to one another. Ignore the dashes (—) in each column.

	(a)	(b)	(c)
Cost of goods manufactured	$?	$630,000	$?
Ending goods in process inventory	80,000	100,000	—
Factory overhead cost	60,000	150,000	?
Direct material cost	55,000	?	50,000
Production cost utilized during period	—	?	150,000
Beginning goods in process inventory	?	120,000	—
Direct labor cost	80,000	300,000	60,000
Total production cost	310,000	—	—
Decrease in goods in process inventory	—	—	10,000

A16-3   *You are given data for the year 19_1 for Gordon Company.*

	19_1
Total manufacturing costs	$500,000
Fixed manufacturing costs	200,000
Units produced (no goods in process inventories)	10,000
Units sold	9,000

Using the relationships from the above data, you are asked to predict costs and expense (cost of goods sold) for the next year (19_2) if production and sales are expected to be 15,000 and 16,000 units, respectively. Specifically, you are asked to determine for the year 19_2 the following (show your calculations):

(a) Variable cost per unit.   (c) Total fixed cost.

(b) Total variable cost.   (d) Cost of goods sold.

A16-4   *You are given below an abbreviated listing of expenditures made by Radosevich Company, followed by some possible ways each expenditure could be classified.*

(1) Payment for three-year rental of factory equipment

(2) Direct materials and labor utilized

(3) Salesmen's travel

(4) Purchase of factory materials

(5) General office salaries

(6) Employer's payroll taxes for factory workers

(7) Overtime paid to factory workers

(8) Factory fire insurance for the fiscal year

(9) Shipping supplies used

(10) Rework of defective product by factory workers

(11) President's salary

(12) Total outlay for advertising allowed

Factory Cost Incurred	Factory Cost Utilized		Expense	
	Variable	Fixed	Variable	Fixed
A	B	C	D	E

List the expenditures by number, and after each number write a letter (A,B,C,D, or E) indicating the classification you think should be selected for that particular expenditure. Also explain why you selected the classification for each expenditure.

A16-5

An incomplete manufacturing overhead distribution schedule for Young Company is presented below.

| | Total Cost | Service Departments | | Producing Departments | |
		Maintenance	Cafeteria	Dept. #1	Dept. #2
Indirect materials and labor	$1,300,000	$90,000	$60,000	$500,000	$650,000
Factory depreciation (based on square footage)	189,000				
Property taxes (based on book value)	100,000				
Insurance	22,950				
Power	2,080				
Sundry factory costs	8,000				
	$1,622,030				
Distribution of service departments to production departments:					
Maintenance	—				
Cafeteria	—				
	$1,622,030				

The above overhead costs can be allocated to the departments based on the data below:

Basis of allocation	Maintenance	Cafeteria	#1	#2
Kilowatt hours used ($.08 per kw. hours used)	5,000	4,000	7,000	10,000
Maintenance hours worked in production departments			4,000	6,000
Book value (5% of book value)	$200,000	$400,000	$600,000	$ 800,000
Value of assets ($.90 per $100 value of assets)	$300,000	$450,000	$800,000	$1,000,000
Number of employees using cafeteria			22	28
Square footage used	2,000	3,000	4,000	5,000
Sundry	1/8	3/8	2/8	2/8

Required:

(a) Complete the manufacturing overhead distribution schedule.

(b) If overhead is applied to the production in the two producing departments on the basis of $15 per direct labor hour used, what is the difference between actual (derived in part (a) of problem) and applied factory overhead for the two producing departments? Assume that 45,000 and 66,000 direct labor hours were used in Departments #1 and #2, respectively.

(c) Show how the rate of $.08 per kilowatt hour was derived.

B16-1

For the year 19_1, Havoc Company manufactured 4,600 finished units of product. There were no goods in process inventories. During the year, $50,000 of raw materials were purchased and $30,000 worth were issued to production. Factory labor costs were $60,000. On January 1, 19_1, new equipment for the factory was acquired at a cost of $200,000. The useful life of the equipment was estimated to be 10 years, with no expected salvage value, and the equipment was to be depreciated on a straight-line basis. On July 1, 19_1, $20,000 was paid for two years' rental service of specialized factory equipment needed by the company. The fiscal period for the company ends December 31.

Required:

(a) What was the total factory cost incurred and the total factory cost utilized for the year 19_1?

(b) If 3,000 units were sold during 19_1 (assume no beginning finished goods inventory), what was the cost of goods sold and the cost of the ending finished goods inventory for the year 19_1?

B16-2

Financial data for Berger Company for the year 19_1 are presented below:

Ending materials inventory	$ 50,000
Equipment	1,000,000
General and administrative expenses	61,000
Income taxes payable	52,000
Ending goods in process inventory	49,000
Retained earnings	219,000
Net sales	700,000
Accounts receivable	300,000
Labor utilized	206,000
Common stock	800,000
Beginning goods in process inventory	100,000
Selling expenses	134,000
Ending finished goods inventory	60,000
Allowance for uncollectibles	55,000
Factory overhead utilized	150,000
Beginning finished goods inventory	40,000
Accumulated depreciation	400,000
Accounts payable	28,000
Materials utilized	35,000
Cash	95,000

Given the above data, you are asked to prepare (a) a statement of cost of goods manufactured, (b) an income statement, and (c) a balance sheet.

B16-3

A fire destroyed most of the accounting records of Sample Company, but the following cost data were saved:

Ending finished goods inventory	$ 50,000
Labor utilized	300,000
Cost of goods sold	890,000
Materials utilized	250,000
Decrease in finished goods inventory	135,000
Ending materials inventory	50,000
Factory overhead utilized	280,000
Materials purchased	240,000
Ending goods in process inventory	180,000

Using the above incomplete data, (a) determine the beginning inventory costs for materials, goods in process, and finished goods, and (b) prepare a schedule of cost of goods sold. Show all of your calculations in arriving at your final figures. (Hint: Try working backwards from the given cost of goods sold figure.)

B16-4

Brooks Manufacturing Company produces one product. The chief accountant for the firm, Bill Woods, is worried that the monthly financial statements are misleading because of seasonal variations in factory overhead costs and in production. He believes that the company should use an estimated *annual factory overhead rate in applying overhead to production. His analysis shows that direct labor hours and factory overhead cost tend to move together; hence, he recommends using an annual overhead rate of $5 per direct labor hour.*

In order to present his case to management, he asks you to (a) compute actual monthly overhead rates (actual factory overhead cost divided by direct labor hours); (b) compute the monthly and the total applied factory overhead cost ($5 rate times direct labor hours); (c) compare the monthly and total applied factory overhead to the monthly and total actual factory overhead; and (d) make recommendations, based on your analysis, as to whether the company should use the annual factory overhead rate.

The accountant provides you with the worksheet below to make your analysis.

Months	Direct labor hours	Actual factory overhead cost	Monthly overhead rate	Applied factory overhead cost	Difference between actual and applied
January	9,000	$ 63,000			
February	11,000	71,500			
March	13,000	81,250			
April	15,000	90,000			
May	17,000	93,500			
June	21,000	105,000			
July	31,000	147,250			
August	41,000	153,750			
September	33,000	140,250			
October	19,000	85,500			
November	15,000	83,000			
December	11,000	66,000			
	236,000	$1,180,000		$	$

B16-5

Simmons Manufacturing Company has been using actual factory overhead cost in costing its two products. However, the chief accountant has pointed out that the monthly financial statements are misleading because of seasonal variations in actual factory overhead cost and in production. The chief accountant recommends that the company use an estimated annual overhead rate for applying factory overhead cost to production. The chief accountant has gathered the following representative data to determine the applied overhead rate to use:

	Production department #1	Production department #2	Total
Factory overhead costs (includes service department costs)	$600,000	$800,000	$1,400,000
Direct labor hours	20,000	200,000	220,000
Machine hours	100,000	20,000	120,000

Required:

(a) Compute factory overhead rates based on direct labor hours and machine hours for each production department.

(b) Compute plant wide factory overhead rates (both departments combined) based on direct labor hours and machine hours.

(c) Present your arguments as to the factory overhead rate or rates that you think Clark Manufacturing Company should use.

MANUFACTURING COST SYSTEMS: JOB ORDER COSTING
CHAPTER 17

PURPOSE OF CHAPTER In the preceding chapter it was pointed out that in accounting for a manufacturing firm the two fundamental purposes of cost data are for product costing and for planning and control. A manufacturing cost system is a method used to collect manufacturing cost data and to assign such data to meet these two basic cost objectives. Cost systems that collect manufacturing cost data within the framework of the general ledger accounts and assign such costs to manufactured products are designed to meet the objective of product costing (i.e., inventory valuation and income determination). The collecting of cost data from original source documents and daily or weekly summaries thereof provide much of the needed cost data for planning and control purposes, even though such data gathering is usually not integrated into the general ledger.

The purpose of this chapter is to describe the job order manufacturing cost system used for product costing purposes and the underlying source documents that can be used to provide cost data for planning and control purposes.

THE NEED FOR COST ACCOUNTING SYSTEMS As a general rule, a manufacturing concern is engaged in the production and marketing of more than one kind of product. Also, as a general rule, several kinds of raw materials are used, and the manufacturing process comprises several distinct production steps. In short, the business activity associated with manufacturing operations often is neither simple nor of the size that would be described as a "small" business. If it were necessary to make a physical count of the inventories and to develop unit cost data each time financial statements were prepared, management would no doubt have some reservations about the adequacy of such an accounting system in any situation of even moderate size and complexity.

The discussion and illustrations in the preceding chapter referred to beginning and ending inventories of goods in process and finished goods. If these inventories are determined by physical count, the *periodic inventory* method is being used. If day-by-day inventory records are kept of the inventory inflows, outflows, and current balances, then a *perpetual inventory* method is being used. Under the periodic inventory method, until the ending inventories are determined by physical count, data needed for the preparation of financial statements are not available. Under the perpetual inventory method, inventory taking need not precede the preparation of financial statements because the required data are available in the accounts. However, physical inventory counts should be made from time to time, at least annually, as a check on the accuracy of the perpetual inventory records.

Because of its advantages, most large manufacturing firms use the perpetual inventory method. Here are some of its advantages:

(1) Perpetual inventory records provide timely cost data for managerial decision making. For example, management decisions with regard to the quantity of materials needed to be purchased, the cash needed for the purchase of materials, and the goods in process and finished goods inventory levels to be maintained are facilitated by up-to-date information about inventories on hand.

(2) The preparation of interim financial statements (statements prepared during the year, e.g., monthly) is facilitated because the inventory figures are readily available without investing the time and expense required for a physical count.

(3) The quantities of inventory that should be on hand are shown, thereby reducing the likelihood of unexplained disappearances in inventories.

(4) As shown later in the chapter, perpetual inventory records provide information about the costs required to make the general ledger transfers from Materials Inventory to Goods in Process, to Finished Goods, and to Cost of Goods Sold.

The fundamental procedures of cost accounting will become apparent from a description of job order accounting in this chapter and of process cost accounting in the next chapter.

JOB ORDER COSTING   Job order or specific order cost accounting is characterized by the accumulation of production costs by separate and distinct jobs. This system is particularly suitable for firms that manufacture according to specific customer orders or for stock (i.e., manufacturing for inventory purposes with sales made out of stock on hand). For example, a furniture manufacturer may receive an order for one custom-made chair, and the company would assign an order number to the job and accumulate costs under that number. Or, the furniture manufacturer may receive an order for fifty of the same custom chairs, and a job order number would be assigned to the entire lot. Note that each product or product lot is sufficiently different so that each job is identifiable.

Specific order cost accounting is used by manufacturing firms that engage in discontinuous production in which a variety of different jobs are going on at once, and in which each job requires different amounts of material, labor, and overhead. Industries using job order cost systems include machinery, furniture, lumber products, and construction.

COST FLOWS   Materials inventory and manufacturing (factory) overhead accounts are set up in the general ledger to accumulate the costs for materials (debit Materials Inventory and credit Accounts Payable) and manufacturing overhead (debit Manufacturing Overhead and credit such accounts as Cash, Accounts Payable, Prepaid Insurance—Factory, and other unexpired factory assets). Because there is no time lag between labor cost incurrence and utilization, a labor cost account need not be used to accumulate labor cost incurred. Instead, a liability account, Factory Payroll Payable, is credited for the cost of labor utilized in production, and the corresponding debit is to Goods in Process. The actual payment of the labor cost is recorded by a debit to Factory Payroll Payable and a credit to Cash (for the present we shall ignore withholding taxes). At the end of the fiscal period, any credit balance in the factory payroll payable account represents the liability for wages earned by employees but not paid. Such a liability arises when the pay date occurs after the end of the accounting fiscal period.

As the services related to direct material, direct labor, and factory overhead are utilized in production, the cost of the services is accounted for in the general

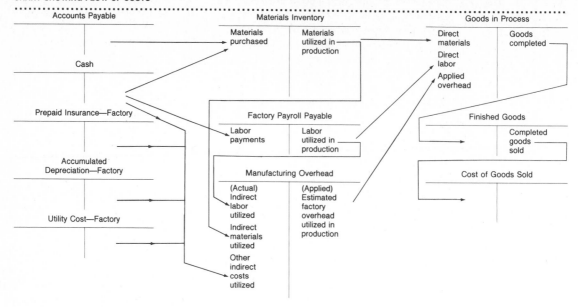

ledger account Goods (Work) in Process. The production costs are transferred from the two basic cost accounts and the payroll account to the goods in process account (debit Goods in Process and credit the respective Materials Inventory, Factory Payroll Payable, and Manufacturing Overhead).

When the goods are completed, the applicable production costs are transferred from the goods in process account to the finished goods account (debit Finished Goods and credit Goods in Process). When the finished goods are sold, the production costs of the goods are transferred to the expense account Cost of Goods Sold (debit Cost of Goods Sold and credit Finished Goods).

The preceding cost entries are facilitated by the use of perpetual inventory records for raw materials (both direct and indirect materials), goods in process, and finished goods. Thus the cost flows can be shown, as above, by arrows (the head of an arrow denotes a debit, the tail represents a credit).

APPLIED FACTORY OVERHEAD COST   As discussed in the preceding chapter, actual factory overhead cost is not directly traceable to particular units of a product, and there is a time lag after utilization before actual factory overhead cost can be determined. Similarly, *actual* factory overhead cost is not directly traceable to particular jobs and it cannot be readily determined as jobs are completed; therefore, applied (estimated) factory overhead cost is used in job order costing. How applied factory overhead cost is determined and used in a job order system is summarized as follows:

(1)   An activity base is selected that tends to vary with factory overhead cost. It is assumed that such a related base reflects the factors that cause changes in overhead costs. For example, if direct labor cost (or direct labor hours or machine hours) tends to vary with overhead cost, it can be used as the activity base needed to derive the applied factory overhead rate.

(2)   The volume of activity for the base selected is estimated for the next fiscal year. Generally it is

either the volume *expected* next year or the *normal* annual volume (an annual average volume estimated over several years). Thus the expected or normal labor cost for next year, say $8,000, would be a measure of the estimated activity volume.

(3) Factory overhead costs are projected for next year at the estimated (expected or normal) activity volume. Assume that this estimate is $4,800.

(4) The estimated factory overhead cost is divided by the estimated activity level to derive an applied factory overhead rate. For example, the estimated factory overhead cost of $4,800 divided by the estimated direct labor cost of $8,000 indicates an applied overhead rate of .6.

(5) As each job is completed during the year, the *actual* direct labor cost for each job is multiplied by the applied factory overhead rate to determine the factory overhead cost to be applied to each job. For example, if Job #80 had direct labor cost of $250, the applied factory overhead cost would be $150 ($250 × .6). Obviously, the cost of a job is the sum of its direct materials, direct labor, and applied factory overhead costs.

(6) For purposes of inventory costing, factory overhead is applied to any uncompleted jobs at the end of the fiscal period. For example, assume that Job #82 utilized $200 of labor and it is not finished. The applied factory overhead would be $120 ($200 × .6).

SUBSIDIARY COST RECORDS   General ledger accounts were used in the preceding section to show cost flows in a job order cost accounting system. The cost data needed to make the entries in the general ledger accounts are provided by subsidiary records. That is, general ledger accounts are summary (control) accounts in which entries are based on total dollar amounts aggregated, usually on a monthly basis, from detailed subsidiary cost records. Subsidiary records are kept (1) to avoid unwieldly amounts of data in the general ledger, (2) to provide a check on bookkeeping accuracy, and (3) to provide easier access to current data (i.e., if the control accounts are being used, the subsidiary records are available for use, and vice versa).

The *job cost sheet* is the basic subsidiary record underlying the goods in process account. For each job there is a job cost sheet, which shows the details of the costs for direct materials and direct labor utilized during production and the applied (estimated) factory overhead cost for a particular job. A job cost sheet is shown below.

Job Cost Sheet

Description: _____   Job Order No. _____

For stock _____   Due date _____
Customer _____   Date completed _____
Date ordered _____   Quantity completed _____
Quantity ordered _____

Direct Materials Cost			Applied Overhead Cost	
Date	Reference	Amount	Date	Amount

Direct Labor Cost			Cost Summary	
Date	Reference	Amount	Direct material	$ _____
			Direct labor	
			Applied overhead	_____
			Total	$ _____
			Cost per unit	$ _____

A file of all the job cost sheets provides a subsidiary ledger to the goods in process account. Consequently, at the end of the fiscal period, the cost of the ending goods in process inventory is merely the sum of the total costs from the cost sheets for all jobs that remain uncompleted. Similarly, the sum of the total costs for all jobs that are completed, as shown by the job cost sheets, provides the data for the entry debiting Finished Goods and crediting Goods in Process (usually done monthly).

In those cases where manufacturing is done by specific customer order, a file of the completed job cost sheets may serve as the subsidiary ledger to the finished goods account. Thus the ending inventory cost for finished goods is simply the sum of the costs from the job cost sheets for those finished goods still on hand at the end of the fiscal period. Instead of job cost sheets, inventory cards or a formal ledger are used as the subsidiary ledger to the finished goods account when goods are manufactured for stock.

Materials Ledger Card

Description _____   Part No. _____

		Received			Issued			Balance		
Date	Reference	Quantity	Unit Cost	Amount	Quantity	Unit Cost	Amount	Quantity	Unit Cost	Amount

Materials Requisition

Job No. _____   Requisition No. _____

Department _____   Date _____

Authorized by _____

Description	Quantity	Unit Cost	Amount

Work Ticket

Employee No. _____   Rate $ _____   Date _____

Operation No. _____   Amount $ _____   Job No. _____

Department No. _____

Time			Pieces		
Stop _____ Start _____ Total hours _____			Accepted _____ Rejected _____ Total _____		
Clock No. _____			Inspector _____		

Besides the job cost sheet, other supporting documents and records are the following:

(1) Sellers' invoices or company receiving reports (a report verifying the quantity and condition of purchased materials received), summarized monthly, provide the data necessary to make the general ledger entry debiting Materials Inventory and crediting Accounts Payable.

(2) Materials (stores) ledger cards (see page 522), which show the detailed inflows, outflows, and ending balances pertaining to materials inventory, serve as the subsidiary records supporting the general ledger account Materials Inventory.

(3) Materials (stores) requisitions (see page 522), which are used as the authority to issue materials to production, provide the material cost data that are recorded in the materials ledger cards and in the job cost sheets. The materials requisitions, or a summary sheet of the requisitions, also serve as a basis for the monthly general ledger entry debiting Goods in Process (direct materials) and Manufacturing Overhead (indirect materials) and crediting Materials Inventory.

(4) Work tickets (see page 522) provide a record of each factory worker's time, pay rate, and total labor cost for each job. Thus the work tickets provide the direct labor cost data that are recorded on the job cost sheets. The work tickets, or a summary sheet of the work tickets, also provide the data needed to make the monthly general ledger entry debiting Goods in Process (direct labor) and Manufacturing Overhead (indirect labor) and crediting Factory Payroll Payable.

(5) Factory overhead analysis sheets (see below), which provide the detailed data pertaining to *actual* factory overhead costs, serve as the subsidiary records supporting the general ledger account Manufacturing Overhead. The factory overhead costs recorded in the analysis sheets are obtained from materials requisitions (indirect materials), work tickets (indirect labor), and miscellaneous invoices. A monthly summary of the overhead analysis sheets provides the data needed for the general ledger entry debiting Manufacturing Overhead and crediting various accounts.

Factory Overhead Cost Sheet

Department _____

Date	Reference	Indirect materials	Indirect labor	Insurance	Depreciation	Taxes	Utilities	Other

A manufacturing company may use a factory overhead cost sheet for each department. In this way departmental responsibility for overhead costs can be maintained. On the other hand, there may be no need to maintain specific departmental records for direct material and direct labor costs because such data can be obtained from the materials requisitions and work tickets.

The preceding financial documents serve (1) to control the use of manufacturing resources (e.g., perpetual materials inventory records provide control over the issuance of materials to production); (2) to provide the stimulus for action (e.g., materials requisitions initiate the action to issue materials to production); and (3) to provide the basis for useful information for decision-making purposes (e.g., the documentation of the cost flows provides the basis for the preparation of financial statements and for comparisons of actual cost data with expected cost data, both of which are useful in decision making).

The general ledger cost entries with the supporting financial documents and subsidiary ledgers are summarized below.

Summary entry in general ledger			Basic document underlying entry	Subsidiary records
(0)	Materials inventory	x	Seller's invoice, receiving report, or purchase requisition	Materials cards or materials ledger
	Accounts payable	x		
(1)	Goods in process	x	Materials requisitions or summary of requisitions	Job cost sheet, factory overhead cost sheets, and stores cards
	Manufacturing overhead	x		
	Materials inventory	x		
(2)	Goods in process	x	Work tickets or summary of tickets	Job cost sheet and factory overhead cost sheets
	Manufacturing overhead	x		
	Factory payroll payable	x		
(3)	Goods in process	x	Applied factory overhead rate	Job cost sheet
	Manufacturing overhead	x		
(4)	Manufacturing overhead	x	Invoices and memos	Factory overhead cost sheets
	Accounts payable	x		
	Cash	x		
	Prepayments—Factory	x		
	Other accounts	x		
(5)	Finished goods	x	Completed jobs cost sheets	File of completed jobs cost sheets, finished goods ledger, or finished goods cards
	Goods in process	x		
(6)	Cost of goods sold	x	Sales invoices or shipping orders	File of job cost sheets associated with goods sold, finished goods inventory cards, or finished goods ledger
	Finished goods	x		

AN ILLUSTRATION OF JOB COSTING   Assume that a furniture manufacturer worked on three jobs (Job #80, Job #81, and Job #82) during the month of August. Further assume that Job #80 and Job #81 were started in July and completed in August, and that the finished product that resulted from Job #80 was sold at the end of August. Finally, assume that factory overhead is applied to production at a rate of 60 per cent of direct labor cost. Because no entries were made for the manufacturing costs utilized during August, you are asked to record the necessary cost entries, given the data below, and prepare a statement of cost of goods manufactured for the month of August.

	Job cost sheets			
	Job #80	Job #81	Job #82	Total
Beginning goods in process	$ 500	$ 800	$—	$1,300
Costs utilized during August:				
Direct materials	200	100	220	520
Direct labor	250	160	200	610
Manufacturing overhead applied	150	96	120	366
Subtotal	$1,100	$1,156	$540	$2,796
Indirect materials (actual)				$ 135
Indirect labor (actual)				180
Various indirect factory costs (actual)				120

Solution:

(1) Goods in process (direct) 520
       Manufacturing overhead (indirect) 135
             Materials inventory 655
       Issuance of direct and indirect materials to production.

(2) Goods in process (direct) 610
       Manufacturing overhead (indirect) 180
             Factory payroll payable 790
       Direct and indirect labor utilized in production.

(3) Goods in process (60% of $610) 366
             Manufacturing overhead 366
       Application of factory overhead at 60% of direct labor cost.

(4) Manufacturing overhead 120
             Miscellaneous accounts (Accounts payable,
               Cash, Accumulated depreciation—Factory, etc.) 120
       To record actual factory overhead cost utilized.

(5) Finished goods 2,256
       Goods in process ($1,100 for Job #80
         plus $1,156 for Job #81) 2,256
       To record completion of jobs #80 and #81.

(6) Cost of goods sold (Job #80) 1,100
             Finished goods 1,100
       To record cost of goods sold.

FURNITURE COMPANY
Statement of Cost of Goods Manufactured
Month Ended August 31, 19__

Direct material cost	$ 520
Direct labor cost	610
Manufacturing overhead (applied)	366
Production cost utilized during August	$1,496
Add beginning goods in process	1,300
Total production cost	$2,796
Deduct ending goods in process (Job #82)	540
Cost of goods manufactured	$2,256

Although the foregoing illustration is simplified because of only three jobs, it does show how the job cost sheets provide the necessary data for recording transfers from Goods in Process to Finished Goods to Cost of Goods Sold. The same method of accounting would be used for a company with 1,000 jobs: sum up the job cost sheets for all jobs uncompleted (ending goods in process), for all jobs completed and still on hand (ending finished goods), and for all jobs of which the finished goods have been sold (cost of goods sold).

The illustration also assumed that each job was the result of a specific customer order, so that upon completion of a job all the units (or one unit) were sold to the specific customer. However, in manufacturing for stock, the units completed for a particular job may not all be sold during the same time period; hence to determine the cost of goods sold it is necessary to calculate an average cost per unit completed in each job. Thus, if Job #190 had total manufacturing costs of $800, and if 20 units were completed, the cost per unit would be $40; if 5 of the units were sold, the cost of goods sold pertaining to Job #190 would be $200 (5 × $40).

UNDERAPPLIED AND OVERAPPLIED OVERHEAD   Note that in the preceding illustration there is a $69 difference between the actual factory overhead cost ($435) and the applied factory overhead cost ($366), as summarized below:

Manufacturing overhead	
(Actual)	(Applied)
135	366
180	
120	
435	

The difference is called the *factory overhead variance,* and in this instance it represents underapplied (underabsorbed) factory overhead: only $366 was applied to production, which was $69 under the actual factory overhead cost of $435. Similarly, if actual factory overhead cost is less than applied factory overhead cost, then the overhead variance represents overapplied (overabsorbed) overhead; in comparison to actual factory overhead cost, too much overhead was applied to production.

In the usual situation there will be month-to-month variation between actual and applied factory overhead cost. This variation should be expected because actual monthly factory overhead cost is affected by fluctuations in actual production volume and seasonal overhead costs. In contrast, applied factory overhead cost for any month (or any interim period) is really an *average* cost (i.e., the estimated average annual applied rate times the actual monthly activity level) that smooths out seasonal variations. On the other hand, by the end of the fiscal year the monthly differences between the applied and actual factory overhead costs should tend to offset one another so that any year-end factory overhead variance should be minor.

If monthly financial statements are prepared, any factory overhead variance should be shown in the balance sheet: underapplied factory overhead would be shown as the last item under current assets and overapplied factory overhead would be shown as the last item under current liabilities. Applied, not actual, factory overhead would be shown on the *monthly* statement of cost of goods manufactured, as shown on page 525, and, therefore, also shown on the *monthly* income statement as part of the cost of goods sold.

The reason for showing a monthly factory overhead variance in the current section of the balance sheet is that the monthly variances largely represent random departures from normal operating overhead costs that should tend to net out and result in a small or zero variance by year end. If monthly overhead variances were shown on the monthly income statements, monthly net income would vary with the random fluctuations in the overhead variance and possibly would mislead investors, creditors, and other readers of the income statement.

At the end of the fiscal year, any factory overhead variance usually is shown in the income statement rather than in the balance sheet. One treatment is to write off any year-end overhead variance to cost of goods sold: underapplied factory overhead is debited to Cost of Goods Sold and overapplied factory overhead is credited to Cost of Goods Sold, as shown below:

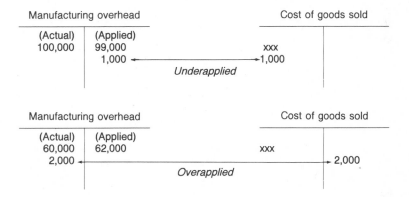

Theoretically, one can argue that any year-end factory overhead variance should be prorated to cost of goods sold, finished goods, and goods in process in proportion to the amount of applied factory overhead contained in the ending balance of each of these three accounts. The contention is that the balance sheet and income statement should reflect *actual* historical overhead cost, which is accomplished by prorating the factory overhead variance to the three accounts. In most cases, however, the prorating is not done because the factory overhead variance generally is small at year end, so that the added accuracy in prorating is not significant.

IMPORTANT TERMS AND CONCEPTS IN CHAPTER 17

Manufacturing cost system—p. 518
Costs for planning and control—p. 518
Perpetual inventory method—pp. 518, 519
Job order costing—pp. 519, 520
Applied factory overhead cost—pp. 520, 521
Job cost sheet—pp. 520, 521

Materials (stores) ledger cards—pp. 522, 523
Materials (stores) requisitions—pp. 522, 523
Work tickets—pp. 522, 523
Factory overhead analysis sheets—p. 523
Underapplied and overapplied overhead—
  pp. 526, 527

DEMONSTRATION PROBLEM FOR REVIEW AND SELF-STUDY Pichler Company manufactures its products for stock rather than by specific customer orders. Job numbers are assigned to each job. The following data pertain to the month of January, and there were no beginning inventories.

1 Materials were purchased on account for $3,000.

2 Three jobs were placed into production:

Job #609 for 10 units of Model W
Job #610 for 5 units of Model X
Job #611 for 20 units of Model Y

3 Materials issued to production were as follows:

Job #609	$400
Job #610	500
Job #611	300
Indirect materials	200

4 Labor utilized in production was as follows:

Job #609	$400
Job #610	750
Job #611	560
Indirect labor	300

5 Factory overhead was applied to production based on direct labor hours used. At the beginning of the year, it was estimated that factory overhead cost would be $500,000 and that direct labor hours would be 100,000. The direct labor hours for January were as follows:

Job #609	100
Job #610	150
Job #611	140

6 Actual miscellaneous factory overhead costs for the month were $800.

7 Jobs #609 and #611 were completed during the month.

8 At the end of the month, cash was paid for the materials purchased and for the labor utilized.

9 At the end of the month, 6 units of Job #609 and 4 units of Job #611 were sold at a 20% markup on cost.

INSTRUCTIONS

(a) Prepare general journal entries from the above data for the month of January.

(b) What was the cost of the ending inventory of goods in process as of January 31?

(c) What was the cost of the ending inventory of finished goods as of January 31?

Note Attempt to solve this demonstration problem before examining the solution that follows.

Solution:

(a) 1.

Materials inventory	3,000	
Accounts payable		3,000
To record purchase of raw materials.		

2. No entry.

3.

Goods in process	1,200	
Manufacturing overhead	200	
Materials inventory		1,400
Issuance of direct and indirect materials to production.		

4.

Goods in process	1,710	
Manufacturing overhead	300	
Factory payroll payable		2,010
Direct and indirect labor utilized in production.		

5.

Goods in process ($5 × 390)	1,950	
Manufacturing overhead		1,950
Application of factory overhead at $5 per direct labor hour.		

6.

Manufacturing overhead	800	
Various accounts		800
To record actual factory overhead cost utilized.		

7.

Finished goods	2,860	
Goods in process		2,860
To record completion of Jobs #609 and #611.		

	Job #609	Job #611	Total
Direct materials	$ 400	$ 300	$ 700
Direct labor	400	560	960
Applied overhead:			
$5 × 100	500		
$5 × 140		700 }	1,200
	$1,300	$1,560	$2,860

8.

Accounts payable	3,000	
Factory payroll payable	2,010	
Cash		5,010
To record payment of materials purchased and labor utilized.		

9.

Accounts receivable	1,310.40	
Sales		1,310.40
To record sales.		

Cost of goods sold	1,092	
Finished goods		1,092
To record cost of goods sold.		

Cost per unit: $\dfrac{\$1,300}{10} = \$130$ $\dfrac{\$1,560}{20} = \$78$

Cost of goods sold:
$$\begin{array}{ll} \$130 \times 6 = & \$ \ 780 \\ \$ \ 78 \times 4 = & \underline{\ \ \ 312} \\ & \$1,092 \end{array}$$

Sales: $\$1,092 \times 1.2 = \$1,310.40$

(b) Only job not completed was Job #610:

Direct materials	$ 500
Direct labor	750
Applied factory overhead ($5 × 150)	750
Total	$2,000

(c)

Job #609: $130 × 4 =	$ 520
Job #611: $ 78 × 16 =	1,248
	$1,768

Questions

1. What is the function of the following cost accounting records?
   (a) Factory overhead analysis sheets
   (c) Job cost sheets
   (b) Materials requisitions
   (d) Materials ledger cards
2. Why is job order costing not used by firms engaged in mass production? Are there any situations where such firms may use job order costing?
3. In the cost flows of a job order system, why are part of the materials and labor costs first taken to Manufacturing Overhead instead of Goods in Process?
4. Why are both general ledger cost accounts and subsidiary cost records kept? For managerial decision-making purposes, which source (general ledger accounts or subsidiary records) of data would be the more useful?
5. Why do firms that manufacture for stock, instead of by specific customer order, not use a file of completed job cost sheets as the subsidiary ledger to the finished goods account?
6. A specific job-order number can refer to the cost of manufacturing one unit of a product or to the cost of manufacturing several units of the same product (a job lot). How does the cost accounting for a job lot differ from the cost accounting for one unit of product?
7. Would the following circumstances result in underapplied or overapplied factory overhead cost? Explain.
   (a) More factory overhead cost utilized than expected.
   (b) An applied overhead rate that is too high.
   (c) Production that is greater than expected.
8. What is the difference between the accounting treatment of factory overhead in monthly as opposed to year-end financial statements? Discuss.
9. Is there any difference between a theoretical approach as opposed to a practical approach in the treatment of the factory overhead variance at year end? Discuss.
10. Note that in the job-order cost flows there is a cost account set up for materials (Materials Inventory) and for factory overhead (Manufacturing Overhead). However, for labor there is a liability account (Factory Payroll Payable) instead of a cost account. Why is no cost account set up for labor? (Hint: Remember the distinction between costs incurred and utilized.)
11. What is the difference between expected annual activity and normal annual activity?
12. Can a company adopt job-order costing and continue to use a periodic inventory system?
13. Is it true that the major advantage in keeping perpetual inventory records is that the need for a periodic count is eliminated?
14. How should the activity base for applying factory overhead be chosen?
15. If direct labor cost is chosen as the base for applying factory overhead, should any overhead ever be applied to a job before the total labor cost is known?

Short exercises

E17-1 *You are given below three multiple-choice statements. Select the correct answers and indicate the corresponding letters on a sheet of paper (e.g., 1-d, 2-d, etc.).*

(1) Which of the following distinguishes perpetual inventory systems from periodic inventory systems? (a) A physical count need never be made. (b) Preparation of the financial statements can be accomplished before a physical count is taken. (c) Inventory items are issued to employees working on jobs throughout the period rather than at the beginning of the period only. (d) Separate accounts are kept for raw materials, goods in process, and finished goods rather than having only one account. (e) None of the above.

(2) Job-order costing is used primarily by firms (a) that manufacture one type of product of which all units are identical, (b) that maintain no stock of finished goods and therefore manufacture only special orders, (c) that manufacture only one item per batch, (d) that sell only to retail customers and not to wholesalers, (e) none of the above.

(3) For firms utilizing job-order costing, the purchase of raw materials is recorded by a debit to (a) accounts payable, (b) purchases, (c) materials inventory, (d) goods in process, (e) none of the above.

E17-2 *You are given below three multiple-choice statements. Select the correct answers and indicate the corresponding letters on a sheet of paper (e.g., 1-d, 2-d, etc.).*

(1) Under a job order system, factory overhead should be applied (a) at the beginning of the period, (b) at the end of the period, (c) at the time the job is completed, (d) at the time the activity base (direct labor cost, direct labor hours, machine hours, etc.) is recorded on the job card, (e) none of the above.

(2) The amount of direct labor cost on a job cost sheet is obtained from (a) work tickets, (b) materials requisitions, (c) materials ledger cards, (d) factory overhead analysis sheets, (e) none of the above.

(3) Theoretically, underapplied overhead should be charged to (a) cost of goods sold, (b) finished goods inventory, (c) cost of goods sold, goods in process, and finished goods, in the ratio of the balances in those accounts, (d) cost of goods sold, goods in process, and finished goods, in the ratio of the amount of overhead in each of those accounts, (e) none of the above.

E17-3 *For the month of September, the costs of Job #18 were as follows:*

Direct materials utilized: 20,000 pounds @ $.35 a pound

Direct labor utilized: 3,000 hours @ $3.50 an hour

Factory overhead applied: $5 per direct-labor hour

Units completed: 5,000

Units sold: 3,500

(a) What was the cost of goods manufactured with regard to Job #18?

(b) What was the cost of the ending inventory of finished goods with regard to Job #18?

(c) What was the cost of goods sold with regard to Job #18?

You are given below the factory payroll payable account for Reese Company for the month of April:

Factory payroll payable

| 20,000 | Balance | 3,000 |
| | | 22,000 |

(a) In general journal form, make the entry for the labor payment.
(b) If direct labor cost utilized was $18,000 during April, make the general journal entry recording the total labor cost utilized.
(c) Why is there a difference between total debits and credits in the above account? Explain.

For the month of January, you are given below the manufacturing overhead account for Gomez Company:

Manufacturing overhead cost

| 6,700 | 7,000 |

(a) The actual factory overhead costs utilized during January consisted of $4,000 equipment depreciation, $500 indirect materials, $1,000 indirect labor, and $1,200 factory insurance. Make one compound general journal entry to record the actual overhead costs.
(b) In general journal form, record the applied factory overhead cost for the month of January.
(c) Why do the total debits not equal the total credits in the above account? Explain.

During the fiscal period, the following charges were made to the goods in process amount for Jo Jo Company:

Goods in process

Balance	—	
Direct materials	200,000	
Direct labor	500,000	
Factory overhead	300,000	

The costs charged to the goods in process account consisted of the following three jobs:

	Units completed	Direct materials	Direct labor
Job #10	10,000	$50,000	$110,000
Job #11	25,000	80,000	200,000
Job #12	20,000	70,000	190,000

(a) If factory overhead was applied to production based on direct labor cost, what was the factory overhead applied rate?
(b) If 4,000 and 8,000 units of Jobs #10 and #11, respectively, were sold during the year, what was the cost of goods sold for those two jobs?

E17-7   The following information was obtained from Handmade Furniture Company:

Job number	Balance—May 1	May production costs
50	$1,000	
51	1,400	
52	600	$ 200
53		1,300
54		1,600

During May, Jobs #52 and #53 were completed and Jobs #50 and #52 were delivered to customers.

Required:

Compute the following:

(a) The goods in process inventory at May 1.

(b) The finished goods inventory at May 1.

(c) The cost of goods sold during May.

(d) The goods in process inventory at May 31.

(e) The finished goods inventory at May 31.

E17-8   Colonial Company has two manufacturing departments—stamping and assembly. The stamping department has few workers because most of the work is done by machine. The assembly department, on the other hand, has few machines because most of the work is performed manually. The following data have been estimated for the upcoming year:

	Stamping	Assembly
Direct labor cost	$ 35,000	$135,000
Factory overhead	150,000	45,000
Machine hours	20,000	1,000

Required:

Using the activity base you deem most appropriate, calculate a predetermined overhead rate for each department.

Problems

A17-1   Joplin Company has two departments—production and assembly. Joplin applies overhead on the basis of machine hours in the production department and on the basis of direct labor hours in the assembly department. The budget estimates for the current year are:

	Production	Assembly
Direct labor hours	40,000	50,000
Machine hours	75,000	15,000
Factory overhead	$150,000	$60,000

During March of the current year, Job #301 was started and completed. The job cost sheet for Job #301 contained the following information:

	Production	Assembly
Direct materials	$500	$ 40
Direct labor cost	$200	$300
Direct labor hours	40	60
Machine hours	70	10

Other information for the month of March is as follows:

	Production	Assembly
Factory overhead utilized	$10,000	$5,000
Direct labor hours	3,000	4,000
Machine hours	5,200	1,100

Required:

(a) Compute the predetermined overhead application rate for each department.

(b) Calculate the total manufacturing cost of Job #301.

(c) Determine the overapplied or underapplied overhead for each department at the end of March.

A17-2

Perry Manufacturing Company uses a job-order cost system. You are required to do the following:

(a) Prepare entries in general journal form for the following transactions that relate to the month of April, assuming no beginning inventories:

(1) Materials costing $60,000 were purchased on credit.

(2) Materials issued to production were as follows:

Job #110	$6,000
Job #111	2,000
Job #112	5,000
Indirect materials	1,000

(3) Labor utilized in production was as follows:

Job #110	$5,000
Job #111	8,000
Job #112	7,000
Indirect labor	3,000

(4) Wages of $20,000 were paid to the factory workers.

(5) Manufacturing overhead is applied to production on the basis of 80% of direct labor cost.

(6) Actual miscellaneous factory overhead costs utilized during the month were $10,000.

(7) Jobs #110 and #111 were completed during the month.

(8) The product from Job #110 was shipped and invoiced at the end of the month at a profit of 20% of cost.

(b) What is the cost of the ending inventory of goods in process? Of finished goods?

(c) What is the overhead variance for the month?

A17-3   The March 1, 19__ inventory balances for Peabody Manufacturing Company are given below:

Materials inventory	$ 6,000
Goods in process	5,000
Finished goods	14,000

The cost transactions for the month of March were as follows:

(1) Materials purchased for cash were $28,000.

(2) Direct and indirect materials utilized were $19,000 and $2,000, respectively.

(3) Direct and indirect labor utilized were $16,000 and $1,000, respectively.

(4) Applied factory overhead cost was $12,800, and miscellaneous actual factory overhead cost was $9,000.

(5) Factory wages paid at the end of the month were $15,500.

(6) The total cost of jobs completed and transferred to finished goods was $30,000.

(7) The cost of the goods sold for the month was $40,000.

Required:

(a) Set up T-accounts and post the beginning balances and the transactions for the month of March.

(b) What was the ending balance in the factory payroll account, what does it mean, and where is it shown in the financial statements?

(c) What was the ending balance in the manufacturing overhead account, what does it mean, and where is it shown in the financial statements?

A17-4   The following data pertain to Title Manufacturing Company.

Cost of goods sold (includes applied overhead cost)	$ 140,000
Net sales	200,000
Stockholders' equity	1,000,000
Net long-lived assets	1,000,000
Selling and administrative expenses	45,000
Actual factory overhead cost	40,000
Current liabilities	190,000
Current assets	180,000
Applied factory overhead cost	30,000

Required:

(a) Prepare a balance sheet and an income statement, assuming that the income statement figures above pertain to the month of January and that the balance sheet figures are as of January 31, 19__.

(b) Prepare an income statement, assuming that the above income statement figures pertain to the year ended December 31, 19__.

(c) Explain the difference between the income statements in part (a) and part (b).

A17-5   You are given some incomplete cost data for Polo Company as of January 31, 19__:

Materials inventory			Goods in process		
Jan. 1 Bal.	20,000		Jan. 1 Bal.	10,000	
	58,000		Dir. matl.	35,000	
			Dir. labor	46,000	

Factory payroll payable		Finished goods		
	50,000	Jan. 1 Bal.	45,000	

Factory overhead cost		Cost of goods sold	
Ind. matl.	10,000	125,000	

In addition to the above data, you find out that the company applies factory overhead at the rate of 80 per cent of direct labor cost, that miscellaneous actual factory overhead costs were $30,000, and that the January 31 ending balance of Goods in Process was $15,000.

Show all computations for:

(1) The total cost of the materials issued to production.

(2) The cost of the indirect labor utilized.

(3) The cost of January 31, 19__ ending materials inventory balance.

(4) The total cost of the goods in process transferred to finished good.

(5) The cost of the January 31, 19__ ending finished goods inventory balance.

(6) The amount by which factory overhead was overapplied or underapplied.

(Hint: *Complete the postings of the T-accounts to solve for unknowns.*)

A17-6   *Hollowtip Manufacturing Company uses a job order cost system. The applied factory overhead rate of 105 per cent of direct labor cost is the same for each job. The incomplete cost data for two jobs are given below:*

	Job #450	Job #451
Direct materials	$ 40,000	$?
Direct labor	?	?
Factory overhead applied	?	42,000
Total	$142,500	$95,000

Required:

(1) What was the direct labor cost for Job #451?

(2) What was the direct materials cost for Job #451?

(3) What was the direct labor cost for Job #450?

(4) What was the applied factory overhead cost for Job #450?

B17-1   *Leather Manufacturing Company uses perpetual inventories. The following data were taken from their accounts:*

	Balances January 1, 19_2	Balances December 31, 19_2
Materials inventory	$ 8,000	$ 12,000
Cost of goods sold	—	180,000
Actual overhead	—	25,000
Applied overhead (at 40% of direct labor cost)	—	24,000
Goods in process	16,000	20,000
Finished goods	49,000	37,000

Required:

(a) What was the cost of goods completed during 19_2? (Ignore any adjustments for overapplied or underapplied overhead.)

(b) What was the cost of materials purchased for 19_2?

B17-2

You are given below cost data pertaining to Downs Manufacturing Company.

Goods in process:	
Beginning inventory balance	$22,000
Direct materials cost	16,000
Direct labor cost	15,000
Applied factory overhead	16,200
Ending inventory balance	25,000
Indirect material cost	6,000
Indirect labor cost	8,000

Required:

(1) Based on the above data, make the cost entries (general journal form) transferring the three cost elements to Goods in Process and from Goods in Process to Finished Goods.

(2) Set up T-accounts and post the general journal entries to them. Number the entries in the T-accounts.

(3) Assuming that it is based on direct labor cost, what is the applied factory overhead rate? Show your calculations.

(4) Make the general journal entry transferring the underapplied or overapplied factory overhead to Cost of Goods Sold.

B17-3

The manager of Clifton Company presents you with the following inventory data for the year 19_8:

	1/1/_8	12/31/_8
Materials inventory	$ 53,000	$ 63,000
Goods in process inventory	90,000	70,000
Finished goods inventory	195,000	175,000

Additional cost data are as follows:

Direct labor hours utilized	30,000
Materials purchased	$30,000
Applied factory overhead rate per direct labor hour	2
Factory supplies used (indirect materials)	1,000
Factory utility costs	4,000
Direct labor utilized	85,000
Factory depreciation	30,000
Factory insurance for the year	10,000
Indirect labor cost	12,000
Miscellaneous indirect costs	1,000

Required:

(a) Using the above data, you are asked to reconstruct the cost entries (in general journal form) for the year 19_8.

(b) What is the amount of the overhead variance at your end? (Show calculations) Explain what the variance means.

(c) Close the overhead variance to Cost of Goods Sold.

B17-4   *The job cost sheets of Weltmer, Inc., for the month of March were as follows:*

	Job #960	Job #961	Job #962	Job #963	Job #964	Job #965
Goods in process, March 1, 19__						
Direct materials			$ 200	$ 125		
Direct labor			300	240		
Applied factory overhead			195	156		
Finished goods, March 1, 19__						
Direct materials	$1,500	$560				
Direct labor	2,000	700				
Applied factory overhead	1,300	455				
Costs utilized in March:						
Direct materials			910	1,100	$3,000	$400
Direct labor			1,200	1,400	3,500	600
Applied factory overhead			780	910	2,275	

Jobs #962, #963, and #964 were completed during March. Based on direct labor cost, applied factory overhead cost was added to the job cost sheets for those jobs completed during March. Actual factory overhead cost at the beginning of March was $3,000 and actual overhead for March was $1,500.

Required:

(a) Prepare a statement of cost of goods manufactured for the month ended March 31, 19__.

(b) Check the cost-of-goods-manufactured figure by adding together the costs of the jobs completed during March. Show your calculations.

(c) Set up a T-account for manufacturing overhead and enter the actual and applied overhead costs as of March 31, 19__.

B17-5   *You are given below some incomplete cost data for Vida Corporation as of January 31, 19__:*

Materials inventory		Goods in process	
Jan. 1 Bal. 7,000	21,000	Jan. 1 Bal. 11,000	

Factory payroll payable		Finished goods	
	45,000	Jan. 1 Bal. 40,000	
		77,000	

Factory overhead cost		Cost of goods sold	
Ind. matl. 8,000	25,000		
Ind. labor 12,000			
Misc. 6,000			

In addition, you are told that the January 31 ending balances were as follows: Materials Inventory $9,000, Factory Payroll Payable $15,000, and Finished Goods $32,000.

Show all computations for:

(1) The cost of the materials purchased.

(2) The cost of the direct materials utilized during January.

(3) The amount of cash paid for factory wages.

(4) The cost of the direct labor utilized during January.

(5) The January 31 ending inventory of goods in process.

(6) The cost of goods sold.

(7) Factory wages owed at January 31, 19___.

(Hint: *Complete the postings of the T-accounts to solve for unknowns.*)

MANUFACTURING COST SYSTEMS: PROCESS COSTING
CHAPTER 18

PURPOSE OF CHAPTER In the preceding chapter a manufacturing cost system was defined as a method used to collect manufacturing cost data and to assign such data to meet the two basic cost objectives of product costing and of planning and control. The purpose of this chapter is to describe the process manufacturing system used for product costing purposes and the underlying source documents that can be used to provide cost data for planning and control purposes.

PROCESS COSTING Process cost accounting is characterized by the accumulation of production costs by specific manufacturing operations, or steps, called *processes.* A manufacturing process generally is associated with a department in which the product costs are uniformly applied to each unit of output worked on in that department. Thus process costing is used by firms that mass produce like products by passing each unit through a series of uniform manufacturing processes until it is completed in the last process. For example, a firm's product may be manufactured by passing sequentially through a preparation department (Process #1), then the assembly department (Process #2), and finally the finishing department (Process #3). Industries using process cost accounting systems include petroleum refining, chemicals, meat packing, ore refining, and canneries.

Since process costing is used for the continuous production of mass quantities of like units, where each unit of product receives the same treatment, broad averages are used to determine the unit costs needed for inventory-costing purposes. The direct material, direct labor, and factory overhead costs utilized in production over the fiscal period, divided by the appropriate physical units produced, provide the unit costs necessary to cost the ending goods in process and the goods completed in a particular process. In contrast, a job order system does not use broad averages because many jobs consist of only one or a few units of the same product, and each job uses varying amounts of material, labor, and factory overhead.

COST FLOWS In process costing, a goods in process account is set up in the general ledger for each manufacturing process or department. Direct and indirect materials may be issued to all or only some of the processes (debit the appropriate goods in process accounts for those processes in which materials were used, debit Manufacturing Overhead for the indirect materials, and credit Materials Inventory), while the labor services usually are utilized in each of the manufacturing processes (debit each goods in process account, debit Manufacturing Overhead for the indirect labor, and credit Factory Payroll Payable). Factory overhead is applied to each process, based on either an overall or a departmental overhead rate (debit each goods-in-process account and credit Manufacturing Overhead).

The cost flows may be such that the product passes through each process in sequence: Process #1 to Process #2 to Process #3, and so on, until the cost of the finished goods is transferred from the last goods in process account to the finished goods account. Sequential process costing is used by manufacturing firms that produce a product or products that receive uniform processing: chemical products, refined ores, and the like. An illustration of sequential process costing is shown below and on the next page, assuming that direct materials are used in all three processes.

In other instances the cost flows may be such that two or more products pass sequentially through different groups of processes: product *A* passes through Processes #1 and #2 and product *B* passes through Processes #3 and #4. Or the products may pass through some processes and not through other processes: product *A* passes through Processes #1, #3, and #4 and product *B* passes through Processes #2 and #4.

SUBSIDIARY COST RECORDS Other than the job cost sheet, the basic cost documents used in job order costing are also used in process costing: sellers' invoices for materials purchased, materials ledger cards, materials requisitions, work tickets, factory overhead cost sheets, and sales invoices. In place of the job cost sheet, a production report is used in process costing to summarize the production costs and units of production in each process. A production report is shown on page 549; however, it contains data that have not yet been explained.

PROCESS COST FLOWS

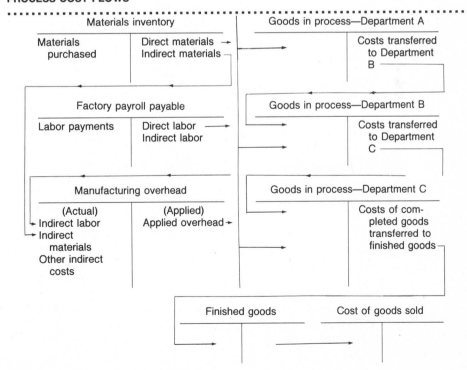

(1)	Goods in process—Department A	x
	Goods in process—Department B	x
	Goods in process—Department C	x
	Manufacturing overhead	x
	Materials inventory	xx
(2)	Goods in process—Department A	x
	Goods in process—Department B	x
	Goods in process—Department C	x
	Manufacturing overhead	x
	Factory payroll payable	xx
(3)	Goods in process—Department A	x
	Goods in process—Department B	x
	Goods in process—Department C	x
	Manufacturing overhead	xx
(4)	Manufacturing overhead	xx
	Various accounts	xx
(5)	Goods in process—Department B	x
	Goods in process—Department A	x
(6)	Goods in process—Department C	x
	Goods in process—Department B	x
(7)	Finished goods	x
	Goods in process—Department C	x
(8)	Cost of goods sold	xx
	Finished goods	xx

ILLUSTRATION—NO GOODS IN PROCESS AT BEGINNING OR END OF PERIOD Assume that, during 19_1 (the first year of its operations), a company produced 8,000 units of commodity X, and that there were no goods in process at the beginning or at the end of the year. The unit cost of the product can be determined as follows:

Direct materials	$ 26,000
(This cost is the total of the materials requisitions.)	
Direct labor	34,000
(Since all direct labor costs in the factory were utilized in the manufacture of commodity X, the entire direct labor payroll for 19_1 may be regarded as a cost of commodity X.)	
Manufacturing overhead	40,800
(Based on an estimated factory overhead rate of 120% of direct labor cost: 120% of $34,000.)	
Total	$100,800

Unit Costs—19_1

Direct materials ($26,000 ÷ 8,000)	$ 3.25
Direct labor ($34,000 ÷ 8,000)	4.25
Manufacturing overhead ($40,800 ÷ 8,000)	5.10
Total cost per unit	$12.60

Assume that, of the 8,000 units of commodity X that were fully completed, 2,000 units were sold during the fiscal period. The above cost of $12.60 per unit is used to cost out the ending inventory of finished goods and the cost of goods sold:

Ending inventory of finished goods (6,000 × $12.60)	$ 75,600
Cost of goods sold (2,000 × $12.60)	25,200
Total	$100,800

EQUIVALENT UNITS (PRODUCTION)   The preceding illustration was simplified by the exclusion of beginning and ending goods in process inventories. With no in-process inventories, the number of units completed was a correct measure of production work accomplished. Because each unit completed received the same manufacturing treatment, the total manufacturing costs utilized could be averaged over the total units completed. However, given the existence of goods in process inventories, the number of units completed may not be the correct measure of the production work accomplished during a stated period of time. In such a case, one cannot derive per-unit costs by dividing manufacturing costs utilized during the period by the number of units completed during the period.

To illustrate the effect of ending goods in process inventories on the computation of unit costs, assume that the actual cost to manufacture one unit started and fully completed during the fiscal period is $10. Further assume that at the end of the fiscal period there are units in process that are only 25 per cent complete in the manufacturing process. What is the cost per unit of the ending goods in process inventory? A solution would be to weight the cost of a partly completed unit in terms of the cost of a fully completed unit. Thus, if it costs $10 to manufacture a unit started and fully completed during the fiscal period, then logically a unit that is 25 per cent complete could be assigned a cost of $2.50 (25% of $10). This assumes, however, that the cost of a unit started and fully completed during the fiscal period has been previously determined.

In order to calculate the cost of a fully completed unit, manufacturing costs utilized over the fiscal period are divided, not by the number of units completed during the period, but by the number of equivalent units produced by the utilization of the manufacturing costs. Equivalent units are physical units weighted by the proportion of work done on them during the current period. Because units started and completed have 100 per cent of the work done on them during the fiscal period, they automatically are in terms of equivalent units. In contrast, goods in process inventories represent units on which less than 100 per cent of the work was performed during the current period. Hence the percentage of product completion during the current fiscal period is used to weight the units in goods in process inventories and thus convert them to equivalent finished units.

For example, if there are 1,000 units in beginning goods in process inventory that are 40 per cent complete, the equivalent units in the beginning inventory are 400 units (40% of 1,000); 1,000 units 40 per cent complete are equivalent to 400 fully completed units. If these 1,000 uncompleted units on hand at the beginning of the period are completed during the period, the equivalent production is 600 units (60% of 1,000); 40 per cent of the work was done last period and 60 per cent (100% − 40%) of the work was done in the current period. Similarly, if there are 2,000 units of uncompleted product in the ending goods in process inventory that are 20 per cent complete, the equivalent production is 400 units (20% of 2,000); 2,000 units 20 per cent complete are equivalent to 400 fully completed units. Finally, if there are 10,000 units started and fully completed during the current period, the equivalent production is 10,000 units (100% of 10,000). These results are summarized below:

	Physical flow	×	Percentage of completion— current period	=	Equivalent units
Beginning goods in process completed during period	1,000		60%		600
Units started and completed	10,000		100%		10,000
Ending goods in process inventory	2,000		20%		400
	13,000				11,000

Assume that the above equivalent units pertain to $220,000 manufacturing costs utilized over the fiscal period. The problem is to determine how much of the $220,000 is assigned to the ending goods in process and to the completed goods. In order to solve the problem, we calculate the cost of a fully completed unit by dividing the manufacturing costs utilized by the pertinent equivalent production:

$$\frac{\$220,000}{11,000} = \$20 \text{ cost per equivalent finished unit}$$

The cost of an equivalent finished unit is then weighted by the percentage of product completion to derive the unit cost applicable to goods in process inventories.

Using the above data, there were 2,000 units in ending goods in process that were 20 per cent complete. If it costs $20 to complete one unit during the fiscal period, then a unit that is 20 per cent complete should be assigned a cost of $4 (20% of $20), and the cost of the ending goods in process would be $8,000 ($4 × 2,000). Or, the 2,000 units in ending goods in process are equivalent to 400 complete units (20% of 2,000) at $20 each ($20 × 400 = $8,000):

Cost of ending goods in process:

(20% of $20 = $4) × 2,000

       or

$20 × 400 units   = $8,000

The same weighting treatment is used to cost the goods completed, assuming that the beginning goods in process will be the first units completed (FIFO):

Completion costs of *current* period:

   From beginning goods in process:

(60% of $20 = $12) × 1,000

       or

$20 × 600 units   = $ 12,000

Started and completed:

(100% of $20 = $20) × 10,000

       or

$20 × 10,000 units   = $ 200,000

                             $212,000

The sum of the cost of the ending goods in process inventory and the cost to complete the units finished during the period total $220,000:

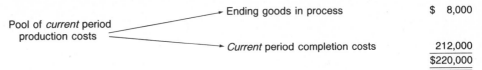

Pool of *current* period production costs	→ Ending goods in process	$ 8,000
	→ *Current* period completion costs	212,000
		$220,000

ILLUSTRATION—MATERIALS AND LABOR AT DIFFERENT STAGES OF COMPLETION

Assume that during 19_2 the company completed 9,000 units of commodity X, that there were no beginning goods in process, and that 400 units were in process at the end of the year. The ending goods in process were in the following stages of completion:

Direct materials	75%
Direct labor	50%

The company's costs for the year were:

Direct materials	$ 28,830
Direct labor	37,720
Manufacturing overhead—120% of direct labor cost	45,264
Total	$111,814

The costs shown above cannot be divided by 9,000 (the number of units completed) to determine the unit costs of completed goods because some of these costs were utilized in the production associated with ending goods in process. Equivalent-production data must be compiled following the procedure discussed in the preceding section. However, in this illustration involving process cost accounting, it is assumed that the stage of completion for the material content of the in-process inventory differs from the stage of completion for direct labor. For example, in the computation on the following page, 75 per cent of the material requirements have been supplied for the 400 units in the ending in-process inventory, leaving only 25 per cent to be supplied during the next period to complete the material requirements. For the labor element, half of the required work has been performed on the goods in process inventory.

The results of the 19_2 production activity are shown by the following T-accounts:

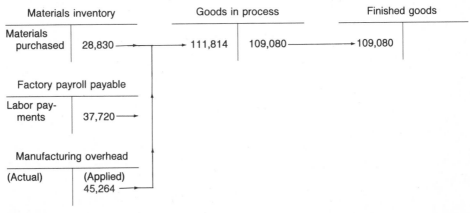

Materials inventory		Goods in process		Finished goods	
Materials purchased	28,830 →	→ 111,814	109,080 —	→ 109,080	

Factory payroll payable	
Labor payments	37,720 →

Manufacturing overhead	
(Actual)	(Applied) 45,264 →

Equivalent Production—19_2

	Physical flow	Equivalent units Direct materials	Direct labor
Units started and completed in 19_2	9,000	9,000	9,000
Add goods in process at end of 19_2	400		
Direct material: 75% of the material requirements have been placed in production, which is equivalent to the material requirements for 75% of 400 finished units, or		300	
Direct labor: 50% of the total labor costs have been utilized, which is equivalent to the labor costs for 50% of 400 units, or			200
Total	9,400	9,300	9,200

Unit Costs—19_2

Direct materials ($28,830 ÷ 9,300) $ 3.10
Direct labor ($37,720 ÷ 9,200)   4.10
Manufacturing overhead (120% of $4.10)   4.92
  Total cost per unit $12.12

Distribution of Total Costs—19_2

Finished goods (9,000 × $12.12) $109,080
Ending goods in process, December 31, 19_2:
  Direct materials:
    (75% of $3.10 = $2.325) × 400 or simply
    equivalent units of 300 × $3.10 $930

  Direct labor:
    (50% of $4.10 = $2.05) × 400 or simply
    equivalent units of 200 × $4.10   820

  Manufacturing overhead:
    (120% of $2.05 = $2.46) × 400 or equivalent
    units of 200 × $4.92 or simply 120% of $820   984   2,734
Total $111,814

ILLUSTRATION—GOODS IN PROCESS AT BEGINNING AND END OF PERIOD Continuing with

the previous illustration, assume that the costs for 19_3 were as follows:

Direct materials	$ 30,600
Direct labor	40,400
Manufacturing overhead—120% of direct labor cost	48,480
Total	$119,480

The company completed 10,000 units in 19_3. There were 400 units in beginning goods in process for 19_3, which were the ending goods in process for the previous period (19_2). There were 500 units in process at the end of the year, in the following stages of completion:

Direct materials	100%
Direct labor	60%

The computation of the equivalent production for 19_3 is shown below:

		Equivalent units	
	Physical flow	Direct materials	Direct labor
Units completed during 19_3:			
From beginning goods in process	400		
Direct materials:			
75% of the material requirements were placed in production last period; therefore, 25% placed in production this period to complete the units, which is equivalent to the material requirements for 25% of 400 finished units, or		100	
Direct labor (50% of 400)			200
Started and completed in 19_3	9,600	9,600	9,600
Ending goods in process:	500		
Direct materials (100% of 500)		500	
Direct labor (60% of 500)			300
Total	10,500	10,200	10,100

To calculate the unit costs for 19_3, divide the production costs by the appropriate equivalent units:

	Unit cost
Direct materials ($30,600 ÷ 10,200)	$ 3.00
Direct labor ($40,400 ÷ 10,100)	4.00
Manufacturing overhead (120% of $4.00)	4.80
Total cost per unit	$11.80

Given the above unit costs and the equivalent production for beginning and ending goods in process inventories, the production costs for 19_3 are distributed as follows:

Completed goods:

To complete beginning goods in process:		
Direct materials:		
(25% of $3.00 = $.75) × 400 or simply equivalent units		
of 100 × $3.00	$ 300	
Direct labor:		
(50% of $4.00 = $2.00) × 400 or simply equivalent units		
of 200 × $4.00	800	
Manufacturing overhead (120% of $800)	960	$ 2,060
Goods started and completed in 19_3 (9,600 × $11.80)		113,280
Ending goods in process, December 31, 19_3:		
Direct materials:		
(100% of $3.00 = $3.00) × 500 or simply equivalent		
units of 500 × $3.00	$1,500	
Direct labor:		
(60% of $4.00 = $2.40) × 500 or simply equivalent		
units of 300 × $4.00	1,200	
Manufacturing overhead (120% of $1,200)	1,440	4,140
Production costs utilized during period		$119,480

The above calculations show the total manufacturing costs for 19_3, but they do not show the total cost of the completed goods. The cost of the beginning goods in process for 19_3, $2,734, which is the same as the ending goods in process for 19_2, must be included.

. . . .

Total cost of completed goods

Beginning goods in process balance	$ 2,734
To complete beginning goods in process	2,060
Goods started and completed in 19_3	113,280
Cost of goods manufactured	$118,074

Using the statement form from Chapter 16 (see page 498), the cost of goods manufactured can be presented as follows:

Direct material cost	$ 30,600
Direct labor cost	40,400
Factory overhead cost	48,480
Production cost utilized during period	$119,480
Add beginning goods in process, December 31, 19_2	2,734
Total production cost	$122,214
Deduct ending goods in process, December 31, 19_3	4,140
Cost of goods manufactured	$118,074

Assuming that the above costs pertain to Department A of a particular company, a production report is shown on the next page summarizing the production costs.

DEPARTMENT A
Production Report
For the Year Ending December 31, 19_3

	Physical flow	Equivalent units	
		Direct materials	Direct labor
Units:			
Beginning goods in process	400		
Units started	10,100		
Units to be accounted	10,500		
Units completed:			
From beginning goods in process	400	100	200
Started and completed	9,600	9,600	9,600
Total completed	10,000		
Ending goods in process	500	500	300
Units accounted	10,500	10,200	10,100

	Total costs	Equivalent units	Unit costs
Costs:			
Beginning goods in process	$ 2,734		
Current costs:			
Direct materials	30,600 ÷ 10,200		= $ 3.00
Direct labor	40,400 ÷ 10,100		= 4.00
Factory overhead applied	48,480 ÷ 10,100		= 4.80
Costs to be accounted	$122,214		$11.80
Ending goods in process:			
Direct materials	$ 1,500 =	500	× $ 3.00
Direct labor	1,200 =	300	× 4.00
Factory overhead applied	1,440 =	300	× 4.80
Cost of ending goods in process	$ 4,140		
Completed and transferred out:			
Started and completed	$113,280 =	9,600	× $11.80
Beginning goods in process balance	2,734		
Complete beginning goods in process:			
Direct materials	300 =	100	× 3.00
Direct labor	800 =	200	× 4.00
Factory overhead applied	960 =	200	× 4.80
Cost of goods completed	$118,074 ÷	10,000[a]	= 11.8074[b]
Costs accounted	$122,214		

[a]Units transferred out.
[b]Average unit cost of goods transferred out.

INTERDEPARTMENTAL TRANSFERS   Most process cost systems involve two or more processes or departments. The goods move from one process to the next until they are completely manufactured in the last process and transferred to finished goods inventory ready for sale. As the goods move from one process to another, the related costs are also transferred. The transferred out costs of one process become the transferred in costs of the next process.

Goods transferred in from a previous process are added to production at the beginning of the receiving process in much the same way as when materials are added at the beginning of a process. Consequently, transferred in costs to a process may be viewed as similar to material costs being added at the beginning of a process. In other words, if the receiving process did not obtain the goods from the previous process, then the receiving process would have to buy partially completed goods from an outside supplier (similar to raw materials), the cost of which would have to be included in the cost of the product. It follows that the receiving process has to account for the process costs transferred in, as well as accounting for any new materials and conversion (labor and overhead) costs utilized in manufacturing.

To illustrate interdepartmental transfers, assume that commodity X is now manufactured in two processes: Department A and Department B. Further assume that the transferred out costs ($118,074, or 10,000 units at $11.8074) from Department A in the previous illustration become the transferred in costs to Department B. Finally, assume that the following data apply to Department B for the year 19_3:

Costs:
Transferred in costs from Department A	$118,074
Beginning goods in process	$ 12,026
Direct materials	$ 55,000
Direct labor	$ 64,500
Manufacturing overhead—120% of direct labor cost	$ 77,400

Units:
Units transferred in from Department A	10,000
Beginning goods in process	2,000
Ending goods in process	1,000
Units completed and transferred out	11,000

Degree of completion:
Beginning goods in process:	
Direct materials—no materials added last period	100%
Direct labor—25% completed last period	75%
Ending goods in process:	
Direct materials—no materials added this period	0%
Direct labor	25%

Direct materials are added at the end of the process when the product is completed. The normal assumption is made that direct labor and factory overhead are added uniformly throughout the production process; hence, these costs are assumed to be utilized in proportion to the degree of product completion.

Given the above data, the equivalent production for Department B for 19_3 can be computed as shown on page 551 (with explanations as to the underlying rationale).

Given the above cost data and the equivalent production, the production report for Department B for 19_3 can be prepared as shown on page 552.

If it is assumed that *actual* manufacturing overhead was $125,000 ($20,000 indirect materials, $35,000 indirect labor, and $70,000 miscellaneous) for 19_3, the summary process cost entries for Departments A and B for 19_3 are shown on page 553.

551

Manufacturing
Cost Systems:
Process
Costing

DEPARTMENT B

	Physical flow	Equivalent units		
		Transferred in	Direct materials	Direct labor

Units completed during 19_3:

From beginning goods in process   2,000
    Transferred in:
      Similar to materials being added 100% at the beginning of the process, transferred in costs are added at the beginning of the process. Since these units were started last period, transferred in costs were applied 100% to them last period, which is equivalent to transferred in costs this period of 0% of 2,000 units, or zero

    Direct materials:
      Materials added at the end of the process means that no materials were added last period when units were only partially completed; therefore, 100% of materials were added this period to complete the units, which is equivalent to material requirements for 100% of 2,000 finished units, or   2,000

    Direct labor:
      Since 25% of total labor cost was utilized last period, 75% was utilized this period to complete the product, which is equivalent to the labor costs for 75% of 2,000 finished units, or   1,500

	Physical flow	Transferred in	Direct materials	Direct labor
Started and completed in 19_3	9,000	9,000	9,000	9,000
Ending goods in process:	1,000			

    Transferred in:
      Since units transferred in are added 100% at beginning of process, 100% of transferred in costs apply to these 1,000 units started, even though uncompleted, which is equivalent to transferred in costs of 100% of 1,000 units, or   1,000

    Direct materials:
      Since ending inventory units have not reached the end of the process, where materials are added in this process, no materials cost has been added, which is equivalent to 0% of 1,000 units, or zero

    Direct labor:
      25% of the total labor costs have been utilized, which is equivalent to the labor costs for 25% of 1,000 units, or   250

	Physical flow	Transferred in	Direct materials	Direct labor
	12,000	10,000	11,000	10,750

DEPARTMENT B
Production Report
For the Year Ending December 31, 19_3

	Physical flow	Equivalent units		
		Transferred in	Direct materials	Direct labor
Units:				
Beginning goods in process	2,000			
Units transferred in	10,000			
Units to be accounted	12,000			
Units completed:				
From beginning goods in process	2,000	—	2,000	1,500
Started and completed	9,000	9,000	9,000	9,000
Total completed	11,000			
Ending goods in process	1,000	1,000	—	250
Units accounted	12,000	10,000	11,000	10,750

	Total costs	Equivalent units		Unit costs
Costs:				
Beginning goods in process	$ 12,026.00			
Current costs:				
Transferred in	118,074.00	÷ 10,000	=	$11.8074
Direct materials	55,000.00	÷ 11,000	=	5.0000
Direct labor	64,500.00	÷ 10,750	=	6.0000
Factory overhead applied	77,400.00	÷ 10,750	=	7.2000
Costs to be accounted	$327,000.00			$30.0074
Ending goods in process:				
Transferred in	$ 11,807.40	= 1,000	×	$11.8074
Direct materials	—			
Direct labor	1,500.00	= 250	×	6.0000
Factory overhead applied	1,800.00	= 250	×	7.2000
Cost of ending goods in process	$ 15,107.40			
Completed:				
Started and completed	$270,066.60	= 9,000	×	$30.0074
Beginning goods in process balance	12,026.00			
Complete beginning goods in process:				
Transferred in	—			
Direct materials	10,000.00	= 2,000	×	5.0000
Direct labor	9,000.00	= 1,500	×	6.0000
Factory overhead applied	10,800.00	= 1,500	×	7.2000
Cost of goods completed	$311,892.60	÷ 11,000[a]	=	28.3539[b]
Costs accounted	$327,000.00			

[a]Units transferred out.

[b]Average unit cost of goods completed.

Goods in process—Department A	30,600.00	
Goods in process—Department B	55,000.00	
Manufacturing overhead	20,000.00	
Materials inventory		105,600.00
To record materials used in processes.		
Goods in process—Department A	40,400.00	
Goods in process—Department B	64,500.00	
Manufacturing overhead	35,000.00	
Factory payroll payable		139,900.00
To record labor used in processes.		
Goods in process—Department A	48,480.00	
Goods in process—Department B	77,400.00	
Manufacturing overhead		125,880.00
To record factory overhead applied to		
production in processes.		
Manufacturing overhead	70,000.00	
Various accounts		70,000.00
To record actual factory overhead costs.		
Goods in process—Department B	118,074.00	
Goods in process—Department A		118,074.00
To record transfer of cost of 10,000 units		
from Department A to Department B.		
Finished goods	311,892.60	
Goods in process—Department B		311,892.60
To record transfer of 11,000 units completed		
in Department B to finished goods inventory.		

ACTUAL FACTORY OVERHEAD In the preceding illustrations an applied factory overhead rate was used because it was assumed that there were seasonal fluctuations in production and in overhead costs. On the other hand, if production is generally uniform and there are only minor seasonal variations in overhead costs, then actual factory overhead can be used in place of applied factory overhead.

PERCENTAGE OF COMPLETION In order to calculate equivalent units, it is necessary to know the extent of completion of the goods in process. An estimate of the degree of completion can be made by having inspectors, such as production engineers, analyze the manufacturing operations to determine how much work needs to be done to complete the goods in process. However, in some industries in which production is uniform, it is assumed that there are no significant goods in process inventories and all production costs are assigned to completed goods. Also, if estimates of the degree of completion are very difficult or very costly to make, the percentage of completion may be based on reasonable assumptions.

ASSUMPTIONS The discussion in this chapter about the accounting for a process cost system was based on the following assumptions:

(1) The percentage of completion for any goods in process inventory is assumed to be either determinable or based on reasonable estimates.

(2) Direct labor and factory overhead costs are assumed to be utilized continuously in production, which means that they are assumed to be utilized in proportion to the degree of product completion.

(3) Direct materials costs are assumed to be added to production based on actual addition in the particular process. Thus materials can be added at the start of the process, continuously, at the end of the process, or at some actual percentage of completion.

(4) Any beginning goods in process inventory on hand is assumed to be fully completed during the current period of production, i.e., FIFO (first-in, first-out) inventory costing is assumed.

(5) Applied factory overhead is used in place of actual factory overhead cost, because it is assumed that seasonal fluctuations in production and in overhead costs exist.

(6) The costs associated with spoilage, scrap, addition or loss of unit weight, joint production, and other complicated cost accounting problems are assumed not to exist. Such problems are discussed in cost accounting courses.

IMPORTANT TERMS AND CONCEPTS IN CHAPTER 18

Process costing—p. 540	FIFO inventory flow assumption—p. 544
Processes—p. 540	Interdepartmental transfers—pp. 549, 550
Process cost flows—p. 541	Actual factory overhead—p. 553
Production report—pp. 549, 551, 552	Percentage of completion—p. 553
Equivalent units (production)—pp. 543, 544	Assumptions—pp. 553, 554

DEMONSTRATION PROBLEM FOR REVIEW AND SELF-STUDY   Stettler Company manufactures a product processed through two departments: Department #1 and Department #2. All materials are started at the beginning of Process #1 except for containers that are added at the end of Process #2. Labor is utilized uniformly throughout the two processes and factory overhead is applied at the rate of 110 per cent of direct labor cost. As the work on the goods are completed in Department #1, they are immediately transferred to Department #2; as the goods are completed in Department #2, they are transferred to finished goods inventory ready for sale.

Data for 19_9 include the following:

	Dept. #1	Dept. #2
Units:		
Beginning goods in process	1,000	4,000
Started or transferred in	12,000	11,000
Completed	11,000	12,000
Ending goods in process:		
20% complete as to labor, 12/31/_9	2,000	
33⅓% complete as to labor, 12/31/_9		3,000
Costs:		
Beginning goods in process:		
40% complete as to labor, 1/1/_3	$ 6,940	
25% complete as to labor, 1/1/_3		$ 37,140
Direct materials	36,000	120,000
Direct labor	66,000	84,000
Actual manufacturing overhead costs:		
Indirect materials—$40,000		
Indirect labor—$50,000		
Miscellaneous overhead—$73,000		

INSTRUCTIONS

(a) Prepare production reports for Departments #1 and #2 for 19_3.

(b) Prepare summary process cost entries for 19_3.

Note Attempt to solve this demonstration problem before examining the solution that follows.

Solution:

(a)

DEPARTMENT #1
Production Report
For the Year Ended December 31, 19_9

	Physical flow	Equivalent units Direct materials	Direct labor
Units:			
Beginning goods in process	1,000		
Units started	12,000		
Units to be accounted	13,000		
Units completed:			
From beginning goods in process	1,000	—	600
Started and completed	10,000	10,000	10,000
Total completed	11,000		
Ending goods in process	2,000	2,000	400
Units accounted	13,000	12,000	11,000

	Total costs	Equivalent units	Unit costs
Costs:			
Beginning goods in process	$ 6,940		
Current costs:			
Direct materials	36,000 ÷ 12,000	=	$ 3.00
Direct labor	66,000 ÷ 11,000	=	6.00
Factory overhead applied	72,600 ÷ 11,000	=	6.60
Costs to be accounted	$181,540		$15.60
Ending goods in process:			
Direct materials	$ 6,000 =	2,000	× $ 3.00
Direct labor	2,400 =	400	× 6.00
Factory overhead applied	2,640 =	400	× 6.60
	$ 11,040		
Completed and transferred out:			
Started and completed	$156,000 =	10,000	× $15.60
Beginning goods in process balance	6,940		
Complete beginning goods in process:			
Direct materials	—		
Direct labor	3,600 =	600	× $ 6.00
Factory overhead applied	3,960 =	600	× 6.60
Cost of goods completed	$170,500 ÷	11,000	= 15.50
Costs accounted	$181,540		

DEPARTMENT #2
Production Report
For the Year Ended December 31, 19_9

	Physical flow	Equivalent units		
		Transferred in	Direct materials	Direct labor
Units:				
Beginning goods in process	4,000			
Units transferred in	11,000			
Units to be accounted	15,000			
Units completed:				
From beginning goods in process	4,000	—	4,000	3,000
Started and completed	8,000	8,000	8,000	8,000
Total completed	12,000			
Ending goods in process	3,000	3,000	—	1,000
Units accounted	15,000	11,000	12,000	12,000

	Total costs	Equivalent units	Unit costs
Costs:			
Beginning goods in process	$ 37,140		
Current costs:			
Transferred in	170,500 ÷ 11,000	=	$15.50
Direct materials	120,000 ÷ 12,000	=	10.00
Direct labor	84,000 ÷ 12,000	=	7.00
Factory overhead applied	92,400 ÷ 12,000	=	7.70
Costs to be accounted	$504,040		$40.20
Ending goods in process:			
Transferred in	$ 46,500 = 3,000	×	$15.50
Direct materials	—		
Direct labor	7,000 = 1,000	×	7.00
Factory overhead applied	7,700 = 1,000	×	7.70
Cost of ending goods in process	$ 61,200		
Completed:			
Started and completed	$321,600 = 8,000	×	$40.20
Beginning goods in process balance	37,140		
Complete beginning goods in process:			
Transferred in	—		
Direct materials	40,000 = 4,000	×	10.00
Direct labor	21,000 = 3,000	×	7.00
Factory overhead applied	23,100 = 3,000	×	7.70
Cost of goods completed	$442,840 ÷ 12,000	=	36.90
Costs accounted	$504,040		

(b)

Goods in process—Department #1	36,000	
Goods in process—Department #2	120,000	
Manufacturing overhead	40,000	
Materials inventory		196,000
To record materials used in processes.		
Goods in process—Department #1	66,000	
Goods in process—Department #2	84,000	
Manufacturing overhead	50,000	
Factory payroll payable		200,000
To record labor used in processes.		
Goods in process—Department #1	72,600	
Goods in process—Department #2	92,400	
Manufacturing overhead		165,000
To record factory overhead applied to production in processes.		
Manufacturing overhead	73,000	
Various accounts		73,000
To record actual factory overhead costs.		
Goods in process—Department #1	170,500	
Goods in process—Department #2		170,500
To record transfer of cost of 11,000 units from Department #1 to Department #2.		
Finished goods	442,840	
Goods in process—Department #2		442,840
To record transfer of 12,000 units completed in Department #2 to finished goods inventory.		

Questions

1   The selection of a job order or a process cost system for a specific manufacturing firm depends on its manufacturing technology. Explain what this statement means.

2   What are the differences between the cost flows of a job order system and of a process cost system? Explain.

3   Manufacturing costs that are direct costs under a process cost system may be indirect costs under a job order system, and vice versa. Explain what this statement means.

4   Job order cost systems emphasize total cost, while process cost systems emphasize average cost. Explain what this statement means.

5   What is equivalent production?

6   Why are separate unit costs calculated for materials and labor?

7   How would service department costs be handled in a process cost system?

8   In a process cost system there is no need to use applied factory overhead rates. Do you agree with this statement? Explain.

9   The basic report of a job order system is the job cost sheet. What is the basic report of a process cost system and why is it important?

10   In a process cost system, the percentage of completion is used to assign cost to a unit partially completed during the fiscal period. Why is this an assumption? Explain.

11   Is the following statement correct? For goods in process at the beginning of the period that are completed during the period, the FIFO process costing method assigns to finished goods only those costs added during the current period.

12   At the end of a specific time period a company has 1,000 partially completed units. Is it possible for the equivalent units of production on these goods with regard to direct materials to be zero?

13   Is the following statement correct? The process costing production report summarizes the production costs of a specific department on a specific date. Explain.

14   XYZ Company consists of Department A and Department B. Manufacturing processing is sequential and all units completed in Department A are transferred to Department B. If Department A's equivalent units for material, labor, and overhead were all 1,000 units, is the cost of goods transferred to Department B 1,000 units multiplied by the total cost per equivalent unit? Assume that an ending goods in process inventory exists.

Short exercises

E18-1

You are given three multiple-choice statements. Select the correct answers and indicate the corresponding letters on a sheet of paper (e.g., 1-d, 2-d, etc.).

(1)   Which of the following is *not* an assumption for the process cost system discussed in this chapter?
(a) Costs associated with spoilage are assumed not to exist. (b) Actual factory overhead is usually

used in place of applied factory overhead because of the assumed seasonal fluctuations. (c) The percentage of completion for any goods in process inventory is assumed to be determinable. (d) Manufacturing costs are usually assumed to be uniformly utilized throughout the production. (e) All of the above. (f) None of the above.

(2) Process costing methods (a) cannot be utilized when there is a beginning goods in process inventory, (b) cannot be used when a manufacturing unit is processed by more than one department, (c) develop a production report and therefore no journal entries are made for cost flows, (d) calculate the cost of a fully completed unit by dividing total costs incurred by the number of units completed, (e) all of the above, (f) none of the above.

(3) Which of the following is *correct?* (a) Transferred in costs are treated in a manner similar to materials added at the beginning of the period. (b) The FIFO method treats the beginning goods in process inventory as though it were completed last period. (c) The number of equivalent units calculated under the FIFO process costing method are the same for both direct materials and direct labor. (d) Material, labor, and overhead are always assumed to be added uniformly as the manufacturing progresses. (e) All of the above. (f) None of the above.

E18-2

You are given below an introductory process costing problem and four related multiple-choice questions. Select the correct answers and indicate the corresponding letters on a sheet of paper (e.g., 1-d, 2-d, etc.).

Process Company production records for 19_7:

Total production costs	$71,000
Materials added (at beginning of process)	$20,000
Direct labor (at a uniform rate)	$34,000
Beginning goods in process inventory	–0–
Units started in production	20,000
Units started and completed	14,000

The ending inventory of goods in process is one-half complete as to direct labor and as to overhead which is applied on the basis of direct labor.

(1) What are the equivalent units of production for materials? (a) 20,000, (b) 14,000, (c) 21,000, (d) 27,000, (e) none of the above.

(2) What are the equivalent units for overhead? (a) 20,000, (b) 14,000, (c) 21,000, (d) 27,000, (e) none of the above.

(3) What is the total cost per equivalent unit? (a) $1.00, (b) $2.00, (c) $3.00, (d) $4.00, (e) none of the above.

(4) The ending goods in process has a cost of (a) $56,000, (b) $6,000, (c) $15,000, (d) $71,000, (e) none of the above.

E18-3

Fill in the blanks.

(a) If 100,000 units were started and completed during the period, they would be equivalent to _____ finished units.

(b) Ending inventory of 2,500 units that is 40 per cent complete during the period is equivalent to _____ finished units.

(c) Beginning inventory of 5,000 units that were 70 per cent complete at the beginning of the period would be equivalent to _____ finished units last period and _____ finished units this period (assuming FIFO).

(d) If materials are added to production at the end of the production process, then ending goods in process of 5,000 units that are 80 per cent complete as to labor and overhead would be equivalent to _____ finished units with regard to materials and _____ finished units with regard to labor and overhead.

E18-4

You are given the following process cost data:

	Physical flow	Equivalent units	
		Materials	Labor & overhead
Completed:			
Beginning goods in process	50,000	—	17,500
Started and completed	150,000	150,000	150,000
Ending goods in process	60,000	60,000	45,000
	260,000	210,000	212,500

The company uses the FIFO process costing method.

(a) Were materials added to production at the beginning of the production process, continuously, or at the end of the production process? Explain.

(b) What is the percentage of completion for labor and overhead with regard to beginning goods in process? started and completed? ending goods in process? Make sure you show how the percentages were derived.

(c) How many units were started in production during the period?

E18-5

You are given below the process flows for Sequential Company:

Materials inventory		
xxx	10,000	

Goods in process—#1	
4,000	12,500
7,500	
6,000	

Finished goods	
25,000	20,000

Factory payroll payable	
xxx	25,000

Goods in process—#2	
12,500	30,000
2,500	
12,500	
10,000	

Cost of goods sold	
20,000	

Manufacturing overhead	
xxx	20,000

Goods in process—#3	
30,000	25,000
3,500	
5,000	
4,000	

(a) In general journal form, make entries to record the above cost flows.

(b) What is the ending inventory for each of the goods in process accounts and for finished goods?

E18-6   *What is wrong with the calculation below? Explain.*

Units of beginning goods in process	3,000
Units started in production	30,000
Total units of production	33,000
Units of ending goods in process	8,000
Units completed	25,000
Beginning goods in process cost	$ 15,000
Production cost utilized during period	285,000
Total production cost	$300,000 ÷ 25,000 = $12.00
Ending goods in process cost ($12.00 × 8,000)	96,000
Cost of goods manufactured	$204,000

E18-7   *Department A uses the FIFO method of process costing. During a cost period 60,000 units were completed and transferred to Department B. There were 12,000 units in the beginning goods in process inventory, which were one-third complete with respect to direct labor and overhead (both utilized uniformly). The ending goods in process inventory was two-fifths complete with respect to direct labor and overhead and 58,000 units were started during the period.*

Required:

Calculate the equivalent units of production for materials under each of the following assumptions:

(a) All material is added at the beginning of the process.

(b) All material is added at the end of the process.

(c) One-half of the material is added at the beginning of the process and one-half is added when the product is 90 per cent complete (as to direct labor).

Problems

A18-1   *Carter Company has a process cost system in which production begins in the preparation process, then moves to the finishing process, and then to finished goods. At the beginning of the year Carter Company had the following beginning inventory balances: materials, $75,000, preparation process, $32,000, finishing process, $40,000, finished goods, $37,500. The following transactions took place during the year 19_5:*

(1) Materials purchased during 19_5 amounted to $225,000.

(2) Materials issued to production were as follows: preparation process, $100,000; finishing process, $75,000; indirect materials, $35,000.

(3) Factory labor utilized was as follows: preparation process, $145,000; finishing process, $180,000; indirect labor, $75,000.

(4) Actual factory overhead costs utilized over the year were: factory utilities, $12,000; factory depreciation, $45,000; factory insurance, $12,500; miscellaneous factory costs, $7,500.

(5) Because factory overhead costs and production are fairly uniform, the firm does not use applied factory overhead. Thus, actual factory overhead cost was distributed to the processes as follows: preparation process, $100,000; finishing process, $87,000.

(6) At year end, there were ending goods in process of $35,000 in the preparation process. The other units were transferred to the finishing process.

(7) At year end, there were ending goods in process of $42,500 in the finishing process. The other units were transferred to finished goods.

(8) The ending inventory of finished goods was $45,000.

Required:

Set up T-accounts. Post the beginning balances and the above transactions.

A18-2

For each of the cases below, calculate the equivalent production for Cap Corporation. Use the FIFO process costing method.

(1) The number of units started was $25,000, ending goods in process consisted of 50,000 units that were 3/5 complete; no beginning goods in process.

(2) Beginning goods in process consisted of 37,500 units 2/5 complete at the beginning of the period; ending goods in process consisted of 50,000 units 1/5 complete; 100,000 units were completed.

(3) Beginning goods in process consisted of 93,750 units in which 80 per cent of the work was done in the current period to complete them; 112,500 units were started; ending goods in process consisted of 31,250 units that were 26 per cent complete.

(4) There were 250,000 units started; beginning goods in process consisted of 25,000 units 4/5 complete as to materials and 1/5 complete as to labor and overhead at the beginning of the period; ending goods in process consisted of 156,250 units 3/5 complete as to materials and 2/5 complete as to labor and overhead.

A18-3

Leaf Company uses a sequential process cost system in which costs flow from Process 1 to Process 2 to Process 3. The following data are provided: Materials A and B were added in Process 1, material C was added in Process 2, and material D was added in Process 3. Assume that costs were added continuously, that there were no in-process inventories, and that actual factory overhead cost was 150 per cent of direct labor cost.

Data for August:

Materials used:		Labor utilized:	
A	$5,600	Process 1	$32,000
B	8,800	Process 2	24,000
C	7,200	Process 3	48,000
D	6,400		

Required:

(a) Set up T-accounts for each process and show the cost flows.

(b) Assuming 20,000 units of finished product were produced, what is the unit cost of the product after it leaves each process?

(c) Prepare a production report indicating, for each process, the total and unit costs.

A18-4

You are given below the cost and the quantity data for Swiss Manufacturing Company. Material is added at the beginning of the process, the FIFO method is used, and completed goods are transferred to finished goods.

Beginning goods in process inventory, April 1, 19_2	
5,000 units, 40% completed:	
Materials	$6,000
Labor and factory overhead	7,500
Costs during April:	
Materials, 15,000 units	19,500
Labor and factory overhead	73,800
Ending goods in process inventory, April 30, 19_2—1,200 units 50% completed.	

Required:

(a) How many units were completed? Show all calculations.

(b) What was the total cost of the goods completed? Show all calculations.

(c) What was the cost of the ending goods in process inventory? Show all calculations.

(d) What was the *average* cost per finished unit?

A18-5

The equivalent production and the manufacturing costs for Number Company for the year ended December 31, 19_2 are presented below:

	Physical flow	Equivalent units	
		Materials	Labor
Ending goods in process	75,000	60,000	37,500
Completed goods:			
Beginning goods in process	15,000	3,000	5,000
Started and completed	85,000	85,000	85,000
	175,000	148,000	127,500

Beginning goods in process cost	$100,000
Materials cost	925,000
Labor cost	860,625
Factory overhead cost—80% of direct labor cost.	

Required (show all calculations and use the FIFO process costing method):

(a) The unit costs of manufacturing for 19_2.

(b) The cost of the ending goods in process and the completion costs for 19_2.

(c) The total cost of the completed goods.

A18-6

Brass Company uses the FIFO process costing method for production analysis. The plating department adds one-half of the materials at the beginning of the process and one-half at the end of the process. Direct labor is utilized when the units are three-fourths completed and overhead is utilized uniformly throughout the process.

    Data for the year 19_8 are as follows:

Goods in process—beginning	12,000 units, seven-twelfths complete, $18,000 (materials, $6,000)
Units completed	50,000
Units started	40,000
Goods in process—ending	2,000, one-half complete
Material cost	$120,000
Direct labor cost	$200,000
Overhead cost	$140,000

Required:

Develop a complete production report for 19_8.

B18-1

Time, Inc., manufactures a product in two production processes. The following transactions took place during January, 19_4.

(1) Purchased material on credit for $100,000.

(2) Materials issued to production were as follows: Process #1, $20,000; Process #2, $30,000; factory supplies, $10,000.

(3) Labor utilized was as follows: Process #1, $40,000; Process #2, $36,000; indirect labor, $16,000.

(4) Applied factory overhead for the month was based on 125 per cent of direct labor cost.

(5) Actual factory overhead for the month was as follows: factory depreciation, $8,000; factory insurance, $4,000; factory machinery repairs, $16,000 (paid to a maintenance firm).

(6) Product costing $60,000 was completed in Process #1 and transferred to Process #2.

(7) Product costing $140,000 was completed in Process #2 and transferred to finished goods.

(8) Product costing $130,000 was sold during the month.

Required:

(a) In general journal form, make entries for the January transactions of Time, Inc.

(b) Compute the ending inventory for the following accounts (show your work): Goods in Process—#1, Goods in Process—#2, and Finished Goods.

B18-2

Assume that Sally Corporation started (i.e., put into production) 80,000 units of product during the fiscal period. For each of the cases below, calculate the equivalent production for Sally Corporation (show your calculations).

(1) The number of units fully completed during the period was 80,000; there were no beginning goods in process.

(2) Ending goods in process consisted of 25,000 units 30 per cent complete at the end of the period; there were no beginning goods in process.

(3) Beginning goods in process consisted of 6,000 units 30 per cent complete at the beginning of the period. Ending goods in process consisted of 10,000 units 80 per cent complete at the end of the period.

(4) Beginning goods in process consisted of 4,000 units 50 per cent complete as to labor and overhead and 90 per cent complete as to materials at the beginning of the period. Ending goods in process consisted of 6,000 units 25 per cent complete as to labor and overhead and 75 per cent complete as to materials at the end of the period.

B18-3

Manufacturing Company has two manufacturing processes. In Process #1 all of the materials were added at the beginning of the process, while in Process #2 all of the materials were added at the end of the process. The percentage of completion with regard to labor and overhead was as follows:

	Process #1	Process #2
Beginning goods in process	75% complete at beginning of period	25% of work done in the current period to complete
Ending goods in process	60% complete at end of period	40% complete at end of period

Given the physical flows on page 565, calculate the equivalent production for the two processes (show your calculations). Use the FIFO process costing method.

	Process #1	Process #2
Beginning goods in process	75,000	50,000
Started or transferred in	625,000	550,000
Units to be accounted	700,000	600,000
Ending goods in process	100,000	75,000
Completed or transferred out	600,000	525,000
Units accounted	700,000	600,000

(Hint: *In calculating the equivalent production for materials, make sure you take into account the time period when the materials were or will be added to production. For example, if all materials were added last period, they would be weighted zero this period.*)

B18-4   *Memory Company uses a process cost system. The company manufactures one product in one process. The cost data for the year 19_2 are given below:*

Goods in process:
Beginning units	—
Units started	30,000
Ending units (100% complete as to materials and 75% complete as to labor and overhead)	6,000
Materials cost	$375,000
Labor cost	$530,100
Manufacturing overhead cost	$313,500

Required:

Prepare a production report for Memory Company as of December 31, 19_2. Use the FIFO process costing method.

B18-5   *Intro Company manufactures a high-quality calculator. The processing consists of a single department which assembles components and then ships the calculators to retail outlets. One-half of the materials are added at the beginning of the process and the remainder at the three-fourths completion point. Labor and overhead are utilized uniformly throughout the process. Beginning inventory was 8,000 units (50% complete, $24,000 of materials, $12,000 of direct labor, and $10,000 of overhead). During 19_6, 60,000 units were completed and shipped and the ending inventory was 10,000 units (40% complete). The costs for 19_6 were materials of $100,000, direct labor of $70,000 and overhead of $40,000.*

Develop the 19_6 production report. Use the FIFO process costing method.

B18-6   *Ag Company opened a new feed plant on March 1. Mixing operations consist of two processes with the following mixing ratios:*

Process 1: Wheat	10 bushels
Milo	10 "
	20 bushels
Process 2: Secret mix	5 "
Feed	25 bushels

There were no beginning inventories of wheat, milo, secret mix, or feed. The two processes had no beginning or ending inventories for the month of March. The month's records indicate the following:

Wheat purchased—60,000 bushels @ $2.90
Milo purchased—60,000 bushels @ $3.60
Secret mix purchased—35,000 bushels @ $4.50
Process #1 direct labor $3,500
Process #2 direct labor   2,000
Factory overhead (150% of direct labor cost)   8,250
Feed produced—130,000 bushels
Feed sold—117,000 bushels

Required:

(a) Set up T-accounts for the three ingredients, for the two processes, and for the feed inventory, and record the cost flows.

(b) Make up a schedule of all the ending inventories.

(Hint: Use the mixing ratios to determine the inputs.)

STANDARD COSTS

CHAPTER 19

PURPOSE OF CHAPTER In the two preceding chapters we discussed two manufacturing cost systems, job order costing and process costing, in which actual production costs utilized in manufacturing products were assigned to these products primarily for product costing purpose (i.e., inventory valuation and cost of goods sold determination). Such cost data are historical in nature in that they are based on past transactions. Carefully compiled and promptly available historical cost data are needed and serve as a starting point for purposes of control. However, there are limitations to the usefulness of historical cost data, especially from the viewpoint of management.

Historical cost data provide an inadequate basis for the measurement of efficiency. It is true that some impressions about efficiency can be obtained through historical comparisons; for example, unit costs for the month just ended can be compared with unit costs for the same month last year. But how is it determined whether or not operations of the same month last year—the basis used for comparison—were efficient? If there have been changes in wage rates, material prices, or the volume of production—to mention just a few of the things that can change—the difference in unit costs is not a reliable indication even for deciding whether recent operations have been more or less efficient. In short, what conclusions about efficiency can be reached from the fact that the unit cost of a given product or operations is $10 above last year?

Moreover, in some industries prices must be announced for the finished product before production is started. This is typical for businesses that make annual model changes. If there is some relationship between costs and selling prices, the costs that are most relevant are not historical costs.

For purposes of controlling costs, management wants to know the difference between planned costs and actual costs and why these differences occurred. In so doing, management attempts to control prices paid and quantities used. Such control is accomplished through standard costs, which can be used with any product costing system such as job order or process costing systems. Consequently, the purpose of this chapter is to discuss control through the use of standard costs.

STANDARD COSTS Standard costs are scientifically predetermined costs that serve as bench marks for comparison with actual costs. They are target costs that should be attained under normal operating conditions.

Standards are used to control costs. Control has to do with achieving conformity to plans, primarily by obtaining useful information feedback on how well the company is moving toward its plans. Based on engineering and accounting studies, standard costs are computed before production occurs, then, as production occurs actual costs are compared with standard costs. Such comparisons provide feedback to management for gauging performance and for placing responsibilities as to the causes of any significant differences.

The degree of difficulty in compiling standard costs is influenced by many factors, such as the size of the business, the complexity of the manufacturing process, and the stability of business conditions. The build-up of predetermined unit costs involves a detailed analysis of the material specifications. Information about the kinds, grades, quantities, and expected prices of the materials is developed. Each step in the manufacturing process is studied in order to determine the class and amount of direct labor required. Wage rates are then considered. The final cost segment to be estimated is manufacturing overhead. Here the accountant often faces a great challenge to his or her ingenuity. It is possible, however, with study and experience, to arrive at predetermined costs for factory overhead that have considerable validity.

Even though great care is used in computing predetermined costs, it is likely that the actual costs will deviate from the standard. Such deviations, or differences, are referred to as *variances*. When actual costs exceed standard costs, the variance is unfavorable. A favorable variance arises when the actual costs are below standard costs. Variances are signals that alert management to seek out the reasons for the variances and, when necessary, to initiate remedial action. In this way, management can improve its decision making by learning how successful its past decisions have been. Moreover, the feedback of actual financial data for comparison with standards aids management in determining whether or not the firm is meeting top management's objectives.

Although variances are signals for management action, the *consistent absence* of variances may also be a signal to management. For example, zero variances may be the result of cost manipulation.

Finally, it must be stressed that unless standards are continually revised, they will be no more effective than a mere comparison of this year's historical costs with past years' historical costs. In other words, the use of a standard cost system assumes up-to-date standards.

BASIC FEATURES OF A STANDARD COST SYSTEM   The use of standard costs and cost variances in the accounting records is called a *standard cost system*. Such a standard cost system can be used in job order costing and process costing. However, some companies do not incorporate standard costs into their accounting records; instead, they use standard costs only for internal reports for management.

Under a standard cost system, standard costs are charged to Goods in Process, Finished Goods, and Cost of Goods Sold. In other words, the standard costs, rather than the actual costs, of direct materials (standard prices times standard quantities), direct labor (standard prices or rates times standard hours), and manufacturing overhead (standard rate times the standard activity level) are charged to these accounts. Any differences between the actual and the standard costs are accumulated in variance accounts, which isolates the variances so that they may be studied for possible remedial action.

The following example will indicate the nature of variances and the distinctive features of the recording procedure when cost standards have been established.

Data:

Standard price per unit of acquired materials	$ 1
Actual cost of acquired materials—400 units @ $.98	392

Accounting entry:

Materials inventory (400 × $1)	400	
Materials price variance		8
Accounts payable		392

The example shows that purchases are charged to the materials inventory account at standard price. Any price variation is isolated in a variance account when the purchase is recorded. By recording the material price variance at the time of purchase, control is facilitated because any corrective action can be taken immediately. This also leads to bookkeeping economy, since the inventory clerk needs only to keep track of quantities of materials. The clerk need not keep track of actual material prices, for the price variances are isolated in the materials price variance accounts and he or she knows the standard prices used to cost out the materials.

A quantity variance may exist if the quantity of materials used in the production of finished goods differs from the predetermined standard quantity.

The several variances that may arise and the factors that determine the dollar amount of each variance follow:

Direct materials:

Price variance = Difference between the actual material price paid (Pa) and the standard material price (Ps) per unit multiplied by the actual quantity of materials purchased (Qp).

$$= (Pa - Ps) \times Qp$$

Efficiency (quantity) variance = Difference between the actual material quantity used (Qu) in production and the standard material quantity (Qs) multiplied by the standard material price per unit (Ps).

$$= (Qu - Qs) \times Ps$$

Direct labor:

Price (rate) variance = Difference between the actual labor price paid (Pa) and the standard labor price (Ps) per hour multiplied by the actual labor hours used (Hu) in production.

$$= (Pa - Ps) \times Hu$$

Efficiency (time) variance = Difference between the actual labor hours used (Hu) in production and the standard labor hours (Hs) multiplied by the standard wage price per hour (Ps).

$$= (Hu - Hs) \times Ps$$

Manufacturing overhead:
Total factory overhead variance = Difference between the actual factory overhead and the standard factory overhead.

Note that the above formulas for computing the variances are established so that positive variances are unfavorable and negative variances are favorable. Also, in the recording of variances, debit variances are unfavorable and credit variances are favorable.

ILLUSTRATION Following is a simple illustration of the operation of a standard cost system. State Company manufactures one product. The following standard unit costs have been established:

Standard cost card

Direct materials—1 unit at $2.80	$ 2.80
Direct labor—2 hours at $6	12.00
Manufacturing overhead—applied per direct labor hour or 2 hours at $2.60	5.20
Standard cost per finished unit	$20.00

Data for the period

Goods in process—no beginning or ending inventories	–0–
Units manufactured	7,500
Units sold	7,000
Direct materials:	
Actual purchase price per unit—$2.75	
Actual quantity purchased	7,700
Actual quantity used in production	7,550
Standard quantity for 7,500 units manufactured	7,500
(Standard cost card shows that it should take 1 unit of material to produce 1 unit of finished product; therefore, the standard quantity is 7,500 × 1.)	
Direct labor:	
Actual hourly labor rate paid—$6.04	
Actual labor hours worked	14,000
Standard labor hours for 7,500 units manufactured	15,000
(Standard cost card shows that it should take 2 hours of labor to produce 1 unit of product; therefore, standard labor hours are 7,500 × 2.)	
Manufacturing overhead:	
Actual factory overhead cost	$39,100
Applied overhead (at standard) for 7,500 units manufactured ($2.60 per hour × 15,000 standard hours)	$39,000

Cost entries:

(1) Materials inventory ($2.80 × 7,700)	21,560	
Materials price variance [($2.75 − $2.80) × 7,700]		385
Accounts payable ($2.75 × 7,700)		21,175
(2) Goods in process ($2.80 × 7,500)	21,000	
Materials efficiency variance [(7,550 − 7,500) × $2.80]	140	
Materials inventory ($2.80 × 7,550)		21,140
(3) Goods in process ($6 × 15,000)	90,000	
Labor price variance [($6.04 − $6.00) × 14,000]	560	
Labor efficiency variance [(14,000 − 15,000) × $6]		6,000
Factory payroll payable ($6.04 × 14,000)		84,560
(4) Goods in process ($2.60 × 15,000)	39,000	
Manufacturing overhead		39,000

(5) Finished goods ($20 × 7,500)	150,000	
Goods in process		150,000
(6) Manufacturing overhead (actual costs)	39,100	
Various accounts		39,100
(7) Manufacturing overhead variance ($39,100 − $39,000)	100	
Manufacturing overhead		100
(8) Cost of goods sold	140,000	
Finished goods (7,000 × $20)		140,000

The cost flows are summarized in the illustration below.

STANDARD COST FLOWS

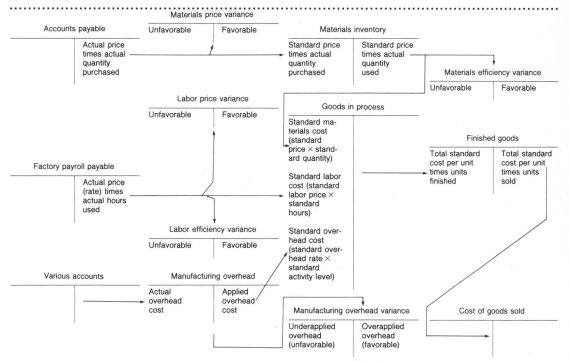

COMMENTS ABOUT ILLUSTRATION To compute standard quantities, actual equivalent production is multiplied by the standard inputs per unit of finished output. The standard cost card indicates the inputs of material and labor that should be used to produce one unit of finished product; hence, to compute standard quantities, actual output is converted into the inputs that should have been utilized to produce that actual output. Because these standard quantities represent the inputs that should have been used to attain the output, they can be directly compared with the quantities of actual input to derive efficiency variances. For example, the standard cost card in the illustration indicates that it should take one unit of material and two hours of labor per unit of finished output. With actual output of 7,500 units, the standard quantity of materials (or more accurately the standard quantity of materials allowed for good output produced) is 7,500 units (1 × 7,500) and the standard labor hours (or more accurately the standard hours of labor allowed for good output produced) are 15,000 (2 × 7,500).

The illustration also points out that the materials and labor efficiency variances are isolated when the costs are transferred to goods in process. The reason for this is that for purposes of managerial control it is desirable to isolate the two variances as soon as possible. Consequently, whenever possible, management should have the materials and labor efficiency variances isolated at the time any excess material and labor are added to goods in process (or at least isolated before the production is completed). For example, the inventory clerk may issue materials based on standard requirements for a job, and any additional materials will be issued only if the production supervisor signs excess materials requisitions, which pinpoint the materials efficiency variances. Such excess quantities of materials are charged at standard prices to the materials efficiency variance account. On the other hand, when the two efficiency variances cannot be reasonably determined until the goods are completed, then the two variances are isolated when the product is transferred from goods in process to finished goods.

Finally, the preceding illustration also points out that to calculate applied factory overhead under standard costing, the *standard* activity level (e.g., standard direct labor hours or cost) is multiplied by the standard factory overhead rate. In previous chapters, the applied factory overhead was the *actual* activity level (e.g., actual direct labor hours or cost) times the standard factory overhead rate. However, the actual activity level may reflect inefficiencies that should not be included in applied factory overhead because, at year end, applied overhead serves as the yardstick for determining, and subsequently analyzing, the total factory overhead variance.

VARIANCE ANALYSIS With the standard cost system isolating the discrepancies between planned and actual costs, management has an excellent opportunity through the use of variance data to seek out the causes for differences between expectation and achievement. However, interpreting variances is not a simple matter. If variances are misinterpreted by management and improper actions are taken, then the standard cost system, a potentially effective managerial device, can in fact prove to be a harmful tool.

There are certain kinds of background information about any standard cost system that, if known, will improve the chances for a correct interpretation of variances. For instance, a causal relationship exists between variances and the level at which standards are set. Standards may be set at *ideal* levels, the attainment of which is only possible at the best operating conditions, since no allowance is made for ordinary machine breakdowns, normal spoilage, normal business interruptions, and the fact that employees do not work at 100 per cent efficiency all the time. Or, standards may be set at *currently attainable* levels, which are "tight" but possible to achieve, since allowance is made for ordinary machine breakdowns, etc. The point is, variances from ideal standards carry different implications from those carried by variances from currently attainable standards.[1]

It should also be recognized that some variances may be an indication merely that external conditions have changed since the standards were adopted. For in-

---

[1]It should be pointed out that most firms do not use ideal standards because they discourage even the most diligent workers, result in variances that have little meaning (i.e., abnormal inefficiency is not isolated because "normal" inefficiency is, in effect, built in), and unlike currently attainable standards are not useful for pricing and other decision-making purposes.

stance, suppliers may have announced new price schedules, or property tax rates may have changed. Under such circumstances it would be desirable to revise the standards to avoid the showing of variances resulting from conditions beyond the control of management or employees.

The standard-setting procedure followed by a company may also be pertinent. If the employees who are in a position to incur costs are excluded from the standard-setting process, they may be inclined to work against the system. On the other hand, if they have participated in the setting of standards and believe that the goals are attainable, the opportunity for management to use variance data as a measurement of performance and to stimulate efficiency may be greatly improved.

The analysis of specific variances should be undertaken for the purpose of locating the reasons for the off-standard results. The reasons set forth in the following paragraphs are illustrative.

Material variances Material price variances may be the fault of the purchasing department. Price variances may be attributable to the ordering of uneconomical quantities of material or the ordering of the wrong quality of material. Improper attention to the location of the supplier may have resulted in above-standard transportation charges. But it is unwise to assume that price variances are always attributable to the actions of the purchasing department. Poor scheduling by the production department may have put such pressure on the purchasing department that it was forced to release purchase orders on unfavorable terms in order to avoid any delay of the manufacturing activities. It is also unwise to assume that a favorable price variance is to the credit of some employee or department. It may merely indicate that market prices have declined.

Material efficiency variances may be traceable to the level of efficiency and skill of the working force, to spoilage from improper handling and storage, or to defective materials. Although efficiency variances generally are more controllable than price variances, efficiency variances may be difficult to analyze if there are several contributing causes. It may be noted at this point that offsetting variances, some favorable and some unfavorable, may cause the net variance to be insignificant and thus possibly lead management to the improper conclusion that no substandard performance exists.

Labor variances Labor variances may be attributable to changes in wage rates, to the wrong category of workers assigned to a task, to improper hiring practices, and to inadequate training programs. An especially difficult analytical problem may arise as a result of the factory working under overtime conditions. The effectiveness of personnel policies can also have a considerable effect on labor variances.

Factory overhead variances In the previous chapter it was pointed out that, during the fiscal period, factory overhead variances may occur because of seasonal fluctuations in production and individual factory overhead costs. However, by the end of the fiscal period, the seasonal variations should tend to average out so that the total factory overhead variance is small or zero, i.e., applied and actual factory overhead should approximate one another. Thus any interim-period factory overhead variance is shown on the balance sheet and any year end factory overhead variance generally is written off, for convenience, to Cost of Goods Sold.

On the other hand, factory overhead variances can arise from other than seasonal factors. For example, actual and standard applied factory overhead costs may differ because of unexpected price changes in individual overhead items, poor cost estimates of individual overhead items, differences between the actual and standard activity level used in applying factory overhead cost to goods in process, and differences between planned and actual production levels.

For purposes of analysis, the total factory overhead variance can be broken down into component parts. Such procedures are discussed subsequently in this chapter.

MANAGEMENT BY EXCEPTION It should be apparent from the above paragraphs that not all variances are signals for action. To treat all so-called unfavorable variances as sufficient reason for some penalty action would, in many cases, be quite short-sighted on the part of management. Thus management is concerned about the unusual and important financial variations from the expected; management is concerned about such exceptions because its time is limited and valuable and should not be spent analyzing all variances. Consequently, management attempts to analyze exceptional variations in order to identify the causes and make remedial decisions affecting the future.

Management by exception necessitates the establishment of criteria to determine whether variances are exceptional enough to warrant analysis by management. For example, the proportion of the dollar amount of a variance to the total standard cost may be used as a criterion. That is, based on past and expected operations, management may ignore all variances of less than 10 per cent as immaterial and random; variances of 10 per cent or more would be exceptions requiring management analysis.

In general, management is more concerned about efficiency variances (material efficiency and labor efficiency variances) than about price variances, because the former are more controllable by management. For instance, unusual material price increases generally are not within the control of the purchasing agent.

Management should be concerned not only about exceptional unfavorable variances but also about unusual favorable variances. Analysis may indicate that standards are out of date or that certain types of management policies that led to the favorable variances should be continued in the future.

DISPOSITION OF VARIANCES When a standard cost system is in use and variances exist, the inventory account balances at the end of an accounting period will not be stated at actual costs. Thus, in theory, the variances should be prorated to the inventory cost accounts and to Cost of Goods Sold in order to reflect actual costs. However, the usual practice is to write off the variances at the end of the annual fiscal period to expense, e.g., Cost of Goods Sold. The practice of writing off variances, for convenience, to Cost of Goods Sold is acceptable so long as the standards are up to date and are not based on unattainable (ideal) performance.

If the State Company data from the previous illustration is used and if annual data are assumed, the variances would be closed to Cost of Goods Sold at year end as follows:

Labor efficiency variance	6,000	
Materials price variance	385	
Labor price variance		560
Materials efficiency variance		140
Manufacturing overhead variance		100
Cost of goods sold		5,585

The labor efficiency and materials price variances are favorable; to close them, therefore, the two variance accounts are debited as shown. Because labor price and materials efficiency variances are unfavorable, they are closed by credits. The manufacturing overhead variance represents underapplied factory overhead cost of $100 ($39,100 actual minus $39,000 applied), which is an unfavorable debit variance. The $100 variance is closed by a debit to Cost of Goods Sold and a credit to Manufacturing Overhead Variance. The standard cost of goods sold of $140,000 less the $5,585 net adjustment for the closing of all the variances results in a $134,415 ending balance for Cost of Goods Sold.

FACTORY OVERHEAD COST CONTROL   Factory overhead costs are controlled by the use of a flexible budget. A flexible budget is used because actual production can vary from expected production, and when this happens certain overhead costs vary with production (variable factory overhead cost) and others do not (fixed factory overhead costs). Consequently, to compare actual overhead costs with budget or planned overhead costs for purposes of evaluating efficiency (the ratio of output to input), the budgeted overhead costs should be at the same level of activity as the actual results. The flexible budget provides such a comparison, since a manager can determine what level of activity was actually attained during a period and then use the flexible budget to determine what costs should have been at that activity level. In other words, a flexible budget is a summary statement of planned costs that is geared toward a range of activity and thereby tells how much cost should be utilized at the level of activity actually attained.

Although the measure of activity or volume used in flexible budgeting varies from company to company, it should be one in which a company's variable factory overhead cost tends to vary with changes in the activity level. A common activity measure is hours, such as direct labor hours or machine hours. Hours, rather than physical units of product, are used since most firms have several products and hours provide a useful common denominator for measuring overall production. Moreover, the hours are normally expressed in terms of standard hours, rather than actual hours, so that the inefficient use of inputs will appear as efficiency variances. In other words, actual hours are affected by variations in performance while standard hours are not; hence, a flexible budget based on standard hours allowed for the output attained focuses on how many inputs should have been utilized at that output level. For example, if two standard direct labor hours are allowed per unit of output, then 800 units of actual output achieved means that 1,600 (800 × 2) standard direct labor hours should have been utilized in production. The 1,600 standard hours are equivalent to 800 units of output.

The construction of a flexible budget assumes that an analysis of a company's overhead cost behavior patterns has been made so that the costs can be separated into variable and fixed components. If such an analysis is assumed, the flexible budget for State Company is illustrated on page 576.

STATE COMPANY
Flexible Budget
For the Month of May 19__

	Budget formula	Various levels of activity			
Capacity level		60%	70%	80%	90%
Units of product		6,000	7,000	8,000	9,000
Standard direct labor hours[a]		12,000	14,000	16,000	18,000
Budgeted factory overhead:					
Variable overhead:					
Indirect labor	$ 60	$ 7,200	$ 8,400	$ 9,600	$10,800
Indirect materials	.50	6,000	7,000	8,000	9,000
Power	.30	3,600	4,200	4,800	5,400
Maintenance	.20	2,400	2,800	3,200	3,600
Total variable	$ 1.60[b]	$19,200	$22,400	$25,600	$28,800
Fixed overhead:					
Depreciation—Machinery		$ 5,500	$ 5,500	$ 5,500	$ 5,500
Depreciation—Building		4,500	4,500	4,500	4,500
Supervisory salaries		3,000	3,000	3,000	3,000
Insurance—Factory		1,500	1,500	1,500	1,500
Property taxes		500	500	500	500
Miscellaneous		1,000	1,000	1,000	1,000
Total fixed	$16,000	$16,000	$16,000	$16,000	$16,000
Total factory overhead	$\left(\begin{array}{c}\$1.60 \times \text{Standard}\\ \text{hours} + \$16,000\end{array}\right)$	$35,200	$38,400	$41,600	$44,800

[a] Two standard direct labor hours are allowed for each unit of output.
[b] Variable overhead rate per direct labor hour.

The important part of the flexible budget is the budget formula. For State Company the formula is:

$$\begin{array}{l}\text{Total budgeted}\\ \text{factory overhead}\\ \text{cost}\end{array} = \left(\begin{array}{cc}\text{Variable} & \text{Standard}\\ \text{overhead} \times & \text{activity}\\ \text{rate} & \text{level}\end{array}\right) + \begin{array}{l}\text{Total fixed}\\ \text{factory overhead}\\ \text{cost}\end{array}$$

$$= \left(\$1.60 \times \begin{array}{l}\text{Standard direct}\\ \text{labor hours}\end{array}\right) + \$16,000$$

By using the budget formula, budgeted factory overhead cost can be determined for any activity level within the relevant range regardless of whether or not it is shown in the flexible budget. For example, assume that State Company had actual production of 7,500 units, which is not shown in the flexible budget. Since output of 7,500 units is equivalent to 15,000 (7,500 × 2) standard direct labor hours allowed, the budgeted factory overhead cost at that level is $40,000 [($1.60 × 15,000) + $16,000]. The $40,000 budgeted factory overhead cost would be compared with actual factory overhead costs for purposes of factory overhead variance analysis, which will be discussed shortly, since both actual and budgeted costs would be at the same activity level.

Note that the flexible part of the flexible budget is really the variable factory overhead costs, since fixed factory overhead costs do not vary with any activity level. In other words, the flexible budget really consists of a flexible variable factory overhead budget plus a static (constant) fixed factory overhead budget.

Consequently, the budgeted fixed factory overhead need not be included in the flexible budget; however, the budgeted fixed factory overhead cost is often included in the flexible budget for the purpose of developing the standard overhead rate.

STANDARD OVERHEAD RATE Management desires to have a stable factory overhead cost per unit for product costing purposes despite month-by-month fluctuations in production. The derivation of such a unit cost is complicated by the fact that part of factory overhead cost includes fixed factory overhead cost that causes factory overhead cost per unit to vary with production. In other words, a given total amount of fixed factory overhead cost spread over a large number of units produced will result in a lower fixed factory overhead cost per unit than if spread over a smaller number of units of product. This problem does not arise with regard to variable factory overhead cost, since it remains constant on a per unit basis regardless of the production level. The variability of unit factory overhead costs because of fluctuations in fixed factory overhead costs per unit is illustrated below using the flexible budget data for State Company.

Volume		Budgeted variable overhead cost			Budgeted fixed overhead cost			Budgeted total overhead cost		
Units of product	Standard hours	Total	Per unit	Per hour	Total	Per unit	Per hour	Total	Per unit	Per hour
6,000	12,000	$19,200	$3.20	$1.60	$16,000	$2.67	$1.33	$35,200	$5.87	$2.93
7,000	14,000	22,400	3.20	1.60	16,000	2.29	1.14	38,400	5.49	2.74
8,000	16,000	25,600	3.20	1.60	16,000	2.00	1.00	41,600	5.20	2.60
9,000	18,000	28,800	3.20	1.60	16,000	1.78	.89	44,800	4.98	2.49

A stable factory overhead cost per unit can be developed for product costing purposes by using a standard factory overhead rate. This is accomplished by choosing one level of activity and dividing it into estimated (budgeted) total factory overhead cost. The single activity level for setting the overhead rate is generally the expected activity level for the coming year. For example, assume that State Company expects production to be 96,000 units for the year, which is equivalent to 192,000 (96,000 × 2) standard direct labor hours, and expects total factory overhead cost to be $499,200 ($307,200 variable plus $192,000 fixed); hence, the overhead rate is $2.60 as shown below:

$$\frac{\text{Standard factory}}{\text{overhead rate}} = \frac{\text{Estimated total factory}}{\text{overhead cost}} \div \frac{\text{Estimated activity}}{\text{level}}$$

$$\$2.60 = \$499,200 \div 192,000$$

In monthly average terms, these expectations are expressed in the flexible budget for State Company (see page 576) at the 16,000 (192,000 ÷ 12) standard hours level, since the $41,600 ($499,200 ÷ 12) expected monthly overhead costs divided by the 16,000 hours equals the $2.60 standard overhead rate.

The standard factory overhead rate can be segmented into a standard variable factory overhead rate and a standard fixed factory overhead rate. If the expected total variable and fixed costs for the coming year are used, the two rates for State Company would be as follows:

$$\frac{\text{Standard variable}}{\text{factory overhead rate}} = \frac{\text{Estimated variable}}{\text{factory overhead cost}} \div \frac{\text{Estimated activity}}{\text{level}}$$

$$\$1.60 = \$307{,}200 \div 192{,}000$$

$$\frac{\text{Standard fixed}}{\text{factory overhead rate}} = \frac{\text{Estimated fixed}}{\text{factory overhead cost}} \div \frac{\text{Estimated activity}}{\text{level}}$$

$$\$1.00 = \$192{,}000 \div 192{,}000$$

Although the variable overhead rate stays the same ($1.60) no matter what the activity level is over the relevant operating range, the fixed overhead rate ($1.00) is based on a single activity level (the expected annual activity level of 192,000 standard hours) in the same manner as is the total standard factory overhead rate. The expected activity level used in setting the fixed overhead rate represents the expected production capability of the plant for the coming year.[2] In other words, the expected activity level is the expected level of capacity utilization; therefore, standard fixed factory overhead cost provides a measure of capacity utilization that can be used for factory overhead analysis. For example, referring to the flexible budget for State Company (see page 576), we see that the monthly expected activity level of 16,000 hours (or 8,000 units of product) represents expected capacity utilization of 80 per cent, which can be compared with the actual capacity achieved. Of course, 100 per cent capacity, which represents the maximum operating level of the plant, is seldom reached because of machine breakdowns, errors in scheduling work, inability to sell all the produced product, and the like.

FACTORY OVERHEAD VARIANCES   As previously illustrated in accounting for State Company under a standard cost system, factory overhead is applied to production at the standard factory overhead cost (standard overhead rate times standard activity level). Then at the end of the period the difference between actual factory overhead cost and standard factory overhead cost is isolated in a manufacturing overhead variance account ready for analysis.

The analysis of the total factory overhead variance takes the form of segmenting the total variance into several variances to determine the cause of and the responsibility for the variances. Similar to analyzing price and efficiency variances for direct materials and labor, the total overhead variance is divided into variable and fixed factory overhead spending (price) variances and a factory overhead efficiency variance, and, in addition, a factory overhead volume (capacity) variance.

For purposes of illustrating the computing of the factory overhead variances in the following pages, assume that the actual factory overhead cost of $39,100 for State Company consists of the following:

---

[2]Instead of using expected annual activity in determining the standard fixed overhead rate, some companies use normal activity. Normal activity is the expected average utilization of plant capacity over several years (e.g., five years). However, it is difficult to make the accurate long-run forecasts necessary for determining normal activity, and there is the question of whether or not normal activity is relevant to the evaluation of current results.

Actual variable factory overhead costs:

Indirect labor	$ 8,500
Indirect materials	7,300
Power	4,400
Maintenance	2,600
Total variable	$22,800

Actual fixed factory overhead costs:

Depreciation—Machinery	$ 5,500
Depreciation—Building	4,500
Supervisory salaries	3,200
Insurance—Factory	1,500
Property taxes	600
Miscellaneous	1,000
Total fixed	$16,300
Total actual factory overhead cost	$39,100

Also remember that State Company produced 7,500 units of product and used 14,000 actual direct labor hours in production (see page 570).

SPENDING VARIANCES Factory overhead spending variances measure deviations from the flexible budget in the amount spent for factory overhead items. Such spending variations arise from changes in prices over those shown in the flexible budget and from waste or excessive usage of overhead items (e.g., indirect materials).

The variable factory overhead spending variance is equal to the difference between actual variable factory overhead costs and the flexible budget at the *actual* activity level (actual direct labor hours), or

$$\begin{array}{l}\text{Variable overhead} \\ \text{spending variance}\end{array} = \begin{array}{l}\text{Actual variable} \\ \text{overhead costs}\end{array} - \left(\begin{array}{l}\text{Standard variable} \\ \text{overhead rate}\end{array} \times \begin{array}{l}\text{Actual direct} \\ \text{labor hours}\end{array}\right)$$

$$\$400^* = \$22,800 - (\$1.60 \times 14,000)$$

*Note that this is an unfavorable variance (a debit variance), since the equation establishes positive variances as unfavorable.

The fixed factory overhead spending variance is equal to the difference between actual fixed factory overhead cost and budgeted fixed factory overhead cost, or

$$\begin{array}{l}\text{Fixed overhead} \\ \text{spending variance}\end{array} = \begin{array}{l}\text{Actual fixed} \\ \text{overhead cost}\end{array} - \begin{array}{l}\text{Budgeted fixed} \\ \text{overhead cost}\end{array}$$

$$\$300 = \$16,300 - \$16,000$$

Factory overhead spending variances are generally viewed by management as providing useful information for control purposes. Normally the price element in the spending variances is small so that attention can be focused on the usage of overhead in production over which the production supervisor has the greatest control.

To determine the causes of the spending variances necessitates analyzing the causes item by item. Such a detailed breakdown of the spending variances is shown on page 581.

EFFICIENCY VARIANCE The variable factory overhead efficiency variance measures the efficiency (the relation of inputs to outputs) of utilization of direct labor hours (or other base underlying the flexible budget) in production. It is equal to the difference between actual hours utilized and standard hours that should have been utilized in production at the variable overhead rate, or

$$\begin{array}{c}\text{Variable overhead}\\ \text{efficiency variance}\end{array} = \left(\begin{array}{c}\text{Actual direct}\\ \text{labor hours}\end{array} - \begin{array}{c}\text{Standard direct}\\ \text{labor hours}\end{array}\right) \times \begin{array}{c}\text{Standard variable}\\ \text{overhead rate}\end{array}$$

$$\$(1,600)^* = (14,000 - 15,000) \times \$1.60$$

*The parentheses mean that that is a favorable variance (credit variance), since the equation establishes negative variances as favorable.

Since the overhead efficiency variance measures the efficiency in the utilization of direct labor hours, the supervisor responsible for the use of labor time in production is responsible for any overhead efficiency variance.

A detailed breakdown of the variable overhead efficiency variance is shown on page 581.

VOLUME VARIANCE The fixed factory overhead volume variance is a rough measure of over or under utilization of expected plant capacity. It is equal to the difference between budgeted fixed factory overhead and standard fixed factory overhead applied (standard fixed overhead rate times standard direct labor hours), or

$$\begin{array}{c}\text{Fixed overhead}\\ \text{volume variance}\end{array} = \begin{array}{c}\text{Budgeted fixed}\\ \text{overhead cost}\end{array} - \begin{array}{c}\text{Standard fixed overhead}\\ \text{cost applied}\end{array}$$

$$= \left(\begin{array}{c}\text{Budgeted direct}\\ \text{labor hours}\end{array} - \begin{array}{c}\text{Standard direct}\\ \text{labor hours}\end{array}\right) \times \begin{array}{c}\text{Standard fixed}\\ \text{overhead rate}\end{array}$$

$$\$1,000 = \$16,000 - \$15,000$$

$$= (16,000 - 15,000) \times \$1.00$$

The volume variance arises when the actual activity level or volume (expressed as standard hours allowed or 7,500 actual units of output times two standard hours per unit) is not equal to the expected or budgeted activity level or volume.[3] For example, State Company has a $1,000 unfavorable volume variance because of the under utilization of planned capacity. It was planned that the plant would be worked 16,000 hours (budgeted hours), or at 80 per cent capacity, and it was worked only 15,000 standard hours, or at 75 per cent capacity.

In general, the volume variance is not considered immediately controllable from a spending viewpoint. The standard fixed overhead rate used in computing the variance is derived for product costing purposes and is not relevant for cost control purposes. Consequently, some companies report the volume variance in physical units, such as hours, only. On the other hand, a large unfavorable volume variance does indicate that further analysis is needed and such analysis could indicate that the failure to achieve planned capacity was the result of sales volume lagging

[3] Remember that the expected or budgeted activity level is that single activity level used in determining the standard fixed overhead rate, as well as the standard total overhead rate. For State Company, the budgeted activity level was 192,000 hours for the year or 16,000 hours per month.

or that there was plant idleness because of machine breakdowns, poor scheduling, failure to deliver materials, and the like.

PERFORMANCE REPORT. A performance report is a control report designed to compare actual performance with what performance should have been and to provide reasons for the difference between actual and expected performance. Such a report for State Company's factory overhead is presented below.

STATE COMPANY
Factory Overhead Performance Report
For the Month of May, 19__

	Actual factory overhead costs (a)	Flexible budget at 14,000 actual direct labor hours (b)	Flexible budget at 15,000 standard direct labor hours (c)	Spending variance (a) − (b)	Efficiency variance (b) − (c)
Variable overhead costs:					
Indirect labor	$ 8,500	$ 8,400	$ 9,000	$100	$ (600)
Indirect materials	7,300	7,000	7,500	300	(500)
Power	4,400	4,200	4,500	200	(300)
Maintenance	2,600	2,800	3,000	(200)	(200)
Total variable	$22,800	$22,400	$24,000	$400	$(1,600)
Fixed overhead costs:					
Depreciation—Machinery	$ 5,500	$ 5,500	$ 5,500	$ —	
Depreciation—Building	4,500	4,500	4,500	—	
Supervisory salaries	3,200	3,000	3,000	200	
Insurance—Factory	1,500	1,500	1,500	—	
Property taxes	600	500	500	100	
Miscellaneous	1,000	1,000	1,000	—	
Total fixed	$16,300	$16,000	$16,000	$300	
Total	$39,100	$38,400	$40,000	$700	$(1,600)

Volume variance:

Budgeted volume level at 80% capacity—budgeted hours	16,000
Actual volume level at 75% capacity—standard hours allowed	15,000
Volume variance in hours	1,000
Volume variance at $1.00 standard fixed overhead rate	$ 1,000

IMPORTANT TERMS AND CONCEPTS IN CHAPTER 19

Standard costs—pp. 567, 568
Variances—p. 568
Standard cost system—p. 568
Direct materials price variance—pp. 569, 573
Direct materials efficiency variance—pp. 569, 573
Direct labor price variance—pp. 569, 573
Direct labor efficiency variance—pp. 569, 573
Total factory overhead variance—pp. 570, 573, 574
Standard quantities—p. 571
Ideal versus currently attainable standards—p. 572

Management by exception—p. 574
Disposition of variances—pp. 574, 575
Flexible budget—pp. 575–577
Standard overhead rate—p. 577
Expected annual activity level—pp. 577, 578
Standard variable overhead rate—pp. 577, 578
Standard fixed overhead rate—pp. 577, 578
Variable overhead spending variance—p. 579
Fixed overhead spending variance—p. 579
Variable overhead efficiency variance—p. 580
Fixed overhead volume variance—pp. 580, 581
Performance report—p. 581

DEMONSTRATION PROBLEM FOR REVIEW AND SELF-STUDY Ruland Company manufactures one product. The standards for one unit of product are as follows:

....

Standard cost card

Direct materials: ½ pound of material Y at $4 per pound	$ 2.00
Direct labor: 3 hours at $7.00	21.00
Factory overhead:	
Variable: 3 hours at $3.00	9.00
Fixed: 3 hours at $2.00	6.00
Total standard cost per unit of product	$38.00

During January 500 units of product were manufactured. There was no beginning goods in process. Actual costs utilized during January were as follows:

Materials purchased: 500 pounds at $4.50 per pound	$ 2,250
Materials issued to production: 230 pounds	
Direct labor: 1,600 hours at $6.90	11,040
Factory overhead costs:	
Variable	4,700
Fixed	2,950

January plant capacity based on expected direct labor hours (budgeted hours) was 1,400 hours, and this was the monthly activity level used to determine the standard fixed overhead rate of $2.00. The flexible budget at the 1,400 hour activity level consisted of $4,200 ($3 × 1,400) budgeted variable overhead cost and $2,800 ($2 × 1,400) budgeted fixed overhead cost.

INSTRUCTIONS Given the above data, prepare (a) journal entries for Ruland Company for the month of January (assume a standard cost system) and (b) a schedule presenting the four factory overhead variances.

Note Attempt to solve this demonstration problem before examining the solution that follows.

Solution:

(a)

Materials inventory ($4 × 500)	2,000	
Materials price variance [($4.50 − $4.00) × 500]	250	
Accounts payable ($4.50 × 500)		2,250
Goods in process ($4 × 250)	1,000	
Materials efficiency variance [(230 − 250) × $4]		80
Materials inventory ($4 × 230)		920
Goods in process ($7 × 1,500)	10,500	
Labor efficiency variance [(1,600 − 1,500) × $7]	700	
Labor price variance [($6.90 − $7.00) × 1,600]		160
Factory payroll payable ($6.90 × 1,600)		11,040
Goods in process ($5 × 1,500)	7,500	
Manufacturing overhead		7,500
Finished goods ($38 × 500)	19,000	
Goods in process		19,000
Manufacturing overhead ($4,700 + $2,950)	7,650	
Various accounts		7,650
Manufacturing overhead variance ($7,650 − $7,500)	150	
Manufacturing overhead		150

(b)

Variable overhead spending variance:

    $\$4{,}700 - (\$3 \times 1{,}600) =$ $(100)^a$

Fixed overhead spending variance:

    $\$2{,}950 - \$2{,}800 =$ 150

Variable overhead efficiency variance:

    $(1{,}600 - 1{,}500) \times \$3 =$ 300

Fixed overhead volume variance:

    $(1{,}400 - 1{,}500) \times \$2$ $(200)^a$

Total overhead variance ($\$7{,}650 - \$7{,}500$) $\$\,150$

[a]Parentheses indicate a favorable variance.

Questions

1   What are the arguments in favor of using standard costs over historical costs? Discuss.
2   Do you think standard costs should be set at *ideal* levels of attainment? Discuss.
3   Why is the difference between actual and standard materials (or labor) costs segmented into *two* variances? Discuss.
4   Some accountants record the materials price variance at time of purchase, while other accountants record the variance when materials are issued to production. What are the advantages and disadvantages of these two different approaches to the recording of the materials price variance? Discuss.
5   Some accountants record the materials efficiency and the labor efficiency variances when the goods are completed, while other accountants record the two variances when materials and labor are put into production. What are the advantages and disadvantages of the two different approaches? Discuss.
6   How is the concept of management by exception related to a standard cost system? Discuss.
7   A materials price variance may be the responsibility of the sales manager or the production manager instead of the purchasing manager. What does this statement mean? Discuss.
8   Is the fixed overhead volume variance uncontrollable? Discuss.
9   If XYZ Company allocates fixed overhead on the basis of some dollar amount per direct labor hour, what calculation is necessary to determine this allocation rate?
10   Is the following statement correct? Variable overhead requires a variance analysis entirely different from the analysis required by direct materials. Discuss.
11   What is done with the cost variances at the end of the fiscal period? Discuss.
12   The standard quantity of materials (or standard labor hours) is based on equivalent production. What does this statement mean? Discuss.
13   The materials price variance and the labor price variance equations are not mathematically sound. In contrast, the equations for the materials efficiency variance and the labor efficiency variance are mathematically sound. What do these statements mean? Discuss. (*Hint:* For an equation to be mathematically correct, only the variable under analysis should vary and the other variable should be held constant.)
14   Why is the treatment of fixed and variable overhead conceptually different?

Short exercises

E19-1

You are given three multiple-choice statements. Select the correct answers and indicate the corresponding letters on a sheet of paper (e.g., 1-d, 2-d, etc.).

(1)   Which of the following accounts is normally stated at standard cost? (a) goods in process, (b) manufacturing overhead variance, (c) accounts payable, (d) net income under the standard cost system, (e) all of the above, (f) none of the above.

(2) Which of the following is correct? (a) When recording variances, debits are favorable and credits are unfavorable. (b) Under a standard cost system, all inventories will be stated at actual cost. (c) Variance accounts usually appear on the balance sheet. (d) Most variances are uncontrollable by management. (e) All of the above. (f) None of the above.

(3) Standard costs (a) are determined at the end of the accounting period, (b) are long-run goals of the firm, (c) must be continually revised, (d) always give rise to variances, (e) all of the above, (f) none of the above.

E19-2   *You are given three multiple-choice statements. Select the correct answers and indicate the corresponding letters on a sheet of paper (e.g., 1-d, 2-d, etc.).*

(1) Direct material efficiency variances may be caused by (a) defective materials, (b) spoilage, (c) inefficiency among plant workers, (d) improper handling, (e) all of the above, (f) none of the above.

(2) Which of the following is correct? (a) Insignificant net variance may lead management to improper conclusions regarding substandard performance. (b) Variances should be prorated to inventory and cost of goods sold. (c) A favorable volume variance for fixed overhead occurs when the budgeted level of activity is less than the actual level of activity. (d) The level of activity does not have to be expressed in terms of direct labor hours. (e) All of the above. (f) None of the above.

(3) Which of the following is correct? (a) The most relevant costs may not be historical costs. (b) Control is a primary purpose for standard cost analysis. (c) The applied factory overhead is equal to the standard hours allowed for units produced multiplied by the standard factory overhead rate (fixed or variable). (d) All variances may not be under the control of the factory supervisor. (e) All of the above. (f) None of the above.

E19-3   *What is wrong with the variance analysis of materials shown below?*

Actual cost of materials ($5 actual price × 1,000 pounds of materials issued to production)	$5,000
Standard cost of materials ($2 standard price × 1,100 standard pounds of materials issued to production)	2,200
Unfavorable materials variance	$2,800

E19-4   *The standard cost card for Top Company is presented below:*

Standard cost card

Direct materials—4 pounds @ $4	$16
Direct labor—2 hours @ $2	4
Variable factory overhead—$6 per direct labor hour	12
Standard cost per finished unit	$32

During the fiscal period 10,000 units of product were manufactured in which 42,000 actual pounds of materials and 19,000 actual direct labor hours were used.

(a) How was the $12 standard variable factory overhead cost per unit calculated? Show all of your work.

(b) What was the standard quantity of materials used in production?

(c) What was the standard cost of materials used in production?

(d) What were the standard labor hours used in production?

(e) What was the standard cost of labor used in production?

(f) What was the materials efficiency variance? Was it favorable or unfavorable?

(g) What was the labor efficiency variance? Was it favorable or unfavorable?

E19-5 *Given the following information, prepare the entry that closes the variances to Cost of Goods Sold:*

Direct labor standard—3 hours per unit at $5 per hour

20,000 units were completed this accounting period requiring 70,000 hours at $4 per hour

Materials price variance	$10,000 (favorable)
Materials efficiency variance	$ 5,000 (favorable)
Variable overhead spending variance	$ 2,000 (unfavorable)
Variable overhead efficiency variance	$ 4,000 (favorable)
Fixed overhead volume variance	$ 8,000 (unfavorable)
Fixed overhead spending variance	$ 3,000 (favorable)

E19-6 *Shell Company uses a standard cost system in accounting for its manufacturing operations. Given the company's cost flows for the fiscal period, as shown below, make general journal entries recording the manufacturing costs.*

Accounts payable		Materials price variance		Materials inventory	
xxx	20,000	500		19,500	11,600

Materials efficiency variance		Factory payroll payable		Labor price variance	
	400	xxx	30,200		1,000

Goods in process		Labor efficiency variance		Various accounts	
12,000	48,400	200		xxx	21,000
31,000					
20,200					

Manufacturing overhead		Manufacturing overhead variance		Finished goods	
21,000	20,200	800		48,400	25,000
	800				

Cost of goods sold	
25,000	

E19-7 *Using the cost flow data of Shell Company (see E19-6), make one compound general journal entry closing out the variance accounts to Cost of Goods Sold. What is the cost of goods sold figure after the closing of the variance accounts?*

E19-8   *Given the following information concerning a standard costing system, in each part find the unknown quantity:*

Standards:

Direct labor—2 hours per unit at $3 per hour

Direct materials—? pounds per unit at $1 per pound

10,000 units were completed during the accounting period

(a) If the direct labor efficiency variance was $30,000 (unfavorable), what was the actual number of direct labor hours used?

(b) If the actual labor rate was $2 per hour, what was the direct labor price variance? Was the variance favorable or unfavorable?

(c) If the direct materials efficiency variance was $10,000 (favorable) and the actual number of pounds used was 30,000, what was the standard number of pounds per unit?

(d) If the actual price for direct materials was $.75 per pound, what was the direct materials price variance? Was the variance favorable or unfavorable? Assume that the actual quantity purchased was 30,000 pounds.

E19-9   *(a) Prepare the flexible budget for Mullinix Company for the month of July. Assume that the following amounts are for the 25,000 machine hour activity level. Use activity levels of 20,000, 25,000, and 30,000 machine hours.*

	Variable	Fixed
Indirect labor	$ 45,000	
Indirect materials	50,000	
Heating and cooling	25,000	
Maintenance	37,500	
Depreciation		$ 62,000
Supervisory salaries		11,000
Insurance		12,000
Miscellaneous		15,000
	$157,500	$100,000

(b) What is the budget formula for Mullinix Company for July?

Problems

A19-1   *Johnson, Inc. provides you with financial data on three types of materials it used in production during March.*

Material E:
  Purchase price per gallon—65.8¢
  Standard price per gallon—67.0¢
  Gallons purchased and used—2,200
  Standard gallons used in production—2,000

Material F:
  Pounds purchased at $2.60—7,500
  Standard pounds used in production—7,400
  Actual pounds used in production—7,000
  Standard price per pound—$2.52

Material G:

    Amount paid for 20 tons—$1,500

    Standard price per ton—$80

    Actual tons used at standard price—$1,200

    Standard pounds used in production—28,000

Required:

(a) Calculate the materials price and efficiency variances for each of the three types of materials. Show all calculations.

(b) Using only the given data, discuss why the variances were favorable or unfavorable for material E.

(c) Make the general journal entries recording the purchase of materials and the issuance to production of material G.

A19-2

Young Company uses a standard cost system. The company's cost data for the month of May were as follows:

Actual direct labor hours used	5,410
Standard direct labor hours used	5,430
Actual direct labor cost—$34,083	
Standard direct labor hour price—$6	

Required:

(a) Make the general journal entry to record the labor cost utilized in production. Show calculations.

(b) Using only the given data, explain why each of the variances is either favorable or unfavorable.

A19-3

Life Manufacturing Company has a standard cost system. The management asks you to provide a schedule showing the variance computations, given the data below.

Budgeted level of fixed overhead	$1,100.00
Actual quantity of material issued to production—200	
Standard direct labor hours used in production—100	
Materials price variance	24.00 favorable
Labor efficiency variance	45.00 unfavorable
Actual quantity of materials purchased—400	
Budgeted level of direct labor hours—110	
Actual labor hours used in production—115	
Materials efficiency variance	30.00 unfavorable
Labor price variance	23.00 unfavorable
Standard price of materials	1.50

    You soon discover that you are missing some data; hence, before you can make up the variance schedule, you have to solve for the missing data.

Required:

(a) From the above data only, find the average actual price paid for materials. Show all calculations.

(b) What was the standard quantity of materials issued to production?

(c) What was the standard labor price (rate) per direct labor hour?

(d) What was the actual labor price (rate) per direct labor hour?

(e) What was the standard fixed factory overhead rate?

(f) What was the fixed overhead volume variance?

The data below pertain to the Seldom Mfg. Co. for the year 19__. The company uses a standard-cost system in its production of one product.

Standard cost card

Materials:	A—4 pounds @ $3	$12.00
	B—1 unit @ $5	5.00
Labor	1 hour @ $3.50	3.50
Overhead:	variable @ $2.00 per direct labor hour	2.00
	fixed—total budget = $75,000	1.00
		$23.50

Goods in process—no beginning or ending inventories

Units manufactured—75,000

Units sold @ $30—72,500

Pounds of material A purchased @ $3.02—320,000

Units of material B purchased @ $4.75—78,000

Actual pounds of material A used in production—310,000

Actual units of material B used in production—76,000

Actual direct labor costs of production—$260,000

Actual direct labor hours used in production—80,000

Actual variable overhead—$165,000

Actual fixed overhead—$74,000

Required:

(a) General journal entries for the year 19__. Use separate variance accounts for materials A and B.

(b) A schedule presenting the four factory overhead variances.

(c) Year-end general journal entries to dispose of all variances. (Close to Cost of Goods Sold.)

(a) Accounting Company uses a standard cost system in which all inventory accounts are recorded at standard cost *(standard rate times standard hours, pounds, etc., allowed for actual production). Given the following information, prepare the necessary journal entries (omit explanations) to record production for January:*

Fixed overhead costs incurred	$8,000
Budgeted level of activity	2,000 units
Standard direct labor hours per unit	2
Budgeted fixed overhead	$6,000
Materials purchased	1,000 pounds @ $1
Materials issued to production	750 pounds
Standard direct material pounds per unit	.2
Standard direct material price per pound	$ .90
Number of units completed in January	2,500
Variable overhead costs incurred	$5,000
Standard rate to apply variable overhead	$ 1.50 per direct labor hour
Standard direct labor hour wage rate	$ 4.50
Actual number of hours worked	5,200
Actual wage rate paid	

There was no beginning or ending goods in process inventory. Omit any closing or cost of goods sold entries.

(b) Prepare a schedule that divides the total overhead variance into four separate variances.

A19-6

The Bill Manufacturing Company produces gadgets. The standards for 100 units of product are as follows:

Standard cost per 100 gadgets

Materials	2.5 pounds sheet aluminum @ $2.80	$ 7.00
Labor	1 hour of direct labor @ $3	3.00
Variable overhead	150% of standard direct labor cost	4.50
Fixed overhead	50% of standard direct labor cost	1.50
		$16.00

Material is added at the **beginning** of the manufacturing process. During May, 2,250 pounds of sheet aluminum were purchased at a cost of $6,255 and 2,000 pounds were issued to production. During the month, 810 direct labor hours were worked at an average wage of $3.02 per hour. Actual variable overhead for May was $3,565.50. Actual fixed overhead for May was $1,400.

The $103.50 beginning goods in process (May 1) consisted of 900 gadgets, 50 per cent complete with regard to labor and factory overhead. During May, 80,000 gadgets were completed. As of May 31, ending goods in process consisted of 700 gadgets that were 50 per cent complete as to labor and factory overhead. The budgeted level of activity for the fixed overhead was 90,000 units (900 standard direct labor hours).

Required:

(a) Compute materials variances, labor variances, and the factory overhead variances. (*Hint:* Use *equivalent units* to calculate standard pounds and hours.)

(b) Set up T-accounts and trace the cost flows.

B19-1

The management of Cost Cutter Company has requested an explanation of the manufacturing variances that occurred during the month of March. The following data are supplied:

Standard labor hours used in production—610

Standard variable overhead rate per standard labor hour—$16.40

Standard quantity of material used in production—4,430 pounds

Actual variable overhead cost—$10,500

Actual labor hours used in production—624

Standard materials price—$24.80 per pound

Standard labor price (rate) per hour—$6.20

Actual materials price—$25.00 per pound

Actual labor price (rate) per hour—$6.10

Actual quantity of materials purchased and used—4,400 pounds

Required:

(a) Prepare a schedule of the factory variances using the format given below.

Variance Description	Calculations	Variance Amount	
		Unfavorable	**Favorable**

(b) Discuss two possible causes for *each* favorable or unfavorable variance.

B19-2   Sally Company uses a standard cost system. The company's cost data for the month of July were as follows:

Pounds of steel purchased	9,000
Pounds of steel used in production	7,750
Standard pounds required for production	8,000
Purchase price per pound of steel—$2.05	
Standard price per pound of steel—$2.00	

Required:

(a) Make general journal entries to record the purchase and issuance to production of the materials.

(b) Explain why the variances are either favorable or unfavorable.

B19-3   Sear Corporation uses a standard cost system. Manufacturing overhead is applied to production based on standard direct labor hours. You are given the following data:

Actual direct labor cost for 4,275 hours	$20,349.00
Actual variable overhead cost	7,468.00
Actual fixed overhead cost	8,500.00
Standard direct labor price per hour	4.80
Standard variable overhead rate	1.70
Standard fixed overhead rate for 4,500 hours	2.00
Standard direct labor hours used—4,300	

Required:

(a) Make general journal entries to record the above data (omit closing entries).

(b) Calculate the four overhead variances. Check to see that they sum to the total overhead variance obtained in part (a).

B19-4   Grinder Company uses a standard cost system for work done in the breaker department. Each breaker requires 2 hours of equipment time (standard). The overhead standards are as follows:

Variable overhead	$3.00 per equipment hour
Fixed overhead	$1.00 per equipment hour

The budgeted number of equipment hours for April was 23,000. The actual performance during April was the following:

Variable costs	$85,000
Fixed costs	$18,000
Equipment hours	25,000
Breakers produced	12,000

Required:

(a) What would you expect fixed costs to be (consider the allocation rate)?

(b) Give the journal entries for overhead (omit explanations).

(c) Calculate the four individual overhead variances.

B19-5   Simulation Company produces one product with the following standards:

Materials	$ 5.00
Direct labor	8.00
Variable overhead	4.00
Fixed overhead	3.00
	$20.00 per unit

During the month 1,000 units were produced and there were no goods in process at either the beginning or end of the month. All inventory accounts are carried at standard (standard cost times standard quantity). Materials purchased during the month had an invoice cost of $8,000. The month-end variances for Simulation Company were as follows:

Fixed overhead volume variance	$1,000 (F)
Fixed overhead spending variance	–0–
Variable overhead efficiency variance	$2,500 (U)
Variable overhead spending variance	$1,000 (F)
Labor price variance	$ 500 (U)
Labor efficiency variance	$ 800 (U)
Materials efficiency variance	$ 200 (F)
Materials price variance	$ 300 (U)

Required:

Reconstruct the standard cost system entries in journal form (omit explanations).

B19-6   Fun, Inc., manufactures a product with the brand name of "Fundo." The company uses a standard cost system.

Standard cost per unit

Materials:	A—4 pounds @ $1	$ 4
	B—6 units @ $2	12
Labor	2 hours @ $5	10
Variable overhead	$1.50 per direct labor hour	3
Fixed overhead	$1.50 per direct labor hour	3
		$32

Material A was added at the beginning and material B was added at the end of the manufacturing process. The beginning goods in process consisted of 800 units that were 50 per cent complete as to labor and overhead. The ending goods in process of 400 units were 25 per cent complete as to labor and overhead. There were 18,000 units started and completed during the fiscal period. The beginning goods in process balance was $9,600.

Forty tons of material A were purchased at a cost of $92,000 and 74,000 pounds were used in production. Material B was purchased for $237,000 (120,000 units), and 112,000 units were used in production. Actual labor cost was $180,320.

Actual labor hours used in production were 36,800. Actual variable overhead was $59,000. Actual fixed overhead was $53,000. Budgeted fixed overhead was $57,000.

Required:

(a) Compute materials variances, labor variances, and the factory overhead variances. (*Hint:* Use equivalent units to calculate standard quantities and hours.)

(b) Set up T-accounts and trace the cost flows.

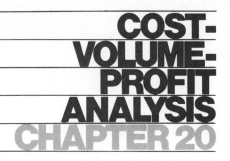

COST-VOLUME-PROFIT ANALYSIS
CHAPTER 20

PURPOSE OF CHAPTER   In Chapter 19 we discussed standard costs as an aid to management decision making with regard to planning and controlling business operations. In this chapter we discuss another aid to management decision making, namely, cost-volume-profit analysis, with regard to profit planning.

The management of a business firm is continually faced with such short-run questions as: What are the total sales needed to earn x dollars of profit? What are the total sales needed to cover total expenses, that is, to break even? Should an attempt be made to increase profits through sales promotion or changing product prices? Is it profitable to enter a foreign market? Should an existing product line be dropped? Is sales territory #4 really contributing toward overall company profits?

To answer such questions, management must know how net income is affected by particular cost and revenue decisions. Management needs to know about the behavior and interrelationships among cost, volume, and profit over the short-run time period. Consequently, the purpose of this chapter is to explain the concept of cost-volume-profit analysis and how such analysis can aid management in short-run decision making.

COST-VOLUME-PROFIT ANALYSIS DEFINED   Cost-volume-profit analysis can be defined as an examination of the effect of changes in costs (expenses) and revenues, and therefore profits, in response to changes in volume (output of product). Such analysis provides management with the means to investigate the possible effects on profits of various short-run management decisions under consideration, as well as providing clues to possible management strategies for increasing profits.

Since many short-run decisions involve an increase or decrease in product output, management is concerned with the variability of cost (expense) with the variability of volume. Consequently, for purposes of cost-volume-profit analysis it is necessary to classify costs into either variable or fixed costs in relation to volume. As discussed in Chapter 16 (see pages 506–507), variable expense is that total expense that varies directly and proportionally with sales volume, while fixed expense is that total expense that does not vary with sales volume, assuming a relevant volume range. Within the relevant volume range, which is the normal operating range of the business, the direct proportionality of variable expense with volume provides a good approximation of actual expense behavior necessary for cost-volume-profit analysis.

It should also be made clear that cost-volume-profit analysis is short-run analysis. As discussed in Chapter 16, the short run is a period of time that is not long enough to permit a company to increase production by acquiring additional capacity. Capacity is the company's upper limit of product output brought about by existing plant and equipment, management, and financing. Over the short run a company operates with given capacity because capacity can be changed only over a long period of time. Since capacity cannot be changed quickly, the costs of providing capacity tend to be fixed costs. Consequently, cost-volume-profit analysis is short-run analysis because the firm is committed to a certain level of fixed costs in the short run and the decision problem is how best to utilize fixed capacity relative to output levels.

A review of the necessary terminology underlying cost-volume-profit analysis is as follows:

(1) Variable expense is that total expense that varies in direct proportion to changes in sales volume, assuming a relevant sales volume range.
(2) Fixed expense is that total expense that remains constant as sales volume changes, assuming a relevant sales volume range and a short-run time period.
(3) Volume is some type of business activity per period of time, and it usually refers to the dollar amount or the quantity of product sold or produced over a time period.
(4) Relevant volume range is the firm's normal operating range of volume during a short-run time period, which excludes extremely high and low levels of volume.
(5) The short run is that period of time that is not long enough to permit a company to increase production volume by acquiring additional capacity; hence, increases in production over the short run result in increased variable costs with fixed costs remaining constant.

CONTRIBUTION MARGIN Contribution margin is defined as the dollar amount that remains when variable expenses are subtracted from net sales and that is available to meet fixed expenses, any positive remainder being net income. Contribution margin is expressed either as a total dollar amount, as an amount per unit of product sold (contribution margin per unit), or as a percentage of sales (contribution-margin ratio):

	Total amount	Percentage	Per unit (7,000 units)
Sales	$140,000	100%	$20.00
Variable expenses	98,000	70	14.00
Contribution margin	$ 42,000	30%	$ 6.00
Fixed expenses	30,000		
Net income	$ 12,000		

Note that if fixed expenses are truly fixed, net income varies with the amount of contribution margin (assuming that sales and variable expenses per unit are constant). For example, if 2,000 more units of product can be sold, contribution margin and profit increase $12,000 ($6 contribution margin per unit times 2,000 units). Similarly, if the sales price per unit is increased $2 and volume remains the same, contribution margin and profit are increased $2 per unit, or $14,000 ($2 × 7,000). The point is that, with known fixed expenses, known sales price per unit, and known variable expense per unit, the accountant can analyze the changes in contribution margin to determine the effects on profits of alternative short-run decisions proposed by management.

THE BREAK-EVEN POINT *Single product case* The break-even point is where total revenue equals total expense and net income is zero. The break-even point is helpful in management planning for new products, new markets, and the like, for it informs management about the minimum sales necessary for these new operations merely to meet expenses. Break-even analysis also provides useful information to management about how well actual volume compares with actual or planned break-even volume.

For a one-product firm or for one product of a multi-product firm, the break-even point can be computed in terms of units of product. In the following illustration it takes sales of 10,000 units of product to break even:

	Amount	Per unit (10,000 units)
Break-even sales	$100,000	$10
Variable expenses	60,000	6
Contribution margin	$ 40,000	$ 4
Fixed expenses	40,000	
Net income	$ —	

Note that, at the break-even point, total contribution margin ($40,000) equals total fixed expenses ($40,000). With a constant sales price ($10) and variable expense per unit ($6), contribution margin per unit is also constant ($4) and total contribution margin at the break-even point equals contribution margin per unit times the number of units to break even ($4 × 10,000). Therefore, the formula for calculating the break-even point in units of product is total fixed expenses divided by the contribution margin per unit:

$$\text{Total contribution margin} = \text{Total fixed expenses}$$
$$\$40,000 = \$40,000$$

Contribution margin per unit	×	Units of product to break even	=	Total fixed expenses
$4	×	10,000	=	$40,000

$$\frac{\text{Units of}}{\text{product to}} = \frac{\text{Total fixed expenses}}{\text{Contribution margin per unit}}$$
$$\text{break even}$$

$$10,000 = \frac{\$40,000}{\$4}$$

The break-even point in units multiplied by the sales price equals the break-even point in terms of dollars of sales:

$$\frac{\text{Break-even}}{\text{sales}} = \frac{\text{Break-even}}{\text{units}} \times \frac{\text{Sales price}}{\text{per unit}}$$

Graphically, the break-even point can be shown in two ways as illustrated below:

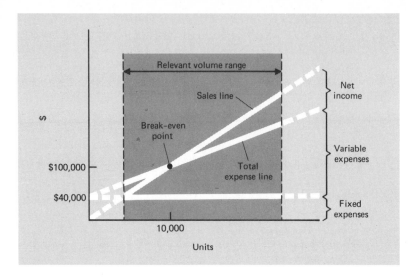

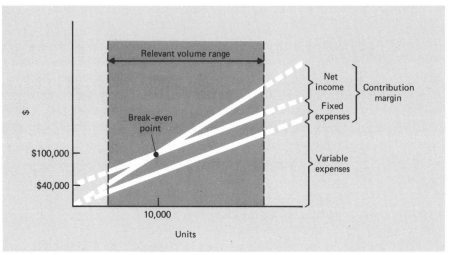

The second graph is preferred because it shows the contribution margin. The first graph is the traditional one.

Multi-product case   For a firm that sells more than one product, the overall break-even point is calculated in terms of dollars of sales instead of units of product. The reason is that units of product are not a common base for calculating the break-even point for a multi-product firm. The break-even point in units of product is usually different for each product because the products are dissimilar, with different sales prices and expenses per unit. The sales dollar, however, is a common denominator for the calculation of an overall break-even point for a multi-product firm.

Assume that the following data are the totals for a multi-product firm:

	Amount	Percentage
Sales (break-even)	$500,000	100%
Variable expense	350,000	70
Contribution margin	$150,000	30%
Fixed expense	150,000	
Net income	$ —	

As with the one-product firm, total contribution margin at the break-even point equals total fixed expense. However, since units of product are not a common base, total contribution margin is the contribution-margin ratio multiplied by the break-even sales. The contribution-margin ratio is the total contribution margin divided by the total sales ($150,000/$500,000 = 30%), or 1 minus the variable-expense ratio:

$$\left(1 - \frac{\$350,000}{\$500,000} = 30\%\right)$$

Consequently, the break-even formula for the multi-product firm is total fixed expenses divided by the contribution-margin ratio.

$$\text{Total contribution margin} = \text{Total fixed expenses}$$
$$\$150,000 = \$150,000$$

$$\begin{array}{ccc} \text{Total} & \text{Contribution-} & \\ \text{break-even} \times & \text{margin} & = \text{Total fixed expenses} \\ \text{sales} & \text{ratio} & \\ \$500,000 \quad \times & 30\% & = \$150,000 \end{array}$$

$$\frac{\textit{Total}}{\textit{break-even}} = \frac{\text{Total fixed expenses}}{\text{Contribution-margin ratio}}$$
$$\$500,000 = \$150,000 \div 30\%$$

Graphically, the break-even point is shown by a sales line drawn at a 45-degree angle and expenses drawn as before. The sales line does not change, for it is a common denominator base that measures dollars of sales regardless of different prices. The vertical axis measures sales and expenses while the horizontal axis measures sales. The horizontal axis is scaled so that it includes the normal operating range (relevant sales range), as shown on page 598.

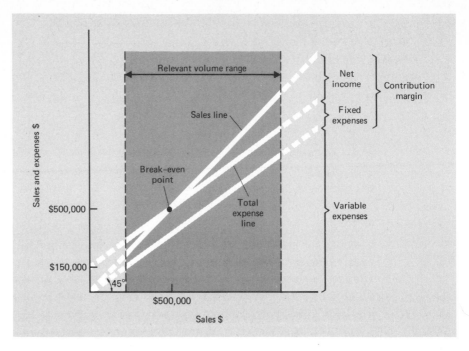

THE MARGIN OF SAFETY When evaluating, for example, the revenue potential of an existing or new product, or a new sales territory, or a different marketing strategy, management is concerned about how much the actual or planned sales can decline before losses occur. Since losses occur when sales drop below the break-even point, the margin of safety is defined as the excess of actual or planned sales over actual or planned break-even sales.

In the example below, actual sales can decline by the $50,000 margin of safety ($250,000–$200,000) before losses occur:

	Actual volume		Break-even volume	
	Amount	Percentage	Amount	Percentage
Sales	$250,000	100%	$200,000	100%
Variable expenses	150,000	60	120,000	60
Contribution margin	$100,000	40%	$ 80,000	40%
Fixed expenses	80,000		80,000	
Net income	$ 20,000	8%	$ —	

Or, in percentage terms, actual sales can decline 20 per cent before losses occur. Thus the margin of safety stated as a percentage is equal to 1 minus the ratio of break-even sales to actual sales:

$$\frac{\text{Margin-of-safety}}{\text{percentage}} = 1 - \frac{\text{Break-even sales}}{\text{Actual sales}}$$

$$20\% = 1 - \frac{\$200,000}{\$250,000}$$

One can find the margin-of-safety percentage also by dividing the percentage of net income to sales by the contribution-margin ratio:

$$\frac{\text{Margin-of-safety}}{\text{percentage}} = \frac{\text{Percentage of net income to sales}}{\text{Contribution-margin ratio}}$$

$$20\% = 8\% \div 40\%$$

TARGET PROFIT   There is more to cost-volume-profit analysis than just determining the break-even point. For example, management may want to know the overall sales necessary to generate net income of $20,000. In the illustration below, it takes sales volume of $150,000 to earn the $20,000 target profit:

	Amount	Percentage
Sales	$150,000	100%
Variable expenses	90,000	60
Contribution margin	$ 60,000	40%
Fixed expenses	40,000	
Net income	$ 20,000	

Note that total contribution margin ($60,000) equals fixed expenses ($40,000) plus the target profit ($20,000). Thus the formula for calculating the sales volume necessary to achieve the target profit for a multi-product firm is the sum of total fixed expenses plus target profit divided by the contribution-margin ratio, as shown below (divided by contribution margin per unit for single-product analysis):

$$\frac{\text{Sales needed for}}{\text{target profit}} \times \frac{\text{Contribution-}}{\text{margin ratio}} = \frac{\text{Total fixed}}{\text{expenses}} + \frac{\text{Target}}{\text{profit}}$$

$$\$150,000 \quad \times \quad 40\% \quad = \quad \$40,000 \quad + \$20,000$$

$$\frac{\text{Sales needed for}}{\text{target profit}} = \frac{\dfrac{\text{Total fixed}}{\text{expenses}} + \dfrac{\text{Target}}{\text{profit}}}{\text{Contribution-margin ratio}}$$

$$\$150,000 = \frac{\$40,000 + \$20,000}{40\%}$$

The target profit is shown graphically below:

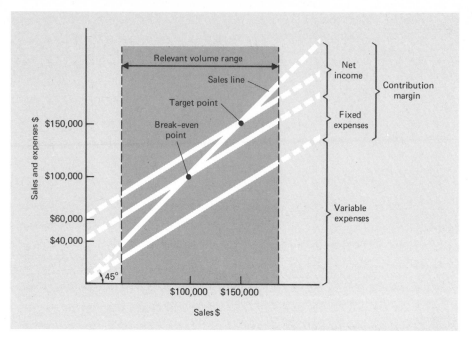

Note that it would be improper to conclude from the graph that an unlimited increase in sales volume will lead to unlimited profits. Conventional cost-volume-profit analysis is applicable only within the relevant volume range. Beyond the relevant range, economic theory indicates that straight-line assumptions are not valid, because of the likelihood of increasing expenses and declining sales.

CONTRIBUTION MARGIN ANALYSIS *Single product case* Contribution-margin analysis allows the accountant to answer quickly the management's questions as to how net income will be affected by changes in selling prices, expenses per unit, or sales volume. The use of contribution-margin analysis means that the accountant does not have to prepare a new income statement each time management asks a question about cost-volume-profit changes. With given fixed expenses, net income tends to vary with changes in contribution margin, and the latter can be analyzed to determine the effects of changes in cost-volume-profit relationships.

Assume that the data below pertain to product *X* and management wishes to know how profits would be affected by certain proposed changes.

	Actual Amount	Per unit (10,000 units)
Sales	$50,000	$5
Variable expenses	40,000	4
Contribution margin	$10,000	$1
Fixed expenses	4,000	
Net income	$ 6,000	

Suppose management asks you what the effect on profits would be if the price per unit were increased $1 and volume remained at 10,000 units. You could immediately state that net income would increase $10,000 because total contribution margin would increase from $10,000 to $20,000 ($2 new contribution margin per unit times 10,000 units). Now suppose that management asks the same question, except that volume would decline 4,000 units. In this instance you could quickly state that net income would increase $2,000 because total contribution margin would increase from $10,000 to $12,000 ($2 new contribution margin per unit times 6,000 units). Similarly, if management asks what the effect on profits would be if there were an increase in variable expense of $.50 a unit, you could point out that at 10,000 units profit would decrease $5,000. That is, contribution margin would decline from $10,000 to $5,000 ($.50 new contribution margin per unit times 10,000 units).

Multi-product case. Whereas the contribution-margin analysis of the single-product case focuses on the change in the contribution margin per unit, the same type of analysis is used in the multi-product case, except that attention is directed toward the change in the contribution-margin ratio. In order to illustrate contribution-margin analysis in the multi-product case, assume the following data.

| | Actual volume | | Break-even volume | |
	Amount	Percentage	Amount	Percentage
Sales	$600,000	100%	$250,000	100%
Variable expenses	480,000	80	200,000	80
Contribution margin	$120,000	20%	$ 50,000	20%
Fixed expenses	50,000		50,000	
Net income	$ 70,000		$ —	

At an overall sales volume of $600,000, suppose management wishes to know what the effect on profits would be if the variable-expense ratio were reduced 1 per cent by an increase in fixed expenses of $2,000. Your instant answer is that net income would increase $4,000 because the increase in contribution margin from $120,000 to $126,000 (.21 new contribution-margin ratio times $600,000 in sales) would more than offset the $2,000 increase in fixed expense.

Assume that management wishes to know how a 20 per cent increase in fixed expenses would affect the $250,000 break-even point. You can immediately state that the break-even sales would also have to increase 20 per cent ($250,000 × 1.20 = $300,000) in order to cover the higher fixed expenses. That is, total contribution margin equals total fixed expenses at the break-even point, and, if fixed expenses increase 20 per cent, then contribution margin must increase 20 per cent (from $50,000 to $60,000) to maintain the equality. Since contribution margin varies with sales, a 20 per cent increase in contribution margin necessitates a 20 per cent increase in sales to break even. Thus, in both the single-product and the multi-product case, an x per cent increase in fixed expenses necessitates an *x* per cent increase in break-even sales. The 20 per cent increase in fixed expenses and break-even sales is shown below:

	New break-even
Sales ($250,000 × 1.20)	$300,000
Variable expenses ($200,000 × 1.20)	240,000
Contribution margin ($50,000 × 1.20)	$ 60,000
Fixed expenses ($50,000 × 1.20)	60,000
Net income	$ —

SALES MIX   For a multi-product firm, the proportion of each product's sales to total company sales is called the *sales* or *product mix.* Cost-volume-profit analysis with regard to the multi-product firm assumes that the sales mix will not change. To illustrate, assume that the total sales of $600,000, total variable expenses of $480,000, and total fixed expenses of $50,000 in the preceding example (see page 601) consist of two product lines (Product A and Product B), as shown below:

	Product A		Product B		Total	
	Amount	Percentage	Amount	Percentage	Amount	Percentage
Sales	$420,000	100%	$180,000	100%	$600,000	100%
Variable expenses	345,000	82	135,000	75	480,000	80
Contribution margin	$ 75,000	18%	$ 45,000	25%	$120,000	20%
Fixed expenses					50,000	
Net income					$ 70,000	
Sales mix	70%		30%		100%	

The sales mix would be 70 per cent for Product A, since it accounts for $420,000 of the $600,000 total sales, and 30 per cent ($180,000 ÷ $600,000) for Product B. The target profit of $70,000, as well as the $250,000 break-even point ($50,000 ÷ .20), assumes a constant sales mix of 70 per cent and 30 per cent. An assumption under multi-product cost-volume-profit analysis is a constant sales mix.

A change in sales mix will change expected profits and will change the break-even point. For example, assume that in the above example the sales mix is exactly reversed (Product A 30 per cent and Product B 70 per cent of total sales) even though total sales remain unchanged at $600,000, as shown below:

	Product A		Product B		Total	
	Amount	Percentage	Amount	Percentage	Amount	Percentage
Sales	$180,000	100%	$420,000	100%	$600,000	100%
Variable expenses	147,600	82	315,000	75	462,600	77
Contribution margin	$ 32,400	18%	$105,000	25%	$137,400	23%
Fixed expenses					50,000	
Net income					$ 87,400	
Sales mix	30%		70%		100%	

The new break-even point would be $217,391 ($50,000 ÷ .23) and the new expected profits would be $87,400. In comparison to the 70–30 sales mix situation, the 30–70 sales mix situation shows a lower break-even point (from $250,000 to $217,391) and higher expected profits (from $70,000 to $87,400) because of the shift in sales mix toward the more profitable Product B. In other words, the shift in sales mix from the lower contribution-margin ratio Product A (18 per cent) toward the higher contribution-margin ratio Product B (25 per cent) causes the overall (average) contribution margin ratio to increase from 20 per cent to 23 per cent. The larger the contribution-margin ratio, the smaller the sales volume necessary to break even and the more profitable the sales (i.e., high contribution-margin sales are more profitable than low contribution margin sales). On the other hand, a shift in sales mix from a high contribution-margin product toward a low contribution-margin product can result in lower profits, or even a net loss, despite total sales staying the same or even increasing.

Multi-product cost-volume-profit analysis depends not only on sales volume and control of expense behavior, but also on sales mix. If a shift in sales mix is expected, then cost-volume-profit analysis should be based on the new sales mix.

GENERALIZATIONS ON COST-VOLUME-PROFIT ANALYSIS After analyzing the cost-volume-profit relationships of a firm, the accountant can make recommendations to management about possible ways to increase profitability. For example, suppose a firm is highly mechanized so that fixed expenses are a large proportion of total expenses, the variable-expense ratio is relatively low, and the contribution-margin ratio is relatively high, as shown below.

In such a situation the accountant can recommend that management attempt to increase profits by increasing sales volume or by reducing fixed expenses. When

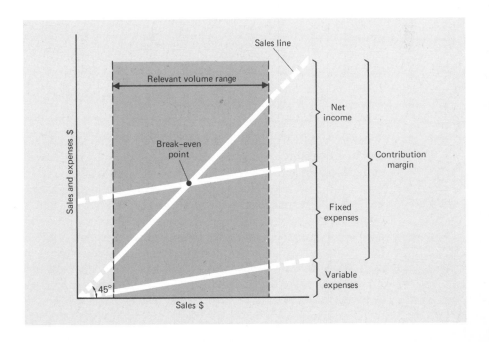

sales volume exceeds the break-even point, such a firm is highly profitable because of the high contribution margin. Note the large gap between sales and total expense beyond the break-even point. Consequently, management should investigate the possibilities of increasing sales volume through advertising and other sales-promotion techniques. Also, management might be able to bring about an increase in profits by a reduction in fixed expenses or by a trade-off of fixed expenses for variable expenses (i.e., reduce fixed expenses more than the increase in variable expenses). Although there are several possibilities, the accountant is saying: "Here are two recommendations that appear to be good starting points in attempting to increase company profits."

Now suppose the accountant is analyzing a firm that has a high proportion of variable expense to total expense, a low proportion of fixed expense to total expense, and a low contribution-margin ratio, as shown below:

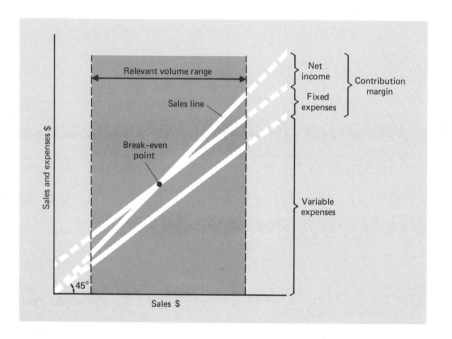

In this case the accountant can recommend to management that two good strategies in attempting to increase profits would be to increase sales price or to reduce variable expense. Note the small gap between sales and total expense beyond the break-even point. That is, the contribution-margin ratio is so low that an increase in sales volume does not increase profits very much; hence, as a starting point, management should attempt to increase the contribution-margin ratio. For example, it may be possible to reduce variable expenses by replacing expensive labor with machinery. Or the firm's markets might be such that an increase in sales prices would not lower sales volume and would thus increase profits.

Finally, suppose management is faced with a problem in that one of its products is not even covering its variable expenses, as illustrated on page 605.

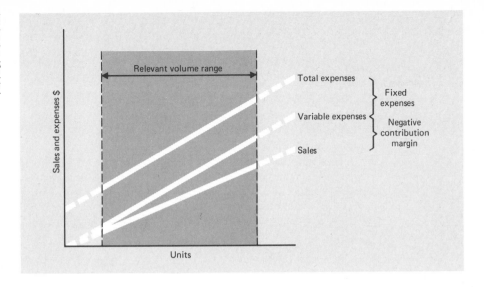

Given the above situation, the firm should drop the product, because it is not providing any positive contribution margin. Losses are minimized at zero volume as shown by the increasing losses as volume increases. On the other hand, if it is possible to bring about changes in the short run that result in a positive contribution margin, then the product could be retained. For example, the sales price might be increased without reduction of volume, or total expenses might be reduced. Also, the recommendation to drop the product is based on the assumption that variable expenses are relevant and fixed expenses irrelevant to the decision; however, the accountant should make sure that this assumption is not distorting the analysis.

Once the accountant has analyzed the cost-volume-profit structure of a firm, recommendations can be made to management that the accountant feels are the most likely to increase company profits. However, this does not mean that the recommendations necessarily will turn out to be the best strategies management can employ. For example, the firm with a high contribution-margin ratio may not be able to increase sales volume in the short run because of a lack of plant capacity. Thus cost-volume-profit analysis is a good starting point, but further analysis, especially of qualitative factors, must be carried on in each situation.

ASSUMPTIONS Short-run analysis of a firm's cost-volume-profit relationships does not provide exact answers to management's financial problems. It provides approximate answers, given the underlying assumptions, and the assumptions have to be kept in mind at all times. Nevertheless, the technique is useful as a starting point in evaluating performance and in planning for the future.

The assumptions underlying cost-volume-profit analysis are summarized:

(1) Revenue and expense are assumed to be linear functions (straight lines) of volume over the relevant range, so that sales prices, variable-expense ratios, and total fixed expenses are constant as volume changes. Cost-volume-profit analysis can be used in a nonlinear case, but then traditional contribution-margin analysis has to be modified.

(2) Variable and fixed expenses can be meaningfully separated. In actuality the separation is a difficult problem. Various approaches to the separation of variable and fixed expenses include judgmental separation based on analysis of the accounting records, the use of scatter graphs, an analysis of the change in total expense over representative high-low volume levels, and the use of such statistical techniques as least squares and multiple regression.

(3) Technological changes and efficiency are assumed to be constant. However, through a series of analyses under different efficiency conditions, the effect of changes in efficiency on net income can be approximated.

(4) Volume is assumed to be the common and relevant base for comparing sales and expenses. Obviously this is a simplification because external factors (wars, business conditions, and strikes) and qualitative factors (trade-union effects or the necessity of maintaining a wide product line to satisfy customers) also influence net income. Thus cost-volume-profit analysis is only a starting point for further analysis.

(5) Variable (direct) costing (discussed in the next chapter), not absorption costing, is assumed to be the proper approach for cost-volume-profit analysis. That is, *actual* fixed factory overhead cost, which is treated as a period expense, is used in cost-volume-profit analysis instead of *applied* fixed factory overhead cost.

(6) For a multi-product firm, the proportion of each product's sales to total company sales is assumed to be constant (i.e., the sales mix is constant). That is, for a particular situation, cost-volume-profit analysis depends on the fixed relationship of high and low sales-mix products. However, the effect of different product sales mixes can be studied by a series of analyses under varying sales-mix conditions.

RELEVANT REVENUES AND COSTS Decision making involves choosing among the alternatives that are perceived to be available. In business decisions the choice among alternative courses of action is choosing that alternative that is expected to lead to the greatest profits. Since revenues and costs (expenses) affect profits, the revenues and costs of each alternative are compared in order to make the choice, provided that the revenues and costs are relevant to the decision to be made.

Relevant revenues and costs are *future* revenues and costs that are *different* under the alternatives being considered. They are expected differential revenues and costs. The essence of business decisions is the comparison of expected differential revenues and costs for each alternative under consideration. The decision process should focus on the expected differences among the alternatives, or so-called *differential analysis.* In fact, cost-volume-profit analysis is a form of differential analysis in which the expected differential revenues and costs are the changes in revenues and costs (variable costs) brought about by changes in volume.

Past revenues and past costs (often called *sunk costs*) are not relevant to a particular current decision because they have already been earned and incurred and cannot be changed by any current or future decision. For example, assume that a company has 10,000 units of a product in the process of being manufactured that are 90 per cent complete at the following costs:

	Total costs for 10,000 units	Per unit
Direct materials	$10,000	$10.00
Direct labor	8,000	8.00
Variable factory overhead	6,000	6.00
Fixed factory overhead (applied at 50% of direct labor cost)	4,000	4.00
Total	$28,000	$28.00

Further assume that because of an unexpected change in consumer demand the product can no longer be sold. Management determines that the product can be sold as is for scrap for $7,000 or the product can be modified at an additional manufacturing cost of $2.50 per unit and then sold for $3.00 per unit. Which alternative should be accepted?

The $28,000 ($28 × 10,000) past manufacturing cost is not relevant to the decision to scrap or remanufacture the goods, since it is a past cost that has already been utilized and cannot be changed. Moreover, note that the $28,000 cost includes variable costs that are not relevant to the decision because they are past variable costs. Differential analysis shows that the company should scrap the product and would benefit by $2,000, as shown below:

	Scrap	Remanufacture	Difference
Expected future revenue	$7,000	$30,000	
Differential revenue			$(23,000)
Expected future costs		25,000	
Differential costs			25,000
Expected net	$7,000	$ 5,000	
Differential profits—advantage to scrap			$ 2,000

Similarly, revenues and costs that are the same for different alternatives are not relevant to a particular decision because they have no effect on deciding between the alternatives. For example, assume that the management of a company is deciding whether to continue to manufacture a part that goes into its final product or to purchase the part from another company—a make or buy decision. Assume that the cost to manufacture the part is the same as that given in the preceding illustration or $28 per part ($28,000 for 10,000 units). Further assume that the company can purchase the part for $27. Should the company make or buy the part?

Note that the expected revenue from the sale of the final product is not relevant to the make or buy decision, since it is the same no matter if the part is produced or purchased. The fixed factory overhead cost is not relevant to the decision if the cost will continue unchanged whether the part is purchased or not, since the cost would not differ between the two alternatives. In other words, the fixed factory overhead cost for the part is the allocated portion of the fixed costs common to all items produced in the factory that will not change. Of course, if some of the fixed cost could be avoided by purchasing the part, then such cost would be relevant to the decision; however, such cost would have to be carefully estimated because fixed overhead costs based on an applied fixed overhead rate would not indicate the avoidable fixed cost. In contrast, the variable costs are relevant costs because they are future costs and they differ between alternatives, since they can be avoided by purchasing the part. Consequently, differential analysis indicates that the company should continue to make the part and benefit by $3,000, as shown on page 608.[1]

[1]The decision to continue to make the part is based on the assumption that the facilities used to make the part would be idle if the part were purchased. If the released facilities could be used to manufacture other products or rented out, then the contribution from the other products or the rent would have to be considered in the decision.

	Make	Buy	Difference
Expected costs:			
Direct materials	$10,000	$	$(10,000)
Direct labor	8,000		(8,000)
Variable factory overhead	6,000		(6,000)
Cost to purchase		27,000	27,000
	$24,000	$27,000	
Differential cost—advantage to make			$ 3,000

The underlying decision model for alternative choice problems is the determination and comparison of the expected future revenues and costs that differ under the alternatives under consideration—the relevant revenues and costs. Examples of such alternative choice problems include:

(1) Whether to sell a product or process it further.
(2) Whether to make or buy a product component.
(3) Whether to accept or reject a special order at a special price.
(4) Whether to produce using one or two labor shifts.
(5) Whether to drop or keep a product line.

NONFINANCIAL (QUALITATIVE) FACTORS IN DECISION MAKING In providing information for managerial decision making, the accountant attempts to express as many decision factors as is possible in terms of dollars and cents—financial (quantitative) factors—such as expected differential revenues and costs. However, nonfinancial (qualitative) factors, which are decision factors not easily measurable in terms of dollars and cents, must also be considered in managerial decision making. For example, assume that differential analysis indicates that a company should manufacture a part instead of continuing to purchase it from an outside supplier. The firm may reject the quantitative analysis and decide to continue to buy the part because of the firm's long-run dependency on the supplier for other strategic parts. In this instance, qualitative factors outweigh quantitative factors.

IMPORTANT TERMS AND CONCEPTS IN CHAPTER 20

DEMONSTRATION PROBLEM FOR REVIEW AND SELF-STUDY Moonitz Company makes and sells 10,000 units of a product per year. The regular selling price is $30 per unit and the unit costs of making and selling the product are as follows:

Variable expenses:

Direct materials	$8.00
Direct labor	7.00
Variable factory overhead	5.00
Variable selling and administrative	2.00
Fixed expenses:	
Fixed factory overhead ($32,000 ÷ 10,000)	3.20
Fixed selling and administrative ($10,000 ÷ 10,000)	1.00

INSTRUCTIONS Given the above data, answer the following independent questions:

(a) Can you prepare an income statement showing the expected contribution margin and net income?

(b) What is the break-even point in units and in dollar sales?

(c) Assume expected sales of 10,000 units. What is the margin of safety in dollars and in percentage terms?

(d) What are the sales in units and in dollars necessary to earn a target profit of $60,000?

(e) The sales manager estimates that by reducing the selling price 10 per cent that the number of units sold would increase 10 per cent. What would be the effect on profits if the sales manager's proposal were adopted?

(f) The sales manager estimates that by spending $10,000 on advertising that sales volume would be increased 10 per cent. What would be the effect on profits if the sales manager's proposal were adopted?

(g) Moonitz Company uses a major part in every unit of finished product. The estimated manufacturing costs for these parts are $5 variable cost per unit and $10,000 additional fixed costs. A firm has offered to supply Moonitz Company with these key parts for $10 each. What would be the effect on profits if the offer were accepted?

(h) A discount firm offers to acquire 4,000 units of the product at $25 per unit from Moonitz Company and then market them under their own brand name. Since Moonitz has unused production capacity, it can supply the 4,000 additional products with no expected change in fixed costs. However, Moonitz would have to spend $5,000 for a special machine attachment to imprint the discount firm's name on the product. Because there would be no selling expense for this product, variable selling and administrative expense per unit would be reduced 50 per cent. What would be the effect on profits if the offer were accepted?

(i) What nonfinancial or qualitative factors should be considered in question (h)?

Note Attempt to solve this demonstration problem before examining the solution that follows.

Solution:

(a)

Sales ($30 × 10,000)	$300,000
Variable expenses ($22 × 10,000)	220,000
Contribution margin ($8 × 10,000)	$ 80,000
Fixed expenses ($32,000 + $10,000)	42,000
Net income	$ 38,000

(b) $\dfrac{\$42,000}{\$8} = 5,250$ units to break even

5,250 × $30 = $157,500 break-even sales.

(c) $300,000 Sales

   157,500 Break-even sales

$142,500 Margin of safety

$1 - \dfrac{\$157,500}{\$300,000} = 1 - .525 = 47.5\%$ margin-of-safety percentage

(d) $\dfrac{\$42,000 \text{ Fixed expenses} + \$60,000 \text{ Target profit}}{\$8 \text{ Contribution margin per unit}} = 12,750$ Units needed to be sold to earn target profit

   12,750 × $30 = $382,500 sales needed to earn $60,000 target profit.

(e) $30 × (1 − .10) = $27 New sales price

   $27 − $22 = $5 New contribution margin per unit

   10,000 × (1 + .10) = 11,000 New volume

   $5 × 11,000 = $55,000 New contribution margin

   $80,000 Old contribution margin

   −55,000 New contribution margin

   $25,000 Decline in profits

(f)   10,000 × .10 =   1,000 Increase in volume

   1,000 × $8 = $ 8,000 Increase in contribution margin

          −10,000 Increase in fixed expense

          $ (2,000) Decline in profits

(g)   Buy ($10 × 10,000) $100,000

   Make [($5 × 10,000) + $10,000*]   60,000

   Differential cost advantage to make because of increase in profits $ 40,000

*Avoidable fixed costs.

(h)   Differential revenue ($25 × 4,000) $100,000

   Differential costs

      Variable manufacturing [($8 + $7 + $5) × 4,000] $80,000

      Variable selling and administrative [($2 × .5) × 4,000]   4,000

      Machine attachment   5,000   89,000

   Differential profits—advantage of accepting

   special order because of increase in profits $ 11,000

(i)   Qualitative factors to be considered are whether or not regular sales would be adversely affected by the sales of the discount firm, whether or not the firm's long-run pricing structure would be unfavorably affected by the special order, and whether or not the lower price would be viewed as unfair price discrimination by the Robinson–Patman Act.

Questions

1 What does cost-volume-profit analysis attempt to do? Discuss.

2 Why is cost-volume-profit analysis referred to as short-run analysis? Discuss.

3 Is break-even analysis synonymous with cost-volume-profit analysis? Discuss.

4 In cost-volume-profit analysis, the *conventional* model used by the accountant is not applicable to volume levels outside of the relevant operating range. What does this statement mean? Discuss.

5 Assuming a short-run time period, why does total net income fluctuate with total contribution margin? Explain and illustrate.

6 Assuming a short-run time period, why does a *y* per cent increase in fixed expenses result in a *y* per cent increase in break-even sales? Discuss.

7 In cost-volume-profit analysis, why does single-product analysis differ from multi-product analysis? Discuss.

8 Graphically, the accountant's model of the firm seems to imply unlimited profits. What does this statement mean? Do you agree with the statement? Discuss.

9 Cost-volume-profit analysis for the multi-product firm implies a constant sales mix. What does this statement mean? Discuss.

10 Does the break-even point indicate the lower limit below which a product line, sales territory, or the like, should be dropped? Discuss.

11 What is meant by the "margin of safety"? Discuss.

12 How does the formula for calculating unit sales needed to break even differ from the formula for calculating unit sales needed to earn a target profit? Discuss.

13 Suppose that two firms are similar in all respects except that Firm No. 1 has higher fixed expenses and lower variable expenses than Firm No. 2. Can you make any generalizations concerning which of the two firms would benefit more by a 10 per cent increase in sales volume? What about a 10 per cent decrease in sales volume? Discuss.

14 What is the importance of relevant revenues and relevant costs? Discuss.

Short exercises

E20-1 *You are given three multiple-choice statements. Select the correct answers and indicate the corresponding letters on a sheet of paper (e.g., 1-d, 2-d, etc.).*

(1) Cost-volume-profit analysis is useful (a) when making long-run decisions, (b) when capacity is not fixed, (c) for all management decisions, (d) for making decisions at extremely low or extremely high operating levels, (e) none of the above.

(2) Contribution margin (a) is not compatible with cost-volume-profit analysis, (b) is defined as total revenue minus total fixed expenses, (c) is defined as selling price less variable expenses, (d) is not useful for making management decisions, (e) none of the above.

(3) The break-even point is the level of output at which (a) total revenue equals total expense, (b) net income is zero, (c) contribution margin equals fixed expenses, (d) all of the above, (e) none of the above.

E20-2   *You are given below three multiple-choice statements. Select the correct answers and indicate the corresponding letters on a sheet of paper (e.g., 1-d, 2-d, etc.).*

(1) A multi-product firm (a) cannot calculate a break-even point, (b) usually calculates a break-even point in terms of dollar sales rather than unit sales, (c) need only make one break-even calculation even if sales mix might vary, (d) cannot use graphical cost-volume product analysis, (e) none of the above.

(2) The margin of safety (a) is the amount by which sales must increase before profits occur, (b) is the excess of planned sales over planned break-even sales, (c) percentage is equal to 1 minus the ratio of actual sales to break-even sales, (d) all of the above, (e) none of the above.

(3) Relevant revenues and costs are (a) future revenues and costs which differ under the alternatives being considered, (b) future costs which are the same under the alternatives being considered, (c) past revenues and costs, (d) the revenues and costs which should be ignored when choosing among alternatives, (e) none of the above.

E20-3   *You are given a cost-volume-profit graph of a firm.*

(a) Identify each number in the graph.

(b) How does the graph differ from the traditional cost-volume-profit graph?

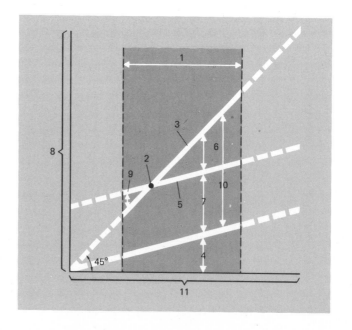

Determine the amounts needed to complete the blanks.

(a) Single-product firms:

	Sales	Variable expenses	Fixed expenses	Net income	Units sold	Contribution per unit
1.	$ _____	$ _____	$ _____	$70,000	5,000	$40 − $20 = $20
2.	300,000	225,000	_____	35,000	5,000	_____
3.	450,000	_____	_____	50,000	30,000	5.00
4.	_____	125,000	50,000	_____	10,000	7.50

(b) Multi-product firms:

	Sales	Variable expenses	Fixed expenses	Net income	Contribution margin %
1.	$300,000	$270,000	$ _____	$25,000	_____ %
2.	200,000	_____	_____	20,000	40
3.	_____	140,000	50,000	_____	30
4.	_____	_____	100,000	10,000	20

Make-or-Buy Company produces and sells several products. One of its products, called Leno, is produced at the following per-unit costs: $4 direct materials, $24 direct labor, $16 variable factory overhead, and $8 fixed factory overhead. An offer was recently received from another company to manufacture Leno for Make-or-Buy Company at a cost of $48. Management has decided to accept this offer since the $48 purchase price is less than the $52 total cost per unit to produce the product. Evaluate the decision.

Assume that One Product Company manufactures a product at a variable cost of $65 per unit. Annual fixed costs are $104,000. The company has an operating capacity of 15,000 units, but annual production and sales have been about 10,000 units. The product is sold for $100 a unit. The company recently received an offer of $70 a unit from a foreign distributor to market 3,000 units of the product. Management rejected the offer because the $73 [($104,000 ÷ 13,000) + $65] average production cost per unit was higher than the $70 price the foreign distributor was willing to pay. Evaluate the decision.

Problems

Answer the following short questions and show all your calculations:

(1) If total fixed expense is $538,125, sales price per unit is $21.50, and variable expense per unit is $11.25, how many units of product must be sold to break even? What is the dollar amount of break-even sales?

(2) Fixed expenses are expected to be $60,000 and variable expenses are expected to be 40 per cent of sales. Sales at 100 per cent capacity are estimated to be $300,000. How would you construct a graph to show break-even sales and target sales if target profit is $37,500?

(3) A company's total fixed expense for the current year is $30,000. Next year the fixed expenses are expected to increase to $31,500. In percentage terms, how will the increase in fixed expenses affect break-even sales? Discuss.

(4) For the current year a company has sales of $400,000, net income of $35,000, and a contribution-margin ratio of 40 per cent. What is the total fixed expense of the company? What is the margin-of-safety percentage?

A20-2

The management of Bettendorf, Inc., has hired you as a management consultant. You are asked to analyze the company's cost-volume-profit relationships in order that management can analyze different strategies in an attempt to increase profits.

You point out to management that, before different strategies can be analyzed, financial data are needed to determine the company's basic cost-volume-profit structure. Thus you ask for a breakdown of expenses into variable and fixed components. Instead you are given the following data for two representative years:

	19_2	19_1
Sales	$600,000	$550,000
Total expenses	520,000	480,000
Net income	$ 80,000	$ 70,000

Given only the above data, answer the following questions (show all calculations):

(1) What is the contribution-margin ratio? (*Hint:* Analyze the changes between the two years.)
(2) What is the variable-expense ratio?
(3) What are the total variable expenses for 19_2 and 19_1?
(4) What are the total fixed expenses?
(5) What are the break-even sales?

A20-3

Fawns Manufacturing produces and sells four products. The operating results for the year are as follows:

	Product #1	Product #2	Product #3	Product #4
Sales	$300,000	$75,000	$100,000	$25,000
Variable expenses	180,000	60,000	50,000	22,500
Contribution margin	$120,000	$15,000	$ 50,000	$ 2,500
Fixed expenses	70,000	13,500	21,500	1,500
Net income	$ 50,000	$ 1,500	$ 28,500	$ 1,000

(1) What is the overall break-even sales?
(2) Using the above data, what is the proportion of *each* product's sales to total sales (sales mix)?
(3) Assume that the sales mix changes to the following: Product #1, 45 per cent; Product #2, 20 per cent; Product #3, 25 per cent; Product #4, 10 per cent. What is the new overall break-even sales?
(4) Explain *why* the break-even sales in part (3) either increased or decreased.

A20-4

Merolis, Inc., produces and sells three products. The operating results for the year just ended are as follows:

	Product #1	Product #2	Product #3
Sales	$250,000	$50,000	$150,000
Variable expenses	200,000	30,000	105,000
Contribution margin	$ 50,000	$20,000	$ 45,000
Fixed expenses	30,000	25,000	27,500
Net income	$ 20,000	$ (5,000)	17,500

Sales consisted of 10,000, 2,500, and 5,000 units, respectively, for Products #1, #2, and #3.

Mr. Skinner, the president of the company, wants to drop Product #2 and undertake a large advertising campaign to push the sales of Product #1. His reasoning is that Product #2 is unprofitable and that Product #1 generates the most profit.

The treasurer of the company contends that Product #2 should be pushed, not dropped, since it has the highest contribution-margin ratio.

The assistant to the president argues that the company should push Product #3, since it has the highest contribution margin per unit.

(1) Evaluate all three positions and state which one you think is the best. Include financial data in your analysis.

(2) What other factors should be considered? Discuss.

A20-6

Chase Company produces and sells one product in the midwestern and eastern markets. The company normally sells 300,000 units of product per year at the following expenses per unit:

Cost of goods sold:	
Direct materials	$ 6.40
Direct labor	8.70
Variable factory overhead	6.20
Fixed factory overhead ($1,410,000 ÷ 300,000)	4.70
Operating expenses:	
Variable selling	2.70
Fixed administration ($390,000 ÷ 300,000)	1.30
	$30.00

(1) Chase Company receives an offer from Blades Company to produce the product for Chase Company's customers in the eastern market. Blades Company is willing to produce and ship the product for $29 per unit. In such a case Chase Company would merely forward its eastern sales orders to Blades Company. Chase Company would still bill the eastern customers at the regular price and collect all receivables. The annual normal sales to the eastern market are 100,000 units of product. If Chase Company were to accept this offer, total fixed factory overhead would be reduced 30 per cent in the production of the 200,000 units and variable selling expense would be cut 40 per cent on the sale of the 100,000 units. Should Chase Company accept or reject the offer? (*Hint:* Try calculating the costs avoided.)

(2) Would your answer to part (1) change if the company were able to rent its idle plant facilities at $800,000 per year, if total fixed factory overhead cost remained the same, and if variable selling expense per unit were cut 40 per cent?

B20-1

Answer the following short questions and show all your calculations:

(1) If total fixed expense is $123,000 and contribution margin is $3 per unit, how many units of product must be sold to break even?

(2) If a multi-product firm has total fixed expenses of $218,080, and the overall contribution-margin ratio is 29 per cent, what total sales are necessary to break even?

(3) If total fixed expense is $405,250, target profit is $80,000, and the overall contribution-margin ratio is 30 per cent, what are the actual sales needed to attain the target profit?

(4) If break-even sales are $42,000, and if actual sales are 10,500 units at $5 per unit, what is the total dollar amount of the margin of safety? What is the margin-of-safety percentage?

(5) If net income is 6 per cent of sales, the contribution margin is 30 per cent, and break-even sales are $352,000, what are the actual sales?

B20-2

McCune Company manufactures and sells one product. The product is sold at $32 per unit. Normal production and sales volume are 120,000 units of product. The expenses associated with one unit of product are as follows:

Cost of goods sold:	
Direct materials	$ 6.40
Direct labor	8.70
Variable factory overhead	6.20
Fixed factory overhead ($564,000 ÷ 120,000 units)	4.70
Selling and administrative expenses:	
Variable	2.70
Fixed	1.30
	$30.00

Management wants to try to increase profits by increasing sales volume. The market-research staff believes sales volume can be increased under four different plans:

(1) To increase annual advertising $80,000 would, it is estimated, increase sales volume 10 per cent. The sales price would remain the same at $32 per unit.

(2) To reduce the selling price by 50¢ a unit and increase annual advertising $12,000, it is estimated, would increase sales volume 10 per cent.

(3) To reduce the selling price $1 per unit should increase sales volume 15 per cent.

(4) To reduce the selling price by $1.50 per unit should increase sales volume 20 per cent.

Prepare an analysis of each of the four plans and show which is the most favorable.

B20-3

Gustafson Company sells pencils to stationery stores on the east coast for $5.00 per box of 200. Last year the company had sales of $1,000,000, fixed expenses of $400,000, and variable expenses of $350,000.

Management wishes to expand its market to the midwest. Since the company has excess capacity, the only additional expenses would be the new salesmen needed for the new market. The estimated expense of the additional sales personnel, who would be paid a fixed salary, is $120,000.

(1) If last year's performance in the eastern market is expected to be the same for the current year, how many additional boxes of pencils must be sold in the midwestern market to provide $75,000 in additional profits over last year? Show all computations.

(2) If the price per box were lowered to $4 for both markets, how many boxes would have to be sold to provide $75,000 in additional profits over last year?

(3) Management estimates that if the price per box is reduced from $5 to $4 in the eastern market, 290,000 boxes can be sold in that market. Given this strategy for the eastern market, how many

boxes must be sold at $5 each in the midwestern market to provide $321,000 in total company profits?

B20-4   *Hickok Manufacturing produces and sells three products. The operating results for the year are as follows:*

	Product #1	Product #2	Product #3	Total
Sales	$100,000	$200,000	$20,000	$320,000
Variable expenses	70,000	160,000	10,000	240,000
Contribution margin	30,000	$ 40,000	$10,000	$ 80,000
Fixed expenses				31,000
Net income				$ 49,000

(1) What is the overall break-even sales figure?

(2) Using the above data, what is the proportion of *each* product's sales to total sales (sales mix)?

(3) Based on total sales of $320,000, assume that the sales mix changes to the following: Product #1, 35 per cent; Product #2, 40 per cent; Product #3, 25 per cent. What is the new overall break-even sales figure?

(4) Explain *why* the break-even sales in part (3) either increased or decreased.

B20-5   *Picker Company manufactures a single product. The company's annual expected production is 437,500 units of output, or, in terms of standard input, 100,000 direct labor hours. The expected plant capacity of 100,000 direct labor hours is based on a single eight-hour-a-day work shift. Last year's internal income statement for the company is presented below:*

G. PICKER COMPANY
Income Statement
For the Year Ended December 31, 19_1

Sales (700,000 units @ $2.50)		$1,750,000
Variable expenses:		
Direct materials	$280,000	
Direct labor (160,000 hours @ $3)	480,000	
Factory overhead:		
Overtime premiums (60,000 hours @ $1.50)	90,000	
Miscellaneous	210,000	1,060,000
Contribution margin		$ 690,000
Fixed expenses		550,000
Net income		$ 140,000

Management is concerned about the overtime premiums (one-half of the normal labor rate) paid last year, and asks the chief accountant to prepare an analysis of the effect on profits on a second work shift. The accountant estimates that the second shift would increase costs as follows: an additional factory supervisor at $15,000 per year, a night-shift bonus of $.30 per direct labor hour, and an increase in fixed expenses (mostly selling and administrative expenses) of $19,800.

(1) Instead of paying overtime premiums last year, would profits have been greater if a second work shift had been used for the 60,000 above-normal direct labor hours?

(2) In comparison to last year, the forecast for this year includes the following: a 20 per cent increase in units sold, a 5 per cent increase in direct materials cost per unit, and a direct labor rate increase of $.16 per hour. Assuming that this forecast is correct, how much can be saved by use of a second work shift?

(3) Assuming that the day shift can best handle the expected capacity of 100,000 direct labor hours, and assuming that the overtime premium is $1.50, at what capacity level above 100,000 hours should the company switch to the second shift? (*Hint:* Find the number of direct labor hours that equate the cost of overtime to the cost of the second shift.)

CONTRIBUTION APPROACH TO INTERNAL REPORTING

PURPOSE OF CHAPTER The purpose of this chapter is to discuss internal reporting to management based on the concepts of responsibility accounting, contribution-margin analysis, and variable (direct) costing. Such internal reporting is designed to provide information useful for management performance evaluation and for facilitating cost-volume-profit type decisions.

RESPONSIBILITY ACCOUNTING Responsibility accounting is the segmentation of the business firm into supervisory areas (responsibility centers) in which only those costs, expenses, or revenues and expenses that are under the control of a supervisor are assigned to that supervisor; they become his or her responsibility. An important point is that those costs or expenses not under the control of a particular supervisor should not be assigned to the supervisor as his or her responsibility.

A segment of an organization can be defined as any unit of the organization for which an accounting is desired. Examples of segments are a product, a product line, a department, a territory, or a division. A segment is also normally a responsibility center in that it is an organization unit headed by a single person who is held accountable for the performance of the segment in terms of costs, expenses, or revenues and expenses over which he or she has control.

Under responsibility accounting, expenditures are accumulated by cost and expense centers, which are segments of the firm for which management desires cost and expense data. Typical cost centers of a firm include factory service and production departments; typical expense centers are the general office and delivery departments. In addition, there are segments of the firm called profit centers for which *both* revenue and expenses are isolated. A profit center is an independent business segment of the firm, and is usually called a "division." A firm, for example, might have two divisions: an electrical appliance manufacturing division and a computer manufacturing division, each having a division manager who is held responsible for revenues, expenses, and assets used in the operation of his or her division.

Ideally, responsibility accounting motivates a manager to control costs, for the manager knows that the costs he or she incurs will be traced to him or her and that the manager will not be charged for those costs not under his or her control. In general, the manager will feel that he or she is being treated fairly if his or her performance is evaluated in terms of those factors over which he or she has control.

TRADITIONAL REPORTING   As pointed out in Chapter 16, direct costs are assigned to production and service departments; indirect costs are allocated to the production and service departments; service department costs are allocated to the production departments; and each production department cost is assigned to the finished product. Thus, to calculate the cost of goods sold (expense) for each product line, the production cost per unit is multiplied by the number of units sold; and, if selling and administrative expenses are allocated to the product lines, the result is an income statement segmented by product lines. The main purpose, generally, is to provide data for financial statements. A traditional report is shown below.

	Total	Product #1	Product #2	Product #3
Net sales	$355,000	$200,000	$30,000	$125,000
Deduct cost of goods sold	200,000	110,000	18,000	72,000
Gross margin	$155,000	$ 90,000	$12,000	$ 53,000
Deduct selling and administrative expenses	98,000	40,000	20,000	38,000
Net income (loss)	$ 57,000	$ 50,000	$ (8,000)	$ 15,000

For purposes of control, the traditional reports are inadequate for two reasons. First is the arbitrary allocations of indirect costs. To achieve cost allocation, indirect costs are prorated to cost centers by means of some rational method of identification. The problem, however, is that there are several rational ways to allocate an indirect cost and that the selection of one allocation method is really an arbitrary choice. For example, note the several possible allocation bases for each indirect cost listed below.

Indirect cost to be distributed	Bases for distribution
Depreciation of equipment	Floor space; value of equipment; direct charge to department using equipment
Machine maintenance	Cost of machines; direct charges to departments where maintenance work is done
Taxes and insurance on building	Value of assets; square feet occupied
Power and light	Kilowatts per meter; capacity of equipment
Personnel department	Number of employees; time spent working on department problems; number of employees hired
Cafeteria	Total number of employees in department; number of employees in department using cafeteria

Second, the traditional report emphasizes the net income from each product after allowing for all expenses associated with the product. When such a report is used to judge performance, product managers normally would be evaluated on the basis of the total product net income, the percentage of product net income to sales, or some other similar measure. However, the emphasis on product net income overlooks the possibility that such reports are based on the allocation to the product lines of indirect expenses that are not under the control of the product manager. For instance, the net loss for Product #2 in the example might be the result of allocations of indirect expenses over which the product manager has no control. The product manager probably has no control over such indirect expenses as top executive salaries, outlays for basic research and development, and the expenses of operating the personnel department that are allocated to the manager's product. Such traditional reports are not compatible with responsibility accounting.

CONTROLLABLE COSTS AND EXPENSES   Controllable costs and expenses are those subject to regulation by a manager because of the manager's direct influence over the incurrence of such costs and expenses, assuming a given time period and a given responsibility center. The latter two assumptions are necessary because controllable costs are affected by (1) the particular responsibility center and (2) the particular time period.

A cost or expense that is uncontrollable with regard to one responsibility center may be controllable at another responsibility center. Thus outlays associated with product research may or may not be controllable by the division manager. Similarly, a cost that is controllable over a long period of time may not be controllable over a short period of time. A division manager may not be able to control the current charge for depreciation of factory equipment, but at the end of, say, five years when the manager buys new equipment, his or her decision will influence subsequent depreciation charges. Given a long enough time period, all costs are at least partially controllable.

As a first approximation, fixed costs are often assumed to be uncontrollable and variable costs controllable; however, the degree of controllability really depends on the particular responsibility center and the particular time period involved. The cost of renting production equipment is an uncontrollable annual fixed cost to the product manager, but it is controllable by the division manager if he or she has the authority to buy new equipment to replace the rental equipment. For this cost the responsibility of the division manager outranks that of the product manager. The cost is uncontrollable at one responsibility center and controllable at a higher responsibility center. Similarly, the product manager may have no control over the annual budget for advertising his or her product, but the manager may have some control in that he or she can decide on the kind of advertising and the spending rate for advertising up to the total amount the manager is allowed. At some higher management level the decision is made to limit outlays for advertising to some fixed amount; advertising expense is controllable at this management level. Thus some costs and expenses are fixed at the discretion of management and are therefore controllable (at least partially) by management: budgeted outlays for advertising and research are examples.

CONTRIBUTION MARGIN   As discussed in Chapter 20, contribution margin is the dollar amount that remains when variable expenses are subtracted from net sales, and is available to meet fixed expenses, any positive remainder being net income. Contribution margin is expressed either as a total dollar amount, as an amount per unit of product sold, or as a percentage of sales:

	Total amount	Percentage	Per unit (7,000 units)
Sales	$140,000	100%	$20.00
Variable expenses	98,000	70	14.00
Contribution margin	$ 42,000	30%	$ 6.00
Fixed expenses	30,000		
Net income	$ 12,000		

Note that, if fixed expenses are truly fixed, net income varies with the amount of contribution margin (assuming that sales and variable expenses per unit are constant). For example, if the sales price per unit is increased $2, contribution margin and profit are increased $2 per unit, or $14,000 ($2 × 7,000). Similarly, if 2,000 more units of product are sold, contribution margin and profit increase $12,000 ($6 contribution margin per unit times 2,000 units). The point is that, with known fixed expenses, known sales price per unit, and known variable expense per unit, management can analyze the changes in contribution margin to determine the effects on profits of alternative short-run decisions.

Contribution-margin analysis is also useful in determining which products, sales territories, and the like should be emphasized or dropped by management. In the short run with given fixed expenses, if a product or sales territory has sales revenue greater than variable expenses (a positive contribution margin), the product is contributing towards the overall profitability of the firm. Even if there is a net loss (fixed expenses exceed contribution margin), so long as the contribution margin is positive, the product should be retained in the short run. Fixed expenses that are truly fixed are irrelevant because they cannot be changed in the short run and are not germane to the decision of emphasizing or deemphasizing products, sales territories, and the like.

Assume that a company sells the following three products and that we are using contribution-margin analysis to determine the profitability of the products.

	Total	Product #1	%	Product #2	%	Product #3	%
Sales	$350,000	$80,000	100%	$70,000	100%	$200,000	100%
Variable expenses	262,000	60,000	75	42,000	60	160,000	80
Contribution margin	$ 88,000	$20,000	25%	$28,000	40%	$ 40,000	20%
Fixed expenses	71,000	12,000		29,000		30,000	
Net income (loss)	$ 17,000	$ 8,000		$ (1,000)		$ 10,000	

With given fixed expenses and plant facilities, contribution-margin analysis shows that Product #2 is contributing $28,000 to overall profits even though there is an apparent net loss of $1,000. If Product #2 were dropped, the $29,000 fixed expense would have to be covered by the other products and there would be a drop in overall profit of $28,000.

	Keep product #2	Drop product #2	Advantage in keeping product #2
Contribution margin	$28,000	$ —	$28,000
Less fixed expense	(29,000)	(29,000)	—
Difference	$ (1,000)	$(29,000)	$28,000

Contribution-margin analysis also shows that Product #2 may have the greatest potential for increasing profits because of its 40 per cent contribution-margin ratio. For every dollar of sales, Product #2 contributes $.40, Product #1 contributes $.25, and Product #3 contributes $.20 to profit. Because it has the highest contribution-margin ratio, management should analyze the market for Product #2 to determine if sales volume can be increased through advertising and other sales promotion techniques. Management should also analyze the possibilities of increasing the contribution margin of Products #1 and #3 by reducing variable expenses per unit or by increasing sales prices. On the other hand, this is not to say that management should always push the product with the highest contribution-margin ratio, because there are other factors that must be considered. Some pertinent considerations might be the total units of each product that can be sold, the production time necessary for producing each product, the capacity of the existing plant to produce the different products, and the social responsibilities of the firm (for example, a drug concern manufacturing vaccines should not base its decisions solely on profits).

CONTRIBUTION MARGIN AND RESPONSIBILITY ACCOUNTING Traditional internal accounting reports prepared for management about segments of the firm tend to follow the functional lines of external accounting statements: sales minus cost of goods sold minus operating expenses equal net income. Such reports as shown on page 620 do not reflect responsibility accounting, nor do they take into account the behavior of expenses via contribution-margin analysis. Thus more useful information can be provided to management if internal reports on segments of the firm are based on responsibility accounting and are designed to set forth the contribution margin. Such a report is presented below, for which data from the traditional internal report on page 620 are classified as controllable and noncontrollable variable and fixed expenses.

	Firm totals	Non-controllable expenses	Sales and controllable expenses					
			Product #1		Product #2		Product #3	
			Amount	%	Amount	%	Amount	%
Net sales	$355,000		$200,000	100%	$30,000	100%	$125,000	100%
Variable expenses	210,000	$ 10,000	140,000	70	10,000	33	50,000	40
Contribution margin	$145,000	$(10,000)ᵃ	$ 60,000	30%	$20,000	67%	$ 75,000	60%
Fixed expenses	88,000	50,000	12,000		11,000		15,000	
Net income	$ 57,000	$(60,000)	$ 48,000		$ 9,000		$ 60,000	

ᵃ( ) denotes negative amount.

Note that the traditional report shows a net loss of $8,000 for Product #2, while the proposed report shows net income of $9,000 and a contribution margin of $20,000 for Product #2. The difference is due to the removal of noncontrollable expenses from the product columns (see the separate column for noncontrollable expenses).

There are some fixed expenses that are fixed by management decision. Such expenses remain constant as sales volume changes because top management plans to spend a certain fixed amount for the current year. However, in some cases the product managers have some control over these so-called "discretionary" fixed expenses, and they, therefore, can be assigned to the product lines (see the $12,000, $11,000, and $15,000 fixed expenses assigned to product lines above). For example, if the product manager can influence spending up to a certain budgeted amount for product advertising and research, the expense would be assigned to the manager's product line. On the other hand, those fixed expenses that are not assigned to the product segments are the result of joint costs that benefit overall operations: top executive salaries, basic research and development expenses, and administrative expenses associated with the central office are examples. These are not identifiable with any segment except under arbitrary allocation methods.

Finally, the proposed report highlights the contribution margin of each product. Product #2 should not be dropped in the short run, for its contribution margin is positive. Also, the total and percentage contribution margins provide a starting point for further management analysis to determine how to increase the firm's overall profitability. For example, note that Product #2, the least profitable product under the traditional report, has the highest contribution-margin ratio.

VARIABLE (DIRECT) COSTING Conventional cost accounting, as explained in Chapters 16 through 19, is primarily concerned with the preparation of financial statements for investors, creditors, and others outside the business firm. Conventional cost accounting for external reporting includes in product cost all those manufacturing costs associated with the production of finished goods: direct material, direct labor, and factory overhead. Such conventional costing is called *absorption costing* because all manufacturing costs, including fixed factory overhead cost, are absorbed into units of product. Since under absorption costing fixed factory overhead cost is applied to production, there is a mixing of variable and fixed costs for the goods produced that is not well suited for the contribution-margin type reporting previously discussed.

Whereas conventional cost accounting generally stresses external reporting, variable costing emphasizes internal reporting to management. Variable costing, when combined with responsibility accounting, facilitates the preparation of internal reports, such as the report proposed on page 623.

Variable costing is a cost accounting procedure whereby production costs are separated into variable and fixed components and only the variable production costs (direct materials, direct labor, and variable factory overhead costs utilized in production) are treated as product costs. Under variable costing, fixed factory overhead cost is immediately expensed (treated as a period expense); therefore, fixed factory overhead cost does not pass through the asset accounts associated with goods in process and finished goods inventories (product costs) as it does under conventional costing. The difference between conventional and variable costing is illustrated below.

	Conventional costing		Variable costing		Difference	
	Amount	Per unit	Amount	Per unit	Amount	Per unit
Direct material cost	$20,000	$20	$20,000	$20	$ —	$—
Direct labor cost	30,000	30	30,000	30	—	—
Variable factory overhead cost	25,000	25	25,000	25	—	—
Fixed factory overhead cost	15,000	15	—	—	15,000	15
Total manufacturing cost	$90,000	$90	$75,000	$75	$15,000	$15
Ending inventory for balance sheet (200 units):						
200 × $90	$18,000					
200 × $75			$15,000		$ 3,000	
Expense:						
Cost of goods sold (800 units):						
800 × $90	72,000					
800 × $75			60,000		(3,000)	
Fixed factory overhead as a period expense	—		15,000			
	$90,000		$90,000			
Income statement effect—Net income	$3,000 higher		$3,000 lower			
Balance sheet effect—Assets and retained earnings	$3,000 higher		$3,000 lower			

Note that since production (1,000 units) exceeded sales (800 units), ending inventory (200 units) was charged with fixed factory overhead cost of $3,000 (200 × $15) under conventional costing, which did not reach the income statement. Under variable costing, all of the fixed factory overhead cost was charged not to ending inventory but to expense. Consequently, both ending inventory and net income were $3,000 lower under variable costing than under conventional costing.

THE CASE FOR VARIABLE COSTING FOR INTERNAL REPORTING The basic argument for variable costing is that it provides more useful information for short-run decision making than does conventional costing. In the first place, variable production costs are closely identified with specific units of production: if production increases (or decreases), variable costs tend to increase (or decrease). Thus variable costs indicate the extent to which factory plant and equipment (physical capacity) are being utilized. In contrast, fixed factory overhead cost is not readily identified with units of production, but it is related to the capacity to produce over a given time period. That is, variable factory costs are utilized because production occurs, while fixed factory overhead cost is utilized over the fiscal period whether production occurs or not. Because fixed factory overhead costs are not closely identified with units of production, the allocation of fixed overhead to production under conventional costing can distort net income and hinder decision making (this is illustrated in the next section). On the other hand, variable costing does not have this problem, because fixed factory overhead cost is treated as a period expense and is not allocated to production.

In the second place, under variable costing a firm's costs and expenses are classified into variable and fixed components; this classification is carried over to the income statement and thereby highlights contribution margin. Under variable costing, cost-and-expense data are recorded and reported in a form that facilitates the use of responsibility accounting and the analysis of cost-volume-profit relationship. On the other hand, conventional (absorption) costing does not distinguish between variable and fixed costs and expenses and does not emphasize contribution margin. Thus it is contended that variable costing provides more useful information for decision making than does conventional costing.

THE CASE AGAINST VARIABLE COSTING FOR INTERNAL REPORTING Those accountants who are against the use of variable costing for internal reporting contend that, if fixed factory overhead costs are necessary for production, then they should be included in product cost. In other words, because variable costing excludes fixed factory overhead cost from product cost, goods in process and finished goods inventories are understated in terms of historical cost.

A second argument against variable costing is that it provides information to management that may be misleading in product-pricing decisions. The contention is that management should set prices so as to cover all costs, including fixed factory overhead costs, and not just the variable costs.

Finally, there is the contention that the separation of costs and expenses into variable and fixed components is not an easy task and that much of the separation ends up being arbitrary. Moreover, even if costs and expenses can be meaningfully separated into variable and fixed components, conventional accounting reports for management can be modified to show variable expenses, fixed expenses, and contribution margin in the same manner as variable costing reports.

THE NET INCOME EFFECT IN INTERNAL REPORTS Conventional cost accounting applies fixed factory overhead cost to ending inventory on hand and to cost of goods sold, while variable costing charges all of fixed factory overhead cost to expense during the current time period, regardless of the quantity of inventory on hand. Thus if, during the current period, production exceeds sales, resulting in an increase in inventory, the profit under conventional costing normally will be higher than under variable costing. The reason is that conventional costing charges part of fixed factory overhead to the increased ending inventory (an asset), which obviously is not expensed (net income higher) during the current period.

The reverse is true if sales exceed production, resulting in a decrease in inventory. Fixed factory overhead cost contained in beginning inventory cost is released as expense (cost of goods sold) under conventional costing, so that net income normally is lower than it would be under variable costing.

An illustration In order to see, for internal reporting purposes, the difference between conventional and variable costing when units produced differ from units sold, assume the following data.

	Year 1	Year 2
Units of product:		
Beginning inventory of finished goods	—	3,000
Finished goods produced	7,000	4,000
Goods available for sale	7,000	7,000
Ending inventory of finished goods	3,000	1,000
Finished goods sold	4,000	6,000

Standard unit costs:	
Variable costs of manufacturing (direct material, direct labor, and variable factory overhead)	$20
Applied fixed factory overhead	30
Conventional cost per unit	$50

Other data:	
Sales price per unit	$80
Actual fixed factory overhead per year	$208,000
Selling and administrative expense per year (assumed to be fixed)	$ 20,000

The above data are used to calculate conventional and variable cost income statements for the two years, as shown below.

During the first year, production (7,000 units) exceeded sales (4,000 units) and resulted in the conventional income statement showing net income $90,000 higher than the variable costing income statement. The difference is explained by the increase in inventory (from 0 to 3,000 units) and the allocation of fixed factory

Year 1

Conventional costing			Variable costing		
Sales (4,000 × $80)		$320,000	Sales (4,000 × $80)		$320,000
Cost of goods sold:			Variable cost of goods sold:		
Beginning finished goods	$ —		Beginning finished goods	$ —	
Cost of goods manufactured (7,000 × $50)	350,000		Cost of goods manufactured (7,000 × $20)	140,000	
Goods available for sale	$350,000		Goods available for sale	$140,000	
Ending finished goods (3,000 × $50)	150,000		Ending finished goods (3,000 × $20)	60,000	80,000
Difference	$200,000		Manufacturing contribution margin		$240,000
Overapplied factory overhead			Fixed factory overhead	$208,000	
[$208,000 − (7,000 × $30)]	2,000	198,000	Operating expenses:		
Gross margin		$122,000	Selling and administrative expenses	20,000	228,000
Operating expenses:			Net income		$ 12,000
Selling and administrative expenses		20,000			
Net income		$102,000			

Year 2

Conventional costing			Variable costing		
Sales (6,000 × $80)		$480,000	Sales (6,000 × $80)		$480,000
Cost of goods sold:			Cost of goods sold:		
Beginning finished goods (3,000 × $50)	$150,000		Beginning finished goods (3,000 × $20)	$ 60,000	
Cost of goods manufactured (4,000 × $50)	200,000		Cost of goods manufactured (4,000 × $20)	80,000	
Goods available for sale	$350,000		Goods available for sale	$140,000	
Ending finished goods (1,000 × $50)	50,000		Ending finished goods (1,000 × $20)	20,000	120,000
Difference	$300,000		Manufacturing contribution margin		$360,000
Underapplied factory overhead			Fixed factory overhead	$208,000	
[$208,000 − (4,000 × $30)]	88,000	388,000	Operating expenses:		
Gross margin		$ 92,000	Selling and administrative expenses	20,000	228,000
Operating expenses:			Net income		$132,000
Selling and administrative expenses		20,000			
Net income		$ 72,000			

overhead ($30 × 3,000 = $90,000) to the ending inventory under conventional costing. In contrast, variable costing assigned all of the fixed factory overhead to expense, which caused the net income figure to be lower:

$$\begin{pmatrix}\text{Difference in profit} \\ \text{between conventional} \\ \text{and variable costing}\end{pmatrix} = \begin{pmatrix}\text{Units} \\ \text{produced}\end{pmatrix} - \begin{pmatrix}\text{Units} \\ \text{sold}\end{pmatrix} \times \begin{pmatrix}\text{Fixed factory overhead} \\ \text{applied per unit}\end{pmatrix}$$

$$= (\text{Change in inventory}) \times \begin{pmatrix}\text{Fixed factory} \\ \text{overhead applied} \\ \text{per unit}\end{pmatrix}$$

$$\$90,000 = (7,000 - 4,000) \times \$30$$

$$= 3,000 \times \$30$$

During the second year, sales (6,000 units) exceeded production (4,000 units), so that part of the goods sold were from beginning inventory (2,000 units) and caused the net income under conventional costing to be $60,000 lower than under variable costing. That is, under conventional costing for Year 2, fixed factory overhead cost in beginning inventory (3,000 × $30 = $90,000) was expensed as part of cost of goods sold, which reduced net income, and part of fixed factory overhead was charged to ending inventory (1,000 × $30 = $30,000), which increased net income; the result was a net reduction of $60,000 in net income.

In contrast, under variable costing for Year 2, beginning and ending inventory included no fixed factory overhead cost because it was charged to expense, instead of ending inventory, in both years:

$$\begin{pmatrix}\text{Difference in profit} \\ \text{between conventional} \\ \text{and variable costing}\end{pmatrix} = \begin{pmatrix}\text{Units} \\ \text{produced}\end{pmatrix} - \begin{pmatrix}\text{Units} \\ \text{sold}\end{pmatrix} \times \begin{pmatrix}\text{Fixed factory overhead} \\ \text{applied per unit}\end{pmatrix}$$

$$\$60,000 = (4,000 - 6,000) \times \$30$$

Net income distortion   Although the foregoing illustration is exaggerated in order to contrast conventional and variable costing, it does point out the difficulty in analyzing net income under conventional cost accounting. Sales increased from $320,000 in Year 1 to $480,000 in Year 2 (a 50 per cent increase), yet the conventional income statement showed a decline in net income from $102,000 to $72,000 (a 29 per cent decrease) despite constant total fixed expense and a constant variable expense per unit. Under such circumstances, it is difficult for management to understand and the accountant to explain what caused the decline in net income. How do you explain to management that net income decreased as the result of the conventional cost accounting allocation of fixed factory overhead cost to finished goods inventory?

In contrast, the net income figure under variable costing is easier to analyze because it tends to change with and in the same direction as changes in volume. In the preceding illustration, the 50 per cent increase in sales from Year 1 to Year 2 was accompanied by a 1,000 per cent increase in net income ($12,000 to $132,000) under variable costing. The large percentage increase in net income is explained by the large contribution-margin ratio (75%), so that, once fixed expenses were covered by sales, every additional sales dollar provided $.75 toward profits. Thus the variable cost statements not only are easier to analyze than conventional statements, they also provide additional information that is useful for managerial decision making.

On the other hand, those accountants who favor conventional costing would contend that the preceding illustration indicates the preferability of conventional costing over variable costing. Those advocating conventional costing would argue that the underapplied fixed factory overhead cost of $88,000 for the second year informs management about the cost of excess capacity (idle plant), which variable costing does not do.

VARIABLE COSTING AND EXTERNAL REPORTING If variable costing provides useful information to management, it would seem that it should also provide useful information to investors, creditors, and others outside the business entity. However, traditionally, accountants have not been willing to use variable costing in the preparation of external financial statements. The basic argument is that fixed factory overhead cost is a necessary cost to produce finished goods and, therefore, it should be included in product cost. If fixed factory overhead cost is excluded from product cost, as in variable costing, then the goods in process and finished goods inventories on the balance sheet are understated and the historical cost assumption is violated. Also, over long periods of time, production and sales volume approximate one another so that net income under variable costing and conventional costing are approximately the same.

IMPORTANT TERMS AND CONCEPTS IN CHAPTER 21

Responsibility accounting—p. 619
Segment—p. 619
Responsibility center—p. 619
Cost, expense, and profit centers—p. 619
Two basic problems with traditional
   reports—pp. 620, 621
Controllable costs and expenses—p. 621

Contribution margin—pp. 621, 622
Contribution margin analysis—pp. 622, 623
Contribution margin and responsibility
   accounting—pp. 623, 624
Absorption costing—p. 624
Variable (direct) costing—pp. 624–629

DEMONSTRATION PROBLEMS FOR REVIEW AND SELF-STUDY Problem 1: L. M. Jones Company produces two different product lines. The company has a manager in charge of each product line. The manager of product line #2 is complaining about the accounting system. The manager feels that the product line has had a better year than last year, but the income statement for the product line shows a $15,000 net loss for the current year.

	Total	Product line #1	Product line #2
Sales	$1,700,000	$900,000	$800,000
Deduct manufacturing cost of sales	1,530,000	790,000	740,000
Gross margin	$ 170,000	110,000	$ 60,000
Operating expenses	137,000	62,000	75,000
Net income (loss)	$ 33,000	$ 48,000	$ (15,000)

You have been asked to analyze the income statements of the two product lines and determine whether the complaint by the product-line manager is justified. In your analysis you find that the overall contribution margins for product lines #1 and #2 are 30 per cent and 40 per cent, respectively. You also discover that variable expenses generally tend to be controllable by the managers, and that noncontrollable fixed expenses for product lines #1 and #2 are $200,000 and $190,000, respectively.

INSTRUCTIONS

(a) Prepare income statements for the two product lines based on responsibility accounting.

(b) Prepare a written explanation supporting or refuting the product-line manager's complaint.

Note Attempt to solve this demonstration problem before examining the solution that follows.

Solution 1.

(a)

L. M. JONES COMPANY
Income Statement
For the Year Ended December 31, 19_

			Sales and controllable expenses			
		Non-	Product #1		Product #2	
	Firm	controllable				
	totals	expenses	Amount	%	Amount	%
Sales	$1,700,000		$900,000	100%	$800,000	100%
Deduct variable expenses	1,110,000		630,000	70	480,000	60
Contribution margin	$ 590,000		$270,000	30%	$320,000	40%
Fixed expenses	557,000	390,000	22,000		145,000	
Net income	$ 33,000	$390,000*	$248,000		$175,000	

*Indicates a negative amount.

Calculation of controllable variable expenses:			
$900,000 × (1 − .3) =		$630,000	
$800,000 × (1 − .4) =			$480,000
Calculation of controllable fixed expenses:			
Total expenses		$852,000	$815,000
Deduct variable expenses		630,000	480,000
Total fixed expenses		$222,000	$335,000
Noncontrollable fixed expenses		200,000	190,000
Controllable fixed expenses		$ 22,000	$145,000

(b) The complaint of the manager of product line #2 is justified. The $15,000 net loss is not indicative of the manager's performance because of the inclusion of noncontrollable fixed expenses. As shown above, if we adjust the statement for noncontrollable expenses, the manager has a net income figure of $175,000, and it is this figure that should be used to analyze the manager's performance.

Problem 2: Flaherty Manufacturing Company has several product lines with a manager in charge of each line. Each product-line manager is paid a bonus based on the net income generated by the manager's product line.

In analyzing one product line, the president of the company noted that sales declined from $800,000 last year to $600,000 for the current year. However, the product-line manager received a larger bonus than last year because net income increased from $90,000 last year to $120,000 for the current year.

Based on the decline in sales, the president wonders whether the product-line manager should have received a larger bonus this year. Also, the president of the company wants to know why net income increased when sales declined. The president asks you to analyze the situation and to prepare a written report explaining how net income increased when sales declined. You are given the following data:

	Year 2	Year 1
Units sold @ $20	30,000	40,000
Units produced	50,000	30,000
Units of beginning finished goods inventory	—	10,000
Standard variable production cost per unit	$ 8	$ 8
Standard fixed factory overhead per unit	5	5
Actual fixed factory overhead cost	200,000	200,000
Selling and administrative expenses (assumed to be fixed)	140,000	140,000
All factory overhead variances are written off to Cost of Goods Sold.		

INSTRUCTIONS

(a) Prepare income statements for the two years using conventional (absorption) costing.

(b) Prepare income statements for the two years using variable (direct) costing.

(c) Prepare a written report, supported by figures, explaining why net income increased when sales declined.

(d) What do you think about the bonus method? Discuss.

Note Attempt to solve this demonstration problem before examining the solution that follows.

Solution 2.

FLAHERTY MANUFACTURING COMPANY
Comparative Income Statements
For the Years Ended December 31, 19_2 and 19_1

(a) Conventional costing	Year 2		Year 1	
Sales		$600,000		$800,000
Cost of goods sold:				
Beginning finished goods	$ —		$130,000	
Cost of goods manufactured	650,000		390,000	
Goods available for sale	$650,000		$520,000	
Ending finished goods	260,000		—	
Difference	$390,000		$520,000	
Factory overhead variance	50,000	340,000	50,000	570,000
Gross margin		$260,000		$230,000
Operating expenses:				
Selling and administrative expenses		140,000		140,000
Net income		$120,000		$ 90,000

(b) Variable costing	Year 2		Year 1	
Sales		$600,000		$800,000
Variable cost of goods sold:				
Beginning finished goods	$ —		$ 80,000	
Cost of goods manufactured	400,000		240,000	
Goods available for sale	$400,000		$320,000	
Ending finished goods	160,000	240,000	—	320,000
Manufacturing contribution margin		$360,000		$480,000
Fixed expenses:				
Fixed factory overhead	$200,000		$200,000	
Fixed selling and administrative expenses	140,000	340,000	140,000	340,000
Net income		$ 20,000		$140,000

(c) Under conventional costing, net income is affected not only by sales, but it is also affected by production because of the application of fixed factory overhead. Thus, even with a decrease in sales there can still be an increase in net income under conventional costing because of an increase in production. For example, in Year 2, Flaherty Manufacturing Company had an increase in inventory of 20,000 units, which resulted in deferring $100,000 ($5 × 20,000) in applied fixed factory overhead to ending inventory. In other words, net income under conventional costing was $100,000 higher than under variable costing because $100,000 in fixed overhead was included in ending inventory instead of being expensed. This treatment of the $100,000 in fixed overhead resulted in net income increasing from Year 1 to Year 2 even though the sales declined over the same period. Also, in comparison to variable costing, under conventional costing net income in Year 1 was understated by $50,000 ($5 × 10,000) because of the expensing of $50,000 applied fixed overhead that was included in beginning inventory, i.e., 40,000 units were sold but only 30,000 units produced. In contrast, net income under variable costing shows a decline from $140,000 in Year 1 to $20,000 in Year 2, which is compatible with the decline in sales over the same period. The reason for this is that variable costing treats fixed factory overhead ($200,000) as a period expense each year.

(d) Because of the production effects of conventional costing on net income, and because responsibility accounting is not being used, the company should change its bonus system. The product-line managers should be paid a bonus based on sales minus controllable expenses.

ASSIGNMENT MATERIAL

Questions

1 Under responsibility accounting, why is the firm segmented into responsibility centers? Discuss.
2 Is the allocation of indirect expenses to product lines useful for managerial decision-making purposes? Discuss.
3 Whether a cost or expense is controllable by a manager depends on the particular responsibility center and the particular time period. What does this statement mean? Discuss.
4 What is meant by a discretionary fixed cost or expense? Discuss.
5 A fixed expense or cost is controllable and a variable expense or cost is uncontrollable. Do you agree with this statement? Discuss.
6 Assuming a short-run time period, what is the decision rule for deciding whether a product line should be dropped or retained? Discuss.
7 The product line with the greatest contribution-margin ratio is the product line that management should emphasize. Do you agree with this statement? Discuss.
8 For purposes of internal reporting to management, why do some accountants prefer variable costing to conventional costing? Discuss.
9 What is meant by the statement that the net income figure reported to management under conventional costing is unduly influenced by production? Discuss.
10 If variable costing is useful in providing relevant financial data for managerial decision making, would it also be useful in providing relevant financial data for investors, creditors, and others outside the business firm? Discuss.
11 How would you respond to an advocate of absorption costing who has just stated that so long as production volume is constant variable (direct) costing and absorption costing will yield the same profit figure?
12 Is the divergence between profit figures computed by absorption costing and variable (direct) costing greater for long periods or short periods?

Short exercises

E21-1 *You are given three multiple-choice statements. Select the correct answers and indicate the corresponding letters on a sheet of paper (e.g., 1-d, 2-d, etc.).*

(1) The least common type of responsibility accounting is one that holds segment managers accountable for their performance in terms of (a) units of output, (b) revenues, (c) expenses, (d) revenues and expenses, (e) none of the above.

(2) Ideally, the result of a responsibility accounting system is to motivate the manager to (a) control the costs of the segment even if it means higher costs for the other segments, (b) maximize the revenue of the segment without regard to the costs, (c) minimize the costs of the segment even

if it means decreasing output, (d) maximize the excess of revenues over costs of the segment even if the total profit of the company declines, (e) none of the above.

(3) Controllable costs (a) can never be assigned to more than one person, (b) might be assigned to a foreman at one level and to a vice-president at another level, (c) never include fixed costs, (d) are not assigned to a specific segment whereas uncontrollable costs are assigned to a specific segment, (e) none of the above.

E21-2

You are given below three multiple-choice statements. Select the correct answers and indicate the corresponding letters on a sheet of paper.

(1) Variable costing excludes from inventory valuation (a) factory overhead, (b) variable factory overhead, (c) fixed factory overhead, (d) conversion costs, (e) none of the above.

(2) Variable costing and contribution margin (a) are not compatible concepts, (b) both separate fixed costs from variable costs, (c) are used for external reporting purposes more than for internal decision-making purposes, (d) are synonymous with absorption costing, (e) none of the above.

(3) Variable costing (a) is acceptable for external reporting, (b) will always yield a different income figure from absorption costing, (c) will usually yield a higher inventory valuation than absorption costing, (d) causes net income to move in the same direction as sales (e) none of the above.

E21-3

Given the cost data below, evaluate the performance of the manager in charge of Production Department #3.

	Production department #3		
	Actual costs	Budgeted costs	Difference
Direct materials	$ 20,500	$ 25,000	$ (4,500)
Direct labor	50,000	51,500	(1,500)
Factory overhead:			
Variable factory overhead	16,000	15,000	1,000
Depreciation of factory building	2,500	2,500	—
Share of service department costs	20,000	10,000	10,000
	$109,000	$104,000	$ 5,000 unfavorable

E21-4

The management of Pea Ridge Company wants to drop product lines #3 and #7. Although the company's overall net income for the fiscal year was $150,000, product lines #3 and #7 incurred net losses of $5,000 and $10,000, respectively, as shown below. The variable expenses for product lines #3 and #7 were $76,000 and $85,000, respectively. Should these two product lines be dropped? Explain, and show your calculations.

	Product #3	Product #7
Sales	$75,000	$115,000
Deduct cost of goods sold	50,000	85,000
Gross margin	$25,000	$ 30,000
Deduct selling and administrative expenses	30,000	40,000
Net loss	$ (5,000)	$ (10,000)

The internal income statement for Parka Company for the year ended December 31, 19_3, is presented below:

	Total	Product #1	Product #2
Sales	$150,000	$50,000	$100,000
Cost of goods sold	85,000	30,000	55,000
Gross margin	$ 65,000	$20,000	$ 45,000
Operating expenses	40,000	10,000	30,000
Net income	$ 25,000	$10,000	$ 15,000

Variable expenses are 70 per cent and 75 per cent of sales from Products #1 and #2, respectively, and an additional $8,000 of the total variable expenses are noncontrollable. Products #1 and #2 have controllable fixed expenses of $2,000 and $3,000, respectively. Given these data and the format below, convert the conventional internal income statement to one based on responsibility accounting.

		Non-controllable expenses	Sales and controllable expense			
			Product #1		Product #2	
	Totals		Amount	%	Amount	%
Sales						
Variable expenses	――	――	――	―	――	―
Contribution margin				═		═
Fixed expenses	――	――	――		――	
Net income	═══	═══	═══		═══	

The management of Markley, Inc., cannot understand why the internal income statement for the year shows net income of $15,000 when only 5,000 units of product were sold out of the 10,000 units produced (no beginning inventory). Management also points out that fixed factory overhead costs were not even covered. In order to explain the situation, the controller of the company prepared a variable cost income statement that could be compared with the conventional income statement, as shown below:

	Conventional costing	Variable costing
Sales ($30 × 5,000)	$150,000	$150,000
Variable expenses	105,000	105,000
Contribution margin	$ 45,000	$ 45,000
Deduct:		
Fixed factory overhead	$ 25,000	$ 50,000
Fixed operating expense	5,000	5,000
Total fixed	$ 30,000	$ 55,000
Net income (loss)	$ 15,000	$ (10,000)

(a) Explain what caused the difference between the net income under conventional costing and the net income under variable costing. Show your calculations.

(b) Which statement do you believe provides the more useful information to management? Discuss.

Problems

A21-1

Newton, Inc., manufactures several different product lines. Each product line is under the responsibility of a manager. The product-line managers are paid bonuses based on the net income of their product lines.

One of the product-line managers is complaining because his bonus will be smaller than last year as a result of a decline in the net income of his product line. He contends that he is not being evaluated fairly because allocations of fixed expenses distort the net income of his product line. He argues that the method of allocating fixed expenses should be changed so that his product line will not be charged with an excessive amount of allocated fixed expense. That is, he feels that the other product lines are not carrying a fair share of the allocated fixed expense.

Required:

(a) Is this allocation of fixed expenses to the product lines consistent with responsibility accounting? Discuss.

(b) Do you agree with the product-line manager's contention that his share of allocated fixed expenses should be reduced in order to provide a more equitable allocation? Discuss.

(c) What is your recommendation as to how each manager's performance should be evaluated? Discuss.

A21-2

McCloud Manufacturing Company produces several products including a plastic jayhawk. Each jayhawk is sold to retail stores for $1.25. The company's cost of manufacturing one unit is $1.15, as shown below:

	Per finished unit
Direct materials	$ .25
Direct labor	.30
Factory overhead (200% of direct labor cost)	.60
Total	$1.15

Both the sales manager and the production manager are unhappy with this product because they both receive bonuses based on net income. With selling expense of $.15 a unit, each plastic jayhawk incurs a $.05 loss.

The sales manager contends that the product should be dropped and states that the price cannot be increased because of strong competition.

The production manager contends that factory overhead cost will remain the same if the product is dropped. Thus the factory overhead rate would have to be increased over the remaining products should the plastic jayhawk be dropped. The production manager suggests allocating factory overhead over a direct materials base because this would reduce the unit cost of the jayhawks and would result in a profit per unit.

Required:

(a) Discuss the sales manager's contention that the plastic jayhawk product should be dropped. Use figures to support your discussion.

(b) Discuss the production manager's contention that the overhead allocation base should be changed.

(c) What do you think of paying bonuses to the sales and production managers based on net income? Discuss.

Tollefson Manufacturing Company produces a number of different products that are classified according to product lines. Each product line is under the responsibility of a manager. At the end of each year, profitability statements are prepared for each product line. Each product-line manager receives a bonus based on the improvement in the product line's return on sales (net income ÷ sales) from the previous year.

The manager of one of the product lines is unhappy because she will not receive a bonus this year, because the product line's rate of return on sales dropped from 8.50 per cent last year to 7.78 per cent this year, as shown below:

	Year 2	Year 1
Net sales	$450,000	$300,000
Deduct cost of goods sold	300,000	185,000
Gross margin	$150,000	$115,000
Deduct selling and administrative expenses	115,000	89,500
Net income	$ 35,000	$ 25,500
Rate of return on sales	7.78%	8.50%

The product-line manager contends that the above statements are misleading and argues that she has no control over the fixed factory overhead contained in cost of goods sold ($58,000 and $140,000 for Years 1 and 2, respectively) and the fixed selling and administrative expenses ($65,000 and $90,000 for Years 1 and 2, respectively). Thus, the product manager feels the rate of return should be based on sales minus controllable expenses divided by sales.

Required:

(a) Assuming that the variable expenses are controllable by the product-line manager, prepare income statements and rates of return on sales based on responsibility accounting.

(b) Present arguments for or against the product-line manager receiving a bonus for Year 2.

(c) What do you think of the bonus method used by the company? Discuss.

Weltmer Liquors, Inc., produces a blended whiskey called Weltmer Dry. The company uses FIFO for costing its inventory and writes off factory overhead variance to Cost of Goods Sold at year end. Operating statistics for 19_5 were as follows:

Cases produced—20,000
Cases of inventory, January 1, 19_5—2,000
Cases of inventory, December 31, 19_5—5,000
Cases sold—17,000

Selling price per case	$37.50
Actual material cost per case	8.00
Actual labor cost per case	$7.00
Actual variable factory overhead per case	5.00
Applied fixed factory overhead per case	7.00
Actual fixed overhead costs	$130,000
Actual fixed selling and administrative expenses	44,375

Actual variable selling and administrative expenses—15 per cent of sales

While costs were the same in 19_5 as in 19_4, materials cost during 19_6 rose 10 per cent and labor cost rose 5 per cent. All other costs remained unchanged. Despite an increase in the selling price of 8 per cent in 19_6, 5,000 more cases were sold than in 19_5. However, production was cut back in 19_6 by 2,000 cases.

Required:

(a) Comparative income statements for 19_5 and 19_6, using conventional (absorption) costing.

(b) Comparative income statements for 19_5 and 19_6 using variable (direct) costing.

(c) For each year, an explanation of the differences in net income under the two methods.

A21-5

Garcia Company manufactures and sells a single product. Data for the first two years of operations are as follows:

	19_2	19_1
Sales	$306,000	$153,000
Cost of goods sold	166,000	99,000
Gross margin	$140,000	$ 54,000
Selling expenses	$ 29,600	$ 18,400
Administrative expenses	30,400	26,800
Net income	$ 80,000	$ 8,800
Selling price per unit	$18.00	$17.00
Units produced	14,000	12,000
Variable costs per unit	$9.50	$9.00

The company uses the LIFO inventory flow.

Required:

(a) Does Garcia use absorption costing or variable costing? How can you tell?

(b) What was the amount of Garcia's inventory at the end of 19_1?

(c) What was the amount of Garcia's inventory at the end of years 19_1 and 19_2 under the alternative costing method?

A21-6

Multiproduct Company wishes to maximize its income for the upcoming year. It has estimated demand for its four products and found that total demand is more than its manufacturing capacity. The following data are available:

Product	Estimated demand	Selling price	Variable mfg. Materials	Labor
A	5,000 units	$5.00	$1.00	$ .80
B	4,000 units	3.00	1.00	.60
C	3,000 units	4.00	1.00	.40
D	2,000 units	7.00	2.00	1.00

Direct labor is paid at the rate of $2.00 per hour. The only selling expenses are a 10 per cent commission based on selling price. Variable overhead will be applied at 50 per cent of direct labor cost. Plant capacity is 2,000 direct labor hours per year.

Required:

(a) A schedule showing that estimated demand exceeds plant capacity.

(b) A schedule computing the contribution margin per unit of each product and the contribution margin per labor hour of each product.

(c) A production schedule that will maximize Multiproduct's income for the upcoming year.

B21-1   Friedman Manufacturing, Inc., produces several lines of chairs in which wood is the basic raw material. The company is segmented into cost and expense centers with a manager in charge of each center.

Paul Jones, the manager in charge of production is unhappy because of the manner in which his performance is evaluated. His performance for last year was rated unsatisfactory; however, he contends that this is the result of being held responsible for costs over which he has no control.

You are asked to evaluate his contention, given the following data:

(1)   The purchase price of wood increased last year.

(2)   A new labor contract had been signed by the personnel department last year in which labor costs went up $.50 per direct labor hour.

(3)   The sales prices of the chairs remained the same.

(4)   The material efficiency variance and the labor efficiency variance last year were below previous years' variances.

(5)   The quantity of chairs produced had increased, but there was no significant change in sales.

(6)   Variable and fixed factory overhead rates were unchanged.

Required:

(a)   Discuss in general the production manager's complaint.

(b)   How would *each* of the six factors above affect the evaluation of the production manager's performance? Discuss.

B21-2   Trylene Company began operations on January 1, 19_1. The following data are available on December 31, 19_1:

Direct material used	$112,500
Direct labor	155,000
Fixed factory overhead	150,000
Variable factory overhead	75,000
Sales revenue	540,000
Selling and administrative expense (all fixed)	60,000
Units sold	15,000 units
Ending inventory	10,000 units

Required:

(a)   The income statement for 19_1 using absorption costing.

(b)   The income statement for 19_1 using variable costing.

(c)   A reconciliation of ending inventory amounts under the two methods.

B21-3   You are given the following financial data for McNish Manufacturing for the last three years.

	Year 1	Year 2	Year 3
Units of beginning finished goods	—	10,000	—
Units produced	40,000	50,000	70,000
Units sold	30,000	60,000	70,000
Units of ending finished goods	10,000	—	—
Net income under variable costing	$400,000	$800,000	$950,000

Standard cost card	
Direct materials	$ 4
Direct labor	2
Variable factory overhead	3
Fixed factory overhead	5
Standard cost per finished unit	$14

The company uses variable (direct) costing for internal reporting to management and conventional (absorption) costing for external reporting. Thus, at year end, it is necessary to convert the cost data from the variable cost system to a conventional cost basis for external reporting.

Required:

(a) Using the above data, convert the net income figures under variable costing to net income figures under absorption costing. Show all calculations for all three years.

(b) For each year, write an explanation as to why net income differed or was the same under the two costing methods.

(c) Would net income in Year 3 be the same under both conventional and variable costing if there were 10,000 units of finished goods on hand at the beginning of the period? Discuss.

B21-4

Aves Company began operations in 19_2 and utilized a manufacturing process with significant amounts of fixed costs. Data concerning amounts produced and sold follow:

Year	Units produced	Units sold
19_2	5,000	4,000
19_3	2,500	3,500
19_4	2,500	2,500
19_5	5,000	2,000
19_6	5,000	2,000
19_7	0	6,000

Production costs were stable for the entire six-year period, but Aves did raise its selling price from $20 to $25 in 19_5. It remained at $25 through 19_7.

Required:

(a) Use the information above to complete the following table:

	Ending inventory level		Higher net income
Year	Number of units	Dollar amount	(Absorption or variable)
19_2	Increased	?	?
19_3	?	Decreased	?
19_4	Same	?	?
19_5	?	?	Absorption
19_6	?	Increased	?
19_7	?	?	Variable

(b) Compare the trend in net income from 19_3 to 19_4 under absorption costing with the trend for the same years under variable costing.

(c) Compare the trend in net income from 19_5 to 19_6 under absorption costing with the trend for the same years under variable costing.

B21-5

The president of a small company, Sherr, Inc., received a letter from a prominent stockholder asking him how reported net income could decline $4,000 when reported sales increased from $60,000 last year to $90,000 this year. The president of the company looked at the income statements for the last two years and could not explain what happened.

The president of the company has asked you to prepare an explanation of why reported net income showed a decline from last year. Because he does not want you to be influenced by the published income statements for the last two years, he asks you to prepare conventional income statements in order to verify the figures on the published statements. You are given the following data:

	19_4	19_3
Units sold @ $15 per unit	6,000	4,000
Units produced	4,000	6,000
Standard variable production cost per unit	$ 5	$ 5
Actual fixed factory overhead	36,000	36,000
Selling and administrative expenses (assumed to be fixed)	5,000	5,000
Standard fixed factory overhead per unit	6	6
Inventory of finished goods	0	?
Overhead variances are written off to Cost of Goods Sold		

Required:

(1) Prepare comparative income statements for the last two years using conventional (absorption) costing. The statements should agree with the published income statements.

(b) Prepare an analysis explaining how net income could decline $4,000 when sales increased $30,000. In your analysis, explain why the $4,000 decline in net income is misleading.

B21-6

The income statements for the last two years for Nichols Company are shown below:

	19_5	19_4
Net sales	$900,000	$600,000
Deduct cost of goods sold	660,000	440,000
Gross margin	$240,000	$160,000
Deduct operating expenses:		
Selling and administrative expenses	$ 54,000	$ 50,000
Underapplied factory overhead	72,000	—
Total	$126,000	50,000
Net income	$114,000	$110,000

Management cannot understand why a 50 per cent increase in sales increased net income by only 4 per cent. You are asked to advise management as to what happened to cause the small increase in net income, given the following additional data:

Units sold		60,000	40,000
Units produced		48,000	60,000
Sales price per unit	$	15	$	15
Standard variable expense per unit (manufacturing)		5	5
Actual fixed factory overhead		360,000	360,000
Standard fixed factory overhead per unit		6	6
Overhead variances are closed to Cost of Goods Sold			

Note Selling and administrative expenses consist of a fixed component and a variable component. The variable rate may be found by dividing the increase in expense by the increase in volume of units sold.

Required:

(a) Prepare income statements by using variable (direct) costing for the two years.

(b) By comparing net income under conventional (absorption) and variable (direct) costing, explain the small increase in net income shown by the conventional income statements.

INTRODUCTION TO CAPITAL BUDGETING
CHAPTER 22

PURPOSE OF CHAPTER Short-run analysis is characterized by financial decision making under conditions of given fixed costs, as previously discussed with regard to cost-volume-profit analysis and responsibility accounting. The short run is that time period which is not long enough to permit acquisition of new capacity, such as plant and equipment. It follows that the long-run time period is that period over which capacity conditions can change. During the long run a company can acquire new plant and equipment, new financing, and new management; hence costs associated with capacity are not constant (fixed) during the long run.

A company's long-run investments in land, plant and equipment, research programs, and the like are extremely important for three basic reasons: (1) long-run investments associated with capacity usually entail large dollar amounts; (2) the decision to acquire plant and equipment commits a company to that decision for several years, with a loss of flexibility (a company cannot afford to buy new plant and equipment every month or year); and (3) the commitment of funds to acquire land or equipment causes those funds to be unavailable for other investment opportunities. Other alternatives are foregone because of the acceptance of particular long-run investments.

An investment is an expenditure of cash or cash equivalents in one time period to obtain enlarged net inflows of cash or cash equivalents in future time periods. The process of planning and evaluating long-term investment proposals is called *capital budgeting*. Capital budgeting provides a scientific and systematic approach to making long-term investment decisions. The term capital budgeting refers to the fact that investment money (capital) is scarce and must be budgeted among competing investment alternatives. The management of a business does not have unlimited investment money available to take advantage of all investment opportunities. Instead, management strives to allocate limited investment capital to those investments that promise the greatest future benefits to the company.

The purpose of this chapter is to provide an introduction to capital budgeting techniques used in determining whether or not long-term investment projects should be undertaken by the management of a firm. Such capital budgeting techniques aid in answering questions such as the following: Should management invest in a proposed project? Should management keep or replace existing equipment? From a set of competing long-term investment proposals, in which one should management invest? If an operation is done manually, should management invest in equipment to do the operation?

ELEMENTS OF CAPITAL BUDGETING A typical investment problem involves a cash outlay made today (a specific current date) to obtain net cash inflows in each of several future years following the investment date. Whether to make the investment or not depends on a comparison of the cost of the investment today with the net cash inflows expected to be generated by the investment over several future time periods. The investment decision is a long-run decision based on relevant cash flows over several future time periods, which is unlike short-run decision making based on single-period relevant cash flows. Relevant cash flows are future cash flows that are different under the given alternatives.

Because the future net cash inflows expected from an investment occur at different points in time, the aggregate net cash inflow (the sum of the future cash inflows) cannot be compared directly to the investment cost because of the time value of money.[1] By converting the future net cash inflows into present value terms (discounting the cash inflows), the present value of the future net cash inflows can be compared directly with the investment cost. If the difference between the present value of the future net cash inflows and the investment cost, called *net present value* (NPV), is positive, the investment is quantitatively acceptable. If the NPV is negative, the investment is quantitatively unacceptable, and if the NPV is zero, management is quantitatively indifferent in accepting or rejecting the investment proposal.

For example, suppose that a proposed investment of $100,000 is expected to generate additional net cash inflows of $25,000, $24,000, $22,000, $18,000, and $17,000, respectively, for the next five years. Further suppose that the firm's minimum desired rate of return (to be explained shortly) is 10 per cent. Despite the fact that the aggregate cash inflow of $106,000 exceeds the investment cost of $100,000, the management of the firm should reject the investment because the negative net present value, as shown below to be $18,060, indicates that the firm would not even earn its minimum desired rate of return of 10 per cent.

	Year	Amount		Present value of $1 at 10% (from tables in Appendix B)		Present value
Investment	0	$100,000				−$100,000
Cash inflows	1	25,000	×	.9091	=	$ 22,728
	2	24,000	×	.8264	=	19,834
	3	22,000	×	.7513	=	16,529
	4	18,000	×	.6830	=	12,294
	5	17,000	×	.6209	=	10,555
		$106,000				
Present value of cash inflows						+$ 81,940
Net present value						−$ 18,060

From the above illustration it can be seen that the elements in a capital budgeting problem are the following:

Estimated initial investment.
Estimated future net cash inflows expected from the investment.
Net present value—the decision criterion.

[1]See the appendix to Chapter 6 for a review of the time value of money, compounding, and present value.

We now turn to a discussion of each of these elements.

INITIAL INVESTMENT   For most investment proposals the initial investment includes the cash or cash equivalent paid to acquire, install, and put in working condition physical facilities such as plant and equipment. For example, an investment in new equipment would include the sum of the purchase price, freight cost, installation cost, any cost of training equipment operators, and any cost of equipment test runs.

In addition to the usual investment costs, there can be equivalent cash outlays for increased working capital and opportunity costs (explained below) that result from the investment and should be included in the initial investment. For example, the acquisition of new equipment may require an increase in working capital to support a larger sales volume expected when the new equipment is in operation. The larger amount of inventory and accounts receivable necessitated by the investment is equivalent to an increased investment in working capital and therefore should be included in the initial investment for capital budgeting purposes.

Similarly, if an investment results in foregone opportunities, then their costs (opportunity costs) should be included in the initial investment.[2] For example, if a firm has idle equipment that would be used with the new investment, then the foregone sales value of the equipment should be added to the initial investment. That is, a cash receipt foregone because of an investment is equivalent to a cash outlay for the investment.

Finally, if a new investment would result in the sale of an existing asset, such as the replacement of old equipment with new equipment, then the cash proceeds to be received from the sale of the old asset should be deducted from the initial investment. The initial investment represents additional funds committed to the investment project and the proceeds from the sale of any existing assets would reduce the cash commitment.

To illustrate the above discussion on the initial investment, assume that Topeka Company is considering the acquisition of some additional equipment. The purchase price of the new equipment is $80,000 and it is estimated that freight costs will be $500, installation costs will be $2,500, and training and test run costs will be $3,000. Also, the firm estimates that the investment in equipment will increase working capital needs by $4,000. Finally, the firm has idle land, with a current sales price of $10,000, that will be used for storage as a result of the investment in equipment. For capital budgeting purposes, and ignoring income tax considerations for the moment, the initial investment in the equipment would be $100,000, as shown below:

Purchase price of equipment	$ 80,000
Freight cost	500
Installation cost	2,500
Training and test run costs	3,000
Increase in working capital	4,000
Sales price of idle land	10,000
	$100,000

[2]An opportunity cost is the contribution foregone by rejecting the next-best alternative. The opportunity cost of an asset is the contribution of the asset foregone in its best alternative use. Opportunity cost is used in decision making as a practical way to reduce alternatives under consideration. Opportunity cost is not used in financial accounting for purposes of external reporting.

TAX CONSIDERATIONS Since we are concerned with the cash or cash equivalent outlays for an investment, we must also consider the income tax effects of the initial investment because income taxes require a cash outlay. The major tax considerations with regard to the initial investment are the investment tax credit, the tax deductible outlays that reduce current income taxes payable, and the tax effects on the gain or loss that would result from the sale of existing assets. We now turn to a discussion of these tax effects in order to derive the after-tax initial investment outlay.

To encourage investment, the tax laws of the United States allow firms to reduce their income tax liability for the year by an amount equal to 10 per cent of new capital investment made during the year, subject to certain restrictions.[3] For example, if the equipment were purchased, Topeka Company would have an investment tax credit of $8,300 [.10 × ($80,000 purchase price + $500 freight + $2,500 installation)], which would be a direct reduction of current tax payments. Consequently, the after-tax outlay on the investment cost (purchase price + freight + installation) of the equipment would be $74,700 ($83,000 − $8,300).

Cash outlays associated with the investment that are fully deductible from taxable revenues reduce current income taxes payable. Thus the net cash effect of a tax deductible outlay is the outlay minus its tax savings. For example, the $3,000 outlay for training and test runs would be fully deductible for tax purposes. If a 40 per cent tax rate for Topeka Company is assumed, income taxes would be reduced $1,200 ($3,000 × .4); hence, the after-tax outlay would be $1,800 ($3,000 − $1,200). Or, merely, the outlay multiplied by one minus the tax rate equals the after-tax outlay of $1,800 [$3,000 × (1 − .4)]. On the other hand, the $4,000 increase in working capital is not tax deductible; hence, there is no tax effect.

Any opportunity costs of the new investment should also be on an after-tax basis. Consequently, if a company would sell an existing surplus asset if the new investment were not made, then making the investment would result in foregoing the proceeds from the sale of the asset, and the proceeds should be on an after-tax basis. When a surplus asset's adjusted basis (book value for tax purposes) exceeds its sales price, there would be a tax deductible loss, which would reduce current income taxes payable. The cash receipts from the sale of the asset would, in effect, be increased by the amount of the tax savings on the loss, which would increase the after-tax opportunity cost. By making the investment, the company would not only be foregoing the proceeds from the sale of the surplus asset but would also be foregoing the tax savings on the loss.[4] For example, if the surplus land of Topeka Company has an adjusted basis of $12,000, then the sale of the land for $10,000 would result in a tax deductible

---

[3]The qualifying base of the 10 per cent credit depends on the estimated life of the asset. If the estimated life is less than three years, none of the cost qualifies for the investment credit; if between three and five years, one-third of the cost qualifies; if between five and seven years, two-thirds of the cost qualifies; and if the estimated life is seven years or more, the entire cost qualifies for the investment credit. Also, Congress may change the investment tax credit, although at the time of this writing the credit is 10 per cent.

[4]Of course, the reverse would be true for a taxable gain (sales price exceeds adjusted basis) on the sale of a surplus asset. The cash receipts from the sale of the asset would, in effect, be reduced by the amount of the additional taxes on the gain, which would reduce the after-tax opportunity cost.

loss of $2,000 ($12,000 − $10,000). At a 40 per cent tax rate, the $2,000 tax loss would result in a tax savings of $800 ($2,000 × .4); hence, the after-tax opportunity cost of the land would be $10,800 ($10,000 + $800).

To summarize the above, the after-tax investment outlay for Topeka Company would be $91,300, as shown below:

	Outlay before tax	Tax effect	Outlay after tax
Purchase of equipment	$ 80,000		
Freight cost	500		
Installation cost	2,500		
	$ 83,000	−$8,300	$74,700
Training and test run costs	3,000	− 1,200	1,800
Increase in working capital	4,000	—	4,000
Sales price of idle land	10,000	+ 800	10,800
Totals	$100,000	−$8,700	$91,300

EXPECTED NET CASH INFLOWS Capital-budgeting decisions are long-run decisions and, as such, they should be evaluated in terms of their effect on the firm's *future long-run profitability*. One can determine how a particular capital-budgeting decision will affect future long-run profitability by making an analysis of the *amount* and the *timing* of the *future net cash inflows* that result from making the investment.

The *timing* of the expected cash inflows from an investment proposal is important because such inflows can be invested and can earn interest over the expected life of the investment. Long-run decisions must take into account the effect of interest. The importance of the timing of net cash inflows from proposed long-term investments means that annual net income should not be used to evaluate such investments. Net income is a short-run measure of profitability that is based on matching revenues and expenses over the fiscal year regardless of cash flows (accrual accounting). Thus net income does not reflect the long-run profitability of capital-budgeting decisions.

Under accrual accounting, the amount of revenue applicable to a given period of time generally differs from the cash receipts generated by the revenue-producing transactions. This condition is attributable to the time lag between the date of sale and the date of collection when sales are made on account. Similarly, the amount of expense applicable to a given period of time generally differs from the related cash disbursements made during the same time period. Depreciation provides the most obvious example of the difference in timing between a cash outlay and the related charges for expense. Usually the cash outlay for a depreciable asset occurs at or near the time the asset is acquired, while the depreciation charges are spread over the useful life of the asset. The aggregate depreciation charges tend to equal the capitalized cash outlays for depreciable assets, but the timing of the two amounts will differ significantly. To repeat, it is the prospective cash flows attributable to an investment, not the resulting revenues and expenses, that deserve attention when investment proposals are being evaluated.

To isolate the prospective relevant cash flows requires considerable analytical skill. The objective is to determine the *change* in cash flows that can reasonably be expected to result from the proposed investment and to assign the change to future time periods. If a company can expect to receive $10,000 a year for the next ten years whether or not a proposed investment is made, that cash flow is irrelevant to the investment decision. Similarly, if a company is committed to spend $5,000 a year for the next ten years whether or not a proposed investment is made, such cash outflow is irrelevant. But if, as a result of a proposed investment, the cash inflow or outflow will change, then the cash flow becomes relevant and the amount of the change should be isolated for analysis. In other words, investment analysis is concerned with relevant cash flows, which are *future* cash flows that are *different* under the given alternatives.

To aid in understanding expected cash inflows, we can conveniently classify them into two main categories:

Operating net cash inflows.
Termination cash inflows.

OPERATING NET CASH INFLOWS   Operating net cash inflows are the expected annual net cash inflows associated with the normal operation of the investment project over its useful economic life. If the investment is expected to increase revenues, such as an investment to expand present operations or to develop new product lines, then the operating net cash inflows are the annual cash revenues minus cash expenses expected from the investment over its expected economic life. If the investment is expected to reduce operating costs with revenue remaining the same, such as an equipment replacement, then the operating net cash inflows are the annual cost savings associated with the operation of the new investment as opposed to the operation of the old investment. That is, the operating net cash inflows would be the expected annual differences between the cash operating expenses of the new and old investments. If the investment is expected to expand revenues and reduce costs, such as equipment replacement where the new equipment is expected to both increase output and reduce operating expenses, then the operating net cash inflows are the differences between the new and old investments annual cash revenues minus cash expenses.

The operating net cash inflows are forecast on an annual basis over the expected economic life of the investment project. The economic life of an investment is the number of years over which the operating net cash inflows are expected as a result of making the investment. However, because it is difficult to predict the future operating net cash inflows precisely, such amounts are often forecast on a formulistic approach, such as constant annual amounts or linearly declining amounts.

Once the annual operating net cash inflows have been forecasted, they must be converted to an after-tax basis. Because income taxes are a cash expense, the additional income taxes must be subtracted from the operating net cash inflows before taxes. It is the operating net cash inflows after taxes that are used in capital budgeting decisions.

Since most investments involve depreciable assets, the operating net cash inflows after taxes must take into account the depreciation tax shield. Although depreciation is not a cash outflow, it is a tax deductible expense that shields income from taxes; hence, depreciation shields pretax cash inflow from the full impact of income taxes. Consequently, annual tax depreciation must be subtracted from the annual operating net cash inflows to derive annual cash inflow subject to tax. The latter multiplied by the firm's income tax rate equals the annual additional income taxes, which are subtracted from the annual operating net cash inflows before taxes to arrive at the annual operating net cash inflows after taxes.

To illustrate the computation of operating net cash inflows after taxes, let us refer to the Topeka Company's investment proposal to acquire additional equipment. Although we have already determined that the after-tax initial investment outlay for the equipment would be $91,300 (see page 647), this is not the tax depreciation base. The base would be the purchase price ($80,000) plus the freight cost ($500) and plus the installation cost ($2,500), or $83,000. If it is assumed that the estimated economic life of the equipment is ten years, that the company uses the double-declining balance method of depreciation, and that the expected salvage amount of the equipment at the end of ten years is $9,000, the expected annual depreciation would be as follows:

Years	Tax depreciation base	×	Double-declining tax rate	=	Annual depreciation
1	$83,000		.20		$16,600
2	66,400[a]		.20[b]		13,280
3	53,120		.20		10,624
4	42,496		.20		8,499
5	33,997		.20		6,799
6	27,198		.20		5,440
7	21,758		.20		4,352
8	17,406		.20		3,481
9	13,925		.20		2,785
10	11,140		.20		2,140[c]

[a]$66,400 = $83,000 − $16,600.

[b]Since the straight-line rate is .10 (1 ÷ 10 years), then the double-declining rate is twice the straight-line rate or .20 (2 × .10).

[c]Since you cannot depreciate below salvage, the last year depreciation is equal to $11,140 − $9,000 or $2,140.

Now that the expected annual depreciation has been determined, and a 40 per cent income tax rate is assumed, the net operating cash inflows after taxes can be derived as follows:

Year	(a) Cash inflow before taxes	(b) Tax depreciation	(c) Taxable cash inflow (c) = (a) − (b)	(d) Income tax (d) = (c) × .4	(e) Cash inflow after taxes (e) = (a) − (d)
1	$17,000	$16,600	$ 400	$ 160	$16,840
2	17,000	13,280	3,720	1,488	15,512
3	17,000	10,624	6,376	2,550	14,450
4	17,000	8,499	8,501	3,400	13,600
5	17,000	6,799	10,201	4,080	12,920
6	17,000	5,440	11,560	4,624	12,376
7	17,000	4,352	12,648	5,059	11,941
8	17,000	3,481	13,519	5,408	11,592
9	17,000	2,785	14,215	5,686	11,314
10	17,000	2,140	14,860	5,944	11,056

Of course, the after-tax cash inflows need to be converted into present value terms before they can be compared with the initial investment, but we will wait and explain this under the net present value discussion.

TERMINATION CASH INFLOWS Termination cash inflows are the cash inflows that the firm receives at the end of the investment project's life. Such cash inflows consist of the future disposal (salvage) amount of the investment facilities at the date of termination of the investment project and the recovery of any working capital that was committed initially to the investment project. These termination cash inflows are viewed in capital-budgeting decisions as future cash inflows in the year of disposal and recovery.

Future disposal amounts may include the resale value of the investment, such as equipment, if it is expected to be still usable in its current form at the end of the project's life. Or if the asset resulting from the investment is expected to be worn out by the project's life, then the disposal amount may be its expected scrap amount (sale of the asset as scrap metal). If the estimated disposal amount is insignificant, because it is a very small dollar amount or it is offset by removal and dismantling costs, then the disposal amount has no significant effect on the capital budgeting decision and can be ignored.

If the initial investment included an increase in working capital, then at the termination of the investment project the working capital is, in effect, released back to the company. This recovery of working capital investment is viewed in capital budgeting as a cash inflow at the end of the last year of the investment project.

Similar to operating cash inflows, the termination cash inflows should be on an after-tax basis. However, there are no tax effects on the recovery of working capital, so that the before- and after-tax cash inflow are the same. With regard to disposal amounts, tax effects would have to be included if there are gains (sale at greater than adjusted basis) or losses (sale at less than adjusted basis) on the disposal of the asset. If the expected salvage is equal to the adjusted basis (cost minus accumulated depreciation for tax purposes), then there is no gain and no loss and no tax effect. As will be explained shortly, in equipment replacement decisions there are usually gains or losses on the disposal of the old equipment that give rise to taxable gains or tax deductible losses that must be taken into account.

For example, the termination cash inflows of Topeka Company consist of the $9,000 expected salvage and the $4,000 recovery of working capital at the end of ten years. Since the adjusted basis of the equipment at the end of ten years is $9,000 (see page 649), which equals the expected salvage amount, there are no expected gains and no losses and therefore no expected tax effects related to the salvage. Since there are no tax effects on working capital, there are no tax effects on the $4,000 recovery of working capital.

Of course, the termination cash inflows must be converted into present value terms, as will be illustrated in the next section.

NET PRESENT VALUE Net present value is a decision criterion for evaluating investment proposals. The criterion allows the management of a firm to make rational investment choices. The reason for this is that the criterion not only takes into account the time value of money, but it also results in choices that are in the best interests of the common stockholders (maximizing common stock price) consistent with efficient resource allocation.

Net present value is the difference between the present value (discounted amount) of the expected net cash inflows to be generated by an investment and the amount of the initial investment (present cash cost). In deciding whether to invest in a proposed project or not (an accept-reject investment decision), the net present value criterion is quantitatively to accept the investment proposal if its net present value is positive and to reject the proposal if it is negative.[5] In deciding between competing investment alternatives in which only one can be chosen (a mutually exclusive investment choice decision), the net present value criterion is quantitatively to accept the investment alternative with the largest positive net present value.

A positive net present value means that the firm is expected to recover its initial investment, earn the minimum desired rate of return on the amount of the investment outstanding, and, in addition, earn the amount of the positive net present value. The total market value of the firm's common stock would be expected to increase by the amount of the positive net present value.

One of the prime advantages of the net present value method is that it takes into account the time value of money and is therefore sensitive to the timing of the future cash inflows associated with the investment. Because the future cash inflows and the initial investment outlay occur at different points in time, it is necessary to convert the future inflows into present value equivalents (discount the future cash inflows), which can then be compared with the initial investment. That is, by multiplying the future cash inflows by the present value of $1 at the minimum desired rate of return, the future cash inflows are restated into present-day dollars that can be compared with the present-day initial investment outlay to derive the investment decision criterion of net present value.

To illustrate the net present value method, let us continue with the Topeka Company example. Up to this point we have determined the initial investment ($91,300), the expected operating net cash inflows (see page 649), and the termination cash inflows ($9,000 salvage and $4,000 working capital recovery). In order to compare the future cash inflows with the initial investment, it is necessary to convert the future cash inflows into present value equivalents, as shown at the top of page 652.

---

[5]If the net present value is zero, the management of a firm is indifferent to accepting or rejecting the investment proposal. In such a situation the firm would be expected to earn only its minimum required rate of return; hence, there would be no expected increase in the firm's common stock price.

Year	Operating net cash inflows after taxes		Present value of $1 at 10% (from tables in Appendix B)		Present value
1	$16,840	×	.9091	=	$15,309
2	15,512	×	.8264	=	12,819
3	14,450	×	.7513	=	10,856
4	13,600	×	.6830	=	9,289
5	12,920	×	.6209	=	8,022
6	12,376	×	.5645	=	6,986
7	11,941	×	.5132	=	6,128
8	11,592	×	.4665	=	5,408
9	11,314	×	.4241	=	4,798
10	11,056	×	.3855	=	4,262

Termination cash inflows

10	9,000	×	.3855	=	3,470
10	4,000	×	.3855	=	1,542
					$88,889

As shown above, the present value of the future cash inflows expected to be generated by the investment in equipment is $88,889. Since the $88,889 is less than the initial investment of $91,300, the net present value is negative, as shown below:

Present value of future cash inflows	$88,889
Initial investment	− 91,300
Net present value	−$ 2,411

and the investment is quantitatively unacceptable. The negative net present value indicates that Topeka Company would not even be able to earn its minimum desired rate of return of 10 per cent on the investment, which is necessary just for the firm to maintain its present financial position. Consequently, if the investment were made, it would be expected that the company's common stock price would decline.

A worksheet is presented on page 653 that summarizes the complete analysis of the equipment investment proposal of Topeka Company.

QUALITATIVE FACTORS   The net present value criterion just discussed involved quantitative analysis in that the elements analyzed were measured in terms of dollars and cents. Consequently, we were careful to state that a positive net present value indicates a *quantitatively* acceptable investment proposal, while a negative net present value indicates a *quantitatively* unacceptable investment proposal. However, long-run investment decisions are based not only on quantitative factors, but also on qualitative factors. Qualitative factors are those which cannot be measured in terms of dollars and cents with an acceptable degree of precision; they are nonmonetary considerations.

To reach a quantitative investment decision, the net present value of prospective long-run investments is calculated. The quantitative decision is either supplemented or offset by the analysis of qualitative factors that influence the investment

Initial investment outlay:

	(a) Outlay before taxes	(b) Tax effect	(c) Outlay after taxes (c) = (a) ± (b)	
Purchase of equipment	$80,000			
Freight cost	500			
Installation cost	2,500			
	$83,000	−$8,300	$74,700	
Training and test run costs	3,000	− 1,200	1,800	
Increase in working capital	4,000		4,000	
Sales price of idle land	10,000	+ 800	10,800	−$91,300

Operating net cash inflows:

Years	(d) Cash inflow before taxes	(e) Tax depreciation	(f) Taxable cash inflow (f) = (d) − (e)	(g) Income tax (g) = (f) × .4	(h) Cash inflow after taxes (h) = (d) − (g)	(i) Present value of $1 at 10%	(j) Present value (j) = (h) × (i)	
1	$17,000	$16,600	$ 400	$ 160	$16,840	.9091	$15,309	
2	17,000	13,280	3,720	1,488	15,512	.8264	12,819	
3	17,000	10,624	6,376	2,550	14,450	.7513	10,856	
4	17,000	8,499	8,501	3,400	13,600	.6830	9,289	
5	17,000	6,799	10,201	4,080	12,920	.6209	8,022	
6	17,000	5,440	11,560	4,624	12,376	.5645	6,986	
7	17,000	4,352	12,648	5,059	11,941	.5132	6,128	
8	17,000	3,481	13,519	5,408	11,592	.4665	5,408	
9	17,000	2,785	14,215	5,686	11,314	.4241	4,798	
10	17,000	2,140	14,860	5,944	11,056	.3855	4,262	+ 83,877

Termination cash inflows:

	Year	(k) Cash inflow	(l) Present value of $1 at 10%	(m) Present value (m) = (k) × (l)	
Salvage	10	$ 9,000	.3855	$ 3,470	
Recovery of working capital	10	4,000	.3855	1,542	+ 5,012
Net present value					−$2,411

proposals. Thus the final investment decision is based on both quantitative and qualitative considerations. Some of the more important qualitative factors to consider are the following:

A company may accept an investment proposal with a slight negative net present value in order to keep its labor force busy and avoid the risks associated with laying off workers and attempting to rehire them later, which might cause labor problems.

A company may accept an investment project that is quantitatively unacceptable because it broadens the company's product lines and thus provides better customer service, which may increase overall company sales.

COST OF CAPITAL The calculation of the net present value of an investment assumes a given discount rate, called the *cost of capital*. The cost of capital is defined as the minimum desired rate of return on investment proposals. It is that rate of return on an investment that must be earned just to maintain present financial position and therefore maintain common stock price. In other words, the cost of capital is the minimum acceptable rate of return on an investment in that the earning of that rate will not depress the price of the company's common stock. Thus an investment proposal is quantitatively acceptable when it has a positive net present value because it is expected to earn a rate of return that is above the cost of capital and is therefore expected to increase the firm's common stock price. Similarly, an investment proposal is quantitatively unacceptable when it has a negative net present value because it is expected to earn a rate of return that is below the cost of capital and is therefore expected to depress the firm's common stock price.

The calculation of the cost of capital is a difficult problem. The traditional approach to its calculation is the weighted average cost of capital method.[6] Under this method, the cost of debt capital plus the cost of equity capital are weighted by the percentage of each individual capital source to total capital (weighted by its capital structure).

For example, assume that Topeka Company's cost of bonds is 3 per cent, cost of common stock is 14 per cent, and cost of retained earnings is 13.5 per cent.[7] Further assume that Topeka Company's capital structure is 40 per cent bonds, 50 per cent common stock, and 10 per cent retained earnings. Thus the cost of capital is 9.55 per cent or, rounded, 10 per cent, calculated as follows:

Source of long-term capital	Book value	Capital structure		Capital cost		Weighted
Bonds	$ 400,000	.40	×	.030	=	.0120
Common stock	500,000	.50	×	.140	=	.0700
Retained earnings	100,000	.10	×	.135	=	.0135
	$1,000,000	1.00				.0955 ≈ 10%

REPLACEMENT DECISIONS   As a firm's long-term operating assets, such as plant and equipment, become outmoded or worn out, management must continually decide whether or not to replace them. Since replacement involves a long-term investment, it is a capital budgeting problem. Consequently, the net present value criterion can be used to evaluate replacement proposals. If the present value of the excess of the net cash inflows of the new asset over the net cash inflows of the old asset (that is, the additional net cash inflows to be generated by the new asset) is greater than the net investment in the new asset, then the net present value is positive and the replacement is quantitatively acceptable. If the net present value is negative, then the replacement is quantitatively unacceptable.

Applying the net present value analysis to replacement cost decisions is basically the same as previously discussed for an investment expansion decision. However, the existence of the equipment being replaced results in some cash flows that are somewhat different from those of the expansion decision. Consequently, the relevant cash flows with regard to replacement decisions are briefly summarized below and then followed by a clarifying illustration.

Similar to investment expansion, the initial investment outlay in replacement analysis includes the purchase price, freight cost, installation cost, any increase in working capital, etc., adjusted for

[6]A second method calculation is the risk adjusted cost of capital that is derived from the capital asset pricing model.

[7]Although it is beyond the scope of this discussion to derive the individual capital costs, it should be pointed out that the low cost of debt (3 per cent) is because it is on an after-tax basis (interest is tax deductible). Also, the cost of retained earnings (13.5 per cent) is slightly lower than the cost of common stock (14 per cent) because it does not include the stock flotation cost that common stocks do.

income tax effect. However, in asset replacement the purchase of a new asset results in the sale of the old asset. Thus the net investment in the new asset is equal to its cost less the after-tax salvage proceeds that would be realized from the present sale of the old asset. The tax effect on the sale of the old asset depends on whether there is a taxable gain (book amount less than the sales price of the old) or a tax deductible loss (book amount greater than sales price), with the former reducing and the latter increasing the proceeds from the sale of the old asset.

The additional annual operating net cash inflows to be generated by the new asset consist of any after-tax additional annual cash revenue and/or any after-tax additional annual cost savings of the new asset, as well as any additional annual depreciation tax savings from the new asset. The additional annual cash revenue would result from acquiring a new asset that would increase volume and therefore increase cash revenue. The annual cost savings would result from acquiring a new asset that has lower annual operating costs than the old asset; hence, the annual cost savings are equivalent to annual net operating cash inflows. Since both additional annual cash revenue and annual cost savings increase annual earnings, there would be additional income taxes that would necessitate adjusting these cash inflows to an after-tax basis. Finally, the additional tax savings on depreciation result from the excess annual depreciation of the new asset over the old asset, which increases the annual depreciation tax shield and is therefore equivalent to an annual cash inflow.

The termination cash inflows consist of any additional salvage if the new asset is acquired, as well as any recovery of working capital as previously discussed. The expected salvage amount of the new asset at the end of its expected useful life is an expected cash inflow. However, the expected salvage amount of the old asset at the end of its expected useful life is equivalent to a cash outflow because it would not be realized if the new asset were acquired. Also, the cash flows from salvage should be stated on an after-tax basis if it is expected that there will be any gains or losses on disposal.

An equipment replacement illustration Assume that management wishes to determine whether or not some equipment should be replaced. The company accountants assemble the following data to be analyzed:

	Old asset	New asset
Expected cash inflow per year	$70,000	$70,000
Expected cash outflows per year:		
Direct material cost	12,000	9,000
Direct labor cost	22,000	15,000
Variable factory overhead cost	10,000	6,000
Fixed factory overhead cost	12,000	12,000
Cost to acquire new equipment today	—	70,000
Expected salvage of new at end of 10 years	—	10,000
Book amount of old equipment today:		
Original cost $50,000		
Accumulated depreciation 15,000	35,000	—
Expected salvage of old equipment:		
Today	15,000	—
At end of 10 years	5,000	—
Depreciation method used—straight line		
Annual depreciation:		
($50,000 cost − $5,000 salvage)		
÷ 15 years	3,000	—
($70,000 cost − $10,000 salvage)		
÷ 10 years	—	6,000

	Old asset	New asset
Expected useful life:		
Old equipment (15 − 5)	10 years	
New equipment		10 years

No investment credit is allowed on new investment
No increase in working capital is expected
Cost of capital is 10%
Tax rate is 40%.

Which cash flows are relevant to the replacement decision? The $70,000 cost to acquire the new equipment is obviously relevant, for it is not the same under both alternatives; the $70,000 cost is not incurred if the old equipment is retained in service. On the other hand, if the new equipment were acquired, then the old equipment would be sold, and the proceeds from the sale would, in effect, reduce the cost today of acquiring the new equipment. However, there is a tax effect on the present disposal of the old equipment because the present book amount (value) of the old equipment ($35,000) is greater than the present salvage or disposal price ($15,000). The result is a tax deductible loss on disposal of $20,000 ($35,000 − $15,000) that results in a tax savings of $8,000 ($20,000 × .4). Consequently, the cash inflow from disposal of the old equipment today would be $23,000 ($15,000 + $8,000), which would result in a net investment in the new equipment of $47,000 ($70,000 − $23,000). The $23,000 after-tax salvage amount today is relevant, for it is realized only if the new equipment is purchased; therefore, the cash inflow from the salvage, in effect, reduces the cost today of acquiring the new equipment.

The expected annual cash revenue of $70,000 and the annual fixed factory overhead cost of $12,000 are irrelevant because they are the same for both alternatives and therefore do not affect the replacement decision. The new equipment results in an annual cost saving of $3,000 ($12,000 − $9,000) for direct material, $7,000 ($22,000 − $15,000) for direct labor, and $4,000 ($10,000 − $6,000) for variable factory overhead. Because the total annual cost savings of $14,000 ($3,000 + $7,000 + $4,000) would increase annual earnings, they would also cause an increase in income taxes. At a 40 per cent tax rate, the annual after-tax cost savings would be $8,400 [$14,000 × (1 − .4)]. In addition, there is also the annual tax saving on the annual increase in depreciation of the new equipment over the old equipment, or $1,200 [($6,000 − $3,000) × .4], because of the additional tax shield provided by the additional tax deductible depreciation expense. Thus the total annual after-tax cost savings would be $9,600 ($8,400 + $1,200), which is equivalent to an annual after-tax cash inflow of $9,600 for the new equipment.

The $10,000 expected salvage of the new equipment at the end of ten years is a relevant cash inflow in favor of the new equipment. The $5,000 expected salvage of the old equipment at the end of ten years is relevant for it is foregone if the new equipment is purchased; hence, it is treated as a cash outflow (a cost) of the new equipment. Since there are no expected gains or losses at time of disposal, there are no tax effects with regard to the salvage amounts and the $10,000 and the $5,000 are the same on a before- and after-tax basis.

The relevant cash flows are summarized graphically below.

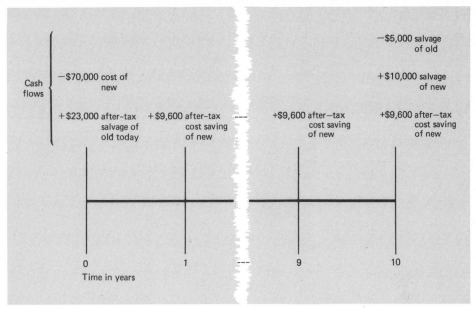

The cost of acquiring the new equipment ($70,000) and the expected after-tax salvage of the old today ($23,000) are both in terms of present-day dollars; no present value computations are necessary. The after-tax cost savings of $9,600 are constant each year and, therefore, can be converted to present value dollars by the use of present value of annuity tables (see Appendix B). The $10,000 salvage of the new equipment and the $5,000 salvage of the old equipment occur in year 10. Therefore, tables for present value of $1 (see Appendix B) can be used to convert the salvage amounts into equivalent dollars today. The present value calculations are summarized below, and the complete analysis is summarized on the worksheet provided on page 658.

Cost today to acquire new equipment	−	After-tax Salvage of old equipment today	=	Net cost of new equipment	Summary
$70,000	−	$23,000	=	$47,000	−$47,000
Annual after-tax cash cost savings	×	Present value of an annuity of $1 at 10% for 10 yrs	=	Present value of annual cost savings of new	
$ 9,600	×	6.1446	=	$58,988	+ 58,988
Cash inflow from salvage of new	×	Present value of $1 at 10% at end of 10 years	=	Present value of salvage of new	
$10,000	×	.3855	=	$ 3,855	+ 3,855
Cash inflow from salvage of old	×	Present value of $1 at 10% at end of 10 years	=	Present value of salvage of old foregone if new purchased	
$ 5,000	×	.3855	=	$ 1,928	− 1,928
Net present value					+$13,915

Initial investment outlay:

Cost of new equipment		$70,000	
Disposal of old equipment:			
Book amount now	$35,000		
Salvage now	15,000		
Loss on disposal	$20,000	$15,000	
Tax savings	×.4	8,000	23,000
Net investment			$47,000

−$47,000

Operating cash inflows:

Year	(a) Cost savings before taxes	(b) Excess depreciation of new over old	(c) Taxable increase in cash earnings (c) = (a) − (b)	(d) Increase in taxes (d) = (c) × .4	(e) Cost savings after taxes (e) = (a) − (d)	(f) Present value of $1 at 10%	(g) Present value (g) = (e) × (f)
1	$14,000	$3,000	$11,000	$4,400	$9,600	.90909	$ 8,727
2	14,000	3,000	11,000	4,400	9,600	.82645	7,934
3	14,000	3,000	11,000	4,400	9,600	.75132	7,213
4	14,000	3,000	11,000	4,400	9,600	.68301	6,557
5	14,000	3,000	11,000	4,400	9,600	.62092	5,961
6	14,000	3,000	11,000	4,400	9,600	.56447	5,419
7	14,000	3,000	11,000	4,400	9,600	.51316	4,926
8	14,000	3,000	11,000	4,400	9,600	.46651	4,479
9	14,000	3,000	11,000	4,400	9,600	.42410	4,071
10	14,000	3,000	11,000	4,400	9,600	.38554	3,701

or   9,600   ×   6.14457   = $58,988   + 58,988

Termination cash inflows:

	(h) Salvage end of 10 years	(i) Book amount at end of 10 years	(j) Taxable gain or loss (j) = (h) − (i)	(k) Tax (k) = (j) × .4	(l) Cash inflow after taxes (l) = (h) − (k)	(m) Present value of $1 at 10%	(n) Present value (n) = (l) × (m)	
New	$10,000	$10,000	0	0	$10,000	.3855	$3,855	+ 3,855
Old	5,000	5,000	0	0	5,000	.3855	1,928	− 1,928

Net present value   +$13,915

The calculations show that the purchase of the new equipment to replace the old equipment is accepted quantitatively, for the present value of the expected cash inflows is greater than the net cost of acquiring the new equipment. That is, there is a positive net present value of $13,915. On the other hand, qualitative considerations must be taken into account before a final decision is reached.

IMPORTANT TERMS AND CONCEPTS IN CHAPTER 22

Long run—p. 643
Importance of long-run investments—p. 643
Investment—p. 643
Capital budgeting—p. 643
Relevant cash flows—pp. 644, 647, 648
Net present value—pp. 644, 651, 652, 657
Initial investment—pp. 645–647
Investment in working capital—pp. 645, 646
Opportunity cost—pp. 645, 646
Investment tax credit—p. 646
Operating net cash inflows—pp. 648–650

Cost savings—pp. 648, 655
Investment expansion decisions—pp. 648, 653
Replacement decisions—pp. 648, 654–657
Depreciation tax shield—pp. 648, 649
Termination cash inflows—p. 650
Expected disposal (salvage) amounts—pp. 650, 653, 656, 657
Recovery of working capital—p. 650
Qualitative factors—pp. 652, 653
Cost of capital—pp. 653, 654

ASSIGNMENT MATERIAL

Questions

1. What is capital budgeting?
2. If accrual accounting is used by accountants in the preparation of financial statements, why not then use accrual accounting data to solve capital-budgeting problems?
3. If the time value of money is such an important concept, why is it not used in cost-volume-profit analysis?
4. What amounts are compared in applying the net present value criterion?
5. What is the decision rule used in the net present value criterion?
6. What amounts are included in the initial investment?
7. Why must tax considerations be included in the capital budgeting process?
8. Given an investment proposal for a new piece of equipment, which inflows and outflows must be adjusted for income taxes in order to arrive at after-tax cash flows?
9. What is one of the major advantages of the net present value method?
10. What is the cost of capital? How is it used in capital budgeting?
11. How is the cost of capital calculated under the weighted average method?
12. How do replacement decisions differ from investment decisions not involving replacements (e.g., expansion decisions)? Can the net present value method be used in both situations?
13. How does a gain or loss on the sale of an existing asset affect its after-tax cash inflow?
14. Why should retained earnings bear a cost of capital?
15. Evaluate this statement: ''It doesn't matter which depreciation method is used because the total income taxes will always be the same over the life of the asset.''

Short exercises

E22-1 *You are given below three multiple-choice statements. Select the correct answers and indicate the corresponding letters on a sheet of paper (e.g., 1-d, 2-d, etc.).*

(1) An investment proposal should be quantitatively accepted if (a) the salvage amount is zero, (b) no increase in working capital is required, (c) its net present value is negative, (d) cost-volume-profit analysis indicates that the firm can operate above the break-even point, (e) none of the above.

(2) Qualitative factors to be considered in a capital budgeting analysis would *not* include the effect of the investment proposal on (a) labor costs, (b) the environment, (c) the economy of the surrounding community, (d) the possibility of a labor strike, (e) none of the above.

(3) The cost of capital is an interest rate equal to the firm's current (a) before-tax cost of debt capital, (b) after-tax cost of debt capital, (c) cost of equity capital, (d) weighted average cost of debt and equity capital, (e) none of the above.

E22-2   *You are given below three multiple-choice statements. Select the correct answers and indicate the corresponding letters on a sheet of paper (e.g., 1-d, 2-d, etc.).*

(1) The initial investment in a capital budgeting analysis would *not* include (a) opportunity costs, (b) increases in working capital, (c) a decrease due to the proceeds from the sale of an existing asset, (d) depreciation on the new asset, (e) none of the above.

(2) No adjustment for income tax effects is needed on (a) the purchase price, (b) changes in working capital requirements, (c) depreciation expense, (d) disposal of an existing asset, (e) none of the above.

(3) The net present value criterion requires that the cost of the investment today be compared with (a) future depreciation expense, (b) future expenses, (c) future revenues, (d) the present value of future net cash inflows, (e) none of the above.

E22-3   *The management of Samson Company has decided to acquire a new piece of equipment. The cost of the equipment is $50,000, and it is expected to generate annual net cash inflows of $10,000 for seven years. The decision to buy the equipment was based on the equipment's net future cash inflows of $70,000 ($10,000 × 7 years) being greater than its $50,000 cost today. Assuming that the amounts above are after-tax cash flows and that the cost of capital is 10 per cent, evaluate management's decision to acquire the equipment.*

E22-4   *As the controller of Yore Company you have been asked to evaluate the following investment proposal. A piece of equipment can be purchased at an after-tax cost of $14,000. It is expected to generate after-tax cash inflows of $2,000 after the first year, $2,400 after the second year, $3,000 after the third year, $4,000 after the fourth year, and $4,400 after the fifth year. If it is desired to earn at least 6 per cent on invested money, should Yore Company make this proposed investment?*

E22-5   *You wish to decide between an after-tax investment of $130,000 in one of two alternatives. The first alternative results in after-tax cash receipts of $20,000 at the end of each year for 10 years. The second alternative results in the receipt of $400,000 at the end of 15 years. If you wish to earn at least 8 per cent on your investment, which alternative should you choose? Would your answer change if you required only a 7 per cent rate of return?*

E22-6   *Segrego Company is considering the purchase of a piece of equipment with an invoice cost of $50,000. Sales tax of 3 per cent must also be paid along with transportation charges of $500. It will cost $1,700 to train current employees to operate the piece of equipment. Also, increased sales will cause working capital to increase by $6,300. Calculate the after-tax investment outlay for Segrego on this piece of equipment. Assume an investment tax credit of 10 per cent and an income tax rate of 40 per cent.*

E22-7   *Flowcash Company has recently purchased a piece of equipment at a cost of $100,000. It is expected to provide a cash inflow of $30,000 per year for eight years, at which time it will be scrapped. Assume that Flowcash uses double-declining balance depreciation for tax purposes for the first four years, at which time (year 5) they switch to straight-line depreciation. Prepare a schedule computing the cash inflow after taxes for the eight-year life of the equipment. Assume an income tax rate of 30 per cent for Flowcash and round all amounts to the nearest dollar.*

PROBLEMS

A22-1

Kompleat Company is considering a proposal to market a new product. The proposal would require an investment of $55,000 in new equipment with an estimated useful life of eight years and no salvage. The new product is estimated to generate after-tax net cash inflows of $10,000 per year for eight years. The firm's cost of capital is 10 per cent.

The marketing manager argues that the investment should be made based on the payback criterion. The manager explains that payback is the number of years that it takes the investment project to recover its initial investment, or

$$\text{Payback} = \frac{\text{Initial investment}}{\text{Annual after-tax cash inflows}}$$

$$5\frac{1}{2} \text{ years} = \frac{\$55,000}{\$10,000}$$

Since the investment can be recovered in only five and one-half years, and since the estimated useful life of the equipment is eight years, the sales manager argues that the investment should be made.

Required:

(a) Using the net present value criterion, determine quantitatively whether or not the investment should be made.

(b) What is wrong with using the payback criterion in capital budgeting decisions?

A22-2

The management of Deciso Company has decided to add a new production line, and the choice is narrowed to either production line A or production line B. Given the data below, determine which production-line alternative is quantitatively better. Is the better alternative quantitatively acceptable?

	Alternative A	Alternative B
Acquisition cost	$500,000	$600,000
Salvage value 8 years hence	60,000	200,000
Estimated annual cash revenues	250,000	300,000
Estimated annual cash costs:		
Direct materials	50,000	60,000
Direct labor	70,000	40,000
Variable factory overhead	30,000	50,000
Maintenance	10,000	60,000
Estimated useful life	8 years	8 years
Cost of capital—10%		
Depreciation method—straight line		
Investment tax credit—10%		
Income tax rate—40%		

(Round all amounts to the nearest dollar.)

A22-3

Ak-Sell Company has just paid $56,000 for some equipment that will have no salvage value at the end of its seven-year life. Net cash inflows before taxes of $11,500 are expected each year from this investment, but no increase in working capital is required. Ak-Sell has a cost of capital of 10 per cent and a tax rate of 40 per cent. An investment tax credit of 10 per cent is also applicable to this equipment.

Required:

(a) Assuming that the straight-line depreciation method is used, prepare an analysis to evaluate Ak-Sell's decision to purchase this equipment. (Round all amounts to the nearest dollar.)

(b) Assuming that the sum-of-the-years'-digits depreciation method is used, prepare an analysis to evaluate Ak-Sell's decision to purchase this equipment. (Round all amounts to the nearest dollar.)

A22-4

Coyote Company is considering the expansion of its facilities. They have hired you to analyze its proposal. Use the following data to prepare a quantitative analysis to defend your recommendation:

Cost of land	$ 10,000
Cost of building	105,000
Cost of equipment	230,000
Employee training costs	15,000
Estimated value of land at the end of 10 years	20,000
Expected salvage amount of building at the end of 10 years	25,000
Expected salvage amount of equipment at the end of 10 years	30,000
Increase in working capital	50,000
Expected net cash inflow (yearly)	50,000
Cost of capital—8%	

Assume that Coyote will use straight-line depreciation for tax purposes on both the building and equipment. An investment tax credit of 10 per cent is allowed on the equipment. Coyote's income tax rate is 45 per cent on both income and gains. The entire amount of working capital can be recovered after 10 years. (Round all amounts to the nearest dollar.)

A22-5

Grant Corporation is considering the replacement of some of its major equipment. Although management has made its choice as to which equipment to purchase, it has not decided whether the replacement is financially sound. Given the data below, advise Alexander Corporation on whether the replacement should be made.

	Present equipment	New equipment
Undepreciated cost	$2,000,000	—
Acquisition cost	—	$10,000,000
Useful life	10 years remaining	—
Salvage value now	$3,000,000	—
Salvage 10 years hence	0	$ 2,500,000
Expected annual cash revenues	$2,000,000	$ 3,150,000
Expected annual cash costs:		
Direct materials	$ 400,000	$ 400,000
Direct labor	300,000	100,000
Variable factory overhead	200,000	300,000
Fixed factory overhead	250,000	250,000
Expected annual cash maintenance	$ 500,000	$ 100,000
Cost of capital—10%		
Depreciation method—straight-line		

Assume that there is no investment tax credit, no expected increase in working capital, and that the income tax rate is 45 per cent. (Round all amounts to the nearest dollar.)

A22-6

Valpo Company is considering replacing part of its manufacturing equipment with newer, energy-saving models. Prepare an analysis of the company's investment proposal. Use the following data:

	Old equipment		New models
Cost to acquire new models			$ 75,000
Expected salvage of new models at			
end of 10 years			20,000
Book amount of old equipment today:			
Original cost	$46,500		
Accumulated depreciation	18,000	$ 28,500	
Expected salvage of old equipment:			
Today		20,000	
At end of 10 years		1,000	
Expected cash inflow per year		100,000	100,000
Expected cash outflows per year		85,000	75,000
Expected useful life:			
Old equipment (13 − 3)		10 years	
New models			10 years
Depreciation method used—sum-of-the-years'-digits			
Investment tax credit—10%			
Income tax rate—45%			
No increase in working capital is expected			
Cost of capital—12%			

(Round all amounts to the nearest dollar.)

B22-1

Montague Company is considering a proposal to market a new product. The proposal would require an investment of $100,000 in new equipment with an estimated useful life of ten years and no salvage. The new product is estimated to generate before-tax cash inflows of $20,000 per year for 10 years. The firm uses the straight-line depreciation method, has a tax rate of 40 per cent, and has a cost of capital of 10 per cent. The investment tax credit would not be allowed and there would be no increase in working capital.

The marketing manager argues that the investment should be made based on the average rate of return criterion. The manager explains that the average rate of return is equal to:

$$\text{Average rate of return} = \frac{\text{Increase in future average net income}}{\text{Average investment}}$$

$$= \frac{\text{Increase in future average net income}}{(\text{Initial investment} + \text{Salvage}) \times 1/2}$$

$$36\% = \frac{\$18,000}{(\$100,000 + 0) \times 1/2}$$

The expected average net income of $18,000 is estimated as follows:

Expected revenue	$80,000
Expected expenses (including depreciation	
of $10,000)	50,000
Expected income before taxes	$30,000
Income taxes ($30,000 × .4)	12,000
Expected net income	$18,000

Since the investment is expected to earn an average rate of return of 36 per cent, which is considerably higher than the minimum desired rate of return of 10 per cent, the sales manager argues that the investment should be made.

Required:

(a) Using the net present value criterion, determine quantitatively whether or not the investment should be made.

(b) What is wrong with using the average rate of return criterion in capital budgeting decisions?

B22-2

Gungo Corporation currently sends its cutting tools to an outside firm for sharpening at an annual cost of $8,500. Gungo is now considering the purchase of a machine to perform the task. The machine could be purchased for $8,000 and would have an expected life of five years with no salvage value. Annual cash operating costs for the machine will be $5,000. If Gungo's tax rate is 40 percent and its cost of capital is 10 per cent, should it purchase the machine or continue to have the task done by outsiders? Assume that a full investment tax credit of 10 per cent applies to this machine even though its useful life is only five years. (Round all amounts to the nearest dollar.)

B22-3

The owners of Ralph Smith Company are considering the expansion of their facilities. The proposed facilities are estimated to have a useful life of 50 years, after which time the salvage value is estimated to be zero. Given the data below, which are assumed to be on an after-tax basis, should the expansion be undertaken?

	Present facilities	Present and expanded facilities
Initial cost	$900,000	$1,400,000
Estimated annual cash revenues	200,000	300,000
Estimated annual cash expenses	100,000	150,000
Remodeling costs—Year 10	75,000	100,000
Remodeling costs—Year 20	100,000	125,000
Remodeling costs—Year 30	150,000	200,000
Remodeling costs—Year 40	175,000	200,000
Cost of capital—8%		

B22-4

Amber Company is considering the purchase of a special piece of equipment. The following information pertains to the investment proposal:

Invoice cost	$28,000
Transportation cost	2,000
Installation costs	3,000
Employee training costs	5,000
Salvage end of 7 years	5,000
Increase in working capital	10,000
Annual cash inflow before taxes	7,000
Useful life—7 years	
Depreciation method—sum-of-the-years'-digits	
Cost of capital—10%	
Tax rate—35%	
Investment tax credit—10%	
Recovery of working capital—end of 7 years	

Using the net present value criterion, determine whether or not Amber Company should invest in the equipment. (Round all computations to the nearest dollar.)

B22-5   The management of D. J. K. Corporation has decided to acquire a new truck, which can be either purchased or leased. Given the data below and that the cost of capital is 7 per cent, should management purchase or lease the truck? Would your answer be different if the rental charge was $1,000 per year plus $.10 per mile? Assume that the cash flows are on an after-tax basis.

Purchase:

Acquisition cost	$27,000
Estimated life	5 years
Salvage 5 years hence	$ 5,000

	Year 1	Year 2	Year 3	Year 4	Year 5
Estimated cash cost savings	$40,000	$50,000	$60,000	$40,000	$30,000
Estimated cash maintenance	1,000	2,000	2,000	4,000	5,000

Lease:

Rental expense	$.10 per mile
Maintenance expense	paid by owner

	Year 1	Year 2	Year 3	Year 4	Year 5
Estimated cash cost savings	$40,000	$50,000	$ 60,000	$40,000	$30,000
Estimated mileage	60,000	90,000	100,000	70,000	40,000

B22-6   Pennysaver Company has been approached by a salesperson for Laborsaver Machine Tools, Inc. The salesperson tries to persuade Pennysaver to replace its manufacturing equipment by making the following sales pitch: "At the low price of $250,000, this equipment will pay for itself twice over its ten-year life by saving you $50,000 per year in labor costs." If you are the controller of Pennysaver and your company's cost of capital is 15 per cent, would you "buy" the salesperson's pitch (and the equipment)? Here are some other facts you may wish to consider:

Book amount of old equipment:		
Original cost (16-year life)		$150,000
Depreciation expense:		
Year 1	$18,750	
2	16,406	
3	14,356	
4	12,561	
5	10,991	
6 (just ended)	9,617	82,681
		$ 67,319
Expected annual cost savings		$ 50,000
Expected salvage of old equipment:		
Today		27,319
At end of 10 years		5,000
Expected salvage of new equipment		10,000
Income tax rate—40%		
No investment tax credit		
No increase in working capital		
Depreciation method—double-declining balance for the new just as it had been for the old equipment		

(Round all amounts to the nearest dollar.)

ANALYSIS OF FINANCIAL STATEMENTS
CHAPTER 23

PURPOSE OF CHAPTER A recurring theme throughout this book has been that the field of accounting exists to provide useful information for decision-making purposes. The discussion now turns to how accounting data in the form of financial statements can provide useful information for persons outside the business firm (external decision makers) who do not have access to internal accounting records. Although financial statements are not specifically designed to aid management (internal decision makers) in decision making, it should be obvious, however, that the information contained in financial statements is also useful to management, especially when used with pertinent internal accounting data.

SOURCES OF FINANCIAL DATA Financial statements and other financial data can be found in annual and quarterly reports prepared and published by business firms. The Securities and Exchange Commission requires certain companies to file detailed annual reports (SEC Form 10-K), which can be obtained for purposes of analysis. Investment advisory services, such as Moody's Investors Service, Inc., Standard and Poor's Corporation, and the Value Line Investment Survey, publish financial statements and analyses of companies. Finally, various financial analyses are published by Dun and Bradstreet, Robert Morris Associates, stock brokerage houses, credit agencies, trade agencies, financial newspapers, and financial periodicals.

COMPARATIVE STATEMENTS In order to determine financial trends, balance sheets, income statements, and statements of changes in financial position for a company should be compared over the last five to ten years. In their annual reports, many companies now show balance sheet, income statement, and SCFP data for several years side by side to facilitate trend analysis. If such comparative statements are not available in an annual report, the data can be obtained from several annual reports and listed side by side on a spread sheet.

From the comparative financial statements, dollar and percentage changes can be calculated for key financial figures to determine: (1) the primary elements that caused the change; (2) whether the trend of the change is favorable or unfavorable; and (3) whether, based on expected business conditions, the trend is likely to continue in the near future.

To illustrate comparative analysis, suppose that your analysis of a particular company shows that net income has been increasing about 4 per cent per year for the last five years. Some conclusions resulting from your analysis of the income data might be:

(1) Much of the recent increase in net income is the result of nonoperating gains which are unlikely to recur in the near future.

(2) The trend is upward, but in comparison to similar companies the rate of increase is below average.

(3) In view of an expected business recession next year, the below-average historical growth in earnings, and no expectation of nonoperating gains, net income next year is unlikely to show any increase.

As an example, some comparative financial statements for "Vivian & Sons, Inc.," are presented below and on page 668. Like most published financial statements, they do not show breakdowns of cost of goods sold, of operating expenses, or of the variable and fixed components of expenses. Generally the lack of detail is rationalized by the desire to avoid bulky financial statements, to avoid giving too much data to competitors, and to avoid confusing the readers of the statements with too much detail.

RATIO ANALYSIS Financial statements contain a maze of dollar amounts that are difficult to interpret when viewed as a whole or individually. Relevant financial relationships may be overlooked in an overall examination because of the complexity of such a large mass of financial data. Similarly, an analysis of each dollar amount by

VIVIAN & SONS, INC.
Comparative Balance Sheets
December 31, 19_1—19_6

	19_6	19_5	19_4	19_3	19_2	19_1
Assets:						
Current assets:						
Cash	$ 5,000	$ 20,000	$ 54,600	$ 37,400	$ 45,000	$ 70,000
Net accounts receivable	400,000	275,000	200,000	170,000	150,000	100,000
Inventory	500,000	300,000	250,000	210,000	200,000	80,000
Total current assets	$ 905,000	$ 595,000	$ 504,600	$ 417,400	$395,000	$250,000
Long-lived assets:						
Land	$ —	$ —	$ 170,000	$ 170,000	$ 80,000	$ 80,000
Plant and equipment	$1,102,000	$1,002,000	$ 802,000	$ 602,000	$500,000	$400,000
Accumulated depreciation	300,400	245,300	195,200	155,100	125,000	100,000
Net	$ 801,600	$ 756,700	$ 606,800	$ 446,900	$375,000	$300,000
Total long-lived assets	$ 801,600	$ 756,700	$ 776,800	$ 616,900	$455,000	$380,000
	$1,706,600	$1,351,700	$1,281,400	$1,034,300	$850,000	$630,000
Equities:						
Current liabilities:						
Accounts payable	$ 125,350	$ 54,800	$ 45,000	$ 40,000	$ 35,000	$ 10,000
Short-term loans	300,000	60,000	35,000	20,000	15,000	—
Taxes payable	79,600	65,200	54,000	46,400	40,000	20,000
Total current liabilities	$ 504,950	$ 180,000	$ 134,000	$ 106,400	$ 90,000	$ 30,000
Long-term liabilities						
Bonds payable—6%	$ 450,000	$ 450,000	$ 450,000	$ 250,000	$100,000	$ —
Stockholders' equity:						
Common stock—20,000 shares	$ 400,000	$ 400,000	$ 400,000	$ 400,000	$400,000	$400,000
Retained earnings	351,650	321,700	297,400	277,900	260,000	200,000
Total stockholders' equity	$ 751,650	$ 721,700	$ 697,400	$ 677,900	$660,000	$600,000
	$1,706,600	$1,351,700	$1,281,400	$1,034,300	$850,000	$630,000
Market price per share of common stock, December 31	$ 80	$ 49	$ 27	$ 19	$ 12	$ 5
Annual dividends	89,450	73,500	61,500	51,700	—	—

VIVIAN & SONS, INC.
Comparative Statements of Income and Retained Earnings
For the Years Ended December 31, 19_1—19_6

	19_6	19_5	19_4	19_3	19_2	19_1
Net sales	$1,210,000	$1,100,000	$1,000,000	$950,000	$900,000	$600,000
Cost of goods sold	806,000	737,000	670,000	646,000	630,000	400,000
Gross margin	$ 404,000	$ 363,000	$ 330,000	$304,000	$270,000	$200,000
Operating expenses:						
Selling expense	$ 115,000	$ 112,000	$ 110,000	$108,000	$100,000	$ 90,000
General and administrative expenses	63,000	61,000	58,000	65,000	64,000	60,000
Total	$ 178,000	$ 173,000	$ 168,000	$173,000	$164,000	$150,000
Net operating income	$ 226,000	$ 190,000	$ 162,000	$131,000	$106,000	$ 50,000
Other expense:						
Interest expense	27,000	27,000	27,000	15,000	6,000	—
Net income before taxes	$ 199,000	$ 163,000	$ 135,000	$116,000	$100,000	$ 50,000
Income tax	79,600	65,200	54,000	46,400	40,000	20,000
Net income	$ 119,400	$ 97,800	$ 81,000	$ 69,600	$ 60,000	$ 30,000
Retained earnings at beginning of year	321,700	297,400	277,900	260,000	200,000	170,000
	$ 441,100	$ 395,200	$ 358,900	$329,600	$260,000	$200,000
Deduct common stock dividends	89,450	73,500	61,500	51,700	—	—
Retained earnings at end of year	$ 351,650	$ 321,700	$ 297,400	$277,900	$260,000	$200,000
Earnings per common share	$ 5.97	$ 4.89	$ 4.05	$ 3.48	$ 3.00	$ 1.50

VIVIAN & SONS, INC.
Comparative Statements of Changes in Financial Position
For the Years Ended December 31, 19_2—19_6

	19_6	19_5	19_4	19_3	19_2
Sources of financial resources:					
Working capital from operations[a]	$174,500	$147,900	$121,100	$ 99,700	$ 85,000
Issuance of bonds	—	—	200,000	150,000	100,000
Sale of land	—	170,000	—	—	—
Total sources	$174,500	$317,900	$321,100	$249,700	$185,000
Uses of financial resources:					
Acquisition of plant and equipment	$100,000	$200,000	$200,000	$102,000	$100,000
Acquisition of land	—	—	—	90,000	—
Payment of dividends	89,450	73,500	61,500	51,700	—
Total uses	$189,450	$273,500	$261,500	$243,700	$100,000
Increase (decrease) in working capital	($ 14,950)	$ 44,400	$ 59,600	$ 6,000	$ 85,000

[a]Depreciation is assumed to be the only nonworking capital expense. Hence, to compute working capital from operations, depreciation expense is added to net income. For instance, working capital from operations for 19_6 equals $119,400 + $55,100.

itself overlooks key relationships because meaningful comparisons are not made. Also, individual dollar amounts by themselves often are relatively insignificant.

So that readers will not be "blinded" by the mass of figures contained in financial statements, financial-statement analysis should entail the use of ratio analysis. A financial ratio is a comparison of two related pieces of financial data of a firm, the ratio being derived from the common fraction of the two in percentage form. An example would be the current ratio of Vivian & Sons, Inc., as of December 31, 19_6.

Current ratio = Current assets ÷ Current liabilities

$$1.79 = \$905,500 \div \$504,950$$

Through the use of ratios, one can focus attention on financial interrelationships:

(1) By relating sections of a financial statement to other sections of the same statement.

    Example: Current assets are compared with current liabilities (current ratio) as an indicator of a firm's ability to meet short-term debts.

(2) By relating financial data in one statement to data in another statement.

    Example: Net income from the income statement is compared with common stockholders' equity from the balance sheet to determine a rate of return on owners' equity.

(3) By relating an evaluation of a particular section of a statement to an overall evaluation of the firm to determine if the latter confirms the former.

    Example: A company may have only a "fair" current ratio, but the overall profitability and financial position may be good enough to offset the current ratio and may lead to the conclusion that the company can meet its short-term debts satisfactorily.

On the other hand, the analyst must be careful to avoid conclusions based on ratio analysis *alone*. Because ratio analysis has certain weaknesses (discussed on pages 679–680, conclusions based on ratio analysis should be checked against flow from operations data (from SCFP), comparative-statement analysis (to determine trends), and the like.

FINANCIAL ANALYSIS FOR INVESTORS IN COMMON STOCKS Varying degrees of risk are associated with investments in common stock. Having determined the risk class of common stock in which one is willing to invest money, the investor is primarily interested in stock-price appreciation and dividend payments. Because both of these factors are influenced by net income, much of the analysis undertaken to determine the attractiveness of an investment in common stock focuses attention on the earnings record of the company under consideration. That is, net income is a measure of operating efficiency and thus provides some indication as to whether a particular common stock is a good investment.

Earnings per share and important relationships The net income of a company minus any dividends on preferred stock equals the amount of income applicable to common stockholders. This divided by the average number of common stock shares outstanding equals the earnings per share of common stockholders.[1]

$$\textit{Earnings per share} = \frac{\text{Net income minus preferred dividends}}{\text{Average number of common shares outstanding}}$$

Although earnings-per-share figures are probably the most widely published and used financial figures, their value is overrated. In the first place, the financial operations of a business cannot really be condensed into one figure called earnings per share. Secondly, comparisons of the earnings per share of different companies can be distorted by the effects of different accounting procedures with regard to inventory, depreciation, capitalization vs. expensing of outlays, and the like.

[1]This is only true for firms with simple capital structures consisting of common stock and ordinary preferred stock. For firms with complex capital structures, the calculation of earnings per share is more complicated. However, the earnings-per-share data can be obtained from the financial statements, since such data must be shown at the bottom of the income statement per *Opinion No. 15*.

The point is, the financial data from which the earnings per share is derived must be analyzed.

Financial analysts compare earnings per share and the related dividends per share to other financial data in the hope of determining key relationships that may indicate the investment merits of a company's common stock. Three such widely used relationships are the price-earnings ratio, the payout ratio, and the dividend yield.

$$Price\text{-}earnings\ ratio = \frac{Market\ price\ per\ share\ of\ common\ stock}{Earnings\ per\ share}$$

$$Payout\ ratio = \frac{Dividends\ per\ share}{Earnings\ per\ share}$$

$$Dividend\ yield = \frac{Dividends\ per\ share}{Market\ price\ per\ share\ of\ common\ stock}$$

From the price-earnings ratio a multiplier is derived that shows the evaluation that investors place on the company's earnings. For example, a common stock with a market price of $100 and earnings per share of $5 has a price-earnings ratio of 20; the stock market values every dollar of earnings twenty times.

A company's payout ratio reflects its management's policy as to whether dividends should be a large or a small percentage of net income. A company that is experiencing substantial growth in earnings (net income) may have a small payout ratio because the management is reinvesting funds in the business. The reinvestment of funds should increase future net income and should be reflected in higher stock prices in the future. An investor interested in stock-price appreciation may well invest in such a company even though the payout ratio is low. In contrast, an investor who is interested primarily in dividends should invest in the common stock of a company with a high payout ratio.

An investor who is interested primarily in dividends can compute dividend yields on proposed investment alternatives in common stock to aid in deciding which is the best. Such an investor probably would be interested in those common stocks that have a high dividend yield and a high payout ratio. However, the dividend yield is not the entire yield, for it does not take into account stock-price appreciation.

From the financial data on pages 667 and 668, the three ratios discussed above are calculated as follows:

		19_6	19_5	19_4	19_3	19_2	19_1
Market price per share, December 31	(a)	$80.00	$49.00	$27.00	$19.00	$12.00	$5.00
Earnings per share (annual net income ÷ 20,000 shares)	(b)	$ 5.97	$ 4.89	$ 4.05	$ 3.48	$ 3.00	$1.50
Dividends per share (annual dividends ÷ 20,000 shares outstanding)	(c)	$ 4.47	$ 3.68	$ 3.08	$ 2.59	—	—
Price-earnings ratio (multiplier)	(a ÷ b)	13	10	7	5	4	3
Dividend yield (per cent)	(c ÷ a)	6%	8%	11%	14%	—	—
Payout ratio (per cent)	(c ÷ b)	75%	75%	76%	74%	—	—

This analysis shows that the company has experienced excellent growth, as earnings per share almost quadrupled from 19_1 to 19_6. The stock market has reacted favorably to the increase in earnings, as shown by the increase in the price-earnings ratio from 3 in 19_1 to 13 in 19_6. Although the dividend yield has been declining, both the yield and payout ratio seem high for a company growing this fast.

If the investor expects earnings to grow at about 20 per cent per year, the estimated earnings per share would be $7.16 ($5.97 × 1.2) for 19_7. If the estimate in growth is correct, the expected growth in earnings should be reflected in an increase in the market price of the stock for 19_7. Suppose that the investor expects the price-earnings ratio to increase to 20 for 19_7, but, to be on the safe side, the investor decides to use the 19_6 price-earnings ratio of 13. Based on the investor's expectations, the valuation of the 19_7 stock would be at about $93 ($7.16 × 13). If the estimates were correct, the stock could be bought today at about $80 and sold next year at $93, a $13 price increase per share.

Profitability ratios   In addition to the calculations pertaining to percentage increases in net income (comparative analysis) and the earnings-per-share figures, the investor should analyze a firm's profitability further by making a comparision of net income to such related financial bases as stockholders' equity and total assets. Even though earnings per share and the percentage increase in net income may both be very favorable, a firm may be unattractive from the investor's viewpoint because its net income is such a small percentage of stockholders' equity. Thus the investor should also analyze net income in terms of the following profitability ratios:[2]

$$\frac{\text{Rate of return on}}{\text{common stock equity}} = \frac{\text{Net income (after taxes) minus preferred dividends}}{\text{Common stockholders' equity}}$$

$$\frac{\text{Rate of return on}}{\text{total assets}} = \frac{\text{Net income (after taxes) + Interest expense}}{\text{Total assets}}$$

The rate of return on common stock equity (Common stock + Capital in excess of par or stated value + Retained earnings) measures the profitability of the capital committed to the business by the common stockholders. Since capital is invested and business is conducted with the object of earning income, the return on equity is a basic test of profitability.

The rate of return on total assets measures the relationship between the after-tax income applicable to *all* those who have supplied funds to a firm and the invested funds themselves as reflected in total assets. This measure is indicative of management's ability to earn a satisfactory return on all funds committed to the business. Because creditors provide funds to the firm, consistency requires that the numerator in this calculation be net income (after taxes) plus interest expense.

The investor in common stock should be aware of the fact that the rate of return on total assets affects the rate of return on common stockholders' equity. If a company borrows money and pays a rate of interest that is less than the

[2]Although not commonly done, the rates of return are sometimes computed on average common stockholders' equity and average total assets instead of on year-end data.

return on total assets, then the return on common stockholders' equity will be increased and it will be higher than the return on total assets. Thus a company may have a relatively low return on total assets but, through low-cost debt financing, may have a relatively high return on stockholders' equity. This is called *trading on the equity* or *leverage:* The excess return accruing to the common stockholders because borrowed funds generate a higher return than their rate of interest cost.

From the data for Vivian & Sons, Inc., the two ratios discussed above can be calculated as follows:

		19_6	19_5	19_4	19_3	19_2	19_1
Net income	(a)	$ 119,400	$ 97,800	$ 81,000	$ 69,600	$ 60,000	$ 30,000
Common stockholders' equity	(b)	$ 751,650	$ 721,700	$ 697,400	$ 677,900	$660,000	$600,000
Rate of return on common stockholders' equity	(a ÷ b)	15.9%	13.6%	11.6%	10.3%	9.1%	5.0%
Net income + interest	(a)	$ 146,400	$ 124,800	$ 108,000	$ 84,600	$ 66,000	$ 30,000
Total assets	(b)	$1,706,600	$1,351,700	$1,281,400	$1,034,300	$850,000	$630,000
Rate of return on total assets	(a ÷ b)	8.6%	9.2%	8.4%	8.2%	7.8%	4.8%

These calculations confirm the substantial increase in earnings per share that were calculated previously. Not only are earnings per share increasing at a fast rate, they are also a favorable percentage in relation to the stockholders' equity base. Although the return on total assets is lower than the return on common stockholders' equity, so long as the return on the total assets remains above the interest expense (6 per cent), the return on common stockholders' equity will be benefited (by the leverage factor).

Finally, another profitability ratio that is used by analysts is the return on sales (net income divided by sales). This so-called *profit margin* indicates the net profitability of each dollar of sales and is supposed to be a measure of overall profitability. However, since it does not take into account the investment used to generate the income, its use as a measure of profitability is questionable. To overcome this problem, some analysts look at the profit margin as one of two primary factors affecting the return on total assets:

$$\frac{\text{Net income}}{\text{Total assets}} = \frac{\text{Net income}}{\text{Sales}} \times \frac{\text{Sales}}{\text{Total assets}}$$

$$= \text{Profit margin} \times \text{Asset turnover}$$

In other words, return on total assets is affected both by profit margin and asset utilization, and these two factors can be analyzed to explain differences in returns on assets.

Debt-to-equity ratio   One measure of the common stockholders' risk in a firm is the relation between the funds supplied by creditors to the funds supplied by owners, as shown below:

$$Debt\text{-}to\text{-}equity\ ratio = \frac{\text{Total debt}}{\text{Stockholders' equity}}$$

Because debt consists of fixed obligations that must be met by the firm in order to avoid insolvency, the higher the debt-to-equity ratio the greater the financial risk that the firm cannot pay its debts. Because of the greater risk, a high debt-to-equity ratio may also preclude a company from obtaining additional debt financing, which results in the loss of financing flexibility.

Although a high debt-to-equity ratio increases financial risk, it can be attractive to stockholders for the following reasons:

(1) It can increase the rate of return on stockholders' equity via leverage.
(2) The voting control of the common stockholders may be maintained by avoidance of new stock flotations.
(3) Because the proportion of stockholders' investment to total financing is small, the creditors are bearing most of the financial risk.

Thus each investor has to weigh the merits of a high debt-to-equity firm by balancing the potential advantages of leverage against the added risk.

The debt-to-equity ratios for Vivian & Sons, Inc., are calculated as follows:

		19_6	19_5	19_4	19_3	19_2	19_1
Total debt	(a)	$954,950	$630,000	$584,000	$356,400	$190,000	$ 30,000
Stockholders' equity	(b)	$751,650	$721,700	$697,400	$677,900	$660,000	$600,000
Debt-to-equity ratio	(a ÷ b)	127%	87%	84%	53%	29%	5%

What the above ratios indicate is that, in order to finance its expanding opera-tions, the debt position of the company was overextended. Debt financing was increased so fast that by 19_4 the possibility of obtaining additional long-term loans was not feasible. Consequently, management increased the firm's short-term debt financing in 19_5 and especially in 19_6 to help finance the company's expansion.

The large proportion of long-term debt and the increased use of short-term debt increase the possibility that the company may not have the funds to meet interest payments and the retirement of the debt. Short-term debt may be more risky than long-term debt because of the frequent need to replace or renew the financing. An important question is whether the company will be able to continue its profitable operations with the heavy burden of debt. To help answer this question, analysis of the statement of changes in financial position (SCFP) is discussed in the next section.

Analysis of SCFP Clues to the general financial approach used by management in providing financing for a firm can be obtained through analysis of where man-agement is obtaining and using its resources. In other words, analysis of resource flows is useful in evaluating managerial efficiency because profitability and finan-cial position are affected by how management obtains financing and by the types of assets acquired by management. Thus analysis of the SCFP is useful not only to common stockholders, but to all those persons who are interested in financial statement analysis.

Since the investor in common stock is concerned primarily with profitability, his or her analysis of working capital via SCFP, via liquidity ratios (discussed on pages 675–676), and via current asset turnovers (discussed on pages 677–678) should attempt to provide answers to the following types of questions: Is the company hurting its future profitability—

(1) By keeping too much cash on hand, some of which could be reinvested at a favorable rate of return?
(2) By not using debt and/or preferred stock to increase the rate of return on stockholders' equity via leverage?
(3) By paying dividends when such cash should have been reinvested in the business?
(4) By neglecting to replace old plant and equipment?
(5) By expanding operations too fast?
(6) By increasing long-term debt too fast?
(7) By overlooking short-term financing opportunities?
(8) By failing to consider the issuance of additional shares of common stock as a means of additional financing?
(9) By tying up cash in excess inventory?
(10) By tying up cash in accounts receivable that should have been collected?

The SCFP analysis confirms the previous analysis of the debt-to-equity ratios. The company's expansion was financed primarily by the issuance of long-term debt through 19_4, by the sale of land in 19_5, and by internal financing obtained from profitable operations (working capital from operations) in 19_6. Also, the balance sheets show a substantial increase in short-term debt the last two years. Considering the size of the long-term debt and the extent of the recent increase in short-term debt, the risk of insolvency has increased.

Up to this point the contention has been that the company has overextended its debt position. However, it was previously pointed out (page 673) that each investor has to weigh the advantages of leverage against the added risk. Thus the analyst may reach the opposite conclusion, that the growth in net income for Vivian & Sons, Inc., indicates management's ability to take advantage of the expansion, and that the company is not really overextended in terms of debt. In other words, two analysts can reach different conclusions based on the same financial data, because some subjectivity cannot be avoided in financial statement analysis.

As the sources of working capital are analyzed, the question arises why management did not issue additional common stock. This strategy would have taken advantage of a rising price for the company's common stock to bring in additional cash. It would have reduced the high debt-to-equity ratio and given management some flexibility in obtaining future financing.

The use of working capital was primarily for new plant and equipment and the payment of dividends. Although the expansion in plant and equipment probably was too fast, management was attempting to expand its facilities in order to take advantage of its growth potential. However, management should refrain from any further extensive plant and equipment expansion until the debt-to-equity imbalance is corrected.

The payment of large dividends was not sound strategy. Because the company was experiencing substantial and profitable growth, the funds paid out in dividends would have been better used if they had been reinvested in the business. The reinvested funds would have earned a good rate of return on equity and would have reduced the need for such an extensive increase in debt. Similarly, management's maintenance of a 75 per cent payout ratio is much too high for a growth company such as this. In fact, 75 per cent is a high payout for a nongrowth company.

The failure to issue additional common stock, the payment of exorbitant dividends, and the small number of common shares outstanding, seem to indicate that the company may be controlled by a small group of stockholders. That is, additional common stock may not have been issued because the small group of controlling shareholders did not want to share voting control with new stockholders. Similarly, the large dividends may have been at the insistence of the small group of controlling shareholders.

The possibility of issuing additional common stock and the expectation of the continuance of funds inflows from operations indicate that sound management of the firm could result in an improvement in the present precarious debt position. The big question, however, is whether the present management is capable of making the necessary decisions to avoid insolvency.

Finally, the SCFPs-flow analysis should be supplemented by an analysis of the composition and movement of the current assets. This subject is discussed next in the section dealing with short-term creditor analysis.

FINANCIAL ANALYSIS FOR SHORT-TERM CREDITORS Short-term creditors are concerned primarily with the ability of the firm to generate sufficient cash to pay current liabilities and to have enough cash left over to meet current operating needs. Consequently, short-term creditors focus attention on a company's cash position and its near-cash resources, that is, the current assets, and their relation to short-term liabilities. Working capital is an indication of the ability of a business to pay its current liabilities as they mature. It is sometimes called a measure of short-term solvency. However, short-term creditors are also interested in the flow of working capital from operations. If the in-flow exceeds the out-flow, there is less concern about a company's ability to meet current liabilities. In the final analysis, whether a company can meet its short-term debts depends largely on whether operating receipts exceed operating outlays as indicated by working capital from operations.

Liquidity ratios Creditors want a firm's working capital to be sufficient to meet current needs. But the amount of working capital is not an adequate measure of sufficiency. Any test of the adequacy of working capital must take into consideration the possibility of shrinkages in the realizable values of the current assets; in the event of forced liquidation, the inventory may have to be disposed of at a loss; and, in the event of a general business recession, it may be difficult to dispose of the inventory and to collect the receivables. Consequently, short-term creditors normally calculate the following two liquidity ratios:

$$\text{Current ratio} = \frac{\text{Current assets}}{\text{Current liabilities}}$$

$$\text{Acid-test or quick ratio} = \frac{\text{Cash} + \text{Marketable securities} + \text{Accounts receivable}}{\text{Current liabilities}}$$

During a business recession, a firm may suffer operating losses (or reduced profitability) and may have difficulty obtaining short-term credit; hence, to meet its operating needs, current assets may be depleted. The current ratio indicates how much current assets can be reduced and still meet the firm's current liabilities. For example, a current ratio of 4 to 1 means that the current assets could be reduced three-fourths and still have sufficient current assets to cover current liabilities. Consequently, a low current ratio, such as 1 to 1 or below, indicates that a firm would have difficulty obtaining cash through a reduction of inventory and accounts receivable and still have cash available to meet normal operating needs. Obviously, a high current ratio is favored by short-term creditors, but from a managerial viewpoint it may indicate excessive cash tied up in current assets that could profitably be used elsewhere in the firm.

In analyzing the current ratio, the short-term creditor should be aware of the practice of many firms to improve their current ratio immediately preceding the end of the fiscal period—so-called window dressing. For example, the firm may postpone purchases of materials until the beginning of next year, or pay off loans at the end of the year with the idea of borrowing again at the beginning of next year. Also, the creditor should be aware of the effect on the current ratio of seasonal fluctuations and general business conditions. For example, many firms end their fiscal period during the slack season when cash and receivables are high and inventory low, which improves their liquidity position.

One of the main shortcomings of the current ratio is that it does not reveal the *distribution* (or composition) of current assets. Normally it takes more time to convert inventory into cash than to convert marketable securities or accounts receivable. Similarly, prepayments are current assets that usually cannot be converted readily, if at all, into cash. In contrast, such current assets as cash, marketable securities, and accounts receivable are called quick assets because they normally can be easily and quickly converted into cash; they are highly liquid. A comparison of the most liquid current assets with the current liabilities is provided by the acid-test or quick ratio.

Using Vivian & Sons, Inc., data, the current ratios and the acid-test ratios are shown as follows:

		19_6	19_5	19_4	19_3	19_2	19_1
Current assets	(a)	$905,000	$595,000	$504,600	$417,400	$395,000	$250,000
Quick assets	(b)	$405,000	$295,000	$254,600	$207,400	$195,000	$170,000
Current liabilities	(c)	$504,950	$180,000	$134,000	$106,400	$ 90,000	$ 30,000
Current ratio	(a ÷ c)	1.8	3.3	3.8	3.9	4.4	8.3
Acid-test ratio	(b ÷ c)	.8	1.6	1.9	1.9	2.2	5.7

The unfavorable trend of both the current ratio and the acid-test ratio confirms the working-capital problem indicated by the SCFP analysis. With a current ratio of 1.8 in 19_6, the company's current assets could shrink 44 per cent $(1 - \frac{1}{1.8})$ and still have current assets available to meet current liabilities. However, the .8 acid-test ratio for 19_6 shows that there are not sufficient quick assets to meet current liabilities.

The movement of current assets Both the current ratio and the acid-test ratio will be misleading if accounts receivable are too high because of slow credit collections. Similarly, the current ratio will be misleading if a firm's inventory is too high because it is not being turned over (sold) as fast as it should be. Because the liquidity ratios overlook the movement of current assets, short-term creditors should also analyze the receivables turnover and the inventory turnover.

$$\text{Receivables turnover} = \frac{\text{Net sales}}{\frac{1}{2} \times \left(\begin{array}{c}\text{Beginning accounts} \\ \text{receivable}\end{array} + \begin{array}{c}\text{Ending accounts} \\ \text{receivable}\end{array}\right)}$$

$$= \frac{\text{Net sales}}{\text{Average receivables}}$$

$$\begin{array}{c}\textit{Average number of} \\ \textit{days to collect} \\ \textit{receivables}\end{array} = \frac{\text{365 days in a year}}{\text{Receivables turnover}}$$

$$\textit{Inventory turnover} = \frac{\text{Cost of goods sold}}{\frac{1}{2} \times \left(\begin{array}{c}\text{Beginning} \\ \text{inventory}\end{array} + \begin{array}{c}\text{Ending} \\ \text{inventory}\end{array}\right)} = \frac{\text{Cost of goods sold}}{\text{Average inventory}}$$

The accounts receivable turnover approximates the average number of times accounts receivable were converted into cash during the fiscal period; therefore, it provides evidence as to the quality of a firm's receivables in terms of liquidity. A declining turnover may mean that the dollar amount of accounts receivable shown on the balance sheet includes "old" receivables that may be difficult to collect. The receivables are not so current (liquid) as they appear to be on the balance sheet.

Dividing 365 days by the receivables turnover will show the average collection period, which can then be compared with the firm's credit terms. For example, if it takes 80 days to collect receivables, and if credit terms are 30 days, this would indicate that the credit department is lax in its collections.

Because cost of goods sold represents the goods transferred out of inventory, cost of goods sold divided by the average inventory on hand during the fiscal period approximates the average number of times the inventory was replaced. Consequently, a declining inventory turnover may mean that:

(1) There is "old" inventory on hand that may not be readily salable.
(2) The firm has too much cash tied up in inventory that could be profitably used elsewhere, which results in a high inventory carrying cost.
(3) The risk of obsolete inventory has increased.

A high turnover of inventory indicates liquidity of inventory. Given a certain percentage of gross margin, the gross margin earned during a year increases as the turnovers increase. However, increasing the turnover by reducing the inventory may ultimately have the disastrous effect of alienating customers who become dissatisfed with the assortment.

The short-term creditor should be aware that both turnovers are only rough indicators of the movement of current assets. Seasonal fluctuations in accounts receivable and inventory may mean that the average figures used in the turnover calculations are not representative data. There is also the problem that some of the turnover data may not be available from the published financial statements. For example, the income statement may not show cost of goods sold, and the analyst would have to estimate inventory turnover by dividing net sales by inventory. Also, the accounts receivable turnover should be based on credit sales, but the financial statements show only total net sales. Finally, the ideal way to determine the movement of accounts receivable into cash is by the preparation of an aging schedule, but an outsider does not have the necessary data to do this.

Using Vivian & Sons, Inc., data, the turnovers are calculated as follows:

		19_6	19_5	19_4	19_3	19_2	19_1
Net sales	(a)	$1,210,000	$1,100,000	$1,000,000	$950,000	$900,000	$600,000
Average accounts receivable	(b)	$ 337,500	$ 237,500	$ 185,000	$160,000	$125,000	$100,000
Receivables turnover	(a ÷ b)	3.6	4.6	5.4	5.9	7.2	6.0
Number of days uncollectible	[365 ÷ (a ÷ b)]	101	79	68	62	51	61
Cost of goods sold	(a)	$ 806,000	$ 737,000	$ 670,000	$646,000	$630,000	$400,000
Average inventory	(b)	$ 400,000	$ 275,000	$ 230,000	$205,000	$140,000	$ 80,000
Inventory turnover	(a ÷ b)	2.0	2.7	2.9	3.2	4.5	5.0

The downward trend of both turnovers provides evidence that the liquidity ratios probably are misleading and are even less favorable than previously indicated. The results tend to confirm the previous SCFP analysis.

Assuming 30-day credit terms, the 101-day average collection period for 19_6 is unfavorable. With the desperate need for working capital, there is urgent need for a revamping of the collection policies of the firm. Also, there is the possibility that the firm may be granting too much credit to customers with low credit standing.

Normally a low inventory turnover and a decreasing trend in the turnover indicates a decrease in the liquidity of the inventory. However, in the case of Vivian & Sons, Inc., sales have been increasing rapidly, and, with a gross margin of about 33 per cent of sales, the net income trend has been favorable. Thus the low inventory turnover must be the result of too rapid inventory accumulation in relation to expanding sales. More than enough inventory is on hand and there should be no substantial increase in the near future; too much cash has been tied up in inventory through failure properly to control inventory levels. Again, this is an indication of inefficiency in the management of the firm.

LONG-TERM CREDITORS   Long-term creditors are primarily interested in whether a company has the ability to meet interest payments over the life of a loan and to repay the loan at maturity. Consequently, the debt-to-equity ratio (previously discussed) is important to long-term creditors because it indicates the margin of safety provided by common stockholder financing. In the event of liquidation, creditors have legal claims to the assets before the common stockholders; hence, the lower the debt-to-equity ratio, the greater the proportion of stockholder financing and the greater the equity buffer protecting the long-term creditors.

Long-term creditors also calculate the number of times interest has been earned as an indicator of the ability of a company to meet its interest payments.

$$\text{Number of times interest earned} = \frac{\text{Net income} + \text{Income taxes} + \text{Interest expense}}{\text{Interest expense}}$$

This ratio measures how much net income before interest and income tax could decline and still provide coverage of the total interest expense. Normally, the greater the ratio the less the risk that the company will not be able to meet its interest payments. Note that the ratio is calculated before income taxes because interest is deductible for income tax purposes; therefore, income taxes do not affect the ability to pay interest.

Using Vivian & Sons, Inc., data, the number of times interest earned is calculated as follows:

		19_6	19_5	19_4	19_3	19_2
Net income		$119,400	$ 97,800	$ 81,000	$ 69,600	$ 60,000
Interest expense	(a)	27,000	27,000	27,000	15,000	6,000
Income taxes		79,600	65,200	54,000	46,400	40,000
Total	(b)	$226,000	$190,000	$162,000	$131,000	$106,000
Times interest earned	(b ÷ a)	8.4	7.0	6.0	8.7	17.7

The times-interest-earned ratios show a favorable trend upward during the last three years and are relatively high. For example, the 19_6 earnings before interest and income taxes could decline 88 per cent $(1 - \frac{1}{8.4})$ and the earnings would still cover total interest expense.

The firm's profitable operations make the times-interest-earned ratios look very favorable. However, it is cash, not net income, that is used to pay interest charges. Whether a firm has the cash to pay interest is better determined by SCFP analysis. As previously discussed, the firm has a favorable generation of working capital from operations, which should be sufficient to meet the interest payments, provided that management refrains from further current expansion of plant and equipment, from paying large dividends, and from carrying excessive inventories and accounts receivable.

WEAKNESSES OF RATIO ANALYSIS The use of ratio analysis is not as popular today as it once was. This decline probably is the result of an expanding awareness of the weaknesses of ratio analysis, some of which are listed:

(1) By the time the outsider has obtained financial statements, the data are out of date.
(2) Ratio analysis uses historical data, and there is some question whether historical data can provide a relevant basis for making predictions.
(3) Diverse accounting treatments of inventory, depreciation, capitalization vs. expensing of outlays, and the like, make meaningful comparisons of companies via ratio analysis difficult.
(4) Ratio analysis by itself overlooks the dynamic aspects of the flow resources through a firm, which is so helpful in evaluating management efficiency.
(5) Ratio analysis normally uses financial data that are not adjusted for changes in the level of general prices, which can distort the analysis.

(6) There has been a tendency to develop a multiplicity of ratios, some of which have little or no significance. If two dollar amounts have little or no significance in relation to each other, a ratio expression of their relation is no more significant. For instance, it is claimed by some that the ratio of current assets to long-term debt is meaningful, but it is difficult to see why.

(7) There are ratios in use that can give misleading results. For example, the turnover of working capital is often regarded as a very significant ratio (net sales divided by the working capital). An increase in the ratio is usually interpreted as desirable. But an increase in turnover may be caused by either an increase in sales or a *decrease* in the working capital. An increase in working-capital turnover caused by a decrease in working capital may be an undesirable trend.

On the other hand, when properly used, ratio analysis can be very helpful in evaluating a company's financial operations. The idea, however, is not to look at each ratio by itself, but to integrate ratio analysis with comparative analysis and SCFP analysis. Comparative analysis and SCFP analysis can indicate favorable or unfavorable trends, but they need to be supplemented by ratio analysis to confirm and determine the reasons for such trends.

IMPORTANT TERMS AND CONCEPTS IN CHAPTER 23

Sources of financial data—p. 666
Comparative statements—pp. 666, 667
Ratio analysis—pp. 667–669
Earnings per share—p. 669
Price earnings ratio—pp. 670, 671
Payout ratio—p. 670
Rate of return on common stock equity—
    pp. 671, 672
Rate of return on total assets—
    pp. 671, 672

Trading on the equity (leverage)—p. 672
Debt-to-equity ratio—pp. 672, 673
Profit margin—p. 672
Asset turnover—p. 672
Analysis of SCFP—pp. 672–675
Current ratio—pp. 675, 676
Acid test (quick ratio)—pp. 675, 676
Receivables turnover—pp. 677, 678
Number of times interest earned—p. 679
Weaknesses of ratio analysis—pp. 679, 680

DEMONSTRATION PROBLEM FOR REVIEW AND SELF-STUDY Following are the financial statements of Bowers Company:

BOWERS COMPANY
Comparative Balance Sheets
December 31, 19_4 and 19_3

	19_4	19_3
Assets:		
Current assets:		
Cash	$ 10,000	$ 14,900
Marketable securities	150,000	70,000
Accounts receivable	100,000	80,000
Inventory	200,000	150,000
Total current assets	$460,000	$314,900
Long-lived assets:		
Plant and equipment	$400,000	$400,000
Accumulated depreciation	300,000	280,000
Net	$100,000	$120,000
Total long-lived assets	$100,000	$120,000
	$560,000	$434,900

BOWERS COMPANY
Comparative Balance Sheets (Cont.)

	19_4	19_3
Equities:		
Current liabilities:		
Accounts payable	$150,000	$ 80,000
Taxes payable	50,000	30,000
Total current liabilities	$200,000	$110,000
Long-term liabilities:		
Bonds payable—6%	$100,000	$100,000
Stockholders' equity:		
Preferred stock—5%	$ 50,000	$ 50,000
Common stock—10,000 shares	100,000	100,000
Capital in excess of par	20,000	20,000
Retained earnings	90,000	54,900
Total stockholders' equity	$260,000	$224,900
	$560,000	$434,900

BOWERS COMPANY
Income Statement
For the Year Ended December 31, 19_4

Sales	$810,000
Cost of goods sold	525,000
Gross margin	$285,000
Operating expenses	183,000
Net operating income	$102,000
Other expense:	
Interest expense	6,000
Net income before income taxes	$ 96,000
Income taxes	38,400
Net income	$ 57,600

Requirements:

Calculate the following ratios for the year 19_4:

(1) Current ratio.
(2) Acid-test ratio.
(3) Accounts receivable turnover.
(4) Number of days uncollectible (assume a 360-day year).
(5) Inventory turnover.
(6) Number of times interest earned.
(7) Earnings per share (common stock).
(8) Rate of return on common stockholders' equity.
(9) Rate of return on total assets.
(10) Total debt to stockholders' equity.

Note Attempt to solve the demonstration problem before examining the solution that follows.

Solution:

(1) $\dfrac{\$460,000}{\$200,000} = 2.3$

(2) $\dfrac{\$10,000 + \$150,000 + \$100,000 = \$260,000}{\$200,000} = 1.3$

(3) $\dfrac{\$810,000}{\frac{1}{2} \times (\$80,000 + \$100,000) = \$90,000} = 9$

(4) $\dfrac{360}{9} = 40$ days

(5) $\dfrac{\$525,000}{\frac{1}{2} \times (\$150,000 + \$200,000) = \$175,000} = 3$

(6) $\dfrac{\$57,600 + \$38,400 + \$6,000 = \$102,000}{\$6,000} = 17$

(7) $\dfrac{\$57,600 - (\$50,000 \times .05 = \$2,500) = \$55,100}{10,000} = \$5.51$

(8) $\dfrac{\$57,600 - \$2,500 = \$55,100}{\$210,000} = 26.2\%$

(9) $\dfrac{\$57,600 + \$6,000 = \$63,600}{\$560,000} = 11.4\%$

(10) $\dfrac{\$300,000}{\$260,000} = 1.15$

Questions

1 Why should one take time to calculate and analyze financial ratios when all of the financial data needed can be simply read from the financial statements? Discuss.

2 Is it possible that a high inventory turnover may be unfavorable? Discuss.

3 In calculating the rate of return on total assets, why is interest added to net income and why are preferred dividends ignored in the numerator of this ratio? Discuss.

4 How does the statement of changes in financial position aid the financial analyst?

5 In analyzing the ratio of total debt to common stockholders' equity for a particular company, why will a common stock investor probably have a view different from a creditor's view of this ratio? Discuss.

6 Suppose that you were analyzing a particular company and found that the profitability trends and ratios were excellent, yet the company badly needed working capital. How could such a situation occur? Discuss.

7 Why might a company want to show short-term investments in government securities as a subtraction from taxes payable on the balance sheet, instead of showing them under current assets? Discuss.

8 The fact that the number of days to collect accounts receivable has been increasing does not necessarily mean that the credit manager is at fault. The fault could lie with the sales manager. What is meant by the foregoing statements? Discuss.

9 What are the implications of an extremely high accounts receivable turnover? What are the implications of an extremely low accounts receivable turnover?

10 Management is bargaining with a labor union over whether there should be a substantial increase in wages. The labor union negotiator contends that the company can afford to pay a large increase in wages because the return on common stockholders' equity has been increasing and is now about 20 per cent. Management argues that the company is not really that profitable, because the return on sales (net income after taxes ÷ sales) has remained constant at 14 per cent. What probably caused the differences between the two rates of return? Discuss.

11 What does the number of times interest earned ratio purport to measure? What specific group of financial statement users would be most interested in this ratio?

12 The current ratio and the acid-test ratio aid financial statement users who are interested in corporate liquidity. Since the ratios are very similar, why would anyone calculate both to analyze the firm's liquidity position?

13 Analysis of the financial ratios of a specific company for a single year may not produce significant insight into key financial relationships of the firm. What modification of ratio analysis would you suggest?

14 What are some of the weaknesses of ratio analysis?

Short exercises

E23-1   *You are given below three multiple-choice statements. Select the correct answers and indicate the corresponding letters on a sheet of paper (e.g., 1-d, 2-d, etc.).*

(1)   Ratio analysis (a) should be used by itself to draw conclusions about financial statements, (b) is a comparison between two or more unrelated pieces of financial data of a firm, (c) can be used only by creditors, (d) is useful, but one must consider other procedures to verify the conclusions indicated by the analysis, (e) all of the above, (f) none of the above.

(2)   Ratios of particular interest to short-term creditors include the (a) current ratio, (b) acid-test ratio, (c) average number of days to collect receivables, (d) inventory turnover, (e) all of the above, (f) none of the above.

(3)   Ratios of particular interest to long-term creditors include the (a) acid-test ratio, (b) debt-to-equity ratio, (c) liquidity ratio, (d) price-earnings ratio, (e) all of the above, (f) none of the above.

E23-2   *You are given below three multiple-choice statements. Select the correct answers and indicate the corresponding letters on a sheet of paper (e.g., 1-d, 2-d, etc.).*

(1)   The earnings-per-share figure (a) is optional on the income statement, (b) attempts to condense the financial operations of a business into one figure, (c) does not depend on different accounting procedures, (d) is also called the price-earnings ratio, (e) all of the above, (f) none of the above.

(2)   An increase in the debt-to-equity ratio (a) increases financial risk, (b) always increases the rate of return on stockholders' equity (c) causes the creditors to bear less financial risk, (d) affects the voting control of the common stockholders, (e) all of the above, (f) none of the above.

(3)   Which of the following is incorrect? (a) High liquidity ratios may also be related to low profitability ratios. (b) A stock investor interested in stock-price appreciation may invest in a company with a low payout ratio. (c) Trend analysis of ratios is useful for long-term creditors only. (d) Integration of ratio analysis with statement of changes of financial position analysis is desirable. (e) All of the above. (f) None of the above.

E23-3   *In the left-hand column at the top of page 685 is a set of common financial ratios numbered one through ten. Opposite each ratio is a set of considerations, identified by letters (a) through (j) to which one of the ratios is applicable. Match the right-hand column to the left-hand column (e.g., 1-a, 2-b, etc.).*

Ratios		Considerations	
(1)	Current ratio	(a)	Rate earned by stockholders on current market price per share
(2)	Earnings per share		
(3)	Number of times interest earned ratio	(b)	Measurement of common stockholders' risk
(4)	Price-earnings ratio	(c)	Measurement of the relative ability to cover current liabilities with current assets
(5)	Receivables turnover		
(6)	Rate of return on total assets	(d)	Earnings applicable to a share of common stock
(7)	Inventory turnover		
(8)	Dividend yield	(e)	Provides evidence on the quality of a firm's receivables in terms of liquidity
(9)	Acid-test ratio		
(10)	Debt-to-equity ratio	(f)	Measures the coverage of total interest expense
		(g)	Measures the relative ability to cover current liabilities with the most liquid current assets
		(h)	Measures the return to all the funds invested in the firm
		(i)	Measures the average number of times the inventory was replaced
		(j)	Shows the evaluation that investors place on the company's earnings

E23-4

A cash dividend was declared during December, 19_2. If the cash dividend was paid during January, 19_3, how would the dividend payment affect the 19_3 current ratio? That is, under the circumstances given below, would it increase, decrease, or not affect it? Explain.

(a) The current ratio was 3 : 2 prior to the dividend payment.

(b) The current ratio was 1 : 2 prior to the dividend payment.

(c) The current ratio was 1 : 1 prior to the dividend payment.

(d) What conclusions can you reach from the effects on the current ratio?

E23-5

(a) If the 19_6 current ratio for Shake Co. was 2 to 1, and if the total working capital was $100,000, what is the dollar amount for the 19_6 current assets and current liabilities?

(b) If the 19_2 number of times interest earned ratio was 5 to 1, income taxes were 40 per cent of net income, and interest expense was $20,000, what was the net income for 19_2?

(c) If the price-earnings ratio was 10, payout ratio was 75 per cent, and dividends were $3.00 per share of common, what was the market price per share of common stock at year end?

E23-6

Assume that a friend of yours wants to invest in the common stock of a company because of the increasing trend of its net income, as shown below. However, your friend is puzzled about why the earnings per share and the market price of the common stock declined in 19_8 in spite of an increase in net income. Write a brief report to your friend explaining what happened.

	19_8	19_7	19_6	19_5	19_4
Common shares outstanding	600,000	200,000	200,000	200,000	200,000
Net income	$900,000	$750,000	$600,000	$522,000	$420,000
Earnings per share	3.00	7.50	6.00	5.22	4.20
Market price per share	62.00	150.00	90.00	66.00	48.00

E23-7   *You are given below some financial data for Lark Company:*

Total assets	$500,000
Income taxes	20,000
Sales	600,000
Interest expense	5,000
Common stockholders' equity	200,000
Preferred dividends	10,000
Net income before income taxes	50,000

(a) Calculate the rate of return on common stockholders' equity. (Show all of your calculations.)

(b) Calculate the rate of return on total assets.

(c) Calculate the rate of return on sales.

(d) Can you make any generalizations about the results of your rate-of-return calculations?

E23-8   *Assume that you are analyzing a company to determine whether you should make a short-term loan. Further assume that you have calculated some ratios, given below, to help you determine whether the loan should be granted. Considering only the ratios given, would you lend the company money? Discuss.*

	19_4	19_3	19_2	19_1
Current ratio	3 to 1	2.5 to 1	2.2 to 1	2 to 1
Acid test	.7 to 1	.85 to 1	.9 to 1	1 to 1
Inventory turnover	5	6	7	8
Accounts receivable turnover	4	5	6	7

Problems

A23-1   *State whether each of the transactions below the three given ratios increases, decreases, or has no effect on the ratio, and then in four or five sentences explain why.*

(1) Current ratio:
  (a) Inventory was purchased on account.
  (b) A cash dividend on common stock was declared.
  (c) An account payable was paid.
  (d) A building was sold at a loss.

(2) Earnings per share on common stock:
  (a) The common stock was split 2-for-1.
  (b) A 10 per cent stock (not cash) dividend was issued.
  (c) A cash dividend on preferred stock was declared.
  (d) A reserve for a pending law suit was appropriated from retained earnings.

(3) Number of days uncollectible.
  (a) An uncollectible account receivable was written off against the allowance account.
  (b) The accounts receivable turnover is increasing.
  (c) An account receivable was collected.
  (d) The entry for estimated bad debts was made at year end.

A23-2   *Following are the financial statements of KBC Company:*

KBC COMPANY
Comparative Balance Sheets
December 31, 19_5 and 19_4

	19_5	19_4
Assets:		
Current assets:		
Cash	$ 10,000	$ 14,900
Marketable securities	150,000	70,000
Accounts receivable	100,000	80,000
Inventory	200,000	150,000
Total current assets	$460,000	$314,900
Long-lived assets:		
Plant and equipment	$400,000	$400,000
Accumulated depreciation	300,000	280,000
Net	$100,000	$120,000
Total long-lived assets	$100,000	$120,000
	$560,000	$434,900
Equities:		
Current liabilities:		
Accounts payable	$150,000	$ 80,000
Taxes payable	50,000	30,000
Total current liabilities	$200,000	$110,000
Long-term liabilities:		
Bonds payable—6%	$100,000	$100,000
Stockholders' equity:		
Preferred stock—5%	$ 50,000	$ 50,000
Common stock—10,000 shares	100,000	100,000
Capital in excess of par	20,000	20,000
Retained earnings	90,000	54,900
Total stockholders' equity	$260,000	$224,900
	$560,000	$434,900

KBC COMPANY
Income Statement
For the Year Ended December 31, 19_5

Sales	$405,000
Cost of goods sold	262,500
Gross margin	$142,500
Operating expenses	91,500
Net operating income	$ 51,000
Other expense:	
Interest expense	3,000
Net income before income taxes	$ 48,000
Income taxes	19,200
Net income	$ 28,800

Depreciation expense for the year 19_5 was $20,000.

Required:

(a) Calculate the following ratios for the year 19_5:

    (1) Current ratio.

    (2) Acid-test ratio.

    (3) Accounts receivable turnover.

(4) Number of days uncollectible (assume a 360-day year).

(5) Inventory turnover.

(6) Number of times interest earned.

(7) Earnings per share (common stock).

(8) Rate of return on common stockholders' equity.

(9) Rate of return on total assets.

(10) Total debt to stockholders' equity.

(b) What was working capital from operations for 19_5?

A23-3

For the years 19_1, 19_2, and 19_3, Wells, Inc., experienced a declining inventory turnover, so that management had been contemplating a reduction of its inventory purchases. However, during 19_4 management increased selling prices and the inventory turnover increased over that of 19_3. Management now believes that the increase in the inventory turnover for 19_4 indicates that there is no need to reduce inventory purchases and that the existing inventory position should be maintained.

Given the data below, evaluate management's policy with regard to maintaining the existing inventory position.

	19_4	19_3	19_2	19_1
Sales	$190,000	$160,000	$180,000	$200,000
Cost of goods sold	114,000	128,000	144,000	160,000
Gross margin	$ 76,000	$ 32,000	$ 36,000	$ 40,000
Inventory	$ 60,000	$ 60,000	$ 60,000	$ 60,000

A23-4

Mr. Rabbit has narrowed down his investment decision to buying the common stock of either Company K or Company U. His stockbroker has provided him with the following financial data about the two companies:

	19_4	19_3	19_2	19_1
Company K:				
Net income after taxes	$ 850,000	$ 740,000	$ 660,000	$ 600,000
Dividends on common stock	510,000	444,000	396,000	360,000
Market price per common share				
(50,000 shares outstanding)	170	118	92	72
Total stockholders' equity	4,250,400	4,106,666	4,125,000	4,000,000
Company U:				
Net income after taxes	$ 89,700	$ 69,000	$ 57,500	$ 50,000
Dividends on common stock	17,940	13,800	11,500	10,000
Market price per common share				
(20,000 shares outstanding)	89.50	52	29	12.50
Total stockholders' equity	598,000	431,250	319,444	250,000

The stockbroker recommends that Mr. Rabbit buy the common stock of Company U because of its growth potential. He points out that the net income of Company U has increased 30, 20, and 15 per cent, respectively, over the last three years. In contrast, the net income of Company K has increased 15, 12, and 10 per cent, respectively, over the last three years.

Required:

Prepare an analysis of each company and discuss your findings in relation to the stockbroker's recommendation. Round ratios to the nearest whole per cent.

A23-5   Given the financial data below, reconstruct the balance sheet and the income statement for Gordon Company.

GORDON COMPANY
Balance Sheet
December 31, 19_9

Assets		Equities	
Current assets:		Current liabilities	$?
Cash	$?		
Marketable securities	?	Long-term liabilities:	
Net accounts receivable	25,000	Bonds payable—6%	$
Inventories	?		
Total current assets	$?	Stockholders' equity:	
		Common stock	$200,000
Long-lived assets:		Retained earnings	400,000
Net plant and equipment	$?	Total stockholders' equity	$600,000
Total assets	$?	Total equities	$?

GORDON COMPANY
Income Statement
For the Year Ended December 31, 19_9

Net sales	$?
Cost of goods sold	?
Gross margin	$432,000
Operating expenses	?
Operating income	$?
Other expense:	
Interest expense	?
Net income before taxes	$?
Income taxes (50% rate)	?
Net income	$?

Other financial data for the year 19_9 include the following:

(1) The total debt to common stockholders' equity was 50 per cent.

(2) The average number of days to collect the accounts receivable was 40 (based on a 360-day year). The beginning accounts receivable balance was $150,000.

(3) The inventory turnover was 3 times. The beginning inventory balance was $335,000.

(4) Gross margin was 20 per cent of net sales.

(5) Interest was earned 18 times.

(6) The acid-test ratio was 2.24. (Use as a check of final answers.)

(7) Operating expenses were 10 per cent of net sales.

(*Hint:* Use the ratio formulas to solve for unknowns.)

Condensed financial data of Scow Company are presented below.

SCOW COMPANY
Comparative Income Statements
For the Years Ended December 31, 19_1–19_6
(in thousands of dollars)

	19_6	19_5	19_4	19_3	19_2	19_1
Net sales	$250	$230	$200	$160	$130	$100
Cost of goods sold	200	180	160	125	100	80
Gross margin	$ 50	$ 50	$ 40	$ 35	$ 30	$ 20
Other expenses	45	40	25	15	7	5
Net income	$ 5	$ 10	$ 15	$ 20	$ 23	$ 15

Note: Other expenses include interest, taxes, depreciation, etc.

SCOW COMPANY
Comparative Balance Sheets
December 31, 19_1–19_6

	19_6	19_5	19_4	19_3	19_2	19_1
Assets:						
Cash	$250	$160	$100	$ 60	$ 30	$ 10
Accounts receivable	70	60	50	15	10	10
Inventory	30	20	30	15	20	10
Net plant and equipment	150	160	180	110	100	70
Total assets	$500	$400	$360	$200	$160	$100
Equities:						
Accounts payable	$ 80	$ 70	$ 60	$ 30	$ 20	$ 10
Bonds payable—10%	240	150	120	30	20	10
Common stock	130	130	130	100	90	60
Retained earnings	50	50	50	40	30	20
Total equities	$500	$400	$360	$200	$160	$100

Required:

(a) Select a set of ratios and compute a five-year trend starting with 19_2.

(b) Analyze and comment on the financial strengths and/or weaknesses illustrated by Scow Company.

The following are the financial statements of Sharp Company:

SHARP COMPANY
Comparative Balance Sheets
December 31, 19_8 and 19_7

	19_8	19_7
Assets:		
Current assets:		
Cash	$ 40,000	$ 60,000
Marketable securities	48,000	40,000
Accounts receivable	120,000	80,000
Inventory	200,000	160,000
Total current assets	$408,000	$340,000
Long-lived assets:		
Plant and equipment	$400,000	$400,000
Accumulated depreciation	320,000	300,000
Net	$ 80,000	$100,000
Total long-lived assets	$ 80,000	$100,000
	$488,000	$440,000
Equities:		
Current liabilities:		
Accounts payable	$ 60,000	$ 40,000
Taxes payable	40,000	80,000
Total current liabilities	$100,000	$120,000
Long-term liabilities:		
Mortgage bonds—5¼%	$160,000	$160,000
Stockholders' equity:		
Preferred stock—6%	$ 40,000	$ 40,000
Common stock[a]	100,000	100,000
Retained earnings	88,000	20,000
Total stockholders' equity	$228,000	$160,000
	$488,000	$440,000

[a]Common shares outstanding were 500 for the years 19_8 and 19_7.

SHARP COMPANY
Income Statement
For the Year Ended December 31, 19_8

Net sales		$480,000
Cost of goods sold:		
Beginning inventory	$160,000	
Purchases	240,000	
Goods available for sale	$400,000	
Ending inventory	200,000	200,000
Gross margin		$280,000
Operating expenses:		
Selling expense	$ 60,000	
General and administrative expense	80,000	140,000
Net operating income		$140,000
Other expense:		
Interest expense		8,400
Net income before taxes		$131,600
Income taxes		59,600
Net income		$ 72,000

Required:

Calculate the following ratios for the year 19_8:

(a) Current ratio.

(b) Acid-test ratio.

(c) Accounts receivable turnover.

(d) Number of days uncollectibles (assume a 360-day year).

(e) Inventory turnover.

(f) Number of times interest earned.

(g) Earnings per share (common stock).

(h) Rate of return on common stockholders' equity.

(i) Rate of return on total assets.

(j) Total debt to stockholders' equity.

B23-2

You are given below an abbreviated balance sheet of Pick Company:

PICK COMPANY
Balance Sheet
December 31, 19_4

Assets		Equities	
Total assets	$2,000,000	Current liabilities	$ 100,000
		Long-term liabilities:	
		Bonds payable—8%	$ 700,000
		Stockholders' equity:	
		Preferred stock—7%	$ 400,000
		Common stock	600,000
		Retained earnings	200,000
			$1,200,000
	$2,000,000		$2,000,000

Required:

(a) Assume that Pick Company had a 6 per cent rate of return on total assets for the year ended December 31, 19_4 and that the 7 per cent preferred dividend was paid. What was the rate of return on common stockholders' equity?

(b) Explain what caused the difference between the 6 per cent rate of return on total assets and the rate of return on common stockholders' equity calculated in part (a).

(c) Assume that Pick Company had a 9 per cent rate of return on total assets for the year ended December 31, 19_4, and that the 7 per cent preferred dividend was paid. What was the rate of return on common stockholders' equity?

(d) Explain what caused the difference between the 9 per cent rate of return on total assets and the rate of return on common stockholders' equity calculated in part (c).

B23-3

Following are condensed balance sheets for Opal Company for the years 19_3 and 19_2:

OPAL COMPANY
Comparative Balance Sheets
December 31, 19_3 and 19_2

	19_3	19_2
Assets:		
Current assets	$ 985,000	$ 550,000
Long-lived assets	4,795,000	5,185,000
	$5,780,000	$5,735,000
Equities:		
Current liabilities	$ 480,000	$ 240,000
Long-term liabilities:		
Notes payable—5%	$1,220,000	$1,660,000
Stockholders' equity:		
Common stock—100,000 shares	$1,500,000	$1,500,000
Additional paid-in capital	1,800,000	1,800,000
Retained earnings	780,000	535,000
Total stockholders' equity	$4,080,000	$3,835,000
	$5,780,000	$5,735,000
Common stock dividends per share	$ 2.00	$ 1.62

For the year 19_2 net income after taxes was $380,000. The common stock was selling for $46.50 and $56.00, respectively, for the years 19_2 and 19_3.

Required:

(a) Calculate earnings per share for both years.

(b) Calculate the price-earnings ratio for both years.

(c) Calculate the pay-out ratio for both years.

(d) Calculate the dividend yield on common stock for both years.

B23-4 *The comparative income statements for Ratio, Inc., are presented below:*

RATIO, INC.
Comparative Income Statements
For the Years Ended December 31, 19_2–19_4

	19_4		19_3		19_2	
Sales		$1,500,000		$1,125,500		$787,500
Cost of goods sold:						
Beginning inventory	$ 175,000		$ 200,000		$150,000	
Purchases	1,250,000		823,750		575,000	
Goods available for sale	$1,425,000		$1,023,750		$725,000	
Ending inventory	225,000	1,200,000	175,000	848,750	200,000	525,000
Gross margin		$ 300,000		$ 276,750		$262,500
Operating expenses		147,500		135,000		126,000
Net income		$ 152,500		$ 141,750		$136,500

A stockbroker friend of yours cannot understand how the sales of Ratio, Inc., increased 47.5 per cent from 19_2 to 19_4 while net income increased only 9.9 per cent. The stockbroker hires you to analyze the above income statements and to tell your friend some possible reasons why net income did not increase more than it did.

Using the financial data at the bottom of page 693 only, prepare a written report for the stockbroker explaining why the great increase in sales did not result in a great increase in net income.

B23-5 Ty Corporation had a fire during January, 19_4, that destroyed most of its accounting records. Management asks you to try to prepare a balance sheet and an income statement for the year ended December 31, 19_3. You have been able to uncover the following accounting data:

TY CORPORATION
Balance Sheet
December 31, 19_3

Assets			Equities		
Current assets:			Current liabilities:		
Cash	$	?	Accounts payable	$	?
Accounts receivable		?	Long-term liabilities:		
Inventory		?	Notes payable—5%	$	?
Total current assets	$	?	Stockholders' equity:		
			Common stock		$200,000
Long-lived assets:			Retained earnings		300,000
Net plant and equipment	$	?	Total		$500,000
Total assets	$	?	Total equities	$	?

TY CORPORATION
Income Statement
For the Year Ended December 31, 19_3

Net sales		$2,250,000
Cost of goods sold		?
Gross margin	$	?
Operating expenses		?
Net operating income	$	?
Other expense:		
Interest expense		?
Net income before taxes	$	?
Income tax (40% rate)		?
Net income	$	?

Other financial data:

(1) Accounts receivable at the beginning of 19_3 were $125,000 and, based on a 360-day year, it took 20 days to collect accounts receivable during 19_3.

(2) Gross margin was 25 per cent of sales for 19_3.

(3) Inventory at the beginning of 19_3 was $237,500, and the inventory turnover for 19_3 was 6.75.

(4) Total debt to equity for 19_3 was 50 per cent.

(5) For 19_3, operating expenses were 8 per cent of sales.

(6) Interest was earned 38.25 times during 19_3.

(7) The acid-test ratio for 19_3 was 3.75.

Required:

Reconstruct the December 31, 19_3 balance sheet and the income statement for the year 19_3 using the financial data at the bottom of page 694 only. (Hint: Use the financial ratio formulas to solve for unknowns.)

B23-6   *Condensed financial data of Sellers Corporation is presented below:*

SELLERS CORPORATION
Comparative Income Statements
For the Years Ended December 31, 19_1–19_6
(in millions of dollars)

	19_6	19_5	19_4	19_3	19_2	19_1
Net sales	$980	$950	$900	$890	$750	$600
Cost of goods sold	730	680	650	600	500	450
Gross margin	$250	$270	$250	$290	$250	$150
Other expenses	220	210	180	150	140	125
Net income	$ 30	$ 60	$ 70	$140	$110	$ 25

SELLERS CORPORATION
Comparative Balance Sheets
December 31, 19_1–19_6
(in millions of dollars)

	19_6	19_5	19_4	19_3	19_2	19_1
Assets:						
Cash	$ 5	$ 10	$ 15	$ 25	$ 20	$ 20
Accounts receivable	100	100	100	60	60	60
Inventory	205	200	190	115	110	100
Plant and equipment	470	470	455	320	310	300
Total assets	$780	$780	$760	$520	$500	$480
Equities:						
Accounts payable	$120	$110	$100	$ 60	$ 60	$ 50
Bonds payable—10%	190	180	170	80	70	60
Common stock	350	350	340	230	230	230
Retained earnings	120	140	150	150	140	140
Total equities	$780	$780	$760	$520	$500	$480

Required:

(a) Select a set of ratios and compute a five-year trend starting with 19_2.

(b) Analyze and comment on the financial strengths and/or weaknesses illustrated by Sellers Corporation.

INCOME TAX CONSIDERATIONS
CHAPTER 24

PURPOSE OF CHAPTER The impact of income tax laws and regulations upon business decisions is very significant. Frequently, such decisions are made with primary emphasis upon the income tax implications. Although the preparation of financial statements for external reporting purposes is not governed by the tax laws, the statements are often affected by accounting methods reflecting a firm's desire to minimize income taxes. This chapter is devoted to a short history of the federal income tax and its purposes, a brief discussion of how tax rules are applied, and a more lengthy discussion of some areas that are of particular concern to both the accountant and the business executive.

THE USEFULNESS OF INCOME TAX KNOWLEDGE Obviously, knowledge of income taxes is a must for the tax specialist—attorney or accountant. But anyone faced with the necessity of making business decisions needs more than accounting data and the ability to evaluate such data; he also needs an awareness of the tax consequences of his decisions. The decision-maker can, and in some complex cases should, rely on the tax specialist for an appraisal of tax consequences. But the better the tax background of managers of business, the greater is their ability to understand and profit from the advice and counsel of the tax specialist.

Those interested in financial statements will find their comprehension level improved by an appreciation of the impact of income taxes on business. Stockholders and investors become more knowledgeable in the pursuit of their interests when they have developed a sensitivity to income taxes. The majority of adults, without regard to occupation or source of income, are involved with income taxes as taxpayers. Furthermore, income tax rules and regulations are such that informed taxpayers often can, through various proper and timely actions, affect the amount of their tax liability.

The magnitude of the income tax collections makes it desirable for the thoughtful citizen to have some familiarity with the subject. There are broad and vital considerations that should concern everyone. For instance, what is the impact of high income tax rates on individual initiative? How does the income tax relate to the size of the federal government and its role in the economic affairs of the nation in such areas as employment levels and price stability? Indeed, the question may well be put, who would not benefit from some exposure to the topic of income taxes?

With such considerations in mind, the remainder of the chapter will be devoted to a short history of the federal income tax and its purposes, a brief discussion of how tax rules are applied, and a more lengthy discussion of some areas that are of particular concern to both the accountant and the business manager.

THE HISTORY OF THE FEDERAL INCOME TAX   Although a federal income tax was proposed as early as 1815 and such a tax was actually collected during the War Between the States, the history of the present law properly begins with the Revenue Act of 1894. In the historic case of *Pollack v. The Farmer's Loan and Trust Company,* the Supreme Court held that the tax under this law was unconstitutional. The Constitution provides that "no capitation or other direct tax shall be laid, unless in proportion to the census or enumeration hereinbefore directed to be taken." Obviously, an income tax cannot be apportioned as required by this provision. For example, no one can say that the amount of tax collected in one state whose population entitles it to 30 representatives will be three times as great as the amount of tax collected in another whose population entitles it to 10 representatives.

The Court found that the income tax at issue was a direct tax in the constitutional sense and hence invalid. Thus it was established that a federal income tax could come into being only through an amendment to the Constitution. The necessary amendment, the Sixteenth, was passed by Congress in 1909 and was ratified by the required number of state legislatures early in 1913. The Sixteenth Amendment gave Congress the "power to lay and collect taxes on incomes, from whatever source derived without apportionment . . . and without regard to any census or enumeration." The government lost little time in tapping this source with the Revenue Act of 1913. Since that time, many revenue acts and other laws containing tax provisions have been enacted. The most recent of these acts at the time of this printing is the Revenue Act of 1978.

The original purpose of the income tax was simply to raise revenue. But over the course of time, the goals of the income tax laws have been broadened to include nonrevenue objectives such as the following:

(1)   Redistribution of national income
(2)   Control of inflation or deflation
(3)   Attainment of full employment
(4)   Encouragement of foreign trade
(5)   Economic stimuli to certain industries
(6)   Granting of subsidies for noneconomic purposes
(7)   Growth of small businesses

Just as the objectives of the income tax have kept expanding, so, too, the rate of taxation has been increasing. Back in 1913, the normal rate for individuals was 1 per cent; the *minimum* is now 14 per cent. The combined normal and surtax in 1913 was only 7 per cent on incomes over $1,000,000; today the rate for an unmarried individual is 70 per cent on taxable income in excess of $108,300. Although there have been many refinements of the tax law through the years, this marked increase in tax rates has been the most significant development.

Almost as significant as the increase in rates has been the broadening of the tax base so that more and more income has been taxed. Broadening the tax base is viewed by many as the most effective means of obtaining greater amounts of tax revenue.

As a consequence of the increase in rates and the broadening of the base, there has been a sharp rise in the number of returns filed and the amount of revenue collected. With the government's increased reliance on the income tax as the prime source of revenue, the federal income tax gives every sign of being with us permanently.

A profile view of federal income taxes

Before the accountant or businessman can appreciate the impact of federal income taxes, he must acquire some general knowledge of basic income-tax concepts. To provide this background, some of the income tax fundamentals—the classes of taxpayers, tax rates, gross income, deductions, taxable income, and other concepts—are briefly presented.

CLASSES OF TAXPAYERS There are four major classes of taxable entities, or kinds of taxpayers: individuals, corporations, estates, and trusts. Each of these must file a tax return.

Partnerships and sole proprietorships are not taxable entities, even though they are separate business entities for accounting purposes. Their income is taxed to the individual owners involved. A partnership has to file a return, but it is for information only, showing how the partners shared the income.

Corporations, on the other hand, are taxed separately. Individual stockholders who receive after-tax profits from the corporation in the form of dividends must report those dividends in their own individual returns. As a consequence, this portion of corporate profits is subject to double taxation.

Corporations that meet certain qualifications can avoid the separate corporate tax by electing to be treated as a partnership for tax purposes. Such partnership-type corporations are commonly referred to as *Subchapter S corporations,* from the portion of the Internal Revenue Code that affords them the election.

INCOME TAX RATES Although there are four kinds of taxable entities, there are only two rate structures, the individual and the corporate. Estates, trusts, and individuals use the individual rate structure.

The federal individual income tax is a progressive tax. This means that those with the lowest taxable income are subject to the lowest rates, while those with higher taxable incomes are subjected to progressively higher tax rates. There is general agreement that the United States income tax rate structure is steeply progressive. Rates go from 14 per cent all the way to 70 per cent. A glance at a schedule of tax rates will show how this works.

INCOME TAX RATES FOR 1979 AND FOLLOWING YEARS FOR MARRIED TAXPAYERS FILING JOINT RETURNS AND CERTAIN SURVIVING SPOUSES

. . . .

Taxable income	Tax (before credits)
$ 0 to $ 3,400	No tax
3,400 to 5,500	14% of excess over $ 3,400
5,500 to 7,600	$ 294, plus 16% of excess over 5,500
7,600 to 11,900	630, plus 18% of excess over 7,600
11,900 to 16,000	1,404, plus 21% of excess over 11,900
16,000 to 20,200	2,265, plus 24% of excess over 16,000
20,200 to 24,600	3,273, plus 28% of excess over 20,200
24,600 to 29,900	4,505, plus 32% of excess over 24,600
29,900 to 35,200	6,201, plus 37% of excess over 29,900
35,200 to 45,800	8,162, plus 43% of excess over 35,200
45,800 to 60,000	12,720, plus 49% of excess over 45,800
60,000 to 85,600	19,678, plus 54% of excess over 60,000
85,600 to 109,400	33,502, plus 59% of excess over 85,600
109,400 to 162,400	47,544, plus 64% of excess over 109,400
162,400 to 215,400	81,464, plus 68% of excess over 162,400
215,400 and over	117,504, plus 70% of excess over 215,400

It should be noted from the tax rate schedule above that there is an important difference between the marginal tax rate on an additional increment of taxable income and the average tax rate on total taxable income. For example, assume that a taxpayer using the table above has taxable income of $60,000. The total tax bill is calculated as follows:

Tax on taxable income of $45,800	$12,720
Tax on taxable income of $14,200	
($60,000 − $45,800): $14,200 × 49%	6,958
Total tax	$19,678

The taxpayer's marginal tax rate, which is the rate paid on the last increment of taxable income, is 49 per cent. However, the average tax rate on total taxable income is approximately 33 per cent ($19,678 ÷ $60,000).

With the enactment of the Tax Reform Act of 1969, Congress provided for a maximum marginal tax rate of 50 per cent on personal service taxable income, now referred to as earned income. For purposes of the maximum tax calculation, earned income includes wages, salaries, professional fees, compensation for services, income from pensions and annuities, and deferred compensation. For example, according to the tax rate schedule above, a taxpayer with earned taxable income of $95,000 would be taxed at a marginal tax rate of 50 per cent, while a taxable income of the same amount, but from sources that did not qualify for the maximum tax rate provisions, would be taxed at a marginal rate of 59 per cent.

The progressive tax is designed to accomplish an equitable distribution of the burden of taxation by distributing the tax load according to the ability to pay. The progressive income tax also helps create economic stability. Inflationary and deflationary trends are minimized; an inflationary expansion of income is dampened by an automatic increase in taxes and a decrease in personal income is softened by an automatic reduction in taxes which results in a smaller decline in disposable income. These are the advantages pointed out by supporters of the progressive tax rates.

The progressive income tax also has many critics. They charge that the progressive tax discourages personal initiative by minimizing incentives. For example, suppose that a married executive is currently earning taxable income of $45,000. The tax bill is calculated as follows, using the tax rate schedule on page 699.

Tax on taxable income of $35,200	$ 8,162
Tax on taxable income of $9,800	
($45,000 − $35,200): $9,800 × 43%	4,214
Total tax	$12,376
Average tax rate ($12,376 ÷ $45,000)	27.5%

Now assume the executive is offered a more responsible position having an annual taxable income of $55,000. The new tax bill is calculated below:

Tax on taxable income of $45,800	$12,720
Tax on taxable income of $9,200	
($55,000 − $45,800): $9,200 × 49%	4,508
Total tax	$17,228
Average tax rate ($17,228 ÷ $55,000)	31.3%

With this small increase in average tax rates, the executive might feel that the salary increase is worth the added work and responsibility. But the executive might feel differently if he or she judges the salary increase in terms of marginal tax rates; every dollar of taxable income that the executive makes over $47,200 will be taxed at a 49 per cent rate. Since the executive could keep only 51 per cent of the raise, he or she might not feel that the new position is worth it. The higher up the income ladder one goes, the more one encounters this situation subject to the previously mentioned maximum tax on personal service income provision. Whether the progressive tax discourages initiative to the degree some claim it does is open to debate, but there is no doubt that it promotes the search for tax-exempt and tax-favored income.

The schedule on page 699 is not the only tax schedule. Married persons filing separate tax returns use a different schedule wherein the dollar amount of the brackets are less than the bracket amounts in the joint schedule.

Further, schedules are provided for (1) single persons and (2) so-called heads-of-household. Some additional relief is granted heads-of-household.

Compared to the individual tax rate tables, corporate taxation is quite simple. The applicable tax rates are summarized below.

Taxable income	Rate
First $25,000	17%
Next $25,000	20%
Next $25,000	30%
Next $25,000	40%
Excess over $100,000	46%

For example, assume a corporation has taxable income of $150,000 for the year. The tax bill calculation is as follows:

First $25,000 × 17%	$ 4,250
Next $25,000 × 20%	5,000
Next $25,000 × 30%	7,500
Next $25,000 × 40%	10,000
Next $50,000 × 46%	23,000
Total tax	$49,750
Average tax rate ($49,750 ÷ $150,000)	33.2%

In the same way that the marginal tax has an impact on individual decisions; it also affects corporate decisions. For example, a corporate taxable income of $55,000 is taxed at a marginal tax rate of 30 per cent and $1,500 ($5,000 × 30%) of the last $5,000 of taxable income must be paid in taxes. If the corporation can somehow defer the $5,000 until a later year when the total taxable income is between $25,000 and $50,000, taxes of only $1,000 ($5,000 × 20%) will have to be paid on the $5,000.

INDIVIDUAL GROSS INCOME As defined in the Internal Revenue Code, *gross income* includes "all income from whatever source derived." This general definition is somewhat misleading; there are many items that do not constitute income for tax purposes. Among them are gifts, bequests, social security benefits, certain money damages, and other items. Of course, most of the money an individual receives is included. Wages, dividends, business income, rents, bonuses, and tips are all subject to the income tax.

DEDUCTIONS Certain expenses can be subtracted from the taxpayer's gross income in computing his net taxable income; these are called *income tax deductions.* These deductions are of two types: (1) deductions from gross income to arrive at adjusted gross income and (2) deductions from adjusted gross income to arrive at net taxable income.

The deductions from gross income are generally of a business nature. They include expenses for salaries and wages paid, advertising, depreciation, expenses attributable to earning rents, losses from the sale of property, and certain other expenses. By subtracting these deductions from gross income, the taxpayer determines his adjusted gross income.

The next step is to compute taxable income by subtracting deductions from adjusted gross income. This involves the deduction of certain nonbusiness expenses such as contributions, taxes, interest, casualty and theft losses, and medical and dental expenses. The zero bracket amount[1] is an important part of this calculation. The zero bracket amount was provided for in the Tax Reduction and Simplification Act of 1977 and replaces the percentage standard deduction previously available to taxpayers. The zero bracket amount is based on the filing status of the taxpayer without regard to the amount of income, as follows:

Filing status	Zero bracket amount
Married, filing jointly, or a qualifying widow or widower	$3,400
Single, or an unmarried head-of-household	2,300
Married, filing separately	1,700

[1]Each of the tax rate schedules referred to previously has a tax rate of zero for the lowest bracket in the schedule. The amount in this lowest bracket is referred to as the *zero bracket amount.* For example, see the schedule on page 699 in which the amount in the zero bracket is $3,400.

All taxpayers are entitled to the zero bracket amount. They may also elect to claim excess itemized deductions in addition to the zero bracket amount.

In addition to the deductions mentioned in the preceding paragraph, every taxpayer is allowed to claim his or her own personal exemption. A taxpayer may be allowed to claim an additional exemption for his or her spouse. Additional exemptions are allowed for dependents (minor children are typical dependents), with additional exemptions for old age (over 65) and blindness. The deduction is presently $1,000 for each exemption.

COMPUTATION OF TAX   The way in which a taxpayer determines the amount of his or her tax was altered by the Tax Reduction and Simplification Act of 1977. The Act introduced the concept of Tax Table Income by providing tax tables that generally must be used by those taxpayers whose tax table income is not in excess of the ceiling amount specified in the table and whose exemptions do not exceed the number specified in the table. Thus taxpayers who use the tables will not have to compute the total dollar amount of personal and dependency exemptions, their taxable income, or the amount of their general tax credits. The major advantage of using the tables is the reduced likelihood of computational errors on the part of taxpayers. Taxpayers not qualified to use the tax tables must use tax rate schedules provided by the Internal Revenue Service.

Once the tax is determined by using either the tax tables or tax rate schedules, this is the amount that must be paid, unless the taxpayer is eligible for certain credits to be subtracted from this figure. Examples include a credit allowed elderly taxpayers equal to a stated per cent of certain classes of "retirement" income, credit for foreign taxes paid, and the investment tax credit, which pertains primarily to machinery and equipment used in a trade or business.

CAPITAL GAINS AND LOSSES   One of the most interesting and important aspects of our tax system is the special tax treatment of gains and losses from the sale of *capital assets.* This special treatment results in a tax that is sometimes one-half (and often less than half) of what the tax would be on a like amount of ordinary income. Because of this special treatment, most taxpayers and their advisers make an effort to get capital gains income instead of ordinary income. Although the ways of doing this are varied and complex, here is a thumbnail sketch of the capital-gains-and-losses situation.

The tax statute defines capital assets. The definition does not correspond very closely with business, economic, or accounting terminology. The capital assets most commonly held by taxpayers include shares of stock, bonds, a personal residence, and land. Business inventories are *not* capital assets.

The next question is how to measure capital gain and loss. Gain (or loss) is measured by the difference between the selling price and the capital asset's "basis." Basis rules are very complicated. For our purposes, we shall use the most common standard of basis, the cost of purchased property.

Another requirement for special tax treatment is that the capital gains must be long-term gains. In tax terms, this means that the assets must have been held for more than one year prior to sale.[2]

Only *net* long-term capital gains are given special treatment. Very specific rules are followed to arrive at net capital gain and loss figures. These so-called "offsetting" rules are necessarily subjects for a tax manual. For our purposes, keep in mind that, in general, long-term gains are offset by long-term losses and short-term gains by short-term losses.

Here is an example of a capital gains situation: The taxpayer buys a share of Big Steel (a capital asset) at $40 (the basis). The taxpayer also buys a share of Telephone at $60 (the basis). Fifteen months later the taxpayer sells Big Steel for $70 and Telephone for $50. Result: Taxpayer has a long-term capital gain of $30 on Big Steel ($70 minus $40) and a long-term capital loss of $10 on Telephone ($60 minus $50). After offsetting these two figures, the taxpayer has a net long-term capital gain of $20.

If capital losses exceed capital gains, so that there is a net capital loss, the loss can be used to offset up to $3,000 of the taxpayer's other taxable income each year.[3] Any net capital losses (subject to the same limitation) that are not used fully can be carried forward and used in succeeding years.

The tax law for capital gains is tailored to meet a certain purpose. By holding down the tax on capital gains, capital investment is encouraged and the whole economy benefits.

CORPORATE TAXATION The corporation is taxed generally in the same way as an individual: Gross income less allowable deductions equals net taxable income. Aside from the deductions which are obviously not applicable to corporations (personal exemptions), there are other important differences:

(1) The capital gain subject to tax is computed differently, but the tax is limited to 28 per cent of the gain.
(2) There is a more stringent limit on corporate deductions for charitable contributions.
(3) Dividends received are treated much more liberally in corporate tax returns than for individuals.
(4) There are also other special deductions that corporations are allowed to take: organizational expenses; a percentage of dividends received from certain foreign corporations; and others.

Aside from these basic differences, corporate taxable income equals gross income minus the usual deductions.

Corporations engaged in a trade or business are permitted to carry back losses or carry them forward. For example, should a company suffer a net loss of $50,000 in 19_8, the loss can be carried back to 19_5 and deducted from the earnings of that year. The 19_5 income tax is refigured and the difference between the tax paid and the revised tax for 19_5 is refunded.

Losses may be carried back and deducted from the earnings of the three preceding years. But suppose that the 19_8 loss is greater than the earnings of the

[2]For many years the asset must have been held for more than six months prior to sale. The Tax Reform Act of 1976 changed the holding period to more than nine months for tax years beginning in 1977 and to more than one year for tax years beginning in 1978 and later.

[3]The $3,000 was effective beginning in 1978. Prior to that time the amounts were $2,000 for 1977 and $1,000 for previous years.

three preceding years? Any unused loss may then be carried forward and deducted from earnings of the next seven years. If a company's losses exceed the earnings of the three preceding years, with the result that the company has a loss carryforward, future earnings equal to the loss carryforward are tax-free. This tax status can be a matter of considerable importance when future earnings prospects of a currently unprofitable company are evaluated.

The operation of the carryback-carryforward provisions is illustrated in the following table, in which a company that was profitable during the years 19_5 through 19_7 turns unprofitable for 19_8 and 19_9.

	19_5	19_6	19_7	19_8	19_9
Taxable income (loss*)	$10,000	$15,000	$5,000	$50,000*	$25,000*
Loss carryback	10,000*	15,000*	5,000*	30,000	
Loss carryforward				$20,000*	$45,000*

If the company should earn $45,000 during the next two years, there would be no income tax on the earnings because of the carryforward privilege.

Business income versus taxable income

Taxable income is a statutory concept that is governed by considerations of public policy; business income follows the generally accepted principles of accounting. Taxable income is computed for one purpose, the payment of taxes; business income is designed to measure the results of operations. Even though both are termed "income," the dissimilar objectives of the two income concepts cause real differences. Many think that there should be greater conformity. For example, a committee of the American Accounting Association stated that "the interest of government, business and the public would best be served if the definition of business income subject to tax were made as nearly as possible coincidental with net income under generally accepted accounting principles." It will be quite some time before these differences are reconciled, if ever.

Tax returns can depart from income statements in two principal ways: (1) some items of revenue and expense that are properly included in the computation of business income are excluded from the computation of taxable income; and (2) a taxpayer can elect to report certain items of revenue or expense in his tax return differently from the way he reports them in his income statement.

The following examples deal more specifically with some of the differences between taxable income and that shown in the books and financial statements.

DIFFERENCES IN CONCEPTS As stated above, the computation of taxable income excludes certain items of business income and expense. These exclusions are dictated by considerations having little relevance to accounting principles. Here is a list of the main exclusions:

(1) Although it is actually business income, interest received on state or municipal bonds is not taxed by the federal government for constitutional reasons.

(2) Only "ordinary and necessary" business expenses are tax deductible. What the Internal Revenue Service means by "ordinary and necessary" does not always coincide with the businessman's interpretation. Result: Some business expenses cannot be deducted for tax purposes.

(3) Only reasonable amounts can be deducted for salaries and other compensation. But for accounting purposes, salaries and wages are considered a business expense no matter how large and unreasonable they are by Internal Revenue Service standards.

(4) Life insurance proceeds are not included in taxable income. On the other hand, deductions for insurance premiums are not allowed.

The government's effort to stimulate investments through tax deductions also contributes to the differences between accounting and taxable income. An example is the percentage depletion allowance. By allowing certain taxpayers a special depletion deduction computed as a percentage of their annual gross income from the exploitation of wasting assets, the government permits these taxpayers to recover more than the original cost of their income-producing property in some cases. This type of depletion has no counterpart in the accounting field.[4]

THE TAXPAYER'S METHOD OF ACCOUNTING   To appreciate how the use of different methods for tax and accounting purposes causes income measurement and reporting problems, we must look into the general rules governing the taxpayer's accounting procedures.

Section 446 of the Code provides that "taxable income shall be computed under the method of accounting on the basis of which the taxpayer regularly computes his income in keeping his books." Generally, the taxpayer uses either the cash method or the accrual method. Whichever one the taxpayer uses, it must "clearly reflect income" or the government will prescribe a method that does. Most businesses use the accrual method.

If Section 446 were the only Code provision dealing with methods of accounting, there would be little problem. The taxpayer's business and taxable income would be kept on the same basis and differences between the two incomes would be confined to the expense and income differences mentioned earlier. But this is not the case.

DIFFERENT METHODS FOR BOOKS AND TAXES   The taxpayer often may, and sometimes must, use an accounting method for tax purposes other than his regular method. In such situations he will use two methods for the same item of income or expense—one method for his books and financial statements and another to determine his taxable income. This practice obviously widens the gap between the two incomes.

Here are two situations in which the taxpayer may be forced to use a different method for tax-computation purposes:

(1) Generally, prepaid income is taxable in the year received; it makes no difference that the taxpayer may be on the accrual basis. For example, advance payments of rent are taxed when received, even though accrual-basis taxpayers do not include them as income in financial statements until the year they are earned.

---

[4]The Tax Reform Act of 1976 curtailed the use of the percentage depletion allowance for oil and gas wells. The current rate is 22 per cent in those situations which now qualify.

(2) Accountants estimate future costs related to current revenue and regard them as current expenses. An example is the cost of performance under warranty and service contracts. In figuring taxable income, whether he is on a cash basis or an accrual basis, the taxpayer is usually not allowed to deduct the future costs until they have become fixed and determinable.

ELECTIVE METHODS The Code also permits the taxpayer to adopt for income tax purposes, with respect to certain specific items, accounting methods that are different from those used in his books and financial statements. These elective methods include the installment sales method, accelerated depreciation, the deferred-payment sales method, various development expenses, and other items.

The LIFO inventory method can be elected for tax purposes, but if it is, it must also be used for accounting purposes.

The installment sales method and accelerated depreciation are two outstanding examples of elective methods.

(1) The installment sales method of reporting income allows taxpayers who receive income from installment sales, and who are using the accrual method in the books and financial statements, to report as income for tax purposes amounts based on collections. This permits an accrual-basis taxpayer, who would otherwise be taxed in the year of sale, to postpone the payment of taxes.

(2) The Code allows a deduction for depreciation in computing taxable income. Two methods of computing depreciation—the straight-line method and the sum of years' digits method—are discussed on page 707. Other accelerated depreciation methods besides the sum of years' digits method are also available. Even though he uses one of the accelerated methods for tax purposes, the taxpayer can continue using the straight-line method in his books. If this is done, there is a difference between taxable and book income.

When one of the elective methods is used, the taxpayer must maintain such records as are necessary to support his determination of taxable income.

FINANCIAL REPORTING PROBLEMS CREATED BY TAX ELECTIONS Whenever a method is elected for tax purposes that is different from that used for accounting purposes, a problem arises in connection with the reporting of net income in the taxpayer's income statement. In particular, the question concerns the proper amount to show for income tax expense. The nature of the problem can be seen if the income of a corporation is computed under two different conditions:

Case A—The company adopts straight-line depreciation for its books and its tax return.
Case B—The company adopts straight-line depreciation for its books and sum of years' digits depreciation for its tax return.

Data for illustration:

Cost of equipment	$150,000
Useful life	5 years
Salvage value	None
Income tax rate[5]	50%

[5]To simplify calculations, it is assumed that all income is taxed at a rate of 50%.

Case A: Same depreciation methods.

	Year					Total for
	1	2	3	4	5	5 years
Net income before depreciation and income tax	$200,000	$200,000	$200,000	$200,000	$200,000	$1,000,000
Depreciation expense— Straight-line	30,000	30,000	30,000	30,000	30,000	150,000
Net income before income tax	$170,000	$170,000	$170,000	$170,000	$170,000	$ 850,000
Income tax expense (50%)	85,000	85,000	85,000	85,000	85,000	425,000
Net income	$ 85,000	$ 85,000	$ 85,000	$ 85,000	$ 85,000	$ 425,000

Case B: Different depreciation methods.

	Year					Total for
	1	2	3	4	5	5 years
Taxable income before depreciation	$200,000	$200,000	$200,000	$200,000	$200,000	$1,000,000
Depreciation—Sum of years' digits	50,000	40,000	30,000	20,000	10,000	150,000
Taxable income	$150,000	$160,000	$170,000	$180,000	$190,000	$ 850,000
Income tax—50%	$ 75,000	$ 80,000	$ 85,000	$ 90,000	$ 95,000	$ 425,000

Income Statement Data
(Assuming for the moment that income tax
expense is the tax shown in the tax return)

	Year					Total for
	1	2	3	4	5	5 years
Net income before depreciation and income tax	$200,000	$200,000	$200,000	$200,000	$200,000	$1,000,000
Depreciation expense— Straight-line	30,000	30,000	30,000	30,000	30,000	150,000
Net income before income tax	$170,000	$170,000	$170,000	$170,000	$170,000	$ 850,000
Income tax expense—per schedule above	75,000	80,000	85,000	90,000	95,000	425,000
Net income	$ 95,000	$ 90,000	$ 85,000	$ 80,000	$ 75,000	$ 425,000

A comparison of the net income amounts in Cases A and B shows that the five-year total is the same, but that the annual amounts have a different pattern. In the Case B situation, investors and creditors would probably be puzzled by the increasing income tax charges and the declining net income, since the income statements would show that the company's business was steady.

In order to avoid such distortion, current accounting practice requires that income tax-allocation procedures be followed.[6] Such procedures require that the

[6]Accounting Principles Board, "Accounting for Income Taxes," *Opinion No. 11* (New York: AICPA, December, 1967).

amount reported on the income statement for income tax expense be determined by applying the current year's tax rate to the pretax income reported in the income statement. For example, in Case B on page 707, the income tax expense reported in the year 1 income statement would be $85,000, determined as follows:

Net income before income tax (per income statement)	*$170,000*
Current year's tax rate	*× 50%*
Income tax expense reported in the income statement	*$ 85,000*

Applying tax-allocation procedures to Case B for each of the five years will remove the earnings distortion and the net income reported in the income statement will agree with that reported in Case A. The accounting for income taxes in Case B, following tax-allocation procedures, is shown by the following entries. Note that in each year the amount credited to the income tax payable account equals the actual tax liability.

Year 1 tax expense:		
Income tax expense	85,000	
Income tax payable		75,000
Deferred income tax		10,000
Tax for year 1 paid:		
Income tax payable	75,000	
Cash		75,000
Year 2 tax expense:		
Income tax expense	85,000	
Income tax payable		80,000
Deferred income tax		5,000
Tax for year 2 paid:		
Income tax payable	80,000	
Cash		80,000
Year 3 tax expense:		
Income tax expense	85,000	
Income tax payable		85,000
Tax for year 3 paid:		
Income tax payable	85,000	
Cash		85,000
Year 4 tax expense:		
Income tax expense	85,000	
Deferred income tax	5,000	
Income tax payable		90,000
Tax for year 4 paid:		
Income tax payable	90,000	
Cash		90,000
Year 5 tax expense:		
Income tax expense	85,000	
Deferred income tax	10,000	
Income tax payable		95,000
Tax for year 5 paid:		
Income tax payable	95,000	
Cash		95,000

The five-year history of the deferred income tax account, which is shown among the liabilities in the balance sheet, is presented below.

DEFERRED INCOME TAX

Year		Year	
4	5,000	1	10,000
5	10,000	2	5,000

The preceding illustration involves differences between accounting income and taxable income due to *timing differences* in the deduction of an item of expense. As noted previously, the total accounting income before taxes for the five-year period is the same as the total taxable income on the income tax returns. However, there is a difference in the pattern of depreciation deductions on the accounting records and the tax returns. In the illustration the timing differences were completely offset over the five-year period. As a practical matter, such differences do not offset each other in total as precisely as indicated by the example.

Many firms have very large credit balances in the deferred income tax account, with the balance increasing steadily over a period of time. One reason for this can be seen by a simple illustration. If the firm in the previous illustration increases its productive capacity by acquiring a larger number of depreciable assets for several periods (one item of equipment in the first year, two in the second year, three in the third year, etc.), this will result in more assets being subject to the higher annual depreciation charge in the early years of asset life than the number subject to the lower charges in later years.

The following question may now be raised: Why would a company want to elect a different method just for income tax purposes if, because of the accountant's use of tax-allocation procedures, the election had no effect on net income? The attraction lies with the difference in timing of cash disbursements for income taxes. The tax payments under Cases A and B are set forth below.

Year	Cash payments for income taxes	
	Case A	Case B
1	$ 85,000	$ 75,000
2	85,000	80,000
3	85,000	85,000
4	85,000	90,000
5	85,000	95,000
	$425,000	$425,000

Given a choice, most businesspeople will select the Case B schedule of payments because it gives them longer use of some of the funds ultimately payable to the government for taxes. Whenever a payment can be postponed without penalty or cost, that alternative will generally appeal to the businessperson.

The impact of income taxes on business decisions

When corporate and individual tax rates were insignificant, businesspeople could afford to make decisions without regard to income taxes. However, for today's businessperson, net income *after* taxes is the primary measure of business success. Therefore, tax economy and planning have become business functions as necessary as marketing, advertising, or sales.

One key fact helps explain why this is so: a tax dollar saved is even more profitable than an extra dollar earned. An extra dollar of income before taxes has to be shared with the tax collector. If, for example, a taxpayer is in the 54 per cent bracket (that is, he must earn a $2.17 profit to retain $1), a tax saving of $1 is worth as much as a $2.17 increase in net operating income. To put it another way, to obtain the same net income effect as that produced by a few hundred or thousand dollars in tax savings, very substantial increases in sales might be required. Assume a tax saving of $10,000. The required increases in sales, assuming various rates of net income, are shown below.

If the company's per cent of net income to sales is	To increase the net income as much as it would be increased by the assumed tax savings, or	The required increase in sales would be
20%	$10,000	$ 50,000
15%	10,000	66,667
10%	10,000	100,000
5%	10,000	200,000
2%	10,000	500,000

With tax dollars at stake in practically every type of business decision, many businesspeople seek guidance from tax specialists. These specialists are usually from the accounting or legal professions. Aside from their importance in terms of dollar savings, tax specialists are often helpful for other reasons.

One reason is that income taxes are sometimes too complicated for the average person. Often it takes a person with time and special training just to fill out the tax return and compute the tax for even a small business.

Another reason is that tax-saving opportunities usually must be recognized when they arise, or they are lost. Again the average businessperson lacks the necessary time and training. If he or she engages a tax specialist, the specialist can plan tax strategies and make sure that no tax-saving opportunities are missed. The businessperson can then implement his adviser's suggestions by making decisions at the right time and in the right way.

EVASION AND AVOIDANCE   Before we go into specific examples of the impact of taxes on business, an explanation of the difference between tax avoidance and tax evasion is in order. Tax evasion is illegal, but tax avoidance is allowed. The whole purpose of tax avoidance is to prevent a needless tax liability coming into existence. Whatever means is used to accomplish this end is unimportant, assuming that it is legal apart from tax considerations. The significant point is that no tax liability is incurred. The tax evader, on the other hand, denies or fails to report a tax liability that is already in existence. Because it is sometimes difficult to know if a tax liability has been incurred, the distinction between tax evasion and tax avoidance is not always easy to make. None of the tax matters covered in this section is based on either a tax-evading "scheme" or a strained interpretation of the tax laws. Tax avoidance, as dealt with here, is both a proper and a profitable activity.

EFFECT OF TAXES ON BUSINESS ORGANIZATION One of the businessperson's first decisions—what legal form the business will have—has income tax overtones. He or she knows the three basic business forms: the sole proprietorship, the partnership, and the corporation. The businessperson also knows that he or she cannot restrict himself or herself to legal considerations but must study the tax consequences of the final choice. Here are some of the points to be considered.

As noted earlier, the sole proprietor must pay a tax on the entire taxable income of the business. The partner must also pay a proportionate share on the taxable income of the partnership. If the businessperson decides to incorporate the business, a new taxpayer comes into existence. The corporation (unless it elects *Subchapter S* treatment) must report and pay a tax on its income, and the stockholders must also include their dividend income in their individual returns. In other words, distributed corporate earnings are taxed twice.

Before he or she decides on the form of the business, the businessperson and his or her tax assistant should estimate how he or she would fare from a tax standpoint under the alternative business forms. For example, suppose that he or she is trying to decide whether to organize the business as a corporation or as a sole proprietorship. He or she plans on receiving $30,000 a year as compensation for services if he or she operates as a corporation. It is expected that the revenue of the business will be $200,000 a year and that operating expenses other than his or her salary will be $80,000. Although most businesses retain some of their earnings for expansion, in this case the plan is to distribute all of its net income. A comparison of the income tax status of the two forms of organization being considered is shown on page 712. It is assumed that the taxpayer, who is married and files a joint return, has total deductions and exemptions of $5,000. Tax computations are based on the rate schedule on page 699.

This example does not prove that the sole proprietorship always has an income tax advantage over the corporation. It merely shows how the comparison between the forms should be made. In the final analysis, many other tax features should be weighed. Following are a few of these features.

In our example, we assumed that the corporation distributed all of its earnings; this is not the usual case. Corporations may retain part of their earnings. Even though there are limits, it still means that a corporation can hold on to some of its earnings and avoid distributing taxable dividends. Unlike a partnership or sole proprietorship, where *all* business income is reported by the owners, the corporation can control the flow of income to its stockholders by retaining earnings.

Other corporate tax features are the various tax-favored pension, profit-sharing, and insurance plans that are designed for use in corporations. Although sole proprietors and partners can set up similar plans, theirs are much more restricted than the plans that can be established by corporations.

Operating Results

	Corporation		Sole proprietorship
Sales		$200,000	$200,000
Deduct expenses:			
Owner's salary	$30,000		$ 0
Other expenses	80,000	110,000	80,000 80,000
Net income before corporate income tax		$ 90,000	
Deduct corporate income tax		22,750ᵃ	
Net income distributed to owner		$ 67,250	$120,000

Owner's Income and Tax Payments

	Corporation	Sole proprietorship
Salary	$30,000	
Dividends	67,250	
Total income	$97,250	$120,000
Deduct income tax	37,308ᵇ	51,128ᶜ
Disposable income	$59,942	$ 68,872

ᵃ$25,000 × 17%	$ 4,250
25,000 × 20%	5,000
25,000 × 30%	7,500
25,000 × 40%	6,000
	$22,750
ᵇTotal income for tax purposes ($97,250 less $200 dividend exclusion)	$ 97,050
Less total deductions and exemptions	5,000
Taxable income	$ 92,050
Tax [$33,502 + ($6,450 × 59%)]	$ 37,308
ᶜTotal income for tax purposes	$120,000
Less total deductions and exemptions	5,000
Taxable income	$115,000
Tax [$47,544 + ($5,600 × 64%)]	$ 51,128

NOTE: The maximum tax on earned income provisions of the tax law has been ignored.

Whatever business form is finally chosen, it is certain that income taxes should play a significant role in the decision.

THE TIMING OF INCOME AND EXPENSES FOR TAX PURPOSES One of the ways income taxes can be controlled is through prudent spending and selling policies. The proper timing of receipts and expenditures is one of the simplest and most effective ways of controlling taxable income. The guidelines for the businessperson are:

(1) Avoid bunching income in one year and expenses in another.
(2) If a big-income year is anticipated, hold off discretionary expenses so that they can be deducted in the high-income year.
(3) If there is to be an increase or decrease in tax rates, accelerate or defer income and expenses accordingly.
(4) Avoid having long-term capital gains and long-term capital losses in the same year. Long-term capital gains are desirable; offsetting losses water them down.

These simple guidelines are among the most effective of all tax-saving devices. They further illustrate the influence of income taxes on basic business decisions.

EFFECT OF TAXES ON FINANCING ARRANGEMENTS If an enterprise is incorporated, the way it is financed can have an effect on its net income and its income tax expense in subsequent years. The reason is that interest on bonds and other forms of indebtedness is deductible while dividends on stock are not. Thus, when a corporation needs funds, it will often find borrowing more advantageous than issuing stock.

A simple example will illustrate this point. Suppose that a company in the 46 per cent tax bracket is considering the following alternatives for obtaining $200,000 on which it expects to earn 12 per cent: (1) issuance of 8 per cent preferred stock, or (2) borrowing at the rate of 7 per cent. The after-tax results of the two alternatives are shown below.

	Issue stock	Borrow
Earnings ($200,000 × 12%)	$24,000	$24,000
Deduct interest ($200,000 × 7%)	–0–	14,000
Taxable income	$24,000	$10,000
Deduct corporate income tax:		
($24,000 × 46%)	11,040	
($10,000 × 46%)		4,600
Earnings after taxes	$12,960	$ 5,400
Deduct preferred dividends ($200,000 × 8%)	16,000	–0–
Earnings available to reinvest or distribute to the common stockholders	$ (3,040)	$ 5,400

Taxes have a major bearing on many other financial-planning decisions. For instance, the decision whether to buy or lease is also affected by taxes. Leasing arrangements may allow rental deductions in excess of the depreciation deductions that would be available to the company if it were to buy property.

TAXES AND INVENTORIES Taxes also influence the choice of method of inventory valuation. Inventory valuation is a major factor in the determination of taxable income. You will recall that the value of goods in inventory at the end of the year affects the company's cost of goods sold. This, in turn, has an effect on the net income figure. To put it another way, the lower the valuation placed on the ending inventory, the lower the taxable income. Thus different methods of inventory valuation can cause substantial differences in taxable income. The last-in, first-out *LIFO* method of valuation has received much attention in recent years and has been adopted by many taxpayers because of its tax advantages.

THE EFFECT OF TAXES ON THE FORM OF BUSINESS TRANSACTIONS Many business transactions are purposely framed in a way that will qualify them for tax-favored treatment. For example, when a taxpayer sells his or her business, he or she will usually try to allocate a large part of the selling price to goodwill. This is done because goodwill is taxed at the lower capital gains rate. On the other hand, a buyer of a business wants a major part of the purchase price allocated to the depreciable assets; total depreciation deductions depend on the price paid for them. Another instance in which terms and conditions are influenced by taxes is the sale of land under an installment contract. If more than 30 per cent of the purchase price is received in the first year, the gain from the sale cannot be prorated over the period during which the installment payments are received. The installment seller must see that the combined down payment and installment collections during the first year do not exceed 30 per cent of the sale price if he or she is to receive tax-favored treatment.

INCOME TAXES AND HOLD-OR-SELL DECISIONS   In reaching a decision about holding or selling income-producing assets, the owner usually should give consideration to income tax consequences. In doing so, the taxpayer would as a general rule, regard the income from the asset as incremental (or marginal) income. That is, the income would be regarded as taxable at the highest rate paid by the owner. To illustrate, assume that an individual in the 54 per cent tax bracket has owned an apartment building for 15 years. Data relating to the building are given below:

Cost	$120,000
Useful life when new	20 years
Present remaining useful life	5 years
Undepreciated cost (tax basis)	$30,000
Salvage value	None
Annual rental income after all expenses except depreciation	$20,000
Depreciation expense	6,000
Income before tax	$14,000
Income tax—54%	7,560
After-tax income from building	$ 6,440
Remaining life of building in years	5
Total prospective after-tax income from building	$32,200

Assume further that the asset qualifies for treatment as a capital asset and that the owner receives an offer of $80,000 for the property. The after-tax gain would be computed as follows:

Sales price	$80,000
Basis	30,000
Capital gain	$50,000
Tax—25% (assumed rate)	12,500
After-tax gain	$37,500

The sale alternative is attractive on two counts:

It offers the larger after-tax income.

The larger after-tax income is available now; if the building is held, the owner must wait up to five years for some of the income.

What are the after-tax earnings prospects of the purchaser if he or she is in the 32 per cent tax bracket?

Annual rental income after all expenses except depreciation	$20,000
Depreciation expense ($80,000 ÷ 5)	16,000
Income before tax	$ 4,000
Income tax—32%	1,280
After-tax income from building	$ 2,720
Average investment in building—$80,000 initially and $0 when asset is fully depreciated gives a simple average of	$40,000
After-tax return on investment ($2,720 ÷ $40,000)	6.8%

CONCLUDING NOTE   This introduction to income taxes will have been worthwhile if opinions such as the following are the result:

> Income taxes cannot wisely be ignored in business affairs.
>
> Income taxes are so complicated that one should never conclude quickly and with supreme confidence that he or she knows and has considered all of the tax consequences of a given course of action.
>
> It is a sign of wisdom in many cases to seek tax advice from those with training and experience in the subject.

IMPORTANT TERMS AND CONCEPTS IN CHAPTER 24

ASSIGNMENT MATERIAL

Questions

1 Mention some of the goals of income tax laws.
2 Name the four major classes of taxable entities.
3 How is the income of a partnership taxed under the federal income tax law?
4 Discuss some theoretical advantages of a progressive income tax.
5 Describe in general terms the operation of the loss carryback-carryforward privilege.
6 Name the two principal ways in which tax return income can differ from the net income before income tax shown in the income statement.
7 May a corporation adopt a different method of depreciation for its books and financial statements from that adopted for income tax purposes?
8 What is the objective of income tax-allocation procedures?
9 Distinguish between tax evasion and tax avoidance.
10 Explain why income taxes may affect the type of business organization used by a businessman.
11 Explain why income taxes may affect the financing arrangements adopted by a business.
12 What is meant by the term "zero bracket amount" as it pertains to an individual's tax deductions?

Short exercises

E24-1
Cordele Company reports taxable income as follows for the first seven years of operation:

19_1	$ 6,000 income
19_2	10,000 income
19_3	4,000 loss
19_4	11,000 loss
19_5	5,000 income
19_6	11,000 loss
19_7	7,000 income

What is the taxable income for each year after application of the loss carryback-carryforward provisions?

E24-2
Dublin Corporation purchased for $20,000 an asset having a useful life of 20 years and zero salvage value on January 1, 19_5. What is the first-year tax advantage (computed to the nearest dollar) of the sum of years' digits method over the straight-line method, assuming a constant tax rate of 46 per cent? What is the tax advantage of the method over the 20-year period?

E24-3
Macon Corporation, which does not use income tax-allocation procedures, uses the straight-line method to depreciate certain assets for income-statement purposes. The use of a different method for tax depreciation resulted in the following differences between the net income reported in the income statement and net income reported in the tax return:

	Net income	
	Income statement	Tax return
19_1	$16,000	$10,000
19_2	8,000	6,000
19_3	15,000	10,000
19_4	10,000	14,000
19_5	14,000	17,000

By what amount would the December 31, 19_5 balance sheet differ if the company had used tax-allocation procedures beginning January 1, 19_1? Assume the corporation's tax rate is 46 per cent.

E24-4

Fred Fern sold for $80,000 a capital asset that cost $100,000 and had accumulated depreciation of $40,000. Assuming that he is in the 54 per cent tax bracket, compute his tax savings as a result of the capital gains provisions of the tax law, assuming that his capital gain rate is 25%.

Problems

A24-1

Don Donald is trying to decide whether to operate his business as an individual proprietorship or as a corporation. Compute the total income tax that will be assessed on the business income earned under both forms of business organization. You may assume that business income is the same as taxable income.

Use the tax rates shown on pages 699–700. Ignore the maximum tax on earned income.

	Corporation		Individual proprietor
Sales		$300,000	$300,000
Expenses:			
Salary to owner	$ 36,000		
Other	200,000	236,000	200,000
Net operating income		$ 64,000	$100,000
Dividends		$ 20,000	
Drawings			$ 30,000

A24-2

Assume that the income tax rate is 46 per cent. Apply the carryback-carryforward provisions to the taxable income data set forth below and calculate the liability for income tax for 19_6 and 19_7.

Year	Taxable income (loss*)
19_1	$20,000
19_2	30,000
19_3	5,000
19_4	75,000*
19_5	25,000
19_6	35,000*
19_7	50,000

Rayburn Company follows income tax-allocation procedures. Data from the company's accounts are shown below.

	Net income	Liability for income taxes
19_1	$100,000	$ 88,000
19_2	90,000	86,000
19_3	105,000	109,000
19_4	110,000	122,000

Deferred income tax

19_3	4,000	19_1	12,000
19_4	12,000	19_2	4,000

Required:

Compute the following: (a) The income tax expense shown in the company's income statements for 19_1, 19_2, 19_3, and 19_4; and (b) the net income that would have been reported if the company had not followed income tax-allocation procedures.

The only income-producing asset of Goodman Company is its patent. The patent has a remaining legal and commercial life of ten years. Under existing legal agreements, the patent will earn a royalty income of $25,000 per annum for the next ten years.

GOODMAN COMPANY
Balance Sheet
December 31, 19_2

Assets			Equities	
Cash and royalities receivable		$ 25,000	Capital stock	$ 70,000
			Retained earnings	55,000
Patent—at cost	$150,000			
Less accumulated amortization	$ 50,000	100,000		
		$125,000		$125,000

Bill Brown has an opportunity to acquire control of the patent (1) by purchasing it from the corporation for $100,000 or (2) by purchasing all of the outstanding capital stock from the stockholders for $150,000 (the receivables are collectible).

If Brown elects to acquire the outstanding capital stock, he will permit the company to continue its ownership of the patent for the remaining life of the patent. At the end of the ten-year period, the corporation would be liquidated.

If Brown acquires the outstanding capital stock, as owner of all of the capital stock he would have the following alternatives:

(a) Have the corporation declare annual dividends equal to its net income for each year.

(b) Have the corporation adopt a no-dividends policy.

Compute total payments for income taxes traceable to Brown's control of the patent under each of the alternative plans described above. Use the following income rates:

Corporation: Use tax rates on page 700.
Individual:

Ordinary income	32%
Capital gains	25%

(Assume that capital losses in excess of capital gains are deductible from ordinary income.)

A24-5 *Refer to Problem A24-4 and compute the aggregate disposable income to the original stockholders of Goodman Company under each of the alternatives set forth therein.*

(a) The patent is a capital asset of the corporation. Any gain on its sale will be taxed at a capital gains rate of 25 per cent. The tax basis of the patent is the same as its book value.

(b) The shares of stock held by the taxpayers have a basis of $75,000. Any excess above the basis received from the disposal of the shares will be taxed at a capital gains rate of 25 per cent.

You may assume further that, if alternative (1) is selected, the stockholders will immediately liquidate the company.

B24-1 *Early in 19_1, Trenton Company purchased specialized production facilities for $500,000. It was anticipated at the time of purchase that the product manufactured by the specialized facilities would be in demand for only five years and that the facilities would have no scrap value thereafter.*

During each of the five years (19_1 through 19_5) the company earned $300,000 before depreciation and income tax. The company used the sum of the years' digits method of depreciation for income tax purposes and the straight-line method for its books, and followed income tax-allocation procedures.

(a) Compute the net income for the years 19_1, 19_2, 19_3, 19_4, and 19_5, following income tax-allocation procedures. You may assume a 46 per cent income tax rate.

(b) Set up a T-account for Deferred Income Tax and show the entries that appeared therein following income tax-allocation procedures.

B24-2 *The owner of a marina has been advised by the controlling governmental agency that his operating license, which expires in three years, will not be renewed. He has received a cash offer of $165,000 for the property and asks you to prepare a suitable analysis to assist him in deciding whether to sell or hold the asset.*

The marina has a tax basis of $90,000. His income from owning the marina, which has been averaging $60,000 a year, is taxed in the 54 per cent bracket. However, any gain from its sale will be taxed at 25 per cent. It seems unlikely that any salvage value will be realized from the property.

Required:

Calculate the after-tax income to the present owner under each of the following alternatives:

(a) The marina will be held by the present owner until expiration of the license. Note: Calculate the total after-tax income for the period.

(b) The marina is sold immediately for the $165,000 cash price.

B24-3 *Salton Company has just been organized. It has depreciable assets that cost $250,000 and have an estimated useful life of 4 years. The management is considering the following alternatives:*

(1) Adopt the sum of the years' digits method of depreciation for both book and income-tax purposes.

(2) Adopt the sum of the years' digits method of depreciation for income tax purposes and the straight-line method for the books.

Assume the following:

	Year		
	1	2	3
Revenues—cash	$300,000	$330,000	$360,000
Cash expenses before depreciation and taxes	165,000	180,000	200,000
Income tax rate	46%	46%	46%

Management asks you to prepare estimates of the following:

(a) Net income for Years 1, 2, and 3 under each alternative, and assuming that income tax-allocation procedures are not adopted.

(b) Net cash inflow from operations for Years 1, 2, and 3 under each alternative, and assuming that the income tax is paid at each year-end.

(c) Net income for Years 1, 2, and 3 under alternative 2, assuming that income tax-allocation procedures are adopted.

B24-4

(a) For each of the following forms of business organization, estimate the amount of gross income that Andy Albers will have to report on his individual tax return. The corporate income tax rate is 46 per cent.

	Corporation	Partnership
Sales	$600,000	$600,000
Expenses:		
Salary to Albers	$ 25,000	
Other	435,000	460,000	435,000
Net operating income	$140,000	$165,000
Income tax expense	64,400	
Net income	$ 75,600	
Dividends	$ 30,000	
Drawings by Albers		$ 25,000

Under the corporate form of organization, Albers will own 50 per cent of the outstanding stock. Under the partnership form of organization, Albers will have a 50 per cent interest in the partnership.

(b) Assume the facts set forth in (a) and that the business is organized as a corporation. Assume further that the corporation can earn 15 per cent before corporate income tax on an additional investment of $100,000.

Albers is willing to make an additional investment of $100,000 in the business and is considering the following alternative arrangements:

(1) A long-term loan of $100,000 at 8 per cent interest.

(2) An investment of $100,000 for an additional 1,000 shares of stock. After issuance of the additional 1,000 shares, 5,000 shares will be outstanding.

Assuming that the corporation will distribute as additional dividends all incremental after-tax income from its use of the $100,000, estimate the increase in Albers' taxable income under each alternative.

PROCESSING REPETITIVE TRANSACTIONS
APPENDIX A

INTRODUCTION   Many types of business transactions occur with considerable frequency within a single firm. In order to reduce the amount of time required in the recording and posting of such transactions, special books of original entry are often used. This chapter discusses the use of these special accounting records.

Manual procedures

SPECIAL JOURNALS   In previous chapters business transactions were recorded in a journal form which required the listing of each amount affected and the amounts debited and credited. A firm could record every transaction in this manner. However, the recording and posting time required would be considerable, even for a firm of only moderate size.

Any procedure that reduces recording and posting time is helpful. Journals specially designed to accommodate different classes of transactions may be used to save time. The special journals to be used in any particular business will depend upon the nature of its operations, and upon whether transactions of a particular kind occur often enough to warrant having a special journal in which to record them. In most firms the following special journals are useful because of the frequency with which certain transactions occur:

(1) Sales journal—for recording sales of merchandise on account.
(2) Purchases journal—for recording purchases of merchandise and other items on account.
(3) Cash receipts journal—for recording all receipts of cash.
(4) Cash disbursements journal—for recording all payments of cash.

Some transactions cannot be recorded in any *one* of the special journals, making it necessary to maintain the two-column journal illustrated in earlier chapters. This journal would also be used to record correcting, adjusting, and closing entries.

ADVANTAGES OF SPECIAL JOURNALS   There are two important advantages of special journals:

Saving of labor   Less time is required in *recording* transactions because it is unnecessary to write the account title for a debit or credit when the heading of a special column indicates the account affected by the transaction. Posting also requires less time because columnar *totals,* which represent several transactions, are posted to the accounts rather than individual amounts.

Division of labor   Special journals allow the division of labor in both the recording and posting of transactions. While one employee is recording sales transactions in the sales journal, another can be recording receipts of cash in the cash receipts journal. The same division is possible for posting.

SUBSIDIARY LEDGERS   The procedure of recording all credit sales in a single accounts receivable account makes it very difficult to determine the amount receivable from each customer. To provide this information an account is needed for each customer who is indebted to the firm. Such individual records facilitate the control of credit limits and the sending of periodic statements to customers. These accounts are kept in a separate accounts receivable ledger, called a *subsidiary ledger*. The accounts receivable account used in previous chapters to show the total accounts receivable from all customers is still used in the *general ledger.*

The accounts receivable account in the general ledger is called a *controlling account* because its balance and the sum of the balances in the subsidiary accounts receivable ledger should be equal. This is so because the transactions affecting the controlling account also affect the accounts in the subsidiary ledger. The controlling account thus serves as a check on the accuracy of the subsidiary ledger. For this relationship to be maintained, the sum of all debits and credits to the *controlling account* must equal the sum of all debits and credits to the *subsidiary ledger.*

The same procedure can be used to maintain a separate record of the amounts owed to individual creditors. A subsidiary accounts payable ledger is established with an account for each creditor. These individual records are useful in providing totals which can be used to check the amounts reported in statements received from the creditor. They also can be used to facilitate timely payment of amounts owed. The accounts payable account in the general ledger then becomes a controlling account.

It should be noted that the subsidiary-ledger-controlling-account arrangement can be used in areas other than accounts receivable and accounts payable. For example, individual accounts can be set up in a subsidiary ledger for each type of equipment owned, with a controlling account in the general ledger entitled Equipment. In any case in which an account requires record keeping in considerable detail, a subsidiary ledger may prove helpful.

REFERENCES TO SPECIAL JOURNALS   When several journals are used, the ledger accounts must indicate the specific journal from which the entries were posted. Thus

  S1   means sales journal, page 1.
  P1   means purchases journal, page 1.
 CR1 means cash receipts journal, page 1.
 CD1 means cash disbursements journal, page 1.
  J1   means journal, page 1.

SALES JOURNAL A single-column sales journal is shown below. Only one amount column is needed because each credit sale results in a debit to Accounts Receivable and a credit to Sales for the same amount.

SALES JOURNAL   (Page 1)

Date	Invoice No.	Name	✓	Debit Accts. Rec. Credit Sales
19__ May				
2	1	R. E. West	✓	800
7	2	G. O. Davis	✓	450
12	3	G. O. Davis	✓	280
18	4	R. E. West	✓	800
23	5	S. E. Bates	✓	600
29	6	R. E. West	✓	300
				3,230
				(10) (40)

GENERAL LEDGER
(Amounts posted at end of month)

ACCOUNTS RECEIVABLE LEDGER
(Amounts posted daily)

Accounts Receivable   No. 10

19__ May 31		S1	3,230		3,230 Dr.

Sales   No. 40

19__ May 31		S1		3,230	3,230 Cr.

S. E. Bates

19__ May 23		S1	600		600

G. O. Davis

19__ May 7		S1	450		450
12		S1	280		730

R. E. West

19__ May 2		S1	800		800
18		S1	800		1,600
29		S1	300		1,900

Posting the sales journal Postings have been made as follows:

Debits:

Posted to the *individual* accounts (West, Davis, and Bates) in the subsidiary ledger. Since the accounts in the subsidiary ledger usually are arranged in alphabetical order and are not numbered, check marks are used (instead of account numbers) to indicate the postings have been made. The frequency of postings to the individual accounts varies. Many firms post the amounts daily in order to spread the posting effort throughout the period. Frequent posting is also necessary in order to maintain control over customer credit limits and to provide statements to customers on a timely basis.

The *total* of the debits to Accounts Receivable for the sales on account ($3,230) has been posted to the accounts receivable controlling account in the general ledger, as indicated by the account number (No. 10) at the foot of the money column.

The posting of column totals to the controlling account (instead of individual entries) is the reason why the use of subsidiary ledgers and controlling accounts does not double the work of posting.

Credits:

The *total* of the sales on account ($3,230) has been posted to the sales account (No. 40) in the general ledger, as indicated by the sales account number at the foot of the money column.

DIRECT USE OF INVOICES Some firms may use sales invoices directly rather than actually recording the invoices in a special journal. One variation of this procedure is to post directly from the invoices to the customers' individual accounts. The amount of the entry in the controlling account is determined by totaling the invoices for the period. For a small firm with few customers, the invoices may even serve as a subsidiary ledger, with the invoices for each customer kept separately.

PURCHASES JOURNAL The purchases journal illustrated below contains only one column for credits: the Accounts Payable credit column. Thus only purchases on account can be recorded in this journal. Provision was made, by the use of the Sundry Accounts section, for debits that cannot be entered in any of the special debit columns.

PURCHASES JOURNAL (Page 1)

Date		Subsidiary Ledger Account Credited	Invoice Date	✓	Credits — Accounts Payable	Debits — Merchandise Inventory	Office Expense	Sundry Accounts — Name	L.F.	Amount
19__ May	1	Price and Holmes	May 1	✓	2,000	2,000				
	9	Henderson's, Inc.	May 8	✓	200		200			
	13	Osborne Company	May 10	✓	2,600	2,600				
	15	Price and Holmes	May 14	✓	650	650				
	20	Henderson's, Inc.	May 19	✓	1,300			Office equipment	15	1,300
					6,750	5,250	200			1,300
					(20)	(12)	(71)			

GENERAL LEDGER
(Amounts posted at end of month)

ACCOUNTS PAYABLE LEDGER
(Amounts posted daily)

Henderson's, Inc.

19__					
May 9		P1		200	200
20		P1		1,300	1,500

Osborne Company

19__					
May 13		P1		2,600	2,600

Price and Holmes

19__					
May 1		P1		2,000	2,000
15		P1		650	2,650

Merchandise Inventory No. 12

19__				
May 31		P1	5,250	5,250 Dr.

Office Equipment No. 15

19__				
May 24		P1	1,300	1,300 Dr.

Accounts Payable No. 20

19__				
May 31		P1	6,750	6,750 Cr.

Office Expense No. 71

19__				
May 31		P1	200	200 Dr.

Posting the purchases journal Postings from the purchases journal are made as follows:

Credits:

These are posted to the *individual* accounts for each creditor (Price and Holmes, Henderson's, Inc., and Osborne Company) in the accounts payable subsidiary ledger. The check marks indicate such postings.

The *total* credits to Accounts Payable are posted to the accounts payable controlling account in the general ledger, as indicated by the account number (No. 20) at the foot of the Accounts Payable column.

Debits:

The *column total* is posted to each general ledger account for which there is a special money column. The account numbers below those column totals (No. 12 and No. 71) indicate the postings.

Debits are posted to the designated general ledger accounts for each entry in the Sundry Accounts section of the journal.

The sundry column total was not posted, and never would be, because the individual amounts therein would always be posted separately.

CASH RECEIPTS JOURNAL The cash receipts journal below is designed to accommodate the two primary sources of cash receipts for most firms—cash sales and cash received on account from customers.

CASH RECEIPTS JOURNAL (Page 1)

| | | | | Credits | | | | | |
| | | | | | Accounts Receivable | | | Sundry Accounts | |
Date	Explanation	Cash Debit	Account Credited	✓	Amount	Sales	L.F.	Amount
19__								
May 1	Issued common stock	25,000	Common stock				30	25,000
3	Cash sale	150				150		
15	Invoice, May 7	450	G. O. Davis	✓	450			
30	Invoice, May 2	800	R. E. West	✓	800			
		26,400			1,250	150		25,000
		(1)			(10)	(40)		

ACCOUNTS RECEIVABLE LEDGER
(Amounts posted daily)

G. O. Davis

19__					
May 7		S1	450		450
12		S1	280		730
15		CR1		450	280

R. E. West

19__					
May 2		S1	800		800
18		S1	800		1,600
29		S1	300		1,900
30		CR1		800	1,100

GENERAL LEDGER
(Amounts posted at end of month)

Cash No. 1

19__					
May 31		CR1	26,400		26,400 Dr.

Accounts Receivable No. 10

19__					
May 31		S1	3,230		3,230 Dr.
31		CR1		1,250	1,980 Dr.

Common Stock No. 30

19__					
May 1		CR1		25,000	25,000 Cr.

Sales No. 40

19__					
May 31		S1		3,230	3,230 Cr.
31		CR1		150	3,380 Cr.

Posting the cash receipts journal   The posting procedure follows the pattern previously described.

Column totals:

Column totals, except the Sundry Accounts column total, are posted to the general ledger accounts
designated by the column headings. In the case of the illustrative cash receipts journal, three
column totals were posted. Specifically, $26,400 was posted as a *debit* to the cash account,
$1,250 was posted as a *credit* to the accounts receivable account, and $150 was posted
as a *credit* to the sales account.

Individual items:

Each amount in the Accounts Receivable column is posted to an individual account (Davis and
West) in the subsidiary accounts receivable ledger. Each amount in the Sundry Accounts
section of the journal is posted to the designated general ledger account.

To repeat, the total of the sundry column was not posted, and never would be, because
the individual amounts therein would always be posted separately.

Posting references in journals:

Account numbers indicate postings to accounts in the *general* ledger.

Check marks indicate postings to accounts in a *subsidiary* ledger.

CASH DISBURSEMENTS JOURNAL   The cash disbursements journal on page 727 is used to
record all cash disbursements of the firm. Special debit columns are provided
for recording the acquisition of merchandise inventory and payments to creditors
on account. It will be noted that the posting procedure is quite similar to the
posting of the cash receipts journal.

THE JOURNAL   When special journals are used, those transactions that cannot be recorded in
a special journal are recorded in the general journal. Two such transactions are
shown below.

JOURNAL   (Page 1)

19__					
May	31	Cost of goods sold	50	2,100	
		Merchandise inventory	12		2,100
		Reduction in inventory for the cost of goods sold			
		during the month of May.			
	31	Notes receivable	11	600	
		Accounts receivable (S. E. Bates)	10/✓		600
		Received 30-day, noninterest-bearing note for balance			
		of invoice of May 23.			

Since the journal does not have special columns for controlling accounts, whenever a controlling account is debited or credited, it is necessary to post such
debits or credits twice, once to the controlling account in the general ledger and
again to an account in the subsidiary ledger. If such double posting is not performed, agreement between the controlling account and the subsidiary ledger

										Debits			
			Cash	Account		Accounts Payable		Merchandise	Sundry Accounts				
Date		Explanation	Credit	Debited	√	Amount	Inventory	L.F.	Amount				
19__ May	1	Cash purchase of merchandise	5,000				5,000			
	1	Rent for May	300	Store rent				61	300
	16	Invoice, May 1	2,000	Price and Holmes	√	2,000			
	21	Invoice, May 9	200	Henderson's, Inc.	√	200			
	26	Cash purchase of merchandise	350				350		
	31	Salaries for May	600	Salesmen's salaries				62	600
			8,450			2,200	5,350		900
			(1)			(20)	(12)		

ACCOUNTS PAYABLE LEDGER
(Amounts posted daily)

Henderson's, Inc.

19__ May	9		P1		200	200
	20		P1		1,300	1,500
	21		CD1	200		1,300

Price and Holmes

19__ May	1		P1		2,000	2,000
	15		P1		650	2,650
	16		CD1	2,000		650

GENERAL LEDGER
(Amounts posted at end of month)

Cash   No. 1

19__ May	31		CR1	26,400		26,400 Dr.
	31		CD1		8,450	17,950 Dr.

Merchandise Inventory   No. 12

19__ May	31		P1	5,250		5,250 Dr.
	31		CD1	5,350		10,600 Dr.

Accounts Payable   No. 20

19__ May	31		P1		6,750	6,750 Cr.
	31		CD1	2,200		4,550 Cr.

Store Rent   No. 61

19__ May	1		CD1	300		300 Dr.

Sales Salaries   No. 62

19__ May	31		CD1	600		600 Dr.

will not be maintained. Thus, in the foregoing illustration, it was necessary to post the credit member of the second journal entry twice:

To the amounts receivable controlling account in the general ledger, as indicated by the "10" in the L.F. (ledger folio) column; and

To S. E. Bates' account in the subsidiary accounts receivable ledger, as indicated by the check mark in the L.F. column.

Notice that the identity of the customer (S. E. Bates) must be included in the journal entry in order that the posting may be made to the subsidiary ledger.

Another use of the general journal is to record correcting, adjusting, and closing entries.

PROVING THE SUBSIDIARY LEDGERS The accounts receivable and accounts payable ledgers after posting from the illustrative journals are shown on page 729. To prove the subsidiary ledgers, schedules of their balances are prepared and the totals compared with the balances of the respective controlling accounts. This proof is presented below.

ACCOUNTS RECEIVABLE   No. 10

19__							
May	31			S1	3,230		3,230 Dr.
	31			CR1		1,250	1,980 Dr.
	31			J1		600	1,380 Dr.

Schedule of Accounts Receivable
May 31, 19__

G. O. Davis	280
R. E. West	1,100
Total (per balance of controlling account)	1,380

ACCOUNTS PAYABLE   No. 20

19__							
May	31			P1		6,750	6,750 Cr.
	31			CD1	2,200		4,550 Cr.

Schedule of Accounts Payable
May 31, 19__

Henderson's, Inc.	1,300
Osborne Company	2,600
Price and Holmes	650
Total (per balance of controlling account)	4,550

ADVANTAGES OF CONTROLLING ACCOUNTS It might seem that when individual accounts are kept with debtors and creditors it is a useless duplication of work to maintain controlling accounts also. However, controlling accounts serve two very useful purposes:

First, controlling accounts make it possible to determine the total accounts receivable and total accounts payable without listing the balances of the individual accounts.

Second, controlling accounts help in locating errors. Without controlling accounts it would be necessary to take a combined trial balance of the general ledger and the subsidiary ledgers. If the combined trial balance did not balance, it might be necessary to check all of the postings in search of errors. With controlling accounts, errors often can be more readily located. For instance, if the general ledger is in balance, but the total of the balances in the accounts receivable ledger does not agree with the balance in the accounts receivable controlling account, an error presumably has been made in the subsidiary ledger.

ACCOUNTS RECEIVABLE LEDGER

S. E. Bates

19__							
May	23			S1	600		600
	31			J1		600	—

G. O. Davis

19__							
May	7			S1	450		450
	12			S1	280		730
	15			CR1		450	280

R. E. West

19__							
May	2			S1	800		800
	18			S1	800		1,600
	29			S1	300		1,900
	30			CR1		800	1,100

ACCOUNTS PAYABLE LEDGER

Henderson's, Inc.

19__							
May	9			P1		200	200
	20			P1		1,300	1,500
	21			CD1	200		1,300

Osborne Company

19__							
May	13			P1		2,600	2,600

Price and Holmes

19__							
May	1			P1		2,000	2,000
	15			P1		650	2,650
	16			CD1	2,000		650

Since, with a few possible exceptions (for instance, the posting of the credit to Accounts Receivable in the two-column journal on page 726, the controlling accounts are produced by the posting of column totals, very little additional work is required to obtain the above-mentioned benefits.

Machine procedures

ACCOUNTING MACHINES The manual procedures discussed up to this point offer the advantages of division of labor and saving of time in the recording and posting operations. However, where the number of transactions to be processed is large, manual procedures are impractical.

Accounting machines can further expedite the processing of a large number of transactions. As an illustration, consider the following sales and billing procedure. It is assumed that orders are secured by salespersons. When an order is obtained, the salesperson completes an order form and sends one copy to the office. This copy ultimately reaches the accounting department, where it is used as a source document for the following:

(1) Preparation of a customer's invoice and a shipping advice. The original of the invoice is sent to the customer, with at least one copy being retained by the seller. The shipping advice is sent to the shipping department, and authorizes shipment of the described merchandise.
(2) Recording of the sales transaction in the sales journal and in the customer's accounts receivable account.

A billing machine can be used to accomplish the above. A new roll of paper, printed in the form of the company's sales journal, is inserted in the machine at the beginning of each month. It is also assumed that the pre-numbered invoice and shipping advice forms are purchased in three-page, carboned packets, assembled as follows:

1st sheet—customer's copy of invoice
2nd sheet—office copy of invoice
3rd sheet—shipping advice

The machine is designed so that a packet of forms and the customer's accounts receivable account sheet can be easily and simultaneously inserted in the machine. The operator can record the facts relating to the sales transaction on the invoice forms, on the shipping advice, in the customer's account, and in the sales journal.

The billing machine just described can accumulate such aggregates as total debits to Accounts Receivable and total credits to Sales. In more elaborate systems, the machine may automatically compute and accumulate such amounts as sales taxes, salesmen's commissions, and shipping charges. Such totals might be printed out at the end of each day, week, or some other period and thus provide data for posting to the general ledger accounts.

As an alternative to posting directly from the machine record, summary general journal entries may be made on the basis of the machine-accumulated amounts. Returning to the sales journal shown on page 723 and assuming that the sales journal had been prepared as a by-product of the accounts receivable billing operation, the data could be used to prepare the following summary journal entry:

Accounts receivable	3,230	
Sales		3,230

Posting to the general ledger would thus be made from the journal.

Other techniques or devices can be designed to accumulate data from which similar summary entries can be prepared. Mechanical accounting devices can be used to accumulate totals affecting other, or all, general ledger accounts, to develop subsidiary records, and to prepare statistical reports—and to do all this speedily and with the expenditure of a minimum amount of human effort.

ELECTRONIC DATA PROCESSING The use of an electronic computer to process accounting data has two important advantages over the use of accounting machines: (1) there is less human involvement once the processing begins and, therefore, less likelihood of error, and (2) data are processed much more rapidly. Hopefully, it will also result in lower costs being incurred to process the data.

The term computer is widely used to describe what is actually a processing system consisting of different but related items of equipment. The equipment in the system can be classified as follows:[1]

(1) Input equipment.
(2) Processing equipment.
(3) Output equipment.
(4) Storage equipment.

These items comprise the physical components of the system and are referred to as *hardware.* The figure below illustrates the components of a typical electronic data processing system.

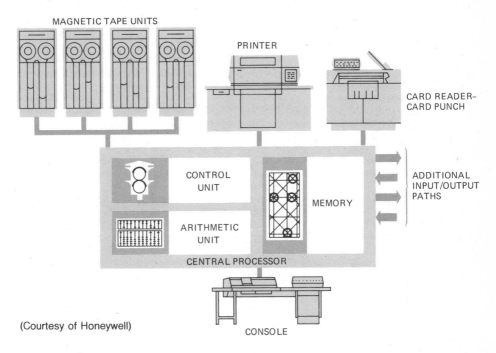

(Courtesy of Honeywell)

INPUT PROCEDURES Input procedures involve translating the data to be processed into a medium that the system understands. The various types of input equipment include card readers, paper or magnetic tape readers, optical character readers, and magnetic ink readers.

Punched cards The computers widely used today are not capable of reading written information. Data to be processed must be presented to the computer in a language it can understand. Punched cards can be used for this purpose. Using a machine known as a keypunch and a predetermined coding system, data are transferred to the cards by a series of holes punched in appropriate places. The information on the punched cards may be checked for accuracy prior to processing by means of a machine known as a verifier.

[1]See Robert B. Sweeney, *The Use of Computers in Accounting* (Englewood Cliffs, N.J.: Prentice-Hall, Inc., 1971).

Card readers are used to scan punched cards and translate the punches into a code the computer understands for processing. Recent electronic data processing systems use punched cards much less than the earlier systems because the speed with which the cards can be prepared and processed is relatively slow in comparison to other input devices.

Paper and magnetic tape   Rolls of tape, rather than punched cards, may be used to provide information to the computer for processing. As with punched cards, a predetermined code is used to place the data on the tapes, which are used as a direct input device for the computer.

Paper tape may offer a relatively inexpensive input medium, but it is used less frequently than magnetic tape. Magnetic tape has three important advantages over paper tape: It can be read by tape readers at a much higher speed, it can accommodate a larger number of characters per inch of tape, and it is reusable.

Optical characters   Optical characters, such as the raised numbers on a gasoline credit card, can be read by an optical character reader. The reader either punches the data into a card for further processing or it may read the data directly to the computer.

Magnetic ink characters   Magnetic ink characters, such as those appearing on a check, can be read by special readers. The process is similar to the use of punched cards except that the reader scans for the characters written in a special ink rather than punched holes in the document. The reader then transfers the data to the computer for processing.

PROCESSING   The processing of data by a computer involves more than just the arithmetical calculations. It will be noted in the illustration on page 731 that the central processing unit of the computer includes control, arithmetic, and memory units. The computer processes data according to a series of instructions, known as a *program*. The *control unit* of the computer is the key to the implementation of the program. If the program is properly written, the control unit will guide the computer through the required processing steps automatically. The *arithmetic unit* performs the calculations involved in addition, subtraction, multiplication, and division. The computer also has a "memory," in that it can store data in a *memory unit* and recall the data when instructed to do so.

These characteristics of the computer enhance its usefulness tremendously. Once data are stored in the computer, additional processing may take place; one needs simply to instruct the computer as to what operations are required. Programmers are highly trained individuals who prepare the programs or instructions given to the computer.

OUTPUT PROCEDURES   The procedures by which processed data are taken from the computer and prepared for those wanting the information are known as *output procedures*. Examples of output equipment are card punches, paper tape punches, magnetic tape recorders, printers, and display devices.

Punched cards Placing the processed information on punched cards offers a distinct advantage when the data require considerable handling after processing by the computer. The cards facilitate changing the sequence of the information for additional processing. The output cards may be the input cards that have been punched with additional data or they may be new cards. Just as with the use of punched cards as an input device, they are relatively slow to process as a form of output.

Paper or magnetic tape If a large quantity of processed data is to be stored, paper or magnetic tape is preferable to punched cards because much less space is needed to store a given quantity of data. Additional processing can also be done more rapidly because of the ability of the equipment to read data from tapes more rapidly than from punched cards.

Magnetic tape is generally preferred over paper tape as an output medium because of its greater speed and the fact that more data can be accommodated in a given space on the tape.

Direct printout Processed data may be prepared in prescribed typewritten form by means of an electric typewriter or line printer connected directly to the computer. A major advantage of this form of output is that the output of the computer is ready for immediate use.

Display Display devices also produce a visual output by retrieving data from the computer and displaying it on a device resembling a television screen. A keyboard is used to signal the computer which information is desired.

ACCOUNTING USES OF THE COMPUTER Computers are most commonly used in those accounting operations that require the routine processing of a great amount of data. Examples are payrolls, inventories, receivables, and payables. The obvious advantages of the computer in these areas are its accuracy and speed. The potential accounting uses of the computer in the future are limited only by the ability of people to discover additional applications and instruct the computer in what is to be done.

The illustration on page 734 shows the operation of a computer in a specific accounting application, the processing of a credit sales transaction.

IMPORTANT TERMS AND CONCEPTS IN APPENDIX A

Operation of a computer in processing a credit sales transaction

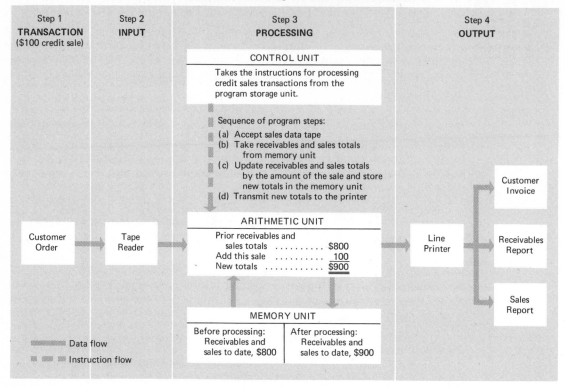

DEMONSTRATION PROBLEM FOR REVIEW AND SELF-STUDY   Newport Company began operations on August 1, 19_6 and uses the following general ledger accounts:

Chart of accounts

1	Cash	40	Sales
3	Accounts Receivable	50	Cost of Goods Sold
4	Notes Receivable	60	Salaries Expense
6	Merchandise Inventory	61	Taxes Expense
7	Prepaid Insurance	62	Office Expense
8	Investments	63	Interest Expense
10	Land	70	Gain on Sale of Investment
11	Buildings		
15	Accounts Payable		
16	Notes Payable		
17	Salaries Payable		
18	Taxes Payable		
25	Mortgage Payable		
30	Common Stock		

Transactions for the month of August are presented below:

August 1—Issued common stock for cash, $40,000.

2—Merchandise was purchased on account from Beaufort Corp., $17,200.

2—Purchased land and buildings for $40,000, giving a mortgage for the amount. The land is estimated to have a value of $5,000.

5—Sold merchandise to Tarboro Company on account, $6,000. Invoice No. 1.

5—Purchased securities as an investment, $700 cash.

5—Office supplies were purchased on account from Burgaw, Inc., $172.

7—Sold merchandise for cash, $1,745.

8—Paid for the merchandise bought on the 2nd from Beaufort Corp.

8—Received payment in full from Tarboro Company.

9—Paid $550 for a three-year fire insurance policy.

10—Sold merchandise to Mayodan Company on account, $7,200. Invoice No. 2.

12—Purchased merchandise from Sylva Suppliers, Inc., on account. Invoice amount, $14,522.

13—Mayodan Company paid its account in full.

13—Sold merchandise to Newry, Inc., on account, $4,675. Invoice No. 3.

14—Sold merchandise to Mayodan Company on account, $1,362. Invoice No. 4.

16—Paid salaries of $1,350.

18—Sold merchandise to Gibsonville Sales Company on account, $5,540. Invoice No. 5.

18—Borrowed $14,000 at the bank, giving a note due one year from date.

18—Cash purchase of merchandise, $927.

20—Purchased merchandise from Glendale Company for $5,620.

22—Sold merchandise to Stevens Point Corporation on account, $1,128. Invoice No. 6.

23—Received partial payment of $980 from Gibsonville Sales Company.

25—Purchased merchandise from Sylva Suppliers, Inc., $4,352.

25—Received a 30-day note from Newry, Inc., in settlement of its account.

26—Sold the securities purchased August 5 for $900.

27—Paid Sylva Suppliers, Inc., half of their invoice of August 12.

29—Purchased securities for $1,700, cash.

30—Sold merchandise to Gibsonville Sales Company on account, $4,254. Invoice No. 7.

31—Cash sales, $542.

31—Paid mortgage installment of $500, of which $114 was interest expense.

31—Paid the semimonthly payroll, $1,400.

31—Purchased merchandise for cash, $2,010.

INSTRUCTIONS

(a) Prepare journal entries for the month. Use the four special journals illustrated in the chapter, plus a two-column journal. Total and rule the journals.

(b) Indicate how the journals would be posted by placing posting references in the journals.

Note Attempt to solve the demonstration problem before examining the solution that follows.

SALES JOURNAL (Page 1)

Date	Invoice No.	Name	Dr. Accts. Rec. / Cr. Sales
19_6			
Aug. 5	1	Tarboro Company	6,000
10	2	Mayodan Company	7,200
13	3	Newry, Inc.	4,675
14	4	Mayodan Company	1,362
18	5	Gibsonville Sales Company	5,540
22	6	Stevens Point Corporation	1,128
30	7	Gibsonville Sales Company	4,254
			30,159
			(3)(40)

PURCHASES JOURNAL (Page 1)

Date	Subsidiary Ledger Account Credited	Invoice Date	✓	Credits Accounts Payable	Debits Merchandise Inventory	Office Expense	Sundry Accounts Name	L.F.	Amount
19_6									
Aug. 2	Beaufort Corp.	Aug. 2		17,200	17,200				
5	Burgaw, Inc.	Aug. 5		172		172			
12	Sylva Suppliers, Inc.	Aug. 12		14,522	14,522				
20	Glendale Company	Aug. 20		5,620	5,620				
25	Sylva Suppliers, Inc.	Aug. 25		4,352	4,352				
				41,866	41,694	172			
				(15)	(6)	(62)			

CASH RECEIPTS JOURNAL (Page 1)

Date	Explanation	Cash Debit	Account Credited	Credits Accts. Rec. ✓	Accts. Rec. Amount	Sales	Sundry Accounts L.F.	Sundry Accounts Amount
19_6								
Aug. 1	Issued common stock	40,000	Common stock				30	40,000
7	Cash sales	1,745				1,745		
8	Invoice of August 5	6,000	Tarboro Company		6,000			
13	Invoice of August 10	7,200	Mayodan Company		7,200			
18	Borrowed money for one year	14,000	Notes payable				16	14,000
23	Receipt of partial payment	980	Gibsonville Sales Company		980			
26	Sold securities	900	Investments				8	700
			Gain on sale of investments				70	200
31	Cash sales	542				542		
		71,367			14,180	2,287		54,900
		(1)			(3)	(40)		

Date	Explanation	Cash Credit	Account Debited	Accts. Pay. ✓	Accts. Pay. Amount	Merchandise Inventory	Sundry Accts. L.F.	Sundry Accts. Amount
19_6								
Aug. 5	Purchased securities	700	Investments				8	700
8	Invoice of August 2	17,200	Beaufort Corp.		17,200			
9	Three-year premium	550	Prepaid insurance				7	550
16	Salaries	1,350	Salaries expense				60	1,350
18	Purchased merchandise for cash	927				927		
27	One-half of August 12 invoice	7,261	Sylva Suppliers, Inc.		7,261			
29	Purchased securities	1,700	Investments				8	1,700
31	Mortgage payment	500	Mortgage payable				25	386
			Interest expense				63	114
31	Salaries	1,400	Salaries expense				60	1,400
31	Purchased merchandise for cash	2,010				2,010		
		33,598			24,461	2,937		6,200
		(1)			(15)	(6)		

JOURNAL (Page 1)

19_6				
Aug. 2	Land	10	5,000	
	Buildings	11	35,000	
	Mortgage payable	25		40,000
	Purchase of land and buildings.			
25	Notes receivable	4	4,675	
	Accounts receivable			
	(Newry, Inc.)	3/✓		4,675
	Receipt of 30-day note in			
	settlement of account.			

TABLES OF AMOUNTS AND PRESENT VALUES

APPENDIX B

AMOUNT OF $1

$(1+i)^n$

n i	½ %	1%	1¼ %	1½ %	2%	2½ %
1	1.0050 0000	1.0100 0000	1.0125 0000	1.0150 0000	1.0200 0000	1.0250 0000
2	1.0100 2500	1.0201 0000	1.0251 5625	1.0302 2500	1.0404 0000	1.0506 2500
3	1.0150 7513	1.0303 0100	1.0379 7070	1.0456 7838	1.0612 0800	1.0768 9063
4	1.0201 5050	1.0406 0401	1.0509 4534	1.0613 6355	1.0824 3216	1.1038 1289
5	1.0252 5125	1.0510 1005	1.0640 8215	1.0772 8400	1.1040 8080	1.1314 0821
6	1.0303 7751	1.0615 2015	1.0773 8318	1.0934 4326	1.1261 6242	1.1596 9342
7	1.0355 2940	1.0721 3535	1.0908 5047	1.1098 4491	1.1486 8567	1.1886 8575
8	1.0407 0704	1.0828 5671	1.1044 8610	1.1264 9259	1.1716 5938	1.2184 0290
9	1.0459 1058	1.0936 8527	1.1182 9218	1.1433 8998	1.1950 9257	1.2488 6297
10	1.0511 4013	1.1046 2213	1.1322 7083	1.1605 4083	1.2189 9442	1.2800 8454
11	1.0563 9583	1.1156 6835	1.1464 2422	1.1779 4894	1.2433 7431	1.3120 8666
12	1.0616 7781	1.1268 2503	1.1607 5452	1.1956 1817	1.2682 4179	1.3448 8882
13	1.0669 8620	1.1380 9328	1.1752 6395	1.2135 5244	1.2936 0663	1.3785 1104
14	1.0723 2113	1.1494 7421	1.1899 5475	1.2317 5573	1.3194 7876	1.4129 7382
15	1.0776 8274	1.1609 6896	1.2048 2918	1.2502 3207	1.3458 6834	1.4482 9817
16	1.0830 7115	1.1725 7864	1.2198 8955	1.2689 8555	1.3727 8571	1.4845 0562
17	1.0884 8651	1.1843 0443	1.2351 3817	1.2880 2033	1.4002 4142	1.5216 1826
18	1.0939 2894	1.1961 4748	1.2505 7739	1.3073 4064	1.4282 4625	1.5596 5872
19	1.0993 9858	1.2081 0895	1.2662 0961	1.3269 5075	1.4568 1117	1.5986 5019
20	1.1048 9558	1.2201 9004	1.2820 3723	1.3468 5501	1.4859 4740	1.6386 1644
21	1.1104 2006	1.2323 9194	1.2980 6270	1.3670 5783	1.5156 6634	1.6795 8185
22	1.1159 7216	1.2447 1586	1.3142 8848	1.3875 6370	1.5459 7967	1.7215 7140
23	1.1215 5202	1.2571 6302	1.3307 1709	1.4083 7715	1.5768 9926	1.7646 1068
24	1.1271 5978	1.2697 3465	1.3473 5105	1.4295 0281	1.6084 3725	1.8087 2595
25	1.1327 9558	1.2824 3200	1.3641 9294	1.4509 4535	1.6406 0599	1.8539 4410
26	1.1384 5955	1.2952 5631	1.3812 4535	1.4727 0953	1.6734 1811	1.9002 9270
27	1.1441 5185	1.3082 0888	1.3985 1092	1.4948 0018	1.7068 8648	1.9478 0002
28	1.1498 7261	1.3212 9097	1.4159 9230	1.5172 2218	1.7410 2421	1.9964 9502
29	1.1556 2197	1.3345 0388	1.4336 9221	1.5399 8051	1.7758 4469	2.0464 0739
30	1.1614 0008	1.3478 4892	1.4516 1336	1.5630 8022	1.8113 6158	2.0975 6758
31	1.1672 0708	1.3613 2740	1.4697 5853	1.5865 2642	1.8475 8882	2.1500 0677
32	1.1730 4312	1.3749 4068	1.4881 3051	1.6103 2432	1.8845 4059	2.2037 5694
33	1.1789 0833	1.3886 9009	1.5067 3214	1.6344 7918	1.9222 3140	2.2588 5086
34	1.1848 0288	1.4025 7699	1.5255 6629	1.6589 9637	1.9606 7603	2.3153 2213
35	1.1907 2689	1.4166 0276	1.5446 3587	1.6838 8132	1.9998 8955	2.3732 0519
36	1.1966 8052	1.4307 6878	1.5639 4382	1.7091 3954	2.0398 8734	2.4325 3532
37	1.2026 6393	1.4450 7647	1.5834 9312	1.7347 7663	2.0806 8509	2.4933 4870
38	1.2086 7725	1.4595 2724	1.6032 8678	1.7607 9828	2.1222 9879	2.5556 8242
39	1.2147 2063	1.4741 2251	1.6233 2787	1.7872 1025	2.1647 4477	2.6195 7448
40	1.2207 9424	1.4888 6373	1.6436 1946	1.8140 1841	2.2080 3966	2.6850 6384
41	1.2268 9821	1.5037 5237	1.6641 6471	1.8412 2868	2.2522 0046	2.7521 9043
42	1.2330 3270	1.5187 8989	1.6849 6677	1.8688 4712	2.2972 4447	2.8209 9520
43	1.2391 9786	1.5339 7779	1.7060 2885	1.8968 7982	2.3431 8936	2.8915 2008
44	1.2453 9385	1.5493 1757	1.7273 5421	1.9253 3302	2.3900 5314	2.9638 0808
45	1.2516 2082	1.5648 1075	1.7489 4614	1.9542 1301	2.4378 5421	3.0379 0328
46	1.2578 7892	1.5804 5885	1.7708 0797	1.9835 2621	2.4866 1129	3.1138 5086
47	1.2641 6832	1.5962 6344	1.7929 4306	2.0132 7910	2.5363 4351	3.1916 9713
48	1.2704 8916	1.6122 2608	1.8153 5485	2.0434 7829	2.5870 7039	3.2714 8956
49	1.2768 4161	1.6283 4834	1.8380 4679	2.0741 3046	2.6388 1179	3.3532 7680
50	1.2832 2581	1.6446 3182	1.8610 2237	2.1052 4242	2.6915 8803	3.4371 0872

AMOUNT OF $1 (CONTINUED)
$$(1 + i)^n$$

n \ i	3%	3½%	4%	5%	6%	7%
1	1.0300 0000	1.0350 0000	1.0400 0000	1.0500 0000	1.0600 0000	1.0700 0000
2	1.0609 0000	1.0712 2500	1.0816 0000	1.1025 0000	1.1236 0000	1.1449 0000
3	1.0927 2700	1.1087 1788	1.1248 6400	1.1576 2500	1.1910 1600	1.2250 4300
4	1.1255 0881	1.1475 2300	1.1698 5856	1.2155 0625	1.2624 7696	1.3107 9601
5	1.1592 7407	1.1876 8631	1.2166 5290	1.2762 8156	1.3382 2558	1.4025 5173
6	1.1940 5230	1.2292 5533	1.2653 1902	1.3400 9564	1.4185 1911	1.5007 3035
7	1.2298 7387	1.2722 7926	1.3159 3178	1.4071 0042	1.5036 3026	1.6057 8148
8	1.2667 7008	1.3168 0904	1.3685 6905	1.4774 5544	1.5938 4807	1.7181 8618
9	1.3047 7318	1.3628 9735	1.4233 1181	1.5513 2822	1.6894 7896	1.8384 5921
10	1.3439 1638	1.4105 9876	1.4802 4428	1.6288 9463	1.7908 4770	1.9671 5136
11	1.3842 3387	1.4599 6972	1.5394 5406	1.7103 3936	1.8982 9856	2.1048 5195
12	1.4257 6089	1.5110 6866	1.6010 3222	1.7958 5633	2.0121 9647	2.2521 9159
13	1.4685 3371	1.5639 5606	1.6650 7351	1.8856 4914	2.1329 2826	2.4098 4500
14	1.5125 8972	1.6186 9452	1.7316 7645	1.9799 3160	2.2609 0396	2.5785 3415
15	1.5579 6742	1.6753 4883	1.8009 4351	2.0789 2818	2.3965 5819	2.7590 3154
16	1.6047 0644	1.7339 8604	1.8729 8125	2.1828 7459	2.5403 5168	2.9521 6375
17	1.6528 4763	1.7946 7555	1.9479 0050	2.2920 1832	2.6927 7279	3.1588 1521
18	1.7024 3306	1.8574 8920	2.0258 1652	2.4066 1923	2.8543 3915	3.3799 3228
19	1.7535 0605	1.9225 0132	2.1068 4918	2.5269 5020	3.0255 9950	3.6165 2754
20	1.8061 1123	1.9897 8886	2.1911 2314	2.6532 9771	3.2071 3547	3.8696 8446
21	1.8602 9457	2.0594 3147	2.2787 6807	2.7859 6259	3.3995 6360	4.1405 6237
22	1.9161 0341	2.1315 1158	2.3699 1879	2.9252 6072	3.6035 3742	4.4304 0174
23	1.9735 8651	2.2061 1448	2.4647 1554	3.0715 2376	3.8197 4966	4.7405 2986
24	2.0327 9411	2.2833 2849	2.5633 0416	3.2250 9994	4.0489 3464	5.0723 6695
25	2.0937 7793	2.3632 4498	2.6658 3633	3.3863 5494	4.2918 7072	5.4274 3264
26	2.1565 9127	2.4459 5856	2.7724 6978	3.5556 7269	4.5493 8296	5.8073 5292
27	2.2212 8901	2.5315 6711	2.8833 6858	3.7334 5632	4.8223 4594	6.2138 6763
28	2.2879 2768	2.6201 7196	2.9987 0332	3.9201 2914	5.1116 8670	6.6488 3836
29	2.3565 6551	2.7118 7798	3.1186 5145	4.1161 3560	5.4183 8790	7.1142 5705
30	2.4272 6247	2.8067 9370	3.2433 9751	4.3219 4238	5.7434 9117	7.6122 5504
31	2.5000 8035	2.9050 3148	3.3731 3341	4.5380 3949	6.0881 0064	8.1451 1290
32	2.5750 8276	3.0067 0759	3.5080 5875	4.7649 4147	6.4533 8668	8.7152 7080
33	2.6523 3524	3.1119 4235	3.6483 8110	5.0031 8854	6.8405 8988	9.3253 3975
34	2.7319 0530	3.2208 6033	3.7943 1634	5.2533 4797	7.2510 2528	9.9781 1354
35	2.8138 6245	3.3335 9045	3.9460 8899	5.5160 1537	7.6860 8679	10.6765 8148
36	2.8982 7833	3.4502 6611	4.1039 3255	5.7918 1614	8.1472 5200	11.4239 4219
37	2.9852 2668	3.5710 2543	4.2680 8986	6.0814 0694	8.6360 8712	12.2236 1814
38	3.0747 8348	3.6960 1132	4.4388 1345	6.3854 7729	9.1542 5235	13.0792 7141
39	3.1670 2698	3.8253 7171	4.6163 6599	6.7047 5115	9.7035 0749	13.9948 2041
40	3.2620 3779	3.9592 5972	4.8010 2063	7.0399 8871	10.2857 1794	14.9744 5784
41	3.3598 9893	4.0978 3381	4.9930 6145	7.3919 8815	10.9028 6101	16.0226 6989
42	3.4606 9589	4.2412 5799	5.1927 8391	7.7615 8756	11.5570 3267	17.1442 5678
43	3.5645 1677	4.3897 0202	5.4004 9527	8.1496 6693	12.2504 5463	18.3443 5475
44	3.6714 5227	4.5433 4160	5.6165 1508	8.5571 5028	12.9854 8191	19.6284 5959
45	3.7815 9584	4.7023 5855	5.8411 7568	8.9850 0779	13.7646 1083	21.0024 5176
46	3.8950 4372	4.8669 4110	6.0748 2271	9.4342 5818	14.5904 8748	22.4726 2338
47	4.0118 9503	5.0372 8404	6.3178 1562	9.9059 7109	15.4659 1673	24.0457 0702
48	4.1322 5188	5.2135 8898	6.5705 2824	10.4012 6965	16.3938 7173	25.7289 0651
49	4.2562 1944	5.3960 6459	6.8333 4937	10.9213 3313	17.3775 0403	27.5299 2997
50	4.3839 0602	5.5849 2686	7.1066 8335	11.4673 9979	18.4201 5427	29.4570 2506

AMOUNT OF $1 (CONCLUDED)
$$(1 + i)^n$$

$\frac{i}{n}$	8%	9%	10%	11%	12%	13%	14%	15%
1	1.080000	1.090000	1.100000	1.110000	1.120000	1.130000	1.140000	1.150000
2	1.166400	1.188100	1.210000	1.232100	1.254400	1.276900	1.299600	1.322500
3	1.259712	1.295029	1.331000	1.367631	1.404928	1.442897	1.481544	1.520875
4	1.360489	1.411582	1.464100	1.518070	1.573519	1.630474	1.688960	1.749006
5	1.469328	1.538624	1.610510	1.685058	1.762342	1.842435	1.925415	2.011357
6	1.586874	1.677100	1.771561	1.870415	1.973823	2.081952	2.194973	2.313061
7	1.713824	1.828039	1.948717	2.076160	2.210681	2.352605	2.502269	2.660020
8	1.850930	1.992563	2.143589	2.304538	2.475963	2.658444	2.852586	3.059023
9	1.999005	2.171893	2.357948	2.558037	2.773079	3.004042	3.251949	3.517876
10	2.158925	2.367364	2.593742	2.839421	3.105848	3.394567	3.707221	4.045558
11	2.331639	2.580426	2.853117	3.151757	3.478550	3.835861	4.226232	4.652391
12	2.518170	2.812665	3.138428	3.498451	3.895976	4.334523	4.817905	5.350250
13	2.719624	3.065805	3.452271	3.883280	4.363493	4.898011	5.492411	6.152788
14	2.937194	3.341727	3.797498	4.310441	4.887112	5.534753	6.261349	7.075706
15	3.172169	3.642482	4.177248	4.784589	5.473566	6.254270	7.137938	8.137062
16	3.425943	3.970306	4.594973	5.310894	6.130394	7.067326	8.137249	9.357621
17	3.700018	4.327633	5.054470	5.895093	6.866041	7.986078	9.276464	10.761264
18	3.996019	4.717120	5.559917	6.543553	7.689966	9.024268	10.575169	12.375454
19	4.315701	5.141661	6.115909	7.263344	8.612762	10.197423	12.055693	14.231772
20	4.660957	5.604411	6.727500	8.062312	9.646293	11.523088	13.743490	16.366537
21	5.033834	6.108808	7.400250	8.949166	10.803848	13.021089	15.667578	18.821518
22	5.436540	6.658600	8.140275	9.933574	12.100310	14.713831	17.861039	21.644746
23	5.871464	7.257874	8.954302	11.026267	13.552347	16.626629	20.361585	24.891458
24	6.341181	7.911083	9.849733	12.239157	15.178629	18.788091	23.212207	28.625176
25	6.848475	8.623081	10.834706	13.585464	17.000064	21.230542	26.461916	32.918953
26	7.396353	9.399158	11.918177	15.079865	19.040072	23.990513	30.166584	37.856796
27	7.988061	10.245082	13.109994	16.738650	21.324881	27.109279	34.389906	43.535315
28	8.627106	11.167140	14.420994	18.579901	23.883866	30.633486	39.204493	50.065612
29	9.317275	12.172182	15.863093	20.623691	26.749930	34.615839	44.693122	57.575454
30	10.062657	13.267678	17.449402	22.892297	29.959922	39.115898	50.950159	66.211772
31	10.867669	14.461770	19.194342	25.410449	33.555113	44.200965	58.083181	76.143538
32	11.737083	15.763329	21.113777	28.205599	37.581726	49.947090	66.214826	87.565068
33	12.676050	17.182028	23.225154	31.308214	42.091533	56.440212	75.484902	100.699829
34	13.690134	18.728411	25.547670	34.752118	47.142517	63.777439	86.052788	115.804803
35	14.785344	20.413968	28.102437	38.574851	52.799620	72.068506	98.100178	133.175523
36	15.968172	22.251225	30.912681	42.818085	59.135574	81.437412	111.834203	153.151852
37	17.245626	24.253835	34.003949	47.528074	66.231843	92.024276	127.490992	176.124630
38	18.625276	26.436680	37.404343	52.756162	74.179664	103.987432	145.339731	202.543324
39	20.115298	28.815982	41.144778	58.559340	83.081224	117.505798	165.687293	232.924823
40	21.724521	31.409420	45.259256	65.000867	93.050970	132.781552	188.883514	267.863546
41	23.462483	34.236268	49.785181	72.150963	104.217087	150.043153	215.327206	308.043078
42	25.339482	37.317532	54.763699	80.087569	116.723137	169.548763	245.473015	354.249540
43	27.366640	40.676110	60.240069	88.897201	130.729914	191.590103	279.839237	407.386971
44	29.555972	44.336960	66.264076	98.675893	146.417503	216.496816	319.016730	468.495017
45	31.920449	48.327286	72.890484	109.530242	163.987604	244.641402	363.679072	538.769269
46	34.474085	52.676742	80.179532	121.578568	183.666116	276.444784	414.594142	619.584659
47	37.232012	57.417649	88.197485	134.952211	205.706050	312.382606	472.637322	712.522358
48	40.210573	62.585237	97.017234	149.796954	230.390776	352.992345	538.806547	819.400712
49	43.427419	68.217908	106.718957	166.274619	258.037669	398.881350	614.239464	942.310819
50	46.901613	74.357520	117.390853	184.564827	289.002190	450.735925	700.232988	1083.657442

PRESENT VALUE OF $1
$$(1+i)^{-n}$$

n \ i	½%	1%	1¼%	1½%	2%	2½%
1	0.9950 2488	0.9900 9901	0.9876 5432	0.9852 2167	0.9803 9216	0.9756 0976
2	0.9900 7450	0.9802 9605	0.9754 6106	0.9706 6175	0.9611 6878	0.9518 1440
3	0.9851 4876	0.9705 9015	0.9634 1833	0.9563 1699	0.9423 2233	0.9285 9941
4	0.9802 4752	0.9609 8034	0.9515 2428	0.9421 8423	0.9238 4543	0.9059 5064
5	0.9753 7067	0.9514 6569	0.9397 7706	0.9282 6033	0.9057 3081	0.8838 5429
6	0.9705 1808	0.9420 4524	0.9281 7488	0.9145 4219	0.8879 7138	0.8622 9687
7	0.9656 8963	0.9327 1805	0.9167 1593	0.9010 2679	0.8705 6018	0.8412 6524
8	0.9608 8520	0.9234 8322	0.9053 9845	0.8877 1112	0.8534 9037	0.8207 4657
9	0.9561 0468	0.9143 3982	0.8942 2069	0.8745 9224	0.8367 5527	0.8007 2836
10	0.9513 4794	0.9052 8695	0.8831 8093	0.8616 6723	0.8203 4830	0.7811 9840
11	0.9466 1489	0.8963 2372	0.8722 7746	0.8489 3323	0.8042 6304	0.7621 4478
12	0.9419 0534	0.8874 4923	0.8615 0860	0.8363 8742	0.7884 9318	0.7435 5589
13	0.9372 1924	0.8786 6260	0.8508 7269	0.8240 2702	0.7730 3253	0.7254 2038
14	0.9325 5646	0.8699 6297	0.8403 6809	0.8118 4928	0.7578 7502	0.7077 2720
15	0.9279 1688	0.8613 4947	0.8299 9318	0.7998 5150	0.7430 1473	0.6904 6556
16	0.9233 0037	0.8528 2126	0.8197 4635	0.7880 3104	0.7284 4581	0.6736 2493
17	0.9187 0684	0.8443 7749	0.8096 2602	0.7763 8526	0.7141 6256	0.6571 9506
18	0.9141 3616	0.8360 1731	0.7996 3064	0.7649 1159	0.7001 5937	0.6411 6591
19	0.9095 8822	0.8277 3992	0.7897 5866	0.7536 0747	0.6864 3076	0.6255 2772
20	0.9050 6290	0.8195 4447	0.7800 0855	0.7424 7042	0.6729 7133	0.6102 7094
21	0.9005 6010	0.8114 3017	0.7703 7881	0.7314 9795	0.6597 7582	0.5953 8629
22	0.8960 7971	0.8033 9621	0.7608 6796	0.7206 8763	0.6468 3904	0.5808 6467
23	0.8916 2160	0.7954 4179	0.7514 7453	0.7100 3708	0.6341 5592	0.5666 9724
24	0.8871 8567	0.7875 6613	0.7421 9707	0.6995 4392	0.6217 2149	0.5528 7535
25	0.8827 7181	0.7797 6844	0.7330 3414	0.6892 0583	0.6095 3087	0.5393 9059
26	0.8783 7991	0.7720 4796	0.7239 8434	0.6790 2052	0.5975 7928	0.5262 3472
27	0.8740 0986	0.7644 0392	0.7150 4626	0.6689 8574	0.5858 6204	0.5133 9973
28	0.8696 6155	0.7568 3557	0.7062 1853	0.6590 9925	0.5743 7455	0.5008 7778
29	0.8653 3488	0.7493 4215	0.6974 9978	0.6493 5887	0.5631 1231	0.4886 6125
30	0.8610 2973	0.7419 2292	0.6888 8867	0.6397 6243	0.5520 7089	0.4767 4269
31	0.8567 4600	0.7345 7715	0.6803 8387	0.6303 0781	0.5412 4597	0.4651 1481
32	0.8524 8358	0.7273 0411	0.6719 8407	0.6209 9292	0.5306 3330	0.4537 7055
33	0.8482 4237	0.7201 0307	0.6636 8797	0.6118 1568	0.5202 2873	0.4427 0298
34	0.8440 2226	0.7129 7334	0.6554 9429	0.6027 7407	0.5100 2817	0.4319 0534
35	0.8398 2314	0.7059 1420	0.6474 0177	0.5938 6608	0.5000 2761	0.4213 7107
36	0.8356 4492	0.6989 2495	0.6394 0916	0.5850 8974	0.4902 2315	0.4110 9372
37	0.8314 8748	0.6920 0490	0.6315 1522	0.5764 4309	0.4806 1093	0.4010 6705
38	0.8273 5073	0.6851 5337	0.6237 1873	0.5679 2423	0.4711 8719	0.3912 8492
39	0.8232 3455	0.6783 6967	0.6160 1850	0.5595 3126	0.4619 4822	0.3817 4139
40	0.8191 3886	0.6716 5314	0.6084 1334	0.5512 6232	0.4528 9042	0.3724 3062
41	0.8150 6354	0.6650 0311	0.6009 0206	0.5431 1559	0.4440 1021	0.3633 4695
42	0.8110 0850	0.6584 1892	0.5934 8352	0.5350 8925	0.4353 0413	0.3544 8483
43	0.8069 7363	0.6518 9992	0.5861 5656	0.5271 8153	0.4267 6875	0.3458 3886
44	0.8029 5884	0.6454 4546	0.5789 2006	0.5193 9067	0.4184 0074	0.3374 0376
45	0.7989 6402	0.6390 5492	0.5717 7290	0.5117 1494	0.4101 9680	0.3291 7440
46	0.7949 8907	0.6327 2764	0.5647 1397	0.5041 5265	0.4021 5373	0.3211 4576
47	0.7910 3390	0.6264 6301	0.5577 4219	0.4967 0212	0.3942 6836	0.3133 1294
48	0.7870 9841	0.6202 6041	0.5508 5649	0.4893 6170	0.3865 3761	0.3056 7116
49	0.7831 8250	0.6141 1921	0.5440 5579	0.4821 2975	0.3789 5844	0.2982 1576
50	0.7792 8607	0.6080 3882	0.5373 3905	0.4750 0468	0.3715 2788	0.2909 4221

PRESENT VALUE OF $1 (CONTINUED)
$$(1 + i)^{-n}$$

n \ i	3%	3½%	4%	5%	6%	7%
1	0.9708 7379	0.9661 8357	0.9615 3846	0.9523 8095	0.9433 9623	0.9345 7944
2	0.9425 9591	0.9335 1070	0.9245 5621	0.9070 2948	0.8899 9644	0.8734 3873
3	0.9151 4166	0.9019 4271	0.8889 9636	0.8638 3760	0.8396 1928	0.8162 9788
4	0.8884 8705	0.8714 4223	0.8548 0419	0.8227 0247	0.7920 9366	0.7628 9521
5	0.8626 0878	0.8419 7317	0.8219 2711	0.7835 2617	0.7472 5817	0.7129 8618
6	0.8374 8426	0.8135 0064	0.7903 1453	0.7462 1540	0.7049 6054	0.6663 4222
7	0.8130 9151	0.7859 9096	0.7599 1781	0.7106 8133	0.6650 5711	0.6227 4974
8	0.7894 0923	0.7594 1156	0.7306 9021	0.6768 3936	0.6274 1237	0.5820 0910
9	0.7664 1673	0.7337 3097	0.7025 8674	0.6446 0892	0.5918 9846	0.5439 3374
10	0.7440 9391	0.7089 1881	0.6755 6417	0.6139 1325	0.5583 9478	0.5083 4929
11	0.7224 2128	0.6849 4571	0.6495 8093	0.5846 7929	0.5267 8753	0.4750 9280
12	0.7013 7988	0.6617 8330	0.6245 9705	0.5568 3742	0.4969 6936	0.4440 1196
13	0.6809 5134	0.6394 0415	0.6005 7409	0.5303 2135	0.4688 3902	0.4149 6445
14	0.6611 1781	0.6177 8179	0.5774 7508	0.5050 6795	0.4423 0096	0.3878 1724
15	0.6418 6195	0.5968 9062	0.5552 6450	0.4810 1710	0.4172 6506	0.3624 4602
16	0.6231 6694	0.5767 0591	0.5339 0818	0.4581 1152	0.3936 4628	0.3387 3460
17	0.6050 1645	0.5572 0378	0.5133 7325	0.4362 9669	0.3713 6442	0.3165 7439
18	0.5873 9461	0.5383 6114	0.4936 2812	0.4155 2065	0.3503 4379	0.2958 6392
19	0.5702 8603	0.5201 5569	0.4746 4242	0.3957 3396	0.3305 1301	0.2765 0832
20	0.5536 7575	0.5025 6588	0.4563 8695	0.3768 8948	0.3118 0473	0.2584 1900
21	0.5375 4928	0.4855 7090	0.4388 3360	0.3589 4236	0.2941 5540	0.2415 1309
22	0.5218 9250	0.4691 5063	0.4219 5539	0.3418 4987	0.2775 0510	0.2257 1317
23	0.5066 9175	0.4532 8563	0.4057 2633	0.3255 7131	0.2617 9726	0.2109 4688
24	0.4919 3374	0.4379 5713	0.3901 2147	0.3100 6791	0.2469 7855	0.1971 4662
25	0.4776 0557	0.4231 4699	0.3751 1680	0.2953 0277	0.2329 9863	0.1842 4918
26	0.4636 9473	0.4088 3767	0.3606 8923	0.2812 4073	0.2198 1003	0.1721 9549
27	0.4501 8906	0.3950 1224	0.3468 1657	0.2678 4832	0.2073 6795	0.1609 3037
28	0.4370 7675	0.3816 5434	0.3334 7747	0.2550 9364	0.1956 3014	0.1504 0221
29	0.4243 4636	0.3687 4815	0.3206 5141	0.2429 4632	0.1845 5674	0.1405 6282
30	0.4119 8676	0.3562 7841	0.3083 1867	0.2313 7745	0.1741 1013	0.1313 6712
31	0.3999 8715	0.3442 3035	0.2964 6026	0.2203 5947	0.1642 5484	0.1227 7301
32	0.3883 3703	0.3325 8971	0.2850 5794	0.2098 6617	0.1549 5740	0.1147 4113
33	0.3770 2625	0.3213 4271	0.2740 9417	0.1998 7254	0.1461 8622	0.1072 3470
34	0.3660 4490	0.3104 7605	0.2635 5209	0.1903 5480	0.1379 1153	0.1002 1934
35	0.3553 8340	0.2999 7686	0.2534 1547	0.1812 9029	0.1301 0522	0.0936 6294
36	0.3450 3243	0.2898 3272	0.2436 6872	0.1726 5741	0.1227 4077	0.0875 3546
37	0.3349 8294	0.2800 3161	0.2342 9685	0.1644 3563	0.1157 9318	0.0818 0884
38	0.3252 2615	0.2705 6194	0.2252 8543	0.1566 0536	0.1092 3885	0.0764 5686
39	0.3157 5355	0.2614 1250	0.2166 2061	0.1491 4797	0.1030 5552	0.0714 5501
40	0.3065 5684	0.2525 7247	0.2082 8904	0.1420 4568	0.0972 2219	0.0667 8038
41	0.2976 2800	0.2440 3137	0.2002 7793	0.1352 8160	0.0917 1905	0.0624 1157
42	0.2889 5922	0.2357 7910	0.1925 7493	0.1288 3962	0.0865 2740	0.0583 2857
43	0.2805 4294	0.2278 0590	0.1851 6820	0.1227 0440	0.0816 2962	0.0545 1268
44	0.2723 7178	0.2201 0231	0.1780 4635	0.1168 6133	0.0770 0908	0.0509 4643
45	0.2644 3862	0.2126 5924	0.1711 9841	0.1112 9651	0.0726 5007	0.0476 1349
46	0.2567 3653	0.2054 6787	0.1646 1386	0.1059 9668	0.0685 3781	0.0444 9859
47	0.2492 5876	0.1985 1968	0.1582 8256	0.1009 4921	0.0646 5831	0.0415 8747
48	0.2419 0880	0.1918 0645	0.1521 9476	0.0961 4211	0.0609 9840	0.0388 6679
49	0.2349 5029	0.1853 2024	0.1463 4112	0.0915 6391	0.0575 4566	0.0363 2410
50	0.2281 0708	0.1790 5337	0.1407 1262	0.0872 0373	0.0542 8836	0.0339 4776

PRESENT VALUE OF \$1 (CONCLUDED)

$$(1+i)^{-n}$$

n \ i	8%	9%	10%	11%	12%	13%	14%	15%
1	0.925926	0.917431	0.909091	0.900901	0.892857	0.884956	0.877193	0.869565
2	0.857339	0.841680	0.826446	0.811622	0.797194	0.783147	0.769468	0.756144
3	0.793832	0.772183	0.751315	0.731191	0.711780	0.693050	0.674972	0.657516
4	0.735030	0.708425	0.683013	0.658731	0.635518	0.613319	0.592080	0.571753
5	0.680583	0.649931	0.620921	0.593451	0.567427	0.542760	0.519369	0.497177
6	0.630170	0.596267	0.564474	0.534641	0.506631	0.480319	0.455587	0.432328
7	0.583490	0.547034	0.513158	0.481658	0.452349	0.425061	0.399637	0.375937
8	0.540269	0.501866	0.466507	0.433926	0.403883	0.376160	0.350559	0.326902
9	0.500249	0.460428	0.424098	0.390925	0.360610	0.332885	0.307508	0.284262
10	0.463193	0.422411	0.385543	0.352184	0.321973	0.294588	0.269744	0.247185
11	0.428883	0.387533	0.350494	0.317283	0.287476	0.260698	0.236617	0.214943
12	0.397114	0.355535	0.318631	0.285841	0.256675	0.230706	0.207559	0.186907
13	0.367698	0.326179	0.289664	0.257514	0.229174	0.204165	0.182069	0.162528
14	0.340461	0.299246	0.263331	0.231995	0.204620	0.180677	0.159710	0.141329
15	0.315242	0.274538	0.239392	0.209004	0.182696	0.159891	0.140096	0.122894
16	0.291890	0.251870	0.217629	0.188292	0.163122	0.141496	0.122892	0.106865
17	0.270269	0.231073	0.197845	0.169633	0.145644	0.125218	0.107800	0.092926
18	0.250249	0.211994	0.179859	0.152822	0.130040	0.110812	0.094561	0.080805
19	0.231712	0.194490	0.163508	0.137678	0.116107	0.098064	0.082948	0.070265
20	0.214548	0.178431	0.148644	0.124034	0.103667	0.086782	0.072762	0.061100
21	0.198656	0.163698	0.135131	0.111742	0.092560	0.076798	0.063826	0.053131
22	0.183941	0.150182	0.122846	0.100669	0.082643	0.067963	0.055988	0.046201
23	0.170315	0.137781	0.111678	0.090693	0.073788	0.060144	0.049112	0.040174
24	0.157699	0.126405	0.101526	0.081705	0.065882	0.053225	0.043081	0.034934
25	0.146018	0.115968	0.092296	0.073608	0.058823	0.047102	0.037790	0.030378
26	0.135202	0.106393	0.083905	0.066314	0.052521	0.041683	0.033149	0.026415
27	0.125187	0.097608	0.076278	0.059742	0.046894	0.036888	0.029078	0.022970
28	0.115914	0.089548	0.069343	0.053822	0.041869	0.032644	0.025507	0.019974
29	0.107328	0.082155	0.063039	0.048488	0.037383	0.028889	0.022375	0.017369
30	0.099377	0.075371	0.057309	0.043683	0.033378	0.025565	0.019627	0.015103
31	0.092016	0.069148	0.052099	0.039354	0.029802	0.022624	0.017217	0.013133
32	0.085200	0.063438	0.047362	0.035454	0.026609	0.020021	0.015102	0.011420
33	0.078889	0.058200	0.043057	0.031940	0.023758	0.017718	0.013248	0.009931
34	0.073045	0.053395	0.039143	0.028775	0.021212	0.015680	0.011621	0.008635
35	0.067635	0.048986	0.035584	0.025924	0.018940	0.013876	0.010194	0.007509
36	0.062625	0.044941	0.032349	0.023355	0.016910	0.012279	0.008942	0.006529
37	0.057986	0.041231	0.029408	0.021040	0.015098	0.010867	0.007844	0.005678
38	0.053690	0.037826	0.026735	0.018955	0.013481	0.009617	0.006880	0.004937
39	0.049713	0.034703	0.024304	0.017077	0.012036	0.008510	0.006035	0.004293
40	0.046031	0.031838	0.022095	0.015384	0.010747	0.007531	0.005294	0.003733
41	0.042621	0.029209	0.020086	0.013860	0.009595	0.006665	0.004644	0.003246
42	0.039464	0.026797	0.018260	0.012486	0.008567	0.005898	0.004074	0.002823
43	0.036541	0.024584	0.016600	0.011249	0.007649	0.005219	0.003573	0.002455
44	0.033834	0.022555	0.015091	0.010134	0.006830	0.004619	0.003135	0.002134
45	0.031328	0.020692	0.013719	0.009130	0.006098	0.004088	0.002750	0.001856
46	0.029007	0.018984	0.012472	0.008225	0.005445	0.003617	0.002412	0.001614
47	0.026859	0.017416	0.011338	0.007410	0.004861	0.003201	0.002116	0.001403
48	0.024869	0.015978	0.010307	0.006676	0.004340	0.002833	0.001856	0.001220
49	0.023027	0.014659	0.009370	0.006014	0.003875	0.002507	0.001628	0.001061
50	0.021321	0.013449	0.008519	0.005418	0.003460	0.002219	0.001428	0.000923

*Tables of Amounts
and Present Values*

PRESENT VALUE OF ANNUITY OF $1

$$p_{\overline{n}|\,i} = \frac{1 - (1 + i)^{-n}}{i}$$

i / n	½%	1%	1¼%	1½%	2%	2½%
1	0.9950 2488	0.9900 9901	0.9876 5432	0.9852 2167	0.9803 9216	0.9756 0976
2	1.9850 9938	1.9703 9506	1.9631 1538	1.9558 8342	1.9415 6094	1.9274 2415
3	2.9702 4814	2.9409 8521	2.9265 3371	2.9122 0042	2.8838 8327	2.8560 2356
4	3.9504 9566	3.9019 6555	3.8780 5798	3.8543 8465	3.8077 2870	3.7619 7421
5	4.9258 6633	4.8534 3124	4.8178 3504	4.7826 4497	4.7134 5951	4.6458 2850
6	5.8963 8441	5.7954 7647	5.7460 0992	5.6971 8717	5.6014 3089	5.5081 2536
7	6.8620 7404	6.7281 9453	6.6627 2585	6.5982 1396	6.4719 9107	6.3493 9060
8	7.8229 5924	7.6516 7775	7.5681 2429	7.4859 2508	7.3254 8144	7.1701 3717
9	8.7790 6392	8.5660 1758	8.4623 4498	8.3605 1732	8.1622 3671	7.9708 6553
10	9.7304 1186	9.4713 0453	9.3455 2591	9.2221 8455	8.9825 8501	8.7520 6393
11	10.6770 2673	10.3676 2825	10.2178 0337	10.0711 1779	9.7868 4805	9.5142 0871
12	11.6189 3207	11.2550 7747	11.0793 1197	10.9075 0521	10.5753 4122	10.2577 6460
13	12.5561 5131	12.1337 4007	11.9301 8466	11.7315 3222	11.3483 7375	10.9831 8497
14	13.4887 0777	13.0037 0304	12.7705 5275	12.5433 8150	12.1062 4877	11.6909 1217
15	14.4166 2465	13.8650 5252	13.6005 4592	13.3432 3301	12.8492 6350	12.3813 7773
16	15.3399 2502	14.7178 7378	14.4202 9227	14.1312 6405	13.5777 0931	13.0550 0266
17	16.2586 3186	15.5622 5127	15.2299 1829	14.9076 4931	14.2918 7188	13.7121 9772
18	17.1727 6802	16.3982 6858	16.0295 4893	15.6725 6089	14.9920 3125	14.3533 6363
19	18.0823 5624	17.2260 0850	16.8193 0759	16.4261 6837	15.6784 6201	14.9788 9134
20	18.9874 1915	18.0455 5297	17.5993 1613	17.1686 3879	16.3514 3334	15.5891 6229
21	19.8879 7925	18.8569 8313	18.3696 9495	17.9001 3673	17.0112 0916	16.1845 4857
22	20.7840 5896	19.6603 7934	19.1305 6291	18.6208 2437	17.6580 4820	16.7654 1324
23	21.6756 8055	20.4558 2113	19.8820 3744	19.3308 6145	18.2922 0412	17.3321 1048
24	22.5628 6622	21.2433 8726	20.6242 3451	20.0304 0537	18.9139 2560	17.8849 8583
25	23.4456 3803	22.0231 5570	21.3572 6865	20.7196 1120	19.5234 5647	18.4243 7642
26	24.3240 1794	22.7952 0366	22.0812 5299	21.3986 3172	20.1210 3576	18.9506 1114
27	25.1980 2780	23.5596 0759	22.7962 9925	22.0676 1746	20.7068 9780	19.4640 1087
28	26.0676 8936	24.3164 4316	23.5025 1778	22.7267 1671	21.2812 7236	19.9648 8866
29	26.9330 2423	25.0657 8530	24.2000 1756	23.3760 7558	21.8443 8466	20.4535 4991
30	27.7940 5397	25.8077 0822	24.8889 0623	24.0158 3801	22.3964 5555	20.9302 9259
31	28.6507 9997	26.5422 8537	25.5692 9010	24.6461 4582	22.9377 0152	21.3954 0741
32	29.5032 8355	27.2695 8947	26.2412 7418	25.2671 3874	23.4683 3482	21.8491 7796
33	30.3515 2592	27.9896 9255	26.9049 6215	25.8789 5442	23.9885 6355	22.2918 8094
34	31.1955 4818	28.7026 6589	27.5604 5644	26.4817 2849	24.4985 9172	22.7237 8628
35	32.0353 7132	29.4085 8009	28.2078 5822	27.0755 9458	24.9986 1933	23.1451 5734
36	32.8710 1624	30.1075 0504	28.8472 6737	27.6606 8431	25.4888 4248	23.5562 5107
37	33.7025 0372	30.7995 0994	29.4787 8259	28.2371 2740	25.9694 5341	23.9573 1812
38	34.5298 5445	31.4846 6330	30.1025 0133	28.8050 5163	26.4406 4060	24.3486 0304
39	35.3530 8900	32.1630 3298	30.7185 1983	29.3645 8288	26.9025 8883	24.7303 4443
40	36.1722 2786	32.8346 8611	31.3269 3316	29.9158 4520	27.3554 7924	25.1027 7505
41	36.9872 9141	33.4996 8922	31.9278 3522	30.4589 6079	27.7994 8945	25.4661 2200
42	37.7982 9991	34.1581 0814	32.5213 1874	30.9940 5004	28.2347 9358	25.8206 0683
43	38.6052 7354	34.8100 0806	33.1074 7530	31.5212 3157	28.6615 6233	26.1664 4569
44	39.4082 3238	35.4554 5352	33.6863 9536	32.0406 2223	29.0799 6307	26.5038 4945
45	40.2071 9640	36.0945 0844	34.2581 6825	32.5523 3718	29.4901 5987	26.8330 2386
46	41.0021 8547	36.7272 3608	34.8228 8222	33.0564 8983	29.8923 1360	27.1541 6962
47	41.7932 1937	37.3536 9909	35.3806 2442	33.5531 9195	30.2865 8196	27.4674 8255
48	42.5803 1778	37.9739 5949	35.9314 8091	34.0425 5365	30.6731 1957	27.7731 5371
49	43.3635 0028	38.5880 7871	36.4755 3670	34.5246 8339	31.0520 7801	28.0713 6947
50	44.1427 8635	39.1961 1753	37.0128 7574	34.9996 8807	31.4236 0589	28.3623 1168

PRESENT VALUE OF ANNUITY OF $1 (CONTINUED)

$$p_{\overline{n}|i} = \frac{1-(1+i)^{-n}}{i}$$

$\frac{i}{n}$	3%	3½%	4%	5%	6%	7%
1	0.9708 7379	0.9661 8357	0.9615 3846	0.9523 8095	0.9433 9623	0.9345 7944
2	1.9134 6970	1.8996 9428	1.8860 9467	1.8594 1043	1.8333 9267	1.8080 1817
3	2.8286 1135	2.8016 3698	2.7750 9103	2.7232 4803	2.6730 1195	2.6243 1604
4	3.7170 9840	3.6730 7921	3.6298 9522	3.5459 5050	3.4651 0561	3.3872 1126
5	4.5797 0719	4.5150 5238	4.4518 2233	4.3294 7667	4.2123 6379	4.1001 9744
6	5.4171 9144	5.3285 5302	5.2421 3686	5.0756 9206	4.9173 2433	4.7665 3966
7	6.2302 8296	6.1145 4398	6.0020 5467	5.7863 7340	5.5823 8144	5.3892 8940
8	7.0196 9219	6.8739 5554	6.7327 4487	6.4632 1276	6.2097 9381	5.9712 9851
9	7.7861 0892	7.6076 8651	7.4353 3161	7.1078 2168	6.8016 9227	6.5152 3225
10	8.5302 0284	8.3166 0532	8.1108 9578	7.7217 3493	7.3600 8705	7.0235 8154
11	9.2526 2411	9.0015 5104	8.7604 7671	8.3064 1422	7.8868 7458	7.4986 7434
12	9.9540 0399	9.6633 3433	9.3850 7376	8.8632 5164	8.3838 4394	7.9426 8630
13	10.6349 5533	10.3027 3849	9.9856 4785	9.3935 7299	8.8526 8296	8.3576 5074
14	11.2960 7314	10.9205 2028	10.5631 2293	9.8986 4094	9.2949 8393	8.7454 6799
15	11.9379 3509	11.5174 1090	11.1183 8743	10.3796 5804	9.7122 4899	9.1079 1401
16	12.5611 0203	12.0941 1681	11.6522 9561	10.8377 6956	10.1058 9527	9.4466 4860
17	13.1661 1847	12.6513 2059	12.1656 6885	11.2740 6625	10.4772 5969	9.7632 2299
18	13.7535 1308	13.1896 8173	12.6592 9697	11.6895 8690	10.8276 0348	10.0590 8691
19	14.3237 9911	13.7098 3742	13.1339 3940	12.0853 2086	11.1581 1649	10.3355 9524
20	14.8774 7486	14.2124 0330	13.5903 2634	12.4622 1034	11.4699 2122	10.5940 1425
21	15.4150 2414	14.6979 7420	14.0291 5995	12.8211 5271	11.7640 7662	10.8355 2733
22	15.9369 1664	15.1671 2484	14.4511 1533	13.1630 0258	12.0415 8172	11.0612 4050
23	16.4436 0839	15.6204 1047	14.8568 4167	13.4885 7388	12.3033 7898	11.2721 8738
24	16.9355 4212	16.0583 6760	15.2469 6314	13.7986 4179	12.5503 5753	11.4693 3400
25	17.4131 4769	16.4815 1459	15.6220 7994	14.0939 4457	12.7833 5616	11.6535 8318
26	17.8768 4242	16.8903 5226	15.9827 6918	14.3751 8530	13.0031 6619	11.8257 7867
27	18.3270 3147	17.2853 6451	16.3295 8575	14.6430 3362	13.2105 3414	11.9867 0904
28	18.7641 0823	17.6670 1885	16.6630 6322	14.8981 2726	13.4061 6428	12.1371 1125
29	19.1884 5459	18.0357 6700	16.9837 1463	15.1410 7358	13.5907 2102	12.2776 7407
30	19.6004 4135	18.3920 4541	17.2920 3330	15.3724 5103	13.7648 3115	12.4090 4118
31	20.0004 2849	18.7362 7576	17.5884 9356	15.5928 1050	13.9290 8599	12.5318 1419
32	20.3887 6553	19.0688 6547	17.8735 5150	15.8026 7667	14.0840 4339	12.6465 5532
33	20.7657 9178	19.3902 0818	18.1476 4567	16.0025 4921	14.2302 2961	12.7537 9002
34	21.1318 3668	19.7006 8423	18.4111 9776	16.1929 0401	14.3681 4114	12.8540 0936
35	21.4872 2007	20.0006 6110	18.6646 1323	16.3741 9429	14.4982 4636	12.9476 7230
36	21.8322 5250	20.2904 9381	18.9082 8195	16.5468 5171	14.6209 8713	13.0352 0776
37	22.1672 3544	20.5705 2542	19.1425 7880	16.7112 8734	14.7367 8031	13.1170 1660
38	22.4924 6159	20.8410 8736	19.3678 6423	16.8678 9271	14.8460 1916	13.1934 7345
39	22.8082 1513	21.1024 9987	19.5844 8484	17.0170 4067	14.9490 7468	13.2649 2846
40	23.1147 7197	21.3550 7234	19.7927 7388	17.1590 8635	15.0462 9687	13.3317 0884
41	23.4123 9997	21.5991 0371	19.9930 5181	17.2943 6796	15.1380 1592	13.3941 2041
42	23.7013 5920	21.8348 8281	20.1856 2674	17.4232 0758	15.2245 4332	13.4524 4898
43	23.9819 0213	22.0626 8870	20.3707 9494	17.5459 1198	15.3061 7294	13.5069 6167
44	24.2542 7392	22.2827 9102	20.5488 4129	17.6627 7331	15.3831 8202	13.5579 0810
45	24.5187 1254	22.4954 5026	20.7200 3970	17.7740 6982	15.4558 3209	13.6055 2159
46	24.7754 4907	22.7009 1813	20.8846 5356	17.8800 6650	15.5243 6990	13.6500 2018
47	25.0247 0783	22.8994 3780	21.0429 3612	17.9810 1571	15.5890 2821	13.6916 0764
48	25.2667 0664	23.0912 4425	21.1951 3088	18.0771 5782	15.6500 2661	13.7304 7443
49	25.5016 5693	23.2765 6450	21.3414 7200	18.1687 2173	15.7075 7227	13.7667 9853
50	25.7297 6401	23.4556 1787	21.4821 8462	18.2559 2546	15.7618 6064	13.8007 4629

PRESENT VALUE OF ANNUITY OF $1 (CONCLUDED)

$$p_{\overline{n}|i} = \frac{1-(1+i)^{-n}}{i}$$

n $\backslash$ i	8%	9%	10%	11%	12%	13%	14%	15%
1	0.925926	0.917431	0.909091	0.900901	0.892857	0.884956	0.877193	0.869565
2	1.783265	1.759111	1.735537	1.712523	1.690051	1.668102	1.646661	1.625709
3	2.577097	2.531295	2.486852	2.443715	2.401831	2.361153	2.321632	2.283225
4	3.312127	3.239720	3.169865	3.102446	3.037349	2.974471	2.913712	2.854978
5	3.992710	3.889651	3.790787	3.695897	3.604776	3.517231	3.433081	3.352155
6	4.622880	4.485919	4.355261	4.230538	4.111407	3.997550	3.888668	3.784483
7	5.206370	5.032953	4.868419	4.712196	4.563757	4.422610	4.288305	4.160420
8	5.746639	5.534819	5.334926	5.146123	4.967640	4.798770	4.638864	4.487322
9	6.246888	5.995247	5.759024	5.537048	5.328250	5.131655	4.946372	4.771584
10	6.710081	6.417658	6.144567	5.889232	5.650223	5.426243	5.216116	5.018769
11	7.138964	6.805191	6.495061	6.206515	5.937699	5.686941	5.452733	5.233712
12	7.536078	7.160725	6.813692	6.492356	6.194374	5.917647	5.660292	5.420619
13	7.903776	7.486904	7.103356	6.749870	6.423548	6.121812	5.842362	5.583147
14	8.244237	7.786150	7.366687	6.981865	6.628168	6.302488	6.002072	5.724476
15	8.559479	8.060688	7.606080	7.190870	6.810864	6.462379	6.142168	5.847370
16	8.851369	8.312558	7.823709	7.379162	6.973986	6.603875	6.265060	5.954235
17	9.121638	8.543631	8.021553	7.548794	7.119630	6.729093	6.372859	6.047161
18	9.371887	8.755625	8.201412	7.701617	7.249670	6.839905	6.467420	6.127966
19	9.603599	8.950115	8.364920	7.839294	7.365777	6.937969	6.550369	6.198231
20	9.818147	9.128546	8.513564	7.963328	7.469444	7.024752	6.623131	6.259331
21	10.016803	9.292244	8.648694	8.075070	7.562003	7.101550	6.686957	6.312462
22	10.200744	9.442425	8.771540	8.175739	7.644646	7.169513	6.742944	6.358663
23	10.371059	9.580207	8.883218	8.266432	7.718434	7.229658	6.792056	6.398837
24	10.528758	9.706612	8.984744	8.348137	7.784316	7.282883	6.835137	6.433771
25	10.674776	9.822580	9.077040	8.421745	7.843139	7.329985	6.872927	6.464149
26	10.809978	9.928972	9.160945	8.488058	7.895660	7.371668	6.906077	6.490564
27	10.935165	10.026580	9.237223	8.547800	7.942554	7.408556	6.935155	6.513534
28	11.051078	10.116128	9.306567	8.601622	7.984423	7.441200	6.960662	6.533508
29	11.158406	10.198283	9.369606	8.650110	8.021806	7.470088	6.983037	6.550877
30	11.257783	10.273654	9.426914	8.693793	8.055184	7.495653	7.002664	6.565980
31	11.349799	10.342802	9.479013	8.733146	8.084986	7.518277	7.019881	6.579113
32	11.434999	10.406240	9.526376	8.768600	8.111594	7.538299	7.034983	6.590533
33	11.513888	10.464441	9.569432	8.800541	8.135352	7.556016	7.048231	6.600463
34	11.586934	10.517835	9.608575	8.829316	8.156564	7.571696	7.059852	6.609099
35	11.654568	10.566821	9.644159	8.855240	8.175504	7.585572	7.070045	6.616607
36	11.717193	10.611763	9.676508	8.878594	8.192414	7.597851	7.078987	6.623137
37	11.775179	10.652993	9.705917	8.899635	8.207513	7.608718	7.086831	6.628815
38	11.828869	10.690820	9.732651	8.918590	8.220993	7.618334	7.093711	6.633752
39	11.878582	10.725523	9.756956	8.935666	8.233030	7.626844	7.099747	6.638045
40	11.924613	10.757360	9.779051	8.951051	8.243777	7.634376	7.105041	6.641778
41	11.967235	10.786569	9.799137	8.964911	8.253372	7.641040	7.109685	6.645025
42	12.006699	10.813366	9.817397	8.977397	8.261939	7.646938	7.113759	6.647848
43	12.043240	10.837950	9.833998	8.988646	8.269589	7.652158	7.117332	6.650302
44	12.077074	10.860505	9.849089	8.998780	8.276418	7.656777	7.120467	6.652437
45	12.108402	10.881197	9.862808	9.007910	8.282516	7.660864	7.123217	6.654293
46	12.137409	10.900181	9.875280	9.016135	8.287961	7.664482	7.125629	6.655907
47	12.164267	10.917597	9.886618	9.023545	8.292822	7.667683	7.127744	6.657310
48	12.189136	10.933575	9.896926	9.030221	8.297163	7.670516	7.129600	6.658531
49	12.212163	10.948234	9.906296	9.036235	8.301038	7.673023	7.131228	6.659592
50	12.233485	10.961683	9.914814	9.041653	8.304498	7.675242	7.132656	6.660515

INDEX